BOB
HAWKE

TROY BRAMSTON

BOB HAWKE
DEMONS AND DESTINY
The Definitive Biography

VIKING
an imprint of
PENGUIN BOOKS

VIKING

UK | USA | Canada | Ireland | Australia
India | New Zealand | South Africa | China

Viking is part of the Penguin Random House group of companies
whose addresses can be found at global.penguinrandomhouse.com.

Penguin
Random House
Australia

First published by Viking in 2022

Front jacket image by Peter Carrette Archive/Getty Images;
back jacket image by News Corp Australia
Author photograph by Shane Reid
Cover design by Alex Ross © Penguin Random House Australia Pty Ltd
Typeset in 11.5/15pt Janson Text by Midland Typesetters, Australia

Printed and bound in Australia by Griffin Press, part of Ovato, an accredited
ISO AS/NZS 14001 Environmental Management Systems printer

 A catalogue record for this
book is available from the
NATIONAL National Library of Australia
LIBRARY
OF AUSTRALIA

ISBN 978 0 14378 809 6

penguin.com.au

MIX
Paper from
responsible sources
FSC® C009448

CONTENTS

Preface   xi
Prologue: 1983   xviii

PART I
DESTINY: 1929–1958

1   Providence   3
2   Son of the Manse   13
3   Rogue Scholar   25
4   Hazel   41
5   Broader Horizons   47
6   Academic Interlude   70

PART II
AMBITION: 1958–1983

7   Advocate   81
8   Rising Star   93
9   Mr President   115
10 The Second-Most Powerful Man in Australia   128
11 Bob and Gough   151
12 All the World's a Stage   173
13 Demons and Decisions   184
14 Enter the Biographer   209
15 The Coming of the Messiah   216
16 Bob and Bill   245
17 Bringing Australia Together   265

PART III
POWER: 1983–1991

18 Taking Power 279

19 Economic Realities 299

20 From Messiah to Mortal 319

21 Hawke Abroad 336

22 Economic Crises 359

23 Let's Stick Together 377

24 Bob and Paul 399

25 In Bed with Bob 410

26 Cold War Conciliator 418

27 Fourth Term 448

28 The View from Yarralumla 475

29 Hawke at War 486

30 Keating Strikes 498

31 End of Days 515

PART IV
STATESMAN: 1991–2019

32 Hawke in Hell 541

33 The Many Lives of Bob Hawke 556

34 The Golden Bowl Is Broken 572

Epilogue: Hawke Reflects 576

Appendix 582

Select Bibliography 588

Note to Readers 591

Notes 592

Acknowledgements 652

Photography Credits 657

Index 659

To John Degen and Kate Degen
And to Ben Heraghty
For decades of friendship, counsel and loyalty

ALSO BY TROY BRAMSTON

The Truth of the Palace Letters:
Deceit, Ambush and Dismissal in 1975 (with Paul Kelly)

Robert Menzies: The Art of Politics

Paul Keating: The Big-Picture Leader

The Dismissal: In the Queen's Name (with Paul Kelly)

Rudd, Gillard and Beyond

The Whitlam Legacy (ed.)

For the True Believers:
Great Labor Speeches That Shaped History (ed.)

Looking for the Light on the Hill:
Modern Labor's Challenges

The Wran Era (ed.)

The Hawke Government:
A Critical Retrospective (ed. with Susan Ryan)

'There is no escape from yesterday. Yesterday is in us. We are part of it. The present is linked with the past and the future with both.'
– Reverend Clem Hawke, unpublished memoir

PREFACE

In February 2019, Bob Hawke sat on the balcony of his sprawling multi-level home at 3 Minimbah Road, Northbridge, overlooking a gleaming Sydney Harbour. The summer sun streaked across his wrinkled face and the blustery wind ruffled his silvery-grey hair. His slim-framed body, tanned and creased, folded compactly into a white plastic outdoor chair. He was slumped and leaning forward, and hardly moved, as if his ageing joints and muscles were fixed. He was not able to get entirely comfortable and the cushion behind his back had to be adjusted several times. But he flashed a smile, cocked an eyebrow and extended his hand in greeting as I sat down to interview him. He smoked a cigar until it extinguished; the stub remained clasped between his fingers. He drained a strawberry milkshake. Hawke loved being outside, soaking up rays like a lizard on a rock. In his final days, it was where he wanted to be. This was to be Hawke's last interview. He knew the end was near.

The image of Hawke in these final days is lodged in my memory. He wore beige golf pants with a shiny tracksuit top over a white polo shirt, and slip-on shoes. His eyes were a duller blue than usual, though still piercing. His hair, once a luxuriant mane, was thinning, whiter and losing its distinctive curl. He was tired and a little irritable. He had lived a long life: he was less than a year shy of his ninetieth birthday. He was fading. It was deeply affecting to see Hawke ready, even eager, to let go. This son of the manse did not know what afterlife there might be. He had long been agnostic, but never an atheist. But he had thought about death, and was coming to terms with it. When I asked how he was feeling, his reply was blunt. 'To be quite honest, mate, I'd be quite happy not to wake up tomorrow morning,' he said. Three months later, Hawke was dead.[1]

Hawke would rather tackle a cryptic crossword or complete a sudoku than answer yet another round of questions for this biography. This was what occupied his days now. There had been a passing parade of former colleagues, rivals, friends and family members in recent weeks, and this would continue until the end finally came. He usually welcomed it, sometimes tolerated it and often enjoyed it, even if it did distract from the brainteasers.

It would be the last time I saw Hawke, and it soon became clear this interview was different. Although increasingly brief in his responses, Hawke was more reflective than usual. He had been thinking about his life. He was concise but thoughtful when recalling his student days, his time in the union movement and his prime ministership. When asked about his parents, Clem and Ellie, or his wives, Hazel and Blanche, or his children, he got emotional. His eyes moistened when he talked about Paul Keating.

There was a jolt of energy when I asked Hawke, again, about his parents. He lifted up in his chair and his eyes sparkled when he spoke about Clem. 'He was a marvellous man, my father, he always looked for good in people and he was a very big influence on me,' Hawke said. 'He was very keen to see that I made the most of what I had. I liked him. I loved him. He was my best mate.' Clem and Ellie Hawke showered their second son with love and fostered in him the belief that his life was destined for a great purpose. Did Ellie crystalise her ambition for her son and believe he would become prime minister? 'I think so,' he replied. 'At least in the back of her mind. Yes, I think it was there.' And Clem? 'Dad was at least as ambitious for me as my mother was.'

Hawke had spoken about how deeply he loved Hazel. He regretted not being a better father to Susan, Stephen and Rosslyn. Or a better husband. He thought he was a better grandfather. He acknowledged his adultery and the impact of the 'demon drink' on their marriage. In this last interview, he described his relationship with Hazel as 'the most important in my life at that time'. When clarification was sought, he became a little tetchy and made it clear he was indeed talking about Hazel. He had always loved her, even if he had not been faithful. He also loved Blanche. He said she was 'the best thing that happened to me'. He had spoken, somewhat awkwardly, about their intellectual, emotional and physical love for each other. She was the light in his life. Her care for him in these later years, as he was slipping away, had deepened their love for one another. Hawke had spent a lifetime trying to convince people that he was a simple, 'dinky-di' Australian, but in truth he was complex. Most people are. He did not see any difficulty loving both Hazel and Blanche. They were the two great love stories of his life.

In recent years, Hawke had repaired any lingering rift with Keating. The mending of this relationship had been a work in progress for a decade; it was not a near-death reconciliation. (I was sitting with Keating in mid-2016, for example, when Hawke rang to talk about a rather routine matter, and they chatted amiably for several minutes.) They were Australia's greatest political duo. They were rivals, and sometimes felt contempt for each other, but there was also admiration and warmth between them. They were like brothers. They never hated one another. Hawke's eyes widened and he smiled when he told me how happy he was that he had seen Keating recently. 'We had a marvellous time,' Hawke said. 'We did a lot of great things together.' He had earlier told me: 'Affection is not an inappropriate word, now, for our relationship.'[2]

After a series of interviews for this book, and many more over the past decade and a half, this was an opportunity to clarify a few things, to plug a few gaps and ask any questions that might help illuminate the life of one of the most remarkable and consequential Australians. Hawke had been interviewed thousands of times since the 1950s – probably more than any other Australian political figure – yet trying to unravel who he really was, what motivated him, how he saw himself, the effect he had on others and the contribution he made to public life still needed exploring. He had been asked the same things over and over again, so my goal was to prompt more revealing responses.

As he neared the end, Hawke was not interested in pushing a legacy or dwelling on regrets. 'I know this probably sounds a bit boastful, but I think I handled the prime ministership very well,' he judged. 'I'm not saying I was perfect – there were some things perhaps I could have handled better – but overall there is nothing I would change.' In his final months, Hawke thought about what he had achieved and not achieved. He thought about those whom he loved and who had loved him. He was at peace with himself and others, and with his legacy. He died a few months later.

—

I first met Bob Hawke at a dinner on 27 May 1994.[3] I was eighteen years old. I have never forgotten it. In a crowded and noisy room, I approached Hawke, caught his attention and extended my hand. He shook it. He looked into my eyes and asked my name. He gave me his undivided attention. The room seemed to blur and the sound dulled. At that moment, for only a few seconds, he was totally focused on me. He had magnetic appeal. For one brief moment, I experienced the Hawke political magic. He was charisma personified.

I lined up with hundreds of other people at Westfield Miranda three months later, on 20 August 1994, to have him sign my copy of *The Hawke Memoirs*. He stood on the stage and spoke about why he wrote the book. What I remember most about that short speech was his unbridled love for Australia, its ancient heritage and its vibrant multiculturalism, and its unlimited potential as a nation and a people. He signed books for several hours, until there was nobody left in the queue.

I spoke to Hawke many times in subsequent years and, with Susan Ryan, co-edited a book of essays about his government published in 2003. It was not until the twentieth anniversary of Labor's 1983 election victory that there was a proper recognition of his place in history. When Keating became prime minister in 1991 and won Labor a fifth election victory in 1993, it was not the right time to celebrate Hawke's life and legacy. He did not help his own cause when he published *The Hawke Memoirs*, which were highly critical of Keating, divorced Hazel and made several public outbursts which diminished his standing. By 1996, Labor was moving away from the Hawke/Keating model. It took time for Hawke to settle into post–prime ministerial life, and for his party to honour him as he – and Keating, too – always should have been.

I interviewed Hawke for my master's thesis in 2004. He launched my edited collection of speeches, *For the True Believers*, at the Trades Hall in Sydney in 2012. As a journalist and author, I interviewed Hawke more than twenty times. These interviews took place at Hawke's office or home, or on the phone. A few queries were answered in writing. I also had the opportunity to talk to Hawke less formally in person and on the phone many times. I usually kept notes of these discussions. And, always, before and after formal interviews, he would talk candidly about politics. This was often when Hawke became most animated.

This is the first full-life single-volume biography of Hawke published since he was prime minister. It follows three conventional biographies of Hawke. John Hurst's *Hawke: The Definitive Biography* was published in 1979. Robert Pullan's *Bob Hawke: A Portrait* was published in 1980. Blanche d'Alpuget published two authorised volumes: *Robert J. Hawke: A Biography* (1982) and *Hawke: The Prime Minister* (2010). A combined edition was published in 2019. I am indebted to these authors for their research and insights.

This new biography draws on a series of interviews I conducted with Hawke between 2017 and 2019 for this book. He gave me access to his personal papers, kept either at his Sydney office or at the Bob Hawke Prime Ministerial Library. Another collection of Hawke's papers from his prime ministerial office, held at the National Archives of Australia, was also made available. The new archival discoveries include letters Hawke exchanged with his parents and Hazel between 1952 and 1956; diaries he kept in 1952 and 1953; letters to and from Hazel in the mid-1960s; his father's unpublished memoir; school and university papers; and notes, diaries, letters and briefing papers kept by Hawke while at the Australian Council of Trade Unions (ACTU) and as Labor's national president. I was also granted access to Hazel's diaries and scrapbooks at the John Curtin Prime Ministerial Library. Most of these records have not been accessible to previous biographers or historians.

An array of new archival material from Hawke's prime ministerial years has also been made available. This includes cabinet papers, departmental documents, letters, and records of meetings and phone calls, Hawke's handwritten notes and speeches, and briefing papers and memos provided by his personal staff. Australian Security Intelligence Organisation (ASIO) memos provided to Hawke were declassified for the writing of this book. I also make use of archival material from the Labor Party's National Secretariat and the records of the Federal Parliamentary Labor Party, including caucus minutes, polling, strategy and campaign documents. A series of interviews that Hawke conducted during his prime ministership with journalist Philip Chubb and solicitor Peter Redlich, not previously made public, have also informed the writing of this biography.

Bill Hayden generously allowed me to access the letters he sent to, and received from, Buckingham Palace as governor-general. Hayden also opened up his personal files, which include the letters he exchanged with Hawke about the Labor leadership in 1983. I make use of diaries kept by Sir William Heseltine, Neal Blewett, Bob Carr and Kerry Sibraa. In addition, this book uses newly available documents from the archives of Ronald Reagan, George H.W. Bush, Margaret Thatcher, John Major and Brian Mulroney, including meeting and phone records, and letters. I was also granted access to extracts from Bush's personal diary which have not yet been published. In March 2020, I travelled to London and was able to view files concerning Hawke at the Oxford University Archives, and also the Rhodes Trust Archive and University College Archive at Oxford University. I have been privileged to access records held by schools that Hawke attended: Perth Modern, West Leederville State School and Maitland Primary School. Most of these records have not previously been available.

I conducted interviews with more than 100 people for this biography. They include Hawke's ministerial and parliamentary colleagues, personal staff, party officials, union leaders, public servants, journalists and business associates. I have spoken to the opposition leaders during the Hawke government: Andrew Peacock, John Howard and John Hewson. I was thrilled to interview several foreign contemporaries of Hawke: George H.W. Bush, John Major, Brian Mulroney, George Shultz, James Baker, Neil Kinnock, Charles Powell and Bernard Ingham. I also interviewed Hawke's children Susan Pieters-Hawke and Stephen Hawke, and his widow, Blanche d'Alpuget. And I have interviewed the prime ministers who succeeded Hawke. I also draw on interviews for previous books and articles.

The result is a fresh look at Hawke's life, from Bordertown to the prime ministership and his years as an elder statesman. As a biography, the spotlight is always on or close to Hawke. The story is often told from his perspective, and that of those who observed him up close, allowing for a broader portrait to be drawn. As with my biographies of Robert Menzies and Paul Keating, I have also sought to analyse and explain Hawke's life, in addition to chronicling it. While Hawke cooperated fully with the book, he asked for no control over the manuscript, nor was this offered. It presents a balanced account of Hawke's many lives. It is, given his substantial achievements, not unfavourable overall. It is impossible to draw any other conclusion. But his considerable personal failings, which have been somewhat sanitised in previous biographies, are not sanitised here. This aspect of the book may shock some readers. But it is necessary to provide an accurate portrait of a complex life.

Hawke is Labor's longest-serving prime minister and the third-longest-serving overall. No prime minister, post-war, has been more popular. No prime minister, other than Menzies, led their party to more election victories. And no prime minister has led a government that so fundamentally transformed Australia's economy, society, environment and international relations. It is my hope that this book will help readers better understand Hawke's life, in public and in private, and the enduring legacy of his government, which brought Australians together and remade the nation for the modern era.

Troy Bramston, December 2021

PROLOGUE

1983

In the summer of 1983, Bob Hawke's destiny edged one step closer to fulfilment. On the twelfth floor of the Commonwealth Government Centre at 295 Ann Street, Brisbane, a deal was made with Bill Hayden to surrender the leadership of the Australian Labor Party. It was done in Hayden's office, with Lionel Bowen, John Button and Don Grimes also party to the agreement. Hayden, who had reluctantly decided to resign, wanted to clarify and confirm the details of the transition, and seal it in writing. Two letters were typed, signed and exchanged. These twin documents were an essential part of the transfer of power within the Labor Party. They were the foundation stone for the Labor government.

The negotiations took place during a morning tea break at a shadow cabinet meeting while their colleagues sat around a table in a meeting room on the lower ground floor waiting for them to return. It was 3 February 1983. The meeting in Hayden's office began just after 10.40 am (Brisbane time). About half an hour later, as they were discussing the terms of the leadership transition, there was a knock at the door. 'Malcom Fraser has gone out to see the Governor-General,' the Labor staff member said. Hawke, Bowen, Button and Grimes laughed. Hayden was speechless. On this day of double drama, there would be a new Labor leader and the announcement of an early election to be held on 5 March. It was time to finalise the leadership agreement.

When the five men returned to the shadow cabinet meeting, their eyes were red and moist, and they were exhausted. Their colleagues were informed of the leadership change, which would be formalised at a caucus meeting within days. Tears had been

shed during this morning of tragedy and excitement. It had been a
gut-wrenching decision for Hayden. It was a moment of triumph
for Hawke that was tinged with sadness but no regrets.

Hayden, with his heart in his throat, had sought to extract
several guarantees from Hawke regarding the futures of his staff,
his colleagues and himself. The letters would be Hayden's insurance. They bound Hawke to a written contract that would last
for years.[1]

'I wish to confirm our discussions of this morning in which
I informed you that it is my intention to stand down as Leader of
the Federal Parliamentary Labor Party,' Hayden wrote to Hawke.
'As I informed you this morning, in standing down as Leader I
will be making a number of sacrifices. I have done this however
for what I and some of my senior parliamentary colleagues believe
to be [in] the interests of the party.'

Hayden outlined the 'agreement' in six points:

1. That you will immediately arrange for appropriate
   employment for all members of my staff who are not
   currently employed in the Australian Public Service.
2. That you guarantee the continuation in their existing Shadow
   Ministries or an alternate Shadow Ministry of equivalent
   status to be agreed upon with them of Messrs John Dawkins,
   Peter Walsh and Neal Blewett.
3. That I will be appointed as Shadow Minister for Foreign
   Affairs until the next federal election and thereafter in
   the event of Labor losing such election until such time as
   agreement is reached on any alternate position between us.
4. That I, as Shadow Minister may be allocated in addition to
   any staff entitlement I shall have a staff member of Assistant
   Private Secretary Grade II. entitlement.
5. That in the event of the Labor Party forming a government
   after the 1983 Federal election, I be appointed as Minister
   for Foreign Affairs, such appointment to be of such period
   as is required to enable me to be appointed Australian High
   Commissioner to London for a period of five years.
6. In the event of the Australian Labor Party not forming
   a government following the 1983 Federal election the

arrangement as referred to in the preceding paragraph is to
apply immediately following the next succeeding election if
at that election the Labor Party is elected to government.[2]

In his signed letter of reply, Hawke acknowledged Hayden had
resigned as leader. He then addressed the 'certain terms and
conditions' that had been agreed:

> On the assumption that at the Caucus Meeting on Tuesday
> 8 February 1983 I am elected Leader of the Australian Labor
> Party I confirm that the matters set out in your letter have been
> agreed between us and as indicated to you verbally I undertake
> to abide by those conditions.[3]

Hayden folded Hawke's letter and a copy of his own, and put them
in his suit pocket. They would later be transferred to a secure place
in his office, and years later to the National Library of Australia,
where they were to remain sealed and not be accessed without his
permission.

The principal figure in persuading Hayden to stand aside was
Labor's Senate leader, John Button. After Labor's failure to win
the Flinders by-election in Victoria in December 1982, Button
decided that Hayden had to go. They spoke about the leadership
in person and on the phone throughout January. But Hayden
initially did not want to quit. Button decided to chip away at his
confidence, targeting Hayden's fatal weakness, and led him to the
edge in the hope that he would jump.

Eventually, on 28 January 1983, Button wrote Hayden a long
letter. This letter was Hayden's death warrant. 'I believe that you
cannot win the next election,' he argued. 'You said to me that you
could not stand down for a "bastard" like Bob Hawke. In my experience in the Labor Party the fact that someone is a bastard (of one
kind or another) has never been a disqualification for leadership of
the party.' Button had tightened the screws. He told Hayden that
he must resign.

Button was also speaking to Bowen, the deputy leader, about a
leadership change. It was Bowen who suggested Button write to
Hayden. Button was also speaking to Hawke. Button, along with
Michael Duffy, met the leader-in-waiting at his Sandringham

home on 16 January. Hawke rubbed suntan lotion on his skin by the pool as he listened to Button outline the plan. Button said Hayden wanted concessions. Hawke already knew this; he had spoken to Hayden directly.

After Hayden received Button's letter on 28 January, events gathered speed. The two men spoke on 30 January on the phone. On the afternoon of 1 February, they talked for two hours in Brisbane. This was when Hayden agreed to make way for Hawke. The plan was that he would resign on 4 February, provided Hawke agreed to his conditions concerning his future, and that of his supporters in caucus and his staff. There would have to be an 'ironclad guarantee' and it would be in writing, signed and witnessed. Hayden was driving a hard bargain. He was leaving nothing to chance.

Bowen, informed by Button of these developments late in the evening of 1 February, was not happy. Hayden wanted Bowen to give up the foreign affairs portfolio. There should be no deals, Bowen said. But a deal was essential to secure a leadership change. Button updated Hawke the next day, 2 February, and told him to get ready to fulfil his destiny. The next morning, on his way to Brisbane, Button told Grimes, the Senate deputy leader, about the deal.

On the morning of 3 February, journalist Laurie Oakes learnt that Fraser was preparing to call a snap election. Fraser wanted to stop Labor changing leaders. Oakes phoned Hayden and told him this might help him hang on. 'So that's what Fraser's up to, is it?' Hayden replied before hanging up. Hayden decided to outsmart Fraser by bringing his resignation forward. But he did not know Fraser was planning to drive out that same day to Government House to recommend an election. Hayden told Button that the deal would have to be finalised during the shadow cabinet meeting that morning. The meeting started late. When Bowen sat down next to Hayden, he was told they would finalise the leadership transition during the morning tea break. Bowen was shocked. Most of the shadow ministers seated around the table had little idea what had been going on and what was about to happen.

At 11.40 am, Hayden informed the shadow cabinet of his resignation. Just ten minutes earlier, at 12.30 pm (Canberra time), Fraser's election gambit had gone awry. When he arrived at Government House with his request for an election, he was told that Sir Ninian and Lady Stephen were lunching with the Polish ambassador, Ryszard Frąckiewicz, and his wife. His written request would have to wait until the Governor-General had finished lunch. Fraser's planned 1 pm press conference to announce the election was cancelled. It would not be until about 5 pm that afternoon that Fraser could inform the nation that it would go to the polls in thirty days.

At the time, Fraser privately boasted to colleagues that he had a Labor source who informed him that Labor was about to change leaders. According to Fraser's senior adviser, Alister Drysdale, that source was Neville Wran, the premier of New South Wales and Labor's national president. 'We got a tip-off from Wran that Labor was about to change leaders,' he recalled.[4] Fraser believed Labor could not change leaders once an election had been called. After all, the shadow cabinet was meeting in Brisbane, and only the Labor caucus meeting in Canberra could change leaders. He was mistaken. It was a monumental blunder.

Meanwhile, Hawke and Hayden fronted separate press conferences in the lower ground floor theatre. Hayden was broken-hearted. 'I believe that a drover's dog could lead the Labor Party to victory, the way the country is and the way the opinion polls are showing up for the Labor Party,' he told journalists. The guillotine fell. Hayden returned to his office and went into the bathroom, locked the door and wept. His staff listened to loud wails of grief and sobbing. 'It hurt like hell revised several times,' Hayden later reflected.[5]

That evening, Hawke was asked by journalist Richard Carleton if he had 'blood on his hands'. Hawke lifted an inch from his chair and fixed his eyes on Carleton. 'You're not improving, are you?' he replied. 'It's a ridiculous question, you know it's ridiculous. I have no blood on my hands.'[6]

It had, in fact, been a bloodless coup. Labor quickly bonded in the ritual of an election campaign with victory in sight. Hawke addressed party members at the Mt Coot-tha Botanical Gardens Auditorium that same night. Many were disappointed by Hayden's resignation, but Hawke won them over. Hawke's leadership would be formalised at a caucus meeting in Canberra on 8 February. It lasted just a few minutes. Hayden told Labor MPs: 'It hurts and it is still hurting.'[7]

Hayden's downfall was ruthless, brutal and sad. But it was the price Labor was prepared to pay for electoral victory. Hayden might lead Labor to power, but the party's research showed that Hawke would guarantee it. 'I felt genuinely grateful for the job Bill had done,' Hawke reflected later. 'It wasn't as though he'd done a bad job, but the question was very debatable as to whether he could win the election. I was fairly certain I could.'[8] A few days earlier, Hayden had attended the funeral of former wartime Labor prime minister Frank Forde. The Labor Party left Brisbane having buried two leaders.

—

Bob Hawke's ascendancy to the Labor leadership, and a month later the prime ministership, was like no other in Australian history. He led Labor back to office with a landslide election victory. Election day was also the birthday of his father, Clem, who had turned eighty-five. 'This is the best birthday present you could give me, son,' he said.[9] Hawke felt he had won the cosmic lottery by having Clem and Ellie as his parents. They had long predicted their son becoming prime minister. The intense love of Hawke's parents gave him an inner confidence. Hawke believed there was a 'guiding' presence that propelled him towards the prime ministership, but downplayed notions of divine intervention.[10] However, when a motorcycle accident nearly killed him at age seventeen, he felt his life had been spared for a reason and he was going to make the most of it. This was a turning point.

It is said the arc of a life reveals its true character, but Hawke's was a life of constant reinvention and redemption. He took time to find his path. As a kid born in the small country town of Bordertown, South Australia, and growing up the son of a clergyman and a schoolteacher, he had thought about becoming a farmer or doctor. He was deeply religious but his faith was shattered in 1952 during a Christian student conference in India, where he witnessed widespread poverty. Hawke had first seriously thought about public service of some kind when he won a Rhodes

Scholarship to commence in 1953. At Oxford University, and later at the Australian National University, where he worked on a doctorate and tutored, he was eyeing a career as an academic. Oxford significantly shaped Hawke's values and outlook. He returned with a heightened sense of his identity as an Australian.

Hawke's rise to power took place outside the political system. He was appointed the ACTU's research officer and advocate in 1958, and within a few years enjoyed a national profile as an intellectual larrikin. In 1969, he won election as ACTU president. Over the next decade, he earned a reputation for resolving intractable industrial disputes, led the union movement into several enterprises and became a prominent contributor to national and international political debates. He was the most brilliant, articulate and effective leader the trade union movement had produced. Hawke had found an outlet for his talents. But the question of when he would go into politics percolated through the 1970s. No political figure has visited themselves upon the imaginations of so many Australians as Hawke in that era; he became a vessel for their dreams. The idea that Hawke could one day be prime minister excited some and repulsed others, but it remained an idea so pregnant with promise that it was fixed in the public mind.

The problem was that Hawke was a notorious drinker, infamous womaniser and prone to angry public outbursts. He was a terrible drunk and could get verbally abusive when inebriated. He was also a serial adulterer. Some women threw themselves at him, mesmerised by his charisma and power, and others he flatly propositioned. When scorned, he would lash out and often humiliate them. He could be selfish and careless. His emotions, whether revealed as tears or temper, were often vividly on display.

He married Hazel Masterson in 1956 and they raised three children: Susan, Stephen and Rosslyn. They lived with the roiling turmoil that most Australians read about or saw on television, and suffered because of it. Hawke personified the very best and worst in Australians. He was a deeply flawed person, and his behaviour would not be tolerated today. He could be vain and arrogant one moment, and then compassionate and inspiring the next. He embodied a mix of contradictions and contrasts but he was an authentic political leader. He never hid who he was or tried to be someone he was not. His life resembled an electrocardiogram, pulsing with soaring highs and dramatic lows.

This explains why Hawke became such a compelling public figure. Television was his premier means for talking to everyday Australians. The secret was that he imagined talking to just one person. If you met Hawke, it was like being struck by lightning. He tried to convey this through the televisual medium. The long, wavy, metallic hair, the tanned, soft, olive skin, the arched eyebrow, the mouth with the corners turned down, and the darting eyes with cigar in hand became legendary. He carried himself with an air of satisfaction and projected confidence. At a moment's notice, like a board being clacked on a sound stage, he could transform to suit the audience. He was a supreme performer who could turn on a range of emotions, as though flicking through index cards until he found the right one: charm, persuasion, indignation, anger, sadness, humour. Voters tuned in because they did not know which Hawke they would get. But to succeed in politics, Hawke's life had to enter yet another phase.

He gave up the booze, moderated the womanising and stabilised his emotions to become prime minister. His life became a reform story of its own. But it was not until 1980 that he was elected to parliament. Just over two years later he was Labor leader, and then prime minister. Although he had been Labor's federal president (1973–78), he was seen as above politics. Hawke made conciliation the centrepiece of his pitch for the prime ministership. He wanted to heal the divisions that defined Malcolm Fraser's government. In 1983, Hawke promised to 'bring Australians together'. The Hawke government was more pragmatic than ideological, and many of its policies were crafted by necessity rather than design. He emphasised the importance of educating the electorate so they would understand and support the need for change. His over-arching vision for Australia was to have a more competitive and productive economy and a compassionate society at home, and to be an independent and respected nation abroad.

The 1980s was an exhilarating decade. Hawke eschewed class war and the politics of envy and worked with business and unions to turn Australia in a new direction. He saw opponents as adversaries, not enemies. The nation became more confident and optimistic, dynamic and brave, with a renewed sense of identity and purpose in a rapidly changing world. The Hawke government smashed the established policy settings and introduced vast economic, social and environmental reforms. Hawke was the last Australian prime minister during the Cold War. He was one of the leaders in the crusade to end apartheid in South Africa and free Nelson Mandela from prison, to safeguard the pristine icy wilderness of Antarctica and to foster greater economic cooperation between nations in the Asia-Pacific region. Hawke played a significant and often unrecognised role as a bridge between East and West by passing on information and sharing his assessments of Chinese and Soviet leaders with Ronald Reagan, George H.W. Bush, Margaret Thatcher, John Major and Brian Mulroney.

As longstanding policy pillars tumbled, and Labor agonised over the ritual slaying of its sacred cows, it was rarely smooth sailing. Cabinet and party disputes were frequent but Hawke managed to keep Labor largely united. In doing so, he changed the party. But he also transcended it. He enlarged Labor's mission, challenged its beliefs and made it fit to govern. He had learnt from the failures of the Whitlam era. Policymaking was invested with rigour and purpose. The public service was encouraged to give frank and fearless advice.

Hawke himself had a unique talent for managing a cabinet and drawing the best out of his staff. He was secure enough in himself that he could share power. He had a strong work ethic and discipline, devoured paperwork and was singularly focused. He articulated the objectives of his government and used his unique rapport with voters to persuade them to keep faith through profound change. He showed Labor could govern for the long term. The voters endorsed the Hawke approach with sustained high approval ratings – which reached an astonishing 78 per cent in 1984 – and four election victories in a row.

Hawke was the brightest star in the political galaxy. He assembled and led the finest constellation of talent in the cabinet room and in the Prime Minister's Office that Australian politics has ever witnessed. He was a strong and purposeful leader, but he was also consultative and collaborative, and unafraid to advance a difficult or unpopular cause or retreat pragmatically when he saw little prospect of success. Hawke, certainly, did not get every-thing right. But the ledger is overwhelmingly stacked on the side of having made the right decisions when tested, and his legacy stands unmatched by that of any post-war prime minister.

In Hawke, Australians saw the mysterious but always recog-nisable alchemy of political leadership. And that is what should be remembered above all.

PART I

DESTINY
1929–1958

I

PROVIDENCE

In the darkness before dawn on Monday, 9 December 1929, in Bordertown, South Australia, Robert James Lee Hawke was born to clergyman Arthur Clarence Hawke and former school-teacher Edith Emily Lee at the Tatiara Soldiers' Memorial Hospital. Located on South Terrace, the district hospital was a single-storey stone building with an iron roof and wrap-around verandahs. It had opened in July 1924, and was the pride of the small country town. Dr Eric Broadbent delivered the baby. On seeing the boy, blinking in the early morning light, the matron of the hospital noted there was something special about him. It confirmed Clem and Ellie's premonitions. This first impression of their son never changed.

It was a 'red letter day' for Bordertown, and for Australia, recalled Clem in his unpublished memoir.[1] The birth of the future Australian prime minister was duly entered at the District Registry Office on 31 December 1929, and recorded in the state's birth registration book as 241A on page 168.[2] A family notice was also placed in *The Advertiser*: 'HAWKE – At the Tatiara Soldiers' Memorial Hospital, Bordertown, to the wife of the Rev. C. A. Hawke – a son, Robert James Lee (Bobbie).'[3] A notice of birth was also placed in *The Chronicle*, and again in both papers the following week.[4] The baby shared the middle name James with his paternal grandfather; a second middle name, Lee, was his mother's maiden name.

Australia was on the brink of the Great Depression. Six weeks earlier, on 22 October 1929, Labor leader James Scullin was sworn in as Australia's ninth prime minister. At the election on 12 October, Stanley Bruce's government was defeated and he suffered the ignominy of being the first prime minister to lose his seat. The Wall Street crash between September and October had marked the end of the Roaring Twenties, a time of post-war optimism, excess and affluence. The world young Robert – or Bobby, as he was now known – was born into was changing fast, and the consequences were unpredictable.[5]

From a young age, Hawke was told that his life was to be lived for a great purpose. Accordingly, he was showered with love by both parents and made to believe that he was unique. Ellie was certain her son would lead the nation one day. When she turned to the Bible in the months before the birth, it always opened at the Book of Isaiah, and her eyes were drawn to a verse that proclaimed, as if with divine intervention, 'For unto us a child is born, unto us a son is given: and the government shall be upon his shoulder.'[6] In his memoir, *Yesterday, Today and Tomorrow*, Clem recalled that his son always had 'a special charm and charisma' about him. Dr Edward S. Kiek, who christened Hawke, said: 'If I were a prophet, I would predict a great future for this child.'[7] The notion that Hawke was destined for greatness became part of the family's mythology.

While Hawke did not see the heavenly hand of God in his journey from Bordertown to the Lodge, he explained in an interview for this book that he did feel a kind of celestial force throughout his life. 'It almost seemed like there was a divine hand guiding my career,' Hawke said. 'Destiny is too strong a word. I didn't say that this is God guiding me, but I did think there was some sort of guidance happening.'[8]

Ellie endowed her son with dynamic energy, conviction and determination. Clem invested in him a profound commitment to serving the public, the values of justice and compassion, and faith in his fellow man and in himself. Although they were devoted to their church and its teachings, Hawke recalled that he did not grow up with 'overt signs of religion' in the home, other than saying a prayer before meals. But the broad concepts of Christianity, essentially the social gospel, had a profound impact on him.[9] Hawke was, he recalled, surrounded by unconditional love. 'I had an absolutely lovely home and they both loved me very much,' he said.[10] His earliest memory was of his parents reading aloud to him – mostly stories from the Old Testament. His parents, recalled Hawke, gave him 'a great sense of security and confidence' and also 'encouraged a precociousness'.[11]

Clem and Ellie were opposites in temperament and comportment, and in their instruction. This may help to explain the inherent contradictions in their son's character, and his struggle to reconcile his competing emotions. Clem, tall and lean, was softly spoken, with a tender nature and a warm heart. He was kind and thoughtful, and had a keen sense of fun. He was easygoing, but disciplined and regimented when it came to his church or Masonic lodge duties. He was not a fire-and-brimstone preacher, preferring to infuse his sermons with homespun wisdom and gentle instruction. Ellie's smaller height belied her energetic, forceful and strong-willed temperament. She could be impatient and belligerent, and was often painfully honest in her opinions of people and in her arguments. She could be intense when gripped by a belief – such as alcohol being the Devil's work – and unrelenting in proselyting it.

Clem and Ellie were blessed with the birth of their first son, John Neil Hawke, at Houghton on 1 March 1921. Ellie longed for a girl, who would be named Elizabeth.[12] She suffered a miscarriage. The belief that having a son was God's will helped assuage any regret she felt at not having a daughter. There was a nine-year age gap between Neil and Bobby. As Neil was boarding at King's College in Adelaide, the brothers did not spend much time together outside of holidays. Bobby looked up to Neil and enjoyed spending time with him when he came home. Clem and Ellie had favourites. Hawke recalled that Neil was 'Mum's boy' and he was 'Dad's boy'. Ellie was utterly devoted to Neil, whereas Clem and Bobby had a deeper bond.[13]

Arthur Clarence Hawke, known as 'Clem', was born on 5 March 1898 in Kapunda, between the Barossa and Clare valleys in South Australia.[14] Clem was the son of James Renfrey Hawke, born 25 September 1862 in Kapunda, and Elizabeth Ann Pascoe, born 13 December 1861 in Blinman, South Australia. A generation before, the Hawkes, like the Lees, had migrated to

Australia from Cornwall, in England. James Hawke mined copper in Kapunda, and later worked in construction for the railways, and as a gardener and carpenter.

Clem had four brothers and two sisters. It was a happy household, with lots of fun and love, but they were poor. The Hawkes were steeped in Labor values. Clem's brother Albert became premier of Western Australia. Clem once imagined a political career and was secretary of the Labor Party's Kapunda Branch as a teenager. Clem left school at age twelve for a series of odd jobs, including carting milk, painting and decorating, and working as a shop assistant and a blacksmith's assistant.

The Hawkes were Methodists and later joined the Baptist Church. Clem became friendly with Baptist minister John Murray and his wife, and was encouraged to take on church roles, including as a deacon. During World War I, the Baptist Home Mission Committee commissioned Clem to go to Parilla, in the Mallee, to undertake work on behalf of the mission. Nine months later, a Methodist minister at Lameroo invited Clem to take up a Methodist ministry at Kalangadoo, 25 miles from Mount Gambier, which he accepted. After twelve months, Clem was sent to Port Neil to conduct church services and administer the sacraments. From there, in 1919, he went to Forster, on the Murray River, to help reorganise churches in that district. After a year there, he decided to further his theological studies and enrolled at the Methodist Training College at Brighton, a seaside suburb of Adelaide. It was while at Brighton in 1919 that Clem was offered a ministry at the Houghton Congregational Church, in the Adelaide Hills. He continued his studies at the Parkin Congregational College. He had been a Methodist, then a Baptist, a Methodist again and was now committed to Congregationalism, a more independent, liberal and less dogmatic church in the Protestant Reformed tradition.

Clem had a unique relationship with his second-born son. 'He's passed on to me the fundamental beliefs I have, and that is: we are in this world not just to advance our own interests but we owe an obligation to our fellow human beings,' Bob Hawke would later say.[15] Clem instructed Bob that if he believed in the 'the fatherhood of God', then he must also believe in the 'brotherhood of man' – the notion that everyone is related to each other, that all should treat one another with respect and dignity, and work together to improve their community. This philosophy became a guiding star in Hawke's life. 'We just loved one another madly,' Hawke said. 'I haven't met a better man. He always tried to see good in people, he was always positive in that sense, and he was genuine about the concept of the brotherhood of man – and it influenced me beyond measure.'[16]

The affection they shared was expressed not only through mutual devotion, and companionship, but also through hugging and kissing. Hawke was always intensely physical, and his need to touch and feel – colleagues, friends, voters, people he had only just met – stemmed from this father/son bonding.

Edith Emily Lee, known as 'Ellie', was born on 1 October 1897 in Green's Plains, on the Yorke Peninsula, South Australia.[17] Her father, the devout Methodist William 'Will' Lee, was a barley and wheat farmer born on 22 February 1859 at Burra, South Australia. Will was also a lay preacher who evangelised with the unshakable rage of the revivalism of that era. Ellie's mother, Matilda Broster, was born on 28 December 1861 at Peachey Belt, South Australia. Ellie had a sister, Lila. Ellie and Lila's grandparents were born in England. The Lees lived an exacting life governed by strict morals and rigid routines at 11 Ashley Street, Torrensville. Ellie graduated high school and teachers' college, and taught at several schools. She also taught Sunday School in Houghton, where Clem ministered when they were married, and at other Congregational churches.

Ellie encouraged Bob to be disciplined, hardworking and focused on whatever task lay ahead of him. Hawke described his mother as 'a woman of passionate commitments'. She profoundly believed in the value and importance of education, and held the view, based on deep religious conviction, that every person had a duty to maximise their talents.[18] 'She was a teacher,' Hawke recalled. 'She was way ahead of her time. She was a woman's liberationist. I remember Dad had a church out in the country in South Australia, Yorke Peninsula, and Mum used to berate the farmers, really knock their ears off, because they would save money to send their sons to college in Adelaide, not their daughters. So these values of equality were very much a part of my upbringing.'[19]

Clem and Ellie met in Forster in 1919. It was a whirlwind courtship. The two families were markedly different. The Lees had known poverty but were now wealthy, unlike the Hawkes. The Lees were politically conservative, whereas the Hawkes were staunchly Labor. Their impending nuptials were announced in a family notice published in *The Chronicle* on Saturday, 22 May 1920. They were to be married at the Thebarton Methodist Church, in Adelaide, at 7 pm on 2 June 1920.[20] Relatives and friends were invited to the ceremony but were advised there would be no reception.[21] Clem's best man was his brother, Albert Hawke. Ellie's bridesmaid was her cousin Lily Lee.

Clem and Ellie settled at the manse in Houghton and had a happy home and community life. The Hawkes moved to New Zealand for several years, living at Trinity House, Lower Hutt, near Wellington. Clem took up a ministry at the Trinity Congregational Church. When Ellie's father, Will, became ill in mid-1924, they decided to return home. A ministry was organised for Clem at Renmark in South Australia. Sadly, Ellie's father died before their return to Australia.

The Hawkes lived in a church manse at Renmark, close to the Murray River, and enjoyed taking picnics, swimming and playing tennis. Clem also played and umpired Australian Rules football and joined the local Masonic lodge. Ellie formed a Girl Guides group and Neil became friendly with boys of a similar age who lived next door. The Congregational church had given the Hawkes use of a Model-T Ford to travel to Murthoo Park and Renmark West for services.

In 1928, the Hawkes moved to Bordertown, where Clem was to run the local Congregational church. They took occupancy of the manse at 63 Farquhar Street, at the top of the hill. It was a comfortable home that had been originally constructed by the National Bank in 1884. The limestone building was purchased by the Congregational Church, to be used as a manse, for £420 in 1897. Clem used the front room as an office and meeting room for parishioners. An extension provided for a kitchen, bathroom and laundry at the rear. There was a small backyard. Along one side of the house was vine that produced white crystal grapes. Across the road were bowling and croquet greens, and tennis courts.

Clem focused on growing the church, located a short walk from the manse on Benjamin and Binnie Streets, which had opened in January 1880. The Congregational church had first been established in Bordertown in May 1874, with services first held in the local schoolroom on the corner of South Terrace and Binnie Street. Improvements were made to the church and an adjoining church hall was built in 1926 – the first in Bordertown. He conducted services, administered the sacraments and offered pastoral care to the community. A Chevrolet supplied by the church enabled Clem to provide services at nearby towns, and also at an Aboriginal reserve two miles out of Bordertown.

To relax, Clem played cricket and Australian Rules football. He joined the Masonic Lodge. Ellie also settled into Bordertown. She had taken time out from teaching when Neil was born and returned to it in Renmark, but she had retired by the time Bobby was born. (She would later return to full-time teaching when the family moved to West Leederville.) She was a leader with the Girl Guides, joined the Women's Guild and played croquet with other women in town. Ellie also taught Sunday School, offered lessons on sewing, organised the children's choir, served on church welfare committees and helped run the Bible Society.

Bordertown was established in the Tatiara district of South Australia in 1852. The location adjacent to the Tatiara Creek had been used as a terminus by Police Inspector Alexander Tolmer, who led the police escort to transport gold mined at Mount Alexander back to Adelaide. There were eighteen successful gold exports between 10 February 1852 and 21 December 1853. The Indigenous people of the region had known this land of creeks, swamps, forests and grasslands for thousands of years, and called it Tatiara, which meant 'good country'.

By the time the Hawkes arrived, the population was around a thousand. There were a few stores, several hotels and a post office. The Congregational church enjoyed the largest attendance at services and social gatherings. The town was thriving, and had a vibrant social life. A railway connected Bordertown to Adelaide. Bordertown was in the centre of a flourishing agricultural district with wheatfields and sheep farms nearby, and plentiful supplies of watermelons, potatoes, onions, cucumbers, tomatoes and marrows.

But within a few years, by 1931, Bordertown was feeling the impact of the Depression as prices dropped, businesses went bankrupt and jobs were lost.

It was not an ideal time to bring a new baby into the world, but the Hawkes were spared the worst effects of the Depression because Clem earned a modest allowance as a minister and lived in the church-owned manse. It is likely the Hawkes also received financial assistance in order to send Neil to boarding school. In Bordertown, Clem, Ellie and Bobby lived a comfortable middle-class existence. Clem and Ellie did not drink or smoke. They lived frugally. Ellie cooked, cleaned and made clothes. Hawke was not, however, shielded from the impact of the Depression. The church's charitable outreach increased, and Ellie made food and clothing for those in difficult circumstances. Those out of work always received a meal if they asked at the Hawke house. And Clem and Ellie loaned money when they could, knowing it might not be repaid.

I visited Bordertown in January 2019. The locals remembered their parents and grandparents telling stories about how Hawke was a chubby and fair-haired toddler who was outgoing, lively and mischievous. In church, he played up, and his parents did little to discipline him. He was popular with neighbours and friends. Clem recalled in his memoir: 'During his childhood days Bob was never without admirers, whether they were men, women or boys and girls. Mrs Hawke had plenty of offers to help from older girls to take Bob out in his little carriage, or to play games with him on the lawn.'[22] In 2019, Prime Minister Scott Morrison announced that the Australian government would provide $750,000 to purchase Hawke's Bordertown home to protect its heritage value and to 'commemorate his life and achievements'.[23]

Hawke often went with his father to visit parishioners at their homes in town or on their farms, and participated in civic events. He was known for standing on a chair and preaching pretend sermons. Visitors to the family home on Farquhar Street recalled seeing him playing with his toys and frequently interrupting with questions and comments. He felt separation anxiety when Clem travelled interstate. 'Bob and I had some sort of special affinity,' Clem recalled. Once, when Clem travelled to Melbourne, Ellie wrote him a letter and mentioned how Bobby was missing his father.

He had told his mother to ask his father to come home immediately, as 'it is terrible without him'.[24]

Ellie believed that idleness was a sin and committed herself to a life of unremitting activity. Whether it was sport or craft or teaching, Ellie was energetic, focused and competitive. These were characteristics that her son would absorb. But what mattered most to her was her faith and her morals, and in this her son did not always follow instruction. Ellie was a prominent member of the Women's Christian Temperance Union. She believed alcohol was evil and campaigned to eradicate it from society. She lectured friends, family, parishioners and even those whom she had just met. She enlisted Neil and Bobby into its youth wing, Band of Hope. Hawke kept his membership certificate for the Loyal Temperance Legion of Australasia. 'Trusting in God's help, I solemnly promise to abstain from any food or drink containing alcohol,' Hawke had pledged on 27 October 1939, when he was nine.[25]

Ellie took her sons to meetings, had them campaign with her and entered them into competitions. Before his tenth birthday, Hawke wrote an essay explaining the emblem for the Independent Order of Rechabites, an organisation that was part of the temperance movement:

> The sun represents light and energy . . .
> The eye on the emblem represents the eye of God . . .
> The hive represents industry and thrift . . .
> The cord represents strength and unity . . .
> The lamb represents purity and innocence . . .
> The Ark is a symbol of safety . . .
> The rainbow represents the promise God made . . .
> The sheaf of wheat is a symbol of plenty . . .
> The serpent represents evil cunning and deceit, and it has been placed on the emblem to warn us to beware of strong drink . . .
> The lifeboat is used to save the lives of those who may be endangered . . .
> The shield was a weapon of defence . . . this reminds us that we are fighting the drink . . .
> Today we are called upon to kill the dragon drink.[26]

While Hawke believed that his mother was far too dogmatic about alcohol, and he struggled to see it as the work of Satan on earth, he lived an idyllic life, surrounded by love and affection, constantly told that he was special, happy and not wanting for anything, and the family did not suffer the shafts of fate that others did in the Depression era.

2

SON OF
THE MANSE

In 1935, the Hawke family moved to Maitland, on the Yorke Peninsula, where Ellie had been born, and where young Bobby – or Bob, as he was now known – commenced his schooling. Clem had been called to minister the local Congregational church. The Hawkes purchased their first car, made possible with Clem's allowance. They lived a relaxed and happy middle-class lifestyle. Tennis courts were attached to the manse and they played against Catholic and Lutheran groups in and around Maitland. Bob, aged five, was excited about the move. Clem and Ellie gave him a small black-and-white fox terrier to make sure he had at least one friend in Maitland. They went everywhere together. Bob was devastated when the dog was run over by a car and was too distraught to go to school.

Bob did not grow up surrounded by extended family. Neil was at boarding school during much of Bob's youth. This had the effect of making Clem, Ellie and Bob especially close. His paternal grandfather, James Hawke, had died on 13 September 1930. He did, however, get to know his paternal grandmother, Elizabeth Hawke, who lived until 27 December 1945. His maternal grandfather, Will Lee, had died on 22 August 1924. His maternal grandmother, Matilda Lee (nee Broster), lived until 18 February 1939. What they did not have in close family they made up for with close community. Hawke recalled being very happy in Maitland. He loved animals, and in May 1939 became a member of the junior branch of the Royal Society for the Prevention of Cruelty to Animals (RSPCA).[1]

Bob enrolled at Maitland Primary School on 4 February 1935.[2] He was a bright student and made an immediate impact because he had already been taught to read by Ellie. The headmaster was known to Clem, as they had been at school together in Kapunda. The headmaster also had a daughter at the school, and a friendly rivalry grew between her and Bob. He was not a particularly studious or dedicated pupil. He was easily distracted and often involved in playground brawls. He was not popular and struggled to make friends. He did not need to, because he had Clem.

Clem and Ellie were too forgiving of Bob. They spoiled him. In a 1978 interview, Clem and Ellie said they never smacked their son. Any disobedient behaviour was resolved by discussion. 'We never used to hit Bob – he was never a difficult child,' said Ellie. She insisted that you have to be firm but reasonable with children and listen to their viewpoints. Clem agreed. 'Bob was never very difficult as a child,' he recalled. 'I don't think we ever had to correct him once.'[3] This was more family mythology.

It is not surprising that Bob was remembered by others as 'a terrible kid'.[4] He was often naughty, but in a cheeky way, which made it tolerable. Hawke's report card for 1937 contained a warning: 'Bob is capable of very good work and would have obtained higher marks but for carelessness.' It worked. By the end of the year, he had gone from third in the class to first and achieved a combined result for reading, writing, spelling, composition and arithmetic of 59 out of 60 marks. 'Bob has done excellent work this term and has improved in all subjects,' wrote his teacher.[5]

In reflecting on his few years living in Maitland, Hawke recalled visiting farms with his father and going to church services and Sunday School. Although he was an energetic and mischievous child, he also learnt from his father how to listen to people, understand and empathise with them, and have them know that he cared. Growing up in a rural community also prompted Hawke, as a child, to think about becoming a farmer when he grew up. But this was hard, backbreaking work outdoors, in the heat and the elements. 'One day I saw them out there in the blazing heat and I abandoned the idea,' he remembered.[6]

In the few years they lived on the Yorke Peninsula, Hawke briefly enrolled in another school, which seems to have escaped his memory in later years. It is not mentioned in his memoir or by previous biographers. According to admission records, Hawke transferred to the remote Tiparra West School on 7 April 1936.[7] In recalling his time at Maitland, years later, Hawke vaguely recollected being briefly enrolled in another school. 'I remember staying on farms and enjoying it,' Hawke said. 'Once Mum and Dad went on a long car trip to the eastern states with a couple of people who were in the church, and for that period I lived out on a farm and went to a tiny little school. I thought that was marvellous, and they were happy, happy days.'[8] The government-run Tiparra West school, which had an average attendance of just fourteen students, closed at the end of 1938.

Clem and Ellie received letters from Neil while he was boarding at King's College in Adelaide. They were both immensely proud of his achievements, and shared this with Bob. But Neil remained somewhat of a mystery to his younger brother. 'It would be fantasising to pretend some close relationship because in the nature of things it couldn't exist,' Hawke recalled. 'But I loved seeing him when he was home and we had a good relationship.'[9]

By his late teens, Neil was six feet tall, with an athletic build and a handsome face. He was an intelligent and sensitive young man, and a keen swimmer, tennis player and cyclist. Clem and Ellie envisioned a bright future. For Ellie, especially, her hopes and dreams were invested in Neil. He could do no wrong in her eyes. Neil had done exceptionally well at school and was awarded a number of merits and distinctions. He had his sights set on joining the public service. After he completed his schooling, obtaining the leaving certificate, he worked as a junior clerk in the Chief Secretary's Office in Adelaide.[10]

In the summer of 1938–39, Australia sweltered through a heatwave. To escape the heat, Neil went swimming at Unley Crystal Pool in Adelaide. Swimming was one of his favourite pastimes. Neil contracted meningitis at the pool and quickly became sick. Ellie's mother had died on 18 February. At her funeral in Adelaide, Neil looked unwell and was reserved. Two days later, after Clem and Ellie returned to Maitland, they received a call to tell them Neil had been rushed to hospital with fever. Clem hurried to Adelaide, and Ellie followed.

Neil deteriorated and life drained from his body. Clem and Ellie prayed at his bedside, hoping that he would be spared by God. Their faith would not be rewarded. Neil died on 27 February 1939, just days before his eighteenth birthday.[11] He was buried at Mitcham General Cemetery in South Australia. Hawke did not attend the funeral or visit the gravesite – which today is run-down and neglected – and never did in later life. A notice was placed in *The Advertiser*: 'HAWKE – On the 27th of February at private hospital John Neil dearly beloved elder son of Rev C A and Mrs Hawke, Congregational Manse, Maitland, aged 18 years [sic].' The Hawkes quoted Ecclesiastes 12:6, signifying that his spirit has returned to God: 'The golden bowl is broken.'[12]

Neil's death had the effect of intensifying Clem and Ellie's love for Bob, who was nine years old. Bob now became the centre of their affections. But the pain of losing Neil never left them. They did not show any outward emotion; they grieved inside. Ellie's deepening devotion to Bob could be overwhelming. Clem asked Bob to be patient and tolerant with his mother. 'Now, son,' he said. 'Some of the great love that you give to me, you have got to see that your mother gets some of it now.'[13]

In November 1939, the grieving family moved to West Leederville, in Perth. The bustling working-class industrial suburb, established in the 1890s, was located in the north-west of the city. They remained terribly upset; as Clem recalled, 'we did not seem to be able to settle down' after Neil's death. Their prayers to save Neil's life had not been answered. It was a time of soul-searching. 'Poor Neil,' Bob would say to his parents again and again.[14] When Clem was asked to take over the Congregational church at Leederville, it was thought the new home, church and neighbourhood might provide some relief from the anguish.

The Hawkes travelled on the express train to Perth to make a new start. For young Bob, the ride was thrilling. It was his first visit to Perth, a thriving city, and he was excited about the next phase of their lives. He peered out the window and spotted kangaroos and emus, rabbits and birds. When the train would stop during the day to take on board supplies, local Indigenous people would line up seeking food and to sell things they had made, such as boomerangs. Bob desperately wanted a boomerang and they indulged him.

On the journey, Clem and Ellie had second thoughts about moving to Perth. They only knew a few people in the west, including Albert Hawke, then a parliamentarian, and some other family and church friends. But they made the right decision. 'There is a divinity that shapes our ends,' Clem quoted from William Shakespeare's *Hamlet*. 'Rough hew them how we will.'[15]

The family moved into a five-room redbrick home at 101 Tate Street. The suburban cottage had an open verandah at the front and an enclosed one at the back, front and back gardens, and small trees. The front door had a stained-glass window with kookaburras inset and a porthole window that looked into the hall. The house on the rise had been vacant for some time, as it was owned by a widow who had moved out to live with her son. The Hawkes rented the house for twelve months and then persuaded the widow to sell it to them. (The church had not provided a rent-free manse.) Clem lived in the house until 1981. In 2020, Western Australia's premier, Mark McGowan, announced that his government had purchased the house for $1.45 million and would maintain it as a state asset, given its heritage value.[16]

The Hawkes soon adjusted to a happy life in Perth. Clem and Ellie ran boys' and girls' clubs attached to the church, and Ellie taught Sunday School. Hawke enrolled at West Leederville State School, located on Northwood Street, on 21 November 1939. He would spend just over two years there. He excelled at school and enjoyed it. His report card at the end of 1940 saw him pass every subject with 'consistently good' effort. Bob's teacher noted that his conduct was good, but he 'talks rather much'.[17] His growing self-confidence was, in part, a result of his parents' devotion to him. By age ten, Bob began to entertain the idea that he might be prime minister one day, without really knowing what it meant. His confidence was also a product of his own success: he did well academically, was a skilled sportsman and was popular with other students.

Hawke had fond recollections of his time at West Leederville. In 1988, on the occasion of the school's ninetieth birthday, he wrote that he had 'mostly happy memories' of his time there from 1939 to 1941. He recalled playing cricket 'with great vigor on a concrete pitch in the school yard'. One thing, years later, still puzzled him. Students who failed to demonstrate decipherable handwriting were given several cuts of the cane on their writing hand. To Hawke's young mind, this was 'not well calculated to improve one's physical capacity for better writing'. He had expressed this view to the teacher as the punishment was being delivered to him. Hawke thought he won the intellectual argument but not the battle, and received a further six lashings.[18]

On 2 January 1941, Clem Hawke went to the Swan Barracks in Perth to enlist in the Australian Army as a chaplain. He was forty-two years old, married with a young son and listed his occupation as 'Minister of Religion'. He was sent to the Army camp at Northam, where he would serve for eighteen months. Clem led church services, administered sacraments and provided counselling services to soldiers. It meant living away from the family. 'This was exciting and traumatic,' Hawke recalled. 'He was both my father and my best friend, and I remember my yearning expectation as I hung over the fence waiting for him to come home on leave.'[19] When Bob saw Clem arriving home, he would 'race down the street' and they would 'embrace one another'.[20] Hawke, though only eleven years old, vividly remembered Australia during World War II and the image of his father in uniform. Sand trenches had been dug around the primary school. During Clem's more than three years of war service in Australia, he attained the rank of captain.[21]

Clem's absence was difficult for both Bob and Ellie. They did not enjoy the comforts they had in Maitland or Bordertown. Clem was now earning more than he had as a minister, but it was still a meagre wage. The wife of a Methodist minister and her son moved into the Hawke home on Tate Street to share the rent; her husband was also in the Army. Ellie was still distraught over Neil, and Bob could still test her patience with his naughtiness. But Ellie, as ever, was busy. She remained active in the Women's Christian Temperance Union, assisted with local church activities and volunteered her time at a refuge for girls. Ellie also returned to teaching in July 1944 to help pay the bills and fund Bob's education. She would continue to teach at various schools until her retirement in December 1961.[22]

Clem, though missing Ellie and Bob, found being an Army chaplain immensely rewarding. He dined with the soldiers, played table tennis and cards, marched and trained with them. He even enjoyed the odd beer. (He drank beer occasionally after the war, which horrified Ellie.) 'Theological colleges are necessary for a clergyman's education but valuable lessons were learned in military camps where chaplains rubbed shoulders with splendid men of all ranks, classes, creeds and conditions,' he wrote.[23] A pipe band would lead a parade before Sunday services in the YMCA hall. He presented each soldier with a Bible before they left for overseas service. In mid-1942, Clem was transferred to an Army convalescent camp outside Fremantle. He also briefly ministered at an Army camp near the Swan River before being transferred to the Artillery Barracks at Fremantle.

In the final year of the war, and after, Clem assisted at several Congregational churches in Cottesloe, East Cannington, Kenwick and Queen's Park. His Leederville parish had been allocated to another minister. Post-war, Clem often travelled interstate to fill in for other ministers who had left the parish or were on leave. On one occasion, in 1947, when Clem went to Melbourne to preach for a fortnight, Bob was so distraught that he begged his mother to send him a telegram saying that he was missed at home. In 1948, Clem became the dedicated minister at the Subiaco Congregational Church, and remained in that role for the next twenty-five years. He also took on a wider leadership role, and was twice elected president of the state body. Clem also increased his involvement in Freemasonry and became Grand Chaplain of the Grand Lodge of Western Australia. The church in Subiaco had a large hall and caretaker's cottage, and also a large tennis court, where Bob played regularly. Clem also served as chaplain at the Hollywood Repatriation General Hospital in Perth for twenty-four years.

In addition to Clem and Ellie, there was another significant figure in Bob's life: his uncle. 'Albert was a big influence on me,' Hawke recalled. 'He was the leader of the Labor Party in Western Australia and became premier. He represented the country seat of Northam but had a flat in the city. He used to come to our place at least once a week for dinner and we would play bridge together – Dad, Mum and myself.'[24] Albert was a fatherly figure to young Bob. With Clem often away ministering, Albert would look in on his nephew. Bob also gained a political education from Albert, who took him to Parliament House to watch proceedings and introduced him to politicians. He became a mentor.

Albert Hawke was two and a half years younger than Clem, born on 3 December 1900 at Kapunda. Albert, known as Bert, won election to the South Australian House of Assembly in April 1924. When he lost his seat of Burra Burra three years later, he worked as a country organiser for the Labor Party. He was elected to Western Australia's Legislative Assembly in April 1933, defeating the premier, James Mitchell, in the seat of Northam. Albert served as a minister in various portfolios. He became opposition leader in July 1951 and led Labor to victory in February 1953. Hawke's was a socially progressive and reformist government, but he often had difficult relations with business. He served as premier until April 1959, when the Labor government was defeated at an election. Hawke continued as opposition leader until December 1966, and exited parliament two years later.

Bob Hawke was reared at a time when children were discouraged, even forbidden, from talking freely about issues with their parents. But this was not the case in the Hawke household. Clem and Ellie encouraged his thinking, exposed him to new ideas and welcomed debates about contemporary issues around the dinner table. When Albert visited, it was an opportunity to discuss politics vigorously, but with respect for differing opinions. Hawke recalled how this approach influenced him:

> I was always encouraged as a child to have my say. I was never
> conscious of any feeling that I was to be seen and not heard.
> I was encouraged to read and to discuss what I read. I was
> encouraged to read newspapers and to understand what was
> happening. That fact, of itself, was important.[25]

Hawke greatly admired wartime prime minister John Curtin. 'I'm not a bloke for heroes,' he said. 'But there is no doubt that Curtin was a hero of mine. We had in common that we both used to drink too much and gave it up. He brought the country together at a time of war, our greatest challenge. What I admired particularly was he wasn't intending to fight that war to restore the Australia of the past; he wanted a new and better Australia.'[26]

Uncle Albert had once introduced Bob to Curtin at a meeting at the Trades Hall in Perth in the early 1940s. It is also likely he saw Curtin speak on 16 August 1943, during the election campaign, at the Leederville Town Hall. This was a fifteen-minute walk from the Hawke home on Tate Street. When Curtin died on 5 July 1945, Albert was approached to stand in his seat of Fremantle, but declined. His nephew thought he may have missed his opportunity to become prime minister.[27]

In his final year at primary school, Hawke sat the statewide examination in the hope of winning a scholarship to the elite, selective and coeducational Perth Modern School. Established in 1909, this was the first public secondary school in Western Australia, and it considerably outperformed fee-paying private schools academically. Its motto was 'Knowledge Is Power', and its emblem was the sphinx, representing knowledge.[28] 'Mod', as it was known, offered entry via examination to 100 students, boys or girls, with half awarded full scholarships and the other half offered entrances. If Hawke was to win a scholarship, he would need a new level of focus and discipline, and with Clem away serving as an Army chaplain, it fell to Ellie to enforce this. Hawke duly won a place among the top fifty students and secured a scholarship.

He enrolled at Perth Modern on 10 February 1942, but his effort and attention did not last. He looked back on his time at the school as wasted years. 'I got good results without working very hard,' Hawke recalled.[29] 'I was just enjoying myself and loved my cricket.'[30]

It was wartime, and the school grounds were dotted with air-raid shelters. Sirens would blare and students would scramble into the trenches dug around the school grounds. During the drills, while they were hiding, it was an opportunity to play around. In the classroom, discipline was firmly enforced by the teaching staff. Hawke found the headmaster, Noel Sampson, to be rigid and stern, and 'not a very likeable person'. While he lacked focus and dedication, Hawke enjoyed French, History and Latin. In later years, he regarded Latin as 'the single most important' influence on his life from his time at Perth Modern. 'It really gave me a pattern of thought and expression,' he said.[31]

Among Hawke's contemporaries at Perth Modern were the future Liberal leader Billy Snedden, Treasury secretary John Stone, Whitlam-era minister Joe Berinson, Labor senator John Wheeldon, businessman Lloyd Zampatti, Olympic athlete and judge Alan Barblett, chief scientist Ralph Slatyer, entertainer Rolf Harris and journalist Maxwell Newton. Hawke participated in speech and debating competitions, which he enjoyed immensely. He also joined the cadet corps, but that held little appeal. And he played, and obsessively watched, cricket and tennis. Hawke made the First XI cricket team in his final two years at Perth Modern. Stone recalled that Hawke was a good wicketkeeper and 'a quite dashing batsman' – and that Hawke would often sneak off 'to have a fag behind the Quartermasters Store' during cadet corps.[32]

Above all, Hawke wanted to enjoy himself at Perth Modern. Accordingly, he liked to flirt with girls. Hawke also gained a reputation for being mischievous, and was involved in playground fistfights. He had several clashes with Sampson, who would punish students for bad behaviour by making them stand silent outside his office for hours. Hawke came close to being expelled in his third year. During an experiment in Chemistry, the teacher left the room to have a cigarette and Hawke blew out the Bunsen burner. The teacher was furious that the experiment was ruined and asked who did it. Hawke fessed up. 'I got taken up to the headmaster, Sampson, who at the best of times had no sense of humour,' he recalled. There was no punishment; Hawke was to be expelled. Clem, at Northam Army Camp at the time, pleaded Hawke's case and the boy was 'given a reprieve'.[33]

Hawke's Student Admission Card for Perth Modern, which recorded his academic progress and behaviour, shows a young man who had academic promise but was easily distracted, disorderly and disrespectful. '[He] is expected to do very well when he settles down to regular concentration,' a teacher wrote in April 1942. His first-year results were 'patchy' and 'below average', and teachers doubted whether he was 'ready enough' for high school. 'Results unsatisfactory – seems irresponsible re his progress [and] inclined to be a nuisance in class – cannot be tolerated – jeopardising his school,' it was reported in August 1943. Hawke passed the year but was subject to 'a number of warnings concerning his conduct'. The next year saw little improvement in behaviour: Hawke had 'a tendency to unsteadiness in class', it was noted in April 1944. He arrived at class one day with a moustache drawn on his face. He was occasionally late to school and did not wear the correct 'attire'. One teacher noted that he was 'anxious to distract others from their work'. By fourth year, there was little change. 'Robert's mediocre results are not to his credit,' it was reported in April 1945. 'He lacks the steady serious application indispensable for his future success.' He was caught 'throwing orange peel' during recess. By the end of that year and through 1946, however, there was some improvement in his conduct, and his work was reported as being 'sound'.[34]

The student magazine, *The Sphinx*, published twice a year, included a gossipy poem titled 'Corridor Chatter'. Hawke made repeat appearances. His flirtations with women were notorious. The November 1945 edition included this sexist line: 'THEY SAY . . . That when Pauline's not Howell-ing she's Hawk-ing.'[35] In November 1946: 'THEY SAY . . . That Joan is fonder of hunting and Hawking than doing Maths.'[36] Several of Hawke's teachers did not think he would amount to much. But the headmaster, Sampson, saw promise in him. 'He has good ability and has made progress with his studies,' he wrote in a reference to support Hawke's application for university. 'He is trustworthy, anxious to succeed and of good moral character.'[37]

Despite his larrikin ways, Hawke was an above-average student at Perth Modern, and performed well in most subjects. For his Junior Certificate, he passed English, Latin, French, History, Geography, Arithmetic and Algebra, Geography and Trigonometry, Chemistry and Drawing B. The results were recorded in *The West Australian*, along with those of 3301 other students, on 16 January 1945.[38] He did not like Chemistry, evidently, and it confirmed in his mind that becoming a doctor was not a realistic aspiration. Hawke matriculated at the end of 1946. He had studied English, Latin, French, History, Mathematics, Industrial History and Economics, and Art of Speech for the Leaving Certificate. The results of the examinations were published on 9 January 1947.

He gained distinctions in three subjects: History, Industrial History and Economics, and Art of Speech.[39]

While at Perth Modern, Ellie decided that Bob needed to improve his elocution. She was appalled by his rough speech, gravelly tones and high pitch, and thought it needed to be smoothed out. Legend has it that she recorded his speech and played it back to him. 'Do I really sound like that?' he asked. 'Yes, you do,' she replied. This was why he enrolled in Art of Speech for the Leaving Certificate. It was not just that the sound of his speech needed elevating, but succeeding in public life required the gift of the gab. Hawke learnt rhetorical techniques but this made little difference to his delivery, and his speech remained far from polished. When Bob phoned Ellie from Oxford University years later, things had not improved. 'You sound as bad as you ever did,' she told him.[40] And it was no better when he returned to Australia. When he got off the ship at Fremantle, Ellie said: 'Oh Bob, you don't sound any different from when you went away.'[41]

For much of his youth, Hawke was thin and gaunt, and under-sized for his age. His parents hoped that the move to Maitland, on the coast, might be a more agreeable climate. But his health got worse. It did not improve when the family moved to West Leederville. Hawke was often unwell at Perth Modern, and had to take time off because of colds, headaches and flu. His shirts were loose and his pants were held up by a belt. A tousle of hair atop a thin face made him look especially underdeveloped. In 1944, Ellie made an appointment for him to see a naturopath. A high-fibre diet with plenty of meat, eggs, milk and cheese was recommended. Hawke gained considerable strength quickly, his health improved and he felt much better.

Family legend has it that this change gave Hawke his distinctive thick, curly mane of hair. It certainly gave him more confidence, not that he needed it. Ellie had long been telling people that her son would be prime minister one day. In his final years at Perth Modern, Hawke often told people he would be prime minister too.

3

ROGUE SCHOLAR

After graduating from Perth Modern, Bob Hawke began his tertiary studies at the University of Western Australia in 1947. He had long given up the thought of farming and had decided against becoming a doctor. (He had initially nominated studying medicine.) In the end, he decided on humanities rather than a science-based degree. 'I wasn't sure what I wanted to do,' Hawke recalled. 'So I thought that I would do law, not with any intention necessarily of practising, but I thought it would provide a good foundation for anything else.'[1]

This was a time of awakening. 'I felt a liberated young man,' he said. 'The regimented authoritarianism of school gave way to the idea that, within certain obvious limits, one was free and expected to run one's own race.'[2] When Hawke arrived on campus at age seventeen, he was energetic, self-assured, arrogant and aloof. 'I was obnoxious in many ways,' he reflected. 'I was self-confident, and that can come out as brashness.'[3] Yet he could also be highly engaging, a good conversationalist and charming. It was his personality rather than his appearance that made him attractive to others. He was still thin, though developing, with green-blue eyes, dark curly hair and soft olive skin. With adults, he knew how to be courteous and respectful, the product of church teachings and the civic learnings of his parents. He was always presentable, wearing shorts or pants with a buttoned-up shirt, blazer and leather shoes. But there was still an immaturity about him, and he lacked focus. This would soon change: these would be years of transformation.

Hawke persuaded his parents to permit him to buy a second-hand 1939 British Panther Model 100 motorbike so he could travel to and from university quickly and directly, rather than rely on public transport. Ellie, ever mindful of Neil's death, reluctantly agreed. On Monday, 11 August 1947, during the university vacation, Hawke rode his bike to the Law Library. After studying for some time, he did not feel well and decided to go to the refectory. There, he had a cup of tea and gulped down a few aspirins before returning home. While riding at high speed through Kings Park, and pushing his bike to the limit, he blacked out and crashed.

Hawke lay in bushland bruised, bleeding and in excruciating pain. A portable metal bike stand tucked inside his windcheater had ruptured his spleen. Hawke was spotted by an off-duty police officer driving through the park. He rushed Hawke to Royal Perth Hospital. He was bleeding, in agony, and fading in and out of consciousness. An operation was conducted the next morning to remove his spleen. He remained on the critical list for several days, and in hospital for three weeks. The crash was reported in local newspapers.[4]

For Clem and Ellie, this was their nightmare. Neil had died at age seventeen. Now Bob, also seventeen, might be taken from them. They prayed day after day, at home, at church and at his hospital bedside. This time, their prayers were answered. Hawke's recovery was confirmation to Ellie of divine providence: her son's life had been saved so that he could one day lead the nation.

Hawke too felt his life had been saved for a reason. The feeling had not yet crystallised into a specific purpose, but he nevertheless decided he would make the most of his life. He had cheated death. It was a seminal moment. Hawke was now driven to fulfil Ellie's ambition by making it his own.

His law studies were interrupted by the motorbike accident, but he only asked for one exam to be postponed. In November 1947 he sat the annual examinations for Constitutional Law, English and Philosophy. He received a Pass B, Pass B and Pass C, respectively. In February 1948, the deferred examination for Legal History took place and he was awarded a Pass C. These were not stellar results. But in the annual examinations held in November 1948, November 1949 and November 1950, Hawke received either a Pass A (known as a distinction) or a Pass B for all subjects. The accident had pushed him to become a better student.

In April 2019, just a month before his death, Hawke recalled how, having pleaded with his parents to allow him to buy the motorbike, after the accident he was overcome with guilt. 'I was well aware of the anguish my parents were going through,' he said. While lying in his hospital bed, Hawke had a moment of clarity that he would never forget. 'In my hazy consciousness, I made a pledge to myself that if I fully recovered, I would repay their prayers for my life to be spared by not wasting my life, but devoting myself to living a life to the full extent of my abilities.'[5]

The crash was so traumatic that Hawke sold the bike a few months after he left the hospital. Many years later, the bike found its way to Bendigo, and was purchased in the mid-1980s at a swap-meet by Peter Matthews for $1500. It was displayed in a museum in Dromana, south of Melbourne, and then sat unused in a garage, where it deteriorated. Tatiara District Council, which includes Bordertown, purchased the bike for $12,000 and paid for it to be restored. It is now on display at the Bob Hawke Gallery in Bordertown.[6]

In his third year at UWA, Hawke won the John Norman Baker Prize for Law, awarded to the best student. He received £3/5/8 – around $580 in relative labour earnings in 2021. Hawke graduated with a Bachelor of Laws (Second Class Honours) on 29 March 1951, having completed the degree the previous year. To graduate with First Class Honours, he needed distinctions in all five subjects in his fourth year, but he got four distinctions (Pass A) and a pass (Pass B). As a student, Hawke did not have a regular study routine; instead, he thrived under pressure, when his back was against the wall and time was running out. It was the thrill, the added danger, the risk that sustained him – and it usually paid off. His main competitor for top honours in Law was his friend John Toohey, a future High Court judge, who received distinctions in all final-year subjects and graduated with First Class Honours.

Hawke enjoyed wider university life. He joined the Student Christian Movement and became state president of the Congregational Youth Fellowship. He joined the Labor Party (Western Australia Branch) on 14 April 1947. On campus, he became active in the Labor Club, but he soon left, uncomfortable with its communist sympathies. In his second year Hawke helped to form the ALP Club and became its foundation president. He also began to involve himself in statewide party affairs and became a delegate to the party's state conference. He played first-grade cricket for UWA, along with hockey and baseball, for which he won a half-blue in 1948.[7] That same year, Hawke saw Don Bradman's Invincibles pass through Fremantle on their way to England.

The Hawke family lived a simple life without extravagance, and prized the virtue of thrift. Hawke received the Hackett Bursary while at university, which was enough to pay his fees. Hawke's applications for the endowment reveal that Clem and Ellie earned a modest income. In 1947, Clem earned £362, while Ellie earned £216. By 1950, Clem's income was £350, while Ellie earned £304.[8] In 2021 value, using a relative labour earnings measure, this represents a family income of around $106,000 per annum.

After finishing his law degree, Hawke began working in 1951 for the Socony-Vacuum Oil Company (now ExxonMobil) as a trainee executive. Further study remained on his mind – he was still enrolled in two subjects part-time towards his Bachelor of Arts – but he was also enjoying earning some money of his own. After about six months, Hawke realised that working full-time was not for him, and quit the oil business. He felt he had more to achieve at university, and focused on completing his Arts degree.

Hawke had decided not to be a lawyer. He saw it as a pretentious profession, and could not imagine arguing a case he did not believe in. Hawke would now major in Economics, seeing it as a more useful qualification. Recommencing full-time studies in 1952, he had two things in mind: winning election as president of the student body, and securing a Rhodes Scholarship.

In September–October 1950, Hawke stood for president of the Guild of Undergraduates (Student Representative Council). Hawke ran against his friend Alan Barblett and John Stone – both also Perth Modernians.[9] In the campaign, Hawke downplayed his Labor links, noting that his nomination was seconded by John Knight, the secretary of the Liberal Club, as well as Frank Malone, the secretary of the ALP Club. He argued that he had been elected Societies Council President and was a member of the

Guild for 1950. He had been a member of the dance committee for the graduation ball. And he was a leader in the Student Christian Movement. In making his pitch to diverse groups on campus – Labor, Liberal and Christian – Hawke expected to win. He made speeches, approached students directly and distributed campaign literature. Stone, academically brilliant and a standout student leader and sportsman, took a more modest approach: he recalled making only one short address to students.[10] Stone's nomination was proposed by Maxwell Newton. When the votes were counted, Stone had won with an absolute majority.[11] Hawke was runner-up and became Guild Vice-President. They would serve during 1951.

When Stone departed for Oxford on a Rhodes Scholarship in August 1951, Hawke became Acting Guild President.[12] In September–October 1951, Hawke again ran for the presidency of the Guild. His opponent was a fellow Christian and sportsman, Bob Leschen. This time, Hawke pulled out all stops to win, and defeated Leschen by 445 to 377 votes. He would serve during 1952 as the Guild's thirty-ninth president, with Barblett as vice-president. The Guild's journal, *The Pelican*, headlined its 5 October 1951 edition 'Close Contest for Presidency – Hawke Swoops Home'. It labelled him 'Czar-Elect' and reported: 'New President Bob Hawke is a Law Graduate now doing Arts. His previous experience appears to indicate that students felt he was well qualified for the position of Guild President.'[13]

As Guild president, Hawke encouraged students to devote themselves to their studies and take advantage of wider campus life. In the April 1952 edition of *The Pelican*, he offered 'a word of advice from one who knows' to the university 'freshers':

> I want sincerely to ask that you realise the significance of your
> entry into the university community. Now I know that this line
> has probably been hammered into you during the past week
> or so. However, accept the fact that it is potentially the most
> important event which has happened in your lives so far. You
> are coming from the somewhat restraining atmosphere of the
> secondary school into an environment which gives you every
> possible opportunity to develop your intellect, character
> and personality.

He asked them to become masters of their fate and be 'your own disciplinarian'. He implored them to 'lead a full life' on campus:

> This is not an exhortation to go to the pub every night after lectures, but to take an active interest in some of the varied activities of the university – sport, social and political clubs, intellectual discussion groups, in addition to putting a decent effort into your academic work. And, most important, take an active and intelligent interest in your own student government . . .

Although he apologised for his 'sermon-like' message, he emphasised that university had changed him and prepared him for the next phase of his life:

> I would ask that you keep an open mind on all things. Rid yourself of bias or preconceived prejudices and accept the intellectual responsibility of thinking clearly. If you do this you will find that at the end of your university career its main purpose will have been achieved – you will be equipped for worthwhile citizenship and to give a lead to those who may be less fortunate than yourselves.[14]

As Guild president, Hawke was the representative of the student body, and required to attend official receptions and social functions. In chairing meetings of the Guild, he was firm, focused and sometimes a little impatient with those who raised frivolous matters or were too meandering in their arguments. In 1953, Hawke served as Immediate Past President of the Guild, and continued to participate in student life. 'I enjoyed it very much, being a representative on the Senate as president of the Guild of undergraduates,' Hawke recalled. 'I like people and it gave me a good opportunity to mix.'[15] Hawke took a wider interest in student politics, attended interstate meetings and conferences, and was elected vice-president of the National Union of Australian University Students.

Neal Blewett, a fellow Rhodes Scholar who would later serve as a minister in the Hawke government, recalled meeting Hawke at a NUAUS meeting in Melbourne. Blewett was a delegate from Tasmania. Hawke was a minor celebrity in the student movement, given the profile he had established in Perth. 'All the women delegates were agog waiting for this man to arrive,' Blewett recalled. 'Then this bronzed, athletic figure strode into the room and there were murmurs of enthusiasm all round.' As they got down to business, Blewett recalled that Hawke was 'a very effective chair of the meeting', but the overriding impression of this fleeting encounter was 'the anticipation in the room' ahead of Hawke's arrival.[16]

Hawke's support for the post-war immigration program of the Curtin and Chifley governments motivated him to become an advocate for the welfare of international students in Australia. Two international students had committed suicide in 1951, and a third had had a breakdown in 1952. Hawke established the International Club (also known as the Australia-Overseas Club), which encouraged students from different backgrounds to socialise together. He also proposed building a student hostel to house 100 students – half from Australia and half from overseas – as many undergraduates from countries such as India, Ceylon, Singapore and Malaya were living in run-down accommodation.

Hawke established the International House Appeal to raise money, seeking donations from the university administration, the state government and community and charitable organisations. He did the rounds of the local media, organised sporting and social events to raise money, and even won the support of the Governor of Western Australia, Sir Charles Gairdner. In a speech to the Country Women's Association in Cunderdin, he said: 'It is very necessary that these students from South East Asia should become good ambassadors for Australia when returning to their own countries, and, therefore, it is our duty to at least ensure their decent living conditions while studying here.'[17]

His aim was to raise £150,000 but only secured £2200 in donations, and the student hostel was never built. Hawke thought he needed more time to sell the idea. Some opposition he put down to racism, or the threat it might pose to existing colleges. Others thought Hawke was too pushy and 'hogged the limelight'.[18] But the students involved in the Australia-Overseas Club were grateful for his advocacy. They presented him with a copy of a Chinese novel set during the Ming dynasty, *Chin P'ing Mei* (The Plum in the Golden Vase), which they each signed.[19]

Hawke was also busy with activities outside university. He had a mix of odd jobs in these years: milkman, gardener, builders' labourer, abattoir assistant and merry-go-round attendant. In March 1953, in his final months on campus, while gardening on the university grounds at Crawley, Hawke was crushed against a gatepost by a horse-drawn cart when the horse suddenly became startled and moved towards him. His right thigh was lacerated and blood poured out. Hawke managed to pull himself up and stumbled to a nearby cricket game, where he was assisted by two touring South African players. One of them, Gary McLean, tore off his shirt and applied a tourniquet, probably saving Hawke's life, and he was taken to Royal Perth Hospital. *The Pelican* had some fun with the incident. 'It has been suggested that Mr Hawke's accident was directly attributable to a preference on his part to be watching cricket rather than horses,' it reported. '[He] is now a wan, pathetic figure, who stomps about the University on a pair of crutches.'[20]

In high school and at university, Hawke read newspapers and magazines daily. This was geared towards a practical purpose: contemporary news and information. He perused journals and books that primarily related to his studies. Beyond this, however, Hawke seldom read for pleasure. He read many books, to be sure, but it was not a favourite pastime to dip into great works of literary fiction or enjoy insights from history, politics or biography.

There was also the social life on and off campus. Hawke was having sex regularly during his undergraduate years. 'He could always line up girls, for himself and his friends,' a university friend remembered. Another said Hawke was 'a great key collector' who 'was always on the look-out for love nests'.[21] He liked to party. But he did not drink in his first or second years at university. It took considerable willpower to not give in to the peer pressure. He drank a glass of beer for the first time at a Law Faculty dinner in 1949 – and took an immediate liking to the amber ale. He drank more and more, every week, and enjoyed it. William Heseltine, a fellow UWA student, recalled Hawke's drinking prowess in an interview years later. 'He had this reputation,' Heseltine said. 'He was a regular of Steve's – a pub on Broadway on the Swan River – and I suppose you would call him a larrikin in those days.'[22]

While there were plenty of drunken nights, and friends would have to help him home and into bed, this did not impact on Hawke's studies. 'I was wild but controlled wildness in that I worked very hard,' Hawke later said. But his wild drinking did cost him the presidency of the National Union of Australian University Students in 1952. Students recalled Hawke increasingly drinking to excess, and often becoming loud and disorderly, sometimes even having to be restrained. Hawke, who had pledged himself to temperance, broke his mother's heart when he told her he had been drinking and would continue to do so. Drinking 'upset my mother no end', Hawke acknowledged.[23] That beer at the Law Faculty dinner would set Hawke on a path to becoming a high-functioning alcoholic by his thirties.

Hawke was still deeply religious while at university. He attended church services several times a week, participated in church social events and was often a speaker at churches in and around Perth. In February 1951, he travelled to Point Lonsdale, Victoria, for a conference of the Congregational Youth Fellowship of Australia and New Zealand. Hawke was elected president. 'Why read the Bible?' Hawke asked at a Christian youth festival held at Winthrop Hall, on the university campus, in October 1951. 'Because it gave God's plan for life.' Every person, he told the 3000 young people in attendance, had an 'intellectual duty' to make up their own mind about the Bible rather than lingering in the 'lazy acquiescence' between belief and disbelief.[24]

In September 1951 Hawke applied for a Rhodes Scholarship to study at Oxford University, in England. The scholarship had been established by Cecil Rhodes to identify emerging young leaders with 'moral force and character' who would undertake study abroad, with the aim of producing scholars who could 'transform the world'. It was originally conceived as part of a grander fantasy to shape the minds of talented and energetic young white men who would further the cause of British imperialism.[25] In Australia, one student in each state was selected as that year's Rhodes Scholar, and would take up a course of study at Oxford the following year.

Becoming a Rhodes Scholar signalled that you were a person of academic merit, community and sporting spirit, and leadership potential. Hawke expected to be selected. He had done well

at university and gained a law degree. He was a student political leader. He was contributing to the community through the
Congregational church. He was a talented cricket player. And,
although he lived a comfortable middle-class existence, he had
connections: his father was a respected clergyman and his uncle
a member of parliament. How could he lose? But he did. It was a
bitter blow to Hawke – the first major setback in his life.

In September 1952, Hawke nominated for a second time. In his
application to be the Rhodes Scholar for Western Australia for
1953, Hawke noted the 'near fatal [motorbike] accident' which had
led him to realise that he should 'lead a full and varied life' and 'do
all things to the very best of my ability'. His improved academic
results were testament to his dedication. He informed the selection
panel about his leadership roles on and off campus in sport, social
and religious activities, and through the Guild. He explained the
International House project and his vice-presidency of NUAUS.
Hawke concluded with a statement about his future: 'At this stage
I am unable to say what my ultimate sphere of study or character
of work in [later] life will be. I know, however, that I want [it] to
be some form of public service either in the academic or other
spheres of public life.'

The Rhodes Scholarship, Hawke argued, would provide him
with a unique opportunity to 'develop' any 'abilities' he may have.
He saw it as an opportunity to 'apply myself to my intellectual
interests under the guidance of outstanding minds and personalities'. He concluded by saying: 'I am sure that I could then return
better equipped to be of service to my fellow men in whatever
sphere of life I follow.'[26]

Hawke's application included six referees. There were four
professors who had taught him at university, along with Dr George
Currie, who was then the vice-chancellor of the University of
New Zealand but had held the same post at UWA, and Dr James
Rossiter, the headmaster at Wesley College. These references,
and another written by Frank Beasley, Dean of Law, which had
been submitted the previous year, recognised Hawke's improved
academic performance, his industriousness and energy, his self-
respect and courtesy in public, his compassion and sympathy, and
his on- and off-campus leadership qualities. They also offered an

assessment of Hawke's character, temperament and values which provide a useful perspective on how others saw him in these formative years.

The referees gave mixed assessments of Hawke's leadership capacity – a requirement of the Rhodes. Most viewed him as a student leader, but others saw only the promise of that, and thought Oxford may provide the spark for Hawke to develop it further. Beasley wrote that Hawke had to 'a marked degree a personal and intellectual honesty', and was one of the most 'conscientious' students he had met. He noted Hawke's 'reserve' and 'almost a brusqueness', which could 'hide his very real qualities from the superficial observer'. His final assessment was, however, deflating: 'He will never be spectacular; but he will always be reliable.'[27]

Mervyn Austin, Professor of Classics and Ancient History, did not see Hawke as possessing 'the outlook or the equipment of a scholar in the strict sense', and saw his 'general qualities of character' as more outstanding than his 'intellectual powers'. But he did see a potential leader: 'I do believe that Oxford and the inspiration of the Scholarship could make something of his raw material and help him to achieve in manhood something which would not disappoint the hopes of those who felt that they discerned some faint signs of a potential Rhodes Scholar.'[28]

Hawke made the shortlist and was invited to be interviewed by the selection panel at Government House. The West Australian Rhodes Scholarship Selection Committee was chaired by Governor Sir Charles Gairdner. The interview started well, but went downhill when Hawke was asked by a panelist what he planned to do with his life. Hawke responded that he could not imagine becoming a lawyer or a civil servant, but wanted to consider some kind of public service. The answer was not well received. He had been too ambiguous, and the question was asked again. This led to a heated discussion, in which Hawke said he had given an honest answer. 'I have answered the question truthfully and to the best of my ability,' he appealed to the Governor. 'I resent the suggestion that I'm avoiding the question and the implication that I'm not being honest.'[29]

Hawke thought he had blown it, and exited the room while the committee deliberated. When he was asked to come back in, he was told that he had been successful. Hawke was elated. The

Governor took him aside, said he thought his written application was the best, and congratulated him for how he had handled the interview. For the Governor, Hawke's suitability for the Rhodes Scholarship had been settled, he said, by 'the way you dealt with that blithering idiot'.[30]

The selection committee's report concluded that Hawke was an 'outstanding' leader who was 'exceptionally adaptable' and would 'take full advantage' of his time at Oxford. They did note, however, that he was older than most scholars. The selection committee disagreed with Austin's reference. Moreover, the selection committee concluded that it was Hawke's interview which had won them over: 'The committee were very impressed with Mr Hawke's record in a number of fields and they considered that his interview, in which he was simple and direct in his replies to questions, amply bore out the high opinion of him expressed by his referees.'[31]

Hawke was announced as the 1953 Rhodes Scholar for Western Australia on Friday, 28 November 1952. Clem and Ellie were immensely proud of their son. A journalist from *The West Australian* went to the Hawke residence to interview the 22-year-old. Hawke posed for the newspaper photographer by pretending to receive a congratulatory phone call and reading a telegram from his uncle Albert, then the state opposition leader. A beaming Hawke, dressed in a smart suit and tie, was also pictured with Ellie packing his bag for a forthcoming trip to India, even though he would not depart for two weeks. 'Good wishes and packing occupy Rhodes Scholar,' read the headline.[32] A more detailed story three pages over noted his academic and extracurricular leadership, and sporting activities. 'Mr Hawke, who has taken an outstanding part in university student affairs, has been the prime mover in launching the appeal for an International House at the university,' the report explained.[33] It was routinely reported that he was Albert Hawke's nephew.[34] The announcement was the talk of Perth.[35]

The following month, Hawke travelled to Kottayam, Travancore-Cochin, in South India, for the Third World Conference of Christian Youth. It was his first overseas trip, and he would be away from home for more than a month. The conference, from 11 to 25 December 1952, included 300 delegates from sixty countries. At the conference, Hawke undertook an intellectual examination of various faiths and creeds. The trip, however, would shatter rather than reinforce Hawke's faith.

On 22 December, Hawke wrote to Clem and Ellie back home. He found India to be utterly fascinating, he told them. The people were 'amazingly friendly', and he enjoyed meeting delegates from other countries. 'India is certainly an interesting country – it is a land of contrasts with some people enormously wealthy and others inconceivably poor,' he wrote. He enjoyed the variety of food and was eating with his hands. But all the delegates had been sick. 'Have had two meals out with private families and they have been tremendous affairs really testing one's digestive organs to the limit,' he wrote. He shared his impressions of Indian politics. The Communists were 'pouring out cheap readable propaganda', Hawke said, which had 'appeal' to poorer Indians, but he doubted the widespread attraction of Marxism, given their strong religious beliefs. He also kept up with Australian politics and was thrilled with Labor's victory at the Victorian state election that month. 'I wonder how old Menzies explained that away,' Hawke wrote. 'I think he'll even be worrying about Kooyong at the next federal elections.'[36]

Although he enjoyed Bible study, and some speakers, the trip did not strengthen Hawke's Christianity. 'I suppose, even before I went there, I was becoming less fervent than I had been,' he later acknowledged. He was shocked, appalled and saddened by the poverty. He could not reconcile students eating, drinking and enjoying hospitality while Indians nearby were starving to death. On Christmas Eve, the Bishop invited delegates to a huge feast at his residence, where they devoured food and wine while poor people peered through the gates. 'Here we were, stuffing ourselves, and these poor bloody people are out there,' Hawke recalled. 'I said, "Fuck this, I'm going." And so I left and I went back to my digs and I got some warm clothing and went down the street and gave them the clothes. They were so happy.'[37] He was appalled that Christians could live in comfort while so many lived in abject poverty. It was the antithesis of Christian teachings. However, Hawke's break with organised religion, and his agnosticism, was not immediate. He had begun to search his soul at university and the seeds of doubt began to flower in India.

In his unpublished memoir, Clem noted that his son's report about the India trip to the National Assembly of Australian Congregational Churches in Adelaide 'was well prepared and colourful and penetrating' and 'touched on some vital matters that seemed to be missing in a youth Christian conference'. To Clem, and others, it was evident that Bob was 'annoyed and irritated' by 'incidentals and trimmings'.[38] But it was much more than this: Bob was turning away from organised religion. However, Christian principles of compassion and community, of helping those less fortunate, and of peace over conflict would continue to guide his life. 'When I went home,' Hawke recollected, 'I told Dad that I just couldn't have the same commitment that I had had, [and] he understood completely.'[39]

Hawke's insatiable appetite for sex did not abate in India, even though he was already engaged to Hazel Masterson at the time. Indeed, it is likely he deepened his understanding of how to maximise pleasure. Two curious pamphlets from Hawke's trip to India were tucked inside a sleeve of his pocket-sized diary. The first promised 'a golden opportunity' to 'take advantage of the latest scientific advancement to eliminate sexual disappointment, troubles and worries'. A 'special consultant' offered services between 8 and 11 am and 3 and 5 pm on how to 'improve your personality enough to make your sweetheart admire and adore you and impel her to be inseparably attached to you'. A second pamphlet advertised a book that held the 'hidden secrets' to 'sexual pleasure' with instructions that, if followed, guaranteed 'complete satisfaction'.[40]

The conference also opened Hawke's eyes to global political issues. There was a growing communist presence in Kottayam (later Kerala), and Hawke went to a large rally they organised. He saw the influence of propaganda first-hand, and the superficial appeal it had to many who were highly literate but also living in poverty. He could not believe that communist literature could be purchased much more cheaply on the street and in shops than Bibles and Christian literature. On his disembarkation in Fremantle on 13 January 1953, travelling on the *Strathnaver*, Hawke told the local media that India was the 'most significant country' in the world. But he offered a word of caution about its political development. 'It is a vital question whether it will remain within Western democracies or succumb to the spell of Communism,' he said.[41]

Hawke kept a diary of his journey home from India.[42] He wrote in cramped scrawl about his train and ferry travels across India, and his passage to Fremantle. When he saw thousands of people getting on and off trains, he diarised: 'Something within me said where do they all come from, go to and what do they think?' He visited religious temples, botanical gardens and local markets. He toured factories and explored the countryside. On a train, with people 'packed in like sardines', he spoke to a businessman about politics, who said: 'Socialists [are a] dying power in India.' Another man told him that India 'will give democracy a go' and, if it fails, 'will then turn to communism'. He wrote about the contrast of poverty and wealth. He spoke to other students also travelling home from the conference. Religion was always a topic of conversation. 'To everyone in India, Nehru is a God on Earth,' Hawke wrote. 'Even enemies say he is a selfless man.' But Hawke asked: 'What after Nehru?' He was told: 'God will produce the man for the hour!'

When Hawke boarded a ferry, he noted that he was 'unable' to secure 'a sleeping berth'. But a 'kind' English 'lady' offered to share her cabin with him. Onboard the final stage of the journey home, Hawke enjoyed the rest and relaxation. He slept late and napped in the afternoon. A cabin steward served him breakfast each morning. He played table tennis, draughts and quoits. He became infatuated with a young girl named Mary. 'What queer things one's thoughts are,' Hawke confided to his notebook. And later, about the women who enjoyed his company: 'More tormenting thoughts.'

Hawke spent most of 1953, after returning from India, continuing his studies towards a second degree, tutoring in Economics and preparing for Oxford. It was also a time of contemplation. Now in his early twenties, he was turning away from some of the principles with which he had been raised by Clem and Ellie. He no longer believed in the evils of alcohol. He was no longer a devout

Christian. And he no longer practised sexual abstinence; indeed, he was becoming a sexual addict, whose desires could not, and never would be, satisfied by just one woman. While Clem and Ellie were disappointed in their son's loss of faith, there was no rupture in their relationship. The devotion he had for them, and they for him, never diminished. Their response could not have been more Christian.

4

HAZEL

During his second year at university, in 1948, Bob Hawke began a relationship with Hazel Masterson. She would become the most important person in his life, after Clem and Ellie, and they formed a deep and abiding love for one another. This relationship was more than just 'mutual attraction and infatuation', as Hawke later put it, but satisfied his desire for a 'companion' who could share his journey towards the fulfilment of his life's ambition, though it was not yet fully formed. Hazel was both passionate lover and purposeful partner. She was intelligent, lively and a shrewd judge of character. Their relationship would, however, always be a roller-coaster ride, a product of what Hawke later called his 'supercharged existence'.[1] There was pressure at times, and they caused each other pain and let each other down. But Bob's serial betrayals of Hazel, with infidelity and alcoholism, and his routinely lying about both, were far worse than anything she ever did to him. Yet Bob respected, admired and loved Hazel, always, even if his actions seemed to indicate the opposite.

Bob and Hazel met through the Congregational Youth Fellowship. Hazel recalled knowing him since they were nine years old, when they both appeared in a church play that was directed by Ellie. In 1946, Hazel and her close friend Joy Albers (nee Woods) joined the youth social group at Leederville Church, of which Bob was also a member. In April 1947, Hazel and Bob attended the annual Easter Camp for teenagers, held at a guesthouse at Roleystone, south of Perth. Hazel noted in her diary that she played doubles tennis against Bob, and lost, and that he 'spoke very well' at one camp event.[2] Through 1947, Bob and Hazel saw each other occasionally when socialising in groups, and became friendly, but were not yet romantically involved.[3]

Things moved quickly after the Easter Camp the following year, when Hazel took a keener interest in Bob. But not everyone saw in Bob what she did. Ellie was a Camp Mother and doted on her son. This generated ridicule and derision from others towards Bob, who was seen as rather aloof and indifferent. But Hazel was not one of them. 'I accepted, even rather liked, that he was, in fact, different,' she remembered. There was also a physical attraction:

> I liked Bob's skin, tending to swarthy, his eyes were a good deep blue, his hair was luxuriously thick, dark brown and wavy. I always noticed hands, and I liked his hands very much – smallish, with the fine fingers I associated with an aesthete, but strong and taut in the way that he used them. Although he was five feet ten and a half inches tall, the impression was of a shorter man, perhaps because posture was not his strong point (I wondered whether it was due to the abdominal injury and surgery after his accident). I also liked the smell of him. He thought it was amusing when I wrote this in a letter to him once – that I looked forward to smelling him again – but for me it was a pleasing part of his close presence.[4]

Bob asked Hazel if she would join him on a motorbike ride. Bob first raised the idea of taking one of the Mount Hawthorn girls out with his mother. Ellie prepared a shortlist of several names. Hazel was the name Bob chose. On Sunday, 4 April 1948, Ellie phoned Hazel's next-door neighbour (the Mastersons did not own a phone) and asked to speak to Hazel. When she got to the phone, Bob was on the line. He proposed she join him for an afternoon motorbike trip to Araluen, 30 kilometres south of Perth. This was a 'pleasant surprise', Hazel recorded in her diary. 'I was excited – went – had lovely time, beautiful weather,' she wrote. 'Went Hawkes for tea, back here church & supper.'[5] They hit it off. The next day, Hazel confided to her diary: 'Thought a lot about Bob, had such a nice time.'[6]

Hazel Susan Masterson was born on 20 July 1929 in Perth. She was the youngest daughter of James 'Jim' Masterson and Edith Laura Masterson (nee Clark). Jim was born in 1898 in Perth. He worked as an accountant and auditor. Edith was born in 1895 in South Melbourne, and her family moved to Perth when she was aged five. She worked at Foy & Gibson, in the shipping department, before marrying Jim in 1923. Jim and Edith met through the Congregational Church in Perth. The newly married couple settled in Mount Hawthorn and built a weatherboard house at 150 Coogee Street, north of Perth. Their first daughter, Edith, known as 'Ede', was born in 1926.

Hazel had thick blonde hair, a short and slim build, and a gregarious nature. She recalled a happy and loving family life while growing up. She slept in a small bed with her sister on the enclosed front verandah. There was a swing in the backyard, near a lemon tree and chook pen, and a rainwater tank. There was a summerhouse with an aviary and a pergola with tangled grapevines. Jim built a backyard cubby house for Hazel and Edith. Hazel took piano lessons from age six. The Mastersons moved into a larger brick house on the same double block when Hazel was nine years old.[7]

Hazel was educated at Mount Hawthorn Primary State School. She was a clever student and came first in her class every year when testing and grading commenced at around age ten. In 1939, when World War II broke out, students helped dig trenches in the playground and practised air-raid drills. Hazel's parents did little to foster her academic ability. 'They expected that I would go to work until I married and live happily ever after in the traditional role,' she recalled. 'I wanted to broaden my experience but there was no one in my world who could guide me, at the age of eleven, to other possibilities.'[8] So, at age twelve, Hazel exited Mount Hawthorn Primary State School as dux and enrolled at Perth Central Girls' School where she could learn typing, shorthand and bookkeeping.

In December 1944, at age fifteen, Hazel completed her schooling, and entered the full-time workforce the following month. She commenced employment as a secretarial assistant at Cheffin's, a small electrical services company. She worked there until 1953.

The Mastersons made their contribution to the war effort. Jim worked in the Munitions Department. Hazel, Edith and their mother knitted socks, organised food parcels for soldiers overseas and volunteered in hostels and canteens. But Hazel also kept up a busy social life. She played tennis with friends and went ballroom dancing on weekends. There were long bushwalks and bike rides, picnics and barbecues. She was active in the Mount Hawthorn Congregational Church, playing the organ, teaching Sunday School and running the Girls' Club, and was increasingly involved in youth activities, where she met Bob.

After her first motorbike ride with Bob, it took a little while for the relationship to develop. On 23 April, almost three weeks later, Hazel recorded in her diary that she went to a church youth dinner, which was very 'enjoyable'. Bob turned up late, after a cricket dinner, and she found him 'a bit queer'.[9] On 11 May, after work, Bob took Hazel to hear a singer at the Capitol Theatre, which was a 'very pleasant surprise' but noted he was a 'bit moody'.[10] They began spending every Sunday afternoon together, followed by dinner at the Masterson or Hawke home, and then going to church. Soon this developed into midweek or Saturday outings to the cinema or the beach, or sporting activities, and socialising with Bob's university friends. The relationship quickly became a passionate romance.

In early 1950, in the lounge room of the Mastersons' home on Coogee Street, Bob asked Hazel to marry him. But Hazel baulked at saying yes. She wanted a few days to think about it. Bob was hurt – an emotional response that would lodge in his memory. Hazel was not concerned about Bob, but about herself. 'How much I wanted to marry him!' she recalled. 'Yet I was afraid that I would not be adequate.'[11] A couple of days later, she accepted his proposal. The Hawkes were pleased but the Mastersons were cautious. Bob had a difficult relationship with Hazel's father, Jim. He was quiet, reserved and conservative, whereas Bob was confident, extroverted and identified with Labor. Bob saw little need to impress Hazel's family. He was respectful and courteous but did not go out of his way to engage them in conversation. He was aloof and often arrogant: his qualifications and accomplishments spoke for themselves, he thought.

Bob and Hazel were inseparable. 'We were very good friends as well as being lovers,' he recollected years later.[12] He watched her play organ at church; she sat in his bedroom while he studied. He visited her at work; she watched him debate politics on campus. While he was state president of the Congregational Youth Fellowship, Hazel was the state secretary. They escaped into the sandhills and spent long nights in Hazel's father's car. They holidayed together. They walked, they fished, they played games, and they talked and talked. They socialised with each other's friends and family. Bob wanted to share and build his life with Hazel, but he still held traditional views about women. Hazel recalled that she felt inadequate because she had not gone to university. 'But if you were,' Bob replied, 'I wouldn't marry you.' Hazel was startled.[13] It reflected how many men thought at the time, and Hawke later recognised he was mistaken in this view.[14]

They would not marry immediately, as Bob would apply for the Rhodes Scholarship in 1951 and again in 1952, and the criteria specified that only single men were eligible. It was a sacrifice Hazel was willing to make for Bob. There was another, far more significant, decision that Hazel and Bob would have to make in early 1952, when she became pregnant. 'The morals of the day dictated that abortion was wrong, full stop,' Hazel recalled. 'Abortion was illegal, full stop. There were no sources of counselling or information that I knew about.'[15] Hazel did not feel guilt or shame but knew she could not keep the baby. She was keenly aware of the 'social alienation' of having 'a child out of wedlock'. Having the baby could also ruin Bob's chances for a Rhodes Scholarship. Hazel and Bob decided to have an abortion in early 1952. It was a wrenching experience. They did not tell their families. Several doctors refused to assist. Eventually a 'mystery man' was found, who emphasised that secrecy was paramount. The abortion took place during Hazel's lunchbreak from work. She went alone. Although Bob was supportive and comforting, it was 'a lonely and agonising experience' for her.[16]

Hazel loved Bob deeply, admired him and was excited about their future together. But she was aware of his hedonistic streak. They had not waited until they were married to have sex.[17] Hawke was having sex with other girls during his undergraduate years, and this concerned her. Hazel was also 'vaguely disturbed' by his drinking. She put it down to youthful exuberance and expected that, as he matured, he would change.[18] But he did not change, and Bob continued seeing other women during his engagement to Hazel.

The Hazel with whom Bob Hawke fell in love in the late 1940s is the same woman with whom Australians would fall in love in the 1980s. In addition to the evident physical attraction, and the companionship and partnership, it was her character that endeared Hazel most to Bob. She was kind and generous, warm and charming, down-to-earth and unpretentious. Hazel drew strength from the church, loved her children dearly and believed in the duty of public service and the rewards that came with self-lessness. She loved to laugh, enjoyed music and liked to smoke and drink (sometimes too much). Hazel was not perfect, and never claimed to be. But she was modest. In her long life, she was loyal to Bob, devoted to her children and a dedicated and dependable friend. It was these qualities, and more, that Bob loved in Hazel always, and which underscored why so many Australians in the coming decades would regard her as a national treasure. Even as dementia robbed her of her final years, and Australians bid a long goodbye, their esteem for her only grew.

5

BROADER
HORIZONS

B ob Hawke departed for Oxford University at 8 pm on Saturday,
15 August 1953. Before he sailed to England, he was a guest
at several farewell functions. At the University Refectory, sixty
overseas students gathered to thank Hawke for his role in establishing the International House Appeal and the Australia-Overseas
Club during his time as president of the Guild of Undergraduates.[1]
The Reverend C. Gordon Jones led the tributes to the departing
scholar at St Andrews Anglican Church in Subiaco. He praised
Hawke's work with the church and his commitment to Christian
values.[2] The Subiaco Congregational Youth Fellowship presented
Hawke with Bertrand Russell's *A History of Western Philosophy*
(1945).[3] There was also a Guild reception, several student parties
and a family farewell. The day before Hawke's departure, he played
three sets of doubles tennis, teaming up with his uncle Albert –
who by now was the premier of Western Australia – against
the state's governor, Charles Gairdner, and the under-secretary
of the premier's department, R.H. Doig. The Hawkes were
'thrashed', the premier said.[4] These farewells demonstrate how
highly Hawke was thought of by family, friends and the community
at the time. He was a minor celebrity in Perth, reported as being in
'the social limelight', and seen as an emerging young leader.[5]

Two years at Oxford would bring about further transformation in Hawke's life. The period shaped his personal relations and
values, fostered his work ethic, stimulated his intellectual capacities, moulded his approach to public life and set him on a course

that would define his career in the labour movement. It would also cement Hawke's interest in global policy, politics and diplomacy. Hawke was already ahead of many Australians in his desire to foster harmonious relations with people from other countries, welcoming them to Australia and recognising the economic and cultural contributions they could make. He was optimistic that Asian students would return home and help persuade their countries of the 'value of democracy' rather than dictatorship.[6]

Hawke travelled in a first-class cabin on the *Dominion Monarch*. He had booked a cheaper passage on another vessel but was awarded a free passage under a scheme for university graduates run by the Australian and New Zealand Passenger Conference.[7] The shipping company which owned the *Dominion Monarch* also allocated notable passengers, such as Rhodes Scholars, a first-class cabin. Hawke would be travelling in style.

But when the ship left Fremantle, he confessed to his parents, he was a 'very sad young bloke' to be leaving them and Hazel, and his friends, behind. '[It's] funny how you tend to take for granted the people and things close to you and it's only when you have to leave them for a time that you come to realise how much they have done for you, how much they mean to you and how much you love them,' he wrote in an emotional letter. He told Clem and Ellie that he 'would never be able to repay' them for what they had done for him: the inspiration, the opportunities and sacrifice. He apologised for sometimes being 'ungrateful and thoughtless'. He would focus on his studies and work hard to 'justify' their efforts, and strive to make them proud of him.[8]

Hawke kept a diary of his journey to Oxford, documenting his daily routine onboard, the places the ship visited, people he met and his impressions.[9] Along with several suitcases, he packed a typewriter, golf bag and cricket kit. It took a month to travel to England. Hawke often slept late, then ate breakfast and lunch soon after, followed by coffee in the afternoon, dinner and games in the evening. He played cards, quoits, table tennis and pool games. He often went to the gym. He worked on his suntan. He listened to the cricket on the radio. He read newspapers, magazines and books, including Nicholas Monsarrat's World War II naval novel *The Cruel Sea* (1951), H.G. Wells' *A Short History of the World*

(1922) and a book by John Maynard Keynes – perhaps *The General Theory of Employment, Interest and Money* (1936). The seas were often rough and Hawke routinely took seasickness tablets. He met other young people onboard and recorded their contact details in his diary. There were late-night and early-morning talks about politics and religion in cabins. And, of course, girls filled the pages, as he often wrote of spending time with Ruby, Jean and Val, among others.

En route to England, Hawke docked in Cape Town, South Africa, on 26 August 1953. There he was met by a family friend, Sister Margaret, also known as 'Mary', from Perth. She gave him a tour of Cape Town. They visited museums, gardens and churches. They went to the Cecil Rhodes memorial and visited his former home. And, most significantly, Hawke witnessed the injustice of racial apartheid. Hawke went to Parliament House and watched a debate on new separate amenities legislation. In his notebook on 27 August, in a statement vested with future consequence, Hawke diarised: 'Didn't see a white man doing manual work – all native labour. There will be a day of reckoning I imagine.' When the ship disembarked, a number of young South Africans – black and white – came aboard. Hawke spent time with them and discussed apartheid. This visit, and these talks, were baked into his memory.

The only setback on the journey was that on one of the final nights, 8 September, Hawke partied above deck and caught pneumonia. He woke up unwell and went to the doctor. He was administered a cocktail of sulphur tablets and three penicillin injections, and told to rest. Hawke insisted that he felt fine on arrival in Southampton the next day, but he had to be helped ashore and the doctor insisted that he go straight to Southampton Hospital by ambulance. 'What an arrival in England!' he wrote to Clem and Ellie. A trip to Edinburgh to visit family was cancelled. 'There is no need for you to worry about me at all,' Hawke reassured his parents. 'I feel good this morning – pulse and temperature are back to normal.'[10] Hawke left the hospital the following day, 11 September.

Hawke then spent several weeks exploring the 'sights of London', after arriving by train on 14 September. It was exhilarating. He was wide-eyed and curious, seized with a sense of energy and adventure as he explored the grand old city. He had arrived just after the coronation of Elizabeth II, and the city was buzzing with excitement about the young Queen, and the dawn of a new era after World War II. Hawke rode the Tube, went to the theatre and visited Buckingham Palace, Whitehall, Westminster Abbey, the Palace of Westminster and the Tower of London. He went to pubs and clubs, visited Madame Tussauds, saw the movie *Moulin Rouge* (1952) starring José Ferrer and Zsa Zsa Gabor, and went to the fictional address of Sherlock Holmes at 221B Baker Street.

Hawke walked to Number 10 Downing Street, the home of the British prime minister, and happened to be there when Winston and Clementine Churchill were returning after a weekend with the Queen at Balmoral. On 16 September 1953, Hawke wrote to his parents, expressing his surprise that there was only one policeman on duty when he spotted Churchill. 'I was within just a few feet of him as he stood in the doorway of No. 10,' Hawke wrote. The prime minister gave the 'v' for victory sign. 'He certainly looks old and bent but still has the look of a man with plenty of fire left in him,' Hawke thought.[11] On 8 November, he wrote to Clem and Ellie noting the 'remarkable' degree of 'respect and even veneration' in which Churchill was held by people from all parties in Britain. He was particularly impressed by the prime minister's answers to questions in parliament.[12]

Hawke continued writing to Clem and Ellie when he arrived at Oxford. He recounted several trips to Dorset, where he stayed with family friends and helped with farm chores and shot rabbits. He saw the Australian cricketers Neil Harvey and Richie Benaud at Piccadilly. He also kept up with Australian news. He gave an assessment of Arthur Fadden's 1953–54 budget. Hawke noted the 'abolition of automatic quarterly basic wage adjustments' and the impact on wages unless 'prices remain virtually static'. He saw this decision as seminal. 'It was certainly a most important decision by the arbitration court and a dangerous one for a period of continually rising prices,' he wrote.[13] By the first week of October, he was eager to 'get stuck in at Oxford'. He missed his parents, and Hazel, and also his cat, 'Boof'.[14] The regular food parcels from Perth – soup, tinned ham and fruit, sugar and cakes – were appreciated, and served as reminders of home.[15]

On arrival at Oxford in the afternoon of 8 October 1953, Hawke made his way to University College, which he had nominated as his first choice. Dating back to 1249, the college had a prestigious political pedigree. Robert Dudley, Earl of Leicester, and a favourite of Queen Elizabeth I, had been a member of the college, along with the brothers Lord Stowell and Lord Eldon, both prominent lawyers in the 1760s. Liberal economist William Beveridge – author of the famous report on the welfare state – was Master of the College from 1937 to 1945. Labour prime minister Clement Attlee had been an undergraduate at the College in 1901. Harold Wilson, also a Labour prime minister, was a Fellow at the College from 1938 to 1945.[16]

Hawke had been allocated a spacious but modest bedroom and lounge/study, with a few pieces of furniture, a washstand and bowl, and a coal fire. Although it had a nice view overlooking the quadrangle, it was cold and damp. He wrote to Hazel that it had a monastic style but he was 'quite happy with it'.[17] In a letter to Clem and Ellie a few days later, he described his new accommodation as 'good' with 'plenty of room'.[18] Hawke was older than most students, and conservative in style, dress and comportment. This would change over time. He quickly fell in love with the majesty of Oxford, its magnificent buildings, the people, and the atmosphere at the most prestigious university there was. He did, however, often find the ancient rituals bizarre. He relayed to Clem and Ellie a ceremony at the home of the College Master, who made new students sign a register and vow to adhere to the rules and regulations of the institution. It took place in Latin, and Hawke's full name and status as an only son was recorded: 'Robertus Jacobus Lee Hawke filius unicus de Clementri Arturi Hawke.' He wrote to Clem and Ellie: 'Whacko for tradition what!'[19]

He was enthusiastic and excited to be at Oxford, and absorbed the culture shock. 'Dear Dad and Mum,' Hawke wrote on 12 October 1953. 'Here's the first letter from the city of spires and long-haired intellectuals – boy oh boy are there some queer characters inhabiting this town?' Still, he found the teachers, staff and fellow students to be welcoming. 'I am going to enjoy myself here I am quite sure,' he told them. '[The] facilities for study are really good, the standard of lecturing promises to be very high, and what a great variety of things there are to do.' He became friends with a Rhodes Scholar from Canada, John Evans. He told his parents that he had purchased an 'ancient bicycle' to get around the university and town, and the requisite academic gown, which he described as 'a proper bum-freezer' as it only hung a short way down his back. He thought the college food was good. He had also found time to attend church services.[20]

Hawke was thrilled to be in the audience to see Clement Attlee, the former prime minister and now opposition leader, speak at the Union Hall, and wrote to his parents about the occasion:

> He is a remarkable man – I went expecting to find a mixture of mediocrity with some element of the outstanding and was not disappointed in my calculations. There is nothing commanding about his appearance, short medium build and bald, but when you get close to him as I did after the end of the meeting you get the impression of an astute man capable of summing up people and situations quickly and having summed them up having the ability and tact to control them.'

Hawke spoke to Attlee and got his autograph.[21]

Hawke found the coursework demanding but interesting. He explained in a letter to Clem and Ellie that his tutors – initially in Economics and Politics – assigned 'a considerable amount of private reading' and expected him to write a weekly essay, which was then critically evaluated. He also attended lectures, which he found to be challenging, sometimes confronting, but always intellectually stimulating.[22]

While settling into student life, Hawke explored Oxford and London to the fullest. He went to the cinema to watch a 1951 French film, *Edward and Caroline*, he joined his new American friends at the theatre to see George Bernard Shaw's 1913 play *Pygmalion*, and he watched Sir Thomas Beecham conduct the Royal Philharmonic Orchestra at the Sheldonian Theatre. Hawke also continued to go to church and smaller chapel services.[23] He enjoyed the fireworks on Guy Fawkes Day. 'You really had to keep your eyes open and look in all directions otherwise you were liable to have a banger down your collar or in some other equally startling and dangerous portion of your person,' he wrote.[24] Hawke hoped that Clem and Ellie might visit him in Oxford, and even looked into Clem taking on a ministry under the Migrant Chaplain Scheme, but neither could be arranged.[25]

Hawke enrolled in a Bachelor of Arts to study Philosophy, Politics and Economics (PPE). He also had to complete a final course for his Bachelor of Arts from UWA. He sat his last UWA exam while at Oxford, and graduated in absentia on 14 April 1955. In his first few months, Hawke felt he was not learning much that was new, so he approached Rhodes House and University College about changing degrees. He had initially considered a doctorate but, given the time left on his scholarship, it was decided he would continue with a Bachelor of Letters with a research focus. Hawke flagged the course change with his parents in a letter on 9 December 1953 – his twenty-fourth birthday. He initially thought he would write a thesis on 'the development of the Australian economy since the war'.[26]

But as he focused on the topic, Hawke decided to write on 'wage determination in Australia' instead.[27] 'It was a natural combination of law and economics,' he explained.[28] The Director of the Agricultural Economics Research Institute, Dr Colin Clark, confirmed to the University Registry on 18 March 1954 that he would be 'glad to act as supervisor' for Hawke's thesis.[29] Hawke was excited. '[I] have been most fortunate in securing Colin Clark as supervisor,' he wrote to his parents. 'He is an Australian regarded as one of the most competent and certainly one of the most controversial economists in the world today.' Hawke envisaged the Bachelor of Letters leading to a Doctor of Philosophy degree.[30]

But Hawke's admiration for Clark was short-lived. He developed an outline and argument for his thesis on the development of the arbitration system and the basic wage. When he met Clark to discuss the framework for research, his thesis plan and proposed argument, the professor responded that it was of no interest to him or the university. Hawke was stunned. 'I thought to myself, that is bullshit,' he recalled.[31] Hawke could not understand why Clark had taken that view. Hawke later discovered that Clark had been an adviser to the Queensland government and had argued for, and succeeded in, ending automatic quarterly adjustments to the basic wage. Clark saw the basic wage as inflationary and advocated for intensive land settlement rather than industrialisation as the key to Australia's economic development.[32]

Hawke took his complaint to Rhodes House and University College. A new supervisor was approached and agreed to take on Hawke as a student: Kenneth Wheare. He was a professor in government and public administration based at All Souls College; he had also been a Rhodes Scholar for Victoria in 1929. Hawke found Wheare to be supportive and encouraging, and enjoyed their discussions about Australia's industrial and political development. 'He said he would be very interested to do it and he said we will learn together,' Hawke recalled. 'He was marvellous.'[33]

Looking back, Wheare liked Hawke very much. 'He used to look quite young and slim,' he said in 1979. 'He was always good at his work, and very interesting. Some pupils are interesting, some are dull, some are very, very boring . . . He was an Australian first. It was the first thing he told people.' Wheare thought Hawke was destined for politics.[34]

Hawke's application to transfer as a full student to a Bachelor of Letters, with his proposed thesis and Wheare as supervisor, was submitted on 24 November 1954 to the Board of the Faculty of Social Studies; it was approved on 2 December 1954.[35] Hawke was granted an extension to his Rhodes Scholarship for a further term on 25 February 1955. The Warden of Rhodes House, Edgar Williams, supported Hawke's application to the Trustees.[36] So did Wheare. 'Hawke, as you know, took a little time to decide what his line of work should be at Oxford,' he wrote to the Warden on 31 January 1955, 'but he has now settled into the piece of research for a B.Litt., and I have little doubt that he will complete it successfully.'[37]

Hawke researched and wrote most of the thesis at Rhodes House. There, in the upstairs library – now the Rosebery Room – sitting beneath the dark brown wooden arches and between the high windows, and surrounded by alcoves of bookshelves, he found everything he needed: arbitration reports, newspaper accounts, Hansard, Constitutional Convention debates, and a range of history and economics books. He commenced writing in early 1954 as a probationer-student with the aim of completing four terms' worth of work during the two non-summer terms. He was

immersed in the research. He would wake early in the morning
and work until sundown, when the library closed. 'I now entered
a period of unique pleasure in my life,' Hawke later recalled. 'For
the first time, I passed over that exquisite line in academic endeavour where study becomes pure joy, free of drudgery and duty.' He
instinctively knew this field of endeavour should be his life's work.[38]

Impressions of Hawke varied among the teaching and administrative staff at Oxford. Williams, a former brigadier in the British
Army, kept a notebook in which he recorded his assessments of the
students; Hawke's is based, it seems, on paperwork and photos sent
ahead of his arrival. Even so, it provides a fascinating perspective
of Hawke at Oxford:

> A strong interesting argumentative face. Dark wavy hair. Lots
> of A's: a few Bs. Nearly killed so had time to think . . . leadership
> in student guild . . . cricket, football, rugby, hockey. Goodish
> cricketer. Keen young Congregationalist . . . churches conf.
> in India. Public service of some sort . . . Adaptable . . . Not
> impressive intellectually – very kind [and] thoughtful about
> new [Australians]. Not outstanding but good raw material.
> Worked as gardener at [university]. Prof. of Econ. thinks when
> not busy with good deeds should mature intellectually. Sharp
> argumentative skill . . . A good man who [should] get a decent
> second if he undertakes fewer good works.[39]

In Hawke's student file at University College, there is a 'Dean's
Card' on which teaching staff shared their impressions. 'Confidence should not blind him from realising that he still has a good
deal to learn,' one academic wrote in the 1953–54 year. Another
assessed Hawke as the 'spoilt son of an Australian politician' (in fact
he was the nephew of a politician, although he was spoilt). They
wrote further: 'Not very clever or industrious, but he improved a
great deal as a person while he was here.'[40]

Reports by Giles Alington, a Senior Tutor, Fellow and Dean of
University College, sent to the Warden of Rhodes House at the
end of each term, show further frank assessments. 'He's here for
the cricket, let's face it,' said a report for Michaelmas term 1953.
'He might be told of the importance of doing a lot now in view
of how little he'll do in the summer. But this isn't to suggest that

he's been idle. It's merely a suggestion which I think couldn't do any harm. But he's a determined man and it may not be necessary.'

At the end of Trinity term in 1954, Alington reported: 'His tutor says that his confidence should not blind him to the fact that he has much far to go & much to learn. I doubt if it will. I don't yet like him enormously but I think I may yet. He's a determined man: a bit grown-up for Oxford life.'

And in a brilliant assessment that would sum up Hawke for-evermore, at the end of Hilary term in 1955 Alington wrote: 'I really can't go on thinking about, writing about, talking about to, and at, this perfectly straightforward, quite nice, rather arrogant, a bit too self-assured, quite intelligent, surprisingly conscientious and reasonably satisfactory van driver.'[41]

Hawke initially found it difficult to adjust to life at Oxford. His feeling on arrival, and in the weeks after, was loneliness. He found Oxford to be intimidating and imposing. He missed his parents and his friends. But he missed Hazel most of all. Their separa-tion was torment for Hawke; he raged and whined and begged her to join him. Hazel had planned to join Bob in mid or late 1954, after his first year of study. In no time, Hawke was exposed to the opportunities for revelry, drinking and sex. He tried to abstain and fought against the demon drink and his carnal desires. He wrote to Hazel on 12 October 1953, just two months after leaving Australia, begging and demanding her to leave work and head to England as soon as she could. He commenced typing the letter at 12.30 am. Hawke was frank about the fact that if Hazel came the following year, he could enjoy the company of other women in the meantime:

> I have been assailed by the thought that young Robert could
> have a more delightful time if his sweetheart didn't come over to
> Oxford until the end of the academic year. I suppose this is only
> reasonably natural and I am not apologising for it but the other
> thoughts which come to mind are much more important and
> the ones which I really want to communicate to you. Invariably
> I come to my senses and remember what you mean to me, how
> much I need you, and how far superior are the qualities of our
> union to the merely passing delights of this other life of mine.

This is Hawke unvarnished. He is communicating his innermost thoughts to his fiancée and revealing his desires, which he finds difficult to restrain. But he goes further. He wants her to come to Oxford and puts the responsibility to tame his sexual cravings onto her:

> In other words I am now telling you that you must come over here as soon as you possibly can – any other arrangement is completely out of the question if our love means anything at all. I have been thrust into an environment which is full of opportunities for the satisfaction of my varied tastes, to which if I succumbed in their entireties, would only succeed in taking me away from you or at least making us more distant from one another.

Hawke tried to emphasise that he was not asking her to come to England 'to help me get over my weakness', but because he had decided Hazel was the one he wanted to spend his life with. But that was exactly what he was doing. The words contained a clear threat: if you don't come, I won't be able to constrain myself and our relationship will be in jeopardy. This is clear later in the letter, when any subtlety vanishes, and he handwrites: 'GET ON THAT SHIP DARLING FOR YOUR SAKE AND MINE.' He wanted Hazel to board the P&O liner *Straithaird*, which departed Fremantle on 16 November 1953. He gave her a month to get to Oxford.[42]

A week after Hawke's demanding letter to Hazel, he wrote to her again: he was 'overworked' and 'intellectually stimulated', he said, but also 'sexually frustrated'. He was 'lacking only those infinite variety of pleasures which continued intimate association' with Hazel brought, and which were now 'an indispensable part' of his complete makeup. Hawke was 'working like a nigger' – an appalling phrase, but one unfortunately common then – but felt a 'purposelessness' and 'lack of motivation'. He emphasised that he wanted Hazel there with him, not only for sexual pleasure, but for intellectual encouragement. 'I need you here my love, always reminding me that the feeling of purpose is necessary for the production of the best results.' He again asked that she do all she could to board the boat leaving Fremantle on 16 November.[43]

Passage was secured for Hazel on the *Strathaird*; the journey would take almost four weeks. Bob felt compelled to give Hazel some advice about fleeting ship romances. He told her to 'watch out for the great number of blokes onboard whose only interest in a woman is to sleep with her'. Referring to his own experience, he noted: 'I know how surprised I was myself at what was behind the seeming natural friendliness of several of the women on the *Dominion Monarch*.' Hazel could tell any 'philanders' that he would be 'provoked to violence' if they tried anything. Finally, Bob advised Hazel to get some rest, acquire a tan, put on some weight and let her hair grow, 'so that when you arrive at Tilbury you will be everything that young Robert waiting on the docks wants you to be'. He was, he explained, 'longing like mad' to be with her again. 'I love you tremendously,' he concluded a 23 October letter, 'and the extent of this love impresses itself on me day by day.'[44]

Hazel had been visiting Clem and Ellie in West Leederville, and they were sad to see her leave for Oxford. In a letter home, Hawke rationalised the decision as both good for Hazel, who could enjoy Oxford, and good for his studies: 'I am perfectly sure that the effect of Hazel being here will be if anything that I will get more work done,' he wrote to his parents. 'There is a constant temptation to be going out with the boys from College or with other people that I am meeting around the place all the time which would be harmless enough in its way but rather detrimental to the amount of work which I would be getting done, whereas when Hazel is here there will not be any question of this.'[45]

But it was too late; he had succumbed to temptation ahead of Hazel's arrival. Rawdon Dalrymple, a fellow Australian Rhodes Scholar at Oxford, recalled that Hawke was already adulterous. 'I don't think for a moment he was particularly faithful, but he was devoted, and Hazel was devoted to him,' Dalrymple recalled.[46] Shortly after arriving at Oxford, Hawke had purchased a small Fordson Ten van for £175 and drove it all over Oxford. It became known as 'the fornicatorium'. Hazel had suspicions about Bob's philandering. A friend, Joy Beck, questioned whether Bob could be trusted to remain faithful to Hazel. Joy, who had known Bob before Hazel arrived at Oxford, advised Hazel 'to beware'. Hazel made a note of this conversation.[47]

Bob could not have been happier that Hazel was to join him at Oxford, and the feeling was entirely mutual. He had driven his friends mad with his excitement at her impending arrival. His letters to Hazel are filled with a mix of love and lust, immature thoughts, subtle threats and intimidation, but above all with the joy that they shared in simply being together. He referred to her as 'darling', 'sweetheart', 'love', 'dearest' and 'chicken'. And he signed off his letters as 'The Lonely Student' and 'The Student Prince'. He wrote about being frustrated that he could not see Hazel, grab her and give her 'a great big hug' – a feeling which was 'growing in ferocity week after week'.[48] He could not wait for the delivery of a 'parcel of one only little Hazel for Bobby who has been enduring this cuddle-control with ever increasing impatience'.[49] On 10 November, Bob wrote about Hazel's arrival: 'what that day will be for both of us – gosh at the very thought of tit as (a typist's faux pas if there ever was one darling)'.[50]

Bob left Hazel in no doubt about his affection for her. 'Hell I'm excited at the thought of seeing you soon my dear – it seems ages since we have been together, fought and had a cuddle,' he wrote. 'I'll have to really bash you up to make up for all the beltings I should have been giving you in these past few weeks.'[51] This was an exceedingly poor joke. It underscores a tempestuous and intense relationship, with Hawke's struggle to control his sexual drive at the centre. Hawke would later acknowledge the narrow-minded and often appalling view of women he had held in his youth. 'I was certainly less than an enlightened male,' he reflected on his early years with Hazel. 'I was a good male chauvinist pig, I think, in my earlier days.'[52]

Hazel arrived in London on 12 December 1953. Bob got up early and drove his van to the terminal so he could collect her belongings when she disembarked. They would then have their own vehicle to explore London. With the assistance of the West Australian Agent-General in London, he secured a pass to board the ship when it berthed at Tilbury Docks. He was first onboard and was thrilled to hold Hazel in his arms again. They explored the sights of London and then escaped to a 'delightful pub' a few miles outside Oxford, where, no doubt, they spent an intimate night together.[53] While Bob continued to live at University

College, as required by his scholarship, Hazel rented a share flat at 42 Lonsdale Road, North Oxford. Bob moved to the flat in his second year at Oxford.

Hazel explored Oxford and London to the full while Bob studied. They rode bicycles together in and around Oxford. They played tennis with friends. They went to the theatre, and visited museums and galleries. Hazel watched Bob play cricket. They also went on camping trips south of Oxford, staying in the van. Bob and Hazel were not prepared for the freezing winter of 1953–54, when Oxford was blanketed in snow. Hawke wrote frequently to Clem and Ellie about how cold it was, and signed his letters as 'The Snowman' or 'The Yeti'.[54]

Shortly after arriving, Hazel secured a job as a stenographer and typist at a local Anglican diocesan office. Later, she found employment at the Oxford Institute of Statistics. She also took an interest in Bob's thesis writing. He wrote to Clem and Ellie explaining how he would read books and Hazel would take down his dictated notes and then type them up for him.[55] Hazel also typed his thesis drafts. Her income enabled the two of them to enjoy a comfortable life at Oxford. While Hawke had to pay dues for accommodation and meals, he also earned an allowance as a Rhodes Scholar. This was initially £500 per year, and it increased to £600 in 1954. (This is the equivalent of around $57,000 in relative labour earnings in 2021.)

Hawke found Oxford's liberal tradition to be in sharp contrast with the heightened fears about communism both in the United States, gripped by McCarthyism, and in Australia, which had recently voted against banning the Communist Party. At a time of Cold War tensions, Hawke later recalled, the geopolitical environment provided 'a breeding ground for intolerance' and 'guilt by association'. Oxford was different. 'I found a place where people and their arguments were treated on their merits,' he said. 'It was regarded as unremarkable that a person holding an academic appointment should be a member of the Communist Party.' There was an emphasis on evidence and argument, rather than on prejudice and fear. It was not a 'soft tolerance', Hawke said, but rather 'contingent liberalism'. The 'framework of a consistent obligation that issues should be discussed on merit' had a profound and lasting impact on him.[56]

Hedley Bull, who later became a professor, was at University College at the same time as Hawke. He recalled Hawke being well known on campus for sport, drinking and girls. 'He had mainly a playboy image, but privately he did a lot of hard work,' Bull said. 'Even then it was clear that he wanted to be prime minister. He advertised the fact that he was a socialist.'[57] But Hawke did not take an active interest in political activities on campus. He wanted to be free of politics at Oxford, and enjoy sport, culture and intellectual stimulation. He felt that, having engaged extensively in campus political activities in Perth, it was time for him to focus on other things.

Much of his spare time was spent playing cricket for University College against other colleges. He was a talented batsman and a reliable cover point fieldsman. In the annual *University College Record*, the Cricket Club's report for 1953–54 noted Hawke's ability with the bat. 'The batting has, on the whole, been the strongest aspect of the side and some very good totals were amassed, due often to good batting by R.J.L. Hawke, a Freshman who was made an Authentic at half-term.'[58] The 1954 team photo features a relaxed Hawke, resplendent in cricketing whites and a blue double-breasted blazer, his head cocked to the right, exuding confidence.

In the English summer of 1954, Hawke went on tour with captain Colin Cowdrey's Oxford XI as the team's twelfth man. (Cowdrey would make his Test debut for England in November that year.) Cowdrey rated Hawke's fielding skills highly. Hawke, nicknamed 'Digger', recalled a pre-match pep talk from Cowdrey before taking the field against the Marylebone Cricket Club at Lord's. He identified the slopes and levels of the ground, and told Hawke to 'get right down to the ball'. But Hawke recalled fumbling the ball when it came to him at cover point. He bent down to scoop it up but it went straight through his legs and away to the boundary. 'Why don't you get a bag!' one of his teammates yelled out.[59] Hawke always lamented not having played against Cambridge, which meant he did not meet the requirement for a university blue.

Hawke gained his solo pilot's licence while at Oxford. In November 1953, he joined the Royal Air Force Volunteer Reserve within the Oxford University Air Squadron. He informed Hazel,

Clem and Ellie that he had decided to fly, and said he understood they might have mixed feelings about it. But in a revealing letter, Hawke explained that he felt God would protect him. 'I don't take the idea of risk seriously as I guess God is looking after you whether it be in an airplane or crossing the street,' he wrote to Hazel. 'Quite apart from these considerations I feel that it is a worthwhile thing to do and to learn is an opportunity which I would never get again.'[60] He sat intelligence tests, was interviewed by an examination board and underwent a rigorous medical examination, discovering that he was partially colour blind. He undertook weekly lectures and flight training. Hawke flew a two-seat, single-engine propeller plane, known as a 'Chipmunk', which was manufactured under licence by de Havilland in the United Kingdom. He was paid an allowance of £60 per year. Hawke clocked thirty hours of solo flying.

Hawke continued to be diligent with his thesis writing, but the larrikin in him could not stay hidden. His ingrained self-indulgent streak manifested itself in sex with other students, excessive drinking and wild partying. Rawdon Dalrymple recalled that Hawke liked to be the centre of attention, enjoyed being in the company of others, and stood out. 'He didn't conceal in any way the fact that he had huge ambitions,' Dalrymple said. 'He had a very high opinion of himself, even then, and he was a bit of a show-off.'[61]

In December 1954, Hawke and his friend Jimmy Allan had driven another friend home after a late-night squadron party, and then returned to the gathering. When they arrived back, two policemen approached Hawke and asserted that he had been driving recklessly and ignored their pleas to pull over. It was claimed that, after stopping, he had reversed into the police vehicle and failed to produce his licence. He was charged with dangerous driving. The matter went to court in January 1955, and he contested the charge. He was represented by F.S. Vaughn, who entered a 'not guilty' plea on Hawke's behalf. In the gallery were his university friends. They saw it as a Town versus Gown matter. The three magistrates ruled that Hawke was guilty. He was fined £20 and disqualified from driving for two months. His friends cried, 'Shame! Shame!' from the public gallery.[62] Hawke took the matter to the Oxfordshire Quarter Sessions Court, and his appeal was upheld.[63]

Then, a short time later, Hawke was busted by police trying to steal a streetlamp, and charged. Hawke engaged barrister Oliver Popplewell when the matter was appealed in court. The police had lied about Hawke winding down his van window and making an inappropriate gesture: the window did not wind down, as part of it was fixed and part of it opened sideways. This destroyed the police's credibility, and Hawke's appeal was upheld. The charges were dismissed, with costs paid.[64]

One night in 1955, Hawke arrived for dinner in the Great Hall at University College without his academic gown. This was one of three offences – the others being arriving early or late – and the penalty was being 'sconced'. This required drinking two and a half pints of beer in a two-handled ancient pewter pot in less than twenty-five seconds. If he failed to do so, Hawke would be liable for the cost of the beer, and another for the person who had 'sconced' him. In the drinking contest, Hawke would be challenged by the president of the Junior Common Room, known as the sconcemaster, who would aim to down the ale in a faster time. A friend of Hawke initiated the sconce by writing a note to the president. The president had no chance against Hawke, who lifted the tankard and swallowed the beer in twelve seconds flat. It was so fast that it earned him a place in *The Guinness Book of Records*.[65] Hawke explained that he had a gullet which could relax and open up, and he could pour the beer down his throat. Nothing he ever did would endear him more to the Australian people, Hawke would say. 'It got me a few votes, I reckon.'[66]

In the summer of 1954, Bob and Hazel embarked on a 'grand tour' of Europe. They were away for a month, from 15 August to 18 September, and visited France, Germany, Belgium, Luxembourg, Austria, Switzerland and Italy. They went to historic sites, and toured galleries and museums. They lived in their small panel van and slept on a mattress with sleeping bags while parked off the main roads. Hazel often cooked eggs, beans, potatoes, tomatoes, spaghetti, and made ham and cheese rolls. They drank wine, coffee and tea. They occasionally splurged on a cafe or restaurant meal. They bathed in local rivers or at camping grounds.

Bob maintained the van as they went. He grew a beard. Bob often purchased newspapers and books, and Hazel enjoyed looking at the markets and shops. They sent letters and postcards to friends and family in Oxford and Perth. Hazel kept a charming diary of the trip, which was sent home to their parents and friends. 'What a wonderful, interesting holiday it was,' she wrote.[67]

Hawke's thesis topic was: 'An Appraisal of the Role of the Australian Commonwealth Court of Conciliation and Arbitration with Special Reference to the Development of the Concept of a Basic Wage'.[68] This was a rather narrow and parochial topic, given Hawke had ready access to some of Oxford's greatest minds and resources. Dalrymple thought it was a wasted opportunity. 'Hawke didn't really get the most out of Oxford,' he said. 'It was all a bit of a waste given he was a Rhodes Scholar.'[69] John Stone, also a Rhodes Scholar at Oxford, recalled that, among students, the degree Hawke had chosen was regarded as 'pretty low grade' with 'a modest thesis', and was referred to as 'a dingo degree'. He added: 'I think he wasted his time.'[70] But Hawke was looking for a practical degree that would satisfy his intellectual curiosity and his desire for a focused field of study.

Hawke's thesis examined the social, economic and political factors in the emergence of the Commonwealth Court of Conciliation and Arbitration. He argued that the evolution of the court from an industrial tribunal to an institution with effective legislative powers was 'probably the most vital question affecting the social and economic welfare of Australia at the present time'. Second, he considered the significant decisions of the court in relation to the development of the basic wage and the Royal Commission on the Basic Wage in 1920. The basic wage was the focus of his study because it was the court's 'primary contribution to the task of preventing and settling industrial disputes', and the basic wage was what had 'made the Court into such a significant institution'. Third, he provided a critical appraisal of the function of the court with regard to the constitution and legislation (*Conciliation and Arbitration Act 1904*). He concluded with suggestions for how the system could be improved.

The thesis is written in a lively and engaging manner, drawing on considerable research and making sharp conclusions throughout. In the final chapter, having traversed the history, role and function of the court, and its expanding influence over the economy, Hawke asked whether it was 'adequate for the discharge of its functions within the role it has acquired'. He concluded that it was not 'competent' to 'exercise wide legislative powers of an economic character' and had failed to adequately prevent and settle industrial disputes.

In the final pages, Hawke turned his mind to the future of the court. It 'should be retained', he argued, but its functions limited to justiciable matters such as union disputes and wrongful dismissal cases. He recommended a focus on conciliation rather than arbitration when resolving disputes. He suggested that a bureau independent of the court – made up of employer and employee representatives, along with government-appointed economists and statisticians – be established to deal with matters such as fixing margins, standard hours and the basic wage, which would then be incorporated into awards.

He thought the basic wage should be determined on the basis of 'a needs minimum' and automatically adjusted in accordance with the cost of living. Moreover, the setting of the basic wage should have regard to 'the productivity or capacity criterion' and 'relevant national considerations'. Hawke saw the distribution of productivity gains as being 'at the centre' of ensuring a 'harmonious and equitable industrial relations' system. He called for the granting of a new 'comprehensive industrial power' to the federal parliament via referendum. These were not original ideas, but they did not have wide currency at the time, nor were they favoured by industry, unions or government. But they would form the building blocks of Hawke's approach to workplace advocacy, industry cooperation and government.

Hawke was influenced by historian Keith Hancock's survey of economic, social and political life, *Australia*, published in 1930.[71] It is referenced throughout the thesis. Hawke wrote:

> Hancock has said that the prevailing ideology of Australian democracy is 'the sentiment of justice, the conception of equality, and the appeal to government as the instrument of self-realisation. The ideology is simple; but the instrument

is not.' The instrument is not simple nor is it immutable. At
the time when it was becoming a nation Australia made a bold
experiment to give effect to this ideology. If the experiment
made in a particular set of conditions has become an inadequate
instrument of self-realisation, Australia should recognise the fact
and, equally boldly, seek to improve the instrument.

The 300-page thesis, typed by Hazel, was submitted for a
Bachelor of Letters degree on 6 December 1955. Hawke asked to
be orally examined by no later than 8 January 1956 because he had
'a passage booked to return to Australia on a ship leaving England
on the 10th of January 1956'.[72] This was supported by Wheare and
agreed to by the university.

Hawke was called to present to the Examination Committee,
comprised of K.G.J.C. Knowles and Hugh Clegg, on 7 January.
Their report found that Hawke had been effective in examining
'the leading decisions' of the court, and in relating them to 'the
original intentions' of the legislation and therefore demonstrat-
ing that it had been unable to establish and maintain consistent
principles. In this main body of the thesis, they said, Hawke had
presented and supported his case 'ably and cogently' in writing
and orally. But in the final chapter, discussing and remedying
these inconsistencies, they found Hawke to be 'less convincing'
and 'his use of material much weaker'. As with his Rhodes application, it was the force of his verbal argument which won them over:
'On balance, however, and particularly after oral examination, we
are strongly of opinion that the work done by the candidate above
named, as embodied in the thesis and as treated by examination, is
of sufficient merit for the Degree of Bachelor of Letters.'[73]

On his return to Perth, Hawke was asked by the *Weekend Mail*
to write an article presenting his 'critical analysis' of the arbitration system and the basic wage, and recommend a way to resolve
this 'national problem'. Hawke did so in an article published on
17 March 1956. He presented the core argument of his thesis,
arguing for the functions of the Commonwealth Court of Conciliation and Arbitration to be limited to essentially justiciable matters.
He urged that in resolving industrial disputes the 'emphasis should
be on conciliation'. And he advocated the establishment of an

independent bureau that would deal with economic matters such as 'fixing margins for skill [and] standard hours', and determining the basic wage. Hawke had wasted no time in taking his ideas into the public sphere. Hawke the advocate had arrived.[74]

Hawke made his mark at Oxford, and Oxford left a mark on him. Journalists liked to compare Hawke with Malcolm Fraser, who apparently made little impression during his time at Oxford.[75] In fact, it was not so much that Hawke was a Rhodes Scholar or a graduate of Oxford that shaped his future industrial and political career, but rather what he had studied. 'Changing from a second-year course to doing research was the foundation of all my subsequent career,' Hawke later reflected. 'I don't think the Rhodes Scholarship as such helped me politically but what came out of being the Rhodes Scholar has set the whole path of my career.'[76]

Hawke made those comments in July 2003, when he returned to Oxford to commemorate and celebrate the centenary of the establishment of the Rhodes Scholarship. He was one of four scholars awarded an honorary doctorate.[77] Tony Abbott, a former Rhodes Scholar, said at the time: 'Hawke was, on balance, a worthy prime minister. For all his flaws, and who hasn't got flaws, he's a larger-than-life character and he's a credit to the Rhodes Scholarship.'[78] Hawke, then seventy-three, was invited by Lord Butler, the Master of University College and a Rhodes Trustee, to repeat his legendary feat of draining a tankard of beer in record time. Hawke took up the challenge, though with non-alcoholic beer, and climbed onto a table as the beer was handed to him. He downed it in one large gulp in a time of thirty-five seconds. Former US president Bill Clinton, also a Rhodes alumnus, was present and cheered Hawke on.[79]

Hawke's experiences at Oxford deepened his affection for Australia. As profound were the elemental virtues he had gained, which would remain prominent for the rest of his life. First, Hawke learned the importance of concentrated intellectual application. Second, he recognised the value of listening to and learning from others. Third, he embraced rational, fact-based, thoughtful argument. Fourth, he understood that conflict could be resolved by finding common ground. And fifth, Oxford affirmed Hawke's belief in 'the brotherhood of man': racial intolerance was not only morally but also intellectually bankrupt. These convictions were embedded within Hawke by the time he and Hazel departed the United Kingdom.

In later decades, Hawke would be remembered as one of Oxford University's most notable graduates. He returned several times to talk to students and give lectures. While portraits and plaques adorned the walls of University College honouring former students – men such as Clement Attlee, Harold Wilson and Bill Clinton – Hawke was missing. Josh Frydenberg, undertaking a master's at University College from 1996 to 1998, thought Hawke should have his own portrait. In early 1999, Frydenberg was an articled clerk at a law firm in Melbourne. He came across Michael Duffy, a former minister in the Hawke government, and asked how he could contact Hawke so he could arrange the portrait. Duffy rang Hawke. 'Bob, I've got a young man here who wants to get your portrait done,' he said.

'Sure,' Hawke replied. 'What do I have to do?'[80]

Frydenberg asked Hawke to select an artist. He rang back and nominated Robert Hannaford. By May 1999, Frydenberg was liaising with Hawke, Hannaford and University College to see the portrait completed.[81]

Hannaford had painted Paul Keating's official portrait. So how did Hawke compare? 'He was a terrific subject,' Hannaford recalled. 'He did six or seven sittings. He turned up on time and sat diligently, and he was good fun to be with. We had interesting conversations.'[82]

The bill came in at $17,000. Frydenberg planned to raise the funds from Oxford alumni. But then, in April 2000, Hawke's racehorse, Belle Du Jour, co-owned with John Singleton, won the $2.5 million Golden Slipper. The two had also backed it to win $1 million. Frydenberg rang Hawke. 'Bob, do you think any of your friends who had a share in the horse might like to chip in?'

'Leave it with me,' Hawke replied.

The next day, Hawke rang Frydenberg. 'It's done,' he said. 'Josh, it's fully paid for.'

Today, the oil on canvas portrait hangs proudly in the University College Hall. 'Thousands of students have seen that portrait and many Australians have felt proud of that portrait,' Frydenberg reflected.[83] Hawke liked it so much that he asked Hannaford to paint another for the Bob Hawke Prime Ministerial Library, which was hung in 2001. Another was painted by Hannaford for The Rhodes Trust in 2003, and it now hangs in Milner Hall at Rhodes House at Oxford University.

6

ACADEMIC
INTERLUDE

Bob Hawke and Hazel Masterson sailed for Fremantle on 10 January 1956. Hawke had been at Oxford for six terms over two years. Onboard, they finalised their plans to be married. The wedding took place just three weeks after their return, on the afternoon of 3 March 1956 at Trinity Church on St Georges Terrace in Perth. It was a sweltering hot day. Clem officiated at the service and was assisted by the minister of the church, John Bryant. Bob's best man was Alan Barblett, his friend from Perth Modern. Hazel's matron of honour was her sister, Edith. Alan and Edith were witnesses for the marriage certificate, which listed Bob as a bachelor and 'university research worker' and Hazel as a spinster and 'stenographer'.[1] Terry Zanetti was master of ceremonies. Albert Hawke and John Toohey, another Perth Modern alumnus, proposed toasts to the newlyweds. The reception in the church hall was a notable event on Perth's social calendar. Leading political and civic leaders, academics and clergy attended, along with family and friends. As a mark of respect to Clem and Ellie, no alcohol was served. The couple stayed the night at the Palace Hotel in Perth, before driving to Caves House at Yallingup for their honeymoon.

Bob and Hazel moved to Canberra on 20 March 1956. While at Oxford, Hawke had applied for a research scholarship in the Department of Law at the Australian National University. In his application, submitted on 6 August 1955, Hawke wrote that he wanted to continue to research 'the regulation of industrial relations in Australia' with a 'detailed and comprehensive study of the

Australian system of conciliation and arbitration'.[2] In his supporting reference, Kenneth Wheare described Hawke as 'a really first
class man' who would be 'an excellent acquisition for the ANU'.
Edgar Williams said Hawke was 'a hard and sensible worker' who
has 'plenty of commonsense, knows how to set about his work
and has great energy'. He added: 'Personally, too, I like him.' F.R.
Beasley offered this assessment: 'He has a lively and penetrating
mind; not given to sudden enthusiasms, when he has chosen a
subject for investigation he will apply himself to it with sustained
effort and keenness.'[3]

Bob and Hazel's arrival in Canberra was heralded in the local
newspaper. Hawke was a Rhodes Scholar, he had been a student
leader and came from a notable Perth family.[4] He had also organised to give four lectures on ABC Radio based on his Oxford thesis;
these would earn him enough money to pay for the honeymoon.
He dictated them to Hazel while in Yallingup. Fellow student
Peter Coleman, writing in 1960, thought Hawke 'was beginning to carry with him an air of coming power' and some people
wondered if 'he had the makings of a future prime minister'.[5]
Hazel secured a secretarial job at the Indian High Commission. They initially lived on campus at University House. When
Hazel became pregnant with Susan in mid-1956, they moved to a
university-owned flat at 12 Masson Street, Turner, since university rules forbade pregnant women to be residents.

Canberra was still underdeveloped. Sheep grazed on paddocks
sandwiched between government buildings. It was a mainly young
population of around 40,000 people, most of whom worked in
the Public Service or at the university. There was little sense of
community or identity. There was no Lake Burley Griffin. The
National Library of Australia, the High Court of Australia and
the National Gallery of Australia were all a decade or more away
from opening. Many roads were dirt or gravel, and there was
little public transport. There were, however, new health services,
schools and sports facilities being built to cater for the growing
population. Susan was born on 19 January 1957. Hawke, who was
playing first-grade cricket for the ACT when Susan arrived, had
wanted and expected a boy, but those thoughts evaporated as he
held her in his arms at Canberra Hospital.

Hawke would spend the next two years working on a PhD. He was to continue examining Australia's wage-fixing system, with a focus on the basic wage, overseen by supervisor Geoffrey Sawer, with whom Hawke developed a close relationship. The academic worked overtime to support and help the student – both to focus his research and in his battles with university administrators. Sawer witnessed Hawke grappling with his demons: chasing girls and excessive drinking. 'He was quite frequently drunk,' Sawer remembered. But he was also an 'admirable student' who 'worked like hell at this subject'.[6]

At University House, where most academics and scholars resided, there was a communal kitchen and dining room, a lounge room, a music room and a billiard room where they often congregated in the evenings. Most nights at Masson Street, or in the local pub, there were also get-togethers with other students and academics. Hawke was popular and well known, and was elected as a student representative to the University Council. Maxwell Newton and John Knight, whom Hawke had known in Perth, and Ron Hieser became regular drinking partners at the Canberra Hotel. Hawke also became friends with several notable academics in these years, including Fin Crisp and Manning Clark.

Coleman, who would later become New South Wales Liberal leader and a federal Liberal MP, had arrived at ANU three days before the Hawkes. Coleman had been awarded a research scholarship in the Department of Social Philosophy. He lived with his wife, Verna, at University House until she fell pregnant and they moved to the flats on Masson Street. Coleman and Hawke became friendly and often socialised. Coleman described Hawke as a mix of 'indiscretions, evasions, strange intensities, blindness and charm', which served to make his days in Canberra 'tolerable'.[7]

Shortly after Susan's birth, Coleman recalled, Hawke found himself back in court. He was double-parked at a shopping centre when a policeman asked him to move on. Hawke explained that he was waiting for Hazel and could not move the car, as Susan would have to be left on the floor and would roll around and likely be injured. He was charged with double-parking. Hawke fought his case, arguing for natural justice, and was fined the nominal amount of £1. He had a moral victory.[8]

Hawke's larrikin personality and hedonist streak had serious consequences. Late on the night of 24 February 1957, Hawke and other students got horribly drunk and, legend has it, decided to swim naked in an ornamental goldfish pond at University House. A group of Anglican bishops were attending a conference at the university, and the raucous behaviour was interrupting their sleep. Professor of Political Science Leicester Webb confronted the students about the noise. This led to a confrontation with Hawke, who abused him. 'I threatened to throw Professor Webb in the pond,' Hawke remembered.[9]

The bishops made a complaint to the vice-chancellor, and the matter was investigated by the university's Disciplinary Committee. In his evidence, Hawke insisted that he had not swum in the pool.[10] After interviewing other students and staff, and the Disciplinary Committee considering the matter, the university registrar wrote to Hawke on 27 February. 'The Committee took an extremely grave view of the matters, especially in view of previous warnings by the Master,' he wrote. Hawke was deemed 'chiefly responsible'.[11] He wrote a letter of apology to the vice-chancellor, Sir Leslie Melville, was fined £15, resigned his seat on the University Council and was banned from University House.

Hawke attended Labor Party branch meetings in Canberra, and during these years got to know many prominent party members. Alan Reid, a journalist in the press gallery, became friendly with Hawke. He met H.V. 'Doc' Evatt several times, and they once had a long debate about the Australian Constitution at the Windsor Hotel in Melbourne in 1958. Hawke was never impressed by Evatt and quickly concluded that he was mad. 'I respected his intellect but not so much his judgement,' Hawke said.[12] In October 1956, Hawke wrote to Clem and Ellie about the factional wars in the local Labor Party in Canberra.[13]

Meanwhile, Hawke imagined a future career as an academic specialising in industrial relations and the law, but had reservations. The quiet, slow, contemplative academic life did not suit the hard-drinking, sexed-up prankster and party boy with a sharp tongue. For now, Hawke was committed to completing his doctorate – his fourth degree – and teaching. He taught Introduction to Legal Method part-time at Canberra University College from 1956 to

1958. He had previously tutored part-time in the Department of Economics at UWA, from March to August 1953, before departing for Oxford. In 1958, Hawke was invited to take up a full-time position as a senior lecturer in law and industrial relations. This would be a step into full-time academia while completing his doctorate. He did not immediately accept.

Hawke considered returning to Perth to contest a seat for Labor at the forthcoming state or federal elections. The suggestion was pushed by the premier, his uncle Albert. Family friend Bill Titterington wrote to Hawke on 17 October 1957 to tell him that nominations for preselection for the next federal election – which would eventually be held in November 1958 – had opened. Titterington had met with Albert and Clem to discuss Hawke's political future. The most likely, and best, scenario was Hawke running for the federal seats of Swan or Perth. But the political climate did not favour Labor, and either seat would be difficult to win. 'I can see that your heart is set on a political career,' Titterington wrote, 'and that you will take the jump sooner or later.'[14] After discussing it with Hazel, Hawke decided against it. He was searching for something else.

Geoffrey Sawer encouraged Hawke to attend a Special Congress of the ACTU which was to discuss union policy and strategy regarding the decision of the Court of Conciliation and Arbitration not to review the ruling in 1953 that abolished the adjustment system. The court had decided to do away with quarterly cost-of-living adjustments to the basic wage, and determined that wages would only increase when the economy had the capacity to pay. Increases would be determined by judges of the court. This gave these judges, led by Raymond Kelly, extraordinary economic power. For workers, it meant their earnings would not be guaranteed to increase in relation to prices, and inflation would erode the value of their wages. In 1956, there had been another significant change to the industrial landscape: the functions of the Court of Conciliation and Arbitration to determine wages and settle disputes would now be carried out by the Conciliation and Arbitration Commission. A new Industrial Court would be responsible for issuing penalties such as fines and imprisonment.

The congress would be an opportunity for Hawke to watch trade unions deliberate on the basic wage, as well as to meet union leaders and share his research. He found it a rewarding experience. He met the ACTU's president, Albert Monk, and secretary, Harold Souter. He was welcomed as a special guest and invited to sit on the platform to observe proceedings. He learnt about the practical application of the basic wage decision in workplaces. He liked them and they liked him. In September 1956, Hawke wrote to Souter offering to assist with the ACTU's preparation for the 1957 Basic Wage Case. 'I would very much like to come down and get an idea of the procedure – and of course, if I can help in any way you know I would be glad to do so,' he wrote.'[15]

Souter took up the offer, and so in November 1956 Hawke attended a conference at the Melbourne offices of barrister Richard Eggleston. Hawke liked Eggleston. He wrote to Clem and Ellie: 'He is an impressive sort of chap who seems to be very much at ease with economic figures and terminology and therefore able to make a good fist of putting the type of arguments to the Court which are the essence of the basic wage hearings.' Hawke attended the subsequent hearings in Sydney and Melbourne, and continued to work with Eggleston. 'I must say that I am enjoying it all immensely,' he told his parents. 'It is good to feel that you are putting your academic and research experience to some practical use which may have some bearing on the Court's decision, and secondly because the union blokes are beaut fellows with whom it is a pleasure to be working.'[16]

The following year, Hawke was again invited to assist with preparing the ACTU's brief for Eggleston, who would appear for the unions in the 1958 Basic Wage Case. It was common for the ACTU to invite academics to help in this way. Keith Hancock, a tutor at the University of Melbourne, also worked on the brief that year. H.P. 'Horrie' Brown, an economic historian at the ANU, had previously advised the ACTU in wage cases. Monk and Souter had sought Brown's advice on who might help them with future wage cases, and he recommended Hawke. Hawke impressed the ACTU with his work, but was irritated when Eggleston and his instructing solicitor, Bob Brodney, did not draw on his research to make an argument more forcefully. Hawke felt he could do better.

In early 1958, following the Basic Wage Case, Hawke was invited to attend a union dinner at Usher's Metropolitan Hotel on Castlereagh Street, Sydney. After dinner, all retired to the lounge bar for drinks. Monk pulled his chair alongside Hawke's and put his arm around Hawke's shoulders. 'Bob, we would like you to come and work with us full-time as our Research Officer and Advocate,' he said. Hawke was touched by the gesture and surprised by the job offer. 'It was just perfect,' he recalled. 'I didn't finish the PhD but I thought what the hell, it didn't matter.'[17] Hawke added: 'The trade unions were terribly important to the life of working people, and I believed that I was uniquely placed, because of my training in law and economics, to help them, as I did in the preparation and presentation of the cases.'[18]

This would be a two-year full-time job. It would require not only giving up his doctoral studies but also moving to Melbourne, where the ACTU was headquartered on Lygon Street, Carlton. This was not the trajectory Hawke thought his career was on. But it was a tantalising offer. Hawke wanted to take the job but decided to talk it over with Sawer and Hazel. Sawer encouraged him to take the job. Hawke asked the university for an extension of time to complete his doctorate, and this was granted. Hazel was concerned about moving to Melbourne with baby Susan, given they were settled in Canberra, but was supportive of her husband's career change.

Hawke also talked to Coleman about the offer at the Lygon Hotel, opposite the Trades Hall in Melbourne. There, beneath the framed pictures of labour leaders, they discussed the options. 'Pugnacious, ambitious, full of confidence, in a hell of a hurry but not certain which way to turn and certainly not listening to anyone who wanted to advise him,' Coleman recalled of Hawke at that time. After their talk, Hawke drove Coleman home, speeding along St Kilda Road, hunched over the steering wheel. When they came to the Junction, which at the time was a large roundabout, Hawke drove around it about ten times, not knowing where to exit. It served as a metaphor for his predicament. 'He had several choices – the Labor Party, the university, the trade unions,' Coleman thought. 'He made the right choice.'[19]

Many on the ACTU executive, however, felt Hawke was not cut from the same cloth as them. He had never worked a full-time manual labour job. He was an an intellectual and an academic – a professional student at age twenty-eight. He had never been a union activist. He had never been a workplace delegate. He had never worked for a union. How could he empathise with working men and women? And he had not practised law, yet he was to be the ACTU's research officer and advocate?

Deep down, Hawke needed little persuading. This was an opportunity to give his academic experience practical expression. Working for the ACTU also accorded with Hawke's social, economic and political values. And so, in March 1958, Bob and Hazel, with Susan, drove from Canberra to Melbourne to start the next phase of their lives.

PART II

AMBITION
1958–1983

7

ADVOCATE

Bob Hawke commenced work with the ACTU, which was located in a small, two-storey, red-brick office opposite the Trades Hall on Lygon Street, in May 1958. He immediately immersed himself in his research and advocacy work, and expanded his knowledge of the unions, their leaders and their members. Hawke's focus was the forthcoming 1959 Basic Wage Case. He began to drink regularly at the Lygon Hotel – later named the John Curtin Hotel – one of two pubs that sandwiched the ACTU's headquarters. The other hotel Hawke frequented was the Dover, which was patronised by the Industrial Groups – known as 'Groupers' – who were part of B.A. Santamaria's shadowy group named The Movement, and supporters of the breakaway Democratic Labor Party.

Melbourne was a maelstrom of political and industrial upheaval. Labor had formally split in Queensland and Victoria over communist influence in the party. The Menzies government was in its tenth year in office and seemed unlikely to be dislodged anytime soon. In May 1958, Henry Bolte's Victorian Liberal and Country Party government was re-elected. Labor, riven with division, would not return to power in Victoria until April 1982. Hawke later wrote:

> This Melbourne was a cauldron of hatred, a witches' brew of loaded labels, mindless epithets and raw sectarianism. Families were split, with brother set against brother or father, officials

within the same union regarding each other as mortal enemies, worshippers in the same Church treated by their co-religionists as lepers, while to be a Mason was to wear a badge of honour in the Victorian branch of the ALP, soon to be guided by the unlovely hands of William Hartley.[1]

Hawke was fascinated by this confluence of events. The men he met, befriended and worked with earned his admiration and respect. They talked politics, economics and philosophy. They were proud men, mostly self-taught, with wisdom that came from years of real-world experience. He admired their integrity and commitment, and the conviction with which they held to their causes. They included communists such as Jim Healy, the general secretary of the Waterside Workers' Union; George Seelaf, secretary of the Victorian branch of the Meat Industry Employees' Union; and Alec McDonald, secretary of the Queensland Trades and Labour Council. 'One of the things that struck me when I went to the ACTU in 1958 was the number of outstanding men – and I say men because there were virtually no women leaders then – who because of their background hadn't been able to finish secondary school, let alone go to university,' Hawke said later. 'So you had people who otherwise would have been doctors, lawyers, executives going into the trade union movement.'[2]

The Australian Council of Trade Unions was established in 1927. It had occupied a corner of the Trades Hall in Melbourne until 1952, when it relocated across the road to its own small building. Power and resources were located in state or regional trades and labour councils, and individual unions. The appointment of Hawke represented a considerable expansion of ACTU resources. Monk, Souter, Hawke, two secretaries and a junior assistant, Jennie McAlpine, were the only full-time staff in 1958. Initially, Hawke was located on the ground floor. McAlpine would assist him, and they grew fond of each other. Souter, however, became 'suspicious' of Hawke's intentions with McAlpine and forbade them to work alone together.[3]

Albert Monk, born in 1900 in England, migrated to Australia at age ten. He undertook clerical studies after completing school and in 1919 joined the Transport Workers' Union as an office clerk. He had served as secretary (1943–49) and as president (1934–43; 1949–69) of the ACTU. He had also served as president of the Victorian Trades Hall Council and the Victorian branch of the Labor Party. Monk was also federal and Victorian president of the Federated Clerks' Union. He was a short, plump, balding man with dark-rimmed glasses. He was reserved, eschewed public displays of emotion and avoided the media spotlight. But he had a shrewd grasp of labour politics, worked assiduously to keep the ACTU a united representative body, and cooperated with governments to advance the interests of working men and women.

By the time Hawke had arrived at the ACTU, however, Monk's best years were behind him. He was approaching sixty, and it was expected that he would retire soon. He was regarded as a largely hands-off president who left most of the work to Souter. Monk spent a lot of time overseas, especially at meetings of the International Labour Organization (ILO). His health was failing and he was an alcoholic. But unlike Hawke, Monk drank whisky alone, darting in and out of the Lygon several times during the day.[4]

Souter did not drink alcohol, nor did he smoke. He was rarely seen at the Lygon. He was lean and fit, quietly spoken, even-tempered and often shy. He was not showy or flashy; he was cautious and conservative in his views and manners. His main hobby was growing dahlias. He was, however, respected for his work ethic and his commitment to industrial labour. Souter had worked as an apprentice fitter and turner in Adelaide before becoming an assistant organiser with the Amalgamated Engineering Union at age twenty-eight. He became an organiser, then district secretary and eventually the union's federal arbitration officer, a role which required him to move to Melbourne in 1947. He was appointed as the ACTU's research officer in 1954. When ACTU secretary Reg Broadby died suddenly in 1956, Souter succeeded him.

Hawke prepared for the 1959 Basic Wage Case with the assistance of economist Eric Russell from the University of Adelaide, along with Horrie Brown and Wilfred Salter from the ANU. He would appear on behalf of the metal trades unions – a claim that would later be joined by 160 other unions – arguing for a 10-shilling increase in the basic wage, plus a 12-shilling cost-of-living adjustment to compensate for the suspension of quarterly wage adjustments. Hawke recalled setting out with a clear purpose: to demolish the argument underpinning the abolition of automatic quarterly adjustments of the basic wage made by the Court of Conciliation and Arbitration, dominated by the presiding judge, Raymond Kelly, in 1953. Between 1953 and 1958, the court and the commission had awarded increases which did not maintain the real value of wages.

Hawke wanted to demonstrate the economic fallacy that employers did not have the 'capacity to pay' increases in salary even though their profits increased, productivity improved and the economy grew. Hawke would argue that the wages of working men and women should reflect the real growth in the economy, and therefore be adjusted based on productivity improvements and prices. Hawke later discovered from Judge Alf Foster that Kelly had developed a close relationship with B.A. Santamaria and Colin Clark, with whom Hawke had had a bitter encounter at Oxford over his proposed thesis. Kelly, Santamaria and Clark advocated intensive land settlement in Australia as the basis of an agrarian rather than industrial economic future. That notion was absurd, Hawke would argue to the bench.

The case opened on Tuesday, 24 February 1959, at the Concil-iation and Arbitration Commission on Little Bourke Street in Melbourne. Richard Kirby, the president, Alf Foster and Frank Gallagher were presiding. The three judges were surprised and somewhat affronted to learn that the ACTU had handed the presentation of their case to Hawke, an academic aged just twenty-nine. The representatives of the Australian Workers' Union – which was not affiliated with the ACTU – were not impressed either. 'From Eggleston to Egghead,' ran a headline in their journal.[5] Hawke was assisted by Ted Deverall from the Amalgamated Engineering Union, Norman Docker from the Waterside Workers' Federation and David Ross from the Feder-ated Ironworkers' Association. They too were unsure about him. But as the first day's proceedings lengthened, the judges, the employer and union representatives, and the industrial reporters were all surprised. The virtually unknown Hawke was arguing the ACTU's case cogently and logically, and with passion and verve. He spoke loud and fast, displaying a nervous energy, while pacing the carpet in front of the bench. One thing was clear: Hawke knew what he was talking about.

The rookie advocate had little time for niceties. Hawke attacked the commission for the decision on wages in 1953, and every year subsequently. Kirby, the only judge who had been on the bench in 1953, was a focus of Hawke's fury. Hawke had interviewed him while a student at the ANU, peppering Kirby with questions about economics, and had less than subtly suggested that the commission had no idea about economic matters. Kirby had found Hawke 'offensive' and cut the interview short.[6] Now Hawke, standing in front of the bench, did not disguise his contempt. This led Deverall, seated at the table, to tug Hawke's sleeve and suggest he use the term 'with respect' if he wanted to call the bench stupid, and 'with the greatest respect' if he wanted to call them something worse than that.[7]

Foster, who was sympathetic to the union's argument, was dismayed that Hawke had replaced Eggleston. A year ago, Hawke was a full-time student. He had no courtroom experience and was not a barrister. Foster thought allowing Hawke to run the case was a grave misjudgement, and made his view known to Monk. 'I am entitled,' Foster wrote in a note to Monk, 'to have senior counsel before me.'[8] But Hawke had won Foster over by the first afternoon. After lunch, Foster conceded the essential validity of Hawke's argument that it was a mistake to suspend quarterly cost-of-living adjustments in 1953. 'I do suggest, with some humility, that judgement was based on a fallacy,' said Foster, with whom Hawke later became friendly.[9]

Hawke recalled that the pivotal moment in the 1959 Basic Wage Case was his demolition of businessman Ronald Truman, who was used as a witness by the employer groups and spoke to why they could not afford pay increases. Truman said his evidence was based on material provided by the Commonwealth Bank. 'I had a lot of doubt about him,' Hawke recalled. 'I rang up the bloke at the bank and asked him about some of the things that Truman had said, and he said that didn't happen. So I had him by the balls.' Hawke said he did not want to 'crucify him' but told the employer advocate, Drew Aird, that Truman's credibility had been shredded. 'There was a discussion with the bench and the employer said they could no longer rely on him,' Hawke recalled.[10]

Throughout the hearings, employer representatives argued that companies did not have the capacity to pay, and asked for the basic wage to be reduced; they also rejected the restoration of quarterly wage adjustments. But Hawke presented evidence that company profits had increased substantially since 1953, while wages had been supressed. He showed that between 1952–53 and 1956–57, Australia's largest 100 companies had increased their profits from £34.9 million to £63.5 million. While profits had increased by 82 per cent, the basic wage had gone up by just 10.6 per cent.

The hearing took place over three months, with forty-four days of hearings, and on 5 June the commission handed down its judgement. The basic wage would increase by 15 shillings, the highest amount since 1950, delivering a huge win for the unions. But Kirby and Gallagher would not overturn the 1953 decision and reinstate automatic quarterly adjustments. The wage boost amounted to more than that would have achieved in any case. In the 1959 Margins Case, held a few weeks later, Hawke further secured a 28 per cent increase in award payments for skills and experience for metal trades workers, above the basic wage. In that case, he was opposed by barrister John Kerr, appearing for the Chamber of Manufactures. Hawke thought Kerr was pompous and arrogant, and deeply hostile to the union cause. Kerr had a perfectly coiffured leonine mane of white hair. 'The Liberace of the law,' Hawke called him.[11]

Hawke was soon being written up in newspapers for his advocacy skills, and interviewed on radio and television. His star was on the rise. By the end of his second year at the ACTU, Hawke had won the respect of the union movement. But employer groups were furious. He was, essentially, responsible for an explosion in the annual national wages bill of some £150 million. Hawke was seen as an enemy of business; wilder claims at the time said he threatened the future of capitalism in Australia. He was known as 'Mr Inflation'. He was accused of being a communist, or at least a communist sympathiser. Within Labor, he was regarded as a larrikin radical on the left wing of the party.

The elements of Hawke's success as an advocate were intellect, determination and passion. He would research matters extensively and prepare copious notes, but rarely read directly from them. He would use logic, appeal to reason and show emotion. His style set him apart from others, and made him – despite his lack of previous court experience – at least the equal of many of the senior counsel who appeared for employer groups or the government. Hawke said his approach was mostly influenced by American lawyer Clarence Darrow: he had 'enormous respect' for Darrow and was 'impressed by him as a man, as a speaker and a thinker'.[12]

—

When they had moved to Melbourne in May 1958, Bob and Hazel purchased a two-bedroom weatherboard cottage at 13 Keats Street, Sandringham, about 20 kilometres south of Melbourne. They paid £4400 at auction for the house, and Hawke used the advance of half a year's salary as a deposit. The ACTU Executive had debated the matter, and some members suggested Hawke should be charged interest, but ultimately £1000 was advanced as a 'salary adjustment'.[13] Bob and Hazel loved the house, which had a big backyard with trees and garden, and was close to the beach. They were blessed with the birth of their first son, Stephen, on 4 February 1959. Rosslyn, their second daughter, was born on 23 November 1960.

Hawke's growing workload and the increasing time he spent away from home travelling and socialising – which he saw as critical to building respect and rapport with his union colleagues – took a toll on the family, and Hazel was effectively mother and father to the children. She also did the grocery shopping and the house cleaning, and paid the bills – almost everything that had to be done to sustain a family and maintain a home. Hazel felt more alone than she had ever been in her life. 'By now Bob was a regular drinker, and patterns which put great strains on our home life became entrenched,' she recalled. 'His working and playing were providing another world for him, and did not leave much time or energy for his family.'[14]

With Hazel having and raising children as the focus of her life and Bob immersed in his work, they were not as intimate as they

once were. The 'sexual pleasure' they found in each other began
to change, and they could not sustain the 'playmates' relationship
they had enjoyed over the previous decade. Hazel knew that Bob
was having affairs.[15] When he was drunk, he would 'descend into
a vitriolic form of verbal abuse'. It was appalling behaviour, often
witnessed by others, yet Hazel remained devoted to Bob – and she
did not fundamentally doubt his love for her.[16]

Hawke was burdened with an immense amount of work in
preparing for the 1959 and 1960 Basic Wage Cases, and was also
running the Margins Case and fulfilling other duties. He would
leave home at around 4 am or 4.30 am, and work at the ACTU
office until around 9 am, when he would then go to court. He
recalled sleeping on the floor during the lunch adjournment and
napping in the afternoon before working late into the night.
'The pressure was unbelievable,' he said. 'In the peak periods it
was seven days a week, eighteen hours a day, for several weeks.'[17]
Learning to take naps was essential in this job, and would be in his
later political career.

In recognition of his immense workload, he persuaded Monk
and Souter to appoint a research assistant, and in late 1959 Ralph
Willis applied for the job. Willis had a Bachelor of Commerce
from the University of Melbourne. Hawke knew his father Stan,
who was a part-time official with the Boilermakers' Union. Willis
got the job and began work in early 1960. 'He was a national figure
of importance at that stage,' Willis remembered. 'Bob had a stellar
year in 1959 and so going to work for him was pretty sensational
for me.'

Willis said Hawke's work ethic was phenomenal. They would
get started early morning, break for a quick lunch, return to the
office in the afternoon, then break again for a few drinks at the
Lygon, and then often return to the office in the evening. Willis
marvelled at how Hawke could be on the phone to officials, chat
effortlessly with unionists at the pub, keep abreast of the latest
political and industrial news, mostly through newspapers, and still
be able to present cases articulately in the court or commission.
Hawke had a unique stamina. He could work effectively with little
sleep. He rarely showed signs of a hangover. And he only occasionally became ill.

Willis was struck by the extent of Hawke's drinking. He would drink a lot and he would drink fast. The Lygon was an essential part of Hawke's day; according to Willis, it was a key meeting place for union officials. But all pubs closed at 6 pm, so there was always a rush for drinks at the end of the day – the so-called six o'clock swill. These restricted trading hours would remain in place in Victoria until 1966. 'There was a quarter of an hour's grace, but there was no serving after six o'clock,' Willis said. 'So you were lining up at six o'clock and you would be looking at five beers, and you would be drinking them before quarter past six.'

Journalists and politicians often frequented the Lygon, which would lead to spirited debates. 'When [Hawke] got a bit pissed he could become fairly abrasive and fairly unpleasant,' Willis said. 'He would react far more aggressively than the situation actually required. We would think, "Oh Christ, we are going to be in for a fight here." And one or two times it did break into a fight, but people broke it up. How he never got his lights punched out a few times I wouldn't know.'[18]

In the 1960 Basic Wage Case, assisted by Willis, Hawke faced off against Eggleston, who was now representing the Commonwealth and the usual employer representatives. It was the first time the Commonwealth had intervened to oppose a pay rise in a Basic Wage Case. This was a measure of Hawke's impact the previous year. Undeterred, Hawke argued for a 22-shilling increase in the basic wage, but the commission, spooked by claims of economic calamity promulgated by Eggleston on behalf of the government, awarded just a 5-shilling increase, and again rebuffed Hawke's push for quarterly adjustments to be reinstated. It was a victory for the ACTU, and did nothing to dent Hawke's standing, but he saw it as a defeat. He steeled himself for the following year's case.

It is not surprising that Hawke's desire to complete his PhD, even remotely, was proving overly optimistic. His ACTU workload was just too big. With Sawer's support, he asked for an extension and, after some deliberation, the ANU gave him two further years. He was asked to submit a draft of his thesis by 1 April 1960. But, in the end, Hawke was forced to acknowledge to the university that he could not complete the PhD.[19] This ended any career he might have had as an academic: Hawke had decided he would make the labour movement his life's work and purpose.

In February 1961, Hawke enlisted the prominent economist Sir Douglas Copland, an adviser to Australian governments during wartime and an ambassador, in his crusade to restore quarterly cost-of-living wage adjustments. Hawke called Copland as a witness in the commission's Wage and Hour Case in Melbourne, having secured his support for overturning the 1953 Basic Wage Case decision. Copland told the commission that since 1953, increases in wages had lagged behind increases in productivity, and to reinstate cost-of-living wage adjustments would not leave employers worse off. Copland was a significant ally for Hawke, who was slowly reshaping the attitudes of the commissioners.

Hawke's opening remarks to the hearing, which began on 14 February, lasted three days. Justices Richard Kirby, Richard Ashburner and John Moore were attacked, insulted and harassed by Hawke. 'You have inflicted hardship upon thousands of people,' he said. He held them responsible for the miserly wage increases. Hawke was unrelenting and unremitting. By the time he made his final address in reply, which stretched over twelve days, he was physically spent. He could hardly stand without gripping the lectern. His feet ached so much that he took his shoes off and stood in front of the judges in his socks, berating them until he had nothing more to give.[20]

On 4 July 1961, the commissioners handed down their unanimous judgement. It represented a stunning achievement by Hawke. The basic wage for adult men would increase by 12 shillings a week, and for adult women by 9 shillings a week. This would affect about 2 million federal award workers in Australia. Proportional increases would flow for junior employees and apprentices. The judgement was estimated to add £60 million to the national wages bill. The commission did not restore automatic quarterly wage adjustments, but it did determine that future variations in the basic wage should be adjusted annually, based on the cost-of-living index, and triennially for productivity increases.

Barrie Unsworth, who became an organiser with the Electrical Trades Union in 1961, remembered how Hawke's achievement thrilled the union movement. 'Hawke was a breath of fresh air in the trade union movement,' he said. 'Appearing for us in the courts, the arbitration tribunals, he was up against the old legal processes that had held the trade unions and the workers back for many years. It was highly legalistic and you were up against employers who had top-rate representatives who were highly paid. But now Hawke was on the union payroll, so we had somebody who would go into the court and represent us in a very effective way.'[21]

From 13 May to 6 June 1962, Hawke won a scholarship to attend the Duke of Edinburgh's Second Commonwealth Study Conference in Canada. His focus of study was Britain's decision to join the European Economic Community – the Common Market – and the trade and investment implications for Australia. Hawke met Prince Philip during the conference. He also travelled to the United States and Europe in July and August, where he met government, business and union officials. Hawke was awarded a Leader Grant, which gave him special status while travelling in the United States and assistance from the Department of Labor with travel and organising meetings. He was paid a per diem of US$20 per day and granted US$40 to spend on books and educational materials.[22] Hawke also travelled to Malaya and Singapore to undertake short periods of study and lecture on industrial relations in Australia.

Hazel wrote regularly to Bob about what was happening in Australia. Her letters show her to be fully engaged in union and party matters. For example, she updated him on a Victorian Labor conference which had debated the White Australia policy, a dispute between unions and management at Ford, and notable articles in magazines and newspapers.[23] She told him about friends and family, and especially the children, and sent along their drawings. They spoke on the phone occasionally – which had to be booked in advance – and Hazel was delighted to read about his adventures abroad in return letters. 'I just devour them,' she wrote, 'and then I can think of them and talk about them.'[24] Her letters, and his, are filled with love and devotion. All the family longed to see him. 'My darling Bob,' Hazel would write. 'How we'd like you home tonight!'[25]

Hawke's successes meant that he had become, unwittingly, the public face of the ACTU, and among the most prominent trade union figures in Australia – a status that agitated Monk and Souter. Hawke had delivered wage increases to millions of working men and women. There would be uproar if his position came under any threat. They needed Hawke. But so did Hazel, Susan, Stephen and Rosslyn. But Hawke was away so much that any parenting in these years was done via phone or letter, and when he was at home he was often asleep, paralysed by exhaustion, or inebriated. Hawke was an absent and inattentive father, yet he valued so highly his own parents who had given him their utmost love and devotion.

8

RISING STAR

After five years at the ACTU, Bob Hawke was persuaded by the Victorian Labor Party to stand as the Labor candidate for the seat of Corio, which included Geelong. Hawke's candidature was confirmed at a meeting of the party's selection committee on Tuesday, 22 October 1963, just five and a half weeks before the election.[1] 'A Rhodes Scholar is strongly tipped to oppose the Minister for Shipping and Transport, Mr. Opperman, for his seat of Corio in the elections on November 30,' *The Canberra Times* reported. Hawke's academic expertise was the focus of the short article, and it was not mentioned until the final paragraph that he worked for the ACTU. But it was undeniably his profile as a union advocate that made him stand out as a candidate.[2]

At the previous election, in December 1961, Labor, led by Arthur Calwell, had come within just two seats of returning to power. The Menzies government had survived even though Labor had won 50.5 per cent of the two-party-preferred vote, and was able to govern with a one-seat majority after allocating a Speaker. There was an expectation within Labor that it would win the next election. Hawke, who had been increasing his involvement in state and federal party affairs as a member of several policy committees, was persuaded to be a candidate. He recalled the principal person urging him to run was Albert McNolty, State and Federal Secretary of the Sheet Metal Workers' Union. McNolty had pressed Hawke to nominate for the seat while sitting next to him at a Labor Party dinner in Melbourne.[3]

Corio had been a Labor seat during the government of Jim Scullin and through the Curtin/Chifley years, when it was held by John Dedman. Hawke's opponent was the sitting Liberal member, and former Olympic cyclist, Hubert Opperman – known as 'Oppy' – who had held the seat since December 1949. The Democratic Labor Party nominated James Mahoney to contest the seat, as it had in 1961. Clyde Cameron, the Labor MP for Hindmarsh, in South Australia, and a leading figure in the Australian Workers' Union, wrote to Hawke, ecstatic to learn of his selection. Corio was a working-class seat and should never have been lost by Labor, he wrote, and predicted Hawke would win. 'Your standing with the workers is almost legendary.'[4]

The Corio campaign was conducted in the shadow of a tragedy for Bob and Hazel. Robert, a second son, died four days after being born premature on 1 August 1963. Both Hazel and Bob were distraught. Hazel turned inward as she coped with her grief; Bob turned outward, looking to union friends and drinking excessively. Bob went to the funeral with Ralph Willis; Hazel was too ill to attend. They never saw their boy. Hawke's preselection took place just months after Robert's death. Willis said it was a 'particularly awful' time for both of them.[5] Hazel, understandably, did little campaigning. Bob got alcohol poisoning, and was still recovering as the campaign began. He had collapsed on a street in Melbourne and Hazel got him to the nearest hospital, quite possibly saving his life.

Corio was to be a generational contest. Opperman was fifty-nine, Hawke just thirty-three. Opperman was no longer the lean and fit Olympic athlete he had once been: he was portly, with thinning hair and looked exhausted. Hawke, with dark, curly hair and piercing blue eyes beneath arched eyebrows, was presented to voters as a young and dynamic man with wisdom beyond his years.

A Labor flyer argued that Hawke 'is one of the most capable men to stand for federal parliament' and had 'the ideal combination of youth and experience'. It noted his marriage to Hazel and their three children: Susan (six), Stephen (four) and Rosslyn (two). It trumpeted his 'outstanding academic career' as a Rhodes scholar with three degrees. It highlighted his success as the ACTU's research officer and advocate, which had delivered increases in the basic wage. And it referred to his 'international experience', with travels to Canada, the United States and Europe. If that weren't enough to win voters over, it also noted his 'armed services experience' in the Royal Air Force Volunteer Reserve at Oxford, and that he was an 'all-round sportsman' who had played first-grade cricket and enjoyed tennis and golf. (Hawke had captained Melbourne Cricket Club's thirds in 1962.) 'All of these qualifications indicate that Bob Hawke is the kind of man Corio needs – he has youth, education, experience, vigor, integrity.'[6] Another flyer focused on Hawke's achievements as ACTU advocate and urged voters to give him the opportunity to serve them in federal parliament. 'Bob is standing for you – give him a seat.'[7]

Before Hawke could win over the voters, he had to win over the party members. Two others had nominated for preselection but were rejected by the Victorian State Executive, which reopened the nominations for Hawke and then promptly selected him. Hawke was not from Corio: he was being imposed on the electorate. Hawke's campaign manager was George Poyser, a former World War II veteran, who at the time was secretary of the Geelong Trades Hall Council. 'There was a lot of resentment that the executive had behaved in this way and a lot of resentment against Hawke,' Poyser recalled. 'We pushed the Rhodes Scholar line and within a week Bob had 100 per cent of the local organisation behind him.'[8]

Hawke campaigned hard. He was at the factories when they opened and when they closed. He spoke from street corners and on shopping strips. He doorknocked houses. He visited bus stops, sporting groups, service clubs and community organisations. He used the local media. He moved Hazel and the children into the electorate as a sign of his commitment. The Hawkes lived in a rental house at Portarlington, enrolling Susan at the local primary school and Stephen at a local kindergarten. Opperman charged Hawke with lacking a record of achievement and with being a carpetbagger. 'Performance not Promises!' the Liberal campaign material read. 'Your man is Opperman.'

Hawke had a stroke of luck when businessman Rod Miller offered both an endorsement and financial assistance. Miller was a critic of Opperman for refusing a licence for his Australian tanker *Millers Canopus*, and had called for him to be sacked as minister for shipping. Hawke chimed in and argued that Australian farmers were being dudded by the Overseas Shipping Conference. When the *Canopus* entered Corio Bay and docked at the Shell Refinery wharf, Hawke was there to greet it with a phalanx of reporters. The ship was clad in Labor campaign slogans. Poyser recalled that Miller paid for Labor's full-page newspaper, television and radio advertisements that attacked Opperman over the handling of his portfolio. These attacks were echoed by Hawke in his speeches and interviews. The money donated by Miller was kept apart from the 'official Labor accounts'.[9]

Gough Whitlam, then Labor's deputy leader, launched Hawke's campaign on 12 November. It took place in front of an audience of about 500 at the Geelong West Town Hall. Before Hawke spoke, Menzies' policy speech was broadcast to the audience from televisions set up around the hall. The major announcement was the allocation of £5 million in grants to state governments to support the teaching of science in secondary schools and scholarships for students to attend the final year of school and enrol in technical colleges. In Hawke's speech, delivered from notes, he accused Menzies of stealing Labor's policies on education, housing, roads, northern development, petrol pricing and child endowment. 'By their deeds shall ye know them,' he thundered.[10] It was a theme continued from Whitlam, who had accused Menzies of belittling Labor policy and then adopting much of it as his own. Hawke said Menzies was 'a millionaire' in words but 'poverty-stricken' in ideas.[11]

Backlighting the campaign was a feverish atmosphere of fear and suspicion. First, there was the scare propagated by Mahoney, and endorsed by Opperman, that Labor and the unions could not be trusted with national security because they had been infiltrated by communists. Many Democratic Labor Party voters gave their preferences to the Coalition. When Hawke was invited by a supporter to walk through the Corio Club, a man stood up and asked, 'Who brought this communist in here?' Hawke's supporter punched the man in the face and he fell to the ground.[12]

Second, echoing Menzies, Opperman accused Hawke of being controlled by a shadowy backroom group of union and party officials known as the 'thirty-six faceless men'. In March 1963, Labor's federal conference – made up of thirty-six delegates – had met in Canberra to decide the party's policy on the United States' naval communications station at North West Cape, in Western Australia. The issue divided Labor. The leader and deputy leader, Calwell and Whitlam, were inclined to support it, provided there was joint oversight. But they were not members of the federal conference, so they waited beneath a lamppost outside the Kingston Hotel while a decision was reached. Journalist Alan Reid organised for them to be photographed, and the picture was published in *The Daily Telegraph*. Although the conference had endorsed Calwell and Whitlam's position, their exclusion from the chief policymaking body of the party was ridiculed by Menzies. It served to confirm his view that Labor was captive to a secretive political machine.

The third factor backlighting the Corio campaign was the fear of a possible war with Indonesia. In September, Menzies had announced that Australia would support Malaysia in its confrontation with Indonesia. In October, he committed Australia to buying two squadrons of F-111 striker bombers capable of carrying nuclear weapons. The implication was clear: they could be used to bomb Indonesia to secure Australia's safety, if needed. Claims that Labor was weak on defence were promulgated in the local press and on local radio, and directly by Opperman in his speeches.

A week before election day, John F. Kennedy was assassinated while riding in a motorcade in Dallas, Texas. Hawke was shaken by Kennedy's death. (When he first heard that Kennedy had been assassinated, he thought it was television personality Graham Kennedy.[13]) He described the president's murder as 'like a family bereavement' and said the world had lost 'a leader of wide and purposeful vision'.[14] The assassination likely led some voters to favour security and stability and not seek to change the government. In the final week of the campaign, foreign-policy issues dominated. Calwell insisted that Labor would maintain the ANZUS Treaty and jettisoned several of the party's defence and foreign policies, such as its commitment to a nuclear-free Southern Hemisphere.

Opperman painted Labor as weak on defence and hostile to ANZUS. He claimed that six members of Labor's federal executive were known to be communists. Hawke responded by demanding Opperman name them and provide evidence, or retreat and apologise. Opperman refused and doubled down. 'Does the ALP deny that there are members of the federal conference who have visited and been honoured in Communist Russia, organised Communist Candidates in union elections with unity tickets, advocated amalgamations of the ALP and the Communist party and been elected by Communist dominated unions?' he asked in a newspaper advertisement.[15] It was disgraceful, but such was politics during the Cold War.

While the political momentum shifted towards the Coalition in the final weeks, Corio was still deemed to be in play. Labor organised for several high-profile visits to the seat: Victorian Labor MP Sam Benson (14 November), former Chifley government minister Reg Pollard (19 November) and New South Wales Labor MP Fred Daly (20 November).[16] Three days before election day, on 27 November, Calwell addressed a public meeting at the Geelong Plaza Theatre. He emphasised that, under a Labor government, there would be no change in Australia's foreign policy and no weakening of the ANZUS alliance, and insisted that the only differences with the Coalition were on domestic policies.[17] Hawke used his speech to lash the government's policy record, accused the Liberal Party of 'McCarthyism', and said Labor would deliver more jobs, wage justice and higher standards of living.[18]

The day before the election, Menzies travelled to Geelong to address two meetings of workers at the Ford Motor Company, a large employer in the city. He argued that Australia's security and defence were the primary election issues.[19] There were concerns for Menzies' safety and he was protected by thirty police officers. However, the only incident was a firecracker in a cigarette box being thrown from one section of the crowd to another.[20] These visits underscored that both the major parties believed Hawke could defeat Opperman. But, as Ralph Willis recalled, Opperman's personal popularity was hard to overcome. 'On election day people handing out cards for Opperman would just say, "This is Oppy's card." They didn't say anything about the Liberal Party. He was a national hero.'[21]

Although Labor lifted its primary vote by 3.7 percentage

points in Corio, and won more votes overall, it was not enough
to secure the seat. Hawke had won 45.6 per cent of the vote
(21,933) to Opperman's 44 per cent (21,185). Most of Mahoney's
votes – 5004 – were distributed as preferences to Opperman,
which enabled him to clinch victory with 53.3 per cent of the
two-party vote. Nationally, Menzies' government was returned
to power with an increased majority. Although Labor's overall
vote had declined, Hawke had increased it in Corio. He may have
been helped by being placed first on the ballot paper, receiving
the so-called donkey vote, but that alone would not explain the
swing in Corio. Opperman compared his victory to winning the
Paris–Brest–Paris cycling race in 1931, when he eclipsed a strong
opponent to claim the best win of his career.[22]

Susan, then age six, recalled moving to Portarlington for
the campaign. 'I still remember watching the ships sail through the
kitchen window,' she said. 'I was always immensely curious, and
out of us three kids probably the most curious about Dad's political and union activity.' She remembered visiting farmers and
knocking on doors, holding her father's hand. He had promised
to wake her with news of the result. 'What happened, Daddy?' she
asked. 'We did okay, love, but we didn't win.' He explained that he
had received more votes than anyone else, but blamed 'the bloody
DLP' as, sitting on the edge of her bed, he took her through the
complexity of preference distribution.[23]

At the declaration of the poll at the electoral office on Malop
Street, Geelong, on 11 December 1963, the animosity between
Hawke and Opperman was barely concealed. They shook hands
and smiled for photos. Opperman said never had so much money
been spent by such a varied group of interests arrayed against
him in so short a time. He predicted that Hawke's campaign for
a seat would not be his last. Hawke said he was 'proud' to have
received the most primary votes, and congratulated Mahoney for
his organisational and campaigning skills, which had delivered the
seat to Opperman. He congratulated Opperman. He predicted
that his party would win Corio next time, and advised Opperman
to make the next three years 'fruitful' ones.[24]

It was, by any measure, a strong performance by Hawke.
Labor's vote locally went in the opposite direction to Labor's vote

nationally. Hawke was an outsider with no connection to the electorate. He was young and had only been working full-time for five years. His opponent was a popular minister and a sporting legend. Hawke should never have been a chance, yet he polled first on primary votes.

Many in the party expected that Hawke would run again in Corio. 'My heartiest congratulations on a magnificent result,' Cameron wrote to Hawke. 'There is not the shadow of doubt that at the next election you will be a member of the federal parliament.'[25] But Hawke did not run for Corio again. In any event, Labor failed to regain the seat at the next election, in November 1966.[26] At every subsequent federal election between 1966 and 1980, Hawke would be approached by Labor figures about again contesting a seat for the party. The overtures came from the party rank and file, too. In August 1965, for example, the secretary of Labor's Wangi Wangi branch, south of Newcastle in New South Wales, wrote to Hawke imploring him to stand as Labor's candidate for Robertson at the next election. 'This seat can be won by a proper Labor candidate,' the secretary wrote, and included the nomination forms.[27] Hawke politely declined. He had other plans.

Hawke never regretted his loss in Corio. 'That was the best thing that ever happened to me,' he recalled.[28] Calwell and Whitlam soon became enveloped in a bitter feud about Labor's future, and the party would remain in opposition for a further nine years. If Hawke had joined Labor's parliamentary team in 1963, he would have spent many years on the back bench and been well down the list of leadership hopefuls. Hazel remarked many years later: 'If Bob had won Corio in 1963, he would have drunk himself to death.'[29]

—

After a brief period of recuperation, Hawke turned his mind to the 1964 Basic Wage Case. He would face off against Jim Robinson, a South Australian barrister, who would represent the Australian Council of Employers' Federation, run by George Polites since 1959. Robinson would spar with Hawke in this and future cases through the second half of the 1960s. They became friends. They kept it mostly polite in the courtroom, and often telegraphed their moves in advance. Each man admired the other's style: Hawke was fast-paced, slashing in attack and indignant; Robinson was more measured, defensive and made his arguments carefully.

After a hearing had concluded, Hawke and Robinson, often joined by Polites and Willis, would adjourn to the Beaufort Hotel. There they would eat and drink, and talk for hours. Willis recalled: 'After a day in court, hammering them away all day and really getting stuck into them, Bob would say, "Let's go down and have a beer together." So we'd go down and have a few beers with Jimmy and George. I found that really odd at first but I got used to it over time.'[30]

The 1964 Basic Wage Case opened with preliminary arguments on 19 February 1964. On 21 April in Melbourne, Robinson, on behalf of the Metal Trades Employers' Association, presented the employers' proposal for a new unified total wage that would replace the existing basic wage and margins system, and allow for increases based on productivity. It was designed to streamline the setting of wages and prohibit unions from gaining increases to the basic wage and then further increases for skills (margins) each year. That was the stick, but there was also a carrot. If the total wage proposal was agreed to, employers would support an increase in wages, and suggested a 2 per cent rise.

The unions, naturally, opposed it because if there were no productivity gains in a particular year, price increases would erode the real value of wages. On 5–6 May, in Sydney, Hawke outlined his opposition: the basic wage was an integral part of Australian social life; the existing wage determination system enjoyed bipartisan support; and it had the solid backing of Australian working men and women.[31] 'The commission must categorically reject any move to abolish this system, which has been approved by both government and public alike,' he thundered.[32] The May Day marches had seen unionists take to the streets to express their opposition to the total wage. Much was at stake. Hawke gave everything he had in his presentations.

The total wage idea was presented in conjunction with the union claim for a £2/12/- a week increase in the basic wage. On 9 June, with Richard Kirby exercising a casting vote, the commission awarded an increase to the basic wage of £1, or 20 shillings, to reflect productivity gains and price rises. Justices Kirby and John Moore prevailed over Frank Gallagher and John Nimmo, who only wanted to grant a 10-shilling rise. The economy was booming, and employers felt confident about their profit margins, so this was a sizeable increase. The commission unanimously rejected both the proposal for a total wage, and the union claim to restore automatic quarterly cost-of-living adjustments, as expected. But, importantly, it had reaffirmed its decision in 1961 that wages should rise in accordance with increases in prices. Hawke was thrilled by Kirby's vote. They had become personally friendly. They often chatted in his chambers, and later swapped horse racing tips and went to the track together.

Flush with his latest success, Bob and Hazel purchased a large two-storey cream-brick house at 25 Royal Avenue, Sandringham, in July 1964. It had a high-gabled roof, and a large garden out the back. It was an upmarket house in an upmarket suburb – a sign that Hawke saw his trajectory as heading upward. Hawke had been eyeing the house and the attached tennis court for some months, but it was beyond his means. In the 1962–63 financial year, Hawke had earned a taxable income of £1616 and gross income of £2227.[33] He purchased the house for £12,250, with an option to buy the tennis court for £5000 within a year. A hefty loan on generous terms was negotiated with the bank. When a Sydney newspaper referred to Hawke as a communist, he sued for libel: the settlement enabled him to purchase the tennis court. The Sandringham abode would be the Hawke family home until they moved to the Lodge in March 1983.

In April 1964, Harold Souter wrote to Hawke to inform him that his salary was increasing to £2600 per annum, in addition to a special allowance of £2000 per annum.[34] In the year after Hawke purchased the house, 1964–65, his income from the ACTU had increased substantially. His tax return for that year showed a gross income of £4448 (about $130,000 per annum, in 2021 value).[35] His total income, before tax, had doubled in two years.

While Hawke was living comfortably, he was still a junior employee at the ACTU. Journalist Alan Trengove visited Hawke in his 'austere' and 'simply furnished' office on Lygon Street in March 1965. 'His desk was covered with files and legal books,' he wrote. 'On a hook by the door was his suit jacket. The floor was littered by a pile of *Financial Reviews*, a box of peaches (to be taken home for bottling), an electric fan, a radiator and a foot rest.' He described Hawke as exuding 'vigor and confidence': he was 'rugged-looking' with 'a thick crop of dark wavy hair'. Hawke spoke in a direct and articulate manner, but his speech was 'twangy' and laced with 'a good deal of earthy colloquialisms'.[36] Hawke was good copy for newspapers.

Hawke's victory in the 1964 Basic Wage Case was short-lived. The following year, on 2 March 1965, Jim Robinson, representing the employers, again presented the proposal for a total wage, which was again to be considered as part of the union claim in the Basic Wage Case. Over the previous year, industrial action had increased as unions sought more for their members at a time when the economy was thriving. The Conciliation and Arbitration Commission bench comprised President Richard Kirby, Deputy President Frank Gallagher, John Moore, John Nimmo and Charles Sweeney. Robinson attacked the commission for submitting to 'militant campaigns' by unions to increase wages, which then flowed on from employer to employer. 'It is our submission that the commission, as a result of these campaigns, has suffered in public prestige and authority,' he argued.

Robinson's opposition to an increase in the basic wage was supported by barrister John Kerr, representing the Commonwealth, who argued that it could be 'fraught with danger'.[37] Hawke was shocked. He demanded the Commonwealth state that it neither supported nor opposed the union's application for a basic wage increase, otherwise his words would be taken as opposition. Kerr declined to comment and said the commission could draw its own conclusion. Hawke was angry. 'We say the Commonwealth has been guilty to this point,' he said, 'of flagrant and blatant dishonesty before the Commission.'[38] Hawke never forgot what Kerr said.

On 18 March, Hawke argued that the employer representatives were tearing at the 'social fabric' by trying to do away with the established system of wage setting. He said this represented an attack on the commission itself, because it challenged the way wages were established. He again opposed the total wage proposal and argued for basic wage rises of between 9 shillings and 13 shillings per week, reflecting productivity and prices. He did not press the commission to reinstate automatic quarterly cost-of-living adjustments.

Over several days, Hawke harangued the judges. He was loud, forceful and unrelenting. Hearings had to be stopped several times due to union protests. Hawke sparred bitterly with Sweeney about previous judgements that he thought strayed into economic policymaking, for which the bench had neither the responsibility nor the competence to determine:

> HAWKE: I think your Honours will see that here is a classic illustration of the sort of stupidity, if I may say so with respect to the tribunal at that time, that they were getting themselves into . . .
> SWEENEY: It is a very difficult thing to say 'with respect'. If you want to be consistent you should delete either the 'stupidity' reference or the 'with respect'.
> HAWKE: In that case, I would prefer to delete the 'with respect'.
> SWEENEY: You please yourself as far as I am concerned.
> HAWKE: Yes, I will please myself, your Honour.[39]

At 10.30 am on 29 June 1965, the full bench handed down its decision. In a shock split judgement, the commission turned its back on the 1961 wage-setting principles and awarded a miserly 6-shilling increase in the margins. There was no increase to the basic wage. The decision repudiated the combination of productivity and prices in setting wages, and reverted to the 'capacity to pay' principle – but based not on productivity but on stability of prices. While the decision did not support the employers' total wage proposal, the commission did resolve to hold basic wage cases and margins cases together, giving them a partial but critical victory. Kirby and Moore, who favoured an 8-shilling increase in the basic wage and the maintenance of existing wage-setting procedures, had been overruled by Gallagher, Nimmo and Sweeney in a 3–2 decision. The judgement was read to the courtroom by Gallagher. It was so sweeping, and so shocking, that newspapers published it in full. It was Hawke's most significant defeat in his time as ACTU advocate.

The argument behind the judgement, much like in 1953, represented a perversion of economics and law which riled Hawke, and
he condemned it in the strongest terms. Hawke asked Kirby to
overturn the decision, made his case in public and then formally
asked the commission to review it. He was rebuffed. There was
no legal avenue for appeal; the only option was to overturn it the
following year. Hawke immediately began preparing an assault
on the decision with the hope of demolishing it. By the end of
1965, he had set himself another goal: becoming president of the
ACTU. He would apply himself to both tasks, and would not give
up until he had achieved them.

—

In the pubs of Sydney, Melbourne, Brisbane and Adelaide, Hawke
began to talk openly to union officials about his desire to become
ACTU president. Monk, who was not going anywhere, was aware
of these casual conversations. In any event, Souter had been
earmarked as the next president. Hawke would not challenge
Monk, but wanted to be ready when he departed. Hawke knew
that he lacked critical support. He had never worked as a workplace delegate, or as an official with a union. He was an academic
turned advocate, with a notable profile and some demonstrable
successes, but it would be an extraordinary step for the ACTU,
which in 1965 represented ninety-seven unions and about 2 million
members, to make Hawke its president.

Hawke had a weapon that could not be wielded by Souter or
any other potential candidate: the media. Hawke had cultivated
relationships with journalists and was always accessible. He
used them and they used him. By the mid-1960s, his profile had
expanded considerably. John Hurst wrote in *The Australian* that
Hawke had rejected offers of a seat in parliament because he felt
he could 'make a greater contribution to the Labor movement in
the industrial field'. Hurst further reported that Hawke 'was being
groomed' to replace Monk as ACTU president. Monk had turned
sixty-five the previous month, the age when most people then
retired. Because of Hawke's 'tremendous prestige' as an advocate,
Hurst said, he could expect to become attorney-general or the
minister for labour, or even treasurer, if he went into parliament.

But Hawke was aiming higher, and it was not an unreasonable ambition. 'Labor circles contend the ultimate prize of the prime ministership would be well within his grasp if he chose a career in politics,' Hurst wrote.[40] It was 1965.

Clever journalists took Hawke to the Lygon Hotel, or another watering hole, or met him there. Interviews, however, often began at the office. In October 1967, Hawke told journalist Elaine McFarling for her 'Talking to Men' column what kind of women he liked. 'When I first meet a woman, I notice her eyes and hair,' he said. 'Then, I would say, her legs. Which is why, I suppose, I do not like those stockings and flat-heeled shoes. They do nothing for the woman with either good or bad legs.' His preference was for women with good legs and wearing miniskirts. 'I have no preference for blondes, brunettes or redheads – my tastes are very catholic – and I think a woman should use wigs or tint her hair if it helps her appearance.' Such comments rolled off Hawke's tongue: he did not hide anything. His wife of eleven years, at home with three children, was likely appalled to read this in *The Herald*. But she might also have been proud because her husband advocated for equal pay and equal employment opportunities for women. Hawke liked women with an active mind, he added, who could have intelligent conversations rather than just inconsequential chatter of the cocktail party variety.[41] Hazel read this article, cut it out of the newspaper and stuck it in her personal scrapbook.[42]

Ralph Willis got to know Bob and Hazel well in the 1960s. He was a regular visitor to the house, and often minded the kids when they went out. 'I remember meeting Hazel on the steps of the commission,' he recalled. 'She came up the steps and Bob said, "Ralph, this is me wife." And she said, "G'day, Ralph," in a broad Aussie accent. My goodness. She was a really friendly decent person.' But, Willis said, Hawke was unable to 'resist the temptations' that were put in front of him. 'Bob certainly loved Hazel but there was nothing stopping him looking elsewhere. Women chased him – the attraction of power – but also he was good-looking and gregarious, and some women would just throw themselves at him. Often he knocked those back, but not always.'[43]

Susan, the eldest of the three Hawke children, thought the tensions in the marriage manifested after Hawke commenced at the ACTU. 'It was after they moved to Melbourne that the fractures and the difficulties started to appear,' she said. 'What changed when we moved to Melbourne was proximity, distance, hours, times and roles with children, but the love remained even though the difficulties were starting.' Hazel and the children missed Bob when he was not around. 'Dad was serially unfaithful, as we know, well before Blanche [d'Alpuget] came along,' Susan said. 'Mum knew, the world knew, it was an open secret, and the drinking was obviously an issue of great distress.'[44]

In the early 1960s, Hawke began an affair with a ballet dancer, Beverley Richards. The relationship went on for years and was well known to Hawke's friends, colleagues and to Hazel. It became destructive and Hawke tried to end the affair. But Richards refused. She travelled to Corio during the election campaign and sat in the front row of his public meetings to upset him. She threw things at the windows of the ACTU offices and shouted for him to come out. She blockaded Lygon Street with her car. And she phoned him at home. Hazel eventually confronted Beverley about it. But Hawke continued to see her. When Hazel said 'nobody will ever know how bad it was', she was thinking of Beverley. It put an enormous strain on their relationship.[45]

The Basic Wage, Margins and Total Wage Case hearing commenced on 8 March 1966. Kirby announced that he would not sit on this case, and nor would Nimmo or Sweeney. Syd Wright, the senior deputy president, would preside in his place. Justices Gallagher and Moore would also sit on the bench. Justice Terry Winter would join the three to hear the employers' total wage claim, which did not deal with the basic wage, and also the unions' margins claim. The unions thought this bench would be more amenable to their claims, while the employer groups were outraged and appealed to the High Court to disqualify Winter, but this was rejected.

In his opening remarks to the judges, Hawke said that the commission's standing in the eyes of the union movement was at stake. 'Never before,' he said, 'have more important issues fallen than those now before the bench.' Hawke, on behalf of several unions, sought an average $4.30 increase in the basic wage per week, and a $5.90 margins increase. (Decimal currency had been introduced on 14 February 1966.) Rallying the evidence and arguments of his Oxford thesis, Hawke told the judges that the fundamental issue before the commission was to determine whether it existed to settle disputes and determine wages, or to be the guardian of the nation's economy. He said the commission did not have the power to take over what was properly the responsibility of parliament: the setting of economic policy.

With much at stake, these hearings witnessed some of the most bitter exchanges between Hawke and the bench during his time as an advocate. He lashed the 1965 judgement as 'not a very sophisticated sort of judgment' and 'outrageous' for overturning the established wage fixing principles. He referred to an aspect of the judgement as a 'cheap and unnecessary jibe' at the minority view held by Kirby and Moore. This led Gallagher, who had been in the majority, to attack Hawke:

GALLAGHER: That is a wanton, reckless statement which should never have come from a senior advocate before this Commission. It is the sort of statement you expect to fall from the lips of some Domain Demosthenes or Hyde Park Cicero. It is absolutely unworthy of you and it is absolutely untrue.

HAWKE: Then it will probably be necessary to pursue that after lunch, your Honour.

GALLAGHER: You please yourself about that.

HAWKE: Yes, I shall.[46]

Hawke objected to Gallagher's assertion that he made reckless statements. Gallagher would not retract. They had more terse exchanges as the hearings continued. Hawke viewed the encounter as a badge of pride. His mother, Ellie, kept a bust of Demosthenes in her kitchen for years.

Brian Buckley, writing in *The Bulletin*, argued that the outcome of the case would 'largely determine the future of both industrial relations in this country and the Arbitration System itself'. That was why Hawke had spent most of the previous three weeks taking apart the 1965 judgement. Hawke had delivered 'a penetrating and trenchant analysis', which had prompted the fiery clashes. Hawke had accused the commission of a judgement that conflicted with the law underpinning industrial relations and the Constitution, that was ignorant of economic reality, and that was contradictory, confused and inherently biased against unions. The risk, Hawke made plain, was that unions would abandon the arbitration system in favour of direct action – industrial unrest.[47]

Jim Robinson, the employers' counsel, began by lavishing praise on the commission for its judgement on the basic wage the previous year. The following day, he summoned the power of the Vernon Committee of Economic Inquiry, established by the Menzies government, to support his views on wages. Its report argued that wages should be adjusted to reflect productivity improvements alone, rather than in combination with prices. Robinson argued that this economic wisdom, the product of some of the finest minds in Australia, should be accepted in wage determinations. Hawke knew this report had credibility with the bench, so his only option was to punch holes in it. On 3 May, Hawke asked for the Vernon Committee to be subpoenaed to appear before the commission so their arguments could be tested. Robinson resisted the request, as did the Commonwealth's counsel, John Kerr. But the presiding judge, Wright, agreed. So did Gallagher. On 6 May, Wright announced that the Vernon Committee would be summoned.

On 27 May 1966, Sir James Vernon appeared before the commission. Much of the morning saw the phalanx of counsel arrayed before Hawke successfully objecting to his interrogation and setting aside his questions. But, after lunch, Vernon agreed to be questioned directly by Hawke. He did not intimidate or bully Vernon, but probed the issues addressed in his report carefully and calmly. He marshalled data to show how his report had been in error. The questioning went on for days. Geoffrey Gleghorn, writing in *The Australian Financial Review*, said the audience was expecting Hawke's questioning to be typically 'fire and brimstone', but instead it was 'largely milk and honey'.

Gleghorn described Hawke's style:

Examining a witness or addressing the Bench, he moves ceaselessly, treading a tight path round his chair, rolling on the sides of his shoes, peering over his glasses at the gallery, leaning on the lectern. Sometimes when putting a proposition to the Bench he appears to gather the concept up and offer it on his cupped hands for the Judge's visual as well as mental inspection.[48]

Hawke's respectful approach paid off. 'By the end of my examination, he had conceded that the committee was wrong on its central point on the stability of the wages share, which had in fact been eroded,' Hawke recalled.[49] When other Vernon Committee members took the stand and agreed with their chair, Hawke knew he had destroyed the 1965 judgement.

On 8 July, the bench handed down their judgement to a packed courtroom. The basic wage would be increased by $2 per week, a modest amount. The real victory was the restoration of factoring in productivity gains and price rises in wage setting. 'I had fulfilled the promise to myself to destroy the 1965 judgment, and in the decision handed down in 1966, the Bench reinstated the principle that wage adjustments must take account of movements in both productivity and prices, a principle never seriously questioned since that time,' Hawke would later write.[50] However, Wright, Moore and Gallagher also gave their support for a single wage (or total wage) – long pushed by employers – to replace the existing basic wage and margins formulation. In other words, there would no longer be a distinction between the basic wage and margins.

Bill Kelty, then undertaking a Bachelor of Economics at La Trobe University, was told 'the best act in town' was to see Hawke in action before the commission. So he went down to Little Bourke Street to see for himself. 'There was Bob Hawke against an armoury of lawyers,' he recalled. 'He was inspiring because he showed no regard to the lawyers, he just beat them up. He kept the bench entertained and informed. He was a crusader.'

After a few days, Hawke approached Kelty and asked what he was doing there.

'I'm here to see you,' Kelty replied.

'Well, what do you think?' Hawke asked.

'It's like a crusade in here,' the young man replied. 'It is you against the world and you are beating them.'

Hawke told Kelty to give him a call if he wanted to work for the union movement one day. Kelty said he had to finish his degree first.[51]

—

Just a few days after the landmark 1966 judgement, Hawke left for Papua New Guinea, where he was to represent the Public Service Association in its claim to increase the wages of 8500 indigenous Local Officers, who were being paid at lower rates by the territory government than their non-indigenous counterparts doing the same work. Port Moresby, where the PSA was based and where Hawke stayed, was a place of entrenched inequality. Racism was ubiquitous. The indigenous officers were sceptical of Hawke. And they were doubtful about the commitment of the PSA.

Hawke immersed himself in the case. He spoke to the indigenous workers who were being discriminated against. He collected evidence. He read reports. He weighed up the best way to prosecute the case. It required an understanding of social norms and traditional customs, of work habits, housing and nutritional needs, of the structure and operation of the public service, of the economic implications, and of the potential impact on all employees. He argued it was morally unjustified to maintain such a large wage discrepancy, and it also risked Australia's standing and security because it fostered resentment. Hawke's commitment to their cause was total.

Hawke was assisted by two officials from the PSA: Rod Madgwick and Paul Munro. 'He was fun to be with,' recalled Munro. 'Bob was never very different in person from what he came across in public. He was light-hearted, ready to joke, brimming with energy and with anecdotes from the world of politics that I did not know.' Munro remembered a 'heavy night' in Wewak ahead of an early-morning flight to Port Moresby for a meeting with Hal Wootten QC, who was representing the Commonwealth in opposing the pay claim. 'I tried to guide Bob into bed away from the bottle and company, but I had no chance of that,' Munro said. 'Around 2 am I adjourned to my motel bedroom and heard them going on. I got Bob out of bed at 5 am to get to the airstrip. I was browned off with him and thought he was not acting responsibly. But he was as bright as a button. When we got into the hearing, he was absolutely astounding and turned the whole conference on its ear.'[52]

L.G. Matthews, the Public Service Arbitrator, heard the case. Employees were called by the PSA to give testimony about the difficulty they faced in looking after themselves and their families. A total of 114 witnesses would give evidence. Hawke also called public servants and economists to test the administration's arguments about its capacity to pay and the impact on the local economy and society if wages were substantially increased. He also, astoundingly, called Wootten himself as his opening witness, forcing him to defend the discriminatory rates of pay. During the hearings, the administration announced it would provide equal pay for male and female local officers and increase some pay scales, but the minimum salary would remain $440 a year. But Hawke pressed on, eager for the tribunal to determine the matter.

In the second half of 1966, when not working on the case, he would spend time with foreign journalists, diplomats and expat Australians. Hawke drank, sang, played cards and bet on horse races. It was in Papua New Guinea that Hawke began punting, and it became a lifetime obsession. Don Hogg, a journalist with *The Australian*, moonlighted as an SP bookmaker. A 44-gallon drum would be loaded with beer at his place by the water near the Koki markets to entice locals to punt and listen to the races on Saturday afternoons. Hawke had a bet on a horse called Pirate Bird. It romped in at an outrageous price and paid handsomely. Hawke was hooked. Hawke wrote to Munro on 26 March 1968: 'Currently among the many reasons I love you dearly is my introduction by you to the noble art of punting.'[53]

Hazel, Susan, Stephen and Rosslyn moved to Papua New Guinea for three months in the second half of 1966, while Hawke worked on the case. The children were enrolled at a small government-run primary school at Ela Beach. They played with local kids, swam in the pool and enjoyed cricket on the beach. The Hawkes visited the homes of local public servants, and mixed with Australian diplomats and foreign journalists. It was an escape from their lives in Sandringham, and they enjoyed the time immensely.

The Local Officers Case was an enormously rewarding experience for Hawke. He gained a detailed understanding of the country, its economy, culture and politics, and spent time with its future leaders, including Michael Somare and Albert Maori Kiki. Munro recalled Hawke's deep commitment to the local indigenous community. 'They believed the sun rose and fell out of him,' he said. 'Wherever he went, Bob got on well with the locals because he was colour blind. His conviviality helped to break down any hostility. He was engaging. He understood what their problems were, and he shared their concerns.'[54]

On 11 May 1967, Matthews delivered his decision to increase salaries for the lowest-paid public servants by just $40 a year. He adopted 'a cautious approach' to the setting of the minimum wage. It still represented only 25 per cent of the wages of comparable white employees. It was a disappointing result. Around 1000 protestors, mostly black, organised a petition and marched in the streets. Hawke was in Port Moresby to hear the decision. Hawke's return caused the Holt government some anxiety. A file kept by the Department of Territories reveals that public servants were eager to know how long Hawke intended to stay, and what ongoing role he would have with the PSA.[55]

Back home, Hawke pressed for a review of the decision, and for wage justice, directly with the Australian government, and made his views known in the media. He said the decision was embarrassing for European and Australian public servants who work alongside indigenous officers. 'The housing conditions of indigenous officers ranges from appalling to very ordinary,' he explained. 'Except for a few who have European-type housing they are unwilling or too embarrassed to invite Europeans into their homes.'[56] He thought the decision just did not reflect the evidence and arguments presented. It defied rationality and logic. In November 1967 he would return to argue for a review, but Matthews said there were no legislative grounds for appeal.

When Hawke returned to Melbourne, he focused on the 1967 National Wage Case. As expected after the judgement in the 1966 Basic Wage Case, the commission decided it would introduce a new total wage, including margins, which employers had long argued for. It represented an end to a system which had operated for sixty years. The commission would now conduct reviews each year and adjust wages in light of economic circumstances. Increases in wages could be awarded in flat monetary amounts or as percentages tied to different parts of the labour force. Hawke made the case for a $7.30 increase in the basic wage, but the days of big annual increases were over. The commission instead increased the total wage by $1 per week for both men and women. The ACTU, following Hawke's recommendation, appealed to the High Court but this was dismissed. In 1968, the commission increased the total wage by $1.35 per week. In 1969, it increased the total wage by 3 per cent. It was clear that the commission was not going to return to automatic quarterly wage adjustments, preferring the flexibility to alter wages each year in accordance with economic circumstances, including the purchasing power of money or prices, and productivity.

While Hawke had been travelling between Port Moresby and Melbourne, the metal trades industry was plunged into its worst period of industrial disputation in two decades. The commission, under Winter, had delayed hearing the claim for an increase in margins until a review of the metal trades' award could be completed. It took more than a year, and workers were granted only small interim margin increases until it was finalised on 11 December 1967. The margins decision was revisited by a new bench the following year, with Kirby presiding. The new judgement, which provided for 70 per cent of the increases to be paid immediately and 30 per cent to be deferred until the next national wage case in August 1968, was attacked by the minister for labour and national service, Les Bury, for its adverse economic impact. It led to further public rows between the government, unions, employers and the commission.

Meanwhile, unions were in conflict with employers and the federal government over the application of penal powers under the *Arbitration Act*. The Industrial Court imposed heavy fines on the unions – about $10,000 in 1967 and $100,000 in 1968. The unions accused the court of doing the bidding of employers. On 15 May 1969, John Kerr, now a judge, jailed Clarrie O'Shea, the Victorian secretary of the Australian Tramway and Motor Omnibus Employees' Association, on a contempt charge. O'Shea, a leading communist, had refused to pay accumulated fines and abide by a summons to produce the union's books. After almost a week in jail, an unknown benefactor came forward and paid the outstanding $8100 in fines. Kerr had no option but to release O'Shea on 21 May. Hawke condemned penal powers as unjust, immoral and discriminatory. It was one of several factors that would influence who the delegates to the 1969 ACTU Congress would elect as their president for the 1970s.

9

MR PRESIDENT

During 1967 and 1968, Bob Hawke was also focused on becoming president of the ACTU. He was surprised when Albert Monk sought, and secured, another two-year term at the biennial ACTU Congress in Melbourne in September 1967. Hawke thought Monk would retire as he was slowing down. But he had been a shrewd and quietly effective president, and had support from affiliated unions to continue. Hawke admired Monk for keeping the ACTU united against potential breakaway groups, especially during the tumultuous years of the split. He also appreciated Monk's role in supporting Australia's post-war immigration program, when many unions were uneasy about the impact of new arrivals on employment. Hawke got on well with Monk but they were not personally close. 'He was always very kind to me if I wanted any advice, but he let me be,' Hawke recalled.[1]

The news of Monk's retirement came on Saturday, 8 March 1969. At a Labour Day dinner at the Melbourne Town Hall, Monk announced that he would not seek a further term as president in September. It was his fiftieth year serving as a trade union official. 'I express the sincere hope that the trade union movement further prospers and solidifies itself in the coming years,' Monk said.[2] But he issued two warnings to the labour movement. First, he counselled unions against 'unjustified' strikes without 'proper planning', saying these only led to harsh penalties. Second, he urged the movement not to succumb to those on the left who wanted to 'capture control of the congress and its organs' for factional purposes, as this would 'destroy the soul and spirit of the labour movement'.[3]

Monk was given a standing ovation. He had dedicated his life to the union movement, having served as secretary or president of the ACTU since 1934. The advances made during this time – including the forty-hour working week, increases in the basic wage, long service leave, and compensation for injury – were legendary. He was a member of the Governing Body of the International Labour Organization, based in Geneva. But Monk's tenure had not been free from controversy. His critics charged that he had not negotiated hard enough with employers or government.

The next day, 9 March 1969, Hawke and Harold Souter both confirmed they would be candidates for the ACTU presidency. Hawke, thirty-nine, had been the ACTU's advocate and research officer since 1958. Souter, fifty-seven, had been its secretary since 1956. Souter would be the candidate of the Right and Hawke was the candidate of the Left. But Hawke immediately began appealing to centrist unions and to those on the Right. 'Should I get the presidency, I would consider it one of my prime duties to continue as Mr Monk has – uniting both Left and Right factions of the ACTU,' he said.[4]

The only obstacle to Hawke's ambition would be Souter. 'Harold Souter was the first Bill Hayden in my life,' Hawke recalled.[5] Souter was respected for his long history with the union movement: he had worked with the metal trades unions and was an efficient manager of the ACTU. But Souter was a teetotaller, and lacked the bonds that Hawke had developed through his afternoon and evening drinking sessions. Hawke believed Souter had become less encouraging of his role as advocate through the 1960s, as his fame grew. Hawke was a mere employee; Souter was an elected official. When there were disagreements, Hawke would appeal to Monk as arbiter, and would usually prevail.

In a statement on 10 March, Souter foreshadowed a bitter contest. He seized on Monk's warning of 'disruptive elements' in the union movement, claiming they were an alliance of the 'New Left Movement', including communists, who were attempting to take over the ACTU. 'This opportunist front is seeking to gain control through dictatorial pressure tactics by dissident groups rebelling against democratic decisions and self-imposed discipline of the trade union movement and attempting to impose conditions to obtain minority control,' Souter said. He warned against 'this senseless thrust for power for individual or sectional gain', which threatened the survival of the ACTU.[6]

Hawke responded in a statement the next day, 11 March. He attacked Souter's statement and questioned the motives of some of his supporters. Some unions that backed Souter would be 'under the control of the extreme Right-wing, including the DLP', Hawke countered. 'I don't expect he will reject that support.' He said their respective supporters did not reflect on the ability of either man to do the job. Hawke called for a campaign that assessed the two candidates on what they would bring to the presidency, rather than a race to the bottom with ill-founded attacks. 'I have always regarded the technique of guilt by association and the tactic of the smear as abhorrent, and I refuse to resort to it myself,' he said.[7] It was a nice idea, but the campaign was always going to be fought hard between the Left and the Right of the union movement, with no quarter given.

According to Hawke, his 'achievements as advocate' and his national 'profile' were the centrepiece of his campaign for president.[8] A twelve-page booklet titled 'Why Bob Hawke should be ACTU president' was circulated. It defended the record of the 1967–69 executive, a majority of whom had endorsed Hawke, with the less active 1965–67 executive. It presented Hawke as an ideas man and an achiever, with a plan to lead the unions into the 1970s. It canvassed hire-purchase and insurance proposals. It outlined a plan to improve cooperation with the 'major white-collar councils' representing professionals and public servants. It lashed Souter's attempt to 'smear' Hawke with 'the communist myth'. It argued that Hawke had 'the talents, the dedication, the loyalty and the youthful vigour to channel the energies of the trade union movement into creating a force for good in the community and into advancing not only the wages and working conditions of employees but the quality of life for working men and women.' It was 'a time of decision', the flyer said. 'It's your choice and your chance.' But Hawke also had drawbacks. He was regarded as arrogant, and some were turned off by his aggression. And his drinking was well known.

Souter thought he had won Monk's endorsement. He was, as he soon found out, mistaken. Monk backed neither candidate, publicly or privately. He supported Souter at executive meetings and continued to drink with Hawke at the Lygon. In presentations to unions, and in interviews, Souter pressed his case against Hawke by linking the younger man's candidacy to extreme elements who wished to divert the union movement away from its industrial focus and towards political campaigns. Souter also pointed to his own administrative skills, his long work for the trade union movement, and his connection with working men. 'I don't consider myself the underdog,' he insisted. Souter acknowledged that he was not dynamic or showy like Hawke, but insisted this was not essential in a president. He said of Hawke: 'Quite a bright intellectual theorist but he hasn't done any practical industrial work of any shape or form.'[9]

The presidency would be decided by delegates to the ACTU Congress held in September 1969 in Sydney. Hawke worked overtime to convince delegates to support his candidature. His support came mostly from left-wing unions, including communist unions, but he also had support from centrist unions and some delegates aligned with the Right. Souter was predominantly backed by unions from the moderate right wing of the movement.

Hawke's principal organiser was Ray Gietzelt – a former member of the Communist Party and the communist-controlled Hughes-Evans Labor Party – who was then federal secretary of the Miscellaneous Workers' Union. Critically, Hawke also enjoyed the support of Charlie Fitzgibbon, the general secretary of the Waterside Workers' Federation, also of the Left. Hawke saw their support as vital in his campaign against Souter. He was not, as he had been accused, a 'red dupe' or an 'extreme left-winger' or a 'communist lover boy'. As journalist Fred Wells perceptively noted: 'Although he is not a committed Left-winger, Mr Hawke was backed by the Left.'[10]

A key step in Hawke's campaign for president was challenging the Right's dominance on the ACTU Executive. Hawke asked Gietzelt – a regular visitor to the Hawke home in Sandringham – to stand for the Services Group position on the ACTU Executive at the 1965 ACTU Congress. Gietzelt had declined, arguing he was too busy, but organised for Fred Whitby, the Queensland secretary of the Miscellaneous Workers' Union, to stand. Whitby would challenge Joe Riordan, federal secretary of the Federated Clerks' Union, the leader of the Right on the ACTU Executive. Whitby lost.[11]

Two years later, at the 1967 ACTU Congress, Hawke again urged Gietzelt to challenge Riordan. 'If blokes like you are not prepared to support me to become president of the ACTU, I might as well pursue a career in academia,' Hawke said.[12] He had been worried that if Monk retired before the 1967 Congress, or before the 1969 Congress, then the Right-dominated executive would appoint Souter as acting president. He would then be difficult to defeat in the election for the presidency at the subsequent congress.

So the Left, at Hawke's insistence, began organising to improve their position on the ACTU Executive. As the 650 delegates gathered for the August 1967 ACTU Congress, held in Melbourne, the Right did not realise just how effective this Left group, supporting Hawke, had been in organising its numbers. The Right had boosted their numbers by sixty-one with the affiliation of the Australian Workers' Union, and thought they could see off any Left powerplay. But they were wrong. Gietzelt defeated Riordan in the Services Group elections for the ACTU Executive by eighty-three votes to fifty-six. Four other Hawke supporters – Charlie Fitzgibbon (Waterside Workers' Federation), Fred Hall (Meat Industry Employees' Union), Jack Devereux (Metal Trades Federation of Unions) and Joe Anderson (Operative Painters' and Decorators' Union) – also defeated their right-wing opponents in their respective sector ballots for the executive.

The upshot was that the new seventeen-member ACTU Executive had eight votes aligned to the Left and nine votes aligned to the Right, including Monk as president. Meetings often saw Monk exercise his casting vote. So the ACTU Executive had shifted to the left, but the Left was not yet in control. It was reported that the newly elected members aligned to Hawke – now firmly regarded as Monk's 'heir apparent' – were 'young Turks' who wanted to 'show their mettle and assert their influence' over their 'older entrenched colleagues' of the Right. 'Like Mr Hawke, they believe the vigor and militancy of the Australian trade union movement must be preserved and fostered,' Geoffrey Barker wrote in *The Age*.[13]

On 12 October 1967, Jim Kenny, the ACTU's vice-president, died. Kenny was secretary of the NSW Labor Council and a key figure of the Right. This reduced the numbers on the ACTU Executive to eight Left and eight Right (assuming Monk supported the Right). The position remained unfilled as the executive could not agree on how Kenny should be replaced. But it was about more than just Kenny's replacement. 'On the surface the meeting was a struggle between the Right and Left wings,' wrote journalist Fred Wells. 'But in reality it was a contest between Mr Hawke and Mr H. Souter for the leadership.'[14]

The following year, on 12 October 1968, Bill Brown, the secretary of the South Australian United Trades and Labour Council, died. He too was aligned to the Right. He was replaced by Jim Shannon, from the Amalgamated Engineering Union, a Hawke supporter who was aligned to the Left. This now meant Hawke's supporters on the ACTU Executive had a 9–7 majority. Souter could not be appointed to the presidency if Monk retired between congresses. The next president would be elected by the ACTU Congress in September 1969, and it was on this which Hawke now focused his attention.

Hawke had effectively launched his campaign for the presidency with a stirring speech at the 1967 ACTU Congress. In presenting a report on economic and wages policy on 29 August, Hawke initially focused on the iniquities in the Holt government's federal budget, delivered just days earlier. 'It is a budget of the privileged, by the privileged, for the privileged,' Hawke said. This boilerplate rhetoric went down a treat. No speech received louder or longer applause. Hawke overshadowed both Monk and Souter, who could not match Hawke for stage presence, intellect or rhetoric. In concluding, Hawke had a message for those who may be wondering whether he could effectively unite and lead the movement, as Monk had done:

> There may be a number of issues which divide us. But let us remember that we are a powerful movement. The substance of economic and wages policies being put before you provide

the opportunity, I suggest, for wielding our power unitedly, progressively and without friction. Those opposed to us have given evidence of their strength and power. Let us unite so as to achieve a rejection of the powers of privilege and, positively, establish that which we are all concerned to establish – a society whose resources will be utilised to the maximum and wherein the reward for labour shall be fair and equitable and the needs of the weak and those unable to fend for themselves shall be our over-riding concern.[15]

It was, as biographer John Hurst said, 'the star turn of the congress'. Hawke was showcasing his leadership qualities. It was a message of pragmatism and cooperation that spoke to the values of the movement they all served. But Hawke was still only the ACTU's research officer and advocate. As one delegate remarked to another, 'It's not his job to tell us how to behave.'[16] Hawke still had a mountain to climb.

Following the 1967 ACTU Congress, Hawke began meeting regularly with members of the Executive aligned to the Left. Although Hawke was not a member of the Executive, this group would run through the business of each meeting and agree on what positions to take on issues and what resolutions to propose. They swapped information about unions and formulated tactics and strategy as they worked towards the ultimate goal: Hawke becoming president.

The Right was also planning. On 10 February 1969, a month before Monk announced his retirement, the Right strengthened their hold on the NSW Labor Council, and flagged that they would be pushing for their 'nominee' – Souter – to be 'elected as president of the ACTU' later in the year.[17] Souter's campaign was supported by the Right-dominated labour councils of New South Wales, Victoria and Tasmania. His key Victorian numbers man was John Maynes, Victorian president of the Federated Clerks' Union, a leading figure in the Industrial Groups. Souter also had strong support from NSW Labor Council secretary Ralph Marsh and assistant secretary John Ducker.

Barrie Unsworth, an organiser with the NSW Labor Council, worked with Marsh and Ducker to support Souter's bid for the presidency. 'We came to the conclusion that we were one hundred votes behind a year before the 1969 ACTU Congress,' Unsworth recalled. The task was to turn delegations around to support Souter, strip single votes from delegations or sign up new unions. Both the Hawke and Souter camps employed all three tactics. Unsworth remembered Ted Innes, Victorian secretary of the Electrical Trades Union, telling the delegates they would all vote for Hawke. But the Right managed to split the delegation in half, with twelve votes for Hawke and twelve for Souter. Unsworth would be the Right's candidate for ACTU secretary if Souter became president.[18]

Hawke's supporters managed to strip votes from Souter too. Bill Kelty began working for the Federated Storemen and Packers' Union in 1970. 'Bill Landeryou changed the votes of the Storemen and Packers' Union when he became secretary in Victoria,' Kelty said. 'They were going to vote for Souter but they shifted all their votes to Hawke. Landeryou stood over the union to get them to vote for Hawke.'[19] Simon Crean, who also joined the Federated Storemen and Packers' Union in 1970, agreed. 'Landeryou was essential to Bob winning because the Storemen and Packers, under Jack Petrie, were going to vote for Harold,' Crean recalled.[20]

The contest between Hawke and Souter received extensive media coverage. Souter tried to restrain Hawke's ability to speak to the media, given he was not an elected official, but Monk overruled him. Souter knew he could not compete with Hawke in the media stakes: he was dour, whereas Hawke was dynamic. In any event, Hawke had rarely missed an opportunity to be interviewed over the previous 11 years – and he was not going to surrender his trump card in the epic contest.

Journalist Scott Henderson from Perth's *Daily News* assessed Hawke as having 'already established a towering image as a brilliant academic and formidable legal opponent'. He would talk about anything and answer any question. 'Hawke has a mind which chews up the complexities of the nation's socio-economic situation, digests it into simple lay terms and dispenses it with absolute conviction,' he wrote. Hawke was happy to talk about his parents and upbringing, his student years and family. He said he earned about $10,400 a year. He was routinely asked about going into parliament and didn't rule out a political career, but said his focus was the union movement.[21]

The ballot to determine the presidency took place on 10 September 1969 at the Paddington Town Hall, in Sydney. The grand two-storey edifice with a clocktower and flag atop had its foundation stone laid by Henry Parkes in 1890. The number of ACTU delegates had swelled by 101 since the last Congress, two years earlier, to 751. There they sat, a mix of union officials and workers, almost all men, many with ruddy faces and rough hands from years of manual labour, and almost all smoking. They were there to listen to speeches, receive reports and move motions. But they were also eagerly anticipating the contest that had been years in the making: between Hawke and Souter.

Bob Carr was then a young journalist working for ABC Radio. He recalled walking into the town hall to interview both candidates. He approached Hawke, who was happy to oblige, speaking freely about why he wanted to be president. When Carr approached Souter, with a tape recorder over his shoulder and his arm extended with a microphone, he was met with stony silence. 'He just stood there and tightened his lips,' Carr recalled. 'He didn't even say, "I'm not talking to the media." He was terrified of the media.' Carr thought Souter was a terrible candidate. 'If Souter was the best that the Right could come up with against Hawke, who had a national reputation and was seen as a brilliant advocate, then the Right had run out of ideas and personnel,' he said.[22]

The Paddington RSL was directly opposite the town hall. Hawke recalled that the delegates were made temporary members for the week-long ACTU Congress. The canvassing for the presidency required going to and from the RSL to press his case. Unsworth remembered walking across Oxford Street between the RSL and the town hall and seeing Hawke coming towards him, who said: 'What are you worried about, Barrie?' He thought Hawke looked relaxed. 'I think he felt he had the numbers,' Unsworth recalled.[23]

Hawke and Souter had an opportunity to address the delegates on the second day of the congress. Hawke gave his report as advocate and research officer, while Souter spoke in support of the economic policy recommendations. Hawke railed against the federal government's budget, against big business and against the wages policy offered by employer groups. He then, as he had two years ago, made a pitch for a united union movement:

> There are undoubtedly a number of issues at this time upon which we do not agree. I suggest that while, with good will and mutual integrity, we pursue our different convictions on those issues we should come together unitedly and progressively on those issues where, in the interests of the people we represent, we should be as one.[24]

Hawke's conciliatory tone was met with applause. Souter, in sharp contrast, missed his moment. He read his economic policy statement word for word, even though it had already been distributed. He lost the attention of the delegates, who began to talk among themselves; some walked out. Souter found it difficult to be heard, and Monk had to call the congress to order several times. Reporter Ray Turner said the Right sending in Souter to speak after Hawke was 'suicidal'.[25] The delegates would vote the following day.

The voting was tightly controlled and monitored. Almost all the unions voted as a group, with organisers appointed to make sure ballots were checked, or filled out as a group, before being put into the ballot boxes. The returning officer was Lindsay North – who was also New South Wales Labor's returning officer and an upper-house MP. After lunch, North entered the main hall and went to the stage. A delegate was interrupted, and North stood in front of the microphone and announced the results. 'Hawke, R . . . 399 votes.' There was a few seconds of silence as the maths was done in hundreds of minds. Then there was cheering and clapping, and the stamping of feet. North continued: 'Souter, H . . . 350 votes.'[26]

Hawke had expected to win by a margin of at least 100 votes, but a concerted effort by John Ducker and Barrie Unsworth saw his support reduced by at least fifty votes. In the end, a change of just twenty-five votes – one union – could have delivered the presidency to Souter. Even so, Ducker knew Hawke would win. Kerry Sibraa, then an organiser for New South Wales Labor, drove Ducker to the conference one day. 'I'm going to have to vote for Souter,' he recalled Ducker saying. 'But I should be voting for Hawke because he is going to win and he is the future for the ACTU.'[27]

Hawke was seated on the platform in the nondescript hall when the election result was announced. He was wearing a light grey suit with a white shirt and thin dark tie. His delegate badge was pinned to his lapel. He wore horn-rimmed glasses but soon took them off. He stood to receive the applause, and accepted the congratulations of those around him. The disappointed Souter extended his hand to Hawke, who shook it. 'I have a whole mixture of emotions,' Hawke said to the delegates. 'One relief is that it's all over. I'm very tired. The presidency is obviously one of the most significant positions available in the whole of Australia.'[28] He paid tribute to Monk, he thanked Hazel and the kids for their support, and he expressed his affection and gratitude for those who worked for his election.

Hawke offered a conciliatory message. 'I will not be the president merely of those who worked for and voted for me,' he said. 'I will be the president of the whole of the ACTU.' He spoke about plans in the areas of hire purchase and insurance, strengthening the ACTU's research capacity and legal services, playing a wider advocacy role, and working with white-collar unions. And, in line with his call for unity, Hawke said the union movement often did not recognise its own strength. He said he would 'mobilise that strength' to improve 'the condition and quality of life of our members and their dependents'.[29]

It was the dawn of a new era for Australia's union movement. Journalist Ray Turner wrote that Hawke's 'militant statements and radical plans' had 'startled both the employer and employee camps'.[30] However, Barry Donovan did not think Hawke would 'launch Australia into the industrial chaos that has been predicted'.[31] Alan Trengove steered a middle path in his analysis, writing that Hawke was a no-nonsense man of strong convictions who would be a more aggressive and proactive president. But he argued that Hawke was intellectual, a scholar, an 'egg-head' who had a common-sense attitude towards things.[32]

The nation's leading mastheads were supportive of Hawke's election to the ACTU presidency. An editorial in *The Age* 'acknowledged a need for fresh ideas' and 'new and creative approaches' to trade unionism. It warned that the decline of blue-collar jobs and more 'enlightened socio-political attitudes' by employers and governments would see membership continue in 'slow decline'.[33] *The Sydney Morning Herald* noted Hawke's backing by left-wing unions but saw his leadership as less an ideological turning point and more a recognition of the need for 'a new style in trade union leadership'.[34] *The Australian* saw Hawke as 'a sharp contrast' to Monk, but nevertheless 'a wise choice' for the ACTU. It hoped that there would be no lingering resentments, or factionalism, and pronounced Hawke 'well equipped' to lead the union movement into a new era.[35]

The first person Hawke called after the result was announced was Hazel, who was at home in Melbourne.[36] He dashed out of the town hall, past well-wishers and journalists, and ran across the road to the RSL club to place the call. She was thrilled and cele-brated with the kids by indulging in champagne, chocolate biscuits and toffee. 'Bob and a lot of other people have worked very hard for this victory,' she told a reporter who knocked on her door.[37] Journalists visiting the Hawkes at Sandringham found a 'gregar-ious' and 'boisterous' household.[38] Susan was twelve, Stephen ten and Rossyln eight. There was also a Siamese cat named Chindi, a kelpie dog named Flash and three mice, along with two parrots and six budgerigars housed in an aviary Bob had built.

The year 1969 was a pivotal one for Hawke. It was also a signif-icant time for many of the men who would play a notable role in his later life. Gough Whitlam led Labor to the first of five general election campaigns in October, winning a remarkable 7.1 per cent swing, but not enough to form a government. Bill Hayden was re-elected in his outer-Brisbane seat of Oxley. He had joined Labor's front bench in opposition and was regarded as one of the party's most promising young MPs. Paul Keating, at just twenty-five, was elected to the federal parliament in the safe Western Sydney seat of Blaxland. He too was already being talked about in the party as a rising star.

On the Coalition side, John Gorton had become prime minister in January 1968, following the disappearance of Harold Holt and the interim prime ministership of John McEwen. In 1971, Gorton would be replaced by Billy McMahon as Liberal leader and prime minister. Malcolm Fraser became minister for defence in November 1969, and Andrew Peacock became minister for the army. And John Howard had stood as the Liberal candidate for the state seat of Drummoyne in the New South Wales election in February 1968, but lost. Now working as a solicitor, he was eyeing a seat in the federal parliament.

As ACTU president in the 1970s, Hawke would bring the union movement's influence and authority to its zenith. He would consolidate his position and, always moderate and pragmatic, forge a close working relationship with the centre and right-wing unions that later became his power base. He wanted to expand the ACTU's membership, particularly by affiliating white-collar unions. He wanted more young people to join unions. He wanted to increase the union movement's profile on national and international political issues. He wanted the ACTU to expand its services to members by establishing insurance and hire-purchase initiatives, which could provide loans at low interest rates. He wanted to boost the ACTU's research staff and create a legal department He wanted to provide educational opportunities for talented children of parents on low incomes. And he wanted the ACTU to play a bigger role in policymaking at the national level, by working with Coalition and Labor governments in the interests of union members.

It was a big agenda.

10

THE SECOND-MOST POWERFUL MAN IN AUSTRALIA

B ob Hawke's presidency of the ACTU began on 1 January 1970.[1] He led a union movement with about 2.51 million members, representing 45 per cent of the workforce – one of the highest membership rates in the world. But union membership was in long-term decline, down from about 54 per cent a decade earlier.[2] Hawke set himself the task of arresting this fall in membership, and actually expanding union representation of the workforce, in overall and proportional terms. He wanted the union movement to lift the wages and improve the working conditions of all men and women. But the ACTU's industrial strategy shifted significantly in these years, using the media to articulate union aims and threaten strikes and bans in parallel to action taken in the Conciliation and Arbitration Commission.

Hawke had ambitions beyond the workplace. He thought unions should no longer confine themselves to issues of wages and conditions, but be concerned with the broader lives of members. First, he wanted unions to play a larger role in improving the quality of life of all Australians: in health, education, the environment, and equality of opportunity. Second, he wanted unions to campaign on issues of national and international importance which accorded with their values. 'The overriding vision that I certainly had when I was president of the ACTU was of a growing economy with rising living standards for all, and increased protection for the least privileged,' Hawke later reflected.[3]

Hawke and his supporters had a narrow 9–8 majority on the ACTU Executive, including his vote as president. But it was a close-run thing. Ray Gietzelt came within three votes of losing his position, which would have handed power to the Right faction.[4] Gietzelt and Charlie Fitzgibbon were Hawke's most reliable supporters on the ACTU executive. Jack Petrie, federal secretary of the Storemen and Packers' Union, and from the Left, was elected senior vice-president. Ralph Marsh, secretary of the NSW Labor Council, from the Right, was elected junior vice-president. Pat Clancy, New South Wales secretary of the Building Workers' Industrial Union, was also a Hawke supporter, and the only communist on the seventeen-member executive.

Hawke had pledged to work with all factions. He was supported by the Left but was never of the Left. He had astutely used their backing to win the ACTU presidency over Souter, and now he wanted the support of both major factional groupings to stay there. When the executive met, Hawke sought to make the group work collegiately, and was available before and after meetings to talk to members. He often invited the executive to Sandringham for a barbecue, a swim in the pool and a sauna (which had recently been put in), and to play tennis or billiards. He discouraged the Left and Right groupings from drinking at different pubs. Over time, he found this strategy helped lessen tensions. He became a member of three unions – aligned to Left and Right – and showed favour to none: the Federated Miscellaneous Workers' Union of Australia, the Federated Clerks' Union of Australia and the Amalgamated Metal Workers and Shipwrights' Union.

Hawke had particular respect for John Ducker, then assistant secretary of the NSW Labor Council, who was emerging as a leading figure of the national Right faction. Ducker had migrated from England to Australia at age eighteen in 1950. He had a thick Yorkshire accent, was staunchly anti-communist, and a devoted Catholic. He joined the Federated Ironworkers' Association as an organiser and was mentored by Laurie Short. He climbed the ranks of the NSW Labor Council, which he had joined in 1961, to become secretary in 1975. He became NSW Labor president in 1970 and leader of that state's Right faction.

Hawke moved into Monk's office at the ACTU headquarters on Lygon Street in Melbourne. He now earned $9000 per annum ($11,000 with allowances). Harold Souter's future as secretary was initially uncertain. Hawke expected Souter to depart but would not force the issue. It was thought he might be appointed to the Conciliation and Arbitration Commission. Souter, in fact, wanted to stay. Hawke felt he had to accept it. 'It was a really difficult period,' Ralph Willis recalled. 'Horrible, actually.'[5] Over time, Hawke and Souter established a working relationship, though it was always cool. But Hawke's magnanimity served to stabilise his leadership. 'We just had to accept the result,' said Unsworth. 'It wasn't as if a communist had been elected president of the ACTU. Hawke was well respected for the work he had done at the ACTU. He won the ballot and once that happened, it was back to business.'[6]

Hawke's authority as president was also established externally. He had just turned forty and was soon being referred to as the second-most powerful man in Australia, after the prime minister.[7] A newspaper profile published in July 1970 argued that he was 'powerful' and 'ambitious' – words that had never been used to describe Monk. In interviews, Hawke outlined his approach to industrial relations and his leadership of the union movement. He promised to work with all union officials, believing more could be achieved as a united and cohesive group with common objectives. It was the beginnings of Hawke's model of 'consensus' – a word he himself used at the time – which would also define his approach to leadership when he became prime minister.[8]

Hawke was recognised as an energetic and exciting advocate, with a mix of intelligence and larrikinism, but some also saw him as intimidating, arrogant and egotistical. It was joked that he was so vain that he took his glasses off for radio interviews.[9] He was viewed as both an asset and a liability for Labor, with some MPs worried he would cost the party votes. The Women's Liberation group welcomed Hawke's support for equal pay for women and his stand against sexual discrimination, but disliked his style. It voted him 'male chauvinist of the month' in June 1971. When he was asked if he had a message for the women of Australia, he responded: 'Tell them I'm glad they're as pretty as they are, and I hope they stay that way.'[10]

Hawke's popularity seesawed through the early 1970s, often in response to industrial action, which the broader public generally disliked. In March 1971, his approval as ACTU president was 42 per cent, while his disapproval was 30 per cent.[11] Five months later, Hawke had the support of only 28.2 per cent, and 41.7 per cent of union members.[12] Yet by February 1972, Hawke's approval rating had increased to 30 per cent.[13] By mid-1972, another poll saw Hawke with a 54 per cent approval rating. Hawke had worked hard to improve his image.[14] And by September that year, Hawke enjoyed the support of 60 per cent of those polled.[15]

Hawke left the day-to-day administration of the ACTU to Souter, preferring to focus on increasing the profile of the movement and negotiating industrial disputes. His workload was exhausting. His desk was routinely covered in paper. He had five phones that rang repeatedly throughout the day. Always a good sleeper, he would typically get up at 5 am and work for around three hours at home before going to the office. He would usually arrive around 8.30 am and work a full day, nap in the afternoon, and continue working into the evening or attend functions. He would typically work 100 hours a week.

In the drab offices of the ACTU, Hawke was supported by his secretary Corinne Millane, aged twenty-one, who was regularly written up by journalists as not only highly efficient but beautiful and stylish. Upstairs worked Ralph Willis, thirty-two, as principal research officer. He was supported by Jan White (later Marsh), twenty-two, who focused on wage cases. Willis and Marsh, like Hawke, were university graduates, and the first to work for the ACTU with such qualifications. They would soon be joined by Peter Matthews as education officer and Geoffrey Gleghorn as press secretary. Along with Souter, there were only about seven full-time staff in 1970, plus several steno-secretaries. The staff would grow considerably over the next decade. In 1972, exasperated by Hawke's failure to be managed in his press relations, Gleghorn resigned. Graham Hardy, a former journalist, took his place.

In 1973, Jean Sinclair was hired to be personal assistant to both Hawke and Souter. She had a degree from the University of Melbourne and had worked at McKinsey's alongside businessman Rod Carnegie. She had a unique ability to turn chaos into order, work collegiately with others and navigate the byzantine world of union and party politics. Sinclair became indispensable to Hawke: she managed his diary, organised his travel, sorted his mail and papers, and became a trusted adviser. Sinclair served Hawke tirelessly and loyally, covering up for his drinking and womanising, rarely with complaint. She would work for Hawke at the ACTU, when he was the member for Wills and a shadow minister, and in government. Sinclair also became Hawke's secret lover. This relationship began while they were at the ACTU and would continue through his prime ministership.

—

Hawke had never been an industrial peacemaker but this became a focus as president. He became widely respected for his ability to resolve protracted disputes between employees and employers. He rejected the suggestion, often made by commentators, that he always waited until the last moment, when both sides were exhausted, to intervene and then took credit for securing a compromise outcome. Individual unions took responsibility for negotiating with employers, and Hawke could only intervene if they requested it or accepted his offer of assistance. It was a good negotiating strategy for unions to say they were calling in Hawke. This seemed to loosen up both sides to prepare to compromise. It was also ACTU procedure for unions to notify the organisation if a dispute it was having would impact on another union. This also gave Hawke an opportunity to intervene.

Hawke's dispute resolution strategy had several elements. First, he took time to understand the respective cases of both employers and unions. Second, he emphasised that he was an honest broker, with integrity, and his word could be trusted and acted upon. He also paid attention to the process. He would allocate time for each side to make their case. He would outline areas on both sides for compromise. And he would ensure both unions and employers felt they had produced an agreement which, if not optimal, they could live with. Hawke felt his father had influenced his approach to disputes, because Clem had 'instilled into me the worth of every person' and he was 'a bloody good listener too'.[16]

In the early 1970s, there were often lengthy disputes in the oil industry that tested Hawke's abilities as a conciliator and brought him into conflict with the Gorton and McMahon governments. Unions were negotiating with employers over the thirty-five-hour week – an idea that Hawke wanted expanded to the rest of the workforce, but which was strongly opposed by the government. In June–July 1972, there was a petrol tanker drivers' dispute, which caused stoppages throughout Australia and led to severe fuel short-ages. The unions refused to negotiate and the companies refused to back down. Hawke, though not directly involved initially, was dragged into the chaos.

Billy McMahon was eager to tie Labor to the ACTU over the threat that petrol stations would not be refuelled and essen-tial services would be severely disrupted. Hawke recalled that McMahon discussed with the industry the idea of deploying the army to run the oil refineries, but was dissuaded. He also consid-ered recalling parliament for an emergency session to deal with the protracted crisis. The ACTU and Hawke personally came under sustained attack from ministers. The government took the side of the oil companies, urging them not to give in.

Eventually cabinet saw that it had to resolve the dispute, and McMahon sent the minister for labour, Phillip Lynch, the minister for shipping and transport, Peter Nixon, and the attorney-general, Ivor Greenwood, to see Hawke. They turned up at Trades Hall and could not find Hawke's office. The media reported every move. When they eventually sat down, Hawke lashed them for taking the side of the companies. They left with their tails between their legs. Billy Snedden, the treasurer, believed that the ministers embarrassed the government, having 'prostrated' them-selves to Hawke and abandoned the oil companies. 'That was the beginning of the end of the McMahon government,' he recalled.[17]

Hawke paid little attention to the sabre-rattling by McMahon's ministers and negotiated directly with industry leaders, chief among them Walter 'Mac' Leonard of Ampol. Hawke was able to reach an agreement whereby some refineries would not face strike action so that essential services could be guaranteed. It led to a new two-year agreement in the commission. The McMahon government opposed this, but by then had been dealt out of the talks and was humiliated. Hawke was viewed as the man who had ended the dispute and, after a period of unpopularity, his favourability ratings began to rise.

One of the most notable disputes in which Hawke was involved was Frank Sinatra's tour of Australia in July 1974.[18] The singer's arrival in Australia on 9 July was greeted with stories about his mafia connections and the string of women in his life. He refused interview requests, and on stage in Melbourne said the media were 'bums' and 'pimps' for hounding him. 'They're parasites who take everything and give nothing,' he said. 'And as for the broads who work for the press, they're the hookers of the press. I might offer them a buck and a half, I'm not sure.' There was uproar. Several unions demanded an apology. Sinatra refused. Hawke intervened, and said: 'If you don't apologise, your stay in this country could be indefinite. You won't be allowed to leave Australia unless you can walk on water.' Sinatra's entourage had scuffles with reporters. Unions threatened bans to stop his tour, and airport workers refused to refuel his Gulfstream jet. Sinatra was under siege.

As the dispute escalated, Sinatra and his entourage escaped on a commercial flight to Sydney. From his suite on the twenty-third floor of the Boulevard Hotel in Sydney, Sinatra appealed directly to Gough Whitlam to intervene. The prime minister said there was only one person who could help him: Hawke. But Sinatra refused to negotiate. He considered asking Jimmy Hoffa and the Teamsters Union for help. Or calling on the United States Navy to save him. Meanwhile, anticipating that Sinatra might need help, the United States' consul general in Sydney, Norman Hannah, phoned John Ducker 'to establish a line of communication'. Ducker said he was already talking to Hawke, who was on his way to Sydney.[19] Eventually, Sinatra agreed to negotiate. On 11 July, Hawke arrived to lead discussions. He met with Sinatra and Milton 'Mickey' Rudin, his manager and lawyer.

Hawke was not introduced to Sinatra at first. He eyed the crooner from across the room and was shocked at how 'fat' he was, and realised he wore a corset in public. Rudin welcomed him.

'Mr Hawke, you can't stop Mr Sinatra going back to America,' he said. Hawke repeated his line about walking on water and said, 'Unless Frank is of that capacity, he can't get out because our people at the airports and ports won't let him out.'

After a while, Sinatra came over and introduced himself. 'How are you going?' he said.

'Well, all we need, Frank, is an apology,' Hawke said.

Sinatra nodded, and gestured to Rudin. 'Well, you work it out with them, Bob.'[20]

Hawke insisted Sinatra issue an apology. Rudin said Sinatra had never apologised to anyone in his life, and he was not going to start now. Hawke sought a compromise. He suggested issuing a statement regretting the remarks on stage and the clash with reporters, and the bans would be lifted. But Sinatra would not budge. They worked on a form of words. After draft after draft, they got nowhere. Hawke made it clear that unless there was a deal, and a statement issued, then Sinatra would not be able to leave Australia. After hours of talks, complete with brandy and cigars, an agreement was finally reached. But it was not an apology.

Sinatra's statement was read out in front of the Boulevard Hotel that afternoon. 'We have produced an honourable result,' Hawke declared. While Rubin suggested there was no 'apology', he did express Sinatra's 'regret' for his remarks impugning the integrity of female journalists, and for any physical altercations with his entourage. The second Melbourne concert had been cancelled, but Sinatra's three Sydney concerts, at the Hordern Pavilion, went ahead. One was televised on Channel Nine for free. Sinatra left Australia as soon as he could, vowing never to return. 'A funny thing happened in Australia,' he said later. 'I made a mistake and got off the plane.'[21]

On 23 March 1983, soon after Hawke became prime minister, Rudin wrote to Hawke to congratulate him:

My client, Frank Sinatra, and I wish to congratulate you on your election. It did not come as a surprise to either of us, since after our meeting in July 1974 I made a firm prediction to Mr Sinatra that eventually you would be elected as the Prime Minister. We were only disappointed that it took you almost nine years.

Somehow, we both feel that we gave you a slight assist on your way to the Prime Minister's office. While some of the other labor leaders created an unwarranted and unnecessary incident, your statesmanship in finding a solution to the problem was perhaps a small step in achieving your ambition.

Rudin's arrogance, like that of his client, knew no bounds. He then suggested Hawke might want to 'admit that Mr Sinatra was unfairly accused' during his tour of Australia a decade earlier, and that 'it was unfair to prevent him from performing his remaining concert in Melbourne'. This 'admission', Rudin suggested, could 'take the form of inviting him back to Australia to perform'. Of course, Sinatra would be there for 'his personal profit' but could also find time for a charity concert. There is no record of Hawke's reply, which might be explained by the 'PS' at the bottom of the letter: 'By the way, Mr Sinatra still believes that the gossip columnists are the "hookers of the press".'[22]

Ol' Blue Eyes would not return to Australia until January 1988, when he was paid $1.4 million to perform at the opening of Sanctuary Cove on the Gold Coast. Sinatra invited Hawke as his personal guest. He declined.

—

A major focus of Hawke's presidency of the ACTU was the establishment of business partnerships with the private sector. Hawke was influenced by the success of Histadrut, the General Federation of Labour in Israel, and West Germany's confederation of unions, the Deutscher Gewerkschaftsbund, known as the DGB. The Histadrut ran a national health fund, nursing homes, training schools, an insurance scheme, a housing construction company, a publishing house, and rural and industrial cooperatives. Postwar, the DGB owned Europe's largest construction companies, which focused on cooperative social housing projects but also built offices, shopping centres, universities and hospitals. It also provided finance and insurance to union members, and had its own bank.

Hawke wanted to replicate this model in Australia. 'Histadrut and the West German union movement have done it. Why not us?'

he said in June 1971. 'Once we have created the apparatus, there's no reason why we should not become involved in other things such as building schools and hospitals.'[23] Asked in August 1972 about the role of unionism in Australia for the next ten to fifteen years, Hawke said: 'The single most important thing, I believe, will be the establishment of trade union economic enterprises.'[24]

Hawke's initial focus, however, was breaking retail price maintenance (also known as resale price maintenance), whereby manufacturers could require retailers not to sell products below a certain price. He explained that workers had to 'justify their claims for increases in wages' through arbitration tribunals, but businesses 'were free to set whatever price the market would bear'.[25] In response to this inefficiency and inequity, he had succeeded in the 1960s in having wages adjusted for prices and productivity. Now he saw an opportunity for workers to save more of their wages by paying lower prices for goods within a more competitive retail industry.

The first step was to take the ACTU into partnership with business owners Lionel and George Revelman to establish the Bourke's-ACTU store on the corner of Elizabeth and La Trobe streets in Melbourne. Bourke's was a well-known discount store. Hawke's aim was to break retail price maintenance and establish a lower retail price structure for consumers. The Revelman brothers approached Hawke with the partnership proposal, and it was finalised in December 1970. In return for helping to bust the manufacturers' boycott on Bourke's, the ACTU would have an equal number of directors, share profits, gain new office space and have an opportunity to buy the store outright after five years. The ACTU Executive endorsed the proposal and the store began trading in January 1971. The following year, the ACTU moved into a spacious fifth-floor office at Bourke's.

With Bourke's-ACTU open for business, Hawke began negotiating with manufacturers but had little success. In March that year, the ACTU took on the Dunlop group of companies, which had refused to negotiate, with coordinated strikes to stop the movement of goods to and from their companies in Victoria. After two days of industrial action, Dunlop relented and agreed to supply Bourke's. Other companies, fearful of industrial action, did the same. Billy McMahon lashed Hawke as the 'bogey man' of Australian politics, and accused him of trying to run the country.[26] But Hawke's campaign led to legislation, introduced by McMahon's own government, to outlaw retail price maintenance, saving consumers millions of dollars with lower prices.

Hawke's vision for Bourke's was never fully realised. On 10 May 1972, Lionel Revelman died at his home while playing tennis with Hawke. They were close friends. Revelman, just fifty years old, died in Hawke's arms. Hawke was devastated. Plans to revitalise the store and expand into other states were shelved. By the end of the decade, the retailer was deep in the red. In 1978–79, Bourke's posted a loss of $276,404. Assessing the venture, Hawke later said it failed to attract a dedicated union clientele and its location counted against it.[27] The ACTU office, however, remained there until 1988. In that time, about $1 million was saved in office rent.

Other ventures had, at best, mixed success. In August 1972, Hawke forged a partnership between the ACTU and Thomas Nationwide Transport (TNT), run by Peter Abeles, to provide cheap travel and holidays. Hawke was chairman of the joint venture, and Abeles deputy chairman. It was a similar arrangement to that struck with the Revelmans. The ACTU had 50 per cent equity, with nothing to contribute up front, and TNT underwrote all costs. ACTU-New World Travel agency opened its doors in March 1973. Five years later, in July 1978, ACTU-Jetset Travel Service was established, with Isi Leibler as chairman. Hawke claimed ACTU-Jetset had saved unionists $1 million in lower-cost travel in its first year.

ACTU-Solo service stations and petrol distribution, a partnership with fuel retailer David Goldberger, began operating in July 1975. The ACTU took 50 per cent equity in the venture but had no liability exposure. ACTU-Solo struggled to take off outside of Victoria. But cut-price fuel did encourage other retailers to lower their prices. Hawke claimed that Australian motorists had saved $100 million thanks to ACTU-Solo.

By the end of Hawke's presidency, in 1980, ACTU-Solo and ACTU-Jetset were providing a regular stream of revenue to the ACTU. But planned forays into insurance, consumer credit, social housing and holiday worker camps were never launched. It is

not surprising that not all unions shared Hawke's vision. At the
September 1973 ACTU Congress, he faced a campaign from
the extreme Right and extreme Left to curtail his consumer
ventures. In a vitriolic debate, Hawke defeated a push by John
Maynes, a DLP member, and John Halfpenny, a communist, to
abandon his union enterprise dreams.

—

During Hawke's presidency, the ACTU became a leading
contributor to economic and social policy debates. He spoke
about education and training, health services, financial support
for families, poverty reduction, and disadvantage faced by Aboriginal Australians. He made an early decision to campaign strongly
against the Gorton government's budget in August 1970. Hawke
initiated a three-hour strike to take place a week after the budget
was delivered. This led to Hawke being savaged by John Gorton in
parliament as 'a would-be dictator' who was trying to incite people
to break the law. Liberal MPs urged Gorton to tie the militant
Hawke to opposition leader Gough Whitlam.[28]

In fact, Hawke met with Gorton several times and liked
him. He admired Gorton's earthy larrikinism, his independent
mind and his promotion of Australian arts and culture. But he
did not rate him highly as a prime minister. 'We just got along
personally but he was not gifted with a great intelligence,' Hawke
recalled.[29] He was stunned by Gorton's downfall in March 1971. It
had been sparked by a disagreement between the departments of
Defence and the Army over civil aid in Vietnam. Gorton backed
the Army. Alan Ramsey, a journalist with *The Australian*, asked
Gorton if Lieutenant-General Thomas Daly had accused defence
minister Malcolm Fraser of disloyalty. Gorton did not deny it.
Fraser resigned from cabinet with a blistering speech that savaged
Gorton. A motion of confidence was moved in the Liberals' party
room and resulted in a tie. Gorton exercised his casting vote
against himself and resigned.

Any regard Hawke had for Gorton was not extended to
McMahon. They often had fiery exchanges in public and never
got on well in person. Hawke thought McMahon lacked the intellectual capacity to lead a government, and regarded him as devious

and untrustworthy. 'He had no judgement,' Hawke recalled. 'He was, no doubt, the least efficient prime minister we have had.'[30] Conversations about industrial and economic matters were 'very barren'. Hawke believed McMahon was a political animal with no regard for anything other than his self-interest, and the worst Australian prime minister in his lifetime.[31]

After less than a year as ACTU president, Hawke was hailed as the 'best known person in Australia'. More people knew the ACTU president than the prime minister.[32] Hawke was in demand to give speeches, appear on radio and television, and be interviewed by newspapers. He could not walk down a street without being stopped by someone wanting to talk to him, shake his hand or pat him on the back. 'Walking anywhere with him is like walking with a film star,' reported journalist Owen Thomson in July 1970.[33] The question of when, rather than if, he would go into politics was perennial. Hawke suggested ten years – 1980 – might be the right time.[34]

While Hawke had never worked in a full-time manual labour job or been a union delegate or official, union members liked, respected and trusted him. The mutual affection between Hawke and working men and women was palpable. He was not one of them, but he was for them. 'He was the most unpopular unionist in the country at one point but union members always loved him,' Bill Kelty recalled. 'People would just come up to him and want to touch him.'[35] In September 1972, Hawke spoke to waterside workers at the Hunter River Hotel, along the 'Hungry Mile' in Sydney. He spoke of his love for the late Jim Healy, federal secretary of their union. The bar was crowded. With a beer in hand, Hawke said: 'I can't remember a happier moment than this since I became president of the ACTU. I love your union and I love your membership.'[36]

For television audiences, and those who read newspapers or saw him in person, Hawke was a familiar sight: of slim build and average height; with soft, tanned skin; dark, thick, curly hair tightly combed back and flattened with Brylcreem; long, dark, bushy sideburns (he briefly grew a beard in 1972); horn-rimmed glasses beneath thick, arched eyebrows (but often removed for television or photos); clothed in a fashionable suit with white shirt and thin dark tie fastened with a Windsor knot; and always wearing suede shoes.

Hawke believed Albert Monk was afraid of the media. By contrast, he cultivated the media and saw it as his principal channel of communication with union members, employers, politicians and the broader public. Journalists could phone him at the ACTU for a 'dial-a-quote' comment. He could be found at the Lygon Hotel or Trades Hall across the road. Journalists rang him at home or turned up on the doorstep for an interview. Hawke often held press conferences at the ACTU offices or outside on Lygon Street. He was a born performer with a sense of the dramatic. 'Gentlemen,' he would say, 'I am here as usual for the convenience of the media.'[37] They would pepper him with questions, and sometimes he could be cranky and irritable, but he rarely lost sight of who he was talking to: the men and women of Australia.

Hawke could be magnetic on television. He was never scripted or overly rehearsed. He knew how to convey his whole personality. He was intelligent and authentic, even if he sometimes came across as vain or snobbish. Hawke was also famous for brash encounters with interviewers when his emotions got the better of him. Whether viewers liked him or not, it always made for compelling viewing. He mastered the medium of TV, which was beginning to have a seismic influence on public opinion at a time when many politicians found it intimidating and preferred radio.

His language was often controversial. Television viewers objected to his use of the words 'For God's sake' or 'Jesus bloody Christ', and studio switchboards would light up with upset callers. At times, some viewers thought Hawke was drunk. When David Frost did a series of television specials in Australia before the 1972 election, he said that many expected it would be a 'confrontation' rather than an 'interview' if he was talking to Hawke.[38] Hawke tried to be less abrasive, but it was a work in progress. During a street meeting in Rockhampton in 1975, Hawke referred to an interjector as a 'silly bastard'. When he discovered that the man had the surname Cocks, Hawke could not restrain himself. He referred to him, and his two sons in the audience, as 'Cocks and his two little cocks'.[39]

The flip side of Hawke's aggression was his tears. He wept on television over his love of Israel, the failures in his marriage and how he missed his children. He sobbed when asked about his parents. 'It's just some physiological thing,' he explained to George Negus in 1978. 'I am emotional in that sense. I'm not proud of it nor non-proud of it; it's just a physiological fact.'[40] This was Hawke: what you saw was what you got. There was nothing phony or inauthentic.

Hawke's growing profile and influence was such that he was being noticed abroad. In a report written by the National Security Council for Richard Nixon on 24 August 1971, he was seen as a potential threat to Gough Whitlam. Hawke was not even in parliament. 'Whitlam faces a potential political rival in Bob Hawke, who is young (41), well-educated (Rhodes Scholar), projects a strong social conscience, and has demonstrated a flair for capturing popular issues,' the report said. 'His power derives essentially from his position as president of the (ACTU).'[41]

During the 1970s, Hawke worked so hard, travelling the length and breadth of Australia, that he often wore himself out. He was frequently exhausted, occasionally hospitalised and often had to spend days recovering. In July 1972, Hawke collapsed from exhaustion as he opened an exhibition at the Munster Art Gallery in Melbourne. A doctor treated him on the scene, and he spent the night at the Southern Cross Hotel with Hazel by his side. There were rumours he had had a heart attack, but the collapse was due to his excessive workload and lack of sleep while negotiating an oil dispute. Hawke regularly took concoctions that promised to cleanse his body, and underwent acupuncture for chronic back problems.

Rob Jolly, who joined the ACTU as research officer and advocate in 1972, recalled that Hawke pushed himself too hard, and often with terrible consequences. 'The combination of workload and drinking too much led to exhaustion,' he said. 'It is not a good combination for your health.' Jolly said Hawke could get aggressive and abusive when he had had too much to drink and was tired. 'Sometimes he would be really ruthless to people and knock the crap out of them verbally, and you would not want to be on the receiving end of his tongue when he was in one of those moods.'[42]

John Stone, a contemporary of Hawke's from Perth Modern, recalled seeing him at the Canberra Rex Hotel in 1972. Stone was then deputy secretary in Treasury. Hawke arrived with Fred Wheeler, the Treasury secretary, at the drinks function hosted by the Chamber of Manufactures. The room was filled with politicians, public servants and business leaders. Wheeler, like Hawke, was known as a big drinker. Hawke saw Stone and made a beeline for him. 'He started attacking me very publicly and very loudly,' Stone recalled. Hawke said: 'When we win the election in a few weeks' time we will bloody well fix you, you know, you're for the high jump. You won't last ten minutes.' Stone was embarrassed and upset. He had had little to do with Hawke since their days together at Oxford.[43]

Word spread about Hawke's outburst, and the next day Stone's phone rang. He recognised the voice: Gough Whitlam. 'Mr Stone,' Whitlam said.

'Oh, Mr Whitlam, yes, sir, what can I do for you?' Stone asked.

'Frank Crean has told me about Bob Hawke's attack upon you last night at the Canberra Rex Hotel,' Whitlam said. 'Well, I just want you to know, Mr Stone, that Bob Hawke will have nothing to do with your position should we win the next election – nothing whatsoever. I will make decisions as to who we continue to employ and who we don't, and I can say to you that your name is not high on my list of people to be sacked.'

Stone was relieved and grateful.[44]

Laurie Oakes joined the staff of *The Sun News-Pictorial* in 1967 and got to know Hawke. 'He was a very bright young bloke,' he recalled. 'Journalists loved him then because he had got a rise for journalists in an important wage case. But it wasn't long before they discovered his faults, and he had a lot of enemies.' Oakes recalled late-night drinking sessions with Hawke that frequently turned ugly. 'He was just a terrible drunk,' he said. 'Hawkey could be pretty horrible, and that was one of the reasons I thought he could never be prime minister.'[45]

While Hawke's drinking and public outbursts were well known, the full extent of his infidelity was only hinted at in the media. Hawke's amatory existence meant that he usually had casual sex with women every week, often several times a week. Some were regular partners. Some were random women who would just throw themselves at him. Women wrote letters to the ACTU, or phoned directly, offering to have sex with Hawke. Some were sex workers, procured by political, union or business figures. Hawke had women in every city, in every state, with their contact details listed in a little black book.

Gillian Appleton became one of Hawke's lovers in 1974. She was working as a researcher on *The Mike Walsh Show* and met Hawke when he appeared as a guest. He contacted her the next day and they met at the Boulevard Hotel in Sydney. 'He was powerful and charismatic, and at the peak of his popularity as ACTU President,' Appleton recalled. She was thirty-two; he was forty-four. They would also meet at an apartment on Park Street, Sydney, owned by a Labor supporter, or at the Canberra Rex Hotel.

After sex, they would talk about politics and books, and sing old hymns together having discovered a shared fondness for favourites of their youth. Hawke liked to imitate British comedians Peter Cook and Dudley Moore. 'When you were in his company, his incredible energy and joie de vivre were infectious,' she said. Hawke liked to be naked and admire himself in the mirror. He was particularly vain about his hair and would whip out a comb at any opportunity. 'He was quite sweet in private,' she recalled. 'I never felt jealous of the fact that he had other women. I was not in love with him, I just found him fun to be with.'

But there was a darker side. 'His behaviour could be terrifying,' Appleton recalled. 'When he drank too much, he would become pugnacious, weird and paranoid. But not violent.' While he did not disparage Hazel to others, he could be contemptuous when speaking to her on the phone. 'I fucking already told you, I'm not going to make it home for the weekend – got it?' he once said to Hazel, within earshot of Appleton. After one incident with hotel guests in the bar, Appleton left Hawke a note saying his behaviour was so appalling that she would not see him again. He rang the next day in tears to apologise, explaining he had no memory of what he had done. The relationship ended when Appleton informed Hawke that she had met someone else, future husband Jim McClelland. Hawke did not take it well.[46]

Hawke travelled to New Zealand for eight days in mid-1975. He was to speak at a conference at Otago University in Dunedin. Tom Lewis and Phillip Ward, from the Diplomatic Protection

Squad, were assigned to look after Hawke. They were briefed that Hawke was a PLO target because of his sympathy for Israel and needed armed protection. While Hawke's address to the conference was a hit, he often swapped sessions for a daytime pub crawl. Lewis and Ward were amazed by his capacity to drink most of the day and night, and still function with just a few hours' sleep. They found Hawke charismatic and great fun to be with.

On arrival, Hawke had insisted on having his own room, and they agreed on the proviso that they could still see inside. What they saw, night after night, was Hawke's philandering turbo-charged as women were regularly escorted to his room. On the final night, they monitored Hawke having difficulty 'disrobing' his companion. She explained that she was happily married and had not done this sort of thing before. 'I'll let you into a secret,' Hawke reassured her. 'Neither have I. Let's relax and help each other.' It was surely a line he had used before.[47]

Not surprisingly, Hawke was rarely at home in time for dinner during the week and often he was in another city. He tried to get home on weekends, and mostly did, but they too were taken up with work and visitors. Hazel ran a busy household: she had children of school age and a husband who was not home regularly, and she often had to facilitate last-minute guests such as journalists or union and party colleagues. In the 1970s, Hazel had the help of Brigitte Warne, who would help clean the house for a few hours each week. Brigitte and her two sons, Shane and Jason, were regular visitors to the Hawke house. Shane would later become one of Australia's greatest cricketers.

While Hawke was an absent father and husband, he was not completely shut off from his family's lives. While travelling, he spoke to Hazel and the kids by phone. They would often pop into the ACTU office or the Lygon Hotel. And Hawke discussed his work extensively with Hazel, and with the children as they grew older. 'I used to think that it would be good to be married to a man with regular hours who would be home every night for a meal with you,' Hazel acknowledged in July 1970. 'But I realise it would be terribly dull. There is an element of excitement in Bob's life that comes through. He discusses everything with me and listens to me in areas where he knows I will be reasonably informed.'

Bob said at the time: 'I would not be able to do the things I do without the wife I have.'[48]

On 1 September 1971, Hawke was named as Victoria's 'Father of the Year'. It was an award bestowed by the Victorian Father's Day Council. The New South Wales Father of the Year was Billy McMahon. Hawke accepted the award, but for those who knew him well it was ridiculous. Hawke corralled Ralph Willis into coming home with him after it was announced to shield him from Hazel. 'Hazel made it very clear she was very unimpressed and took the opportunity to list Bob's shortcomings as a father,' Willis recalled. 'I just stood there and watched her tear strips off him.'[49] Bob was quick to credit Hazel with being both mother and father to Susan, then fourteen, Stephen, twelve, and Rosslyn, ten. 'The award really should be made to my wife, Hazel,' he said at the time.[50]

Many years later, Hawke acknowledged his failings as a father and husband. 'I put my life in the trade union movement as number one, and it didn't get the priority that it should have got,' he said about fatherhood. He paid tribute to Hazel. 'She made up for my many absences from home,' he said. 'She was a marvellous mother and the kids respected her enormously. I was always travelling and spent a lot of time away from home as president of the ACTU, and that made for some difficulties.'[51]

Hawke's failures as a father, of course, did not mean that he did not love Hazel or Susan, Stephen and Rosslyn. 'He genuinely loved the kids and wanted to do what he could for them,' Willis said. 'But his lifestyle involved drinking in the pub after work and not getting home until late, when the kids were already in bed or going off to bed, and there wasn't much time for them. But in terms of him having a regard for and concern for, and love for, his kids, I think it was all there as much as any father.'[52]

Susan and Stephen have mostly happy memories of these years, but did witness tensions between their parents. They recall Hawke working on papers in the dining room, sitting on the lounge or sunbaking in the backyard, and often being on the phone. They would usually greet him at the airport after an overseas trip and run into his arms when they spotted him in the arrivals hall. There were family holidays, including to Yugoslavia and Greece in 1975. The Hawkes had a half-share in an eighteen-foot sailing boat, *Jackpot*, that was moored at the Sandringham Yacht Club. Taking that out was a fond memory. Hawke loved fishing, too: in September 1973 he caught a 155-kilogram black marlin while fishing on the Great Barrier Reef, off Cairns.

Susan engaged her father on political issues. If she thought he was unconvincing, she did not hesitate to tell him. Stephen was quieter and thoughtful. He also liked to talk to his father about issues, especially as he got older, and there were expectations that he would go on to university. Rosslyn was cheeky, warm and loving. Hawke loved to scoop her up into his arms and cuddle her tightly. Susan and Stephen were used to the public spotlight that followed their father. Rosslyn, as time went on, was less accepting, more vulnerable; she suffered the most of the three children.[53]

Susan remembered playing with her father in the backyard at Keats Street or Royal Avenue. She recalled various union and political people coming and going, especially on weekends. 'It was convivial, there was a barbecue, there was laughter, there was beer and it was a great environment for kids,' she said. 'We were not brought up to be seen and not heard.' Bob and Hazel were not strict disciplinarians, and the kids were always welcome, no matter who was visiting.[54]

Stephen also has fond memories. 'Dad was a pretty absent father a lot of the time but not totally absent,' he recalled. 'He used to throw me thousands of cricket balls and play tennis, and when he was around he was usually loud and boisterous.' Nevertheless, work was always a priority. 'There was an acceptance among the family that his work was important and was good work to be doing, and that it required putting in extraordinary hours,' he said. But the Father of the Year award should never have been accepted. Stephen said his father should have said to the organisers: 'I don't think this is a good idea.'[55]

—

Hawke took a strong interest in international issues, and was well known in the United States, Europe and the Middle East in the 1970s. He marshalled the union movement to oppose French nuclear testing in the South Pacific, with unions banning the servicing of planes and ships visiting Australia during this period. He participated in public demonstrations against Australia's involvement in the Vietnam War. But Hawke was not initially on the frontline of the anti-war movement, which was one of many challenging establishment thinking in the 1970s. But in June 1971, in conjunction with the third mass moratorium marches, Hawke spoke at a rally at the Sydney Town Hall, along with Gough Whitlam and Jim Cairns.

The most significant international issue in which Hawke played a role during this period was apartheid – institutionalised racial segregation in South Africa – which many Australians found repugnant. The six-week Australian tour by the South African rugby union team from June to August 1971 was met with protests, as the Springboks were all white. In Perth, Adelaide, Melbourne and Sydney, the demonstrations turned violent. Activists were beaten and arrested by police, and a state of emergency was declared in Queensland by Premier Joh Bjelke-Petersen. Australians had mixed views about the protests.

Meredith Burgmann was co-convenor of the Anti-Apartheid Movement and the 'Stop the Tours' campaign. She met Hawke to discuss a ban on the Springboks, and was surprised by his immediate support. 'This was at a time when basically the only political action being taken by unions was by the communist-dominated unions in the maritime, mining and construction industry,' Burgmann recalled. 'To have a political ban on an international issue put on by the ACTU was quite a surprise. We'd never actually seen him take an overtly radical position on a non-industrial issue.'[56]

Hawke encouraged unions to protest the tour. Taking its lead from the International Confederation of Free Trade Unions, the ACTU Executive endorsed the protest but did not insist that unions impose bans. The divisiveness of the protests led to Hawke being abused by politicians, sporting administrators and commentators. This, he accepted, was the price for taking a stand. Far more significant were the threating phone calls made to his mother, Ellie, the black paint poured on Hazel's car in the middle of the night, and the abuse yelled at Susan, Stephen and Rosslyn at school. Security protection was arranged for the Hawkes' home.

Hawke felt strongly about apartheid. More than a decade earlier, while visiting Cape Town, he had been appalled by the racial segregation he saw. He thought that appeals to emotion and reason could sway views. Many Australians just wanted to see rugby and cricket, and thought politics had no role in sport. It was a view that Sir Don Bradman put to Hawke directly. 'Bob, I believe very strongly that politics shouldn't interfere with sport,' he said.

Hawke replied that he could not agree more. 'It's the government of South Africa which introduced politics into sport,' he told Bradman. 'They have made the decision that if a person is not white, they cannot represent the country.'

Bradman looked at Hawke and said, 'I've got no answer to that.'[57]

Billy McMahon vigorously supported the Springbok tour, pledging to do whatever it took to see it proceed, and lashed Hawke for his opposition. He promised the use of the Royal Australian Air Force to transport the Springboks around Australia if need be. McMahon even accused the union movement of being 'prejudiced' against the Springboks. He sought to tie the unions to the Labor Party – which also opposed the tour – and gain political mileage. But this only had the effect of aligning the McMahon government with the apartheid government of South Africa, even though McMahon had said sport and politics should not mix. 'How more completely can you bring politics into sport?' Hawke asked.[58]

There was far from universal support within the unions for disrupting the Springbok tour. The Transport Workers Union believed it should go ahead, and threatened to black-ban Hawke if he travelled to Perth. Laurie Short, from the Federated Iron-workers Association, said: 'It is not good for the union movement to be too much involved in political strikes.'[59] Joe Riordan, secretary of the Federated Clerks Union, agreed. He also opposed the Vietnam moratorium marches, and the strike against the federal government's budget.[60]

The Stop the Tours campaign was a success. The Springboks were the last racially selected sporting team to tour Australia. A scheduled tour by the South African cricket team was cancelled. Burgmann said the union ban was a 'crucial' part of the campaign.

'Once the ACTU and the churches came out in opposition to the tour, it made a huge difference,' she said. 'It went from being a series of fragmented student demonstrations on a fairly peripheral international issue to being a human rights dilemma for the whole country.'[61]

The attempts to clip Hawke's wings by restraining future 'political strikes' at the August–September 1971 ACTU Congress in Melbourne failed. Hawke also won endorsement for union enterprises in the areas of retail, consumer credit, insurance and housing. He secured a 50 per cent increase in affiliation fees, even though the executive had recommended 100 per cent. And he emerged from the congress with a 10–7 majority on the ACTU Executive. The Hawke era was just beginning.

11

BOB AND
GOUGH

Prior to the November 1966 election, deputy Labor leader Gough Whitlam arranged to meet Bob Hawke at the ACTU in Melbourne, and urged him to run again for the seat of Corio. But Hawke was not interested. Robert Menzies had retired on 26 January 1966 and the Coalition government had a new prime minister, Harold Holt. In any event, Hawke was focused on succeeding Albert Monk as ACTU president. Labor did not pick up Corio at that election; in fact, its election performance was disastrous, and the party lost seats. Whitlam succeeded Arthur Calwell as Labor leader on 9 February 1967. When Hubert Opperman retired later that year, causing a by-election in July, Whitlam again urged Hawke to run. Again, Hawke declined. But he did say that if he failed to win the ACTU presidency, he would seek to enter parliament.

In the 1960s, Hawke and Whitlam were among Labor's most promising figures. Whitlam was the first Labor leader born in the twentieth century. Like Hawke, he represented a new style of leadership for a new age. By 1970, both men were leaders of the industrial and political labour movement, even though neither had worked on the factory floor or could be described as blue-collar. Aside from this, they could not have been more different in background, character or style. They were generally united, however, on the policy and political direction that Labor needed to adopt. But they were competitors, never friends, and over the years to come would express a mix of admiration, hostility and disdain for one another. They were, as journalist Paul Kelly said, 'the two great prima donnas of Australian politics'.[1]

Whitlam was born in July 1916; Hawke in December 1929. Whitlam was a big man; Hawke was short in stature. Whitlam was an intellectual who devoured books on ancient history, politics and literature; Hawke was a sports fanatic, preferring to play or watch tennis, cricket and Australian Rules football. Whitlam's upbringing was urban and middle-class, and his parents spoke about politics, history and literature at home; Hawke's upbringing was rural and suburban, and his parents preferred moral teachings from the Bible and small-town news. Whitlam was a big eater but not a drinker; Hawke never had much interest in food but drank to excess. They were alive to each other's political skills and capabilities, and equally aware of their flaws and eccentricities.

Whitlam was waging war against the moribund Victorian branch of the Labor Party. Following Labor's split in Victoria in 1955, and the formation of the Democratic Labor Party, it had become the most militant and doctrinaire branch. It paid a price for this with a long period out of power. Hawke too saw Victoria as a handbrake on Labor nationally. At the 1969 election, Labor won 46.9 per cent of the vote nationally but only 41.3 per cent in Victoria. Federal intervention to wrest control from the Socialist Left faction was essential. Bill Hartley (secretary) and George Crawford (president) opposed the intervention, which dismissed the Victorian Central Executive, formally dissolved the branch and installed Mick Young (federal secretary) and Tom Burns (federal president) as administrators of the party in Victoria.

Hawke was cautious about intervention. He feared that militant unions would form a breakaway Industrial Labour Party. Clyde Cameron, who played a critical role in the intervention, recalled that Hawke urged a conciliatory approach. 'Bob sees himself as the great compromiser, a great consensus man, and he did not want us to take the drastic steps we were planning,' Cameron later said.[2] Hawke disagreed with Whitlam's approach to dismiss the executive 'very drastically' rather than 'get changes' in a more cooperative manner. It was a subtle, yet important difference. According to Whitlam, Hawke opposed intervention and had tried to let the executive 'off the hook'.[3] Whitlam was a 'crash through or crash' politician; Hawke never was.

However, after intervention on 14 September 1970, Hawke supported it. He had made it clear that if the Victorian branch refused intervention and formally split from federal Labor, he would remain with the federal party. This was interpreted, correctly, as a break with the 'extremist trade unionists' who were hoping for a breakaway party to be established.[4] Hawke's support for intervention put him on the outer with several left-wing unions in Victoria, and marked a turning point in his shift towards the Right. Hawke was appointed to a twelve-man advisory council to help administer the party in Victoria. He and Frank Crean were also appointed as temporary Victorian delegates to the federal executive, replacing Hartley and Senator Bill Brown.

Hawke was formally elected to Labor's federal executive the following year, 1971. He was federal Labor's junior vice-president (1970–71) and senior vice-president (1971–73). He played a key role in promoting Labor ahead of the 1972 election, but he would not be a candidate. Ahead of the election, former leader Arthur Calwell did not recontest his seat of Melbourne. Calwell said Hawke could be prime minister by 1981 if he went into parliament.[5] 'My father would have liked Hawke to succeed him,' said Mary Elizabeth Calwell. 'He wanted a successor who had the qualities and should be able to make a significant contribution to the ALP and Australia.'[6]

On the night of 13 November 1972, the Bowman Hall in the Blacktown Civic Centre was buzzing with excitement. About 1500 Labor supporters, including MPs and union leaders, along with entertainment and sporting stars, waited for Whitlam to launch Labor's election campaign and outline his policy manifesto for government. Those who could not find a seat peered through the windows; hundreds more were stuck outside. The room was festooned with black-and-orange 'It's Time' banners, posters and balloons. The true believers had 'It's Time' badges pinned to their lapels. Australia had never seen anything like it. The carnival atmosphere resembled a scaled-down version of a United States presidential nominating convention.

The stage was set with a triple archway of bright flashing lights from floor to ceiling. A dozen girls wearing 'It's Time' T-shirts and barely anything else danced as Hawke and Whitlam walked up to the stage. Whitlam, wearing a light-grey suit with a white shirt and dark tie, was cool and relaxed. Hawke, dressed in a darker suit with a striped shirt and tie, and wearing his glasses, appeared overwhelmed by the charged atmosphere. He glanced at the girls and danced a little jig. He looked up at Whitlam, who towered over him, in awe. Hawke and other party figures sat on the stage as Whitlam delivered his speech, which was broadcast live on radio and television. 'Men and women of Australia!' Whitlam began. 'The decision we will make for our country on 2 December is a choice between the past and the future, between the habits and fears of the past, and the demands and opportunities of the future . . . It's time for a new government – a Labor government.' The audience clapped and cheered and stomped their feet.

Hawke was in huge demand to campaign for Labor's candidates. Graham Richardson was Hawke's driver in the campaign. 'He was a living Labor hero,' Richardson recalled. 'Everyone loved Hawkey. This was still the era of the town hall meetings. Sometimes his speeches were appalling because he was so pissed, and they would just go on and on, sometimes for forty-five minutes. But it did not matter because they loved him.'

Richardson recalled dropping Hawke at a Labor fundraiser at the APIA Club in Leichhardt while he ducked home for dinner. When Richardson returned, there was a commotion and he had to quickly usher Hawke out the door. He asked Hawke what had happened and he explained that television personality Hazel Phillips was at the same table and he had simply said that she had 'great tits'. Phillips took offence but Hawke could not see the problem. 'Some bloke wanted to biff him and take his head off,' Richardson recalled.[7]

Hawke addressed thirty-one public meetings and made seventy-one other appearances, including factory gate meetings, lunches and dinners. NSW Labor's general secretary, Geoff Cahill, thought Hawke was one of the 'main contributing factors' in the party's nationwide vote surge.[8] The Liberal Party tried to paint Hawke as the man behind Whitlam who was secretly running the party. Newspaper advertisements showed Hawke holding a mask of Whitlam in his hand. 'When Labor speaks who's really talking?' it asked. This was foolish: Hawke was a popular figure, not the 'bogey man' that McMahon had made him out to be. Whitlam/Hawke was a winning combination for Labor.

Two days before polling day, Whitlam and Hawke shared the stage at St Kilda Town Hall. Around 4000 true believers filled the room, and hundreds crowded outside. The mood was electric. Before Whitlam and Hawke walked onto the stage, they shared a private moment with their wives, Margaret and Hazel. They listened to the roar of the crowd humming through the corridors. At the microphone, Hawke introduced Whitlam, who paid tribute to unions, party members, candidates and state and federal MPs. 'The central ambition of an Australian Labor government will be to unite all sections of our great community in a common resolve, to forge a new spirit of common purpose that will let us meet the challenges ahead,' Whitlam said. The crowd cheered, clapped and stamped their feet. Then confetti poured down from above and streamers were thrown on the stage.[9]

Labor's primary vote lifted to 49.6 per cent and it claimed sixty-seven seats in the House of Representatives – a majority of nine. The Liberal Party's vote had collapsed to 28.1 per cent. Labor won 52.7 per cent of the two-party preferred vote. Whitlam wasted little time getting to work. With Labor having been out of power since 1949, the expectations were huge. Three days later he formed a temporary duumvirate government with his deputy, Lance Barnard, and for fourteen days they ruled the nation alone, making some of the most far-reaching decisions in Australian political history. These included withdrawing Australia's remaining forces from Vietnam, prohibiting racially selected sporting teams from coming to Australia, and formally recognising the communist government of China.

Bob and Hazel were thrilled by the election result. In the heady early days of the Whitlam government, Hawke thought the future for both his party and his country was bright. The two men consulted each other on critical matters. Whitlam invited the Hawkes to stay overnight at Kirribilli House in Sydney, and at the Lodge in Canberra. 'We put them up in the nuptial suite formerly occupied by the McMahons,' Whitlam indiscreetly recalled. 'They later complained about the fleas which bit them when they were disporting themselves on the carpet.'[10]

Hawke was elated but also cautious. He recalled pulling Whitlam aside at the last federal executive meeting of the party before the election. 'You will do some marvellous things in government in the fields of education, health and internationally,' Hawke said. 'But, Gough, your government will live or die on how you handle the economy. So, when you get elected, I'll organise for senior economists from the ANU to spend some time with you. It won't take too long, two or three months, a few hours a week and you'll get the basics of it.' Whitlam, often impervious to advice, flattered Hawke in response. 'Oh, thanks, comrade,' he said. But he had no intention of doing as Hawke suggested. Hawke raised it a few times but Whitlam ignored him.[11]

Hawke was elected Labor's federal president, succeeding Tom Burns, on 6 July 1973. He would hold the position, elected annually by the federal executive, until 1 August 1978. Jack Egerton, the Queensland Labor president, was elected senior vice-president, and John Ducker, the New South Wales Labor president, became junior vice-president.

Hawke was now wearing two hats as head of the labour movement and head of the party. The majority of voters – 71 per cent – said he should only hold one job.[12] Hawke wanted to bring the political and industrial wings closer together. But this was often the nub of the conflict. 'The main responsibility of the president is to use his or her best influence to see that the party is pursuing fundamental Labor policies consistent with the changing circumstances over time, and to ensure to his or her best ability that the party organisation machine is in the best possible shape to provide assistance to the parliamentary party,' Hawke reflected.[13]

Hawke could usually be relied upon to support the Right and Centre positions on the federal executive, which also accorded with Whitlam's views. Hawke played this role shrewdly. For example, when Left faction heavyweights Senator Lionel Murphy and Senator Arthur Gietzelt pushed for an investigation into New South Wales Labor, controlled by the Right, as a likely step towards intervention in July 1973, Hawke made sure that he was absent for the vote, which was tied and therefore lost.[14]

Despite being Labor's federal president, Hawke frequently clashed with the government on policy and political strategy.

An early flashpoint was appointing the president of the Conciliation and Arbitration Commission to succeed Sir Richard Kirby. Clyde Cameron, the minister for labour, promised the position to Sydney barrister Jack Sweeney. Hawke thought the best candidate was Justice John Moore. Hawke took it up with Whitlam, and Moore was appointed. It was a setback for Cameron, who did not forget. The ACTU's relationship with Cameron continued to go downhill. Cameron introduced changes to the *Conciliation and Arbitration Act* without consulting the ACTU. Harold Souter was incensed. 'We were better off under the Liberals,' he fumed. 'At least they used to talk to us first.'[15]

On 18 July 1973, the Whitlam government announced a 25 per cent cut in tariffs across the board. The economy was buoyant, with strong demand causing supply shortages, risking inflation. Reducing tariffs was seen as a means of easing these inflationary pressures. A committee chaired by Alf Rattigan, the chairman of the Tariff Board, was asked to consider the idea and reported back to Whitlam in just three weeks. Again, there was no consultation with the ACTU. Nor was there any reference to the Tariff Board. And no consultation with industry. The decision would see decades of protection removed by the stroke of a pen. Many sectors simply could not compete. Rattigan estimated that around 30,000 jobs would be lost as industry adjusted.

Unions were outraged. Hawke, whose instincts were to gradually remove protection to make industry more competitive and efficient, was furious. He phoned Whitlam to express his anger about being blindsided. When he fronted the media, Hawke said he 'agreed with the principle' of removing protection.[16] But he also made it clear, channelling union anger, that he was 'appalled at the government's political ineptitude' by announcing its decision without notice or prior consultation, and an appropriate adjustment package for industry.[17]

On 22 September 1973, a by-election for the seat of Parramatta was held. Nigel Bowen, the former Liberal MP, had accepted an appointment to the New South Wales Court of Appeal. There was a chance that Labor could win the seat, which it had narrowly lost by 0.3 per cent in December 1972. But the Liberal Party held the seat with a 7 per cent swing in its favour. The new Liberal

MP was Philip Ruddock. Prior to the by-election, Whitlam said it was 'a very strong probability' that Sydney's second major airport would be built at Galston, which adjoined the Parramatta electorate.[18] Hawke was furious and blamed the by-election loss on the Galston announcement, which he called an 'act of political insanity'.[19]

On 8 December 1973, Australians voted on two referendums that would give the Commonwealth power over prices and incomes. In the previous year, prices had risen by 13.2 per cent. Revaluations of the dollar, an across-the-board tariff cut and the establishment of the Prices Justification Tribunal had not arrested rising prices or escalating inflation. The Coalition opposed both referendums. The ACTU advocated a 'Yes' vote on prices but a 'No' on incomes. This put the ACTU in direct conflict with the government.

Hawke argued that if the government was granted power over incomes, it could be used to freeze wages. Whitlam gave Hawke a guarantee it would not do so, but Hawke feared a future Coalition government might. Whitlam wrote to Souter and argued that a new power over incomes could be used to restore cost-of-living adjustments to the basic wage. The ACTU was not persuaded.

Voters are usually suspicious of granting the federal government more power, and rejected both referendums. Indeed, neither received a majority of votes in any state. Jim Spigelman, Whitlam's principal private secretary, said the electorate could be forgiven for being confused, but doubted whether the referendums were ever viable. 'The referendum never had a chance so the impact of the ACTU was nil,' he said. 'Incomes policy was a global debate of the era. Gough seized on it as an opportunity to expand Commonwealth power.'[20] But Whitlam had no doubt who was to blame: he accused Hawke of 'sheer sabotage'.[21]

The Whitlam–Hawke relationship was under severe strain by the end of the Labor government's first year. When questioned at the National Press Club about Hawke's pro-Israel stand, and his attempt to shift Labor policy in that direction, Whitlam barely disguised his contempt for Hawke. After responding to a volley of questions, he sat down and said, in an audible whisper, 'And fuck him anyway.'[22]

When Hawke suggested in November 1973 that taxation should be increased to fund public services, Whitlam responded ferociously. 'The president of the federal executive of the ALP does not determine such matters, he doesn't speak for the party on such matters,' he said. 'And I doubt if in this matter he speaks on behalf of the trade union movement.'[23] Whitlam would rage up and down the corridors of his office fuming at public statements by Hawke that contradicted government policy.

An attempt was made to get the relationship back on the rails at the start of 1974. The Australian Labor Advisory Council – made up of union officials, party officials and MPs – met at the Canberra Rex Hotel on 15 January. The discussion was scheduled to begin at 2 pm. Hawke, Cliff Dolan, Harold Souter and Ralph Marsh were on time, and so was Labor federal secretary David Combe. But there was no Whitlam. He did not arrive until 4 pm. Hawke tore into Whitlam, who just sat there nonplussed. 'Oh well, I'm here,' he said. The ACTU representatives were infuriated. The meeting broke without discussing any of the agenda items. ALAC would not meet again until 11 November 1975.[24] Whitlam's speechwriter, Graham Freudenberg, explained: 'Hawke's mistake was to put the entitlement to consultation too high. Whitlam's mistake was to put the political advantages of consultation too low.'[25]

By mid-1974, the Whitlam government had implemented far-reaching reforms that touched almost every aspect of the economy and society. But the voters were growing tired of the galloping speed of government, its disregard for the economy and its apparent lack of concern about spending. Several of Whitlam's landmark reforms, including the introduction of Medibank and 'one vote, one value' electoral laws, had met with opposition in the Senate. So Whitlam called a snap double-dissolution election for 18 May 1974, designed to secure a fresh mandate. Hawke campaigned strongly for the return of the government and often shared a stage with Whitlam. At the main Melbourne rally before election day, the applause for Whitlam was the longest, but the cheers for Hawke were the loudest. In his election campaign report, David Combe said Hawke had made a 'tremendous campaign contribution' by giving 'everything he had in the cause of securing the re-election of the Whitlam government'.[26]

Hawke's speaking style was now established. He wrote speeches in longhand, with key passages in capitals or underlined several times. He quoted extensively from newspaper articles. They were not polished performances, but freewheeling and extemporaneous, and would often be more effective than a written speech because they were authentic. He would parry interjectors and dispatch noisy hecklers with ease. He would get fired up, angry and indignant. He would plunge his hands into his pockets and take them out again. He would swivel from side to side on his heels and lunge forward. He would point a finger in the air or raise his clenched fists to either side of his face and then throw them down again. He would run his fingers through his hair, adjust his glasses, pull his tie and examine his fingernails. It was, above all, a visual performance. And the crowd was always enraptured.[27]

Whitlam became the first Labor prime minister to lead the party to back-to-back election victories. With a swing of just 1 per cent against the government on the two-party preferred vote, and the loss of just one seat, Labor still claimed a relatively high primary vote of 49.3 per cent. On 6 and 7 August, a joint sitting of the House of Representatives and the Senate took place for the first time. Labor secured the votes to bring into law a universal health scheme, Medibank, and changes to electoral laws.

But any euphoria from the election result was short-lived, and Whitlam's government rolled from policy blunder to policy blunder and from scandal to scandal. The ministry and caucus became more unruly, and the government more chaotic. Whitlam suffered a setback after the election when the caucus refused to support Lance Barnard remaining deputy leader, and he was defeated by Jim Cairns in a ballot, 54–42. Cairns, from the Left, became deputy leader and deputy prime minister.

Hawke was alarmed by the government's lack of attention to unemployment and inflation, and critical of its budget management. Spending had risen by 20 per cent in 1973–74 and would rise by a further 46 per cent in the 1974–75 budget. Treasurer Frank Crean could not win support in cabinet for reducing the deficit and fighting inflation. Crean would be sacked as treasurer and replaced by Cairns, who soon became engulfed in a love scandal with his staffer Junie Morosi. Ultimately, Cairns would be dismissed from cabinet in July 1975 for misleading parliament over the loans affair. Unemployment had increased from 2 per cent to near 5 per cent by the end of 1974. Hawke said Labor could lose the next election and urged Whitlam to abandon a planned five-week overseas trip. He was, as ever, rebuffed.[28]

The Whitlam government never had a workable prices and incomes policy. Jim Spigelman recalled that Clyde Cameron strongly advocated the 'cost plus inflation process' for the public service. 'No doubt that originated with the union movement, but Clyde was convinced that the policy was correct,' he said. 'It contributed to inflation and that was a problem for the government.'[29] Cameron delivered huge increases in public servants' wages and increases in salaries and entitlements for MPs. The increase in public-sector wages led unions in the private sector to seek higher salaries in 1973 and 1974. This wages explosion led to increases in inflation. Whitlam blamed Hawke for this. 'The industrial wing of the Labor movement worked against its own long-term interests and those of the parliamentary wing,' he wrote. 'It inadvertently hastened the electoral demise of my government through the promotion of wage-push inflation.'[30]

But Hawke defended unions seeking, and gaining, wage rises. He argued that the economy had been 'recessed' in 1971 and 1972, and when growth increased over the next few years, workers sought higher wages. When some unions achieved large pay increases, this led other unions to seek 'catch-up' wage increases. During 1973 and 1974, award wages increased by 48 per cent for bank officers, 64 per cent for metal trades workers, 78 per cent for truck drivers, 55 per cent for builders' labourers and 45 per cent for postal workers. There was enough blame to go around.

In January 1975, Whitlam was widely castigated for returning from an extensive overseas trip to tour the ruins caused by Cyclone Tracy in Darwin and then promptly resuming his travels abroad. The government's image worsened the following month. Labor's thirty-first federal conference was held at the Florida Hotel in Terrigal in February 1975. Between proceedings, delegates, party officials, union leaders, staffers and journalists relaxed poolside in their swimming costumes, short dresses and Hawaiian shirts. Hawke was photographed drinking beer and cavorting with bikini-clad women with his shirt off. Hawke had an affair with Jim Cairns' secretary, Glenda Bowden, during the conference. He was 45; she was 23. Bowden admitted the affair two decades later, recalling Hawke's 'voracious sexual appetite' and described him as 'one of the most charming, intelligent and sexually attractive men' she had known. But she said he was an 'average lover'.[31] Cairns had also been having an affair with his staff member, Junie Morosi. He told journalist Toni McRae that he felt 'a kind of love' for Morosi during the conference.[32]

On 23 June 1975 Whitlam appointed Barnard as ambassador to Sweden, Finland and Norway, which prompted a by-election in his Tasmanian seat of Bass. Hawke was on his way to an ILO meeting in Geneva. The news of Barnard's appointment reached him while he was scaling the ancient slopes of Delphi. He did not need the oracle to tell him this was a bad sign. The media tracked Hawke down. He trashed the appointment, hoping Whitlam and Barnard might reconsider. On arriving in Geneva, Hawke further told the media that Barnard's appointment defied 'rational under-standing' and characterised it as one of 'insanity' and 'stupidity'. He was incensed that, as Labor's federal president, he had not been consulted, and nor had anyone else in the party organisation.[33] Hawke knew the Whitlam government was doomed.

Bill Hayden became treasurer following Cairns' sacking. The 1975–76 budget – which would soon be at the centre of a constitutional crisis – helped to restore some of the government's economic credibility. Cameron was dumped from the labour port-folio in June 1975, his duties passing to Jim McClelland.

Hawke used his address to the ACTU Congress in Septem-ber 1975 to argue for a change in industrial strategy in response to the changed circumstances. He argued for greater cooperation between the Whitlam government and the union movement, and suggested unions limit their wage claims in return for govern-ments not increasing taxes and charges. A more conciliatory and moderate Hawke was emerging as the Whitlam government cascaded towards oblivion.

But Hawke could not get through to Whitlam. In the spring of 1975, Whitlam's principal private secretary John Mant recalled, Hawke strolled into the prime minister's office at the end of a sitting week. 'Would you please ask if Mr Whitlam would see me,' Hawke requested.

Mant went into Whitlam's office and found him lying on the lounge reading and signing papers. 'Prime Minister, Mr Hawke would like to see you,' he said.

Whitlam peered over his papers. 'I don't want to see Mr Hawke,' he said. 'Tell him to go away.'

Mant went back to Hawke. 'Sorry, Mr Hawke, the prime minister is unable to see you.'

Hawke's eyes narrowed. 'Listen, you little shit. Tell him I want to see him.'

Mant went back in. 'Prime Minister, Mr Hawke is insisting on seeing you.'

Whitlam was irritated. 'Tell him to go away,' he said.

By this time Hawke had helped himself to a beer in the fridge, adding to those he had already consumed. He was furious. He finished the beer and then left. Hawke did not see Whitlam that night.[34]

Exactly one month before the Whitlam government was dismissed, Bob Hawke sat down with Paul Kelly, political correspondent with *The Australian*. They talked about the 'post-Whitlam era' and the future of the party. 'I would think that we've got lessons to learn from Gough's contributions,' Hawke said. 'Part of politics is bringing people along with you, consulting with them, understanding them, learning from them, and I think that Gough, particularly in office, once he saw enormous responsibilities in what he had to do, and the pressures of the time upon him, perhaps fell down somewhat in that area.'[35] Hawke was already thinking about the future.

—

In the evening of 13 December 1974, Labor's federal executive met at the Lodge. Hawke pressed Whitlam to be more consultative with unions on economic and industrial matters. But Whitlam's focus was elsewhere. In another room, the federal executive council was also meeting. Senior ministers approved minerals and energy minister Rex Connor's request to raise a US$4 billion loan for 'temporary' purposes to invest in national resource projects.

The loan would be raised via a middleman, Tirath Khemlani, a Pakistani commodities trader and money broker. The money would be raised in the Middle East, not via London or New York, and neither the Treasury nor the Reserve Bank would be involved. On 7 January 1975, the loan was revoked. But, at Connor's urging, it was reinstated at US$2 billion on 28 January. It was then revoked altogether on 20 May 1975.

Connor refused to let his dream die and continued to deal with Khemlani, even though he no longer had the authority to do so. When this became public, and Connor was found to have misled parliament, he was forced to resign on 14 October 1975. This provided the justification for the Coalition to delay passage of Labor's budget in the Senate. Malcolm Fraser had become Liberal leader on 21 March, replacing the hapless Billy Snedden, and forced a constitutional crisis. The budget was denied passage on 16 October. It became a contest of brinkmanship. Would Fraser capitulate and pass the budget, handing Whitlam a victory? Or Whitlam buckle under the pressure and go to an early election? The opposition's strategy, in the event of Whitlam not backing down, was to have the governor-general, Sir John Kerr, intervene to dismiss the government and dissolve the parliament for an election.

Hawke later met Khemlani on a Pan Am flight from Bangkok to Europe. Sitting in the first-class cabin, he asked the hostess to invite Khemlani to sit next to him. Hawke told Khemlani he was 'a two-bit fraud' and a 'shyster', and could not believe he had raised billions of dollars for another government. 'It is a mystery how otherwise intelligent men could have allowed this charlatan to be the instrument of their destruction,' Hawke thought.[36]

On Monday, 10 November 1975, Hawke met with Whitlam in Melbourne. They discussed the supply crisis and Hawke pressed upon Whitlam the strategy of calling a half-Senate election. Whitlam agreed with Hawke, but this was a flawed strategy for resolving the crisis. The crisis was about supply. Funding would run out during the election campaign. Nor was there any likelihood the government would secure the Senate votes it needed to pass the budget. The time for a half-Senate election would have been at the start of the crisis. And so Whitlam never had an effective strategy, and did not have any contingency plans in the event of his dismissal.

At lunchtime the next day, 11 November 1975, Hawke was seated at the Hotel Cecil in Melbourne with Jack Kornhauser, the brother of his friend Eddie Kornhauser, and Jean Sinclair. He had enjoyed the onion soup and was about to tuck into a T-bone steak and wash it down with a bottle of claret. Then news arrived by phone that Kerr had dismissed the Whitlam government. 'I was staggered,' Hawke recalled. 'My mind immediately turned to what were we going to do.'[37] He left the restaurant and arranged to fly to Canberra. Meanwhile, Whitlam returned to the House of Representatives. Denise Darlow, Whitlam's personal secretary, recalled that when he came back to the office at around 3.15 pm, he instructed that word be sent to Hawke to 'quieten the masses'.[38]

When Hawke arrived in Canberra, he went straight to a meeting of the Australian Labor Advisory Council at the party's headquarters at John Curtin House. Whitlam joined them. Hawke was under pressure from Labor MPs and union leaders to call a national strike. Former minister Tom Uren pushed hard in caucus for a national stoppage, and thought the ACTU had betrayed the party by not agreeing.[39] Eric Walsh, who had been Whitlam's press secretary, felt Hawke's approach to the strike was opportunistic. 'Hawke opposed it because he didn't want to do anything that might revive Gough,' he said. 'He was pretending that he was being proper and responsible, but he did not want to help Gough.'[40]

In reality, Hawke thought cooler heads should prevail, as the country was at a dangerous tipping point. John Mant remembered listening to Whitlam's speech on the steps of Parliament House on a radio in the prime minister's office with Hawke and press secretary David Solomon. Conversation turned to a national strike. 'All three of us thought that the political thing to do was to look constitutional,' Mant recalled. 'Gough wanted to maintain the rage, but rage against the abuse of the Constitution by the Liberals. A strike would therefore be counterproductive.'[41] This was precisely the view Hawke took. 'We were complaining about proper processes not being followed in determining the course of constitutional events,' he recalled. 'It didn't make sense in those circumstances to talk about national stoppages.'[42]

When Hawke gave an afternoon press conference, he surprised journalists with his measured tone. There would not be a national strike. It was a message he reiterated the following day at a rally on the lawn outside Parliament House. Hawke said it was not a time to 'substitute violence in the streets for democracy'. There had already been violent demonstrations in several cities, and acts of vandalism. Hawke told the journalists that Australia 'could be on the verge of something terrible'.[43] He could have incited protests, strikes and stoppages. He was being urged to. But he did not. Hawke, after all, was an advocate for conciliation. He wanted harmony, not conflict. He preached consensus, not confrontation.

Hawke had never liked Kerr. The two men had opposed each other before the Conciliation and Arbitration Commission. Hawke feared Kerr would be hostile to Labor. He knew he had been a supporter of the Democratic Labor Party. 'His interests were anti-Whitlam, anti-Labor,' Hawke recalled. 'To appoint a supporter of the DLP to that position just didn't make any sense at all.' Hawke recalled telling Whitlam that he opposed Kerr's appointment as governor-general. 'What are you doing appointing this bastard?' he asked. He suggested barrister Richard Eggleston was better suited. 'He had a great traditional Labor background,' Hawke argued.[44] Hazel recalled Bob's 'anger' when Whitlam had phoned to inform him of the Kerr appointment.[45] After the dismissal, Hawke recalled, Whitlam told him: 'You were right, you bastard, weren't you?'[46]

A federal election was to be held on 13 December 1975. For Whitlam, it was about 'the survival of Australian democracy'. He urged voters to return Labor to power to continue its reform program. For Fraser, the election was all about passing judgement on a scandal-plagued government that had mismanaged the budget and the economy. Labor was defeated in a landslide. The party's primary vote fell to 42.8 per cent and it secured just 44.3 per cent of the two-party vote. It was one of Labor's worst ever election results. The party was shattered, left with just thirty-six seats out of 125 in the House of Representatives. After twenty-three years in the wilderness, Labor had returned to power for less than three years. While its achievements were significant and lasting, so were its failures.

Hawke spent election night in the National Tally Room in Canberra. He watched with profound sadness as Whitlam arrived and conceded defeat. Whitlam, he thought, had been essential in Labor returning to power, and had achieved extraordinary things in government. But his dreams of a Labor government of longevity were shattered. While the dismissal had been the cause of Labor's ultimate destruction, he knew that voters had decided not to return it to power because of its political ineptitude, its economic failures and the chaos and scandals that had pockmarked its brief time in power.

The day after the election, Hawke received a phone call from Labor's federal secretary, David Combe: Whitlam wanted to see him at the Lodge. Sitting by the pool, Whitlam urged Hawke to come into the parliament and immediately lead the party. Whitlam had already asked Bill Hayden to take over the leadership, but he had declined in exasperation. 'Jesus fucking Christ, Gough, I don't even know if I'm going to be in the bloody parliament,' Hayden replied. 'Leadership is the last fucking thing I'm interested in.'[47] Hayden was so shell-shocked by the election result, and by almost losing his seat, that he refused to serve on the party's front bench. He would not rejoin the shadow ministry until March 1976.

Hawke agreed to think it over and consult with party figures. But before he could decide, the plan leaked. In any case, Hawke was lukewarm on the idea, and no seat was readily available. Some in the Labor caucus blamed Hawke for the turmoil of the previous three years, as he had often been the government's most biting critic. In any event, this was no way to manage a leadership transition. 'Gough was pretty devastated and I don't think he was thinking as clearly as he might,' Hawke reflected. 'It was a chalice that I was quite happy to see pass by.'[48]

There was another prominent Labor figure outside parliament who was often talked about as a future federal leader: Don Dunstan. The South Australian premier was also encouraged to come into the parliament and take the leadership after the 1975 election. Hawke met with Dunstan to talk about the federal leadership in 1974. Hawke said he would support Dunstan becoming leader if he made it to federal parliament first. If not, Hawke hoped to secure

Dunstan's support when he entered the parliament. Dunstan told Hawke he was not interested. 'The situation won't arise,' he said. 'I'm going to stay put. I don't believe that a federal government can implement social democratic reforms; it must be at the state level.'[49]

On 27 January 1976, the Labor caucus met in the opposition party room. Whitlam decided to continue as leader, but he was challenged by Frank Crean and Lionel Bowen. He defeated them both, winning an overall majority of thirty-six votes, to Bowen's fourteen and Crean's thirteen. But Whitlam's wings were clipped, as caucus resolved to revisit the leadership in eighteen months' time. In the ballot for deputy, there were eight candidates, and when preferences were distributed, Tom Uren defeated Paul Keating by thirty-three votes to thirty. It marked Keating as a future leader of the party.

On 12 February, Hawke was briefed by Ken Bennett, Labor's assistant national secretary, and Jack Egerton, a member of the federal executive, about an attempt to secure a $500,000 gift to Labor from Iraq's Ba'ath Socialist Party. Bill Hartley had tried to arrange the funds with the knowledge of Whitlam and Combe. Whitlam was told on 16 November 1975 – before the election – about the madcap plan, and did not discourage it. Hartley's intermediary was a shady businessman named Henri Fischer, who promised he could secure the loan. Whitlam met Fischer on three separate occasions, but Hartley and Combe handled the negotiations. The Iraqi government was a barbaric authoritarian regime. Hawke was shocked that the three of them could ever countenance such an idea. Although the money was never procured, Hawke thought the scandal would finish Whitlam as leader.

The story about the Iraqi 'loan' would be first revealed by journalist Laurie Oakes on 25 February 1976. Days later, Hawke entertained journalists at home. He made several highly critical off-the-record comments about Whitlam. Hawke highlighted several paragraphs quoting an unidentified federal executive member in an article on the front page in *The Australian* on 1 March 1976, and kept it in his files. The remarks were his:

Gough's gone. Gone a million. He's had it. I'd give him inside two weeks before we get his resignation one way or another. He can't have double standards. He can't sack ministers for various indiscretions and not apply the same ethic to himself. He's got to sack himself or be sacked. Nothing else will do.

The quotes appeared alongside a portrait of Hawke playing snooker at home.[50]

Hawke had initially given a press conference in his front yard and then invited the journalists around the back for a beer, where he made the off-the-record comments. A telex was sent by journalist Barry Watts to Phil Cornford, acting news editor in Sydney. This telex was subsequently leaked, and circulated to party and union figures, and journalists. Hawke was sent a copy by Egerton. It is clear Watts intended the damaging Hawke quote as off-the-record and non-attributable in any way. The telex further included Hawke saying that Whitlam's leadership was 'dead'.[51] The upshot was that it was widely suspected to be Hawke, and the telex confirmed it. This was highly damaging for Hawke, who made a formal complaint about Watts to the Australian Journalists' Association. Watts, in turn, launched defamation action against Hawke. Both matters were eventually settled.

A special meeting of the federal executive was convened, and Hawke pushed for Hartley to be expelled from the party and Whitlam and Combe to be censured. Instead, after considerable debate, the federal executive decided to reprimand the three of them. The scandal was discussed several times in caucus during February and March 1976. Keating told Whitlam, during a caucus meeting, that he should 'consider his future role' as leader.[52] Clyde Cameron wrote in his diary that Keating said Whitlam's 'credibility' was being 'questioned in the electorate'. Whitlam was stung. When the wounded Whitlam passed Keating in the corridor, he called him a 'sneaky little cunt'.[53]

Meanwhile, Combe spent the money that never arrived. After the election, Labor was saddled with $350,000 in debt. The party lent on Hawke – one of the few figures in the party who had credibility – to help repay it. Hawke appealed directly to unions, business leaders and party members to raise funds.

The defeat of the Whitlam government prompted thinking about Labor's future. On 3 August 1976, Hawke made his most important contribution to this debate when he delivered the Arthur Calwell Memorial Lecture. Labor had to recognise the innate conservatism of voters, Hawke told the audience, and embrace 'gradualism' in implementing a reform agenda. In a systematic deconstruction of Whitlam's failures, he outlined a strategy for Labor's revival: the party must address its weaknesses in economic and budget policy, establish a better relationship with the public service, improve decision-making processes, and more effectively communicate with voters and the union movement.[54] He was assembling the building blocks for the next Labor government.

—

During the 1970s, Hawke gained a valuable education in Australia's economic, social and industrial policy settings through his appointments to a variety of national and international boards and advisory bodies. He served on the board of the Reserve Bank of Australia (1973–80) and was a member of the Immigration Planning and Advisory Council (1970–80), the Australian Population and Immigration Council (1976–80), the Australian Refugee Advisory Council (1979–80) and the Monash University Council (1970–73).

Hawke's membership of the Reserve Bank board was particularly important. He impressed Treasury secretary Sir Frederick Wheeler, who thought Hawke 'behaved himself superbly' on the board, and said it was a 'triumph of common sense' to have him there because it influenced how he ran the ACTU. It exposed Hawke to a range of economic data and analysis, and gave him boardroom experience. Hawke treated the board's work seriously, never used it for grandstanding, and always took an economy-wide view rather than a narrow union focus.[55]

Two other appointments convinced Hawke that industry needed to become more productive, efficient and competitive. On 18 July 1974, Whitlam appointed Hawke to a committee to advise the government on manufacturing to be chaired by businessman Gordon Jackson. In its report the following year, delivered on 30 July 1975, the Jackson Committee concluded that tariffs should be reduced in incremental steps over a period of five to fifteen years; assistance should be provided to business to become more export-oriented; and federal and state industry councils should be established to advise on the adjustment process. On 6 September 1977, Malcolm Fraser announced the establishment of a study group on manufacturing to examine the adjustment challenges of the most protected industries. It was chaired by Sir John Crawford, and Hawke was made a member. Its report to government, released on 6 March 1979, identified the need for further taxation concessions to encourage investment, funding for research and development, and initiatives to facilitate market access abroad.

After the defeat of the Whitlam government, Hawke began to seriously contemplate whether he should stand for election to the national parliament. In the second half of the 1970s, it was referred to in the media on an almost daily basis. Hawke was a popular figure. In November 1973, Gallup found his approval rating to be 50 per cent.[56] Among union and party members, his popularity was unrivalled. Only Don Dunstan and Neville Wran could challenge Hawke for the affections of the voters, and especially the true believers.

Ahead of the 1974 election, it had been speculated that he might run for Scullin, held by Harry Jenkins. Or that he would challenge Billy Snedden in Bruce. Another option was nominating in Isaacs, taking on David Hamer, which Hawke came close to accepting. In 1975, there was the prospect of him succeeding Jim Cairns in Lalor. The closest Hawke came was succeeding Frank Crean, after he had been stripped of the Treasury portfolio, in the seat of Melbourne Ports. Hawke was the number-one ticket holder for the South Melbourne Football Club, so it was an ideal seat, argued journalist Neil Mitchell.[57] Crean had offered to resign the seat for Hawke to contest in a by-election in October 1974. This had Whitlam's support, but Hawke doubted whether Labor would retain the seat.[58]

Journalist Allan Barnes, like everyone else, was sick of the speculation. 'For years, the mercurial Mr Hawke has been promising to make his talents available to the nation,' he wrote. 'But he always has declined to say when that time will come.'[59] Hawke, however, argued that journalists kept asking him about a parliamentary career and he was simply answering their questions honestly.[60]

One thing, however, was clear: if Hawke did go into parliament, he would want to be leader. He said it repeatedly. 'If I did go across to the parliamentary side of things, being the sort of human being I am, I'd aim for the top,' he said in January 1974.[61]

12

ALL THE WORLD'S
A STAGE

Labor's dismissal and electoral drubbing in 1975 marked
a turning point in Bob Hawke's presidency of the ACTU.
The times dictated a new approach. The economy was sluggish
as unemployment and inflation increased. With union members
losing their jobs and seeing the value of their wages erode, it was
time to rethink widespread industrial action. The firebrand of the
1960s and early 1970s had morphed into the fireman by the middle
of the decade as he was often called in to douse industrial disputes.
He was, after all, a man who preached compromise and consensus. There was another factor in Hawke's changed approach: he
was eyeing an eventual entry into parliament, with the goal of
becoming Labor leader and prime minister.

Hawke continued to focus the union movement on quality-
of-life issues, pursuing union enterprises and pushing the Fraser
government to act on unemployment, inflation, education and
training, poverty reduction and health policy. Hawke continued
to defend so-called 'political strikes' – a term he did not like –
and among the most important concerned Medibank. Labor's
universal health scheme was being slowly dismantled by the Fraser
government. In 1976, it introduced an additional 2.5 per cent levy
to fund Medibank. Hawke negotiated directly with Fraser, but
when no headway was made, a nationwide general strike was held
on 12 July 1976. Around 2.5 million workers left their jobs. Never
in Australia had there been a twenty-four-hour protest stoppage
on any issue. Hawke argued that this was an issue directly relevant

to unions because it concerned the interests of working men and women, and their families.

The three major political strikes that Hawke initiated – protesting the Springbok rugby tour, French nuclear testing in the Pacific, and Medicare – were never broadly popular with voters. Hawke's approval rating dipped as the country ground to a halt. 'These were the biggest political disputes in the history of Australia,' recalled Bill Kelty. 'They were very unpopular, and people forget this. But it was militancy for a purpose.'[1]

By the mid-1970s, Hawke was one of the best-known Australians abroad. The premier vehicle for his international engagement was the International Labour Organization. He attended his first conference, held on the shores of Lake Geneva, in 1970 as a workers' representative. Two years later, Hawke was appointed to the ILO's Governing Body. He was one of three Australians on the tripartite body – representing employees, employers and governments – which met three times a year. In 1977, he was approached to nominate for the position of chair of the Workers' Group at the ILO. Leading the Governing Body or even becoming director-general were also possibilities for Hawke in these years, and when later prime minister, but he was never seriously tempted to seek these positions.[2]

The ILO gave Hawke the opportunity to meet other political and industrial leaders, and to play a role beyond Australia. He had extensive contacts in the United States, throughout Europe and the Middle East. He was even received by Pope John Paul II at the Vatican in June 1979. But the work of the ILO was bureaucratic, procedural and technical. Hawke had little interest in spending lengthy amounts of time on meetings, negotiations and resolutions. Nor did he particularly enjoy the social functions that took place almost every morning, afternoon and evening. Hawke liked attending the ILO, but making it his career was not something he ever seriously contemplated.

In July 1974, *Time* magazine's cover story was on '150 Rising World Leaders'. It profiled the brightest stars in the United States, Canada, Latin America, Europe, Asia, Africa and the Middle East. Three leaders from Australia featured: Andrew Peacock, Bill Hayden and Hawke. 'Robert Hawke, 44, is brash and abrasive – useful qualities for a man who, as president of both the Australian Council of Trade Unions and the Australian Labor Party, is the most prominent champion of his country's workers,' it said. 'An outback-reared lawyer and Rhodes scholar, his aggressive intellectual socialism has invigorated the labor movement.' It noted that Hawke had turned down the job of ILO director-general and was expected to go into politics soon.[3]

Foreign diplomats in Australia were keen to develop a relationship with Hawke. British diplomat Brian Barder visited Hawke at the ACTU on 27 June 1974. Hawke gave an unvarnished assessment of the Whitlam government. He said several MPs were 'better qualified' than some ministers in cabinet and he thought the leader should appoint the ministry rather than the caucus. Hawke said he got on 'very well' with Whitlam even though they had disagreements, and he said the prime minister had acted 'rather silly' over the prices and incomes referendums. Hawke said that Whitlam wanted him to be his 'successor'. But Hawke was reluctant. 'Where I sit, I am always the government,' he said. If he did go into parliament, he 'would have to make a drastic change in his lifestyle'. Hawke explained that he could 'go off and get drunk, and have a few extramarital affairs, without this being in any way disastrous'. But if he became a politician, he would probably have to moderate his behaviour. Barder appreciated his candor. 'Hawke struck me as a man of natural authority, with a quick and perceptive mind and a ready tongue,' he reported. 'He clearly sees himself, not without justification, as a man with a special destiny and as the most probable successor to Mr Whitlam.'[4]

Hawke was also frank with diplomats from the United States in private talks.[5] He said he would resign as Labor's federal president if the party did not accommodate his support for Israel, according to a cable sent to Washington, DC on 21 February 1973. Later that year, in a cable sent on 26 November, Hawke lashed Whitlam as 'egocentric', and called his conduct 'beyond belief'. In a 24 January 1974 cable, Hawke said he was going to challenge Whitlam's 'immoral' position on Israel. The Labor Party lacked 'money and momentum' to mount an effective re-election campaign, he said, according to a 5 April 1974 cable. Hawke shared his estimation of the likely seat losses for Labor at the forthcoming May 1974 election. In a 12 November 1974 cable, it was reported that Hawke had made it 'crystal clear' to Whitlam that he 'was not pursuing [an] economic program with due regard for its obligations to the people who had elected' him. He spoke of Whitlam's 'inadequacy' as prime minister. On 12 August 1975, a cable reported that Hawke said Labor faced a 'parliamentary disaster' by the end of that year, and Whitlam's 'personal image' had been diminished.

Unsurprisingly, American diplomats were impressed with Hawke. By the mid-1970s they saw him as a reliable supporter of the ANZUS alliance and a future leader worth building a relationship with. In a 31 May 1974 cable, diplomats reported: 'While Hawke is an unusual figure, with noticeable ups and downs, there is little doubt he has major potential as a Labor Party leader.' Marshall Green, the United States' ambassador, emphasised that Hawke's forthcoming trip to Washington, DC and New York was important. 'He has every prospect of being a major figure on the political scene for the next 20 years or so, and it will be worth our while to make a real effort to develop a worthwhile program for him.' It was an astute judgement.

The Americans, like the British, were cultivating Hawke, and he was happy to be cultivated. This is what diplomats do. Hawke was not the only Labor or union figure who shared information with foreign diplomats; so did Liberal and Country Party figures. His assessments were no more candid than what he said in private, and often in public. Hawke knew these relationships could pay dividends later, as he continued to build contacts abroad. Nor was it a one-way street. Information was regularly traded by diplomatic and security agencies, and the Australian Security Intelligence Organisation was a frequent recipient and dispatcher of political and union information in these years. Hawke was not a spy or a mole, or a leaker. While he shared information with diplomats, like many others, it is misleading to describe him as an 'informant'. His commitment to Labor, and to Australia, was total.[6]

ASIO had been keeping an eye on Hawke since the mid-1950s. On file was material going back to when Hawke was flying planes at Oxford. Vetting checks were carried out when he won the Duke of Edinburgh scholarship in 1962. A 'Secret' three-page ASIO

Records Review from the mid-1970s shows 'no adverse information was recorded' concerning these matters. ASIO kept a file on Hawke's dealings with certain people, namely communist union and party figures. ASIO agents reported mentions of Hawke at Communist Party meetings. Intercepts of phone calls and telegrams chronicled Hawke's rather routine dealings with Soviet diplomats. The actual files containing this material were – curiously – destroyed by ASIO in the 1970s, in accordance with a policy that people who posed 'no security concern' and were not 'persons of interest' should not have material kept on them.[7]

—

In early 1971, Hawke was invited by former senator Sam Cohen's widow, Judith, to travel to Israel and return to Australia to give a lecture in her deceased husband's honour. And so in June and July that year he travelled to Israel under the auspices of the Sam Cohen Memorial Foundation, and delivered a lecture in Melbourne on 6 October 1971. This was the beginning of an intellectual and emotional journey that saw Hawke became a passionate defender of Israel. Hawke fell in love with Israel, a place he had read about in the Bible as a child. He admired and respected the Israeli people. He was deeply committed to the international community's support for the creation of the state of Israel, and its right to exist, after the horrors of the Holocaust during World War II. He drew inspiration from former Labor leader H.V. 'Doc' Evatt, who had been president of the United Nations General Assembly and played an important role in the creation of the state of Israel. And he had formed a bond with leaders of the Israeli trade union movement, the Histadrut.

Hawke's passionate commitment for Israel was fostered by friendships he developed in the Melbourne business community, such as that with Isi Leibler. 'My relationship with Bob in the 1970s was extremely warm on both personal and political grounds,' Leibler said. 'I recollect Bob telling me he had been engaged in an anti-Semitic act that nauseated him to such an extent that he was determined to compensate for this by showing his friendship to Jews.'[8] That incident took place at Perth Modern. Hawke used anti-Semitic language and beat up a Jewish boy. 'It was nothing other than the accumulated prejudice of the uneducated,' Hawke recalled. 'When I was at university and started to think a bit, I remember being horrified at what I had done. I sought that boy out and he was gracious enough to understand.'[9] Hawke's love for Israel was, in part, an atonement for past sins.

Hawke admired the Israeli people for defending their state, and historic homeland, under repeated attack from Arab states and the Palestine Liberation Organization. He criticised the Arab states and the PLO for having 'paraded the plight of the Palestinians' rather than taking up the United Nations' mandate from November 1947 to establish their own state of Palestine. He blamed Palestinian leaders, not the Palestinian people, for this failure. 'I have always felt a deep concern for the plight of the Palestinians,' he reflected.[10]

Hawke befriended many senior Israeli politicians. The leader with whom he formed the closest bond was Prime Minister Golda Meir. He met her several times, first in July 1971. He was in awe of her toughness, her intellect, her dedication and drive, and her compassion. They hit it off. Meir sat behind her desk, smoking cigarettes the whole time. She and Hawke were scheduled to meet for about fifteen minutes but talked for over an hour. Meir found Hawke intriguing. Susan, age fourteen, was travelling with her father at the time, and after spending a few weeks in a kibbutz she had joined her father for the meeting with Meir.[11] When they finished their talks, they embraced.

Hawke returned to Israel after the Yom Kippur War of October 1973. He was the first non-Israeli to visit the Golan Heights, and to travel into Syria when it was still a battle zone strewn with busted Soviet tanks with dead bodies inside. He recalled an emotional discussion with Meir in her office in Jerusalem as she recounted the dilemma she had faced: whether to make a pre-emptive strike in an attempt to shorten the war. She had not ordered the attack and blamed herself for the deaths of thousands of Israeli soldiers.[12] Together they wept in her office. After returning to Australia on 24 November 1973, Hawke arranged a press conference in Perth. He showed the media photographs given to him by Meir with young Israeli soldiers, captured by Syrians in the Golan Heights, shot in the head with hands tied behind their backs. Hawke broke down on television. He attacked Labor's policy of 'even-handedness' – neutrality – in the Middle East as 'not an intelligent approach to the situation'.[13]

Hawke's commitment to Israel was sharply at odds with Labor's policy on the Middle East. The Labor Left, especially in Victoria, identified with the PLO. Whitlam made it clear Hawke's views did not reflect any change in Labor policy. Hawke was unbowed. On 26 January 1974, Hawke addressed the Zionist Federation in Sydney. Standing at a podium with a yarmulke on his head, Hawke had the audience hanging off his every word. In a highly charged atmosphere, Hawke said Labor's policy was 'morally repugnant'.[14] He said: 'I do not speak here for my party or for the industrial movement which I lead. But as an individual Australian I know that I am not an island and I know that if we allow the bell to be tolled for Israel it will have tolled for me, for all of us, and we will all to that extent again have been diminished.'[15] Many in the audience were in tears as they stood and applauded. Hawke was so overcome that he broke down and wept, again, for Israel.

The Left's Bill Hartley was outraged by Hawke's speech, and wanted him reprimanded by Labor's federal executive. Whitlam was also irritated, and he and Hawke exchanged tough words. Indeed, Hawke was so wound up about Labor's stance towards Israel that he contemplated resigning as national president. On 20 April 1975, speaking at the Sydney Opera House on the anniversary of Israeli independence, Hawke took on Israel's critics. 'The Arab States and the PLO are not talking about peace with Israel but without Israel,' he said. 'We should be bending every endeavour to see that there is obtained from the relevant Arab States and the PLO an unequivocal recognition of Israel's right to exist with appropriate international guarantees provided to back up such recognition.'[16]

On 27 December 1976, a forest of 10,000 trees on the southern side of Mount Carmel in northern Israel was named in Hawke's honour. He travelled to the Holy City with Clem, Ellie and Hazel. A delegation of Australian Jews accompanied them. The Australian ambassador to Israel, Richard Smith, attended. Also present was Yeruham Meshel, the secretary-general of Histadrut. A plaque was unveiled recognising Hawke for his 'outstanding humanitarian endeavours, his exemplary stand for individual freedom and international justice, and his courageous support of Israel and the national liberation of the Jewish people'. It was deeply humbling for Hawke, who said he had not been given a greater honour.

Three days earlier, on Christmas Eve, Bob, Hazel, Clem and Ellie met with Golda Meir, who by now had left the prime ministership, at her office in Tel Aviv. Clem wrote in his unpublished memoir: 'We were impressed by her personality, vitality and knowledge of world affairs.'[17] The mutual affection between Bob and Golda was evident. She handed him her recently published memoir, *My Life*, and inscribed it: 'To my friend Bob Hawke – A man of principle and courage. In admiration, Golda Meir.'[18]

Over multiple trips to Israel – he made five between 1971 and 1976 – Hawke met, befriended and corresponded with other leading political figures, among them Yitzhak Rabin and Shimon Peres. They discussed the peace negotiations with Egypt, relations with the PLO and the fraternal bonds between the Israeli and Australian Labor parties. 'His passionate support of Israel was of course welcomed by his many Jewish admirers,' Leibler recalled. 'He was highly regarded in Israel by all political parties.'[19]

The same year that Hawke travelled to Israel for the dedication of the forest in his name, he was a high-profile target for assassination by a Palestinian terrorist on Australian soil. ASIO briefed Malcolm Fraser that Hawke was at risk of being murdered, along with Isi Leibler and Sam Lipski, for their outspoken support of Israel.[20] Hawke had already lived with such threats for years. In late 1973, a telephone call was made to the ACTU from a man who claimed to be part of Black September – the Arab terrorist organisation responsible for the massacre of Israeli athletes at the 1972 Munich Olympics – who said he would kill Hawke and his family. When Hawke was told of this, he collapsed. It may have been a prank call, but no chances could be taken. Bob, Hazel and the children were put under immediate police protection.[21] Hawke cancelled all meetings for the next fortnight and did not return to full-time work until January 1974. For several years, Hawke travelled with a bodyguard, Chris Crellin.

In 1971 and 1973, Hawke tried to ply his negotiating skills on the world stage. He travelled to the Soviet Union to press for the release of Jews, known as Refuseniks, who wanted to settle in

Israel. The idea of Hawke as a negotiator came up during his first meeting with Meir in 1971, and he travelled to Moscow for talks. He contacted Alexander Shelepin, the head of the Soviet Union's trade union movement and a member of the Central Committee of the Communist Party, and arranged to meet. Hawke had first met him on a two-day trip to Moscow in 1970.

Hawke arrived in Moscow on 21 July 1971 for talks. After several hours debating geopolitical issues, Hawke made the case for allowing Soviet Jews to emigrate. He appealed on humanitarian grounds, urging Shelepin to accept that Israel's desire for its territorial integrity and security was no different to the Soviet Union's. Shelepin listened and understood. He then raised Hawke's plea with Soviet officials. These talks may have helped to hasten the emigration of Jews from the Soviet Union in that and subsequent years. Between 1971 and 1972 the number of Jews allowed to emigrate increased from 13,000 to 32,000.[22]

Following further talks during 1973, Hawke returned to the Soviet Union in May 1979 to again argue for more lenient treatment of Soviet Jews. Hawke met and talked with Refuseniks in their homes. He negotiated with Alexei Shibaev, the new head of the Soviet Union's trade union movement. With copious amounts of vodka and cognac, their discussions extended over several days and eventually, Hawke thought, an agreement was reached. Twelve Jewish dissidents, including scientist Anatoli Scharansky, would be released from prison, and restrictions on about 2000 others who wanted to emigrate would be eased. Hawke phoned friends in Rome and issued a statement summarising the agreement, prepared by Alexander Lerner on behalf of the Refuseniks. It was made public.

Bob and Hazel then departed for Rome – and arrived to a media storm. Newspapers around the world were reporting that Hawke had achieved an extraordinary breakthrough in negotiations with the Soviet Union. He was praised for succeeding where others had failed. Sydney's *The Daily Telegraph*, for example, said: 'Hawke has shown that he can handle himself in the most delicate of international negotiations. In short, that he has the capacity to be a statesman.'[23] In Rome, Bob and Hazel met with leaders of the international Jewish community, including Isi Leibler, and celebrated the outcome.

But when Hawke went on to Geneva for the annual meeting of the ILO, he realised something was not quite right. Piotr Pimenov, the secretary of the Trade Unions' Council in the Soviet Union, issued a statement saying Hawke had 'misunderstood' what was agreed in Moscow. Hawke was told by the Soviets they had decided to tie the agreement to the successful passage of the Salt II agreement, signed by Jimmy Carter and Leonid Brezhnev days earlier in Vienna, through the US Senate. But this was never confirmed through official channels. Hawke thought he had been played. 'I had been the victim of vicious duplicity by Soviet authorities,' he recalled.[24] The deal concerning the Refuseniks was a bust. Hawke recalled being driven to 'black despair' by the thought that he had raised their hopes, only to see them cruelly dashed. Hawke, who had never known depression, contemplated suicide for the only time in his life.[25]

But was Hawke really duped? 'The Soviet Union never reneged on a promise to Hawke,' reflected Leibler. 'Bob was seduced by the KGB operatives in lengthy drinking sessions and was completely drunk when he reported that he had achieved the release of Refuseniks. When he told me this on the telephone from Moscow, I was very concerned that he was inebriated and was being manipulated. I was very pessimistic about the outcome. False hopes were raised among the Refuseniks.'[26]

Rawdon Dalrymple, Australia's ambassador to Israel from 1973 to 1975, revealed that Israeli leaders cultivated Hawke. 'They regarded Bob as a bit naive,' he said. 'They saw him as someone who is not a fool but swallows a line.'[27] This view is backed up by a dispatch sent from the British High Commission to London after Hawke became prime minister. 'Hawke seems to me to have been the archetypal sucker upon who the Israelis are always ready to seize, and to con, feeding uncritical minds with skilful Israeli propaganda,' John Mason wrote. 'The Russians deceived him into thinking that he had succeeded, and he foolishly said in public that he had done so.'[28]

Back on surer ground, Hawke's relationship with several Israeli leaders led to him becoming 'an unofficial conduit' between Israel and the Arab states. In 1978, Hawke travelled to Jordan as a guest of the Crown. He had 'lengthy and constructive' discussions with Prince Hassan. Hawke took a clear message back to Israel: that Jordan accepted Israel's right to exist behind safe and secure boundaries alongside a Palestinian entity. Jordan also held out the prospect of improved economic relations with Israel.[29] This encouraged Hawke's belief that he could play the role of peace negotiator into the future.

In autumn 1978, Hawke travelled to China as a guest of its government. It was the dawn of Deng Xiaoping's program of 'reform and opening up' to the world. By embracing elements of a market economy, albeit with restrictions, millions of Chinese were lifted out of poverty. Hawke regarded this as a landmark decision for China and the world, and recognised the significant economic opportunities for Australia. At the time of his 1978 visit, he said: 'The overwhelming important impression one gets of China is of the intensity and determination of the Chinese government and people to pursue new paths.' He thought there was room for 'significant development' in the Australia–China trading relationship, particularly in minerals and energy.[30] He was thinking about the role that he could play in forging that new path.

13

DEMONS AND DECISIONS

In the second half of the 1970s, Bob Hawke spent more time in Canberra. He often met with the government's leaders, particularly Prime Minister Malcolm Fraser, Treasurer Phillip Lynch, and Minister for Industrial Relations Tony Street. Fraser's ruthless demolition of the Whitlam government, forcing its dismissal and routing the party at the ballot box, made him a powerful but divisive figure for many voters. He was regarded as aloof and arrogant, and Australians never warmed to him. Fraser was a Cold War warrior. His government made limited economic reforms to free up the setting of interest rates, foreign bank entry rules and exchange controls, but never delivered a budget surplus. He was a believer in multiculturalism, opposed apartheid, supported Indigenous land rights and was welcoming towards refugees.

Although Hawke got on well with Street and Lynch, the Fraser government initially adopted a confrontational approach to industrial matters. Legislation such as the *Commonwealth Employees (Employment Provisions) Act 1977* aimed to restrict the capacity of unions to take industrial action. An Industrial Relations Bureau was to be established to provide greater oversight of unions. The government intervened in national wage cases to urge restraint or reject increases, demanding wage decisions take into account economic consequences, and attacked the Conciliation and Arbitration Commission when it failed to do so.

John Howard, who was minister for business and consumer affairs from 1975 to 1977, recalled discussions with Hawke about amending the *Trade Practices Act 1974* to prohibit secondary boycotts by unions. Hawke was not averse to verbal confrontation. 'If you go ahead with this, there will be blood in the streets,' he said. Howard accepted this was not a real threat but a figure of speech, and the legislation was enacted with Fraser's support. But he did not get Fraser's support to abolish the Prices Justification Tribunal. 'We are going to have to soft-pedal on getting rid of the PJT,' Fraser told Howard. 'We've got to give Hawke a win.' Howard was stunned.[1] (The PJT was eventually abolished in 1981.)

Street also talked tough about cracking down on unions but compromised. Street told cabinet he wanted powers to enforce compulsory secret ballots for union elections, strengthen essential service provisions to get around strikes, and authority to freeze union assets and deregister unions. But Street was also willing to give Hawke a victory. An insight into Hawke's negotiating style is provided in a paper Street submitted to cabinet on 16 May 1977. Street outlined how, during talks on proposed amendments to the *Conciliation and Arbitration Act*, Hawke was almost entirely opposed. But then Hawke offered a compromise: the ACTU would not resist the establishment of the Industrial Relations Bureau, and would support the existing framework for penalties, provided that a tripartite National Labour Advisory Council was established which would review the legislation.

Moreover, Hawke had already won the support of major employers for his proposal, who warned Street that it represented 'a very substantial shift in trade union attitudes' and urged the government to give it 'serious consideration'. Street had been blindsided. Hawke said 'confrontation' should be avoided. The employers said the government could not expect 'a great deal of real support' if there was a 'confrontation' with unions over the bill. Street recommended the cabinet support Hawke's proposal, and it did. It was a masterful negotiation with a mix of verbal threats, compromise, appeals to the national interest and support from employers. Hawke comprehensively outplayed Street.[2]

Howard judged the Fraser government as too timid on industrial relations. 'The mindset of the Coalition was not a deregulatory one,' he explained. 'It was all about finding the middle ground. It was not about winding back union power, although there were

rhetorical flourishes to that effect.'[3] David Barnett, press secretary
to Fraser, thought the government was too soft on Hawke. 'He
destroyed the Whitlam government and he destroyed our government too,' Barnett said. 'He was relentless in pushing for higher
wages and supporting strikes. He did not care about the economy.
He did it all for his own ambition. He knew what he was doing all
the bloody time.'[4]

Hawke had got to know Fraser when he held the shadow industrial relations portfolio. A degree of mutual respect developed.
Hawke felt that Fraser, as prime minister, was 'well briefed' for
meetings and able to 'make informed contributions' to discussions. But he found Fraser guarded and uneasy when it came to
informal conversations.[5] While Hawke began to recognise the
need to reform the economy, Fraser remained wedded to the old
protectionist model. Howard, who became treasurer in November
1977, said Fraser was not the free-market ideologue that many
thought. 'Malcolm belonged to a generation that believed government intervention in the economy worked,' he said.[6]

In June 1976, Fraser invited Hawke and other union leaders to
meet the cabinet. This had never happened under Whitlam. The
talks were constructive but little progress was made. Fraser then
invited Hawke, Cliff Dolan and John Ducker, along with Street,
to the Lodge for dinner. As the evening wore on, only Fraser and
Hawke were left. They drank several bottles of port until interrupted by Tamie Fraser. 'Dear, it's time you went to bed,' she told
her husband.[7] And so Fraser did, and Hawke left.

Hawke offered Fraser the opportunity to develop a more cooperative approach to wages and prices. He proposed wage restraint
in return for tax reductions and more effective control of prices.
If the real wages of employees could be gradually improved, there
would be less need for inflationary wage increases. 'I had argued
with him that the system of wage and price indexation was out
of kilter, and we should try and do something together to fix it,'
Hawke recalled. 'But he wasn't prepared to discuss that issue at
all.'[8] Fraser advocated wage freezes without any trade-offs. His
government experimented with wage indexation, a wages pause
and a shift to enterprise-level bargaining – there was no consistent
or coherent approach. The result was double-digit inflation and

unemployment – otherwise known as stagflation – and a deepening recession.

Hawke also advocated a high-level summit between government, business and unions. This was Hawke's central idea in public life. But Fraser was not interested. 'I'd said to Fraser that if not a summit, he should be prepared to sit down and talk with us,' Hawke recalled. 'There was no use him trying to belt the unions and us just saying, "Well, if you're going to say that wages are the only price you are going to try to control, well, fuck you."' So Hawke told Fraser: 'Why don't we sit down and try to get a broader canvass where we recognise the legitimacy of claims on both sides.' But Fraser was unmoved. 'He wouldn't even entertain that sort of approach,' Hawke said.[9]

The Fraser government's unwillingness to deal with Hawke on these matters would have consequences. David Kemp was Fraser's senior adviser in 1975–76 and became director (or chief of staff) of his office in 1981. 'It was the wage explosion of 1981–82, of course, that gave Hawke such seemingly powerful arguments against the Fraser government in 1983,' he recalled. 'Hawke had little respect for Fraser intellectually and Fraser had little respect for what he saw as Hawke's inability to give priority to the national interest. Hawke wanted Fraser to accept the unions' position of power, and Fraser would not do this, so agreement between them was almost impossible.'[10]

—

In 1969, Hawke had been the candidate of the left-wing unions, including communist unions, for ACTU president. He was associated with the Left faction of the Labor Party. Nationally, he was now regarded as a member of the Right faction. In Victoria, Hawke became a leading figure in the Centre Unity faction. Hawke's relationship with those on the left wing of the party and the union movement became increasingly acrimonious through the 1970s.

Many of the Left could never forgive Hawke for supporting federal intervention into the Victorian Labor Party. His passionate support for Israel further alienated the Left. His bitter feud with Bill Hartley, whom he tried to expel from the party in January 1979, did not help matters. Nor did Hawke's refusal to call a national strike after the dismissal in 1975. But the issue that antagonised the Left faction more than anything else was Hawke's support for uranium mining. In the post-Whitlam years, no policy issue dominated party and union forums more than uranium. Hawke was a key figure in this debate.

The Whitlam government supported and promoted the mining and export of uranium. Jim Cairns, from Labor's Left faction, was an enthusiast for selling uranium abroad and travelled the world to extol its virtues. But by the mid-1970s, uranium had become the new moral evil for the Left, who campaigned against nuclear energy and the proliferation of nuclear weapons. The party and the unions divided on these issues and struggled to settle on a clear position.

In November 1976, Tom Uren advocated a total ban on the mining and export of uranium. He was challenged by Paul Keating, the party's minerals and energy spokesman, in a bitter debate that took place in caucus and at the party's federal executive. Keating won this round, with the party agreeing to support existing contracts for export while an inquiry examined the future of the industry. At Labor's July 1977 national conference in Perth, the party voted to oppose the mining and export of uranium, and not honour existing contracts if returned to government. This decision was opposed by Hawke and Keating, who advocated for supporting at the very least any existing contracts for mining and export. At Labor's July 1979 national conference in Adelaide, the party maintained its moratorium on uranium mining and again pledged to cancel contracts for mining and export.

The union movement was just as divided over uranium as the party. At the September 1977 ACTU Congress, Left unions pushed for a total ban on the mining, transportation and export of uranium. This motion was opposed by Hawke, and was defeated by 493 votes to 371. Hawke proposed and secured support for what he called a 'referendum' – more accurately a plebiscite – on the future of uranium mining in Australia. It was aimed at lessening tensions within the union movement by insisting that voters have a say. But the idea was dead on arrival: the Fraser government said it would never support it, and neither would the Whitlam opposition.

Ahead of the September 1979 ACTU Congress, Hawke advocated a pragmatic position. He argued that it was irrational and illogical to ignore the existence of uranium, and Australia could mine and export it with the highest safety standards. Australia's export of uranium was, in accordance with the Non-Proliferation Treaty, only for power generation, and specifically not for the development of nuclear weapons. As union members would continue to work in the industry and the government would continue to support them, a resolution by the ACTU would have zero impact. Such rational views were not universally supported within the union movement or at home. Hawke discussed uranium extensively with his teenage children Susan and Stephen, who urged him to ban mining and export. Susan joined the protests outside the ACTU Congress.

On 14 September 1979, Hawke opened and closed the debate on uranium. This was the critical moment of Hawke's presidency. Standing on the stage of the Dallas Brooks Hall in Melbourne, he delivered a speech that betrayed everything he had learnt about the art of persuasion. Instead, the delegates witnessed an enraged, intemperate and abusive firebrand. 'You may luxuriate in your morality but you will have done nothing positive,' he thundered to his critics. 'You will have destroyed the credibility of this great organisation.' Hawke went over the top. He was met with boos and hisses. The more he raged, the more he lost the debate. He became angry and lashed out at certain union leaders. He shouted, hectored and abused. He thumped the podium.

The result was a humiliating defeat for Hawke, the most significant during his presidency. The Left amendment placing bans on uranium mining was carried by 512 votes to 318.[11] According to Bill Kelty, the ACTU's assistant secretary, he and Hawke were entirely to blame. 'We had not done the hard work with our own groups, let alone others,' he recalled. 'We didn't even get all the Storemen and Packers' onside. We misjudged the numbers. Emotion overtook the reality of the situation, so we lost. We probably deserved to lose.'[12]

———

Hawke's role as an industrial peacemaker was the aspect of the ACTU presidency that he enjoyed the most. Among the many disputes in which Hawke was involved during the 1970s, several stood out: the State Electricity Commission (1972); the oil industry (1972); air traffic controllers (1976); Telecom (1978); and live sheep exports (1978). His reputation as a strike-breaker and conciliator was now firmly established. He was called on by unions, employers and the government – even by Malcolm Fraser – to intervene and resolve disagreements. This meant that Hawke was rarely blamed for a strike, and generally got the credit for resolving it.

ACTU advocate Rob Jolly said Hawke would talk to both the employer and union during a dispute, before getting involved. 'He had that knack of understanding where the point of exhaustion was,' Jolly recalled. 'He would only come into a dispute when he thought it was the right time to settle.'[13] When he became involved, Kelty said, Hawke was always well prepared. He would simplify and focus the issues. He would sympathise with both the union and the employer positions. Critically, he knew that resolving a dispute meant compromising. 'The easiest thing was to say no, but the hardest thing was to say yes,' Kelty said. 'A lot of other union leaders just couldn't do this.'[14]

In 1976 Hawke explained to The Age, not immodestly, why he had been successful. First, he had expertise and experience. Second, he had authority. Third, he had integrity and his word was trusted by all parties. Fourth, he was often called in when negotiations had stalled and both parties were eager to settle. And fifth, he believed that he could identify options that had not been thought of or followed through.[15]

By the mid-1970s, the ACTU Executive was evenly divided into three groups. In 1975–76, the Left were: Ray Gietzelt (Miscellaneous Workers Union), Pat Clancy (Building Workers Industrial Union), Dick Scott (Australian Manufacturing Workers Union), Bob Gregory (South Australian Labor Council), Peter Cook (West Australian Labor Council) and Jim Roulston (Amalgamated Metal Workers Union). The Right were: Edgar Williams (Australian Workers Union), John Ducker (NSW Labor Council), Ken Stone (Victorian Trades Hall Council), Bill Wood (Federated Ironworkers Association), John Morris (Liquor Trades Union) and Harold Souter (ACTU). The Centre were: Charlie Fitzgibbon (Waterside Workers Federation), Fred Peterson (Clothing and

Allied Trades Union), Jack Egerton (Queensland Labor Council), Cliff Dolan (Electrical Trades Union) and Peter Nolan (ACTU). Hawke could now usually rely on most of the Right, the Centre group, plus Gietzelt and Clancy, giving him majority support drawn from all factions.

In October 1977 Harold Souter retired as ACTU secretary. It had been more than seven years since his defeat by Hawke for the presidency. Souter had been in the role since 1957. He was succeeded by Peter Nolan, who was then ACTU assistant secretary. Nolan, described as 'a gentle giant', was respected for his role as an administrator, negotiator and advocate. But he was completely overshadowed by Hawke, and Kelty was increasingly taking on his responsibilities.[16]

Kelty was elected ACTU assistant secretary. He had been research officer and advocate for the ACTU since November 1974. He had previously worked as a research officer for the Worker's Education Office in Adelaide (1973–74) and as industrial officer for the Federated Storemen and Packers' Union (1970–73). Kelty thought Nolan was 'a very nice person' and committed to the union movement, but not up to the job of being secretary. 'It was just beyond his capacity,' Kelty said. 'He just could not get anything done and he was always causing problems.' So Kelty worked closely with Hawke and others, such as Charlie Fitzgibbon, to ensure the ACTU ran effectively. It was not in Hawke's nature to move Nolan on.[17]

Rob Jolly had been advocate and research officer since 1972. He had an academic and public-sector background. He was immediately struck by how intelligent, fast-thinking and hardworking Hawke was. 'He was far from a micro-manager,' recalled Jolly. 'He thought outcomes were what was important and so it was up to you how you presented and argued a national wage case.' He worked with Hawke on developing policy and advocating it to government. 'He had this charisma which was infectious,' Jolly explained. 'He respected people's values, he was always supporting the underdog and he fought for the rights of workers.'[18]

Jan Marsh was elevated to the role of ACTU advocate in March 1979. Softly spoken and shy, but nevertheless formidable, she was a trailblazer for women in the union movement. She secured a major win with the maternity leave test case in 1979, which guaranteed workers six weeks' compulsory and twelve months' unpaid maternity leave. It split the union movement, was opposed by employers and regarded by some non-working women as a concession to careerists.[19] Hawke gave his full support to the test case but left the running of it to Marsh and Kelty. 'There were so many views on it in the union movement because it was seen as a women's issue, but Hawke was very supportive,' Marsh recalled.[20]

—

Hawke was considering contesting a seat at the next federal election, which was due in 1978. Bill Landeryou was investigating potential seats for him in Victoria, while Mick Young did likewise in South Australia. There was an expectation that Hawke would run for a seat and seek to become leader in the next term. But on 16 September 1976, Hawke ended months of speculation by announcing that he would not be a candidate, after preselections had been called. Hawke told a packed press conference that he would be a lame-duck ACTU president if he was chosen as a candidate perhaps two years before the election was held.

But there was more to the decision. First, no federal Labor MP was retiring, nor did any offer to stand aside for Hawke. Among those the Centre Unity group hoped would make way included Frank Crean, Jim Cairns and Gordon Bryant. Second, the Socialist Left in Victoria were now in open warfare against Hawke. Bill Hartley made it clear he would oppose Hawke's entry into parliament at all costs. By mid-1976, Centre Unity was strengthening within the party but was engaged in a fierce battle against the Socialist Left for dominance. Centre Unity was controlled by party chairman Peter Redlich, Victorian opposition leader Clyde Holding and Hawke.

Malcolm Fraser called an early election for 10 December 1977. It was an election that few in the party thought Labor could win, especially with Gough Whitlam as leader. Labor's campaign was launched at the Sydney Opera House on 17 November. Hawke had the task of introducing the opposition leader. He spoke about Whitlam's achievements in government and lashed Fraser's record as one of division, distrust and disastrous economic management. Journalist Ian Warden thought Hawke was 'as good at making speeches as Mozart was at writing music'. In his policy speech, Whitlam focused on those who had been left behind: young people, the elderly, the unemployed, small-business owners and migrants. 'The task before us is to restore parliament as an instrument for progress and reform,' he told the audience.[21]

The result was a disaster for Labor. The party's primary vote fell to 39.7 per cent. Labor gained two seats – Capricornia and Griffith in Queensland – but still held just thirty-eight seats out of 124 in the House of Representatives. Significantly, the Coalition won an outright majority in the Senate. On election night, Whitlam announced that he would resign as party leader.

On 22 December 1977, Labor MPs met in Canberra. Bill Hayden nominated to lead the Labor Party. On 31 May 1977, at the midterm caucus elections, Hayden had challenged Whitlam as leader. The Left mostly locked in behind Hayden, while the Right mostly stuck by Whitlam. The result was thirty-two votes for Whitlam and thirty for Hayden. Now, seven months later, Hayden faced Lionel Bowen in a ballot for the leadership. He defeated Bowen by thirty-six votes to twenty-eight.

The new leader wasted little time developing an ambitious strategy to revitalise Labor for an election expected in 1980. Hayden flagged recruiting new candidates, rejuvenating the front bench, overhauling policies, developing a modern mission statement for the party, and reforming the organisation so that it better reflected the community, and was more transparent and accountable.

A National Committee of Inquiry was established. Jointly chaired by Hayden, Hawke, John Ducker and John Button, it reviewed every aspect of the party. During the next year, forums were held with party members, written submissions were received, ten discussion papers were issued, and an interim report was released. A final report was published in March 1979. This was the springboard for a series of reforms that included doubling the size of the party's national conference to ninety-nine delegates, establishing a more representative national executive body and conducting a review of the party's moribund 'socialist objective'.

Hayden had made an impressive start. Even so, for most voters he was not the leader they wanted. That person was Hawke, who remained the most popular political figure through the second half of the 1970s. In March 1976, his approval rating was 62 per cent. In June 1977, it was 57 per cent. In May 1978, it was 59 per cent. In contrast, Hayden's approval rating was 47 per cent in May 1978. Whitlam's final approval rating, according to Gallup in December 1977, was 36 per cent. Fraser's approval rating in May 1978 was 44 per cent.[22]

There was no other person in greater demand to campaign for Labor candidates than Hawke. These visits always drew out the voters and received local media coverage. But they did not always go to plan. John Kerin recalled Hawke campaigning with him in his seat of Macarthur in 1977. 'He was drinking too much,' recalled Kerin. 'He arrived terribly late and we had to cancel the first three events. He insulted the Shoalhaven Shire Council. But then he gave two big speeches to the workers and it was absolutely brilliant. We had a big fundraiser lined up at the Albion Park RSL, and when he got there he just collapsed so we had to put him to bed. The next day he went on to address a big meeting at Dapto, and it was quite a brilliant presentation.'[23]

Kerry Sibraa, by now a senator, organised for Hawke to present the winning trophy at the 1978 Australian Surf Life Saving Championships at Kingscliff, in northern New South Wales. This was conservative territory. 'The reception that Hawkey got on that beach was amazing,' Sibraa recalled. 'People came from everywhere to slap him on the back. That is when I thought, "I've seen a future prime minister." I think they saw someone who was strong, who was no-nonsense, there was no bullshit about him.'

A few years earlier, Sibraa had picked up Hawke from the Boulevard Hotel to take him to Bankstown for a function. 'It was quite obvious he had had a long lunch and I thought, "This is not going to go well,"' he recalled. As they drove along the Hume Highway, Hawke said: 'Let's go and have a beer.' Sibraa replied: 'Mate, you're kidding.' Hawke was persistent. They called into a pub and found a group of workers who had just finished a shift. 'The next minute they were slapping him on the back and shaking his hand,' Sibraa said. 'It was like recharging his batteries. At the function, he made a great speech, everybody was happy, and then he collapsed in the car and slept on the way back to the hotel.'[24]

Ros Kelly invited Hawke to campaign with her in the seat of Canberra in 1980. It did not go to plan. 'I was driving him around in my little yellow Mazda and I pulled up at the lights at Hindmarsh Drive, just near Woden Valley Hospital, and next to us were two young women with the hood down in a VW,' recalled Kelly. 'They noticed Bob and they screamed out – "Bob, come and join us!" – and he jumped out of my car and into the back of their VW and disappeared for two hours. He later joined me at a shopping centre as if nothing had happened.' Hawke then asked the local pharmacist about the best shampoo for his hair.[25]

Hawke was a media sensation. He frequently made the front page, led the radio news and appeared on television programs. He was always interesting, often controversial and never dull. 'He drinks like a fish, swears like a trooper, works like a demon, performs like a playboy, talks like a truckie – and acts like a politician,' wrote Craig McGregor in May 1977. 'Almost your cliché Aussie. Except in this case it's Bob Hawke, and the only typical thing about him is the way he's larger than average in almost everything. Bob Hawke is your typical Australian, oversize.'[26]

Almost everybody knew Hawke. He was photographed at home, in his dressing gown, on the phone while patting the family cat, Mr Tich, which sat on his lap. Journalists interviewed him poolside as he rubbed suntan lotion on his legs and offered his opinions on Whitlam or Fraser, or talked about whether he might go into parliament. Ever the egotist, Hawke enjoyed being naked. He would swim in the pool at home naked and then climb out to talk to union or party colleagues without rushing to reach for a towel. In hotels, he would greet waiters, colleagues and journalists stark naked when opening the door, and then proceed to talk to them with his penis dangling between his spindly legs. Hawke's ACTU staff regularly saw him naked while travelling.[27]

Journalists often witnessed such displays of masculinity and exhibitionism. On one occasion, while staying at the Canberra Rex, Hawke was phoned by the manager: a group of journalists had arrived to interview him. 'Send them up,' he said. But Hawke had a young woman in his room, and the manager, trying to be discreet, suggested that might not be a good idea. Hawke insisted. 'That's alright, mate,' he said. When he opened the door, Hawke was still dressing, and told the journalists to take a seat. The young woman slid down the bed and pulled the sheet up over her head. 'Righto, you blokes,' he instructed the photographers. 'Head shots only. You know the rules.' This happened regularly.[28]

One of the most extraordinary interviews Hawke did in this period was with Toni McRae from *The Sun* in Sydney in March 1977. Over a bottle of Veuve Clicquot at the Boulevard Hotel, he loosened his tie and kicked off his suede shoes and spoke about his children, his propensity to cry, his parents, and his sleeping and eating habits. He was frank about the failures of the Whitlam government. He stayed out of the looming Hayden–Whitlam leadership contest, but predicted Fraser would lose the next election. And he did one-arm push-ups while ruminating on being prime minister one day. 'I'm not asking or expecting that the prime ministership of Australia should be offered to me on a platter,' he said, switching arms. 'But if the circumstances were such, and I were asked and I became prime minister of Australia, I'd do it bloody well.'[29]

Hawke's celebrity status had reached its zenith. There had never been anything like it. Hawke revelled in his superstardom. He was in demand as a guest speaker at union and business conferences, he was often a guest at charity functions, he was seen regularly at sporting events, and he appeared on television and radio, and in the morning and afternoon newspapers. Hawke was even 'flogged' at Old Sydney Town ahead of Labor's federal conference at Terrigal. He mixed fun with seriousness. Hawke was also a regular election night commentator. For this, and for certain interviews, he asked for and received a fee. Channel Nine paid Hawke $1000 for his election night commentary in 1980.[30] He received the same amount for a *60 Minutes* interview earlier that year.[31]

Hawke engaged the public consciousness like no other national political or union figure. He had a connection with everyday Australians. He was at the epicentre of a great celebrity drama in which he was the dominant figure: the drinking, the womanising, the emotional reactions, the critical assessments, the audacious idea of consensus and conciliation, the man with the ear of politicians, union leaders and business titans, and the never-ending speculation about whether and when he would go into politics.

He was original, authentic and compelling. He thrived on the media and craved public attention. It was a grand drama produced and scripted by Hawke, with himself as the star.

Often, Hawke's ego got the better of him. Ahead of Labor's July 1977 national conference, in Perth, Hawke had to fight to secure a fifth one-year term as president. The Left's Tom Uren and Arthur Gietzelt hatched a plan to topple Hawke and replace him with Mick Young. Uren, then deputy leader of the party, and Gietzelt thought they could marshal twelve votes on the national executive. At the Sheraton Hotel on 30 June, they told David Combe to suggest to Hawke that he give the presidency away and not contest the ballot that was due to take place the following morning. Hawke refused. With John Ducker and Combe, he rang the national executive members, knocked on their doors and buttonholed them in the lobby and corridors. Hawke then pre-recorded an interview with John Highfield for ABC Radio's *AM* program, in which he announced that he would be standing for another term as president. It went to air just before the national executive met. Uren and Gietzelt soon realised their plan had been thwarted, and Young decided not to nominate. Hawke was elected unopposed for what would be his last term as ACTU president.

The re-elected president, rather pleased with himself, then spoke at a lunch organised by the Perth Press Club. After delivering a speech, he answered questions for half an hour with a glass of wine in his hand. He called Premier Charles Court 'a hopeless out-of-touch bastard' and Malcolm Fraser 'a hypocritical bastard'. He said he would be available to lead the party if his colleagues wanted him. Hawke made it clear that if he went into parliament, he would not want to put his 'bum on a back bench' – it was leader or nothing.[32] Many observers thought he had blown his chance.

Drinking was a big part of Hawke's life. He could not go into a bar without somebody wanting to buy him a beer. It became a badge of honour to say you had drunk with him. Hawke, of course, never shouted the bar. His Oxford beer-drinking record was now a fixed part of his legend. In December 1972, the Storemen and Packers' Union purchased the Phoenix Hotel in Brunswick, Melbourne, for $120,000 and renamed it 'The R.J. Hawke'.[33] It was opened by Gough Whitlam in May 1973. Hawke and Whitlam took turns trying to down a yard of ale.[34] 'The Bob Hawke Drinking Song' was released as a record single in August 1975. Paul Jennings impersonated Hawke. The song featured the words: 'Remove the caucus and drink to Bob Hawke, the wonder of the down-under dog. Let's all drink to Bob Hawke.'[35] The legend was amplified.

The public often saw Hawke drinking in public. In October 1975 he began three days of electioneering in Queensland with a pub crawl in Brisbane. He was cheered and patted on the back as he drank and drank and drank.[36] It perplexed many how he did not get fat. Unlike a lot of unionists who celebrated their victories with the amber ale, and drowned their sorrows with it too, becoming portly and pudgy, Hawke had a cast-iron stomach, a fast metabolism and remained lean and fit. He did not have a big appetite for food, and fancy restaurants never held much appeal.

Especially when travelling, Hawke was known to go on lengthy benders. He could drink from lunchtime until late, catch a few hours' sleep, and then appear on time and fresh the next morning to chair a meeting. Colleagues were astonished at his ability to function without a hangover. 'Bob would drink, he would fuck somebody and he would gamble until 2.30 am or 3.30 am in the morning, and then when the ACTU Executive started at 9 am in the morning, he was the second one there and he was fine,' recalled Bill Kelty.[37]

But sometimes he was in no state to attend meetings, and would arrive late or not at all. Hawke was known for having to take spells to dry out, often at home or at the farm of his family doctor, Brian Woodward, in South Gippsland. Woodward would help Hawke to recover.[38] Sometimes Hawke could not be reached by phone for days. When the media reported that Hawke was not available for comment, it was code for a period of detoxification. But then, as ever, he would resurface and the cycle would begin again.

Col Cunningham, one of Hawke's closest friends, said he was 'the worst drunk' when he was out on the booze. 'He was a pisspot, a drunk, you couldn't handle him,' Cunningham recalled. 'It was just awful to see the guy, as beaut as he is, belittling himself in front of people, and people saying, "Look at that drunk." It used to make me bloody sick. He'd be making a fool of himself. Jesus.'[39]

Kelty said Hawke was 'a drunk' who might have twenty beers

in one session. Hawke could get loud, argumentative and abusive. During one drinking session, Hawke said he would not proceed with the appointment of Alan Boulton as the ACTU's legal officer. 'What do you mean we're not appointing him,' Kelty raged. 'We have already appointed him.' Hawke said, 'I don't fucking care. I'm not fucking appointing him.' Hawke threw something at Kelty. He responded by throwing a set of keys at Hawke, which shattered the glass in his hand and the beer spilled out and soaked his pants. 'That was a fucking good throw,' Hawke said. The next day, Hawke apologised and said Boulton's appointment was fine.[40]

In July 1976, Hawke addressed the National Press Club in Canberra. It was an impressive performance. He surveyed Australia's unique form of government, a 'marriage' between the United Kingdom's Westminster system and the United States' republic, and outlined ways it could be improved, such as by allowing men and women of great talent to serve in cabinet without having to be members of parliament. He spoke mostly from notes. The journalists were impressed. But it then went downhill: he made several sexual allusions about people, told a reporter they were talking 'bullshit' and stood behind the podium sipping a glass of wine as he tersely answered questions.[41]

Barrie Unsworth recalled attending a conference with Hawke in Adelaide in 1978. Before a dinner with premier Don Dunstan on the Saturday evening, they spent the day at the racetrack and then went to Mick Young's pub in Port Adelaide. Hawke had been loaned a car by General Motors. Hawke played snooker with patrons in the pub and they gave him a pool cue as a memento. Hawke asked the publican if he had any bottles of Grange. He opened the cellar trapdoor, went downstairs and returned with a box of Grange covered in cobwebs. 'I'll box them up for you, Bob,' he said. Hawke 'nearly fell over' when the cost was over $100, as he expected them to be two or three dollars a bottle. They left the pub and headed to the dinner. Hawke propositioned a woman at the restaurant, which led to an altercation with her boyfriend. An Australian Workers' Union official flattened the boyfriend. Unsworth had had enough and retired to the hotel.

The next morning, Unsworth looked out the window and saw Hawke's car parked ten feet from the curb, jutting out onto

North Terrace. He went to the reception to check out. 'Are you a friend of Mr Hawke?' the man behind the counter asked. 'Yes, I'm travelling with him. Why?' Unsworth replied. 'Well, he asked for a wake-up call, and when we went to wake him up, he threw a punch, and we're not going back in there,' the hotel worker said. Unsworth went to Hawke's room, opened the blinds, got him out of bed and dragged him into the shower. They got a flight to Melbourne. Before Unsworth headed on to Sydney, he saw Hawke out to the arrivals hall, where Hazel was waiting. 'Hawkey's got his bag, the dozen bottles of wine and a snooker cue, and you could tell that Hazel was not impressed,' he recalled.[42]

Hawke's drinking threatened to destroy any future political career. A key flashpoint was Labor's national conference in Adelaide in July 1979. This was Bill Hayden's big opportunity, a year before an election was expected, to remake the party in his name. 'Australia's got the future – Hayden's got the team' read a huge banner across the stage of the Space Theatre. Labor was ahead in the polls and Hayden was more popular than Fraser. He made 'responsible economic management' a key theme of his speech and said: 'We cannot achieve social reform unless we competently manage the economy.'[43]

A focus of the conference was settling a new policy on prices and incomes. Hawke, as chair of the party's economic policy committee, proposed that Labor pledge to hold a referendum to secure powers to regulate the setting of prices and incomes. Hayden gave Hawke his support for this idea, which had the backing of the Right faction. But at lunchtime on Tuesday, 17 July, Hayden changed his mind. He supported the Left's proposal that Labor commit to maintain real wages with quarterly adjustments and productivity increases. Hayden did not want to make an enemy of the Left by supporting the Right, and allow Hawke to claim a conference win.

Meanwhile, Hawke had gone to lunch with Mick Young, and learned about the deal between Hayden and the Left when he returned. The Right faction shared Hawke's view that Hayden had betrayed them. Hawke was seething. Hayden had won a significant victory. The conference was seen as the making of Hayden as a leader: he had delivered a good speech and won a vital

conference vote. That is how the media reported the conference –
until that evening.

Hawke walked into the Rotunda Bar at the Gateway Inn at
9.10 pm. It was full of Labor MPs, party and union officials, and
journalists. Hawke was already well lubricated. He spoke to a few
people and then sat down on one of the plush red chairs with a
group of journalists. Paul Kelly knew that Hawke would be 'a great
story', so he quickly engaged him in 'a provocative conversation',
hoping to elicit a response to the day's events. Journalists continued to buy him drinks. 'He just went berserk about Hayden,' Kelly
recalled.[44]

Hawke then offered, in full earshot of much of the bar, a with-
ering assessment of the Labor leader: 'As far as I'm concerned Bill
Hayden is dead. Hayden is a lying cunt with a limited future.'[45]
The next day, the conference was abuzz with Hawke's bar-room
declaration. When Hawke arrived at the conference, he was set
upon by reporters. 'For Christ's sake, fuck off,' he said. 'I'm trying
to make a private call.'[46] Not for the first time, journalists wrote
off Hawke's future in politics.

Hawke looked for opportunities to show he was capable of
being Labor leader. In November–December 1979, he delivered
the Boyer lectures for the ABC, with the title *The Resolution of
Conflict*. He spoke about consensus, called for a national economic
summit, expressed support for 'alternative lifestyles', and advocated abolishing state governments and allowing ministers to be
drawn from the public without having to be MPs. Hawke said
there is 'ultimately a desire for harmony rather than conflict' in
the community and the 'resolution of conflict' should be Australia's goal.[47] Hawke was paid $1750 for the lectures.[48] However, he
did not win many plaudits. Some wondered whether Hawke was
all that he thought he was. His ideas were deemed to be unoriginal
and implausible.

Earlier that year, Hawke was made a Companion in the General
Division of the Order of Australia on 26 January 1979.[49] It was
recognition of the high regard many Australians had for Hawke,
regardless of his personal flaws, and he accepted the honour as an
acknowledgement for his work as ACTU and ALP president. He
celebrated with a quiet dinner at a restaurant in Melbourne with

Hazel and several party and union colleagues. But there was shock among some of Hawke's friends, colleagues and admirers that he accepted the award even though it was not a British imperial honour but an Australian honour, introduced by the Whitlam government.

Writer Xavier Herbert was gobsmacked. 'I am reeling, as if the life has been knocked out of me for good. I'm not joking! Never in my life have I felt so dismayed,' he wrote to Hawke. 'Dear, dear Bob – what have you done?' Herbert urged Hawke to renounce the honour, as Patrick White and H.C. 'Nugget' Coombs had done. 'Until you do my heart will bleed – not for you, but for my poor hopeless, helpless country.'[50] Hawke kept the honour and wore the insignia proudly for the rest of his life.

Governor-General Sir Zelman Cowen bestowed the AC on Hawke at a ceremony at Government House, Yarralumla, on 14 March 1979. Hawke was invited to dine that evening with Sir Zelman and Lady Cowen. Clem and Albert Hawke attended as Bob's guests. Ellie was unwell and in hospital. For Clem, it was another sign that his son was destined for greater things. '[He] has outstanding qualities of leadership,' he told a journalist in May 1980. 'He's very much a man of the people. When Bob walks into a room, you can't miss him. He has great charisma.' The father had no doubt the son would be an outstanding prime minister.[51]

—

Hazel did not attend the Yarralumla dinner, as by this time her marriage was under serious strain due to Bob's ongoing infidelity and excessive drinking. She worried deeply about his 'monster drink' problem, which she described as a 'demon' inside of him.[52] Hawke always downplayed his drinking and did not fully accept that he had a problem. He referred to drinking as a 'social lubricant' and only gradually came to see its negative effects.[53] Blanche d'Alpuget wrote: 'The difficulty was not that Hawke drank but that he was and had been for years a loathsome drunk – poisoned, savage, a man possessed.'[54]

It is remarkable that, given Hawke drank so much, it didn't kill him. Hawke was an alcoholic, although he never acknowledged this. He was addicted to alcohol and struggled to give it up. Hawke was also what medical experts would diagnose today as a highly functioning alcoholic. D'Alpuget agreed with this assessment. 'Oh yes, no doubt,' she said.[55] It was only when Hawke realised that it threatened to derail his political career that he contemplated giving it up. He did not need a doctor or a support group or rehabilitation – the fires of ambition were sufficient.

At 7 pm on 29 July 1975, Hawke sat down with Michael Schildberger for a live interview on Channel Nine's *A Current Affair*. The interview probed Hawke's views on a range of issues, and then turned to the personal. Schildberger asked Hawke if he had any weaknesses. 'I tend to take too much refuge in taking a drink,' Hawke conceded. He had never acknowledged the problem in such a direct, confessional manner. Hawke said that if he went into parliament, and became prime minister, he would abstain from drinking. But it would be a struggle. 'I would not want to do that because I get joy and relief out of having a drink,' he said.[56]

Hawke's confession was big news. He said after the interview that he felt he had to be honest, given Schildberger had asked such a direct question. But his friends were shocked. Politicians and journalists thought it showed poor judgement. Whitlam, unable to resist, poked fun. 'I intend to turn over a new leaf and undertake steady drinking from now on,' he joked to journalists. He added that meetings of Labor's federal executive would be like 'gatherings of Alcoholics Anonymous'.[57]

Hawke's womanising, however, remained largely unreported and certainly unconfessed. Bob Hogg, the Victorian Labor state secretary (1976–83), said Hawke had an active extramarital sex life in the 1960s and 1970s. 'He rarely missed an opportunity, and he had many.'[58]

Graham Richardson, state organiser with New South Wales Labor (1971–76) and later general secretary (1976–83), recalled Hawke travelling to Armidale, in New South Wales, to help Labor campaign in a state by-election in February 1973. 'The Australia Party candidate [Joan Kersey] had not indicated where she was going to allocate her preferences,' he said. 'So Hawke and I got this woman to come to our motel suite and talk about it. Then, after we talked for a while, he signalled and I left the room. They emerged an hour later.'[59]

Bob Carr, then a journalist with *The Bulletin*, recalled wanting to interview Hawke about uranium ahead of the 1979 ACTU Congress. Hawke told Carr the only spare moment he had was on the way to Sydney airport. So Carr joined Hawke and they headed to the airport, only for the interview to be interrupted by an unscheduled stop on a residential street in Woollahra. For thirty minutes, Carr waited while Hawke was inside with one of his mistresses. He then emerged and returned to the car, and they resumed the interview on the way to the airport.[60]

In October 1974, journalist Mamie Smith asked Hawke how he coped with women who found him 'attractive' and would 'flutter' around him. Hawke saw the question as provocative and asked why she did not simply ask: 'Are you a womaniser?' Journalists knew about Hawke's serial infidelity, but feared being sued for libel if they reported it. Hawke was notoriously litigious in these years. Moreover, there was a convention that the private lives of public figures should remain private. Smith did not report his infidelity. Astonishingly, she later confessed to Hawke biographer Robert Pullan a desire to have sex with Hawke. Smith was not only covering up Hawke's sexual desires, she wanted to satisfy them.[61]

Hawke was a sexual magnet. When Craig McGregor wrote a profile of Hawke in mid-1977, he witnessed this first-hand. After speaking at a conference in Melbourne, Hawke was stopped by a pert young girl in a bosomy sweater. 'Mr Hawke! Can I touch you? Are you human?' She ran her hands over his chest. 'I'm just an ordinary citizen and I can't believe you are real.' Later, when they arrived at the Windsor Hotel, Hawke was stopped by a middle-aged woman, who rushed up and gave him a hug. 'Bob!' she said. 'I just wanted to tell you, I thought you were marvellous last night. You keep it up, Bob, keep giving it to them.' McGregor asked Hawke who she was. 'Never saw her before in my life,' he replied.[62]

Hawke's womanising was often too much for his colleagues. Ahead of a federal executive meeting in North Queensland in the late 1970s, several party figures were scheduled to go on a boat trip on the Great Barrier Reef, hosted by Jack Egerton. Hawke arrived with a bikini-clad girl on each arm. Egerton said: 'Listen, Bob, we all know Hazel, so you just can't do this. I'm sorry. It is not on.' Hawke promptly sent the bikini-clad women away and got on the boat.[63]

When he was drunk, Hawke could treat women appallingly, often in full view of others. Hawke would proposition women for sex.[64] 'Do you find me attractive?' he would say. He could be even blunter: 'How about a fuck?' Sometimes women would oblige. Sometimes they would reject the outrageous suggestion, which would prompt Hawke to lash out like a scorned lover with a stream of verbal abuse.

Journalist Gay Davidson recalled interviewing Hawke in his hotel room during Labor's federal conference in Terrigal in 1975. He stripped naked and lay on the double bed, then asked her to join him. When she refused, he insisted she at least take her shoes off and sit on the edge of the bed. She did. But when it became evident that she would not be taking her clothes off and getting into bed with him, he became angry. 'God, you've got ugly feet, Davidson,' he said.[65]

John Button told Bob Carr about a Christmas drinks function at Holding Redlich. 'There was a woman serving drinks and Hawke turned on her and snapped, and said: "Get off my back. Don't hang around me. Look, I'm not interested in you. I fucked you last year at this event and I'm not doing it again."' Carr recalled Button saying he had never seen a woman so humiliated in front of other people.[66]

When Senator Susan Ryan came across a drunk Hawke one night during Labor's federal conference in Perth in 1977, he propositioned her. When Ryan declined, he said: 'Anyway, you've got a scraggy body.'[67] At the same conference at the Sheraton Hotel, Hawke was approached by a group of young men and women who asked for an autograph. 'I don't give autographs in hotel foyers, only hotel bedrooms,' he replied. Ryan recalled that Hawke's affairs were well known, and many women were 'boastful' of having had sex with him. She once said to another Labor woman: 'I think you and I are the only women in the Labor Party that haven't had an affair with Bob.' Ryan added: 'He wasn't a sexual predator. Women were quite attracted to him and often persuaded him. He emanated power and sensuality. Women found that very attractive.'[68]

While Hawke skirted around the issue of womanising in interviews, he did speak frankly – too frankly – to Mamie Smith about his marriage to Hazel. 'I have an operating marriage,' he said. 'I would not be telling the truth if I denied there were problems.' He said one of the reasons he wanted to continue the relationship was the children. He had 'wondered whether marriage is producing all the things I want', but had decided nothing could replace 'the positive things' in the marriage.[69]

Hazel was increasingly unhappy. She neither sought nor enjoyed the spotlight. She began receiving letters from women, some anonymous, who claimed they had had sex with Bob. Others attacked her as weak for staying with him.[70] Hazel felt the intrusion into their private lives was too much. 'I do find being Bob's wife inhibiting,' she told *Woman's Day* in March 1976. 'I'm never seen as myself. I'm always seen as Bob Hawke's wife.'[71] Hazel began drinking too much in the mid-1970s. She sought refuge at home with cask wine, and slid into a 'deep funk'.[72]

Susan, Stephen and Rosslyn witnessed as teenagers the tensions between their parents, which sometimes turned ugly. Hawke was spoilt by Hazel. He rarely did any cleaning, cooking or maintenance at home. He could not work the oven or the washing machine. He expected to be waited upon, and when he was not, he became frustrated and angry. He preferred to lie in the sun by the pool rather than help Hazel run the household. Hawke was a legend in the eyes of the public, but his celebrity status had no currency at home.

The children were almost always on their mother's side. 'His treatment of Mum was not always wonderful,' Stephen recalled. 'They fought like cats and dogs at times.' His father's 'infidelities' were not 'unnoticed' or 'unremarked' upon – they were front and centre.[73] As a result of 'serial infidelity' and excessive drinking, Susan acknowledged, 'there were night-time arguments and drunkenness' that they witnessed.[74] This 'ugly behaviour had been going on for years', and led Susan, Stephen and Rosslyn to be detached from their father by the late 1970s, even though there was 'a strong and mutual love' between them all.[75] Stephen explained: 'In those dramas between Mum and Dad, I was on Mum's side emotionally. I stood with her in the troubles that were going on.

So certainly, in those years, I was the least close to my father. But that is not to my memory a period of estrangement – it was a period of distance, you might say.'[76]

It was obvious to Hawke's union and party colleagues that his marriage was not good. Simon Crean, who became secretary of the Federated Storemen and Packers' Union in 1979, often visited the home in Sandringham. 'The best you could say is that it was strained; it wasn't a very good relationship,' he recalled.[77] Bill Kelty thought Hawke deserved the 'Arsehole of the Year' award rather than 'Father of the Year', given his 'terrible' behaviour. 'When you are drinking at the pub all the time and your wife is raising your kids, that is no way to be a father,' he said.[78]

Bob and Hazel's marriage was on the rocks. In 1979, she consulted a lawyer about divorce. She did not tell Bob at first. He was also looking into divorcing her. In 1980, Hawke consulted lawyer Arnold Bloch about divorce.[79] One morning in 1979, in the bedroom, Bob told Hazel that two women wanted to marry him. He confessed his infidelity and raised the prospect of divorce. It plunged Hazel into despair. Susan worried that she might suicide. Hazel was hurt, and felt 'futile and irrelevant'. But she loved him and wanted to save the marriage. Her friends rallied and she saw a counsellor, and emerged stronger.[80]

There were more family difficulties. By the late 1970s, Ellie's health was failing. She had a second stroke in May 1978. Ever since he had left home to go to Oxford, Hawke had written to his parents or spoken to them on the phone almost every week. Whenever he went to Perth, he visited them in West Leederville. Clem had kept him informed of Ellie's deterioration: she was now living in a nursing home. Hawke recalled a visit in her final year. Kneeling by her bedside, he said: 'Thank you, Mum, for every-thing you've done for me.' Ellie replied: 'It was a pleasure, son.'[81] It was the last thing she would say to him.

On Saturday, 8 September 1979, Ellie died. Hawke was in Melbourne preparing to address the 1979 ACTU Congress on the difficult issue of uranium mining. Bob and Hazel flew to Perth on Monday evening, arriving at 10.30 pm. The cremation service was held the next morning, at 9.30 am. Clem, Bob and Hazel arrived early to say their farewells before the coffin lid was fixed. 'Edith looked very peaceful and we kissed her a last goodbye on her forehead,' Clem wrote in his memoir.[82]

Ellie's death occurred before her son had fulfilled her expectation that he would become prime minister. A critical first step, of course, was winning a seat in parliament. Before Hawke could jump from one wing of the labour movement to the other, he had to exorcise the demons of his past. It was time to atone for his sins. He needed a way to put the past behind him, and a clean slate for the future. An authorised biography would provide the catharsis he was looking for.

14

ENTER THE
BIOGRAPHER

In 1970, Bob Hawke travelled to Jakarta and stayed at the home of Australian diplomat Rawdon Dalrymple and his wife, Rossie.[1] Hawke and Dalrymple were contemporaries at Oxford University. Former journalist Blanche d'Alpuget was not that long married to Tony Pratt, who worked in intelligence at the embassy; D'Alpuget herself worked in the embassy press office. There was a lunch at the Dalrymples' house. Bob came and sat next to Blanche on a swing seat on the balcony. She was wearing a white linen dress sewn by her mother, and patent-leather platform shoes. 'You look like a movie star,' he said. He was forty; she was twenty-six. They talked about Indonesia. Later that evening, back at the ambassador's residence, they played table tennis until the early hours of the morning. They chatted later that day as they toured Jakarta, and again in the embassy swimming pool. 'He was perhaps a bit smitten with me,' D'Alpuget recalled.[2] Hawke remembered the beautiful, tanned and blonde woman years later. 'I was very taken,' he said.[3]

The following year, Hawke stopped at Jakarta on his way to Geneva for meetings at the ILO. There was a party at Blanche and Tony's place. Susan Hawke was travelling with her father, and they went along. There was a lot of drinking, music and discussion. There was an argument about the Vietnam War. Then, in a loud voice, in front of about twenty people, Hawke looked at Blanche and said: 'I want to fuck you.' Susan was almost certainly within earshot. Tony was seated next to Blanche. She recalled being 'shocked and taken aback' by the comment and, given the awkwardness of the situation, everybody 'pretended nothing had happened, and the conversation went on'.[4]

In 1976, D'Alpuget flew to Melbourne to interview Hawke for her biography of Sir Richard Kirby. 'The interview ran over the morning and then it was time to go to lunch, so we went down to the local pub and we sat there talking,' she recalled. 'By then there was a very strong sexual attraction between us. I was going back to Canberra that afternoon or evening, and as it happened so was he. We didn't say anything more than that but word-lessly it was agreed between us that we would become lovers in Canberra, and we did.'[5] The love affair – both intellectual and physical – began.

'He was charming, funny and straightforward,' D'Alpuget recalled. 'What he loved was sex. He was a busy man; I was a playmate. That suited me – I wanted a playmate too.' While both were married at the time, Hawke also had other lovers in other Australian cities, and D'Alpuget understood this. There was also Paradiso, who lived in Switzerland, whom Hawke would visit when he was attending meetings of the ILO. 'His love life was a kind of freewheeling, decentralised harem, with four or five favourites and a show-sale queue of one-night stands,' she recognised.[6]

Over the next few years, the love affair continued as they both pursued other relationships. They would meet in hotel rooms in Canberra and Sydney every few weeks. Hawke's union and politi-cal colleagues, and journalists, often saw D'Alpuget when she was ushered up to his hotel room. She would contentedly wait until their business was finished. D'Alpuget acknowledged a degree of jealousy about his other women. 'He was a philanderer,' she said. 'He was a sailor with a girl in every port, or a few of them, and it took me a little while to realise that.'[7]

In November 1978, Bob proposed to Blanche that they get married. The night before, he had a dream. It involved Blanche and Paradiso standing on a spinning roulette wheel. The ball landed on Blanche. It meant that he must choose her to marry.[8] But it was also, the dream suggested, a gamble.[9] It might explain why he seemed half-hearted about it. They were staying the night in a Canberra motel. 'He was drinking very heavily and his own marriage was really going down the tubes,' D'Alpuget recalled. In the early hours of the morning, he 'leaned his head back' against the exposed brick wall and said: 'I'd like you to marry me.' She was still married, and with a son, Louis. She would think it over. D'Alpuget decided she would leave Tony and marry Bob.

But the following year, in September 1979, Hawke changed his mind. D'Alpuget had moved out of the marital home in preparation for being with Hawke. They were speaking almost daily. Then the calls stopped. She was concerned. He eventually rang. It had been a difficult month: Ellie's death, the ACTU debate over uranium, and his wrestle with whether or not to go into parliament. Hawke told her he could not get divorced because he thought that if he became Labor leader, it would cost the party 3 per cent of the vote. He also suspected, wrongly, that he had a brain tumour. 'It just couldn't go ahead because of my emerging political career,' Hawke recalled.[10]

'I cried for three days,' D'Alpuget said. 'I thought I would commit suicide and then I pulled myself together and I thought, "No, I'll kill him." I didn't stay with that thought for very long.' Nevertheless, the relationship cooled. She decided to kill one of the lead characters in her novel *Turtle Beach* instead.[11]

Meanwhile, in the Hawke household, Hazel and the children knew that divorce was being discussed, and a marriage to Blanche. Even Clem Hawke knew what was going on; he raised it with Hazel.[12] By now Hawke had decided to seek preselection for the Melbourne seat of Wills ahead of the election due in 1980, but he was still weighing up whether to divorce Hazel and marry Blanche. Susan suggested that her father 'essentially contrived to have Mum leave him', because then it would not be 'the handicap either emotionally or morally or politically' if he had left her.[13]

It was a stressful time for everyone, with Hawke's career at a turning point, a toxic marriage and a possible divorce, and a lover whom he wanted to make his wife. Hawke was also 'extremely worried' about Susan, who was smoking marijuana, and Rosslyn, who was then injecting heroin, and he was distant from Stephen, who was living and working thousands of miles away.[14] Hawke was anxious and uncertain, and drank himself into 'a bad way', only to be rescued, as ever, by Hazel.[15]

By the late 1970s, no one was talked about as a future prime minister more than Hawke. Two other writers were engaged in writing his biography: John Hurst and Robert Pullan. D'Alpuget would be the third. Her biography of Kirby, *Mediator*, had been published in 1977. (Hawke launched it.) After initially intending to write a biography of Albert Monk, D'Alpuget had turned her focus to Hawke. There was no better way, she thought, than to deal with her grief than to 'write it out'.[16] She began working on the biography in November 1979.

Hawke's reaction, D'Alpuget recalled, was 'positive' but not 'enthusiastic'. Hawke gave his blessing to the project, sat for interviews, and encouraged others to speak to her. He wrote Blanche a handwritten letter confirming she was his 'official biographer'.[17] There was a roadblock, however, in the form of Jean Sinclair, his personal assistant, who was not a fan of the project. Sinclair was also one of Hawke's lovers. 'She knew all his secrets, she was wonderfully discreet, but she picked immediately his attraction to me and so that made organising times to meet him rather difficult,' D'Alpuget recalled. Still, Sinclair passed on details for Hawke's family, union, political and business contacts.

It was widely assumed in political, union and journalism circles that Hawke was having an affair with D'Alpuget while she was writing his biography. D'Alpuget was respected for her journalism, and fiction and non-fiction books, and to have an affair with her subject would bring the literary integrity of her work into question. For decades, D'Alpuget denied they were lovers while she was writing the biography. She did so before and after the book was published. In truth, they were lovers before, during and after she was writing the book. Interviewed for this book, D'Alpuget was asked if she was in an intimate relationship with Hawke while writing the biography. 'No,' she replied. When pushed, she said: 'Maybe.' And then: 'Yes.'[18]

In a rare confession to journalist Janet Hawley in February 1998, D'Alpuget had already conceded that she did indeed have sex with Hawke while writing his biography, but stressed that it did not mean the book lacked credibility. 'We continued to be intimate,' she said. 'Look, I was still having sex with Bob occasionally, but that does not mean the book was not also highly professional.'

D'Alpuget is stung by the allegation that some people thought she could not be an honest biographer while also being a lover.[19]

D'Alpuget began extensive research into Hawke's life. She did not think much of Hurst or Pullan, and disparaged their work in writing to those she sought interviews with.[20] She spoke to family, friends, and union and political colleagues. Some interviews were granted on background only and others insisted they must remain anonymous. The result was a well-written, well-researched and almost warts-and-all account of Hawke's public and private life.

One key person Blanche had to interview for the book was Hazel. This was, of course, an intolerable idea. Hazel knew that Bob was having an affair with Blanche. And Blanche knew that Hazel knew. Moreover, Hazel knew that Bob had thought about leaving her for Blanche. 'It wasn't easy for either of us,' D'Alpuget recalled. 'He had talked her into the fact that it would be a good idea. It would be important that she did take part.'[21]

In May 1980, D'Alpuget knocked on Hazel's door. Hazel was uneasy. 'I was not in favour of the biography,' she said. 'Although Bob had authorised the book, it had been embarked upon without my approval even though it would clearly need to refer to myself, the children and Bob's personal life.'[22] Hawke had asked his wife to agree to an interview with the woman he was having sex with, and thinking about marrying, and who was probing their private life. It was humiliating. Susan thought her father put her mother in an impossible position. Hazel's choice was to 'either cooperate or be a bitch with the biographer'.[23]

D'Alpuget remembered the mood being uneasy. Hazel made her some toast, which helped ease the tension. 'I realised that this is a very caring woman,' Blanche recalled of Hazel. 'She was sort of the opposite from me. Not that I was uncaring about people, but she was a genuine nurturer and mother. When I realised that, it made it much easier to interview her, and she became less hostile once she had shown that soft side of herself. She was very cold up until then.'[24] Blanche's notes from her interview with Hazel reveal they had an extensive discussion about almost every aspect of Bob's life, his parents, education, academic and union work, and their marriage and the children. Much of it made its way into the book.[25]

In January 1982, Bob and Hazel were provided the manuscript so they could read it and suggest corrections before publication. Hazel objected strongly to several personal references to herself and the children, and demanded they be removed. One reference involved Rosslyn, who had turned to drugs as a teenager. Another reference was to Susan and Stephen taking 'refuge in assumed names' to avoid the public spotlight.[26]

Blanche composed a letter for Hazel when the manuscript was completed for her review. 'I hope you find the book interesting and, within the bounds of respect for privacy, honest,' she wrote. 'It would have been sheer foolishness, for example, to remain silent about Bob's womanising in view of the fact that it's been discussed on national television and in the press. And, as I suggest – and believe – it's a thing of the past, something that has been lived out, and that Bob is "normal" now in that respect.' This was plainly not true.

Blanche continued, astonishingly, by asking for forgiveness:

> I hope, too, that you and I can let bygones be bygones. I've always found you an attractive character, as I've said before – and, for all I know, you may have in one part of your mind thought I was quite OK – but there was this mountain of hostility between us. Now this whole project is drawing to a conclusion I hope you will feel (as I do) that the mountain has vanished. I apologise for those letters I wrote you: I can't remember what I said but I'm sure they were silly and malevolent. I hope you will forgive me. I can't offer to forgive you: you did nothing nasty to me. So it's a bit of a bum request, I suppose. Anyway, I've tried to do a good – in numerous senses – portrait of you in the book. Perhaps you will accept that as restitution.[27]

Hawke was horrified when he read the manuscript. 'He was genuinely shaken,' D'Alpuget recalled. 'He sat down and he read it with that usual intensity he had with everything he did. He was shocked.'[28] Hawke suggested several changes, particularly sections that referred excessively to his infidelity.[29]

When *Robert J. Hawke: A Biography* was published, it was a sensation. It was launched by Sir Richard Kirby on 5 October 1982 at the Lakeside International Hotel in Canberra. The book not only chronicled Hawke's roller-coaster life story, it also detailed his angry outbursts, his extensive drinking and mentioned his womanising. Hawke's friends and family were aghast. Hawke's political colleagues thought he had killed any chance he may have had of becoming Labor leader, let alone prime minister. But they were not surprised about the revelations. 'They were appalled and embarrassed that he had cooperated in having his personality so intimately exposed,' journalist Michelle Grattan wrote at the time.[30]

The book was cathartic. His skeletons were now out of the closet. He could present himself to the Australian people as a man who had bared all. He had no secrets. Whenever questions about his moral values, his personal flaws or his marriage came up, he could simply refer them to the book. It was a brilliant strategy, and it worked. Even Hazel thought, on reflection, that she was 'glad the book was written' because voters now had 'an understanding of the man they were considering for election'.[31]

D'Alpuget's book, however, was a sanitised version of the real Hawke. It was circumspect about his infidelity. No sexual partners were named, and nor did anybody speak on the record about it. The book also argued that Hawke was, in his way, 'a faithful man, devoted to Hazel'.[32] The truth was that Bob was not faithful to Hazel. He never had been. Even as the book was being written, he was having an affair with its author. Hawke later divorced the woman who had given everything to his life and married the woman who had written the story of his life as he wanted it written.

15

THE COMING OF
THE MESSIAH

At 3.03 pm on Sunday, 23 September 1979, the boardroom at
ACTU headquarters was packed. Bob Hawke had called a
press conference. He strode into the hot, crowded room wearing
a grey suit, light blue shirt, and red and blue striped tie. It was not
his usual weekend attire. Hazel walked to the back of the room
and stood behind the sixty reporters. Hawke had a prepared statement. The journalists expected him to announce that he would
remain ACTU president.

Hawke said he was concerned about 'the condition of our
country' and wanted to use his talents to help bring Australians
together. He was committed to the Labor Party. And for those
reasons, he said, 'I will be a candidate for preselection for the seat
of Wills'. It was described by journalist Malcolm Colless as the
most important development in Australian politics since Gough
Whitlam's dismissal.[1] Hawke was the coming man.

With the 1980 election looming, Hawke resolved that it was
time to move on from the ACTU. But the decision weighed heavily
on his mind. Journalist Michael Gordon recalled watching Hawke
days earlier sitting at the red cedar table by his pool at home, writing
down the pros and cons on a notepad. On the table was Frederick
Scott Oliver's three-volume biography of British prime minister
Sir Robert Walpole, *The Endless Adventure*.[2] The first volume of
that work begins with a lengthy essay on politics, which Hawke
described as the most 'brilliant' he had ever read.[3] Oliver urged
readers to accept that politicians are people with flaws and faults,

much like themselves, and what matters most is not their 'morals' but rather their 'craftmanship'. Oliver writes: 'In taking stock of a politician, however, the first question is not whether he was a good man who used righteous means, but whether he was successful in gaining power, in keeping it, and in governing.'[4] This *realpolitik* approach to leadership and public life appealed to Hawke.

It was, he told the media, 'probably the biggest decision of my life'. He was reluctant to give up the ACTU presidency. He had status, prestige, influence and power. But Hawke was in pursuit of a greater prize: the prime ministership. Hawke's uncle Albert had missed his own opportunity to enter federal politics when John Curtin died, and asked: 'Is another Hawke going to squib it?'[5] Hawke was questioned about the Labor leadership. He insisted that Bill Hayden had his support. Hawke said he had phoned Hayden earlier that morning to inform him that he would nominate for Wills, and the leader had welcomed the news.

How had Hayden really reacted? 'Here comes bloody trouble,' he recalled. 'One of the most popular blokes in Australia. I was under no illusion there would be a lot of pressure.'[6]

In the preselection contest for the northern Melbourne seat of Wills, Hawke would be the candidate of the Centre Unity faction. He would leave almost all the canvassing to his supporters, including Bill Landeryou, who was then Labor's opposition leader in the Victorian upper house. 'I haven't spent one microsecond of my own time counting numbers,' Hawke said at the press conference. 'I understand from those who have been doing the exercise, the numbers are there for me.'[7] Bill Kelty said Hawke needed a warrior, and that was Landeryou. 'Hawke realised that what Landeryou had he did not have, and that was a good sense of organising numbers,' Kelty said. 'Landeryou was Machiavellian tough.'[8]

Hawke's eleven years as president were analysed and assessed as he prepared to vacate the ACTU.[9] He had massively expanded the profile and influence of the union movement since 1970. Hawke was always in the media, pressing union issues, and his contribution to public policy debates and dispute resolution earned him many plaudits. After a rocky start, he became a phenomenally popular figure, but he was seen by some as divisive and unnecessarily aggressive.

Hawke had fulfilled his central promise: to increase the number of union members in overall terms and as a proportion of the work-force. Union membership had increased from about 2.51 million to 2.56 million members over the decade, lifting density from 45 per cent to 50 per cent. This was a remarkable achievement, given membership had been in long-term decline. When Hawke left the ACTU, this upward trajectory was reversed, and union membership reverted to its long-term decline. Hawke succeeded in affiliating the two major unions representing white-collar employees – the Australian Council of Salaried and Professional Associations (ACSPA) in 1979 and the Council of Australian Government Employee Organisations (CAGEO) in 1981 – to the ACTU.

Hawke had also transformed the operations of the ACTU. Full-time staff increased from about seven employees to about forty. He introduced specialised departments with a focus on legal representation, policy research and advocacy, and services to members. The annual income of the ACTU increased from $162,000 in 1969 to $1 million by 1980, through a combination of increased affiliation fees and income from services and invest-ments. The Trade Union Training Authority was established by the Whitlam government.

Concerning wages and employee entitlements, however, Hawke's scorecard was mixed. While automatic quarterly wage indexation was not reinstated, the Conciliation and Arbitration Commission granted partial indexation, and many wage increases were secured through direct bargaining and negotiation. Austra-lian workers secured significant wage increases during the 1970s, but in real terms these were partly eroded by inflation. Penal sanctions were not abolished but had not been used since 1969. Hawke's promised thirty-five-hour week was not achieved for all workers, but was granted to some mining and energy workers. The principle of equal pay was delivered by the Whitlam govern-ment. Paid maternity and paternity leave was introduced by the Whitlam government, and in 1979 the ACTU secured six weeks' unpaid maternity leave for women in the private sector.

Hawke's foray into union enterprises and cooperatives did not fulfil his initial hopes. ACTU-Bourke's initially had modest success, but by 1979 it was deep in the red. The following year the store was closed. The real impact of ACTU-Bourke's was that it forced the abolition of retail price maintenance, saving consumers millions of dollars. ACTU-Jetset and ACTU-Solo were turning a profit by the time Hawke exited the ACTU. But they, like Bourke's, would not last. There was no hire-purchase company, no insurance company, no housing finance company, no consumer credit scheme. But over a ten-year period, factoring in these enterprises, free office rent and the sale of several radio stations, Bill Kelty estimated the ACTU had made a net profit of about $20 million.[10]

—

Hawke lodged his nomination for preselection for the seat of Wills at 12.35 pm on 1 October 1979.[11] The preselection took place two weeks later, on 14 October. A thirty-member panel of local members and a forty-member panel of party members from outside the electorate would select the candidate. The outside panel component was drawn by lot from a group elected by the party conference. The seat was deemed a Socialist Left stronghold, but Centre Unity worked hard to maximise Hawke's vote and the result was expected to be close.

Hawke was opposed by Gerry Hand, a former union official from Warrnambool who was then working as a party organiser in Melbourne. Hand, then thirty-six, was a rising star in the Socialist Left faction. There were two reasons why Hand contested the preselection: first, to represent Wills, where he lived, and second, to stop Hawke.[12] The Socialist Left faction despised Hawke, and its leadership pledged to do everything they could to prevent his entry into parliament. In an article in *The National Times*, the Left was asked to spell out the reason for its antipathy for Hawke. In a nutshell, a Left faction leader said, they saw Hawke as 'another Whitlam'.[13]

The candidates had an opportunity to address the preselection panel. Hawke gave a rundown of his twenty-one years of service to the industrial movement, as ACTU advocate and president, and his contribution to the party as an executive member and federal president. 'I believe the time has come when I can best put all this accumulated experience to the service of the party and the community in the federal parliamentary sphere,' he said. Hawke said he would focus on serving the electorate and play a national role in the party. He rejected claims propagated by the Left that he was a 'Labor rat' because of his cross-party dealings as ACTU president, or that he was elitist, insisting that he mixed with working men and woman about as much as anyone else.[14]

The voting took place at the Trades Hall in Melbourne. Hawke waited in a corridor with other party members while the votes were counted. Hawke had a comfortable win, but it was far from a landslide. Hawke received thirty-eight votes, Gerry Hand twenty-nine, and Ruth Reddall three. The draw for the outside panel had been critical. 'If the draw had gone bad, he would have lost,' recalled Robert Ray, who would be elected to the Senate for Victoria in 1980.[15] Hawke was now the endorsed Labor candidate for Wills. 'It is a fairly good win given the circumstances,' he said after the result was announced. Hand had hoped for a closer result, but congratulated Hawke. Hayden also welcomed the result and said Hawke would be minister for industrial relations in a Hayden Labor government.[16]

Mimi Tamburrino worked on Hawke's campaign for Wills, and later on his electorate staff. 'The constituency was overwhelmed with Hawke as the candidate,' she recalled. 'They absolutely adored him. It was almost like the Messiah had arrived. Everywhere he went, people came up to him. He thrived on it. He would hug people, he would kiss the ladies, particularly when we went to different ethnic groups, and they just loved him. There was a magnetism that drew people to him. He did not come across as arrogant. He spoke to people as if they were his mum or dad, a relative or a friend. It was amazing.'[17]

In the 1970s, Hawke's popularity rested with the public rather than the party. While he was devoted to Labor, it riled many that his principal mission in public life was consensus, which denotes compromise, rather than winning for the Labor side. He was willing to work with business to secure better outcomes for workers. He was willing to meet with Malcolm Fraser to talk about policy issues. He spoke about forming cabinets with talent drawn from all sections of the community. He spoke about wanting more bipartisanship. Hawke was never into tribalism, the politics of envy or class warfare.

Hawke had trusted, reliable colleagues in the unions and the party, supporters and backers, but no real friends. The people he really called his friends were business leaders such as Isi Leibler, Roderick Carnegie and Eddie Kornhauser. Hawke was especially close to Peter Abeles, and he regarded George Rockey as like a father. Jockey Roy Higgins and Col Cunningham, a businessman, were also reliable friends. Cunningham was pro-Labor but Higgins was not. These were the men he could rely on. Hawke drank with them. He went to the football, cricket and races with them. He played snooker and tennis with them. They came to his home and he went to theirs. Hawke's business mates were also his patrons and financial guarantors. These corporate links led some in the party to question the strength of his fidelity to the Labor cause.

Gareth Evans was friendly with Hawke in the 1970s, and an occasional visitor to Sandringham. 'He was blokey, larrikinish, tight as a duck's arse – short arms and deep pockets – but everybody wanted a piece of him, his star was ascendant,' Evans recalled. 'Bob was never a bloke you went out to dinner with, because he just saw food as fuel. He was utterly uninterested in the normal association you develop with someone over time which involves going out to dinner and chatting over things. His interests were having a beer, sex, sport, gambling, making a buck. Bob had no interest in history, art, literature.'[18]

Hawke's business friends – especially Abeles and Rockey – provided him with financial support. They paid his hotel bills, picked up the tab at the Boulevard Hotel – Hawke usually occupied the Lady Nelson suite, which had entrances onto different corridors – provided him with chauffeur-driven cars, and plied him with drinks, cigars and women. Some hotels let Hawke stay for free. Hawke relied on Abeles to employ several former girlfriends at his transportation company, TNT. Abeles also paid Hawke's mortgage and his children's private school fees.[19] There was speculation that Melbourne's Jewish community had established a fund for Hawke to ensure that he had whatever he needed to make the transition into parliament. It was referred to as a political 'nest-egg'. He could use it for travel, accommodation and meeting policy experts.[20] Abeles also bailed Hawke out of several gambling debts over the years.[21]

Hawke simply could not afford the lifestyle he was leading in the 1970s without other sources of income. He never made much money out of gambling and was sometimes in debt to book-makers. One means he found of supplementing his income in the 1960s and 1970s was suing newspapers for defamation. Hawke was accused of being a communist, of taking bribes from Zionists, of using foul language in public, of doing deals for a seat in parliament and of wanting to use nuclear weapons against Arab states. He usually relied on Peter Redlich to handle his libel cases. By one rough estimate, Hawke won over $100,000 in damages between 1970 and 1980.[22] (This would equate to around $500,000 in 2021.)

In the mid to late 1970s, Abeles urged Hawke to leave Labor and establish a new political party under his own leadership. In a meeting with the US Department of Labor attaché Edward Labatt on 12 November 1974 in Melbourne, Hawke mentioned Abeles and the new party. '[Abeles] has recently sounded out Hawke's availability for a leadership position in such a new political unit. Hawke reported this flatly to Labatt without indicating whether or not he favoured such an idea,' said a cable sent to Washington, DC.[23] Abeles raised it again when Hawke was considering running for preselection for Wills. He urged Hawke not to run, and said he would bankroll a new party with $250,000.[24]

Hawke also had good relations with Rupert Murdoch and Kerry Packer, Australia's two leading media moguls at the time. In an interview with *The Bulletin* in December 1979, Murdoch said Hayden was 'a very nice man' but also 'a very weak man'. Asked by Trevor Kennedy who should be leading Labor, Murdoch said: 'Neville Wran or Bob Hawke would make a very good success of leading the Labor Party. Obviously Neville Wran would, Bob Hawke probably would.'[25]

But many still doubted that Hawke could make a successful transition into politics. His success at the ACTU did not guar-antee success in parliament. Hawke's Boyer lectures had been criticised as lacking intellectual depth or practical application. But his pathway to the prime ministership was never about policy: it was about his personality, character and style. Hawke was seen as authentic, unscripted and honest about his virtues and his flaws. He was involved in the pursuit of power and the promulgation of grand ideas, but he was also at home at the pub or the footy or the cricket. Although many thought he was a magnetic leader, some saw him as polarising. Indeed, Hawke was a paradox: a larrikin and a scholar, a healer and a divider, a drinker with a foul tongue who aspired to unify the nation, a womaniser and a husband and father.

Hawke was so ill-disciplined in his personal life and so emotionally volatile that journalists frequently predicted he would never successfully transition into politics. Hawke's 'self-destruct syndrome' was frequently on display. Yet he always recovered, and another wave of 'when will Hawke go to Canberra?' stories would roll around. But many journalists who saw Hawke up close in the 1970s just did not think he would make it. 'I didn't think he would be prime minister,' Laurie Oakes said. 'His lack of self-control ruled it out.'[26] Michelle Grattan agreed. 'The conventional view was that Hawke's womanising and drinking was a limitation on his ambitions,' she said.[27] Paul Kelly was of the same view. 'He couldn't succeed in the parliament or as Labor leader carrying on the way he carried on that night at the Gateway Inn,' Kelly said.[28]

Hawke knew he had to change. He moderated, though did not cease, his infidelities. He became more careful in his public language. In May 1980, he told *Playboy*, rather ironically, that he had developed more respect for women. 'We don't treat women as equal human beings, and I hope I have become more conscious about that,' he said.[29] That same month, he decided to give up alcohol. He was on his way to Geneva to attend his last meeting of the ILO. He became a teetotaller, and mineral water became his new staple. Hawke was reluctant to give up drinking, but once he had decided, he did so and never relapsed. He had an iron will. 'I had done many silly things when I'd had too much to drink, and I simply couldn't afford as prime minister to disgrace my country, so I gave it up completely,' Hawke recalled.[30] His discipline and repentance increased his popularity. It would also have made his mother proud.

With Hawke on his way into parliament, the future leadership of the party began exercising the minds of powerbrokers. Barrie Unsworth, the secretary of the NSW Labor Council, thought Hawke should meet Paul Keating. 'I see Hawkey is going to be our future minister for industrial relations,' Unsworth recalled.

'Keating, of course, is our man in Canberra, and I just thought they should be working together. Keating obviously saw Hawke as a potential threat to his leadership ambitions. But I still thought that they had common interests they should discuss.'[31]

Keating had been eyeing Hawke for some time. 'I was never attracted to Bob in his more swashbuckling days as the beer-swilling, girl-chasing ACTU president,' he said.[32] He saw Hawke as a rival who wanted to be leader but had not toiled away, as Keating had, in the long dog years of opposition and through the travails of government. Keating was opposed to Hawke becoming leader.

Keating enlisted his friend Bob Carr of *The Bulletin*. Keating told Carr he had a duty to 'expose' Hawke and reveal him to be 'a charlatan'.[33] In April 1978, Carr wrote an article surveying Hawke's time as ACTU president. The article was headlined: 'Is Hawke finished?'[34] In June 1979, Carr cast doubt on Hawke's preselection chances in Wills and argued that even if he was elected to parliament, Lionel Bowen was 'most likely' to succeed Hayden as leader if Labor did not win the next election.[35] In January 1980, Carr speculated that if Hawke was elected to parliament, he could find himself 'a raging failure of Australian politics'. If Hayden resigned, Carr suggested, Hawke would be 'overwhelmingly' defeated by Bowen or Keating in a leadership contest.[36] Many years later, Carr felt 'ashamed' of these articles.[37]

Hawke already had good relations with Labor's New South Wales Right faction. He knew Unsworth, and was close to John Ducker and Graham Richardson. He understood that the faction would be important in any future leadership contest. On 21 September 1979, Keating had been elected president of New South Wales Labor at an administrative committee meeting, succeeding Ducker in the role. Keating had long been regarded as a rising star. Journalist Neil O'Reilly profiled Keating when he became state president, and marked him out as a future prime minister.[38]

In September 1979, before the Wills preselection, Hawke phoned Keating twice. He wanted to talk about the leadership of the Labor Party. Hawke told Keating they should work together. He suggested a 'Hawke–Keating leadership ticket' at some time in the future.[39] Hawke's message was twofold: he made it clear that he wanted to lead the party and that Keating would be the junior partner. Keating was not impressed and made it plain that any support for a future tilt for leader would depend on how he performed. 'Bob,' he said, 'you can't ask me for automatic support.'[40]

In early 1980, encouraged by Unsworth, Hawke met Keating twice in Sydney to talk about the leadership. Hawke was eager; Keating was not. 'I didn't want to meet Hawke,' he recalled. 'I had not known him industrially. I didn't like him much. He was always abusing people when drunk. I regarded him as, basically, an empty-headed pisspot.'[41] Nevertheless, they met first at the Hyatt Hotel, in Kings Cross. But the pivotal meeting took place in Hawke's suite at the Boulevard Hotel, on William Street.

At this meeting, Hawke outlined his intention to become leader and stay for two terms in government, then defer to Keating. 'I made no secret of my hope to lead the party, and at some point in our discussion observed that in about two terms as prime minister we should have gone a long way in laying the basis for the reforms we sought to achieve,' Hawke recalled. 'I was outlining a loose chronology against which Paul could measure his own leadership aspirations.'[42] Hawke saw this as a goodwill gesture, not a firm agreement with a specific timetable.

Keating saw it differently. 'Bob said that Hayden's got no chance of beating Fraser and that only he could,' Keating recalled. 'He needed the support of the New South Wales Labor Party, of which I was the president, and in the event that I supported him and he became leader, he would only want to stay a couple of terms and then he would defer to me.' Keating did not give Hawke a commitment but took the conversation as an 'understanding' regarding the future leadership of the party.[43] He was not willing to give up on Hayden that easily and surrender his own ambitions to Hawke. Keating gave Hawke his own message: 'The first Labor leader I tear down will be the one I replace.'[44]

Malcolm Fraser announced an election for 18 October 1980. Hayden appointed Hawke to Labor's front bench as spokesperson on industrial relations, employment and youth affairs on 17 September.[45] Hawke formally finished up as ACTU president on 30 September, having given notice in writing a month before.[46] He had organised support for Cliff Dolan to succeed him.

Now Hawke threw himself into the election campaign and the next phase of his life.

Hawke and Neville Wran featured alongside Hayden in Labor's election advertising. Wran, the New South Wales premier, had recently succeeded Neil Batt as the party's national president. This so-called 'troika' was aimed at bolstering Hayden's leadership. Some thought it might raise doubts about Hayden's capacity to be prime minister, but David Combe, Labor's campaign director, thought this 'team' approach enhanced Hayden because he could demonstrate the quality of people around him. Moreover, Combe argued, keeping Wran and Hawke 'in the shadows' would have invited 'more troublesome speculation on Bill Hayden's confidence and security'.[47]

Defeat for Labor would open the way for Hawke to become leader in the next term, while a Hayden victory would put Hawke's ambitions on ice. His future would then depend on how Hayden and his government performed. There was also no guarantee that Hawke would be Hayden's successor. After a few terms in government, it would be impossible to predict who might emerge as a potential leader: Lionel Bowen, Mick Young and Paul Keating, for instance, could all be in the mix.

Hayden launched Labor's campaign in Brisbane on 1 October. He promised to 'bring Australians together' and 'unite our country' with policies that restored equality of opportunity and renewed national pride. Hawke campaigned with Labor candidates around Australia. He also had to campaign in Wills. Mostly this involved walks down busy Bell Street and Sydney Road in Coburg, and visiting community, business and sporting groups. Hawke loved the multicultural vibrancy of Wills, where migrants from Greece, Italy, Lebanon and Turkey had settled. The suburbs came alive on weekends with markets, singing and dancing. As Hawke toured the electorate, women would thrust their children into his arms and steal a kiss for themselves, while men shook his hand and patted him on the shoulder. 'G'day, how are ya?' he would say.[48]

Hayden fought the election campaign valiantly. He had to spend a lot of time trying to convince voters that, contrary to media reporting, Labor had a realistic chance of winning. It was only in the final weeks that 'the possibility was given any credence', Labor's election campaign report later found.[49] But Labor MPs thought any hope of regaining government slipped away in the final week, when frontbencher Peter Walsh said during a television interview that Labor might introduce a capital-gains tax. Fraser seized on the remark to reinforce doubts about Labor's economic credentials – the key issue that Hayden had tried to neutralise over the previous three years. Both Hawke and Keating thought Walsh's blunder cost Labor the election.[50]

On the eve of the election, Hayden sent Hawke a telegram. 'My sincere thanks for your hard work and support throughout the campaign,' he said. 'We are going to win . . . I look forward to working with you in the Hayden Labor government.'[51] But the Fraser government was returned to office for a third term with a reduced majority of seats. Labor gained thirteen seats and lifted its primary vote to 45.15 per cent. The two-party result saw Labor with 49.6 per cent of the vote to the Coalition's 50.4 per cent. In Wills, Hawke lifted Labor's primary vote to 65.1 per cent, a swing of 7.5 per cent, and he gained 69.9 per cent of the two-party vote. Hawke was finally a member of parliament.

Mimi Tamburrino managed Hawke's electorate office in Coburg, while Jean Sinclair focused on shadow ministerial duties and headed up his Parliament House office. When he was not interstate or overseas, Hawke worked from the office from Mondays to Thursdays. He continued to live at Sandringham and would drive his Mercedes to the office. He was not a very good driver – Tamburrino and Sinclair held their breath every morning hoping he arrived safely. Hawke focused on seeing constituents, responding to mail, talking to the local media and attending functions. He also used his negotiating skills to help settle disputes between local employees and employers. 'They would come to our office and he would not let them leave until a deal was sorted out,' Tamburrino recalled.[52]

Hawke was elected with a singular purpose: to become prime minister. He would have to defeat two others to get there: Bill Hayden and Malcolm Fraser. This was the task he set himself over the next three years. Hawke's political rise seems inevitable in hindsight, but at the time it was anything but. There was suspicion and hostility towards him from within his own party. He had arrived in Canberra like no other person before him with a claim on the prime ministership. Perhaps Robert Menzies (1934), H.V. 'Doc' Evatt (1940) or Garfield Barwick (1958) could be said to have been eyeing, perhaps even expecting, the top job. But none of them matched Hawke's arrival in 1980.[53]

—

The new decade witnessed a new Bob Hawke and a new chapter in his life. Hawke in the 1980s looked very different to the Hawke in the 1960s and 1970s. Partly this was due to changing fashions, but Hawke made a concerted effort to look more – as he saw it – prime ministerial. A new look would be phased in: he cut his salt-and-pepper hair shorter, he trimmed his sideburns, he gave up glasses for contact lenses, he swapped his suede shoes for leather, and he wore only tailored suits. He no longer drank alcohol and he tried to smoke cigars only in private. He allowed himself fewer displays of temper with journalists. And any womanising was done behind closed doors.

Hawke found the transition from the ACTU to the opposition benches difficult. 'It was a bit of a comedown in status,' he reflected.[54] He attended his first caucus meeting on 7 November 1980. It was anything but a rock star's welcome. He was introduced as the new Labor MP for Wills, along with a host of other new members in the opposition party room. In the elections for the front bench, Hawke polled twelfth out of eighteen. He was being sent a message: the new boy would have to earn his stripes. Hawke was formally appointed as the shadow minister for industrial relations.

Hawke was allocated a small corner office on the first floor of Parliament House. Sinclair was joined by David McKenzie, an economist, to help with shadow ministerial responsibilities. Hawke wanted Bill Kelty to join his staff, but he had dedicated his life to the union movement. Hawke never liked the cramped working conditions in Parliament House, which was designed as a temporary building, but had been extended and renovated several times. Although he was a social animal, he could not down beers in the Non-Members' Bar like other MPs, staffers and journalists.

In anticipation of his election to parliament, he had purchased a two-bedroom townhouse in Kingston for $50,000.

At 8.53 pm on Wednesday, 26 November 1980, Hawke gave his maiden speech to parliament. (It was not, however, the first time he spoke in parliament: he had asked Fraser a question about wages the day before.) He began with a joke to the deputy speaker, noting that he was 'one of the tardier maidens'. He paid tribute to his predecessor in Wills, Gordon Bryant, and then thanked the union movement:

> The only societies where one does not have such movements with the right of men and women freely associated together to withdraw their labour are the dictatorships of the Left or the Right. That movement in Australia has been extremely generous to me in providing unique opportunities to develop whatever intrinsic talents I may possess. I place on record my appreciation for being given those opportunities.

He thanked the people of Wills for sending him there, acknowledged his shadow ministerial predecessor, Mick Young, and pledged both to oppose the government when its decisions went against the best interests of the Australian people, and to propose positive and constructive policy alternatives. This was how he saw the role of opposition: to oppose and propose. The more interesting part of Hawke's speech was his criticism of the government's policies which had set Australian against Australian, left people behind and failed to address the pressing problems facing the nation:

> As we have moved into the 1980s under this government, we have moved inexorably towards that destabilised and dangerous position described by Disraeli as 'two nations', the nation of the privileged and the nation of the poor. There can be room for legitimate argument between competing policies when the country is confronted with times of economic difficulties. But there can be no room for the attitude of this government and its leader who have accepted with complacency this increasing division in our society and indeed have done so much to foster divisiveness.

He warned that, 'in these tortured times of compounding economic complexity', there was a danger that some might turn to 'the insidious forces of the extremes of the Left and of the Right' for solutions. They provided only false hope. The remedy, he said, was to come together as a nation to better understand and respond to the challenges facing the country. It was a call for consensus and unifying leadership:

> Our tragedy is not that we, as Australians, do not have the capacity to meet this challenge; it is that we have a prime minister and a government whose natural instincts are not for cohesion but confrontation, not for truthful exposition to serve as a basis for mutual understanding but for partisan propaganda calculated to set Australian against and apart from Australian. We on this side of the House do not feel ourselves powerless in the face of that tragedy. We will, from this day, work to provide Australia with an alternative government.[55]

It was a fine first speech.

While Hawke was a competent speaker and debater, he never fully adjusted to speaking in the House of Representatives. He was used to delivering speeches in town halls, at union conferences or outdoors to workers. His style of debate had been honed before the Conciliation and Arbitration Commission. There he could speak for days on end, shaping and sharpening his argument, in an effort to convince the bench. Parliament was totally different. 'One of the reasons why people hold parliament and parliamentarians in contempt is the actual process of parliament itself is a total charade,' Hawke said. 'I never enjoyed parliament myself. I was used to appearing in full courts and commissions where the quality of the argument won the decision or lost it. Here, whichever side is in power, the decisions have been made beforehand in the government party room.'[56]

Hawke surprised his colleagues when, on 29 October 1981, he broke down and cried in parliament. During a debate over Australian participation in a Sinai peacekeeping force, the Liberal MP for Phillip, Jack Birney, accused Hawke of betraying Israel. Shaken, Hawke fled from the chamber in tears. He had been explaining why he supported Labor's opposition to Australia taking part in the force. Hawke later spoke to the media, saying the attack cut him to the core. 'After I had done the best I could for the country, all I get are claims that I sold them out,' he said. It was 'politics at its lowest level'. Hawke may have won some public sympathy, but in the hard world of politics many doubted if he could handle the rough and tumble of parliament.[57]

As shadow minister, Hawke focused on attacking the Fraser government over its confrontational approach to industrial relations. He regularly put questions to Fraser and his ministers for industrial relations, Ian Viner and Ian Macphee, and participated in debates on legislation and matters of public performance. None of this, however, made Hawke stand out in parliament. He strongly disliked Viner, and claimed credit for his being moved to the lesser portfolio of defence support after a year in the job.

With Ralph Willis and Paul Keating, Hawke prepared a discussion paper that examined the resources boom. The paper reads like a bridge between the old economy and the new economy yet to come. Their recommendations included 'maximisation of Australian ownership' of the minerals and energy industry, monitoring of 'pricing practices', a new approach to export controls, the abolition of 'excessive' tax concessions, and a new tax on super profits of mining ventures to be called 'a resource rent tax'.[58]

But Hawke's focus was becoming prime minister. There would be no apprenticeship. If there was a leadership queue, he believed he belonged at the front. 'He was thinking all the time about what he would be doing as prime minister and he was totally devoted to that end,' recalled Kim Beazley, who was also elected to parliament in 1980.[59]

Hawke soon began stalking Hayden's leadership in earnest. He did little to discourage media speculation that he wanted to be leader. Indeed, Hawke himself said it again and again. On 21 April 1981, for example, the front page of Sydney's *The Daily Mirror* bore the headline 'Hawke: Why I'd like to be PM'. Hawke outlined his ambition and 'how he would work for a better Australia' over two pages inside. He spoke about economic recovery, unemployment, poverty reduction and filling cabinet positions with 'talent' from outside parliament. Part two of the interview with Hawke ran the following day, with further ruminations on policy and politics.[60]

Hawke's principal tool in his crusade to become leader was the polls. At almost any opportunity, with colleagues or journalists, he would mention the polls. He was always preferred as Labor leader over Hayden. In May 1981, a poll showed Hawke had the support of 61 per cent as leader, compared to 31 per cent for Hayden.[61] In April 1982, a poll showed Hawke leading Hayden by 56 per cent to 28 per cent. Among Labor voters, Hawke was preferred by 62 per cent to 27 per cent for Hayden. It was clear that Labor was more likely to win the next election with Hawke as leader.[62]

More lethal was Labor's internal research, carried out by Labor's pollster, Rod Cameron, who judged that Hawke should be leader. Hayden was viewed as smart, competent, decent, honest and modest. He had rebuilt Labor's economic credibility. But he was also seen as uncharismatic, awkward, weak, wishy-washy and a whinger.[63] It was not surprising that Fraser had a leadership edge as preferred prime minister. Cameron sent these reports to Hawke. Graham Richardson, a member of Labor's National Campaign Committee, leaked Cameron's polling to the media.

In a display of audacity, Hawke even made the case directly to Hayden that he should vacate the leadership. One night in late 1981, Hawke strolled around to Hayden's office in Parliament House. He relaxed into a lounge chair and whipped a poll out of his suit jacket pocket, then argued it was indisputable evidence that Hayden should 'stand down' from the leadership. Hayden promptly told Hawke to 'go and get stuffed'.[64]

Cameron and Margaret Gibbs, who ran focus groups for the party, often had to brief Hayden on the bad news. 'I had several very unpleasant sessions with Hayden, and he did not take it well,' Cameron recalled. Hayden dismissed Gibbs' focus groups as 'seance sessions'.[65] Gibbs said voters were hopeful about a Hawke-led Labor Party. 'He was always seen as a great potential leader as soon as he was in the parliament because voters thought he was genuine, authentic and strong,' she said. 'He was not seen as a politician.'[66] Cameron and Gibbs assessed that a Hayden-led Labor Party was in a 'potentially' winning position, but it was not a firm position.[67]

Bob McMullan, the party's national secretary, was in a difficult spot. 'I had two competing obligations,' he explained. 'One was to continue to support the existing leader, which I did to the best of my ability. The other was to maximise the party's chances of getting elected, which meant that we needed to change to Bob, and I made it as clear as I could that this was my view.' Hayden knew McMullan supported a change of leader.[68]

Still, not all Hawke's parliamentary colleagues were persuaded that his talents outweighed his failings. On 28 July 1981, Hawke attended a party fundraiser with 600 guests at the Southern Cross Hotel in Melbourne. A focus of the evening was telling jokes. The line-up also included Clyde Holding, David Combe, Ros Kelly, John Button, Joan Child, Bill Hayden, Lionel Bowen, Tom Uren, Margaret and Gough Whitlam, Mick Young and Barry Cohen. The jokes were not very funny. Several were tinged with racism, but Hawke took it to another level. He began, in an Indian accent, explaining that an adviser to Indian Prime Minister Indira Gandhi had come up with the idea of a 'national lottery' with 'three mystery prizes' to revive her government's fortunes:

> Tens of millions of people bought tickets. When the day came to draw the monster Indian national lottery, the host, Mr Mukagee, was surrounded by tens of thousands of people in the stadium and millions more in the surrounding mountains.
>
> And when he called out the winner of the 'turd prize', way out into the distance this little man came rushing up, thrusting his hand into his dirty little dhoti to pull out the winning ticket. He won a first-class ticket around the world on glorious Air India, with the free food and the free drink and the unlimited spending money.
>
> Then the winner of the second prize came running up. He won a fruit cake. The man shouted at Mr Mukagee: 'But the third prize was an around the world ticket on glorious Air India, with the free food and the free drink and the unlimited spending money. And second prize is a fruit cake?' But, Mr Mukagee said, 'It's not just any fruit cake. It's a fruit cake baked by our glorious Prime Minister, Mrs Gandhi.' And the little man said, 'Fuck Mrs Gandhi.'
>
> And Mr Mukagee said, 'Oh, no, no, no, you'll be wanting the first prize!'

There was laughter mixed with groans. It was a terrible joke. Despite the huge audience, the joke did not make it into the media. A tape, however, began circulating in party, union and journalism circles. It was not until many weeks later, on 3 September, that Niki Savva reported Hawke's joke in *The Sun News-Pictorial*. Savva's source was Alan Ramsey, Hayden's press secretary and a virulent Hawke hater.[69] But the joke was censored by Savva's editors. Hawke apologised on ABC Radio, acknowledging it was in bad taste, but insisted he was not racist. Days later, Brian Toohey revealed Hawke's joke in more detail in *The National Times*.[70]

The joke led many to question Hawke's suitability for leadership. It fuelled the lingering doubts about Hawke. He had not adjusted well to a parliamentary career. In his first year in parliament, he was a shrunken figure. Labor MPs, party and union officials, and journalists often questioned whether Hawke had what it took to become leader. When he would tell people that he wanted to be leader, and would be leader, many were not convinced he could achieve his ambition.

Moreover, Hawke was not the only leadership alternative to Hayden. Neville Wran, the popular New South Wales premier who had led the party to a one-seat majority victory in May 1976, followed by two 'Wranslides' in October 1978 and September 1981, was considering a move into federal politics. He had a stylish intellectual larrikinism and a shrewd understanding of politics and power. Wran could have presented a serious threat not only to Hayden but to the ambitions of both Hawke and Keating. In 1980 the New South Wales Right faction leaders approached Dick Klugman (Prospect) and John Armitage (Chifley) to vacate their seats for Wran, both in Western Sydney, but neither would stand aside. When Billy McMahon retired in January 1982, Wran considered running in Lowe, but Michael Maher was preselected and Labor won the seat from the Liberals.

Wran eyed Hawke cautiously. 'There was not a real friendship,' recalled Wran's press secretary, Brian Dale. 'Competitors more likely, as in the years prior to 1983, Neville and Bob both had their eyes on the same prize. The chips didn't fall Neville's way.'[71] Denise Darlow, Wran's principal private secretary, recalled that Wran and Hawke did not speak often. 'Wran was not in awe of

Hawke,' she said. 'Wran did not see Hawke as an impediment to any (fleeting) federal ambition he may have had.'[72]

Stephen Loosley, who was New South Wales Labor's assistant secretary at the time, said the New South Wales Right faction had 'three important players on the chessboard' in this period: Wran, Keating and Hawke.[73] Another option for Wran was the Senate, and becoming attorney-general in the next Labor government. He liked the idea, but after his voice was damaged in a throat operation, it lost its appeal. On 4 August 1982, Wran put the speculation to bed. He drank half a bottle of Rosemount Estate Gold Medal Chardonnay and announced he would stay in New South Wales politics and lead his government at the next election.

—

In June 1980, Hawke had spent two weeks in Washington, DC, meeting union and political figures. During these discussions, Hawke told them that he expected Labor to lose the next election. Hawke also said that he would replace Hayden and lead the party to victory, with Keating as his deputy, in 1983.[74] The US State Department officials were stunned by his frankness. The talks leaked and Hawke was forced into an embarrassing (and untruthful) denial.[75]

In Washington, Hawke was accompanied at some official meetings by the Australian embassy's first secretary, Graham Evans. Hawke was impressed by Evans and during the week pulled him aside for a confidential discussion. Hawke said he had 'higher ambitions' and asked Evans if he would like to be 'associated' with him if that were to happen. 'At that stage it was a completely hypothetical issue,' Evans recalled.[76]

A year later, Evans was studying at Johns Hopkins School of Advanced International Studies in Washington. 'I am still very much interested in the matter we discussed when you were in Washington,' he wrote to Hawke on 28 June 1981.[77] Hawke replied, confirming their understanding, and said that he expected a leadership spill to happen by the middle of 1982. Hawke said some MPs felt he 'had a significantly better chance of getting Labor into office' than Hayden. 'The calculations seem to show that in the event of a spill I would have the numbers but getting the spill is a different question.' He wanted to make sure Evans would be ready to join his staff when he became leader.[78]

Evans transferred from the Department of Foreign Affairs to Treasury in early 1982. Hawke and Evans met again face-to-face in September 1982. At this meeting, Hawke specifically mentioned the principal private secretary role. To help quell concerns among some Labor MPs about Hawke's lack of ministerial experience, he wanted to be able to reassure them that he would appoint a middle-ranking public servant with experience in economic and foreign policy to head his prime ministerial office. Hawke did not want to repeat the mistakes of the Whitlam government. 'Hawke felt that relations with the public service under Whitlam were not good and had been an obstacle to pressing ahead with the policies and the programs they wanted,' Evans explained.[79]

Hawke was assembling a prime ministerial staff. He also approached Geoff Walsh, a former journalist who was then Labor's communications director. 'I intend to challenge, and when I succeed, I would like you to become my press officer,' he told Walsh in April or May 1982. Walsh replied: 'If that came to pass, that would be a terrific thing to do.' An understanding has been reached.[80]

In mid-1982, Hawke met with Bob Hogg at Peter Redlich's home in Melbourne. Hawke asked Hogg if he would join his staff if he became leader. Hogg did not agree then, but Hawke kept him in mind. Hawke also asked: 'What has the Left got against me?' Hogg said they were concerned that he surrounded himself with 'fuckwits' like Bill Landeryou inside the party and 'spivs' like Peter Abeles outside the party.[81]

During 1982, Peter Barron was also sounded out about joining Hawke's staff if he became leader but only for the duration of an election campaign. Barron, a former tabloid journalist, was then on the staff of Neville Wran. It was understood that Barron would be 'borrowed' by Hawke.[82]

There was another person Hawke expected to join his staff: Graham Freudenberg. This conversation occurred many years before. They were part of a group celebrating Labor's 1972 election victory at the Four Seas restaurant in Sydney. Amid the revelry, Freudenberg proclaimed: 'Bob, one day you will be prime minister and I will be your speechwriter.' Another understanding had been reached.[83]

—

With Hawke now in federal parliament, Hazel was going in her new direction. She began volunteering for the Brotherhood of St Laurence, initially working at the Family Centre for Low Income People and later at the head office, which became full-time work. She had completed a night-school course in English, and another on politics through the Council for Adult Education. In 1980, Hazel began a two-year full-time course of study for a Diploma of Welfare Studies.

Bob and Hazel wanted Stephen to go to university, but it was not for him. In 1977, he escaped to Tasmania with friends. He lived in a shepherd's hut in the bush and worked on conservation issues. Hazel and Bob visited him that year. Stephen then worked in Darwin as a journalist for *Nation Review*. He wrote under the name of Steve Masterson. 'I just didn't want to be known as Bob Hawke's son,' he explained. 'I wanted to be my own person. It didn't last very long. I became known as Steve – wink, wink – Masterson.'

By November 1978, Stephen was living and working among the Noonkanbah Indigenous community in the Kimberley, Western Australia. He was supporting their struggle to protect their land from mining. 'I was completely and utterly absorbed in the work,' he recalled. The Noonkanbah dispute was a turning point in the push for land rights. They won the support of unions in Western Australia, who placed a ban on drilling, and Stephen engaged his father. 'It was his last big thing at the ACTU,' Stephen recalled. 'He went into parliament within a week or two of that dispute coming to a head.'[84]

Rosslyn had left school at age fifteen, which troubled her parents, and lived in several communes with friends in New South Wales and Queensland. 'I worried a great deal about her,' Hazel recalled.[85] In these years, Rosslyn became addicted to heroin. It had taken a toll 'physically and psychologically', D'Alpuget recalled. 'Bob had gone with Peter Abeles around the squats in Kings Cross and finally found her sitting with a group of naked hippies and loaded her into Abeles' Rolls-Royce, and had her cleaned up and brought her home.' Hawke mistakenly believed that Rosslyn had overcome her addiction by the late 1970s.[86]

Rosslyn claimed that in 1983 she was sexually assaulted by Bill Landeryou, then a Victorian government minister. Landeryou was a close friend and union and political ally of Hawke's, and she was then working on Landeryou's staff. She feared that Landeryou had made her pregnant. Rosslyn said that when she told her father, he responded by urging her not to go to the police because he was 'challenging for the leadership of the Labor Party' and it would be too controversial. This allegation was made as part of a $4.2 million legal claim against Hawke's estate in December 2019. The affidavit, filed with the NSW Supreme Court, sought $2.5 million for a property in Sydney's eastern suburbs along with funeral costs, dental implants, kitchen and bathroom items, a computer, sewing machine, furniture and clothing.

These allegations are damaging for Hawke. They cannot be proven or disproven. Rosslyn, who struggled with drug and alcohol addiction, and continues to suffer chronic health problems along with depression and anxiety, has lived a tragic life. These accusations were made after her father and Landeryou had died. They cannot respond. Several of the claims in the affidavit do not add up: Landeryou never lived in the suburb of Sunshine, Hawke challenged for the leadership in 1982 not 1983 and Rosslyn was already pregnant with her son David by the time she joined Landeryou's staff in 1983. Nevertheless, Susan said she was aware of the allegation at the time and the family provided support to her sister. Hawke was not close to Landeryou after he became Labor leader. His former colleagues believe they had a falling out. The sexual assault may be the reason. Taking legal action at the time may have compounded Rosslyn's pain, something Bob and Hazel would not have wanted. But, in doing so, she claims her father covered up a crime for political advantage. Rosslyn does not allege that her father did not believe her. 'She did tell people at the time,' Susan said. 'I believe there was a supportive response, but it didn't involve using the legal system.'[87]

———

Bill Hayden had done much to change the Labor Party and position it to regain government. He was respected for his time as a minister in the Whitlam government, when he had established

Medibank and helped restore a degree of economic credibility in the Treasury portfolio. He had recruited new candidates, remade the front bench, reformed the party to be more democratic and accountable, and overhauled the party's policies and philosophy. This had paid off with a close result at the 1980 election. But Hayden remained suspicious of his colleagues. He was guarded, cautious and never fully trusting. He lacked self-confidence. As the next election neared, many in the party were questioning whether he should remain leader.

A key issue was Hayden's ability to articulate Labor policy. He often lacked cut-through with voters. On 9 June 1982, Hayden fumbled an explanation of Labor's policy on a nuclear-free South Pacific by suggesting American ships would not be able to dock at Australian ports. This was untenable for the United States. Lionel Bowen, the deputy leader and shadow foreign minister, had to correct Hayden. Malcolm Fraser pounced, arguing that a Hayden-led Labor government would mean the end of the ANZUS alliance. A fortnight later, after concerns were raised by visiting US government officials, Hayden acknowledged he had mangled Labor's policy. On 25 June, Hawke visited New South Wales Labor secretary Graham Richardson in his Sussex Street office and told him it was time to challenge Hayden's leadership, and he wanted the New South Wales Right faction with him.[88]

Hawke had been preparing to strike at Hayden's leadership. 'There were three or four meetings to plan the leadership challenge,' revealed Robert Ray, who had joined the caucus in 1981. 'The people involved included Mick Young, Kim Beazley, Bill Landeryou, Clyde Holding, Simon Crean, Ralph Willis, myself and probably a few others. We discussed when would be the best time to challenge.' The calculation was simple: Hayden was a 'possibility' of leading Labor to victory but Hawke was a 'certainty'.[89]

Hayden's stumble over US ships came just weeks before Labor's national conference at the Lakeside Hotel in Canberra, which opened on 5 July 1982. Prior to the conference, Hayden signalled a plan to shift Labor's policy on uranium. He proposed that a Labor government would honour existing contracts that allowed for mining and export. This was a reversal of decisions taken by the party's previous two national conferences. The ACTU had in 1981 changed its position to no longer ban the export of uranium. Moreover, a new uranium mine at Roxby Downs (Olympic Dam) in South Australia had been greenlit, and the Ranger uranium mine in Darwin was now operational. Hayden's position was pragmatic.

Hayden was supported by the Right faction, including Hawke and Keating. His proposal would permit mining at Roxby Downs, Ranger and Nabarlek in the Northern Territory. This became known as the 'three mines policy'. Hayden won the conference vote. But it enraged Labor's Left faction. Tom Uren called Hawke prior to the conference to express his indignation. Uren was no Hawke supporter, but he felt betrayed by Hayden. 'At least we know where you bloody well stand on the issue!' he told Hawke. Hayden's phalanx of support from the Left began to crack. 'Hayden is finished, he's a dead-duck leader,' Uren said.[90]

Not surprisingly, the national conference was gripped by leadership speculation. Hawke did little to quell it. On Wednesday, 7 July, in response to a poll in *The Bulletin* showing Fraser leading Hayden as preferred prime minister by 50 per cent to 31 per cent, Hawke told journalists that if he was made leader, there was 'no doubt' Labor would win the next election.[91] Hayden had had enough. The following afternoon, he announced that a special caucus meeting would be held at 11 am on 16 July to determine the leadership. The party had eight days to make their decision. 'No leader can tolerate such insidious destabilisation of our team effort,' Hayden said.[92]

Hawke said he would nominate for leader. 'It was time for the party to fish or cut bait,' he thought.[93] Caucus members who were believed to be open to voting for Hawke were summoned to his suite. Hawke argued he was better placed to lead Labor to an election victory. Some, such as Neal Blewett, were not convinced. 'I told him that I thought Hayden had restored the party's electoral position after the catastrophes of 1975 and 1977 and that he deserved the opportunity to lead the party into the election, which I believed he would win,' he recalled. 'It was made clear to me by Hawke's allies that retribution would be exacted.' Blewett recalled Richardson and Evans making this threat.[94]

The big issue for Hawke was where Keating would stand – with him or with Hayden. Keating talked it over with Richardson as they drove from Canberra back to Sydney. 'He didn't like Hawke and he didn't like Hayden,' Richardson recalled. 'He didn't think anyone should be leader except him.' Keating thought Hawke had not served enough time in parliament and he saw himself as Hayden's eventual successor. Richardson told him that the New South Wales Right faction had to support Hawke, and most of its MPs would anyway, but they needed him to switch camps.[95]

That same day, 8 July, Keating confided his thoughts to Blewett, who recorded them in his diary:

> Keating spoke to me advising against any shift to Hawke at this time. (Apparently he had heard of my interview with Hawke.) Paul is clearly determined to move only if the strength moves to Hawke – his basic conviction is that whoever wins must win strongly. Given Bowen's commitment to Hayden, it is fairly obvious that Keating will only move if the Left or the Centre shift to Hawke – particularly the Left as they have the bigger battalions.[96]

Keating's hope was short-lived.

Hawke was slow to begin campaigning. He was holding out for a bloc of votes to come from Uren and the Left. By Sunday, 11 July, he had not phoned a single caucus member. Robert Ray could not believe it. 'Hawke's convinced he can bring Uren over the line,' he recalled. 'I went down to Hawke's electorate office and made sure he rang every member of caucus. He was a long, long way behind.'[97]

On Tuesday, 13 July, the Left met and reaffirmed their support for Hayden. Uren had been duplicitous in signalling his support for Hawke. More important was that two days before the ballot, Keating had still not switched to Hawke. Keating had rung around and knew Hawke would fall short of the numbers he required. Hawke and his key lieutenants – MPs Gareth Evans, Clyde Holding and Mick Young, and Simon Crean from the Storemen and Packers' Union – met with Keating and Richardson in Hawke's suite at the Boulevard Hotel at 8 am on Wednesday, 14 July.

As breakfast was delivered to the suite, Keating said he did not want the New South Wales Right faction attached to a losing challenge. Hawke insisted he would defeat Hayden. 'Paul's essential concern was that if anyone were to replace Hayden, it should be him,' Hawke later said.[98] Keating needed convincing if he was going to desert Hayden. 'He certainly wasn't buying the Messiah argument over loyalty,' Crean recalled.[99] Ray, who had spoken to Keating on the phone but was not at the meeting, thought he had to back Hawke because he risked 'his power base disappearing from under him'.[100] Several New South Wales Right faction MPs, including Doug McClelland, Les Johnson, John Brown and Barry Cohen, were going to support Hawke in any event.

Evans recalled Keating's 'sentimental attachment to Hayden' and his lack of 'enthusiasm' for Hawke being the sticking points.[101] But eventually they persuaded him. 'I did not think that Bob would beat Bill Hayden,' Keating recalled. 'But I did believe that he could beat Fraser. To not support him would leave him with no opportunity to challenge again. So, reluctantly, at the very end, I switched the New South Wales camp in its entirety across to Hawke.'[102] Keating rang Hayden from the hotel to tell him the news. Hayden was disappointed but not surprised, given he never trusted the New South Wales Right faction. He told Keating that he would beat Hawke.

Evans drafted a statement for Keating to read to journalists in the lobby. Reports that Hayden's leadership was being supported by Laurie Carmichael, a communist, and John Halfpenny, a former communist, provided Keating with the opportunity to distance his faction from Hayden. 'The Centre Unity group respects Bill Hayden's capacity and contribution to the Labor movement and will support him absolutely, without reservations, in the event that he wins Friday's ballot,' Keating told the journalists. 'I believe, however, that the New South Wales members will take the view that the best interests of the Labor Party, and the millions of Australians who deserve and need a Labor victory and the end of Fraserism, will be best served by Bob Hawke now becoming leader.'[103]

Hawke had drawn up several lists to assess where he thought the numbers might fall in the caucus ballot. On one sheet of paper,

Hawke listed thirty-eight names beneath a column listed as 'yes' and thirty-four names under 'no'. Another seven names were listed as 'maybe'. Another list had Hayden with forty, Hawke with thirty-four and five MPs doubtful. Hawke looked like he was going to fall short, but it promised to be close.[104]

Hawke had been leaked a polling report by Labor's pollster, Rod Cameron, which showed he was preferred as prime minister by 43 per cent of voters over Fraser (20 per cent), Peacock (11 per cent) and Hayden (7 per cent). Hawke quoted the figures to MPs in an attempt to persuade them.[105] Bob Carr, with *The Bulletin*, recalled being in Hawke's suite at the Boulevard Hotel as he dialled caucus members for an hour before rushing to the airport. 'Have you seen the party's polling?' Hawke would say.[106] Carr audaciously wrote this up, after the ballot, reporting that Hawke 'was imbued with the excitement of a man convinced' he would be leader within days.[107]

The Labor caucus began at 11.05 am on Friday, 16 July 1982 in Canberra. Hayden resigned as leader to allow a secret ballot to take place. There were two nominations: Hayden and Hawke. A ballot box was set up in the corner of the opposition party room, and the returning officer drew up and issued ballot papers to MPs. One by one, they dropped them in the box.

While the votes were being counted, Hayden returned to his office with John Button, Peter Walsh and John Dawkins. They were informed of the result before it was announced to the caucus: forty-two votes for Hayden and thirty-seven for Hawke. It was a narrow margin: a change of just three votes would have delivered the leadership to Hawke. 'Is that enough?' Hayden asked. Walsh said, 'Yes.' Dawkins said, 'Yes.' Button shook his head and said, 'No, I don't think so.'[108]

They returned to the meeting and the result was announced. It was 11.45 am. Hayden thanked the caucus and called for their 'loyalty and unity'. Hawke supported Hayden's comments.[109] The news made its way to the cabinet meeting that was taking place around the corner. Ministers clapped when they learned that Hayden was still leader.[110] Gough Whitlam was pleased that Hayden had defeated Hawke, and telegrammed his 'warmest congratulations' and welcomed the fact that his 'numeracy [had] improved'.[111] Hawke was magnanimous towards Hayden, and the two of them, along with Bowen, faced the media. They laughed, smiled and shook hands. But Hawke was startled by the result. 'Hawke was surprised he didn't win,' recalled Ray.[112]

The polls continued to be on Hawke's side. A Gallup poll the following month showed that 55.3 per cent thought Hawke would be a better Labor leader than Hayden, who attracted 44.7 per cent.[113] Labor was not accustomed to executing leaders. Whitlam had led the party to five elections; before him, Calwell and Evatt had three elections each. The caucus had a long history of sticking with leaders. But Hawke was determined to strike again. Destiny still called, and the fires of ambition burned stronger than ever. 'I wasn't going to give up,' Hawke said.[114] Hayden knew it too.[115]

16

BOB
AND BILL

While Bob Hawke's determination to wrest the leadership from Bill Hayden never diminished, he knew that he could not force another showdown, as that could have the effect of reducing his support in caucus. Hawke's key lieutenants settled on a strategy of letting events take their course. The aim was to quell talk about a further leadership challenge. They wanted the party to come to Hawke. Hayden would make mistakes, they believed, now that he was under intense pressure from within and without the party.

Hawke's pledge of loyalty soon rang hollow, however, during an interview on ABC Radio on 5 November 1982. Hawke said there was 'concern' about the performance of the opposition and that voters did not 'seem to be thoroughly approving' of the party. He said he was not planning to challenge Hayden again, but then said: 'What my party colleagues may or may not do is a matter for them.' It was provocative, self-indulgent and ill-disciplined. Hawke was forced to kill the leadership speculation by sending a grovelling letter to all caucus members in which he said he stood by his commitment that there would be 'no further challenge' before the next election.[1]

Meanwhile, with Labor divided, Malcolm Fraser continued planning for an election by the end of the year. The Liberal Party undertook extensive quantitative and qualitative research, and consulted with MPs, party officials and business leaders about calling a snap election in September, October, November or

December 1982. Although Fraser was unpopular and seen by voters as arrogant and aloof, the party assessed that he had a leadership advantage over Hayden. The economy, with high unemployment and inflation, was the government's principal weakness, although there were also concerns about Labor's spending and taxation plans, and about union influence.

Dr Jim Forbes, the party's federal president, was keen to avoid an early election.[2] So was federal director Tony Eggleton. A 'personal and confidential' brief was provided to Fraser, assessing the option of going to an election in December: over the past eighteen months, Eggleton said, Labor had been 'polling better than the 1.4 per cent it needs to win government'. A survey of state directors forecast the 'probable' loss of sixteen seats, and the 'possible' loss of six more. Only three seats were 'possible' wins from Labor. The party was uneasy about an early election and the business community was equivocal. 'The degree of risk at this time is too great,' Eggleton wrote. 'It could look like an opportunistic, panicky scramble to the polls, and it is not possible to be entirely confident in such a volatile and cynical political climate.'[3]

Two factors influenced the decision not to go to an election in 1982. Firstly, the release of the report of the Costigan Royal Commission on 12 October, established to investigate crime in the Victorian Ship Painters' and Dockers' Union, had uncovered widespread corporate tax avoidance. This was an embarrassment for Fraser. Secondly, Fraser's chronic back problems saw him admitted to hospital on 31 October. He underwent surgery and it took him weeks to fully recover.

For Hayden, finalising an agreement between the party and the union movement on a new prices and incomes policy was a key priority. The work was left primarily to Ralph Willis, with Hawke assisting. Several meetings were held with the ACTU during 1981 and 1982, and a working paper had been prepared by April 1982. Hayden was surprised work had progressed that far. 'My impression had been,' he wrote to Willis, 'that consultations you and Bob had been taking had been fairly informal.' Now he sought to slow the process down. 'There needs to be some substantive consideration of the draft paper before too much additional progress is undertaken,' he wrote.[4] This was a mistake. Hawke now put the go-slow on finalising an accord.

Eight months later, on 2 December 1982, Hayden, Hawke, Bowen and Willis began a two-day meeting with the ACTU Executive in Melbourne aimed at finalising the accord. The previous month, Fraser had announced a twelve-month wage freeze, and the ACTU expressed a willingness to accept a six-month pause under certain conditions, including a 6 per cent minimum wage increase afterward. This showed the ACTU was prepared to deal with Fraser. Hayden's natural paranoia and suspicion was elevated. Cliff Dolan, who had succeeded Hawke as ACTU president, made it clear he thought Hawke should be leading the party. So the meeting was held in an atmosphere of mutual distrust. There were heated exchanges and no agreement was reached, but the party and the unions agreed to work towards concluding an accord in the coming months.

Labor needed to demonstrate to voters that it could forge a cooperative relationship with unions on prices and incomes, given the explosion in wage claims in 1973–74 and 1981–82. But many unions were unsure about an accord, recalled the ACTU's advocate at the time, Jan Marsh. 'There was a lot of scepticism about the way to go,' she recalled. 'It had to be sold to every union, each with their own agenda on wages, at a time of high inflation and unemployment. It would be a major undertaking to get consensus within the union movement for that policy.'[5]

On 4 December, voters in the Victorian seat of Flinders voted in a by-election. It was a key test for Hayden. Although the Liberals had a margin of 5.5 per cent, with high unemployment, inflation and interest rates, and in the wake of the Costigan Royal Commission, a Labor gain was possible. But Labor had preselected a gaffe-prone candidate named Rogan Ward, a controversial local real-estate agent. A few days before election day, Hawke visited for a scheduled street walk. In the campaign office, he saw New South Wales party official Stephen Loosley. 'Gee, it's bad, isn't it?' Hawke said, with a grin on his face. 'We both knew what it meant,' recalled Loosley.[6] Flinders was won for the Liberal Party by Peter Reith. Hawke later said the by-election was 'fatal for Bill'.[7]

Labor's doubts about Hayden intensified. The by-election loss also undermined Hayden's confidence in himself, and encouraged

Fraser to think he could beat Hayden in a general election. The day after, Hawke flew to Sydney and lunched with Graham Richardson, who impressed upon Hawke the need to remain disciplined. The strategy they had to follow was one of 'private pressure and public silence'.[8] The next day, 6 December, Richardson phoned John Button. They agreed the party had to think afresh about the leadership. Richardson and Button continued to talk over the next few weeks.

When Hayden addressed the caucus after the Flinders by-election, he faced an avalanche of criticism over the campaign, and about Labor's overall political strategy. He said new policies would be developed in response to the wage freeze and unemployment. He urged the party not to 'drop its bundle', even though the by-election result was 'a disappointment'. He called on everyone to lift their game. His speech did not inspire confidence. 'The leader had limitations in the Labor Party in what he could do,' Hayden told MPs.[9]

—

Although John Button, Labor's Senate leader, was personally close to Hayden, he had decided by the end of 1982 that Hayden should resign. In December, Button spoke with Lionel Bowen, Labor's deputy leader. 'What do you think?' Button asked.

'We're not in the race with Bill,' Bowen replied. 'He can't win. You made him, you ought to unmake him.'

So Button talked to Hayden about the leadership and suggested he quit. But Hayden refused to go.[10]

With the issue unresolved, Button left for a holiday in Fiji. On Christmas Eve, there was media speculation in Australia that his support for Hayden was 'wavering'.[11] His talk with Bowen leaked. On 30 December 1982, Button sent a telegram to Hayden:

> I was thinking about you on the beach in Fiji but that was
> because it was the season of goodwill . . . I will be in Queensland
> staying with [Michael] Duffy for a day or two in early
> January . . . perhaps I can then take you and hopefully Dallas
> [Hayden] to dinner and we can discuss the future of the great
> institution we all adore in a leisurely way.[12]

Button included others in the discussions. He had already spoken with Richardson, the New South Wales Labor secretary. Now, while still in Fiji, he phoned Bob Hogg, the Victorian Labor secretary. 'We need a change of leader,' Button said. Hogg agreed. He arranged a meeting of the Socialist Left in Victoria, and at that meeting, 'a sizeable portion of the Left decided there had to be a change of leader'.[13]

Button stayed with Duffy, the member for Holt, and his family at Kirra Beach on the Gold Coast. Duffy knew what was happening. It weighed heavily on Button, and he was not in the mood to talk much about it. Duffy recalled his teenage daughter saying, 'What's the matter with you and Mr Button? You haven't said more than a couple of words to each other since he got here.' Duffy replied that their guest had things on his mind. At the beach, they went for a swim. Button was thrashing about in the wild surf. 'You're getting a bit far out there, John,' Duffy yelled out. Button replied: 'I'm wondering if I should keep going.'[14]

On 6 January 1983, Button met with Hayden in Brisbane. He wrote a four-page memo of their discussion over lunch. Hayden said he only had an hour to spare because he was busy renovating his bathroom at home. Button said party morale was low and he did not think Hayden could win the next election. He should stand down as leader. It was a ridiculous suggestion, Hayden replied, given the good polls, and in any event, he would not make way for a 'shallow man' like Hawke. The conversation continued:

> I then said that if he lost the next election, I felt he would
> be finished in politics, but that if he stood down in favour of
> Hawke, and perhaps became deputy leader after the election,
> he would be in a much better position to influence events,
> and would be the heir-apparent in the event of Hawke not
> succeeding for any reason.
>
> He said he thought that Keating would be the heir-apparent,
> and I said I thought this unlikely. Hayden said that in any event,
> what would Lionel Bowen think about that, and I said: 'I'm not
> sure, but if you were agreeable, I would be prepared to put it to
> Lionel.' He said: 'Oh no, I would not want to put Lionel out of a
> job.'

Hayden speculated that he might get out of politics altogether and become a lawyer. But for now, he was thinking about a shadow ministerial reshuffle. Hayden said he might move Willis to the portfolio of economic development. But the big question then was who to make shadow treasurer. He had two names: Keating and Hawke. He favoured Keating, as there was nobody suitable to take Hawke's portfolio of employment and industrial relations. Maybe Mick Young, but he was not sure. Button also raised the matter of Hayden's staff. They were not well regarded, he said, especially Alan Ramsey, the press secretary, who when approached by journalists, often told them to 'fuck off'. The result of this rambling lunch was that Hayden was not resigning. 'I could never stand down for somebody like Hawke,' he told Button.[15]

A week later, on 13 January, Hayden acted. He used a shadow ministerial reshuffle to shore up his leadership by making a shock announcement: Paul Keating as shadow treasurer. Willis would be shifted to the portfolio of 'economic development', which would include taxation and federal–state relations, and he would retain responsibility for developing the accord. When Hayden phoned Willis to tell him he was being removed from the Treasury portfolio, he felt like he had been punched in the stomach. 'I had been doing the hard yards for five years and then to be dumped at this time was really upsetting,' he recalled. Willis saw it as Hayden currying favour with the New South Wales Right.[16]

Keating 'vigorously resisted' the appointment, Hayden remembered. Yet Keating had asked for the portfolio after the 1980 election and Hayden had raised it with him in 1981 and 1982. Hayden said Ramsey had been pushing for Keating to be given Treasury.[17] Keating took the call from Hayden in Bill Bradshaw's antiques shop in Woollahra, where he had been tracked down. He expressed his concerns to several union and party colleagues, and eventually spoke to Hawke, who was equally stunned. 'He's fucked us all,' Hawke said. 'He's fucked you by giving you the job. He's fucked Ralph, and he's fucked me.' Hawke remembered Keating's call. 'Oh, God. What should I do? Should I take it?' Keating asked. After analysing the situation, Hawke told Keating he should take the position.[18] Keating accepted the appointment as shadow treasurer and it was announced the next day.

On Sunday, 16 January, Button and Duffy met with Hawke at his Sandringham home. They were ushered outside, where Hawke was sitting in his swimming costume by the pool. 'While we talked he kept reaching for the sun lotion, basting himself so he glistened like a turkey gobbler about to go into the oven,' Button recalled. He told Hawke he should become leader and was talking to Hayden to encourage him to step aside.[19]

Button pressed Hawke to ensure there would be no negative consequences for Hayden, his supporters in caucus or his staff. This was critical to ensuring a smooth leadership transition and a harmonious team in government, should Labor win the election. 'People will go along with the leadership change but they are not avid supporters of yours,' Button said. Hawke pledged to treat Hayden and his close supporters respectfully if he became leader. Hawke emphasised to Button and Duffy that he was not 'vindictive' as it was not part of his 'nature'.[20]

Later that day, Button wrote a note for the record:

I concluded during this period that [Hayden] has no idea about leading a team, that he is obsessed with personal vindication and lacks generosity of spirit and understanding. He is profoundly distrustful of others and is incapable of delegating. All these personality flaws have been present all along: but they have become profoundly worse since August 1982.[21]

Button knew he had to nurse Hayden to the point where he would quit. Another leadership challenge would not work. Hayden had to pull the trigger himself. Button would become both therapist and assassin.

Hayden, having remade his frontbench, looked for a major policy announcement to further shore up his leadership. On 19 January, the shadow cabinet met and finalised the party's economic policy. Hayden was planning to release it as a major pre-election statement. Hawke, however, engineered to have it delayed. A plan was hatched to have the ACTU tell Hayden that the outline of a proposed accord, which was part of the economic policy, could not be made public until a conference of unions had endorsed it. This was weeks away. Hawke raised it with Dolan, who then spoke to Mick Young, who proposed it at the party's national campaign committee meeting on 20 January. It was agreed. Hayden had been blindsided. Hawke planned to release it when he became leader.

On 27 January, Button again flew to Brisbane to meet Hayden. A fortnight had passed since their lunch. They only had a brief discussion; Hayden was not in the mood. He would not quit. On his way back to Melbourne, Button stopped over in Sydney and phoned Bowen. It was about 9.30 pm. Bowen drove to the airport. They agreed he should write a letter to Hayden. 'He's going to step down,' Button reassured Bowen. But it would take time. Bowen recalled there were suggestions within caucus that Hawke should challenge Hayden again.[22] The pressure was building.

The next day, 28 January, Button wrote to Hayden. He valued Hayden's friendship, he said, and admired and respected what he had done as Labor leader, but he felt a duty to put the party first. Button believed that Hayden could not win an election and urged him to resign for Hawke:

> The alternative leader (created as such by the last leadership ballot) is, of course, Bob Hawke. You said to me that you could not stand down for a 'bastard' like Bob Hawke. In my experience in the Labor Party the fact that someone is a bastard (of one kind or another) has never been a disqualification for leadership of the party. It is a disability from which we all suffer in various degrees.

While Button expressed reservations about Hawke's 'capacities to lead the party', he believed a leadership change would give Labor 'a better chance' of winning the next election.[23] It was a hammer blow for Hayden.

Michael Costello, who joined Hayden's staff as principal private secretary in 1981, revealed that, around this time, Hayden talked directly to Hawke and outlined the key 'condition' for stepping aside was that he be made foreign minister in the next Labor government. Hawke listened and was open to this. He would not play a lead role in the negotiations; he would let Button do the work.[24]

Events moved fast. On Sunday, 30 January, Hayden phoned Button and asked him to come to Brisbane. On Tuesday, 1 February, following the funeral of former Labor prime minister

Frank Forde, they spoke for two hours. It was at this meeting that Hayden agreed to step aside for Hawke. Button's handwritten notes disclose that Hayden planned to resign on Friday, 4 February. But he had conditions: he wanted the foreign affairs portfolio in opposition and in government; he wanted an 'ironclad guarantee' that Neal Blewett, John Dawkins and Peter Walsh would keep their positions on the front bench; that his staff would be assisted to find jobs; and that he would be appointed Australian high commissioner in London for five years. These 'principles should be set out in writing [and] signed by myself [Hayden] and Hawke – Bowen + Button witnesses', Button noted.'[25]

That evening, 1 February, Button met with Bowen again in Sydney and told him what had been agreed. Bowen was not happy about a portfolio change. Nor was he happy about making a commitment to give Hayden an overseas posting. He thought there should be no deals. But Bowen made it clear he would not stand in the way of a portfolio change to ensure Hawke became leader. In the days prior, Bowen had repeatedly declined to give a full-throated endorsement of Hayden's leadership when asked by journalists.

The following day, Wednesday, 2 February, Button met with Hawke in Melbourne to tell him that he expected Hayden to resign and to prepare himself to become Labor's new leader. Button was tight-lipped about the arrangements. The only people on the front bench who knew the details were Hayden, Hawke, Bowen and Button. But word began to spread. John Dawkins recalled speaking to Hayden from London. 'I urged him not to resign,' he said. Hayden raised the issue of taking Bowen's portfolio of foreign affairs. 'Don't worry about that,' Dawkins told him. 'He hasn't been much help to you – he hasn't been much help to anyone.'[26]

Button decided to bring his Senate deputy, Don Grimes, up to speed on what had transpired. Grimes was told on the morning of Thursday, 3 February, in Sydney, before they both flew on to Brisbane for the shadow cabinet meeting. When Grimes arrived in Brisbane he spoke to Hayden, who confirmed that he would stand down for Hawke. 'I was disappointed, but Bill was a pretty straightforward bloke and said that is the way it is,' Grimes recalled. 'I accepted that that was going to happen and so there wasn't a big kerfuffle about it.'[27]

Politics swirled with rumours that Fraser would rush to an early election to prevent a Labor leadership change. Just six days earlier, on 28 January, Fraser announced that he would travel to the United States and meet with Ronald Reagan on 5 March 1983.[28] Now, he decided to junk the meeting with the president and have an election on that day instead. That this meeting had been scheduled and announced, and then cancelled, shows Fraser's panicked frame of mind.

Journalist Laurie Oakes, the king of scoops, got wind of Fraser's plan for a snap election. On the morning of 3 February, Oakes confirmed the story and filed it for the 7 am radio news bulletins. Oakes then phoned Hayden in Brisbane and told him about Fraser's plan. 'If you want to hang on to the leadership, this will help you,' Oakes said. Hayden listened and replied, 'So that's what Fraser's up to, is it?' Oakes recalled that it was clear Hayden was about to tap the mat: 'Instead of me giving him the reason to stay on, he had made up his mind that he was going to go for the good of the party.'[29]

Michael Costello recalled that Hayden felt under siege. 'We were almost certain that we were going to win the next election with Bill, but it was pretty clear that Bob was much more likely to win and win bigger,' he said. 'If there had been another challenge, Bill would have won by more. However, it became clear that the destabilisation was not going to stop. They set out to psychologically destabilise Bill, but they did not succeed in that. The reason he stood aside was for the good of the party and the country.'[30]

As Fraser made plans in Canberra to call an election, Hayden decided to bring his own plan forward. Hayden thought he would beat Fraser's announcement by one day; he did not know that Fraser was already speaking to cabinet ministers, the party organisation and his department in order to make the announcement that same day. But the arrangements for a leadership transition were not yet finalised. The deal Hayden wanted would have to be negotiated directly with Hawke. And, most importantly, it would have to be witnessed by others and put into writing and signed. He would leave nothing to chance.

The shadow cabinet meeting was to take place that morning on the lower ground floor of the Commonwealth Government Centre in Brisbane. Hayden spoke to Button and said the resignation would be brought forward and take place that day, during the morning tea break. Shadow ministers began arriving at 9.15 am (Brisbane time).[31] Hawke arrived at 9.30 am. He met with Button and learned that the plan was being accelerated. Hawke would be the leader-elect of the Labor Party within the next few hours, provided the transition could be agreed. At 9.45 am, Hayden arrived.

Due to a plane delay, Bowen arrived twenty minutes later, at 10.05 am, and made his way to the conference room. He sat next to Hayden. Bowen had understood from Button that Hayden would relinquish the leadership the next day, Friday.

'I'm going to make that announcement today,' Hayden told Bowen.

'Today?' Bowen said, startled.

'Yes,' Hayden confirmed.

'I thought you weren't going do it till tomorrow,' said Bowen.

'No,' Hayden said. 'I decided to do it today because it's virtually out now. I want to have a discussion in the morning tea break about my future. We'll have a meeting upstairs. It will be Grimes, and yourself, myself, and we'll get Hawke in, and Button.'[32]

The shadow cabinet meeting began at 10.10 am, with Hayden in the chair. Willis gave an update on the accord. Keating spoke about economic policy. The mood was tense. They all knew something was happening, but only a few knew exactly what. Hayden had told MPs that he would never resign for Hawke. If need be, he would call another leadership ballot to settle the matter.

Keating revealed that Button had kept him informed about his talks with Hayden. 'I was president of New South Wales Labor and I commanded the largest group in the parliamentary party, the NSW Right,' Keating said. 'Button was talking to me. In the party, I could hear the ants change step.'[33] But most of the other shadow ministers were clueless. 'I didn't know what was going to happen, and several of the others didn't know,' said Susan Ryan.[34] John Kerin recalled: 'I didn't know what was going on behind the scenes. I didn't know about the factional manoeuvring and the bastardry.'[35] Neal Blewett remembered a meeting with several Hayden supporters the night before which was 'pretty gloomy' and a worry that Hayden was in 'real danger'. But it was unclear if Hayden was going to stand down or if Hawke was going to challenge.[36] Chris Hurford recognised a change to Hawke 'probably was inevitable' but not then. 'I thought Hayden had a bit of time left,' he recalled.[37]

At 10.40 am, Hayden announced there would be a short break. Hayden, Hawke and Bowen took the lift to Hayden's twelfth-floor office. Button and Grimes soon joined them. Hayden asked to become shadow minister for foreign affairs, with a promise to hold that portfolio in government. He wanted a guarantee that his supporters in the shadow ministry would retain their portfolios, and his staff would be found new jobs. Hayden also asked to be appointed Australia's high commissioner in London after serving a period as minister for foreign affairs. Hawke agreed. To Bowen, Hayden said: 'I want your job.'

'Well, you've got no bloody right to my job,' Bowen replied. 'I ought to fight you for it.' Bowen did not think Hayden should be appointed high commissioner either. 'That is utterly ridiculous,' he said.[38]

Shortly after 11.15 am, a Labor staff member interrupted the meeting: 'I want to tell you that Malcom Fraser has gone out to see the governor-general.'[39]

This interjection prompted laughter from Hawke, Bowen and Button. But not from Hayden, who stood there in stunned silence. They all knew what this meant: Fraser was calling an early election. The tension lifted. Bowen, Button and Grimes left. Hawke and Hayden stayed behind and finalised the agreement with an exchange of letters.

Bowen did not sign any letter, and neither did Button or Grimes. Bowen did not think there was an agreement about Hayden becoming high commissioner, or an exchange of letters with Hawke. Interviewed in 1990–91, Bowen said: 'Can you imagine what public opinion's going [to] think if it ever comes out that we're stupid enough to give you a letter saying that as and when we win government . . . you will become high commissioner?'[40]

But that is exactly what they did. Hawke was not concerned about the integrity of promising Hayden the diplomatic posting. 'At the time I didn't think that would eventuate; nor did it,' he said.[41]

By 11.40 am, the five men had returned to the shadow cabinet meeting. Hayden had bloodshot, red-rimmed eyes and his jaw was clenched. Hawke was also red-eyed. Bowen, Button and Grimes were grey and grim.[42] Hayden informed the shadow cabinet that he had agreed to resign the leadership and Hawke would take over. He thought he could lead Labor to victory but, evidently, others did not. Hayden then left. Hawke, though not yet officially party leader, took the chair. He asked everyone for their support and, focused and businesslike, resumed the meeting. Then another messenger came into the meeting to confirm that Fraser had indeed requested an election, but it had not yet been granted. The meeting broke up for a lunch hosted by the local Chamber of Commerce.

Ryan recalled the atmosphere in the meeting as tense and somewhat bitter. It was far from euphoric. She recalled being abused by a member of Hayden's staff. 'It was one of the worst days of my life – still,' she recalled. 'Bill's eyes were all red and the others looked like death.'[43]

The news spread like wildfire. Peter Beattie, Queensland Labor's secretary, recalled being aware of the pressure building over the previous few days. 'We knew there were all sorts of machinations going on but not to the extent that we thought there would be a change that day – we were stunned like everyone else,' he said. 'I was disappointed for Hayden but also knew that Hawke would revive our fortunes.' Beattie and Denis Murphy, Queensland Labor's president, spoke briefly to Hayden before he fronted the media. 'He was breaking down and he was very emotional,' Beattie recalled. 'I wish I could find the Celtic spirit of my ancestors to go and do what I have to do,' Hayden told them.[44]

Hayden's resignation was announced at a press conference at 12.25 pm. 'Well, today I advised the shadow cabinet of the Labor Party, the parliamentary Labor Party, that I would be resigning as leader,' he said. 'I didn't take this decision with any sense of joy, but it did seem to me as a matter of responsibility to my party, a party in which I have great faith, which really has an historic mission, that the situation confronting us was that there was an inevitable conflict coming up in caucus.' He said he may have been able to win a leadership ballot but only by a narrow margin. Then, with tears in his eyes, he said: 'I want to say this. I am not convinced the Labor Party would not win under my leadership. I believe that a drover's dog could lead the Labor Party to victory the way the country is, and the way the opinion polls are showing up for the Labor Party.'[45]

Shortly after, 12.40 pm, Hawke announced to the media that he would nominate for the leadership of the party at a caucus meeting the following week, and he did not expect to be opposed. 'Bill Hayden has done a remarkably courageous thing,' Hawke said. He announced that Hayden would serve in a senior shadow portfolio and occupy a senior ministerial position in government. When asked if he had been undermining Hayden, he cut short the press conference and walked out. 'Nonsense,' he said.[46]

Events were moving so fast that Bob could not reach Hazel by phone before the news broke; she was out with Rosslyn. Hazel found out that Hayden had resigned when she arrived home and was besieged in the driveway by journalists and photographers.

Meanwhile, Hayden's supporters were not happy. 'I was deeply depressed,' Blewett recalled. 'I believed then, and have always believed, that Hayden would have won the 1983 election, but was equally convinced that a bitter and divisive leadership ballot between him and Hawke would ruin the party's electoral chances.' Blewett and Button later exchanged harsh words. Blewett said he did not think much of his colleague's 'methods'.[47] Button was minded to tell Blewett to 'fuck off', but resisted the temptation.[48]

Yet Button's strategy was effective. Hawke did not have to challenge, risking a divided caucus and fostering resentment. Hayden was not heavied by faction bosses with a tap on the shoulder to resign. He was not called to a meeting and told, humiliatingly, that he had lost the support of his colleagues. There were no demands that he quit, and no public calls for him to stand down. Button chipped away at Hayden's confidence in himself. In the end, it was Hayden who decided to quit. This was a perfect political execution: the leadership transition was essentially seamless.

Hayden recalled that it was difficult for him to relinquish the leadership, but once he had made up his mind, he resolved to go through with it regardless of Fraser calling an election. 'I was in personal turmoil about stepping down as leader,' he said. 'It hurt a lot. I worked hard. I was away from home a lot. It caused a lot of grief with my two daughters and my wife, who had given a lot to support me. The youngest, Ingrid, protested one morning. She picked it up and said, "You are going to resign, aren't you?" She was cranky. I said I was doing the best I can.'

Hayden recalled the phone call from Oakes. He felt he could not fight to remain leader, even though he knew an election was about to be called. 'It had been agreed,' he said. 'The election would have become about the Labor leadership, and it would have been a wipeout for Labor. It would have broken the hearts of the true believers of the party and the candidates. It struck me pretty hard when I stood down because I felt like a total failure. It really hurt. But I couldn't hang on. Malcolm was tough and unforgiving. He would have given me a hard time.'[49]

As Hawke realised the leadership would be his, he felt 'elated'. While he was mindful of Hayden being upset, he made no apologies for the toughness of politics. 'There was a sense of sadness as Bill had done so many good things for the party,' he said. 'But I was absolutely convinced that I had a better chance of winning the election and that was a view shared by a majority of my colleagues. Political parties are not there simply to provide opposition for ever. They are about winning government. It would be a dereliction of their duty if they failed to do all they could to win an election. That would be a negation of everything that politics is about.'[50]

The Labor caucus met on 8 February 1983 to make Hawke's leadership official. After the meeting, Stephen Loosley went to the opposition leader's office and spoke to Hawke. The room was piled high with boxes. 'I'll guess you'll have to start unpacking those,' he said.

'No, no,' Hawke replied. 'These will go straight to the prime minister's office after the election.'[51] Hawke had a rendezvous with destiny.

—

Fraser thought Labor would stick with Hayden once the election had been called, because a challenge from Hawke would require a caucus meeting in Canberra, and take days to organise. He did not anticipate that Hayden would resign in Brisbane. It was not the first time Fraser had tried to stop Labor changing leaders. He had called an early election in 1977, amid rumours that Whitlam was about to step aside or face another challenge. That was to stop Hayden becoming leader. Now, in 1983, he was trying to stop Labor removing Hayden as leader.

Fraser had been tipped off by a Labor insider.[52] Speculation fell on two former ministers: Clyde Cameron and Tom Uren.[53] Neither liked Hawke, and each had a relationship with Fraser. The other mentioned was Alan Ramsey, Hayden's press secretary, who despised Hawke. It was suggested that Fraser's information had come from a Hayden staff member.[54] Alister Drysdale, who had returned to Fraser's office as a senior adviser ahead of the election, said Fraser's source was Neville Wran. 'We got a tip-off from Wran that Labor was about to change leaders,' he said. 'As is often the way with Liberal and Labor leaders, Malcolm got on better with Wran than he did with [Victorian Liberal premier] Dick Hamer. I am pretty certain that Nifty was the tip-off.'[55]

Brian Dale, Wran's former press secretary, cannot challenge Drysdale's claim. 'I am surprised,' he said. 'My only proviso is: what did Neville gain by doing this? It is possible they were just sharing political gossip.'[56] Hayden had long suspected Uren was Fraser's source. But he was not surprised to learn that it was likely Wran. 'He could easily have done that,' Hayden said. 'I remember going to talk to him once and he leaked a story about how he had given me a lecture. So, I tended not to trust him.' Hayden thought Button likely told Wran, who was talking more widely to people than has been previously understood. 'If Wran knew, he'd know because Button told him,' Hayden thought. 'He was a mercurial fellow. He went out of his way to declare his faithful support to me, but in the end, he was leaking stories all over the place.'[57]

At 3.30 pm, Governor-General Sir Ninian Stephen contacted Fraser to ask for clarification about the bills being used as the trigger for a double-dissolution election. At 4.55 pm, Stephen phoned Fraser to inform him that he had granted an election, and a formal letter was being couriered to Parliament House. And so it was not until about 5 pm – four hours after he had planned – that Fraser was able to announce that Australia would have an election on 5 March 1983.

John Howard, the treasurer and deputy Liberal leader, said Fraser had wanted to go to an early election since the beginning of 1982. 'He wanted to fight an election against Hayden,' Howard said. 'Malcolm was at his best when waging political war. But I was against an early election.' And what was his reaction when he heard Fraser had called a snap election but would face Hawke, not Hayden? 'I thought we were done for,' Howard said.[58]

Tony Eggleton, the Liberal Party's federal director, was in Sydney meeting with the party's campaign advertising agency, D'Arcy MacManus Masius, when the election was called. They were planning a campaign against Labor led by Hayden. 'We were astounded to hear that Labor had changed its leader,' he recalled. 'We had no doubt that Hawke, with a political honeymoon, would be a formidable adversary. Fraser was aware that Hawke, as a popular and well-known figure, would be a very different proposition to Hayden. That is why he wanted to move quickly for an early election.'[59]

Drysdale, who monitored events as they unfolded from Fraser's office in Canberra, was of the same view. 'I think we all knew the day Hawke became leader that the game was over,' he said. 'He was trying to get in before Hawke was actually made leader. I think a Fraser–Hayden election contest would have been a fifty-fifty prospect. The government had been around for a while and he had taken power in difficult times.'[60]

David Kemp, who had left Fraser's staff but was tapped to work on the election campaign, was also at the advertising agency when Labor changed leaders. He spoke to Fraser. 'It was a disaster for Fraser, but I recall trying to give him an assurance that all was not lost,' Kemp said. 'Apart from the inflation and unemployment, it was a bad time for Fraser. His health was not strong, the bushfires were shocking, and he had also lost some support within the Liberal Party because of his 1982–83 budget. I think, and he thought, he would have beaten Hayden. Hawke was just too popular.'[61]

When Tamie Fraser heard that her husband had called an election and would face Hawke, she thought, 'We're a goner.'[62] Days later, on the ABC's *Nationwide* program, she conceded that most women 'quite like' Hawke and agreed that he had 'sex appeal'.[63] Tamie was not alone in that view.

Margaret Gibbs ran focus groups for the party the night Hawke became leader-elect. 'There was a complete change in the mood in the electorate,' she said. Rod Cameron, Labor's pollster, said Hawke's sex appeal manifested in his charisma. 'It was magnetism,' he explained. 'Whenever Hawke would come into a room it was almost like there was a halo around him and there would be a gravitation towards him.' Gibbs added: 'He liked people and you would see it when he worked a crowd. The way he would smile at people, he would hold their hand, he would hug them.'[64]

Fraser told the media he was not fazed about the prospect of facing Hawke rather than Hayden. 'It will be the first election when two Labor leaders were knocked off in one go,' he said. Fraser was not intimidated by Hawke. He was not intimidated by anyone. Fraser knew Hawke was a tougher opponent that Hayden, but he had destroyed two previous Liberal leaders (John Gorton and Billy Snedden), and seen off two Labor leaders (Gough Whitlam and now Hayden).

But on reflection years later, Fraser conceded he made a mistake. 'I made a stupid decision about the timing of the election,' he said. 'If I had left it to the end of the year, the drought would have broken, the economy would be looking up, and Hawke would have been tested in parliament. It may not have altered the outcome, but it would have made for a closer contest.'[65]

Hawke thought that if Fraser had realised he was too late, he would not have called the early election. 'I am sure that if Fraser knew he was fighting me and not Bill, then he wouldn't have called the election,' Hawke judged. 'But the die had been cast.'[66]

Hawke's central pitch to voters was first articulated in the 1960s: to bring Australians together by consensus on the major issues facing the country and come to agreement on how to deal with them. This reflected Hawke's personality as a conciliator. With Australia in a recession, gripped by drought, ravaged by bushfires, and pessimistic about the future, Hawke would articulate a better and brighter future under Labor. He would be a unifying leader, in contrast to Fraser's divisiveness. He wanted to repair and reconstruct the economy so that the recovery from recession would be lasting. He projected an optimistic view of the future.

Labor's campaign committee had already settled on much of the strategy for the election. The party was planning to use the election slogan 'A New Direction' but Graham Richardson thought 'Australia Deserves Better' would be more effective.[67] Labor's research showed that voters felt the Fraser government had not managed the economy well and a 'fairer system' was needed. A 25 October 1982 strategy paper outlined two key policy focuses for Labor: a 'rescue' program and a 'reconstruction' program. This became a strategy for economic 'recovery' and 'reconstruction'. This was developed by Hayden's former private secretary, Clem Lloyd.[68]

But Hawke, not yet leader, felt there was something missing. At a meeting of Labor's campaign committee on 20 January 1983, he suggested adding 'reconciliation' as a central theme. Hawke prepared a four-page typewritten document and presented it to the committee:

> The essential malaise to be identified with the period of the Fraser government is the increasing erosion of any sense of common national purpose . . . In this new environment of uncertainty and fear there is, I believe a growing conviction that what has underlaid the Fraser government's approach in the past i.e. the pursuit of self-interest, the politics of confrontation and divisiveness, is now not appropriate. There is a desire for healing, for a sense of common purpose . . . Most of our important, and somewhat esoteric, policies can be placed squarely within the framework of this approach – most obviously the prices and incomes policy, but similarly others as, for example, health and housing . . . this concept of the reconciliation of strategy has three advantages:
> (a) it is right;
> (b) it represents what the electorate wants;
> (c) in itself, it is cost-free.[69]

This document was written for Hayden, but it is pure Hawke.

On 4 February, Labor's campaign team met at the New South Wales Labor Party's headquarters on Sussex Street in Sydney to finalise its strategy. The triple-themed Labor campaign – 'reconciliation, recovery, reconstruction' – was formally adopted at this meeting. The same concepts would guide Labor's policymaking in government. It is what Hawke wanted and had argued for. The principal campaign slogan was also agreed at this meeting: 'Bob Hawke: Bringing Australia Together.' But there was scepticism, especially from Neville Wran. 'If the greedy bastards wanted spiritualism, they'd join the fucking Hare Krishnas,' he said.[70] But it seemed the voters were looking for a messiah after all.

17

BRINGING AUSTRALIA
TOGETHER

On 16 February 1983, Bob Hawke launched Labor's election campaign at the Sydney Opera House. The Opera Theatre was packed, and another thousand or so true believers assembled outside on the steps. Neville Wran introduced Hawke. 'The first pledge I now make, a commitment which embraces every other undertaking, is that everything we do as a government will have the one great goal: to reunite this great community of ours, to bring out the best we are truly capable of, together, as a nation, and bring Australia together,' Hawke said. There was thunderous applause.

Hawke's speech, drafted by Graham Freudenberg, took forty-six minutes to deliver. Unlike in 1972, there were no dancing girls, balloons or streamers. Hawke stood alone: he was Labor. The image was of a sophisticated, modern party. Accordingly, Hawke's delivery was somewhat subdued. Gone was the passion, the thumping of the podium and the finger pointing. Journalist Peter Bowers said Hawke was now the 'quiet persuader'.[1] Hawke acknowledged being disciplined. 'I was confident we were going to win,' he reflected. 'I didn't want to appear cocky and triumphal.'[2] But at the end, he was overcome with emotion. The Opera House had a special significance for Hawke. He had taken his mother as his guest to the opening on 20 October 1973. Now, at the end of his Hawke's speech, he was joined on stage by his father. They embraced with tears in their eyes.

Hawke's central promise was reconciliation, recovery and reconstruction. He pledged an accord with unions, and offered

personal income tax cuts, increases in pensions and family allowances, and money for employment programs. The speech reflected
some of the old Labor agenda. The deficit would increase by
$1.5 billion, and there would be tighter regulation for banks and
additional protection for industry. But the election was not about a
sweeping reform program. Where many voters were drawn to and
identified with Gough Whitlam's vision and goals, finding him
inspirational, more were drawn to and identified with Hawke on
a personal and emotional level. At the heart of Hawke's leadership
model was the inner Hawke: a man who had reformed himself and
now wanted to reform Australia.

The leadership change dramatically reshaped the dynamics of
the election campaign. The Liberal Party commissioned detailed
qualitative research over four days, from 3 February to 6 February.
The results were not encouraging. It found the 'most critical' issue
for voters was unemployment. There was also concern about rising
prices, taxation and home loan interest rates, and scepticism about
a wage pause. While the research picked up 'strong anti-union
feelings', and partly blamed the unions for the 'economic plight',
there was difficulty pinning this on Hawke. Some voters thought
Hawke might handle the unions better as he 'talks their language'
and 'might have the answers'.

The leaders were an important factor for uncommitted voters.
The following attributes, positive and negative, were identified in
the Liberal research:

> Hawke Positives: Energetic, More Human, More
> Understanding, Won't Give in to Unions, Clear Thinker.
> Hawke Negatives: Unproven, Emotional, Hot-Tempered, Not
> a Good Ambassador, Over-Ambitious, Only Experienced in
> Industrial Relations.
> Fraser Positives: Hard-Working, Strong, Proven Statesman,
> Steady.
> Fraser Negatives: Aloof, Arrogant, Opportunist.

The report found a mood that 'perhaps Hawke should be given
a go'. But there were concerns about his inexperience in government and his emotionalism. The Liberal Party advised Fraser
to establish clearly in the minds of uncommitted voters 'that it

is too critical a time to hand over the reigns [sic] of office to a learner driver'.[3]

Rod Cameron found that Hawke's elevation to the leadership cemented Labor's lead in the polls. 'Even though Hayden restored Labor's economic credibility, and despite a very credible effort in 1980, he was never going to beat Fraser,' he argued. Cameron explained Hawke's appeal to voters. First, Hawke was a 'non-politician' at a time when disillusionment with politics was growing, and he was seen as 'a real Australian'. Second, he had character traits not usually found together in politics: he was 'strong' but also 'compassionate'. He was tough but could bring people together to compromise. Hawke's sex appeal was a 'big factor' too. Third, Hawke had nullified his negatives. He had dealt with his drinking by going on the wagon and admitting indiscretions. Doubts about his 'statesmanship' were quelled by his becoming the 'sober statesman'. And his union links were dealt with by emphasising his consensus approach.[4]

Labor's campaign director was the party's national secretary, Bob McMullan. Hawke made several appointments to his personal staff, announced on 8 February.[5] Bob Hogg was named as an adviser. Geoff Walsh was press secretary. Peter Barron was also appointed as press secretary but was essentially a political adviser. Graham Freudenberg was appointed as adviser and speechwriter. Barron and Freudenberg were borrowed from Wran's office with the premier's encouragement. Jean Sinclair continued as private secretary. Geoff Evans was appointed as policy adviser and Peter Simmonds as economic adviser. Richard Farmer worked out of the Sydney headquarters on Hawke's schedule. Legendary agency Forbes MacFie Hansen handled the advertising.

Hawke also announced changes to the shadow ministry.[6] He would keep the industrial relations portfolio for the campaign. Lionel Bowen remained deputy leader and took on the trade portfolio. Hayden, as agreed, had foreign affairs. Mick Young was given employment, youth affairs, immigration and ethnic affairs. Stewart West was allocated finance.

Hawke travelled to every state during the campaign. He was mobbed everywhere: street walks, shopping centres, town hall meetings and functions. He shook hands, kissed babies and hugged his way around Australia. He joked with the media pack trailing him. He backslapped Labor candidates. He posed for photos. He signed autograph books. Hawke was a dream candidate. He loved meeting people and they loved meeting him. He basked in the adulation, cheers and applause. It fed him, nourished him and sustained him. He drew energy from it.

Hawke was disciplined and focused, and there were no angry clashes like he had had with Richard Carleton after the election was called. He had been counselled by Barron and Hogg to banish that version of himself for the campaign. 'If you keep behaving like that, you will lose the election, you will fuck it up,' Hogg told him. The party's research showed voters wanted to be sure that the prime minister they chose would be fit to meet the Queen. Hawke had to reassure the doubters that he could be prime ministerial.[7] He got the message.

Fraser was on the back foot from the start of the campaign, and never recovered. He was guarded and reserved, and had several sharp interactions with journalists. He complained that Hawke was getting a charmed run in the media. The Liberal campaign slogan, insisted on by Fraser, was 'We're Not Waiting for the World'. It featured in a television commercial with a message about Australia's greatness – we were better than everyone else. John Howard, the treasurer, had been arguing that Australia's economic problems – double-digit inflation and unemployment – were functions of the world economy. In other words, we were not immune from the rest of the world. Yet here was the Liberal campaign arguing that Australia was not 'waiting for the world'. It was a confused message.[8]

Senator Kerry Sibraa acted as Hawke's 'advance man' in Queensland, South Australia, Western Australia and Tasmania. The response from the public was overwhelming, and halls and function centres hosting a Hawke appearance were often so full that people had to be turned away. There was a surge in donations to Labor. Candidates who did not think they had a chance of winning their seats now believed they could. But when Sibraa walked into Hawke's office in Parliament House at the start of the campaign, they were far from ready. 'It was chaos, as no staff, no nothing [and] Jean Sinclair trying valiantly to cope,' he wrote in his diary. But Hawke becoming leader was like a surge of energy for Labor. 'A great lift in party morale is evident since Hawke's leadership took place,' Sibraa wrote.[9]

Walsh recalled 'the sense of optimism and anticipation' among candidates, staff and party members. He remembers the 'palpable public upsurge in interest and attachment' to Hawke.[10] Sibraa thought he was 'brilliant' on the campaign trail. 'Some of the people who would line up to meet him were the little old ladies – the 'blue rinse set' – and Hawkey used to woo them by telling them how beautiful they were. He was a magical campaigner.'[11] Wendy Fatin, who was elected to parliament in 1983, likened Hawke to the Pope being on the campaign trail. 'People just wanted to touch him,' she recalled. 'We took him to the big shopping centres and he was friendly and laughing, and would look at people in the eye when they talked to him. This is a skill that not many politicians have, but he had it.'[12]

Journalist Paul Kelly followed Hawke on a streetwalk through Brisbane at the start of the campaign. 'It was a revelation,' he said. 'Women in their forties, fifties and sixties came up and wanted to touch him. Some had tears in their eyes. The degree of emotional engagement with Hawke was extremely high, particularly from women.' Later in the campaign, after a press conference, Hawke signalled to Kelly to talk to him in another room. 'Putting his face very close to my face and gazing directly at me,' Kelly recalled, 'he wanted me to know that he was totally confident of his ability to respond to the challenges facing the country. It was an intimate, personal message, and I've always remembered that.'[13]

The manifestation of Hawke's consensus approach was the accord between the unions and the party on prices and incomes. The idea was to implement wage restraint to reduce inflation in return for social-wage benefits, such as universal healthcare and increased investment in education. Hawke emphasised that the agreement would be a key election policy. But when Keating attended a meeting with union leaders at the Waterside Workers' Federation in Sydney, he discovered the accord had not been finalised. The ACTU wanted 'catch-up' wage claims 'over time', given the wages freeze. Keating would only agree to this being 'an objective over time'. Bill Kelty, who became ACTU secretary in 1983, said Keating regarded the accord as an election strategy, not a policy for government. 'He made it clear he didn't support the accord,' Kelty said.[14]

Keating conveyed his scepticism to John Laws on Sydney radio station 2UE on 24 February. 'All I can say is that if we are elected to office, we'll do our best to make it work,' he said. Fraser said it showed the accord was a 'fraud'. Howard said Keating had made a telling 'admission' about Labor's policies.

Hawke was furious; it raised doubts in his mind about Keating's suitability for the role of treasurer.[15] He tried to mop it up. 'All I can say, on the basis of my unrivalled knowledge of both sides of industry in this country and my faith in the Australian people, I am certain the policy will work,' Hawke said.[16] That evening, recorded Sibraa, Hawke and his staff discussed the 'Keating gaffe' in his motel room. Hawke spoke to Keating 'for a long time' about the error.[17] McMullan, Labor's national secretary, said it was clear Keating was 'struggling' as shadow treasurer.[18] Barbara Ward, an adviser to Keating, said there were doubts about whether he would be appointed treasurer. 'Hawke threatened it, there is no doubt,' she said.[19]

The Hawke/Keating partnership had not got off to a good start. Keating was nervous and seemed to lacked confidence. The key task was to convey to voters that Labor would foster a growth-led economic recovery to lift Australia out of recession. On 10 February, Labor's economic policy was launched by Hawke, rather than Keating, at the Wentworth Hotel in Sydney. It was a typical tax-and-spend economic policy that promised a massive increase in outlays, to the tune of $2.75 billion, coupled with personal income tax cuts and the creation of 500,000 jobs over the next three years. Hawke said he would convene a national economic summit and create an Economic Planning Advisory Council to assist the government in the longer term.

On 14 February, Keating said that Labor would use Treasury bonds and notes to help fund its election promises. He said there were 'massive savings locked up in the banking system' that could be used for government spending. It was another gaffe. Fraser said Labor would be 'robbing' bank accounts to finance its election policies. Voters' savings would be at risk. 'Under Labor, it'd be safer under your bed than it would be in the banks,' he charged.

But Hawke quickly defused the issue: Fraser was 'a desperate man', hoping to breathe new life into an old scare tactic. 'They can't put [their savings] under the bed,' Hawke responded, 'because that's where the commies are!'[20]

The most difficult issue for Labor during the campaign was its opposition to the construction of the Franklin Dam in Tasmania. Environmental activists had clashed with construction workers and local communities through 1982. It was one of the largest environmental protests in Australian history. At Labor's national conference that year, the party resolved to oppose the building of the dam, which would flood parts of the Gordon and Franklin rivers and cause huge environmental damage. Hawke promised to use federal powers to halt construction of the dam, while further promising that Tasmanian workers, their families and communities would not be disadvantaged.

When Labor's national conference narrowly voted in support of the 'no dams' motion, Hawke let environmental campaigner Bob Brown know that he was on their side. 'There had been the blockade of dam works, which attracted national and international publicity, but suddenly it could be determined by an election because Labor now had a leader who was in favour of no dams,' Brown recalled. 'Bob came to the "Save the Franklin" rally in Melbourne with 15,000 people and said he would stop the dam and Hazel put on the yellow triangular "No Dams" earrings, and the crowd roared with approval.'[21]

Although Labor's pledge to stop the dam was popular on the mainland, it was deeply unpopular in Tasmania, where a majority of voters supported the dam's construction. Hawke was not risk-averse: he went to Hobart twice during the campaign and made the case, on environmental grounds, that the dam should not be built. His staff thought this a waste of time. But Hawke believed he had a responsibility to put Labor's policy to the people of Tasmania and allow them to judge the party on it. It also reinforced his message of conciliation and cooperation. At Hobart Town Hall, Hawke said the choice was not between 'environment and development', and insisted that, with 'sensible policies, and a willingness to resolve problems through negotiation and consensus, Australia can have both'.[22]

As the election campaign entered its final stages, Hawke reached for the mantle of economic responsibility. He simultaneously buried the legacy of fiscal profligacy of the Whitlam years and torched Fraser's claim to fiscal rectitude. The 1982–83 budget deficit was an estimated $1.6 billion, but it was expected to have increased to about $4 billion due to new spending and a fall in revenue. On 19 January, Howard was advised by Treasury that the 1983–84 budget deficit might be $8 billion. But on 21 February he said the deficit for the following year could be about $6 billion. On 28 February, Howard was advised by Treasury secretary John Stone that the projected deficit for 1983–84 was now about $9 billion. Howard contacted Fraser and said this figure should be made public. Fraser rejected the idea.

When Hawke spoke at the National Press Club days later, he said, relying on a tip-off, that the deficit might be larger than the government was letting on. And if the budget was worse than the government was admitting, then Labor reserved the right to revisit its policy promises. This was audacious. He was signalling to voters that Labor might junk some of its own policy agenda. It underscored his confidence that voters trusted his judgement. Hawke was right. The day before the election, Howard was told the projected 1983–84 deficit was now $9.6 billion. Howard told Fraser it should be revealed before election day, but again he was rebuffed.[23]

In a suite on the thirteenth floor of the Lakeside Hotel in Canberra, Hawke monitored the results on election night with Labor's campaign team, and a few friends and family – about twenty people in total. Susan and Rosslyn were there, as was Col Cunningham. Hawke's father, Clem, was celebrating his eighty-fifth birthday. Richard Farmer was asked to say a few words of appreciation. 'I was surprised because I did not know his father,' Farmer recalled. 'Hazel asked me to speak, being a bit of a wordsmith, so I did. Bob was very focused on the election, but he joined in and it was very nice for the old man.'[24] A chocolate cake was brought out and they sang 'Happy Birthday', and Clem blew out the candles.

Jill Saunders, who had worked in Hawke's Canberra office during the campaign, recalled the atmosphere. 'It was one of quiet excitement but also quite subdued,' she said. 'Bob was wanting to watch the television and talk on the phone so there wasn't a great deal of whooping going on in the background, that's for sure.'[25] He sat casually on a plush chair, cigar in hand, close to the single television set, watching the results come in. Geoff Walsh recalled that Hawke was confident of victory. 'The polling was telling us we were going to win, the mood on the streets was telling us we were going to win, and now, as the numbers were coming in, it was clear we were going to win,' he said.[26]

The results began to be reported on television at around 9 pm. Hawke's staff phoned party officials in different states for more up-to-date figures. The signs were promising. By 9.30 pm, Labor was not doing well in Tasmania, but the rest of the country was looking good. In the television tally, Labor was ahead of the Coalition by twenty seats. Hawke was engrossed in the coverage. He drank mineral water and black coffee; his staff began cracking open cans of beer. There were swings to Labor in Victoria and New South Wales. By 9.35 pm, Hawke told the room: 'It looks definite. We'd have to do very badly in Queensland and Western Australia not to win.' The results slowed but Labor was picking up seats in every mainland state. At 11.05 pm, a strap on the television said: 'LABOR WINS GOVERNMENT.' There was a cheer and applause. The staff hugged and shook hands. At 11.20 pm, Hawke sat next to his father on the lounge and put his arm around him. The election was over.[27]

In the end, it was not even close. Labor's primary vote increased by 4.34 per cent to 49.48 per cent. Labor won 53.23 per cent of the two-party vote to claim seventy-five seats to the Coalition's fifty. This gave Labor a twenty-five-seat majority in parliament, which represented the party's greatest electoral triumph since John Curtin's victory in August 1943. Across the mainland, city and rural, young and old, male and female, voters swung to Labor. Labor won six seats in Victoria, five each in New South Wales, Queensland and Western Australia, and one each in South Australia and the Northern Territory – twenty-three in total. Labor also won Flinders in Victoria, the seat it had lost in a December 1982 by-election, setting in train the events that led to the leadership change. In the Senate, Labor won thirty seats in the sixty-four-seat chamber, an increase of three. The Australian Democrats held the balance of power. The Liberals held all five seats in Tasmania.

In his election campaign report, McMullan noted that the victory had been the result of years of planning. The first draft strategy was prepared in July 1981, and a contingency plan for a March 1983 election had been approved in January that year. Labor's candidate selection, marginal seat strategy, research and advertising had been first-rate. The campaign team worked effectively together. The short campaign was an advantage as it forced the team to make 'tough decisions' and prioritise 'discipline'. These would not be factors when the government faced re-election.[28] Tony Eggleton said in his report that 'after seven years, the government had very little going for it' and battled an 'anti-government atmosphere'. But he also concluded: 'Hawke gave new relevance to Labor promises and generated a fresh spirit and confidence of a kind that we could not match.'[29]

In assessing Labor's campaign, Cameron said Hawke's campaigning 'struck the right note' with voters and was 'the dominant factor in Labor's victory'.[30] He conducted a post-election survey in capital cities. He found the net swing to Labor by January 1983 was 2 per cent. When the leadership changed, and until election day, a further 2.5 per cent was added to Labor's swing. This constituted: 0.5 per cent due to the Labor campaign, 0.5 per cent due to the Liberal campaign, 0.5 per cent due to other factors, and 1 per cent due to Hawke. Labor's support was particularly strong with young families in the suburbs, women, and people under twenty-five. When asked what the best feature of the Labor campaign was, 38 per cent said Hawke.[31]

By 11.25 pm at the Lakeside, Hawke had changed into a fresh suit and tie. He had a cup of tea. Just before 12 am, Bob and Hazel headed to the National Tally Room at the Canberra Showgrounds. Before the Hawkes arrived, they first stopped at the ABC studios on Northbourne Avenue. It was there, interviewed live on national television, that Hawke first claimed victory. It was 12.06 am.

'I want to say first of all to the people of Australia: thank you for the confidence which they have entrusted in me and my colleagues in forming the next government of Australia,' he told the nation.

'I want also particularly to say to those who have voted another way that this is going to be a government for all Australians, irrespective of how they cast their vote ... So I say that from this moment I commit myself, I commit our government, to undertaking from this moment the task of national reconciliation ... We have a magnificent country. If we all work together, we can see, I believe, no bounds in what we can do.'[32]

The Tally Room was filled to the brim with poll workers, journalists, commentators and a large public gallery. Hundreds of people were crowded around outside. At 12.30 am, Hawke took Hazel by the hand and stepped into the room. There was huge applause and cheers, and the chant went up: 'We want Bob! We want Bob!' Hawke waved and shook hands. He spoke to Paul Keating, Mick Young and Andrew Peacock. And then he did the rounds of the television networks.

Fraser was at the Southern Cross Hotel in Melbourne. He was surprised by the scale of the defeat, and could not hide his emotions. Although regarded as stern, aloof and arrogant, caricatured as an Easter Island statue, he was visibly upset. Fraser's face was flushed as he took 'total responsibility' for the election result. Tears welled in his eyes and his lower lip quivered. Fraser had bottled up his emotions as prime minister; now they poured out. It was just before 1 am.

Hawke finished up in the Tally Room and exited to the car. The media followed. They drove back to the Lakeside. Hawke talked to Hazel in the car about Fraser's breakdown. They had been told about it by journalists, but had not seen it. Hawke felt personally sorry for Fraser, but he also thought he had squandered his prime ministership. 'Fraser had come to office with big majorities,' Hawke reflected. 'He had the opportunity to make all the reforms that I made, and he didn't.'[33]

The party in Hawke's suite continued until 3 am. The staff celebrated further at Juliana's restaurant downstairs and at Charlie's Restaurant in Civic. Finally, the sun came up heralding the dawn of a new Labor government.

Clem Hawke was up early to celebrate his son becoming the twenty-third prime minister of Australia. He could not have been more elated. In the lobby of the Lakeside Hotel, as his son began the task of forming a government and the transition of power, Clem was shaking hands with anyone he could find, boasting about the election victory and declaring that his son would be a great prime minister. He had been saying it for more than fifty years.

PART III

POWER
1983–1991

18

TAKING
POWER

The day after the election, Sunday, 6 March 1983, Malcolm Fraser met with Governor-General Sir Ninian Stephen. His prime ministerial car, with the Australian flag flapping on the bonnet, drove through the gates at Government House at Yarralumla at 5.30 pm. Fraser returned his commission as prime minister, and recommended Stephen call upon Bob Hawke to form a government. Fraser agreed to continue in a caretaker capacity, as he had done in November and December of 1975. A short time later, Fraser's car sped through the gates and he waved to the assembled journalists. The flag had been removed.

Hawke's office was phoned, and he was asked to call upon the governor-general. He had an appointment with destiny. Hawke arrived at 6.38 pm. They met in Stephen's study, where Gough Whitlam, the last Labor prime minister, had been dismissed by ambush at lunchtime on 11 November 1975. After offering his congratulations, Stephen invited Hawke to begin forming a new government. He was now the prime minister designate. They spoke for just over ten minutes. At 6.52 pm, Hawke's car sped through the gates and took him back to Parliament House.

Hawke, of course, had no direct contact with Queen Elizabeth II. But he did receive a letter from Prince Philip, the Duke of Edinburgh, who broke royal protocol to congratulate him in writing. Hawke had attended the Duke of Edinburgh Study Conference in Canada in 1962. 'When the Commonwealth Study Conferences first started, it never occurred to me to speculate about what the members might be doing in the future,' Philip wrote from Windsor Castle on 20 March. 'Even if I had indulged in a little speculation, I am sure I would never have dreamt that any of you might become a prime minister! Well you've made it and many congratulations on your achievement.'[1]

Hawke wasted no time getting to work. He gave a lengthy press conference, where journalists questioned him about the make-up of his ministry, the swearing-in of ministers, his meetings with departmental heads, and the specifics of several policies. Hawke said he had already spoken to Sir Geoffrey Yeend, the secretary of the Department of Prime Minister and Cabinet. He had also spoken to Treasury secretary John Stone and requested a written update on the state of the budget. Hawke also confirmed that Keating would be treasurer.

Yeend had met with Hawke in his suite at the Lakeside Hotel at 3 pm that afternoon. Jean Sinclair and Gareth Evans, who had prepared Labor's transition plan, also attended. Yeend congratulated Hawke on his election victory, and they got down to business. Hawke told Yeend he wanted him to remain as head of the department. 'I would be very happy to continue and look forward to getting the new government into operation,' Yeend would write in his note for file. Hawke informed Yeend that Graham Evans from Treasury would lead his private office. Hawke said there would not be widespread changes to department secretaries. They canvassed Hawke's personal security arrangements and agreed staff would need security clearances. Five volumes of briefing material covering government operations, the machinery of government, economic and non-economic policy matters, and election commitments were handed over.

Hawke and Yeend then discussed the forthcoming visit of Prince Charles and Princess Diana, the visit of the Chinese premier, Zhao Ziyang, and the resumption of parliament. The most important matter discussed was Hawke's Economic Summit. Other matters were canvassed: taking possession of the prime minister's office, moving into the Lodge, the use of VIP aircraft, the swearing-in of ministers, the declaration of private interests, decisions made during the caretaker period, and appointments to the public service. Hawke said he did not want to press Fraser on 'departure arrangements'. He could leave his office and the Lodge when he was ready.[2]

The contrast with the previous Labor government was total. There were no quick ministerial swearings-in, no urgent removal of public servants, no rapid changes to policy, no rush of announcements. This was a focused, methodical, process-driven government. Hawke trusted the public service and wanted to work with them. It set the tone for the next nine years.

At 2.30 pm, in the closed saloon bar, Paul Keating met with Stone and Treasury deputy secretary Dick Rye. Keating's staff – Barbara Ward, Barry Hughes and John Langmore – joined them. The incoming treasurer was briefed on the state of the budget and the outlook for the economy. Keating and his staff then took the lift upstairs to Hawke's suite to tell him the grim news. Stone and Rye joined them shortly after. The incoming prime minister and treasurer were given Treasury's official briefing book.

The budget figures were much worse than imagined. The Fraser/ Howard budget deficit for 1983–84 had blown out to a projected $9.6 billion. Australia was still in recession and drought. Inflation and unemployment remained stubbornly high. Company profits were low, and excess capacity, coupled with a lack of confidence, meant that businesses were not investing. 'They were inheriting a bloody mess,' Stone recalled.[3] In a subsequent memo, Stone said there was 'uncertainty' about the precise forecasts, but noted that with Labor's proposed spending, the deficit for 1983–84 could be up to $12 billion – the largest since the end of World War II.[4]

Labor's landslide election victory powerfully influenced the dynamics in which Hawke sought to lead. He now possessed considerable authority in the new government, and he set his mind to establishing his first cabinet and outer ministry. Hawke decided to test his authority by exploring the idea of dumping Keating as treasurer. A few days after the election, Hawke met with a delegation from the ACTU at his home in Sandringham. Bill Kelty told Hawke that Ralph Willis should be the treasurer in the new government, not Keating. 'I put a fair amount of pressure on him,' Kelty recalled.[5]

Hawke was sympathetic to Kelty's view. '[Kelty] wasn't anti-Paul,' Hawke recalled. 'He was pro-Ralph. He knew Ralph's economic competence, which was unquestioned.'[6] So Hawke raised it with his staff. 'I want Ralph as treasurer, not Paul,' he said. 'See if we can fix it.'[7] Peter Barron, Hawke's political adviser, confirmed Hawke did consider replacing Keating with Willis.[8] So did speechwriter Graham Freudenberg who, like Barron, was close to Keating's NSW Right faction.[9] Keating was aware of Hawke's ruminations on his future and made it clear, via Graham Richardson, that he would not tolerate being moved from the Treasury portfolio. But he did not discuss it directly with Hawke.

In the end, Hawke decided to stick with Keating. 'He was close to Ralph, but I think he wanted somebody who was a bit more dynamic,' Kelty recalled. 'The greatest supporter of Keating was Hawke.'[10] Hawke had actually 'confirmed' to Treasury secretary John Stone at 1.45 pm on the Sunday after the election that Keating 'would be the Treasurer'.[11] But Hawke turned the idea over in his mind for several weeks. He still lacked confidence in Keating. In late March, Hawke told Richardson that Keating 'wasn't up to the job' and he wanted Willis to take over. Richardson told him to give Keating time. 'He will be fine,' Richardson said. It was a discussion they would return to throughout 1983.[12]

The swearing-in of ministers took place in the governor-general's study at Government House on 11 March 1983. It was televised for the first time. The initial thirteen-member cabinet included deputy Labor leader Lionel Bowen (deputy prime minister and minister for trade), Senate leader John Button (industry and commerce), Senate deputy leader Don Grimes (social security), Gareth Evans (attorney-general), Bill Hayden (foreign affairs), Paul Keating (treasurer), Susan Ryan (education and youth affairs), Gordon Scholes (defence), Peter Walsh (resources and energy), Stewart West (immigration and ethnic affairs), Ralph Willis (employment and industrial relations) and Mick Young (special minister of state).

The outer ministry of fourteen comprised John Dawkins (finance), John Kerin (primary industry), Kim Beazley (aviation), Peter Morris (transport), Chris Hurford (housing and construction), John Brown (sport, recreation, tourism and administrative services), Neal Blewett (health), Barry Jones (science and technology), Michael Duffy (communications), Barry Cohen (home affairs and environment), Clyde Holding (Aboriginal affairs), Brian Howe (defence support), Tom Uren (territories and local government) and Arthur Gietzelt (veterans' affairs).

The construction of the ministry was a little messy. Hawke's notes show he originally had Dawkins in cabinet, but then moved him to the outer ministry to accommodate Scholes because he felt he could not leave out the defence minister. It meant the finance minister was not originally in cabinet, but Dawkins attended most meetings anyway and was a member of the Expenditure Review Committee. Hawke decided to allocate what he deemed was the 'pecking order' based on how many votes ministers received in the caucus ballot. After the four parliamentary leaders – elected separately by caucus – this resulted in Willis (106 votes) being ranked higher than Keating (105). It also meant that the minister for foreign affairs, Hayden (101), was ranked lower than the minister for resources and energy, Walsh (102).[13] The factional make-up was less important in the first two terms. There were originally five from the Right (Hawke, Keating, Bowen, Willis, Evans); five from the Centre Left, officially formed in 1984 (Hayden, Button, Young, Ryan, Walsh), just one from the Left (West) and two unaligned (Grimes, Scholes).

There was little change in the cabinet and ministry in the government's first two terms. On 4 November 1983, West resigned from cabinet, but remained in the ministry, because he could not support uranium mining at Roxby Downs. He returned five months later, on 3 April 1984, after promising to maintain cabinet solidarity. Mick Young resigned over the Combe–Ivanov scandal on 14 July 1983. He was only in the sin bin for a short period, though, and returned to cabinet on 21 January 1984. Dawkins joined the cabinet when Young was ejected, and remained. John Kerin joined cabinet when West left, and he too remained. The size of Hawke's cabinet gradually increased to seventeen members by April 1991. There were only ever two women – Susan Ryan and Ros Kelly – but they were not cabinet members at the same time.

The first cabinet was extraordinarily diverse in background, education and work experience. There were unionists (Hawke, Keating, Willis, Young, West, Scholes), a shearer (Young), a doctor (Grimes), a farmer (Walsh), a policeman (Hayden), lawyers

(Bowen, Button), a schoolteacher (Ryan) and an academic (Evans). Several already had ministerial experience (Keating, Hayden, Bowen) or had served on the back bench in government (Willis, Scholes, Grimes, Walsh, Young). In time, the ministry would include three Rhodes Scholars (Hawke, Beazley, Blewett). Bowen had served in World War II, Young had been Labor's national secretary, and Scholes had been speaker of the House of Representatives. Most had working-class or middle-class backgrounds.

Hawke thought his ministers comprised 'without any doubt the most capable cabinet since Federation'.[14] He was especially pleased with John Hewson's 1987 assessment in *Business Review Weekly*: 'The Hawke government was very professional and is probably the best front bench since World War II.'[15]

—

How Bob Hawke governed for the next eight years, nine months and ten days was established in the early days. He worked long hours, was disciplined and focused, had a clean-desk policy, devoured paperwork, and was always well briefed on every item before cabinet. He would sleep only four or five hours a night. He would begin the day once or twice a week with nine holes of golf at 5.30 am or 6 am. He would eat breakfast at the Lodge – usually muesli and fruit, plus a cup of tea – and scan the newspapers. He would speak to his media advisers about what was making news, and identify stories that might need responding to. Hawke would chat with staff at the Lodge, his drivers and security personnel. He would be driven to Parliament House, sitting in the front seat, usually arriving between 8 am and 9 am. As Hawke was on the low-fat, high-fibre Pritikin diet, meals prepared by Hazel would be sent from the Lodge, but he would often swap these for more palatable options prepared by his Italian butler, Osvaldo Meneghello, known as 'Ossie'.

In between meetings with ministers, public servants and staff, and outside visitors such as ambassadors and union and business leaders, Hawke would read through cabinet documents and policy papers, and look at cables from overseas posts. He would talk to staff about the forward calendar. He would consider speeches and provide instructions to be passed to Graham Freudenberg or

Stephen Mills, or speak to them directly. He liked quiet uninterrupted periods of time to think. He had a large folder for Question
Time, with anticipated questions and suggested responses. During
a parliamentary sitting week, between 12 pm and 2 pm, he would
blaze a cigar and sit alone in his office reading this folder, occasionally calling in an adviser to answer queries. Sometimes he
would have a larger group discussion.

The daily program had to be flexible to allow for Hawke to give
interviews or press conferences, and to respond to events. Meetings
would be scheduled to speak to policy or political advisers, or see
senior public servants, if they deemed it time sensitive. Hawke
often saw Kim Beazley at the end of the day for a Villiger cigar.
Depending on his program, Hawke would usually depart the
office at around 9 pm or 10 pm. A few journalists or colleagues
might join him in the evening at the Lodge, where Hawke would
drink non-alcoholic beer imported from Germany.

The Hawkes moved into the Lodge the weekend after the
election, on Sunday, 13 March. Hawke enjoyed living there. As
he had done in the 1970s, he often greeted staff and ministerial
colleagues while sunning himself on a banana lounge by the pool;
sometimes he was naked during these discussions. Hawke was also
known to use the shower in his prime ministerial suite while talking
to staff. In hotel rooms, he would freely walk around nude in front
of staff. On a Friday afternoon, staff would prepare him a briefcase
full of briefing papers, cabinet submissions and letters to sign, and
this would be returned on Monday morning. Hawke would mostly
spend Saturdays betting on and watching horse races. On Sundays
he would play tennis, and later golf, and then focus on preparing for
the coming week, usually at the Lodge, where staff, public servants
and ministers would join him. Any chance Hawke got, he escaped
to Kirribilli House. There, with the magnificent lawns sloping
down towards Sydney Harbour, he could soak up the sun, breathe
the fresh harbour air and watch the boats go by.

When Hawke took possession of the prime minister's suite in
Parliament House on Wednesday, 9 March, Graham Freudenberg had already reclaimed his office. Freudenberg had last been
there on 11 November 1975, when the Whitlam government
was dismissed. Asked what it was like to return, he replied: 'It was

like Winston Churchill pissing into the Rhine.' Freudenberg, who would also spend time working from Sydney, recalled there was not much that was different about the way Whitlam and Hawke worked. 'Access was very easy,' he recalled, 'and they both stocked the fridge very well.'[16]

Hawke positioned his desk with his back to the large windows that looked across the lawn and the Aboriginal Tent Embassy to the Australian War Memorial. A wooden cigar box sat permanently on his desk. On the far wall, where Whitlam had placed his desk, was a lounge and coffee table. A television sat on top of a credenza so Hawke could watch horse races or the cricket, and news coverage. A peephole through a bookcase allowed staff to see if Hawke was busy without disturbing him. There were few paintings, photos or mementos. Hawke could call ministers directly from his desk, but often had calls placed by staff. He rarely left his office other than to talk to staff; ministers were usually summoned. He had a small private bathroom with a toilet and shower. Few ministers had walk-in rights – Paul Keating was one exception, and Graham Richardson (a backbencher until 1987) another. Staff would usually speak to the principal private secretary to arrange a time to see Hawke, and it would be scheduled.

Hawke was the last prime minister in what became known as Old Parliament House, and the first in the current building. Since 1973, the prime minister's suite of offices had been located on the north-eastern corner of the main floor. It opened onto a hallway that led directly to the House of Representatives on the left, and out to King's Hall straight ahead. Keating's office was located directly underneath. Hawke would usually enter the building through a set of fire escape doors on the side of the building that led directly to his suite. Occasionally, he walked up the front steps into King's Hall, then turned left and walked down the lobby to his office, which was guarded by a security post.

Hawke had thought about how he wanted his office to be structured and managed. He maintained a clear division between its administrative, policy, media and political functions. He wanted well-defined responsibilities and lines of accountability. He appointed career public servants as his principal private secretaries (chiefs of staff): they would lead the office, attend to administration, liaise with the public service and manage the business of cabinet. Hawke had four principal private secretaries: Graham Evans (1983–86), Chris Conybeare (1986–88), Sandy Hollway (1988–90) and Dennis Richardson (1990–91).

Evans recalled that he read an article in *The Australian Financial Review* predicting he would be appointed PPS. Hawke had already informed Yeend. But Evans had not discussed it with Hawke since the election. Evans spoke to John Stone, who encouraged him to take the position. Evans phoned Hawke's office and they invited him to come in and meet the prime minister designate. There Hawke formally offered Evans the role, but Evans baulked. 'I'm not entirely comfortable about Labor's economic policy,' he said. Hawke reassured him. 'I think you will find that we will need to review quite a bit of that.' He asked Evans to find a foreign policy adviser and an economic policy adviser. Evans quickly recommended career diplomat, and sport and music enthusiast, John Bowan for the former, and Australian National University economist Ross Garnaut for the latter.

Evans presided over a well organised and highly efficient office. He set the template for the next nine years. No prime ministerial office has operated more effectively. 'My main role was managing a very capable and highly intelligent group of people,' Evans recalled. 'Hawke was always open to contestable ideas and frank conversations. He was a good listener but it would be unwise to turn up with a poorly thought-out view that was not evidence-based. Anybody who wanted to see him could do so, but it had to be arranged with regard to his other responsibilities.'[17]

Conybeare said Hawke could get angry about an issue but never humiliated a staff member or held a grudge, preferring to learn from it and move on. 'Everyone knew their role and everyone was respected,' he said. 'It was a very open and consultative office. Hawke was totally consumed with the job. He was a workaholic. He was very focused on working through issues, managing the paper flow and being attentive to the policy, political, administrative and media needs of the office.'[18]

Hollway saw his role as managing the flow of advice and ensuring the machinery of government ran smoothly. 'Each day would involve a continuous but organised interaction across the corridor, going from my office into his or him into mine, working conscientiously,' he recalled. 'I took a lot of time to consider how his day needed to be structured and would present issues to him according to their priority and importance throughout the day. The key was staff having clearly defined roles.'[19]

Richardson said Hawke took a methodical approach to the prime ministership. 'He worked very hard – all prime ministers work very hard, but he was especially assiduous,' Richardson said. 'Hawke had oral briefings but he also read his briefs very carefully, he prided himself on never going into a meeting and shooting from the hip, he prepared for everything. He always had politics in his mind but, as a discipline, he mostly separated the politics from the policy.'[20]

The administrative and secretarial work of the office was managed by the principal private secretary, and these staff initially included Jeff Townsend (senior private secretary), Jean Sinclair (personal secretary) and Jill Saunders (assistant private secretary). They managed Hawke's diary, cabinet papers, parliamentary liaison, correspondence and travel schedule, and handled visitors. There were a range of other administrative and staff over the years. Geoff Yeend and then Mike Codd, along with their staff, had a small four-room suite of offices located just a few steps from Hawke's.

Political advice was dispensed by Peter Barron and Bob Hogg, who had agreed to join Hawke's prime ministerial staff, and later by Bob Sorby, Geoff Walsh and Colin Parks.[21] They were encouraged to tell Hawke difficult news and argue against a proposed course of action if they thought it was wrong. Barron, Hogg and Sorby often spoke to Hawke in the most robust language. 'Hawke was never afraid of the truth,' Barron said. 'He was always accepting of tough advice. Sometimes he did not like it, but he was never afraid to receive it.'[22] Hawke was in regular contact with Bob McMullan, as Labor's national secretary, and Rod Cameron, as the party's pollster, along with Margaret Gibbs, who reported on focus group research.

Media liaison was handled by seasoned media professionals, including Walsh, Parks, Paul Ellercamp, Barrie Cassidy, Grant Nihill and Bob Bowden. In Old Parliament House, they worked out of an office located in the Press Gallery.

Policy advisers were almost always drawn from the public service or academia. The two key initial appointments were Garnaut and Bowan. Hawke's subsequent principal economic advisers were Steve Sedgwick, Rod Sims and Malcolm Gray. Hugh White later succeeded Bowan as foreign policy adviser. Craig Emerson and then Simon Balderstone handled environmental policy. Freudenberg was speechwriter and later shared the role with Stephen Mills, who joined the staff in 1986: they became known as 'the old bull and the young bull'.[23]

Hawke's electorate secretary, Mimi Tamburrino, effectively became the member for Wills. She worked closely with Sinclair to manage local party and electorate matters. Hawke would usually visit every month or two for citizenship ceremonies, major community functions and sporting events. Many Wills constituents felt a sense of pride that the prime minister was their local member of parliament, recalled Tamburrino.[24]

Hawke got on well with his staff, quickly establishing a rapport based on the immense privilege they felt to be serving their country, their commitment to the reformist program of the government, and their respect for each other. He treated his staff like family and was loyal towards them. He knew their names, their families and interests. Hawke remembered the original core of staff – Evans, Walsh, Barron, Hogg, Garnaut, Bowan and Freudenberg, known as the 'gang of seven' – with particular affection. Hawke's staff would increase from about sixteen in 1983 to about thirty by 1991.

In the early years of the government, the only way Hawke could communicate with his staff when not in the office was via landline. There were no mobile phones, car phones, pagers, fax machines or emails. Graham Evans recalled escaping to Point Lonsdale for a family holiday over Christmas in 1984. He gave Hawke the phone number of the motel. One morning the manager told him he had received a call. 'It was some bloke pretending to be the prime minister,' he told Evans. 'Never mind, I told him where to get off. We're always getting prank phone calls here.'[25]

—

The lessons learnt from the Whitlam government remained at front of mind in the first days of the Hawke government. 'I had

witnessed the absolute chaos of the way the Whitlam government had operated,' Hawke said.[26] He was highly critical of the
poisonous relations that often existed between ministers and
their departments. While Whitlam distrusted much of the public
service, and introduced personal advisers to second-guess the
public service, Hawke believed a cooperative and respectful relationship with public servants was essential for good government.

Frank and fearless advice from public servants was expected.
Public servants across the board were respected for their knowledge and policy advice, and worked seamlessly with the Prime
Minister's Office and other ministerial offices. Hawke wanted
to appoint Ted Evans, a deputy secretary in Treasury, to succeed
Yeend as head of his department in February 1986. Evans declined,
believing he was not as suited to the role as other potential candidates were. Graham Evans suggested Mike Codd, who was then
running the Department of Community Services. They would
form a respectful and effective relationship.

In Hawke's Garran Oration, delivered in 1988, he explained that
the Department of Prime Minister and Cabinet was 'substantially
less interventionist, with greater concentration on its fundamental
role as a coordinating agency', than it had been under Fraser. He
said this reflected a change both in concept and in the character of
the prime minister.[27] Hawke reshaped the focus of his department
to suit his own political and policy style. He reduced its policymaking role, and instead used it to coordinate policy work and
undertake specialist initiatives.

The Office of the Status of Women, headed by Anne Summers,
was re-established in the department. Other specialist units
included the Office of Multicultural Affairs, the Aboriginal
Reconciliation Unit and the Office of the Chief Scientist. Hawke's
department also managed the Economic Planning Advisory
Council, and organised the 1983 National Economic Summit,
the 1983 South Pacific Forum, the 1983 and 1985 Constitutional
Conventions, the 1985 National Taxation Summit, the Council
of Australian Governments (COAG), and the 1988 bicentennial
projects. The International Division was upgraded to manage the
work of the Asia-Pacific Economic Cooperation (APEC) forum,
the Cambodian peace process and the Antarctic Treaty.

There would also be broader changes to the public service, initiated by John Dawkins. The purpose was to make the public service more responsive to government and more accountable for decisions. This was characterised as the adoption of private-sector management techniques, known as 'managerialism', which placed a premium on efficiency and effectiveness. Among these reforms were the introduction of the Senior Executive Service, the removal of permanency for departmental secretaries and an emphasis on merit-based promotion under the *Public Service Reform Act 1984*. 'We were not going to end our days complaining about the public service not supporting us, as Malcolm Fraser did when he lost,' said Dawkins.[28]

The Whitlam government had had a toxic relationship with the Australian Security Intelligence Organisation (ASIO). The election of a new Labor government represented an opportunity for the agency and the party to reset their relationship. Harvey Barnett, ASIO's director-general, met with Hawke for the first time at Kirribilli House at 3.30 pm on Tuesday, 8 March 1983. Hawke initially greeted Barnett in his swimming costume while farewelling his old friend George Polites, and quickly changed into more suitable attire. Barnett's briefing paper and subsequent record of the discussion, now declassified, reveal that he reassured Hawke that ASIO was a 'bipartisan' and 'loyal organisation' which acted 'within the ASIO Act', and there were no 'dirty tricks'. The past difficulties between the agency and the Whitlam government were discussed. Barnett briefed Hawke on espionage activities and the threat of terrorism, which was deemed low. He said there were KGB and GRU (Soviet military intelligence) officers operating in Australia. Hawke said some Trotskyists were 'probably' working within the Labor Party. Hawke asked for information on his old nemesis, Bill Hartley.[29] A report was subsequently provided on his relationships, predominantly with Iraq and Libya, and the sizeable payments he received.[30]

The most difficult aspect of the conversation concerned the Communist Party links of Labor MPs Arthur Gietzelt, Tom Uren and Bruce Childs. 'The person of most concern because he was a member of the shadow cabinet was Senator Arthur Gietzelt,' Barnett told Hawke. 'He was probably a CPA [Communist Party of Australia] member as far back as 1940 and had been on the Sydney District Committee between 1952 and 1955. He operated under the party name of "Arthur James". CPA members were urged to keep his identity secret.' ASIO's files on Gietzelt's CPA links included audio and video recordings, photographs, intercept reports, agent assessments and eye-witness testimony. ASIO believed Gietzelt had been a dual member of the Labor Party and the CPA, and acted as an operative inside Labor.[31] The US State Department viewed Gietzelt as a national security risk because of his close relationship with the CPA in the 1970s.[32] Barnett told Hawke that Gietzelt could still be a member of the CPA. Uren and Childs were deemed to have had 'close relations' and a 'long association' with the CPA, but ASIO's assessments were less definitive about the extent of their involvement.[33]

Gietzelt, Uren and Childs denied their CPA links. But Uren revealed in one of his final interviews that he believed Gietzelt had been a CPA member. 'I think he was,' Uren said. 'Arthur did some silly things but I'm pretty sure he wasn't a member of the [Communist] party when he was a minister. He used to go regularly into the Communist Party headquarters. I think he was a silly bastard in many ways, dogmatic, all those things.' Uren also said that Childs was a dual member of the Labor Party and the CPA. 'In my mind, I respected them very much and they were both probably Marxists – I never was,' he said.[34]

Bill Hayden was also briefed by ASIO about Gietzelt's links with the CPA. 'I did receive a briefing from ASIO on Gietzelt when I became foreign minister,' Hayden recalled. 'I knew they had caught him out in a couple of clandestine operations. ASIO was on the ball. Obviously, they picked him up and knew what he was up to.' Hayden said his 1983 briefing followed an earlier briefing in 1975. 'Whitlam had organised for me to be briefed by ASIO,' he said. 'Gietzelt was raised by the ASIO representative. I must say, Gough was devastated. He knew what the political consequences would be if it got out.'[35]

The revelation that Gietzelt was suspected by ASIO of having extensive and long-running CPA links would have been a national security scandal if revealed in 1983. Hawke accepted what ASIO said about Gietzelt, but felt he could not deny him a ministry. He suspected Gietzelt's CPA links were behind him. He made the further point that Gietzelt was not in cabinet, nor was Uren, and he did not deal with foreign policy, defence or national security matters. So Hawke decided to leave it. 'I dealt with my ministers as they were,' he explained.[36]

Hawke was secure enough in himself that he could share power. He was regarded as a good chair of cabinet by all ministers. He had extensive experience chairing meetings of the ACTU Executive and Congress, as well as Labor's national executive and conferences, and had been a member of many boards. He was on time for meetings and across all aspects of business. He could distil complex issues and summarise debates well. He went to great lengths to achieve consensus-based outcomes – a style that could lead to debates that continued for inordinate lengths of time – but his efforts to be consultative and inclusive were usually appreciated by those around the table.

Hawke trusted his ministers and respected them to do their jobs with little interference. He recalled what he told ministers: 'I will leave you to run your area. I won't be an intrusive prime minister. But there are two circumstances in which I will be involved. One is if you come to me and ask for my involvement. Secondly, if something arises in your portfolio which I think has a significance for the government as a whole, beyond your portfolio, then I will become involved.'[37]

Susan Ryan, unique as the only female minister, had gained the respect of the male-dominated caucus and cabinet. Meetings in both forums could be robust. But Ryan could be a tough and wily operator, and she was able to build critical alliances to advance her policy agenda. Ryan acknowledged it was sometimes 'difficult' being the only woman in cabinet. 'I honestly find it hard to say how much of the difficulty was down to what I was pursuing as education minister and women's minister as opposed to just being the only woman,' she recalled. 'I just accepted it as my lot. Getting into a position of power was so extraordinary that I just thought I've got to make this work.'[38]

It was only a short walk from Hawke's office to the cabinet room. Dark-wood panelling lined the walls. In the centre was a large, square oak table with a huge hole in the middle; it had been built to seat all ministers during the Whitlam government. One side of the room was a large window, where light streamed in through sheer curtains. Public servants would sit in the corners of the room at small tables. A thick layer of smoke hung in the air, as several ministers smoked cigarettes. Button later wrote that Hawke smoked his cigars 'stylishly and with pleasure', much 'like a successful Mississippi riverboat gambler'.[39]

Outside was an anteroom where public servants or non-cabinet ministers would wait to be summoned. Food and drink would be served by Hawke's butler, Ossie, from a kitchenette during short breaks in cabinet business. Ministers could also summon Ossie or another attendant with a button if they wanted something to eat or drink during meetings. Snacks were usually sandwiches, party pies, lamingtons or scones. Sandy Hollway recalled that Hawke was very focused on cabinet business and gave it his undivided attention. He did, however, recall Hawke once briefly adjourning one cabinet meeting, walking across the corridor and into his office, and closing the door. Hollway was curious. He looked at the closed-circuit television that monitored Hawke's office: the PM was turning on the television to check the winner of a midweek horse race.[40]

Hawke used the committees of cabinet, with the wider input of other ministers, to initiate and determine policy. He chaired the three coordinating committees dealing with parliamentary and budget matters, and also the seven functional committees on policy. The Expenditure Review Committee – initially comprising Hawke, Keating, Willis, Walsh and Dawkins – was responsible for overseeing government outlays and became the engine room of economic policy. Decisions of the ERC were unlikely to be revisited in cabinet. The ERC had immense authority, given the status of its members, and some ministers found the process of submitting proposals to scrutiny intimidating.

Hawke benefited from two key administrative changes that caucus denied to Whitlam. First was having an outer ministry. This served to consolidate decision-making among a smaller group of senior ministers in cabinet. Second, cabinet ministers were bound by the principle of solidarity, which meant they could not challenge cabinet decisions in caucus. And once senior ministers representing different factions had agreed to a position, there was little chance that caucus would override it. This was a departure from Labor tradition, which held that caucus, not cabinet, was supreme, and that all ministers were equal.

Hawke formed a good working relationship with Lionel Bowen. He would consult his deputy on all important matters across government, policy and political, and respected his counsel. 'There were no fits of temper or outbursts of any kind,' Hawke recalled of Bowen. 'He was calm, moderate and a thoroughly decent man.'[41] John Button was leader of the government in the Senate for the entire Hawke prime ministership. Hawke did not have a close relationship with Button, but thought he was 'a very good minister' and consulted him on major policy and political decisions.[42]

The critical partnership, which was fundamental to the government's overall policy achievements and electoral dominance, was that of prime minister and treasurer. Keating saw Hawke as 'chairman of the board' and himself as 'chief executive officer'.[43] While personally very different, they had a natural synergy in their approach to politics and in their policy goals. The seeds of the destruction of their relationship lay not in policy differences but in ambition. Nevertheless, a mutual respect and affection developed that was both public and private. Hawke would often use the intercom to buzz Keating at his desk and invite him up for a conversation or to join a meeting. Keating would often wander into Hawke's office, take a seat and chew over the issues of the day. There would be weekend lunches at the Lodge with Paul and Annita Keating, and their children.

Hawke was attentive to caucus and his office was accessible to MPs. He often relied on the party leaders Bowen, Button and Grimes in the early years to deal with tricky issues. Later, this leadership group included Keating and Evans. Few were prepared to challenge Hawke's authority in the caucus, not only because of his personal popularity and authority, but also because any differences were usually sorted out among faction leaders and senior ministers prior to caucus meetings. As the factional system became more organised and disciplined, Hawke used faction leaders to communicate with the caucus, maintain unity and divide the spoils of power: ministries, committee appointments and overseas trips. He enjoyed good personal relations, for most of the time, with leaders from the Right (Graham Richardson and Robert Ray), the Left (Gerry Hand and Nick Bolkus) and the Centre Left (Peter Cook).

—

Hawke's rise to a position of public prominence and power had taken place outside the political system. His celebrity-like status meant that he was typically more 'presidential' than any other prime minister, and the government traded on his personal standing with voters. Occasional flashes of vanity and arrogance, or tears, never seemed to do lasting damage. Hawke continued to revel in his folk-hero status and seemed to embody the national spirit. Australians saw him sing, dance, hold a bat, kick a football, throw a frisbee, kiss women on the cheek, shake hands with children and pat animals. The Hawke persona was brilliantly satirised by actor Max Gillies, who exaggerated Hawke's distinctive voice and familiar mannerisms: tugging an earlobe, adjusting his ring, eyes darting around with a cheeky laugh followed by a serious scowl. Hawke joined in the celebration of sporting triumphs, cheered Australia's achievements in the arts and sciences, and appeared on popular television programs such as *Countdown*, *A Country Practice* and *The Comedy Company*. He handed out Logie Awards. And he featured in *The Phantom* comic book.[44]

Hawke was an egotist but not a narcissist. Critics argued that he was the latter, and that his narcissism was fired by a sense of destiny and sustained by conceitedness. But a consensus leadership style is intrinsically at odds with narcissism. Hawke maintained broad support in cabinet and caucus for the government's policy direction. His above-average approval rating underscored his ability to broadly empathise with Australians. Nevertheless, Hawke could be vain and arrogant, and he enjoyed the attention and the accoutrements of office. It would be odd for a prime minister not to believe they have special talents. But it is exaggerated to think that Hawke, like Narcissus, drowned in his own reflection.

Hawke's guiding political philosophy – consensus – was also his central idea in public life. He had identified a policy challenge (economic crisis and social division) and a framework within which to address it (consensus). It was not about winning total agreement; it was the search for common ground between competing ideas. It was a desire for 'a unity of understanding and purpose' as a means of achieving lasting reform.[45] The National Economic Summit and the Prices and Incomes Accord reflected this approach. Hawke established the Economic Planning Advisory Council (EPAC) to assist policy development.[46] Another initiative was to re-establish the Australian Labor Advisory Council – bringing together government, unions and the Labor Party – which had foundered in the Whitlam years.

Consensus politics underscored Hawke's disdain for class warfare and the politics of envy – approaches in Labor's past and its future – that never appealed to most Australians. Hawke believed in national unity and common purpose. 'Class warfare does not resonate with me,' Hawke explained.[47] 'Employers have a legitimate ambition to grow their businesses. Unions have a legitimate ambition to improve the wages and conditions of employees. They are both more likely to achieve these legitimate ambitions if they sit down and talk and work together'[48]

—

During the first year of the new government, Australians got to know Hazel Hawke better, finding her warm, generous and modest. They also glimpsed the other side of her: a lively and articulate woman with strong opinions. Hazel felt her marriage to Bob had entered a new phase. Her friend Wendy McCarthy recalled these years as one of adjustment. 'There was a happiness in their relationship that had not been there for a long time,' she said. 'Clearly they had a great foundation for the marriage but it went off the rocks in the middle and now it was back together.'[49] Daughter Susan also saw a change in the relationship. 'There was a high level of companionship and contentment between them in these years and the fact that the grandchildren were coming meant a new phase of family life,' she said.[50]

But these were still challenging times for the three Hawke children. Stephen had watched his father claim the election victory on television at a friend's place in Derby, in Western Australia.

He was thrilled. 'There is a bit of a myth about me and Dad not getting on at all and being hostile to each other,' he explained. 'I had a life, and my life was in the Kimberley, which was a fucking long way from Canberra, and I was quite glad of that. But there's never been an estrangement.' He recalled spending Christmas at Kirribilli in the early years of the government.

Stephen fell in love with Lesley Corbett, and they had two sons, Kel and Sam, who took their mother's surname. Their paternal grandfather was hurt by this. 'I'm Hawke and I'm not ashamed of it,' Stephen said. 'But it does affect your life. People react to you in a different way. They don't take you as you are.'[51] It was a lesson he had learnt himself.

19

ECONOMIC
REALITIES

The press conference on Tuesday, 8 March 1983, was packed when Bob Hawke and Paul Keating took their seats. As Hawke revealed to the nation that the budget deficit had deteriorated significantly, and that this had been kept secret by the Coalition before the election, his righteous indignation was turned up for maximum political effect. 'It is just unbelievable that what the Australian people, and we as the alternative government, have been faced with is a proposition of being told that the deficit on existing policies in 1983–84 would be $6 billion when in fact they knew it was $9.6 billion,' Hawke said. The Coalition's economic credibility was shredded.

While much of Labor's election manifesto would be jettisoned – leading some to complain of policy backflipping and electoral betrayal – Hawke insisted that reforming and reconstructing the economy was a central element of his pitch to voters in 1983. What stuck in Hawke's mind was Lee Kuan Yew's warning about Australia in 1980: 'If Australia keeps going the way it is, it is going to end up the poor white trash of Asia.'[1] And so, as would be the story of the Hawke government, events forced its hand. The budget had to be repaired.

At their first meeting, on Sunday, 6 March, John Stone advised Hawke and Keating about the flight of capital out of Australia. A decision had to be made about devaluing the currency. Stone suggested a 5 per cent devaluation. But Reserve Bank governor Bob Johnston suggested a 10 per cent devaluation. The next day, there had been a flight of capital to the tune of $200 million. Hawke had taken possession of Kirribilli House in Sydney. There, in the drawing room, it was decided to devalue the currency by 10 per cent. This was announced on Tuesday, 8 March. It worked. The dollar fell from 94.15 US cents to 85.49 US cents, and by the end of that week around $3 billion had returned to Australia.

While economic policy took centre stage in the first few days of the Hawke government, another significant decision was to determine Stone's future. It was widely anticipated within the party, and speculated in the media, that Stone would be dumped. He was seen as a conservative spear-carrier unacceptable to Labor. Stone and Hawke knew one another from their time at Perth Modern and Oxford. Stone had risen fast through the Treasury ranks to become deputy secretary in 1971 and secretary in 1979.

Ross Garnaut, economic adviser to Hawke, argued against sacking Stone.[2] 'Treasury is one of the greatest institutional offices of this country and you don't have politicians arbitrarily changing the secretary,' Garnaut said. 'If he had been incompetent or had other weaknesses then obviously you would do something about it but changing a secretary of Treasury without good reason was bad governance.'[3]

The treasurer was also committed to keeping Stone. At a time of fluctuating currency and exchange markets, and being new in his job, Keating did not seriously countenance sacking him. 'If the first action of the government was to execute the Treasury secretary, who had been essentially our emissary to the world, then this would go down very badly in foreign capitals,' Keating said. 'I didn't want it looking like *The Beverly Hillbillies* were back in town and the first thing we do is shoot the sheriff.'[4]

Stone had voted Labor in 1983. He did not think John Howard had been a successful treasurer, regarding him as 'weak' and 'overshadowed' by Malcolm Fraser, and believed he had left the nation's finances 'in a very bad way'. But Stone had doubts about Labor's agenda. He saw little point in the proposed National Economic Summit, was sceptical of the accord, and thought Labor's tax-and-spend proposals would not be effective in reducing inflation and unemployment. Keating and Stone quickly established a mutually respectful relationship. Stone found Keating to be 'self-confident' but also 'hardworking' and 'good fun to be with'.[5]

Meanwhile, the shattered Liberal Party met to select a new leader. Howard had been Fraser's deputy. Andrew Peacock had staked a claim on the leadership when he challenged Fraser in April 1982, losing by fifty-four votes to twenty-seven. Now the leadership contest was between Howard and Peacock. The result of the ballot was that Peacock defeated Howard by thirty-six votes to twenty. Peacock wanted to steer his party in a new direction. 'I wanted to put it in a position to win an election and to have a platform which was somewhat more liberal in the classic sense,' he recalled.[6]

The National Economic Summit, held on 11–14 April 1983, was the highpoint of Hawke's consensus policymaking. This was an idea he had talked about since the 1970s. It held out the promise of a grand bargain between government, business and unions on economic reform. Held in the House of Representatives and broadcast live on television and radio, it brought together representatives from business, unions and welfare organisations, along with state governments and members of parliament. This was a new style of policymaking. Hawke wanted participants to be informed of the true state of the Australian economy and then agree on a series of measures that would constitute the building blocks of a program of reform.

Having the summit in the House of Representatives gave it status and authority. But Hawke recalled Sir Geoffrey Yeend, the head of his department, trying to veto the idea. 'Oh you can't do that, Prime Minister, it has never been done,' Yeend said.

'Well, this is a new government, and that's what we're going to do,' Hawke replied, 'unless you can tell me there is some legal reason for not being able to do it.'

Yeend conceded: 'No, there is nothing to stop you doing it.'[7]

Hawke's opening address sought to focus minds on the economic challenges facing the nation, concrete steps that could be taken to address them and the need, above all, for cooperation. Hawke appealed to high principles, patriotism and public duty. 'We meet here today as the representatives of the Australian people, in a time of Australia's gravest economic crisis in fifty years,' he said. 'They have imposed a high trust on us. We must try our very best not to let them down.' The deliberations would 'shape the future of Australia' in the decades ahead. It was a call to action at the beginning of a new era. In a memorable assessment, journalist Peter Bowers said Hawke left 'the chamber steaming in consensus like a cow paddock after a rain shower'.[8]

The summit communiqué supported an accord between government and unions (but not business) that provided for a return to centralised wage fixation coupled with wage and dividend restraint. There was to be a focus on new job-creation programs, industry assistance, welfare reform, better use of technology and upskilling the workforce. Union amalgamations were agreed to. The Economic Planning Advisory Council was established. All participants – except Queensland premier Joh Bjelke-Petersen – signed the communiqué. Hawke was enthusiastic when he briefed cabinet. 'The conference is a central part of the government's more open and consultative approach to economic management,' he noted. 'There was a willingness on the part of all participants to acknowledge that we all bear some responsibility for our current economic malaise and that all have a part to play in overcoming our current difficulties.'[9]

The summit, Hawke argued, provided the springboard for the economic reforms of the coming decade: floating the dollar, deregulating the financial system, slashing tariffs, overhauling the tax system (with big reductions in company and personal tax rates), and privatising government assets. These reforms were the foundation stones for three decades of economic growth. The budget was repaired structurally, with spending cut in real terms, and returned to surplus. The accord with unions moderated wage claims in return for social wage benefits.[10]

It also heralded a shift in the nation's mood and ambition, thought Peter Barron. 'Almost everything Hawke achieved as prime minister had its foundation in that week,' Barron said. 'What happened that week, and the flow from it, changed Australia as much as any other event in our history. But it was proactive, not reactive. It was not only the economic reforms but the summit itself that did more for the nation's self-confidence than anything else. This was all Hawke. And it was about the national interest.'[11]

Ross Garnaut agreed. 'Talking things over on the basis of shared information and knowledge was how Hawke thought economic policy should work,' Garnaut said. 'The symbolism of doing that was even more important than the actual content. It was tremendously important.' Stone, though, thought the summit was a waste of time. Garnaut recalled having a pee in the toilet next to Graham Evans when Stone walked in. 'You two blokes should be ashamed,' he remembered Stone saying. 'This is not how policy should be made.'[12]

On 29 March 1983, Keating and Dawkins informed cabinet that spending would have to be reduced in order to meet a deficit target of $8.5 billion. Ministers with dreams of new programs were shocked. Keating and Dawkins made it clear existing programs would have to be substantially trimmed or abolished, and some new proposals would have to be deferred.[13] On 19 May, Keating delivered an economic statement. The result was that $985 million was cut from existing programs, and after allowing for $557 million in new programs, the deficit was reduced by $428 million. New savings measures included reductions in depreciation allowances and subsidies, a new lump-sum tax on superannuation, and an assets test on pensions as an important equity principle.

It was not what many in caucus expected when briefed by Hawke and Keating earlier in the day, but it was the new reality.[14] During the campaign, Labor had seized the mantle of fiscal responsibility and now they had to deliver. 'The big driver was the Whitlam legacy,' Keating explained. 'It was instilled in us that this was not how to run an economy. Then along comes Fraser and Howard who compounded the spending of the Whitlam government. So, you had one group of fiscal fools compounding the work of an earlier group of fiscal fools.'[15]

The first budget of the Hawke government, delivered by Keating on 23 August, witnessed a more confident treasurer who locked in the principal economic strategy of reducing inflation and unemployment while growing the economy and cutting the budget deficit. 'This government sought and received a very clear mandate from the Australian people to put the country back on the path to economic prosperity and to deal with inflation and unemployment simultaneously – with a spirit of consensus and fairness,' Keating said.[16] There were further reductions in spending programs, new taxes and levies, and funding provided for new programs such as Medicare, a boost to unemployment and family welfare support, and increases for universities, defence, the arts and the ABC.

The Hawke government was more pragmatic than ideological; Hawke believed ignorance was the enemy of good public policy. He wanted to inform the electorate, help them to understand the need for change, and then persuade them of the merits of the government's policies. Hawke saw this continual process of education as one of the hallmarks of his government. 'We didn't just come in with proposals for economic reform, we brought the Australian people along with us,' he said. 'We had the most economically literate electorate in the world. We had an educative process. People came to understand that what had been appropriate in the past was inappropriate now.'[17]

The result was that the Hawke government changed the nation and the Labor Party. A new governing framework was established that blended market-based economic reform with a targeted social safety net. It was not a hijack of Labor, as some from the academy claimed, but a recognition that while the goals of equality and opportunity remained, the tools to achieve them had to change. Labor's mission had always been to civilise capitalism and achieve social harmony.[18] Hawke had no doubt about his government's fidelity to Labor values. He knew Labor could not be a prisoner of its past. 'Fuck the past or the past will fuck you,' Hawke said.[19]

An important policy innovation was the accord struck between the government and unions. This tied both the political and industrial wings of the labour movement to the economic success or failure of the government. Hawke saw the accord as a way of fostering industrial harmony and repairing and reconstructing the economy. It was another tool of consensus politics. Simon Crean, who became ACTU president in 1985, said the partnership was born out of the ashes of the Whitlam government. 'We lent credibility to a Labor government in terms of economic management because we delivered on where we had previously struggled,' he argued. 'We showed what the labour movement could do for the nation when it shared the economic agenda.'[20]

As treasurer, Keating took the lead on negotiating the Prices and Incomes Accord. Although a sceptic in opposition, he became a convert in government. The combined authority of Hawke and Keating with Kelty and Crean underpinned it. There were six iterations, known as Mark I to Mark VI, during the Hawke government. In addition to moderating wage increases in return for a combination of real wage and social wage benefits, which eased inflationary pressures in the economy, monthly working days lost to industrial disputes per thousand employees fell from forty-nine between 1976 and 1982 to nineteen between 1983 and 1991.[21]

In the first two years, from October 1983 to October 1985, there was a half-yearly indexation of income to inflation (CPI) under Accord Mark I. An effective wage pause was followed by a 4.1 per cent boost to wages in April 1984 and another 2.6 per cent increase, in line with the CPI, in April 1985. A wage-tax trade-off in the August 1984 budget was designed to boost the economy as inflation and unemployment fell. Accord Mark II, inked in September 1985, demonstrated its flexibility as a tool of policy-making. The indexation of wages was discounted by 2 per cent, there was a trade-off with superannuation and a commitment to future income tax cuts. In September 1987, Accord Mark III adopted a two-tier approach to wage increases. This meant wage adjustments in line with inflation and further increases negotiated in return for productivity gains. Employers could negotiate with employees at the enterprise level within the accord framework.

—

The Hawke government faced one of its most serious challenges within its first month, when Soviet diplomat Valery Ivanov was expelled on 22 April 1983 after it was revealed he had tried to cultivate former Labor national secretary David Combe. By then a lobbyist, Combe was hoping to open doors for business leaders by trading on access to his friends and former colleagues in the government. ASIO believed that Ivanov, the first secretary at the Soviet Embassy, was an intelligence operative working for the KGB. Ivanov met Combe at an Australia-USSR Society function at the Canberra Labor Club during 1982. Combe was given a fully paid trip to Moscow to attend a conference organised by the society. Contact between Ivanov and Combe steadily increased. On the day before the 1983 election, they had a lengthy conversation over dinner that was recorded by ASIO as part of Operation Bushfowl. Combe canvassed the possibility of being appointed as a consultant or ambassador to the USSR to improve relations with Australia.

ASIO Director-General Harvey Barnett met with Hawke at his Parliament House office at 4.45 pm on 20 April to inform him that Ivanov was a spy, and that Combe (codenamed EPIC) may have been compromised. Hawke was shocked. Barnett said Combe:

> (a)   intended to enrich himself over the next two years and then seek a 'job-for-the-boys' from the ALP – he mentioned Ambassador to Moscow. He indicated that multinationals requiring his services for entrée to the ALP machine and its leaders would have to pay highly for the service. He discussed with IVANOV the prospect of an arrangement to be cleared with Moscow whereby his information would reach the CPSU and/or Politburo. IVANOV agreed to take this matter further.
> (b)   he spoke at length on an anti-American theme based on his belief that the CIA had engineered the downfall of the Whitlam government.

Ivanov told Combe that he was under surveillance and their relationship had to become 'more clandestine' to 'evade' detection. Hawke thought Combe was greedy and stupid, but did not immediately decide what to do about him. Barnett favoured expelling Ivanov, which would be a triumph for ASIO. After forty minutes, the meeting ended. Hawke told Barnett to stand by at the Lakeside Hotel; he would be summoned later that evening.[22]

Graham Evans, the only member of staff at that point who had a top-secret security clearance, was briefed by Hawke. Sir Geoffrey Yeend was called. 'It was a very dangerous issue for the government,' Evans recalled. 'The immediate issue was how to manage Combe. The issue was how culpable is Hawke if, knowing what Barnett has told him, he allowed Combe to continue as a lobbyist.'[23]

Jeff Townsend, Hawke's senior private secretary, recalled the reaction. 'Combe was a good bloke and he had been a good national secretary, but by this time he had become a bit unhinged,' Townsend said. 'On the tapes he came across as a greedy drunk. He said he was going to make a fortune from his former colleagues. So that didn't go down well. The ASIO guys were trying to get Ivanov but they got Combe by accident. Hawke was torn between his long-term friendship with Combe and the national interest, but he knew he had to act decisively.'[24]

At 9 pm, Hawke convened the National and International Security Committee of cabinet with Bill Hayden, Gareth Evans and Mick Young. They were briefed by Barnett. There was unanimous agreement that Ivanov should be expelled. Hayden suggested it be done quietly. The others disagreed. They quizzed Barnett about whether there was concrete evidence that Combe had been recruited by the KGB. There was no evidence of this, but clearly Combe was being cultivated. Evans was sceptical of ASIO and troubled by how quickly Hawke was acting. It also rankled with Evans, understandably, that Barnett had not gone to him first as attorney-general. 'ASIO was totally Cold War counter-espionage obsessed with the Soviet threat and agents of influence and all the rest of it,' he recalled. 'Maybe I could have stood up to Hawke but I didn't try hard enough.'[25]

At 8.30 am the next morning, 21 April, the NISC reconvened with Lionel Bowen and Gordon Scholes, who had not been available the previous evening. Bowen, who had spoken to Hawke the night before, asked Barnett about details of other surveillance operations. It was an odd detour. The result of the meeting was that ASIO officers, together with their files, were summoned from Melbourne and the NISC reconvened for a third time, at 12.30 pm, in the cabinet room. Parts of the Operation Bushfowl transcript were quoted, and questions answered. Hayden, however, said 'there was not enough hard evidence to expel IVANOV' and suggested he be further monitored. Hawke disagreed. He said Ivanov would be expelled, and it was agreed that Hayden would inform the Soviet ambassador the following day. Andrew Peacock, the opposition leader, was briefed by Barnett in Hawke's office at 5.15 pm.[26]

Hawke acted promptly to expel Ivanov and told ministers to break off contact with Combe. Hawke believed this scandal could have threatened the government's survival. 'If I had shown any weakness at all in regard to that, the opposition would never have left us alone,' he said. 'We had to be absolutely tough and it was the right thing to do. They had no business interfering in our affairs in the way they did.'[27]

The government still had to decide how to handle Combe. The cabinet was due to meet in Adelaide on 26 April. Hawke met with Barron, Hogg and Walsh at a cafe and told them the news. 'We were all a bit stunned by it,' recalled Walsh. 'It was not clear what or when it would emerge. But it was clear this was quite a big test for the government.'[28] Hogg's first reaction was to wonder if this was a repeat of the Whitlam years. 'Oh, here we go again,' he thought. Hogg told Hawke: 'Are you sure they haven't fucked up? David can be silly but he's not a crook.'[29]

When cabinet was informed about the Ivanov–Combe scandal, there was shock and dismay among ministers. It was decided to cease ministerial contact with Combe. He was *persona non grata*. At 11.35 pm on 10 May, Barnett met with Hawke, Gareth Evans and other officials to finalise the terms for a negotiated outcome with Combe. Hawke said Combe needed to acknowledge that he accepted the decision to bar him from contact with government. In return, the government would say that he was not a spy, he would not be prosecuted and the decision related partly to his relationship with Ivanov. Hawke, having now examined all the evidence, was furious with Combe, who had gone public to profess his innocence after being labelled a spy by the media.

At 11 am on 11 May, Barnett and Gareth Evans met with Combe at the attorney-general's department. Barnett briefed Combe on the surveillance of Ivanov and the recording of their conversation over dinner on 4 March. Barnett said he felt it necessary to inform Hawke of the danger to both Combe and Australia's national security. 'I told EPIC that he appeared to us to be standing on a cliff edge with one foot dangling over the edge and about to plunge,' Barnett noted. The ASIO man then read long extracts from the Bushfowl transcript to Combe, and flagged the warning signs that Combe was being cultivated. Combe responded that he was only talking about trade, and Barnett pointed out that Ivanov only wanted to talk about politics. Barnett left it to Evans to work out the 'terms of settlement'.[30]

On 12 May, Hawke announced the establishment of the Royal Commission on Australia's Security and Intelligence Agencies. Justice Robert Hope would examine the Ivanov expulsion, the cultivation of Combe and the actions taken by ASIO and the Hawke government. Hawke was cross-examined for three days during August. Combe protested his innocence and said his civil liberties had been trampled upon. He also claimed that ASIO had concocted an elaborate sting operation to entrap him. Canberra swirled with rumours that the royal commission would show that Hawke had been mistaken, that ASIO had overstepped its authority and that Combe would be cleared.

ASIO, while trumpeting its success in catching a KGB spy, had made a significant error, but not one concerning Combe. On 3 May, Hawke was informed that Hogg had had breakfast with Combe the day before. Combe, then under surveillance, had suggested to Rod Cameron they invite Hogg to breakfast at the Lakeside Hotel. But not only did Hogg not attend, he was never even invited. Hawke was furious and gave Barnett a dressing-down. On 4 May, Hawke told Barnett that it was 'intolerable and inexplicable' that the prime minister had been given 'untrue information'.[31] Barnett apologised to Hogg. Hawke subsequently took it upon himself to review the tape recordings and transcripts at his office at Treasury Place in Melbourne on 8 May. 'Although I did find some minor mistakes, they were not exculpatory of Combe,' he concluded.[32]

Mick Young became collateral damage when he let slip to Gough Whitlam's former press secretary, Eric Walsh, that a Soviet diplomat was about to be expelled. The conversation had taken place on 21 April in the carpark of the 19th Hole Motel in Canberra. This conversation did not become known until months later. Hawke felt he had no option but to insist Young resign from cabinet, as he had broken solidarity. Young resigned on 14 July. Hawke said this was the hardest decision of his prime ministership. 'We were great mates but that certainly hurt the friendship,' he reflected.[33]

Some ministers felt Hawke's handling of Combe was heavy-handed. It showed that Hawke would put probity before sentimentality, nation before party, and the public interest above all else. Justice Hope's royal commission reported on 6 December 1983. It found that Combe had been cultivated by Ivanov, but had not compromised national security, and nor had there been any breach of intelligence. Combe did not know any secrets; he traded in influence, not intelligence. But Hope did conclude that Ivanov had a good chance of succeeding in turning Combe into an agent of influence for the Soviet Union. The Hawke government and ASIO were also cleared of any wrongdoing towards Combe. Barnett thought that what had motivated Combe was 'greed'.[34]

Gareth Evans thought Hawke had mishandled the saga. 'I'm ashamed of myself,' he reflected. 'Combe was shockingly treated. The notion of him being a bloody threat to national security was laughable. I was appalled by the way Hawke had just bought the ASIO version of it, lock, stock and barrel, and immediately excommunicated Combe. He was determined to establish his national security credentials. He was desperately worried this would tarnish the government. I was really troubled by it.'[35]

During the research for this book, a former senior ASIO official confided to the author that ASIO had considered recruiting Combe to work against the Soviet Union. In other words, he would be a double agent. But this sort of Cold War game playing was deemed too risky for ASIO, which was trying to build a good relationship with the Hawke government. Apparently, Barnett planned to meet with Combe to discuss the idea, but then changed his mind. ASIO instead took the easy win by identifying Ivanov as a spy.

Combe had been Labor's national secretary during the Whitlam and Hayden leaderships, from 1973 to 1981. He was damaged by his involvement in the madcap plan to accept US$500,000 from Saddam Hussein's Ba'ath Socialist Party. But Combe survived. With Whitlam's backing, he ran for preselection in the Sydney seat of Barton in 1983, only to be beaten by Gary Punch in a rank-and-file ballot. When Hawke led Labor to power in 1983, Combe thought he would get rich as a lobbyist. The scandal dashed those hopes.

Although Combe was later made a trade commissioner to Canada (1985–89) and Hong Kong (1990–91), and would have a successful career in the wine industry, he never fully recovered from the the scandal. In his last interview, in 2019, Combe said the scandal evoked bitter and difficult memories. 'I was unfairly treated by Hawke,' he said. 'It ruined my reputation, my livelihood and hurt my family. It marked the destruction of civil liberties in Australia, even though I regard Hawke as the best prime minister we have had.' Combe died, at age seventy-six, the following month.[36]

—

When the Hawke government came to power, it inherited an arrangement whereby a small group of government officials met to set the value of the dollar within a range established by cabinet.[37] This was known as a 'crawling peg'. Since the end of World War II, the Australian currency had been tied to the United States dollar, British pound sterling, gold or a trade-weighted basket of currencies. The Fraser government, like its predecessors, did not support allowing market forces to determine the value of the currency. Treasury remained opposed to a 'floating' currency, but the Reserve Bank, led by Bob Johnston, supported the idea. The problem was that the Australian dollar was often overvalued, and speculators could bet on devaluations and pocket windfall gains. Moreover, an overvalued dollar placed upward pressure on inflation and contributed to some industry sectors being uncompetitive.

The landmark decision to float the dollar on 9 December 1983, abandoning the managed exchange rate system, was taken after extensive deliberations over a nine-month period. The float was perhaps the most important economic decision made by any Australian post-war government and would become a central battle in the history wars between Hawke and Keating.

Hawke was always inclined to float the dollar and argued that Keating had to be convinced. 'It was tough because the Treasury was dead against it,' he said. 'Paul had to be brought along. To be fair to Paul, he had a steep learning curve when he became treasurer. He had no experience. He relied very much on Treasury, and he was very much under their influence. We had to bring him along, but he came along, and it was part of his development into becoming a very significant treasurer.'[38]

Garnaut thought a more flexible exchange rate was necessary for structural reform of the economy. 'The first thing was to make sure we did not have an overvalued exchange rate and devaluation was essential,' he explained. 'The second thing was to move towards a float. From April, we all thought in the Prime Minister's Office that this is something the government should do. Stone was adamantly opposed to a float. Paul didn't want to hurry it along. And Bob didn't want to hurry Paul. Above all, Bob respected good governance and so he respected that Paul wanted Treasury onside.' Asked if Keating was opposed to a float, Garnaut said: 'No, but I don't think he was strongly supportive. I think he was weakly supportive.'[39]

When Keating first met with the Reserve Bank governor on 8 March 1983 in Sydney, he asked about the fluctuations in capital flows and questioned the viability of the exchange rate mechanism. 'Should we float the rate?' Keating asked. 'I think it is a waste of time, really, what we are doing,' Bob Johnston replied. 'We are a big enough economy now, and strong enough on the monetary front for the rate to set itself.' Asked in 2016 what Keating's attitude was in 1983 to floating the dollar, Johnston was certain: 'He was in favour of it. He accepted from me that I thought the rate should be altered now.'[40]

But Keating's department, led by John Stone, preferred an 'evolutionary' approach to the float.[41] The Treasury secretary confirmed to Johnston on 6 September 1983 that he favoured 'incremental' change.[42] Yet Keating was talking to others in Treasury through 1983 about a float. Ted Evans, who became Treasury deputy secretary in 1984, disagreed with Hawke's view that Keating needed to be brought along or opposed a float.[43] So did senior Treasury official David Morgan. 'I recall him being a supporter of floating the dollar from quite early on,' Morgan said.[44] Stone was not informed of these discussions, nor was he aware of Johnston talking to Keating about these issues.

On 13 October, Keating, Stone and Johnston met at the Reserve Bank in Canberra. A 'dirty' float – providing for limited government intervention – was considered.[45] Johnston pushed for a full float. Stone instead supported 'some change in the system' and argued it 'should be undertaken in stages'. On 16 October, Stone sent a minute to Keating: 'A complete and wholesale leap to a full market system overnight would be an act of faith to which the government has no need to commit itself at this time and the consequences of which cannot clearly be foreseen.'[46]

On 27 October, Hawke and Keating, along with Treasury officials and personal staff, met in the prime minister's office. It was decided to float the forward rate, which meant the Reserve Bank would no longer intervene in the forward exchange market. This was announced the following day. Hawke and Garnaut both thought it was time to float the dollar but decided to wait, given the concerns raised by Treasury.

Recalling this meeting, Hawke said Keating was 'nervous' and expressed 'reluctance', and Stone offered 'vociferous opposition'.[47] Floating the forward rate reflected Treasury's gradual approach. 'I said we should not have a revolutionary approach to it but an evolutionary approach,' Stone recalled.[48] Keating said he was predisposed towards a float but it was a matter of 'picking the right moment' to act and ensuring everyone was onboard.[49] In any event, the government had now made an important decision, and both Hawke and Garnaut thought it was 'inevitable' the spot rate would also be floated.[50]

On 1 November, Keating informed the cabinet that it was no longer viable to maintain strict controls over the setting of the exchange rate. He flagged the 'possibility of a floating exchange rate with a quantity, as distinct from price, intervention in markets'.[51] On 30 November the Reserve Bank was given the 'green flag' to proceed. John Phillips, a senior Reserve Bank official, had spoken directly to Keating and to his principal private secretary, Tony Cole. A note prepared by Phillips reveals that Hawke and Keating had spoken about 'rate management', and the Reserve Bank was instructed to revise and distribute the 'war book', which outlined how the move to a market-determined exchange rate system would take place.[52]

Events now moved fast. In the first week of December, there had been a capital inflow of $1.4 billion, with a further $1.5 billion booked for the following week. By 8 December, the last parliamentary sitting day for the year, a series of meetings and phone conversations took place about closing the foreign exchange market and floating the dollar. The floating of the forward rate had not eased speculative trading activity. Hawke was ready to float. Keating wanted to make sure there was agreement across government. He consulted Hayden, Dawkins and Willis. The Reserve Bank governor was on board but the Treasury secretary was not. Eventually, between 1 am and 2 am on 9 December, the decision was made in Hawke's office to float the dollar. The Reserve Bank was alerted, and the markets would be closed that day.

At about 10.20 am on 9 December, the door to the cabinet room opened and in filed Hawke, Keating and their senior staff, along with officials from the Department of Prime Minister and Cabinet, Treasury and the Reserve Bank. Hawke, on his fifty-fourth birthday, chaired the meeting. He invited Keating to speak. He methodically went through the options, from maintaining the existing system to a float. Hawke assumed everyone was 'agreed in principle on the desirability of allowing market forces to have more rein' and said 'he had no philosophical problem with a float'. Johnston was gung-ho but conceded he was unsure about the immediate impact on the value of the dollar. Stone reiterated his opposition to a float at that time and concern about the economic impact. But Hawke said 'there was a clear majority view for a float' and this was 'the appropriate course'.[53]

These debates had been extensively ventilated over the previous weeks and months, and it was time to decide. 'That's it,' Hawke said. 'We're going to do it.' Stone said: 'Prime Minister, you will live to regret this. It is a great mistake.' At this, Hawke smiled.[54] Stone argued that Treasury, under his leadership, did not 'formally oppose' the float. 'I didn't oppose the float in the post-October period,' he said. 'But I did believe on the day that they actually took the decision it was an unnecessarily rash decision.'[55]

The final decision was taken by the economics committee of cabinet, which met at 3.40 pm that afternoon.[56] '[The] government [has] got to do something,' Hawke said, according to the cabinet notebook. Johnston spoke at length. Only Willis expressed concern and suggested maintaining controls over the rate. Hayden said the value of the dollar could not be predicted when it floats. The meeting ran for just over an hour. 'Agreed step[s] [should] be taken to float [the] exchange rate,' Geoffrey Yeend noted.[57] The decision was announced at a press conference fronted by Keating and Johnston just after 5 pm. The float and the abolition of most exchange controls would take effect on Monday, 12 December 1983.

This decision, more than any other in the 1980s and 1990s, joined Australia to the global economy. Market forces, not bureaucrats, would now set the value of the currency. Banks, corporations and individuals could buy and sell foreign exchange in an open market. It made industry more competitive and the economy more productive. The currency would act as a shock absorber for the economy when faced with strong economic headwinds. 'The nation has now come of age,' said *The Australian*.[58] It is understandable that Keating was cautiously supportive through 1983. This was a decision for which both Hawke and Keating could share credit. It could not have been made without both supporting it. Hawke gave the decision his authority, while Keating announced it and took political responsibility for it.

The Coalition did not enthusiastically embrace the deregulatory reforms of the Hawke government, including the float of the dollar. Opposition leader Andrew Peacock gave only cautious support. Doug Anthony, the National Party leader, opposed the float. Malcolm Fraser, the former Liberal leader, opposed the float. John Howard was virtually a lone voice in support.[59] Asked if the Liberal Party would have supported a float of the dollar if Fraser was opposition leader, Howard said: 'Probably not.'[60]

Even before the government was sworn in, Keating had decided to revisit the inquiry into the deregulation of the financial system chaired by Keith Campbell, initiated by the Fraser government and handed to Howard on 28 October 1981. Keating raised this with Johnston at their first meeting, on 8 March 1983.[61] Hawke and Keating were both supportive of the Campbell inquiry, which had been considered by Labor's shadow cabinet. 'I think it would be a mistake to let the Campbell report simply collect dust on the shelf,' Keating told journalist Ross Gittins in April 1983.[62] That same month, Hawke wrote to Keating asking him to commission a group to revisit the Campbell report. Keating established a review group led by businessman Vic Martin on 29 May 1983.

In opposition, Labor had opposed the broad thrust of the Campbell report, including the introduction of foreign banks. Howard announced that the Fraser government would permit the entry of foreign banks, but much of the report was not implemented. Labor's Left faction was uneasy about deregulating the financial sector. 'The Left were barracking for the four major Australian banks, and here I am, with Hawke, on the right of the party, barracking for the competition from foreign banks,' Keating recalled.[63] Martin's review group reported on 22 February 1984. It would pave the way for the deregulation of the financial sector, including the entry of foreign banks. Ahead of the party's July 1984 national conference, Hawke and Keating steeled themselves for battle against the Left faction.

———

As 1983 drew to a close, Australians were increasingly optimistic and upbeat. The country was emerging from recession and the drought had broken. The Fraser government, marked by confrontation and division, had been terminated. Hawke projected a sunny, positive and hopeful prime ministership compared to the aloof, stern and dour Fraser. Labor's internal polling found Hawke to be very popular, with particular appeal to 'middle Australia', and with a yawning gap over Peacock as preferred prime minister, 60 per cent to 22 per cent.[64]

Nothing seemed to better encapsulate the mood than *Australia II* winning the America's Cup yacht race. The contest with America's *Liberty* was tied at 3–3 after six races. The seventh and final race took place in the early hours of 27 September 1983. The cabinet had met in Perth the day before. Hawke watched the final race in the pre-dawn in his hotel suite. When *Australia II* crossed the finish line, forty-one seconds ahead of *Liberty*, it was the first time in 132 years that the trophy had been won by the non-American team. Hawke was so ecstatic that he wanted to go to the Royal Perth Yacht Club to join in the celebrations. 'The coppers were terrified because they were not prepared,' recalled Jeff Townsend. 'So we all piled into two cars and went to the

Yacht Club. We get there and it was mayhem. Everybody was pretty pissed, apart from the prime minister, who had been drinking tea all night and eating chocolates.'[65]

As Hawke made his way into the club, he was mobbed. There were cheers and applause. Champagne corks flew through the air and his silvery grey suit was drenched. His hair was dripping wet. The crowd was electric. Amid the throng, university student Paul Burnham was wearing a white suit jacket with the words *Australia* diagonally emblazoned in blue, along with a flag superimposed inside the map of Australia. It was custom-made while he was on holiday in Kuala Lumpur. The design was based on a popular tea towel pattern.

Hawke was interviewed live via satellite link on *The Today Show*. He was overjoyed and said it was one of the greatest days in Australian sporting history. 'I just feel so proud to be an Australian,' he said. While being interviewed, a member of the yacht club gave Hawke the garish blazer to wear. He pulled it over his suit jacket. Hawke was asked if Australians should have a day off work to celebrate. He demurred. But when asked again, Hawke said: 'Any boss who sacks anyone for not turning up today is a bum!' The room exploded with cheers, applause and laughter. That sentence seared itself into popular memory. 'Of all the things I've said in my life, that is what is remembered most of all,' Hawke later said. 'It was not just a great sporting achievement. Here was little Australia, up against the mightiest nation on earth, and we beat them. It was great for the Australian spirit.'[66]

Tributes to the *Australia II* team – funded by Alan Bond, skippered by John Bertrand and using a unique winged-keel design by Ben Lexcen – flooded in from world leaders. Ronald Reagan sent a generous message to Hawke. 'If the America's Cup had to leave the United States, I am delighted that its home will be Australia – at least until the next race,' the US president wrote.[67] Former president Richard Nixon was another notable person who wrote to Hawke. 'I was naturally pulling for our boat, "Liberty", but if we had to lose there was nothing more heart-warming than to have Australia win,' he said.[68]

When it was time for Hawke to leave the yacht club, he took the jacket off and handed it to Townsend. 'The police were very keen to get us out of there because it was totally uncontrolled and you couldn't move,' Townsend recalled. 'The kid asked for his jacket back. We were trying to leave. I figured this jacket had some significance and it had been given to the PM, so I thought I would take it with me.' But Burnham wanted it back. His mother later phoned the hotel where Hawke was staying and said, 'Somebody from the prime minister's office stole my son's jacket. Tell them to look inside and you'll find his wallet and keys.' Townsend organised for Burnham to get the jacket back.[69]

20

FROM MESSIAH
TO MORTAL

As he approached his second year as prime minister, Bob Hawke was riding high. *The Australian* named him as its Australian of the Year.[1] Hawke's approval rating reached 73 per cent in January 1984, far outpacing the highest ratings achieved by Malcolm Fraser (57 per cent), Gough Whitlam (62 per cent), Billy McMahon (55 per cent) and John Gorton (64 per cent).[2] Two months later, in March, Hawke's approval rating reached an astonishing 78 per cent.[3] Not since the wartime government of John Curtin had Australians given a prime minister so much support.[4] The idea of an early election to capitalise on this wave of popularity remained a tempting option for the party during 1984.

While Hawke's focus was on economic and foreign policy, the social policies of his government were also transformative. School completion rates – students staying on for Years 11 and 12 – would increase from 35 per cent in 1982 to 77 per cent by 1992. University and college sectors were overhauled and enlarged. University enrolments increased from 357,000 in 1984 to 559,000 in 1992. Vocational education and training enrolments increased from 832,000 in 1984 to 1,043,000 in 1992. Hawke made support for multiculturalism, with programs to foster community understanding and harmony, integral to his government. Welfare spending was better targeted to those most in need, with the assets test on pensions being an important early initiative, followed by substantial increases in family assistance, pensions and other allowances. Low-income families with children were better off at the end of the decade, while any increase in overall inequality was offset by tax changes and payments.[5]

The massive increase in school completion rates – which Hawke preferred to call 'retention rates' – was achieved by two key reforms. First, funding was provided to schools for curriculum development and teacher training to design subjects that encouraged students to remain at school after the end of Year 10. Second, student allowances were changed so that kids in Year 11 and Year 12 would now be eligible for income support through the AUSTUDY program. This was a financial incentive to stay at school that was welcomed by low-income families. Susan Ryan, the minister for education, recalled Hawke being 'totally supportive' of her in cabinet against Peter Walsh, who was arguing that schools were a state government responsibility.[6]

No social policy reform was more important than Medicare. Labor had promised to reintroduce universal healthcare. This policy was developed, advocated and implemented by Bill Hayden in the Whitlam government as Medibank and by Neal Blewett in the Hawke government as Medicare. Hawke, like all Labor MPs, was deeply committed to this totemic policy. He had led a national strike in 1976 in support of Medibank. Hawke pledged that all Australians would again have access to 'health services according to their medical needs'. A year later, on 1 February 1984, Medicare was introduced. It is now woven into the social fabric of Australian society and is sacrosanct. But at the time, Medicare was opposed by the Liberal and National parties, and by the medical establishment.

The opposition to Medicare reflected the original struggle over Medibank. The Whitlam government's Medibank scheme did not commence until 1 July 1975 – Labor's third year in government. A double dissolution election and a joint sitting of parliament was needed to pass the legislation required to establish Medibank. Although the Coalition promised to maintain Medibank during the 1975 election campaign, in government it systematically weakened accessibility. The Fraser government eventually abolished Medibank in 1981.

The fight over Medibank left the medical profession bruised and fragmented, and there was no desire for a second protracted battle over Medicare. Nevertheless, Medicare's pathway into law would not be easy. 'Australia had had six different national health schemes in the 1970s, and no doubt many expected that volatility to continue,' Neal Blewett, the minister for health, recalled. 'No one would have predicted in February 1984 that a generation later Medicare would still be in place with all its key elements intact.'[7]

Medicare provided for emergency and basic hospital care, bulk-billed medical and treatment services by doctors, and subsidised pharmaceuticals. The scheme was partly funded by a 1 per cent levy on most taxpayers. It formed part of the government's social wage concept within the Prices and Incomes Accord framework, offered in return for moderating wage demands. Blewett recalled that Hawke saw Medicare as a critical element of the accord, and urged him to get the universal health scheme established by the beginning of 1984.[8] A green and gold Medicare card would become part of everyday life. Hawke featured in a national television advertisement applying for the card and then receiving it in the mail. His popularity helped build confidence in Medicare.

Another major health initiative was the government's response to the HIV/AIDS epidemic. The government saw it as a public health risk that required both a medical response and a public education and prevention response. A national strategy was established at a series of ministerial meetings between November 1984 and April 1985. The 'Grim Reaper' advertising campaign in 1987 was revolutionary. It featured a menacing Reaper rolling a bowling ball down an ally towards human pins and knocking them over. When Blewett showed it to Hawke, he was a bit startled. 'It's a bit dramatic, isn't it?' he said. But that was the point. Hawke approved it with little hesitation.[9] Yet it was not enough. By 1989, the government estimated that 15,000 Australians were infected with HIV, and the World Health Organization estimated that up to 10 million people were infected worldwide.

Blewett recognised that HIV/AIDS had to be depoliticised, and that a systematic national response was required. The government had to play a role in alleviating fear about the disease – for which there was no cure or treatment – and prejudice towards gay men, the community most affected. The policy response needed to be coordinated across jurisdictions. Encouraging the use of condoms was a key element, as was access to clean and disposable syringes. Public education was critical. Ita Buttrose was appointed chairperson of the National Advisory Committee on AIDS, which brought together medical experts, government and community leaders to guide the government's response.

A national strategy for dealing with AIDS in the decade ahead was agreed by cabinet on 21 July 1989. 'An HIV epidemic is Australia's biggest public health risk,' Blewett warned ministers. This strategy focused on public education; prevention programs; treatment, care and counselling; enabling people with HIV to live without fear of discrimination or prejudice; biomedical, scientific and social research; and international cooperation with nations in the region.[10] There was, however, some educating of ministers required. Don Grimes, as minister for community services, first raised AIDS in cabinet. 'I had lots of conversations about AIDS,' he recalled. 'Hawke and Keating, and some others, initially were very suspicious about the seriousness of AIDS and HIV. We talked it over and, as a government, we handled that issue very well.'[11]

Another pioneering area of reform was removing legal barriers that discriminated against women. The lead advocate was Susan Ryan, a trailblazer for women in politics. Ryan had a critical ally around the cabinet table, which otherwise was comprised entirely of men, and that was Hawke. 'Hawke's active leadership ensured its success,' Ryan said. The *Sex Discrimination Act 1984* made it illegal to discriminate 'on the ground of sex, marital status or pregnancy' in a range of areas such as employment, education, accommodation, property, clubs, and in the administration of Commonwealth laws and programs. The Human Rights Commission would be the principal body to put the measures into effect, and the position of Sex Discrimination Commissioner would be established. Prior to the passage of the legislation, women could find themselves forced to leave employment because of marriage or pregnancy, unable to rent housing or obtain housing loans without a male guarantor, or without access to certain training courses or postgraduate education. Often they were denied superannuation.

Some in cabinet, however, thought Ryan was moving too fast. 'A few cabinet colleagues thought I could leave it a while,' she recalled. 'I didn't.' Ministers were concerned about wild claims from some business and conservative lobby groups that the laws would pose a threat to the family unit, to marriage as an institution and to Christianity. At the other end of the spectrum, Ryan had to manage advocacy groups that wanted to move further and faster. 'Removing blatant discrimination against women was underestimated at the time by more radical voices from the feminist movement, which wanted more severe penalties, more criminal convictions and massive fines,' Ryan said.

The original proposal coupled anti-discrimination provisions with affirmative action measures. 'That bill contained requirements that large employers take positive steps to ensure fairness in the hiring, training and promotion of women,' Ryan said. 'Opponents asserted that they would be forced to employ quotas of women regardless of merit, and sack men to make way for these incompetents.' In response to the backlash, cabinet decided to split the bill in two. There would not be quotas, but firms with more than 100 staff were required to introduce affirmative action programs. Separate legislation to provide for affirmative action in employment was enacted in 1986.[12]

Ensuring women had equality of opportunity was a priority for the Hawke government. 'Bob understood the importance of equal opportunity for women and support for women who were bringing up children,' Ryan said. 'I never had to argue the case with him.'[13] Ryan recalled discussing the public service appointment of Anne Summers as head of the Office of the Status of Women with Hawke, who was supportive. Summers said Hawke understood that his election victory was, in part, due to the votes of women and the promises he had made to them. 'He always read any briefs I sent over, and often wrote supportive or friendly comments in the margins before sending them back,' Summers recalled. 'He was intellectually disposed to understand and agree with the need for any civilised society to ensure that women were not discriminated against and could pursue any opportunities of their choosing,' she said.[14]

In addition to Ryan and Summers, others were also blazing new trails for women to follow. Mary Gaudron became the first woman appointed to the High Court in February 1987.[15] Joan Child became the first woman speaker of the House of Representatives, serving from February 1986 to August 1989. And Helen Williams was the first woman to head a federal government department, as Secretary of the Department of Education from January 1985 to July 1987.

Childcare was another important initiative of the Hawke government, and Summers helped overcome bureaucratic resistance to expanding the role of government in this area. 'It was a protracted fight,' Summers recalled. 'But what Hawke did was to take to the 1984 election the biggest ever – at that point – expansion in childcare funding.'[16] The goal was not only to improve access to childcare and reduce costs for young families, but also to lower barriers for women who wanted to enter the labour market. As the government encouraged women to stay on at school and undertake a university or college education, it was important to help them to make the most of these skills in the workforce. Subsidised childcare places massively increased over the decade, beginning with a landmark announcement of 20,000 places in the election policy speech in November 1984.[17] Within five years, the Hawke government had directly funded 64,000 additional child care places.[18] And by 1991, federal government funded child care places had increased by 77,500 – more than doubling the number of places since 1983.[19]

During the 1980s, the Hawke government made decisions that helped define Australia as an independent sovereign nation while retaining the monarchy. These initiatives helped to strengthen national identity. 'Advance Australia Fair' was made Australia's national anthem in April 1984. That same month, green and gold were formally recognised as Australia's national colours.[20] The golden wattle became Australia's official floral emblem in August 1988.

The *Australia Acts* were adopted and commenced in March 1986, ending the capacity for the United Kingdom to legislate with respect to Australia, interfere in Australia's government or hear legal appeals to the Privy Council. This was a milestone in Australia's legal and constitutional development. Queen Elizabeth II proclaimed the legislation when she visited Australia for a royal tour that month. Her private secretary, Sir Philip Moore, wrote to Hawke to convey the Queen's appreciation for his having handled

Baby Bob Hawke, born in 1929, bathes in a washing tub in the backyard of the church manse at 63 Farquhar Street in Bordertown, South Australia.

Young Bob Hawke lived an idyllic life, surrounded by love and affection, and constantly told that he was special. Bordertown locals recall a toddler who was outgoing, lively and mischievous.

The Hawke family: Congregational minister Clem, Bob, schoolteacher Ellie and Neil, who was then a boarder at King's College in Adelaide. Neil was 'Mum's boy' and Bob was 'Dad's boy'. Neil died, at age seventeen, after contracting meningitis in 1939.

In 1941, Clem enlisted in the Australian Army as a chaplain and, after three years of service in Australia, attained the rank of captain. Clem was Bob's best friend, and he missed his father terribly when he was away.

Bob Hawke in India for the 1952 World Conference of Christian Youth, which shattered his faith and hastened his break with organised religion after witnessing widespread poverty.

After being announced as a 1953 Rhodes Scholar, Bob is pictured with Ellie at home at 101 Tate Street in West Leederville, Perth. He would graduate with a Bachelor of Letters from Oxford University.

Bob Hawke and Hazel Masterson sitting on Bob's British Panther motorbike. Bob crashed the bike in 1947 and nearly died. Bob felt he had been spared death and decided to make the most of his life.

Bob put enormous pressure on Hazel to join him at Oxford as he fought the demon drink and his carnal desires. In the summer of 1954, they embarked on a month-long grand tour of Europe in this small van.

Hazel began dating Bob in 1948 and they fell deeply in love. Hazel was a passionate lover and purposeful partner for Bob. They married in Perth in 1956.

The Hawke family – Bob, Rosslyn, Hazel, Susan and Stephen – photographed in 1963 for Hawke's campaign for the federal seat of Corio, in Victoria, as he tried to defeat Liberal MP Hubert Opperman.

ACTU President Bob Hawke meets Labor leader Gough Whitlam in 1970. They were among Labor's most promising figures and represented a new style of industrial and political leadership for a new age.

At his desk at the ACTU, as advocate and president, Bob Hawke worked exhausting hours. His desk was routinely covered in papers with a bulging in-tray. He would typically work 100 hours a week in the 1970s.

Bob and Susan Hawke meet Israeli Prime Minister Golda Meir in 1971. Hawke had a passionate commitment to Israel in the 1970s. He formed a close bond with Meir and was in awe of her intellect, toughness and compassion.

Being a highly functioning alcoholic threatened to derail Bob Hawke's political ambitions. Hawke, pictured here with Gough Whitlam in 1974, earned a place in *The Guinness Book of Records* for an Oxford drinking record. 'It got me a few votes,' Hawke thought.

The closest friendship Bob Hawke formed was with businessman Peter Abeles in the 1970s. He provided Hawke with financial support, paid his bills, bailed him out of gambling debts, and supplied him with cars, drinks and women.

Gough Whitlam and Bob Hawke at the Terrigal conference. Hawke and Whitlam frequently clashed over policy and political strategy during the Whitlam government. Hawke learnt vital lessons, though, for Labor's return to power in 1983.

A life-long adulterer, Bob Hawke did little to hide his sexual appetite. One of his most notable, yet brief, affairs was with Glenda Bowden, secretary to Jim Cairns, at Labor's federal conference in Terrigal in 1975.

Bob Hawke had good relations with employers and judges. At the ACTU's fiftieth anniversary dinner: Justice John Moore, ACTU Secretary Harold Souter, Hawke, Employers' Federation chief George Polites, Gough Whitlam and Justice Richard Kirby.

Blanche d'Alpuget with Richard Kirby at the launch of her biography of Bob Hawke in 1982. D'Alpuget, a journalist and author, had an affair with Hawke before, during and after the writing of the book.

In 1980, Bob Hawke was elected in the seat of Wills. Since failing to win Corio in 1963, Hawke was perennially talked about as a Labor candidate. He finally took the plunge, leaving the ACTU behind.

Stephen, Rosslyn and Susan with Bob and Hazel at Sandringham in 1982. Hawke was an absent and inattentive father, and there were often disagreements and disappointments, but they loved each other deeply.

From the moment Bob Hawke arrived in parliament, Bill Hayden's leadership was under siege. Hawke had the support of voters, and party members, to lead Labor as this badge demonstrates. But he had to convince Labor MPs.

In 1983, Bob Hawke finally wrested the Labor leadership from Bill Hayden in a bloodless coup. That same day, Malcolm Fraser called an election. Hawke pledged to bring Australians together and to reform and reconstruct the nation.

Bill Hayden and Bob Hawke shake hands after the leadership challenge in 1982. Hawke expected to defeat Hayden. He was determined to strike again. 'I wasn't going to give up,' he recalled. Leading Labor, and the nation, was his destiny.

A victorious Bob Hawke arrives at the National Tally Room at the Canberra Showgrounds late on election night in March 1983. He was met with cheers and applause, and the chant: 'We want Bob! We want Bob!'

Bob Hawke blazing a cigar on his campaign plane, with (left to right): journalist Colin Parks, who later joined Hawke's staff; Senator Kerry Sibraa; journalist Peter Logue; press secretary Geoff Walsh; and Labor staff Kate Moore and Janet Willis.

Treasurer Paul Keating and Bob Hawke formed a highly effective partnership, but their relationship fractured over competing ambitions. NSW Premier Neville Wran, here with Hawke and Keating in 1984, provided a model for Hawke's approach to government in the post-Whitlam years.

The happiness in Bob and Hazel's relationship was renewed during the prime ministerial years, pictured here in 1990. Hazel was admired, respected and loved by Australians and became a national treasure.

Public servant Graham Evans became Bob Hawke's first principal private secretary (chief of staff) in 1983 and established the model for an efficient and effective prime ministerial office.

Deputy Prime Minister Lionel Bowen (1983–90) was consulted on all key matters and Bob Hawke recalled him being a calm, moderate and thoroughly decent friend and colleague.

The first Hawke ministry sworn in at Government House in 1983. Front row (left to right): Peter Morris, Mick Young, Paul Keating, Don Grimes, Governor-General Ninian Stephen, Hawke, John Button, Lionel Bowen, Ralph Willis. Middle row (left to right): John Brown, Michael Duffy, Arthur Gietzelt, Stewart West, Neal Blewett, John Kerin, John Dawkins, Tom Uren, Gareth Evans, Brian Howe. Back row (left to right): Susan Ryan, Peter Walsh, Clyde Holding, Gordon Scholes, Barry Jones, Chris Hurford, Kim Beazley, Barry Cohen, Bill Hayden.

A degree of mutual respect developed between Malcolm Fraser and Bob Hawke, pictured here in 1978, but Hawke thought Fraser led a divisive government of missed opportunities. Hawke supported Fraser for diplomatic appointments in retirement.

Andrew Peacock faced Bob Hawke at the 1984 and 1990 elections, the latter Peacock expected to win and nearly did. Hawke and Peacock, pictured here in 1988 opening an extension to the press gallery, occasionally exchanged tips at the racetrack.

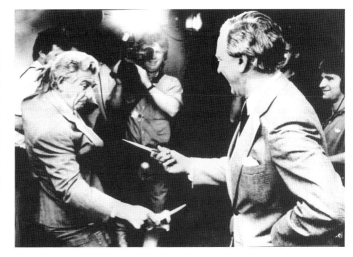

John Howard and Bob Hawke led their respective parties at the 1987 election. Hawke thought Howard was the most substantial Liberal leader after Robert Menzies and, while they disagreed on issues, respected his tenacity and longevity.

When *Australia II* won the America's Cup in 1983, Bob Hawke was at the Royal Perth Yacht Club and was asked if Australians should have a day off work to celebrate. 'Any boss who sacks anyone for not turning up today is a bum!' he said.

In response to the crackdown on pro-democracy protests in and around Beijing's Tiananmen Square in 1989, Bob Hawke shed tears at Parliament House. Hawke's staff referred to his occasional public tears as the 'optic nerve'.

During the annual cricket match between the Prime Minister's XI and the press gallery in 1984, a ball caught the top edge of Bob Hawke's bat and smashed into his face and shattered his glasses, with splinters going into his eye.

Bob Hawke meets Ronald Reagan at the White House in 1983, with George H.W. Bush, George Shultz (left) and Paul Keating (right). Hawke told Reagan he wanted to strengthen the alliance, but they may disagree from time to time.

George H.W. Bush had a 'close personal relationship' with Bob Hawke, the president recalled. They spoke regularly. Bush wrote in his diary that when he saw Hawke on the backbench after addressing parliament in 1992, he 'choked up'.

To Prime Minister Bob Hawke
With Friendship Geo Bush

Margaret Thatcher and Bob Hawke, pictured here in 1986, respected each other despite clashing over apartheid in South Africa. They shared information about the Soviet Union and China in an effort to improve East–West relations.

Bob Hawke built a rapport with Chinese Communist Party General Secretary Hu Yaobang. They toured an Australia–China joint mining venture in Western Australia in 1985. Hawke had visited China in 1978 and saw the economic opportunities for Australia.

Mikhail Gorbachev welcomed Bob Hawke to Moscow in 1987. They spoke for two-and-a-half hours conducting a *tour d'horizon* of geopolitics. Hawke said it was one of the most fascinating meetings he had ever had.

Bob Hawke was a leader in the global effort to end apartheid. Hawke said Nelson Mandela, pictured here on a visit to Australia in 1990, was the most impressive person he had met during his time in politics.

Australia's worst-kept secret was finally revealed in 1995 when Bob Hawke and Blanche d'Alpuget were together in public. They were married at the Ritz-Carlton Hotel in Sydney six months later. Bob was deeply in love with Blanche, and they formed an abiding intellectual, spiritual and physical bond.

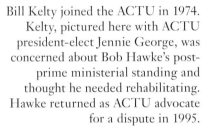

Bill Kelty joined the ACTU in 1974. Kelty, pictured here with ACTU president-elect Jennie George, was concerned about Bob Hawke's post-prime ministerial standing and thought he needed rehabilitating. Hawke returned as ACTU advocate for a dispute in 1995.

Bob Hawke wanted Kim Beazley to succeed him as prime minister and, when that was not possible, to lead Labor back to power. Hawke thought Beazley, pictured here in 2006, would have been a great prime minister.

In his final years, Bob Hawke liked nothing more than doing the daily crossword and sudoku puzzle as he smoked a cigar, sipped coffee or drained a strawberry milkshake. Here, at the Woodford Folk Festival in 2014, the daily ritual was uninterrupted.

Bob Hawke allowed his name to be used for a beer brand, Hawke's Brewing, with one proviso: that his royalty be donated to Landcare Australia. He is pictured here at The Clock Hotel in Sydney's Surry Hills in 2017.

Paul Keating saw Bob Hawke for the last time in late 2018. It was not a reconciliation, but a recognition of their partnership, Keating recalled. 'We completely changed the country,' Keating said. 'It was a very sweet and generous moment.'

the 'long and difficult negotiations' so 'astutely'. He added: 'The Australia Act has established The Queen in what is her proper relationship with Australia and it has been encouraging to find that the Act has been widely welcomed wherever we have gone.'[21]

Also in 1986, the government removed knights and dames from the Order of Australia, which had been reinstated by the Fraser government. Hawke told the Queen he did not support the awarding of imperial honours to Australian citizens, nor did he support Australian state governments recommending such honours to the Queen. The Queen agreed she would no longer award such honours. In February 1990, the Queen's private secretary, Sir William Heseltine, advised the governor-general and the state governors that the Queen had decided that Australians should be recognised exclusively by an Australian system of honours. The Queen could, however, continue to personally honour Australian citizens within her personal order, the Royal Victorian Order, or bestow other awards on them.

The Hawke government secured a mandate to stop the construction of a hydroelectric power station with the Franklin Dam in Tasmania. On 16 March 1983, cabinet resolved that if the Tasmanian government refused to halt construction, it would use its external affairs power under the Constitution to make regulations under the *National Parks and Wildlife Conservation Act 1975*. The Royal Australian Air Force was instructed to fly reconnaissance missions over the dam site on 8–9 April. Gareth Evans joked to journalists, 'Don't call me Biggles.' It was unnecessary and provocative, and Hawke was 'enraged' when he found out. Evans pleaded the streaker's defence: 'It seemed, your worship, like a good idea at the time.'[22] The case went to the High Court, which on 1 July ruled in the Commonwealth's favour by a 4–3 margin.

This decisive action had strong support within Labor. But party members and supporters were not happy with everything the government had achieved after its first year in office. On 10 July 1984, at Labor's national conference in Canberra, Hawke told the delegates that they had an obligation 'to the party and to the people'. He drew on Labor history and argued that his government, like those of Andrew Fisher and John Curtin, faced a national 'crisis' that required 'planning and thinking' anew. It was a call to embrace a party being remodelled for the modern era. 'We have made the reconciliation,' Hawke said. 'We are achieving the recovery. Let us now complete the reconstruction.'[23]

Hawke and Keating engaged in a battle with the Left faction on several policy fronts. The most critical of these was financial deregulation. The pivotal debate took place on 9 July. The treasurer argued that consumers would benefit from a more competitive banking system. He demanded to know from the Left why the government should support the financial establishment – the big four banks – rather than new entrants to the marketplace. On the issue of foreign bank entry, an alliance between the Right and the Centre Left factions defeated the Left by fifty-six votes to forty-one. Neville Wran, the party's national president, said the party had been remade: it was 'the equivalent of stealing the holy water from the church'.[24]

While the Right and Centre Left alliance also secured the endorsement of the float of the dollar and interest rate deregulation, and support for the government's policies on uranium mining, joint defence facilities and East Timor, it was always a close-run thing. The Left could rely on 40 per cent conference support. Yet a majority of ministers and MPs could win the day in cabinet, caucus, the national executive and the national conference to support the government's policies. There would be no repeat of the bitter divisions prevalent during the Whitlam years.

Keating was now firmly established in the Treasury role, quelling any doubts Hawke had, and they worked together effectively. In August 1984, John Stone announced he was resigning as secretary of the Treasury. While he was complimentary towards Keating, he took several swipes at the government over policy and processes, and with his resignation coming a week before the budget, it was seen as damaging.[25] The resignation, however, led to one of the most important public service appointments of the decade. Hawke and Keating approached Bernie Fraser and Chris Higgins to write essays about what they would do as secretary of Treasury. The two men also dined separately with Hawke and Keating at the Lodge. The upshot was that Fraser, then deputy secretary, was appointed to head the Treasury.

—

Towards the end of the government's second year, Hawke's popularity continued to astound Labor strategists. His approval rating was 66 per cent, while Andrew Peacock's was just 25 per cent. Hawke enjoyed a leadership edge as preferred prime minister over Peacock by 73 per cent to 15 per cent. Labor enjoyed a primary vote of 50 per cent, compared to the Coalition's 42 per cent.[26] But Labor's internal polling was even better. Hawke's satisfaction rating among swinging voters was 74 per cent in September 1984. He was seen as 'strong', 'in touch' and had 'proved himself' as prime minister.[27] Labor envisioned securing an even larger majority of seats in parliament. Hawke was eager to go to an early election at the end the year.

The Liberal Party's research judged the Hawke government's re-election to be 'a virtual certainty':

> During [this] term, the Hawke government has adequately
> demonstrated leadership capabilities: the state of the economy
> has improved; inflation and unemployment have fallen; industrial
> unrest has abated. Not only are these factors in favour of a Labor
> victory, there is widespread agreement that there exists no strong
> alternative.

The research also judged Peacock harshly. 'During his days as Minister for Foreign Affairs there was a strong feeling that he would one day make a great leader,' the report noted. 'Yet, this has not come to pass; reality has not matched expectation.'[28]

On 8 October, Hawke announced that he would seek a 'reinvigorated mandate' to continue the work that had begun twenty-one months earlier.[29] An election for the House of Representatives and half the Senate would be held on 1 December 1984. There would always have to be an early election, given the fixed Senate term would expire on 30 June 1985. This meant a separate half-Senate election – which had not been held since 1970 – or a normal election for both houses of parliament. Hawke's other option was to hold a general election in the first half of 1985. But he gambled, hoping his personal popularity would deliver Labor another historic election victory.

The election would be for a larger parliament. On 5 October 1983, Kim Beazley, then in the outer ministry, presented to cabinet a proposal to increase the size of the House from 125 seats to 148 seats. The Senate would be expanded to seventy-six seats. There was opposition within cabinet, and it became evident that Beazley's submission was not going to be supported. 'Oh God, the boys aren't going to be happy,' he said.

'What do you mean?' asked Hawke.

'Well, Richardson and Ray are supporting this,' replied Beazley.[30]

Hawke adjourned the meeting and had a note sent to Graham Richardson and Robert Ray asking them to address the cabinet. At 8.13 pm, according to the cabinet notebook, the meeting resumed. Even though they were not ministers, Hawke asked them to express their view and assess the implications.[31] They made it clear they supported expansion of the parliament. 'Well, we've heard from the boys,' Hawke said in summing up the debate. 'I take it that it is now unanimous that we do this.'[32]

Personally, Hawke was in no position to wage a fifty-three-day election campaign. On 9 August, Hazel had told him that the full extent of Rosslyn's heroin addiction had been revealed when she gave birth to a son by caesarean section the previous month. There had been extensive tissue degeneration and wastage of Rosslyn's lower limbs. Her life expectancy had been shortened to just a few years. Hazel had taken the extraordinary step of ringing Graham Evans from Melbourne to tell him that she needed an appointment to see Bob as soon as she arrived in Canberra.

After hearing this grim news, Hawke's next meeting was with the Malaysian prime minister, Dr Mahathir Mohamad. He broke down during the talks. Keating, who was in the meeting, was supportive and understanding but felt Hawke had sunk into a depression. A month later, on 20 September, Hawke was quizzed at a press conference about Susan's conviction for cannabis possession and usage, which had been set aside. He began crying. The tears streamed down his face, and he caught one with a side swipe of his tongue and sucked it into his mouth. Hawke was emotionally wrecked. He considered resigning as prime minister but Hazel talked him out of it.[33]

Hawke's staff were concerned. When Hawke returned from the press conference, he stopped by Peter Barron's office and asked if the tears would have any negative political impact. 'It does not really matter, I don't think, but don't let it happen again,' was the cool-headed advice. 'It's not something you want to make a habit of because there will be a price.'[34] The office agreed that Hazel should front the media. 'It was felt that unless there was a frank account of what was behind this, it would continue to be a problem,' recalled Geoff Walsh. 'Hazel was the best person to put this matter into the public domain.'[35] On 24 September, she appeared on *Terry Willesee Tonight*. She revealed that Rosslyn and her son-in-law, Matt Dillon, had a heroin addiction. This, she said, explained Bob's tears days earlier. 'It is very much a family process, and it just so happens that I am the spokesman,' Hazel said.[36] Rosslyn and her two sons, David, born in April 1983, and Paul, born in August 1984, lived at the Lodge with Bob and Hazel between 1985 and 1987. Rosslyn and Matt divorced in April 1986.

Bob Hogg thought Hawke wanted to go to an early election because it would allow voters to pass judgement on the family tragedy. 'It was his way of eliminating the guilt,' Hogg thought. 'It was his way of asking for forgiveness. It was his way of being judged – I hate giving the pop psychology, but it certainly had something to do with it.'[37] McMullan supported the early election decision. 'We thought we could virtually win two elections at once,' he said. 'We could get such a majority we would be unbeatable at a subsequent election.' But it was Hawke who made the final call.[38]

It had been a torrid few months. High Court judge Lionel Murphy became embroiled in the '*The Age* Tapes' scandal, which purported to reveal telephone conversations illegally taped by New South Wales police claiming he had links to organised crime and may have tried to influence court proceedings concerning solicitor Morgan Ryan. Murphy's conduct became the subject of two Senate inquiries.[39] Mick Young was found to have not declared a Paddington Bear in his luggage when returning from overseas, and temporarily stood down from the ministry until an inquiry could clear him. And when the Costigan Royal Commission concluded its work and parliament debated the establishment of the National Crime Authority, Peacock lashed out at Hawke, claiming he was a 'crook' who had associated with 'criminals'. It was an absurd allegation without any evidence and he later withdrew it, but Hawke was upset by it.

During the election campaign, the annual cricket match between the Prime Minister's XI and the press gallery was held at Kingston Oval, Canberra, on 14 October 1984. Hawke put on his cricketing whites and went to the crease. He was batting when a fast-paced delivery from journalist Garry O'Neill caught the top edge of his bat and smashed into his face, shattering his glasses and sending splinters into his eye. Hawke was taken to Royal Canberra Hospital and was discharged after having his eye patched up. He had scored twenty-seven runs before retiring hurt, and the Prime Minister's XI had won by six runs.

'It was just the worst period of my life,' Hawke recalled. He was in 'physical agony' with his eye and in 'emotional' pain over Rosslyn.[40] The campaign, however, had to go on. Hawke travelled to every capital city and every state. He walked down busy streets. Visited shopping centres. Talked to schoolkids. Hawke was still immensely popular with voters. Roger Martindale, the head of Hawke's VIP protective service detail within the Australian Federal Police, recalled managing his interaction with crowds: 'He would be swamped by people wanting to meet him. We had to ensure one of us held onto his belt because we were very worried about being able to control certain situations.' There were few incidents where Hawke was ever in danger. A Right to Life activist once burst through a crowd in Melbourne hoping to kick Hawke in the nuts, but Martindale leapt in front and absorbed the blow. 'That was the most courageous thing anyone has ever done for me,' Hawke said, 'protecting my crown jewels.'[41]

The party's campaign committee made economic management the centrepiece, with the Hawke/Keating partnership emphasised, and with a focus on creating jobs and reducing inflation.[42] One of the challenges for the government was a degree of voter angst over the assets test on pensions. But overall, as the polls showed, the government was seen as better able to manage the economy than the opposition, by a margin of 54 per cent to 25 per cent.[43]

Tax reform was, inadvertently, made an issue by Hawke. Interviewed by Bob Maumill on radio station 6PR in Perth on 19 October, Hawke said the government would hold a summit on taxation if re-elected. Keating, who had not been consulted, thought it was policymaking on the run. On 31 October, following a meeting at the Lodge, Hawke outlined a framework for taxation reform, including nine principles to guide the process. It was enough to defer the issue until after the election campaign.[44]

There was another prime ministerial fiat during the campaign. To cement the government's claim to fiscal prudence, Hawke announced there would be no increase in taxation revenue, the deficit or expenditure as a proportion of GDP in the next term. This became known as the 'trilogy' of commitments to guide fiscal policy. Keating had not been consulted about this either, and afterwards privately expressed his doubts about its viability.

Hawke retuned to the Sydney Opera House to launch Labor's election campaign on 13 November. He asked for a mandate to 'consolidate, sustain and build upon the great gains' achieved; to 'build a new decade of national unity, national purpose and national progress'; to ensure the economic benefits 'are fully shared'; and to make Australia 'a nation foremost among the nations of the world in freedom and fairness'. No choice facing voters, he said, was more important. He asked voters to 'continue to put Australia first' by re-electing his government.[45] This central campaign message was encapsulated in a jingle developed by Forbes MacFie Hansen:

When Aussies work together
We're unbeatable, unstoppable,
invincible, incredible, undeniable,
When we put Australia first.

Australia's first ever televised leaders' debate took place on 26 November. Malcolm Fraser had refused Hawke's challenge to debate in 1983, so Hawke could not credibly refuse to debate Peacock. The 'great debate' was held at the National Press Club in Canberra, and televised on the ABC, Nine and Seven from 7.30 pm to 9 pm. Hawke and Peacock looked nervous and uncertain as the debate commenced. For ninety minutes they answered questions from a panel of journalists moderated by Ken Randall. The questions dealt with the economy and industrial relations, allegations of corruption in New South Wales, and even what make-up the leaders were wearing. The consensus among journalists was that Peacock performed better. He was more assertive, confident and on top of issues, whereas Hawke was mostly on the defensive and seemed irritated by the attacks. Phone polls showed Peacock winning by various margins.[46]

Peacock ran an energetic, focused and disciplined campaign. He quickly defied expectations with his dogged and tenacious pursuit of Hawke. He was well briefed, self-confident and strong. The Liberal Party made 'Stand Up for Your Family' their key theme, with a focus on youth unemployment, health costs and the assets test on pensions. Peacock was also effective in hammering Hawke for cynically going to an early election – not to capitalise on his popularity, but to avoid internal party problems.

Despite Hawke's patchy performance during the lengthy campaign, Labor managed to win a slew of newspaper endorsements for its economic achievements. The newspapers that backed the Hawke government's re-election included *The Australian*, *The Australian Financial Review*, *The Age*, *The West Australian*, *The Sun News-Pictorial*, *The Courier-Mail*, *The Sydney Morning Herald* and the Melbourne *Herald*. Not since 1972 had Labor won this degree of support from the print media.

But Labor's hopes of a landslide election victory had evaporated by election day. The mood in Hawke's suite at the Regent Hotel in Melbourne was glum. His staff, family and friends were disheartened. During the evening, Hawke retreated into the bedroom and could not face the result. Peter Barron found him watching the World Gymnastics Championships on television. He told Hawke to pull himself together, recognise that he had been re-elected and prepare to claim victory on television. 'Don't worry, mate, you are going to get home,' he said.'[47]

The Hawke government won a second term, but the result was disappointing. Labor gained seven seats in net terms but the Coalition gained sixteen, and Labor's majority of twenty-five seats was reduced to sixteen. Labor lost Flinders (Victoria), Macquarie (New South Wales), the Northern Territory seat and Petrie (Queensland), plus four new notionally Labor seats. Dreams of a forty-seat Labor majority were dashed. Labor's primary vote fell by almost two percentage points to 47.55 per cent and the

Coalition secured 45.01 per cent. On a two-party basis, Labor secured 51.77 per cent to the Coalition's 48.23 per cent, a swing of 1.46 per cent away from the government.

As part of a series of electoral reforms – including establishing the Australian Electoral Commission, ending the alphabetical listing of candidates on ballot papers, public funding for election campaigns and new donation disclosure laws – the voting process for the Senate was changed. But allowing voters to number a single square above the line (in order to vote for a group) led some to think they could vote the same way for the House of Representatives, where all squares had to be numbered for the allocation of preferences. The informal vote increased from 2 per cent to almost 7 per cent, and Hawke believed this robbed Labor of many votes.[48]

Two referendums also failed to be carried. First, to alter the Constitution to allow for the interchange of powers between state and federal governments. And second, to change the terms of senators so they were no longer fixed and to require elections for the House of Representatives and the Senate to be held on the same day. The government had considered putting five referendums to the voters earlier, on 25 February 1984, but abandoned this idea after polling showed there was little public awareness of the issues.[49] In March 1984, cabinet endorsed a charter of rights and freedoms – essentially a bill of rights. It was revived by Lionel Bowen in September 1985, winning cabinet approval, and was passed by the House of Representatives later that year. However, unable to win passage in the Senate, it was dumped in November 1986. 'Hawke had no interest whatsoever in the law reform agenda, human rights, civil liberties,' Gareth Evans recalled.[50]

Rod Cameron called the early election gambit a 'ridiculous decision' which 'completely destroyed Hawke's "above politics" reputation'.[51] McMullan was equally scathing. 'It was a terribly wasted opportunity,' he recalled. 'Bob did not perform well, but none of us did. It was the worst election campaign I ever ran.'[52] McMullan's report to the party's national executive recognised the lack of leadership and vision for Australia's future as key factors in the defeat. The party was complacent about the outcome. McMullan did not believe the high informal vote had a major impact, as the party's vote fell during the campaign, according to polling.[53]

Tony Eggleton, the Liberal Party campaign director, concluded that the Coalition and Peacock as leader had 'out-manoeuvred' and 'out-performed' Hawke and Labor. Although they failed to regain government, the Coalition had won the campaign, and were now in a strong position to win the next election. 'The outcome was a stunning rebuff for Labor,' Eggleton reported. 'The election transformed a somewhat embattled opposition into a revitalised Coalition with every prospect of being perceived as a meaningful alternative government.'[54]

Peacock was pleased with the result. He did not expect to win but thought the Coalition could take seats off Labor. 'I had a feeling that Hawke didn't have the support the newspapers said that he had,' Peacock recalled. 'I never thought he was invincible. Although we got on well, he was a trifle thin-skinned, and he really would react personally to political criticism.' Even though the campaign was long enough, Peacock thought a few more weeks campaigning might have seen more Labor seats fall. 'I was wishing we had another week or two,' he reflected.[55]

Hawke rejected the suggestion that it was a mistake to go to an early election. 'No,' he said. 'We got a working majority.' However, a great election victory – perhaps the party's greatest ever – had been in prospect. Hawke's performance was far from optimal, but he grumpily rejected this suggestion too. 'Andrew Peacock was only able to do better because he wasn't up against Bob Hawke,' he insisted.[56] In other words, Hawke was not at his best and this explained Peacock's superior campaign. But it is a poor rationalisation for the result. In truth, the messiah was made mortal.

—

It had been a difficult year for Hawke. Learning the extent of Rosslyn's drug addiction shook him to the core. He blamed himself. He had not been this emotionally distraught since the disastrous negotiations over the Soviet Refuseniks in 1979. It was Hazel who comforted him, reassured him and helped him deal with it. She not only saved Rosslyn and Matt, she saved Bob too. It would take him months to regain his equilibrium. Michelle Grattan wrote a perceptive column about Hawke in September, which Hazel cut out and stuck in her scrapbook. 'The fact that he, in common with most other MPs, almost certainly would not sacrifice the pursuit of power for the sake of family if he had his life to live again, does not reduce the guilt: it increases it,' Grattan wrote. Hazel circled this sentence.[57]

Bob could not deal with family pressures and the responsibilities of running the country without Hazel. It was widely reported that her dignity, reserve, honesty and generosity had 'won the heart of a nation'. She showed courage and resilience in the face of family adversity.[58] Hazel was already an electoral asset, and now became even more so. 'This country is very lucky to have a First Lady of such strength,' said a caller to 2GB in Sydney.[59] She was a tower of strength for Hawke.

It did not take long for Hazel to adjust to her new life. She had music, yoga and friends in Canberra, Sydney and Melbourne. She started studying music and had a Schimmel piano brought into the Lodge which had been found in government storage. She was a devoted grandmother. As well as having Rosslyn's boys living with her during these years, she remained in close contact with Susan and Stephen and their young families.

2 1

HAWKE ABROAD

B ob Hawke wanted Australia to be a creative middle power that punched above its weight on the world stage. He favoured a personal approach to diplomacy and working through international forums to achieve outcomes. His priorities were strengthening the alliance with the United States, working through the Commonwealth Heads of Government Meeting (CHOGM) to end apartheid in South Africa, and building closer trade relations in the region by establishing the Asia-Pacific Economic Cooperation (APEC) forum. While pursuing these initiatives, and others, Hawke saw an opportunity to ply his negotiating skills and act as a mediator between East and West.

Hawke's first overseas trip was a nineteen-day tour of seven countries and eleven cities in June 1983. In Papua New Guinea, he met with Prime Minister Michael Somare. In Indonesia, he met with President Suharto. In London, he met with the Queen. In Paris, he met with President François Mitterrand and Prime Minister Pierre Mauroy. In Canada, he met with Prime Minister Pierre Trudeau. And in the United States, Hawke met with President Ronald Reagan and Vice President George H.W. Bush, along with cabinet secretaries George Shultz (state), Caspar Weinberger (defense) and Donald Regan (treasury). Hazel travelled with him, as did Paul and Annita Keating, who joined the party in Geneva, where Hawke addressed the International Labour Organization and met with Director-General Francis Blanchard.

The most important of Hawke's meetings, he believed, were

with Reagan and Bush. Hawke was determined to demonstrate that he was different to Gough Whitlam and had no truck with the anti-American sentiment that still existed within some sections of the Labor Party. It was widely reported, from *The Wall Street Journal* to *Playboy*, that American political analysts thought Australia had taken a leftward turn and the Hawke government could be thrown out of office after one term.[1] Hawke wanted to position Australia as a dependable, not compliant ally of the United States. 'While you had an alliance with the United States, you had to maintain the reality and the appearance of Australia as an independent, sovereign, decisionmaker in terms of its foreign policy, which would be decided according to its own assessment of Australia's national interest,' he explained.[2]

Reagan had written to Hawke on 5 March 1983 to offer his 'warm congratulations' for the election victory. Reagan emphasised that the United States and Australia had 'shared interests and values' that underpinned the relationship. He said the ANZUS alliance 'transcends military and security needs' and encompasses 'a broad range of political, economic and cultural interests'. Reagan wanted to work 'closely' with Hawke and invited him to visit Washington.[3] Hawke replied, agreeing with the sentiments in Reagan's letter, and said his government would be 'that of a constructive ally'.[4]

The Central Intelligence Agency assessed that a Hawke government 'would not result in a major realignment of bilateral cooperation in security and defense'. The CIA recognised Hawke's 'moderate' approach to foreign policy but thought there was a 'remote possibility' that the 'radical Left wing' of the Labor Party might try to exert 'influence'. The ANZUS alliance and continuation of the joint defence facilities were not under threat. Hawke would position Australia as 'a more active and ideologically independent participant in world affairs'. Pursuing nuclear disarmament policies, acting as a mediator in Indochina and increasing aid to the Asia-Pacific region were identified as changes in emphasis from the Fraser government. 'Concern that a Labor government under Hawke would be a repeat of the 1972–75 Gough Whitlam government is, we believe, unfounded.'[5]

Shultz was not concerned about Hawke. He had known Hawke

since the 1970s, when he was an executive with Bechtel and
Hawke was ACTU president and they had negotiated disputes in
the construction industry. Shultz regarded Hawke as a friend. 'He
was a pleasure to deal with,' Shultz recalled. 'He was tough and
strong in representing [workers] but he was fair and you could work
with him and come to a solution. I admired him and I got to like
him.' He did, however, acknowledge that some in the administration were nervous about Hawke. 'I said, "Settle down, this guy is
going to be great." I told that to the president and we went ahead
on that presumption and I knew our relations would be wonderful.'[6]

James Baker, chief of staff to Reagan, was also not at all
concerned about Hawke or the election of a Labor government.
'Bob was a steadfast ally of the United States and a good friend of
ours, someone that we could always in my view count on – a really
strong ally,' Baker remembered. 'We had a wonderful relationship with him in both the Reagan and the Bush administrations.
I found him fine to deal with. He said what he meant and meant
what he said. He was a no-nonsense kind of guy.'[7]

At 11.30 am on 13 June 1983, Hawke walked into the Oval
Office of the White House and shook hands with Reagan. Paul
Keating joined Hawke for the meeting, along with senior staff
and officials from both countries. Hawke and Reagan spent two
hours together, which included a further meeting in the Cabinet
Room and lunch in the Red Room, followed by joint remarks on
the South Grounds.

Hawke recalled the key message he gave Reagan: 'I said to
Reagan that I would be supportive of the alliance but there would
be occasions when I didn't agree with him and I would talk to him
about those issues. I said I wasn't from the left wing of the party
and I didn't come with any fixed attitude.'[8] Reagan wrote in his
diary about his meeting with Hawke: 'Visited by Bob Hawke new
P.M. of Australia. We got along fine & quietly just between the
2 of us he let me know he did not represent the left wing of
the labor party.'[9] The message was received.

A more expansive discussion was had in the Cabinet Room.
Hawke recalled this was where 'the personal chemistry' really
began. Hawke asked about the economy and prospects for growth.
Reagan shuffled through cue cards and when he found the right

one offered some perfunctory remarks, and then asked Donald Regan, the Treasury secretary, to continue. 'The most powerful man in the world sat there and said nothing,' Hawke recalled. 'As we were going out, some of my blokes were very critical of him. I said, "What would you rather? A bloke who doesn't know very much about things rabbiting on?" What he really liked was the meal and telling jokes. So we went to lunch and told some jokes, which he enjoyed enormously.'[10]

George H.W. Bush recalled the high importance the United States placed on the relationship with Australia at the time. 'The bilateral relationship between allies as historically close as the United States and Australia has always been a priority,' he said. 'Because of the many things we shared – basic values such as our commitment to democracy, freedom and human rights – I do not recall any major fires that needed to be put out. I hope it is not revisionism to suggest our consultations always seemed to be working more on refinements to an already extraordinarily good and productive partnership.'[11]

The Americans did want reassurance that ANZUS and the joint facilities at Pine Gap, Nurrungar and North West Cape would continue. A CIA briefing paper advised that Hawke wanted 'to reassure the US that Australia remains a reliable ally' but cautioned he may propose 'making some adjustments', including 'control' of the facilities.[12] Labor had announced a review of ANZUS but Hawke reassured Reagan it would not lead to any diminution in the alliance framework; rather, it would strengthen it. They agreed, however, to work towards disclosing details about the role and functions of the joint facilities, and Hawke gave a detailed statement to parliament about this the following year, on 6 June 1984.

Bill Hayden was sceptical of the United States, especially the Reagan administration. The new minister for foreign affairs had questioned the value of ANZUS and was concerned the joint defence facilities undermined Australian sovereignty. 'I am sceptical of big powers,' Hayden recalled. 'They will always want things to suit themselves. I thought Hawke was too quick and heavy-footed in supporting Reagan and Bush.'[13]

Some CIA assessments of Hayden were illogical and irrational, even verging on the comical. The CIA believed the Centre Left faction – which had Hayden as a key figure, along with Young, Dawkins and Blewett – represented a threat to Hawke's 'tight control' of the party. They suggested Hayden might launch a 'leadership bid' to wrest the prime ministership from Hawke.[14] Hayden regarded this as nonsense. 'I wasn't looking for a return to the leadership,' he recalled. 'Bob was too popular with the public. He was winning elections. If I took him on, I would have been beaten in the caucus.'[15] Michael Costello, principal private secretary to Hayden, said the idea never crossed his mind. 'Hayden never thought he was going to be leader again.'[16]

Hawke sensed the concern about Hayden within the Reagan administration. It is telling that he did not take Hayden with him to meet Reagan in June 1983, but Keating. 'I had on occasion to reassure George Shultz that Bill was not anti-American,' Hawke recalled. 'Bill was a bit touchy at the edges at times about them, but he was committed to the alliance. So I talked to Bill and he listened, and any initiatives I undertook he was very supportive of.'[17]

Kim Beazley, who became minister for defence in 1984, reflected on the Hawke–Hayden relationship. 'Hayden was enormously careful of what Hawke's views were,' he said. 'He had his own views, and he made those known, but he always assumed that foreign policy was an area where the prime minister would have a large role. Hawke was always mindful of Hayden, cautious about offending him and anxious to ensure he was always respected.'[18]

Costello said Hawke and Hayden got on well together. 'Bill was not the smooth, sweet, charming diplomat,' he explained. 'He was a politician, and a good combination of realist and idealist. He had the proper balance between being a strong ally of the United States but also having an independent foreign policy. He was able to push to one side those in caucus who wanted to get rid of the joint bases.'[19]

Hayden saw an opportunity for Australia to help broker peace in Indochina, which unsettled the United States. Labor's pledge to resume aid to Vietnam was criticised by the United States and some ASEAN members, and it was dropped. It was Hawke who asked Hayden to take the lead on a Cambodia peace initiative. Hayden felt Australia owed 'a moral debt' to Indochina. 'Hayden's diplomatic efforts culminated in a meeting with foreign minister

Hun Sen in Ho Chi Minh City in 1987,' recalled Costello. 'That meeting upset ASEAN and so Hayden had to back off.' But the initiative was taken up again by Gareth Evans in 1989. By then, the geopolitics had changed; the Soviet Union was no longer providing support for Vietnam and China was no longer supporting the Khmer Rouge. Evans and Costello went on to play a lead role in negotiating a peace agreement that was signed in Paris in 1991.[20]

During the Hawke–Reagan meeting, the president discussed the development of the Strategic Defense Initiative (SDI), known as 'Star Wars', which ludicrously included space-based lasers shooting down nuclear missiles launched by the Soviet Union. Reagan pressed for the Australians to be involved in the development of the program. Hawke declined. Labor was elected on a promise to advocate nuclear disarmament, and remained committed to this goal. The government pushed for the adoption of the Chemical Weapons Convention, helped to create the South Pacific Nuclear Free Zone, worked through the United Nations on the Nuclear Non-Proliferation Treaty and the Comprehensive Test Ban Treaty, and appointed Richard Butler as ambassador for disarmament.

The United States objected to the South Pacific Nuclear Free Zone initiative, which was formalised with the Treaty of Raratonga in 1985. This had the support of South Pacific Forum members. Hawke insisted to the United States that he would maintain the agreement, which banned nuclear testing, storage and waste disposal in the region. He reassured the United States that it was primarily directed towards France. Moreover, Hawke would not let Australia go down the path of New Zealand, which had banned United States ships from docking in its ports – a decision that led to New Zealand being consigned to the diplomatic freezer. The United States would no longer facilitate military exercises, reciprocal military placements or the sharing of intelligence with New Zealand.

Hawke renewed the commitment given to the United States by the Fraser government that Australia would allow the use of its airfields to monitor the testing of the controversial MX intercontinental ballistic missile. The splashdown of the MX – without a nuclear warhead – would be 220 kilometres off the east coast of Tasmania. Hawke negotiated to shift the splashdown area into international waters, but its planes would still be allowed to land in Australia. On 29 January 1985, the security committee of cabinet met to discuss how it would 'explain its position on the MX missile test program', should it become a public concern. Hawke was due to head to the United States the following week. It was agreed that he would make it clear that there was no guarantee Australia would provide assistance for 'further tests'.[21]

When news that Australia had agreed to support the testing of the MX missile became public, on 1 February 1985, it was met with significant caucus opposition. The context is important. At the December 1984 election, the Nuclear Disarmament Party won 7 per cent of the vote. Public support for peace initiatives was high – 250,000 Australians joined Palm Sunday peace marches in April 1984. Some Labor MPs were alarmed by Hawke's closeness to Reagan's Republican administration.

Hawke, who was in Brussels, strongly defended both the testing program and his promise to the Americans. He instructed Hayden and Beazley to defend the government's policy, and not to buckle to caucus threats. Beazley recalled telling Hawke months earlier that 'all hell will break lose' if the MX promise became public. As the heat rose in caucus, Beazley thought it was better just to get the test over and done with. He rang up his counterparts in the Pentagon and told them: 'Just fire the fucking thing.' He was told they could not do that because it would take twelve to eighteen months to set up. 'You mean to say we are going to have to put up with this crap for twelve to eighteen months while you get your act together?' he replied. It was not tenable. Once Hawke was told by Graham Richardson that he would not survive a caucus revolt, he had to retreat.[22]

Hawke travelled on to Washington, DC. He used his personal relationship with Shultz to free himself from the MX commitment. On 6 February, Hawke told Shultz the backlash in Australia was due to elements of 'anti-Americanism' and 'emotional garbage' about uranium mining and nuclear weapons that 'fused' around the MX missile.[23] They issued a joint statement announcing the test would not require the use of Australian facilities. Hawke had raised 'community concerns in Australia' over the MX. Shultz said that 'there are a variety of ways to monitor an MX test', and it 'need not involve the provision of Australian support'.[24] Shultz understood Hawke's political problem and worked out a way to resolve it. 'He was very clear that he couldn't do it, and I would say in a sense I could tell that he wanted to do it, but there was no way he could do it,' Shultz recalled. 'There was no point in ratcheting it up when he couldn't do anything about it.'[25]

Hayden and Beazley thought Hawke's execution of a backflip without damaging the alliance relationship or his personal relations with the White House was extraordinary. Beazley reflected: 'Hawke got the Americans to do something they would never do for anyone else.'[26] Hayden recalled: 'It was a huge embarrassment. I don't know how he got out of it. He must have kissed a few bums in Washington.'[27]

Shultz and Weinberger recognised that, given the opposition within Labor, the alliance might come under greater strain if they applied too much pressure on Hawke. The bigger picture for the Americans was the future of the joint defence facilities. They were not going to do anything to jeopardise that. So they let Hawke off the hook, and he was able to quell the concerns within caucus.

Bush confirmed the MX missile controversy did not hurt Hawke's standing at the White House. 'Bob and President Reagan, I believe, had a similar close and friendly relationship,' he said. 'I do not believe there could have been any lasting ill will. In my experience, Bob was a straight shooter as prime minister, always telling you what was on his mind, and always doing so in a spirit of friendship looking for solutions. He could be tough, but with Bob Hawke it was never his way or the highway.'[28]

Shultz agreed the MX missile retreat did not damage Hawke with Reagan. 'He was my friend,' Shultz said. 'We had a lot of fun together. We trusted each other. When he told me something I believed it and if I told him something he believed it. There are matters of big-time international diplomacy and there are a lot of smaller things, but trust is the coin of the realm. He trusted me and I trusted him, and that was the main thing.'[29]

At 11.30 am on 7 February 1985, Reagan greeted Hawke in the Oval Office. It was Reagan's first meeting with a head of government in his second term. Photographers were invited in. One journalist asked Reagan: 'Mr President, does the ANZUS alliance have any future given the lack of cooperation we have been getting from our South Pacific allies?' Hawke sat still and smiled. 'Well, the only thing that's happened that disturbs that is the New Zealand position on our vessels there,' Reagan replied. 'Other than that, I think our ANZUS alliance is very sound and very solid.' Asked specifically about the MX backdown, Reagan said he was concerned because it was the United States' 'idea' but they had other 'options' available. When the media exited, Hawke said: 'I didn't know they were going to throw questions at you.'[30] If Hawke was wondering about what Reagan might say about the MX issue, he need not have worried.

Reagan and Hawke met for about fifteen minutes and then moved to the Cabinet Room for a broader discussion. Cocktails were served in the State Dining Room. Then Reagan took Hawke next door to the Family Dining Room for a private lunch. After-wards, they exchanged departure statements before Hawke left. Much of the discussions concerned the ANZUS alliance and the fallout with New Zealand. Reagan wrote in his diary about Hawke's visit: 'Rest of morning & lunch with Bob Hawke – P.M. of Australia. He's a good man. We're both upset about New Zealand – refusing to allow our destroyer to use the port. Has to do with N.Z.'s ban on ships powered by or carrying anything nuclear. We've cancelled the Anzus war games.'[31]

In February 1985, Paul Dibb was commissioned to review Australia's defence planning. His report, delivered in March 1986, recommended an abandonment of the forward defence posture that had been adopted in the 1950s and 1960s. This report led to a Defence White Paper, adopted in February 1987, which initiated a major reorganisation of the Australian Defence Force, and the adoption of a self-reliant posture focused on areas of Australia's direct interest, especially in the South-West Pacific region and South-East Asia. It confirmed Australia as an important member of the Western alliance structure, and endorsed the joint facilities with the United States and the cooperative defence relationship. Importantly, the report concluded there was no direct military threat to Australia.

The government agreed to $25 billion in spending on new initiatives, including new fighter and reconnaissance planes and helicopters, submarines and radar stations. The development of the *Collins*-class submarine would be plagued with design defects, production delays and cost overruns. Beazley said he had only a few ministers supporting him in cabinet when the decision was made to proceed with the initiative, but he had Hawke's backing. He rejected criticism of the submarine decision. '*Collins* has turned out to be the best conventional submarine in the world,' he insisted. 'There has never been a new weapons system developed and first built for a country that has ever produced a perfect outcome. But in so far as we could, we came close to it with the *Collins*.'[32]

Hawke was back in the United States the following year, with Australia's defence planning a topic of discussion during his third Oval Office meeting with Reagan, on 17 April 1986. After photographs were taken and a few questions asked by journalists, they had a brief discussion before heading to the Cabinet Room, where officials joined them. At the commencement of their talks, Reagan asked if Hawke had brought the America's Cup back. Hawke said they would have to earn it. Reagan moved to the official business. 'I'm pleased with the security cooperation that we've had with the ship and aircraft visits that help us maintain a presence in the Indian Ocean, and the joint facilities that provide a deterrence and certainly intelligence gathering,' he told Hawke. 'I recognise, too, the political burden that you bear in helping us in that way.' Differences on foreign policy, or any other issue such as agricultural trade, could be discussed 'as good friends', Reagan said.[33]

Refreshments were served in the State Dining Room, before Reagan escorted Hawke to the Family Dining Room for a working lunch. They both addressed the media in the East Room and then Hawke departed from the South Grounds. The personal chemistry between Hawke and Reagan was now cemented. 'Main part of day was visit & lunch with P.M. of Australia Bob Hawke,' Reagan wrote in his diary. 'We have a good relationship both as individuals & as countries.'[34] The following year, on 11 July 1987, Reagan phoned Hawke to congratulate him on his third election victory. 'The victory shows the confidence the Australian people hold in [your] imaginative leadership,' he said.[35] The call, like the meeting, was a testament to the growing mutual regard between the two men.

Rawdon Dalrymple, Hawke's friend from Oxford, took up the post of ambassador to the United States in June 1985. He sat in on Hawke's meetings with Reagan. 'Hawke was much more successful with the Americans than Whitlam or Fraser,' he recalled. 'Hawke got on very well with Reagan who is a much more complex character than a lot of people understood. Hawke was a master at all that male bonding stuff and telling each other jokes. Hawke had a great capacity to make himself liked.'[36]

After meeting with Reagan and Bush in February 1985, Hawke travelled to Ottawa. He had been invited by Canadian prime minister Brian Mulroney, who was holding his own national economic conference, modelled on Hawke's 1983 initiative. Hawke, who was the keynote speaker, forged another critical Cold War partnership. 'He spoke in his own very straightforward way, and he contributed largely to making a great success of our national economic conference,' Mulroney recalled. 'We got along very well, and we were together, I guess, for almost eight or nine years, and I cannot say that I ever had an unpleasant moment in his company.' Like Hawke, Mulroney had advocated for the abolition of apartheid since the 1960s. Ahead of the CHOGM meeting in Nassau later that year, they decided to work together to try and force change in South Africa.[37]

—

Hawke thought the Fraser government had lacked a coherent foreign policy, and was too focused on the United States and Europe, without paying sufficient attention to the Asia-Pacific. In November 1983, Hawke travelled to Thailand and met with Prime Minister Prem Tinsulanonda and the Thai king and queen. In January–February 1984 he travelled to Japan and met with Prime Minister Yasuhiro Nakasone; in South Korea he met with Prime Minister Chin Iee-chong; he sat down with Prime Minister Lee Kuan Yew in Singapore; and he visited Dr Mahathir in Malaysia.

The most important visit of this trip was to China. Hawke was an enthusiast for the 'reform and opening-up' of China, having first visited in 1978, because he recognised the economic benefits for Australia. 'I was extraordinarily lucky in the timing of my relationship with China,' Hawke recalled. 'When I was president of the ACTU a lot of the left-wing union leaders had been up there and come back with invitations to say they wanted to see me. I refused to go until the Gang of Four was out of power. My relationship with Chinese leaders coincided with that historically unparalleled transformation.'[38]

From his earliest days as prime minister, Hawke built a rapport with senior Chinese leaders trusted by Deng Xiaoping: premier Zhao Ziyang and party secretary Hu Yaobang, along with officials Hu Qili and Wan Li. The pivotal event was Zhao's visit to Australia from 17 April to 23 April 1983. Hawke was immensely impressed by Zhao's breadth of understanding of international issues. He was unassuming and understated in his formal dealings, and a mutual regard developed between the Chinese and Australian leaders.

Ross Garnaut thought this visit was critical for the Australia–China relationship. 'Bob had an unusual capacity to strike very close relationships, trustful relationships, across cultural barriers,' he recalled. 'He had the early view that the changes in China were going to change its place in the world. He thought, first, that we had to understand them. Second, be closely linked to them. And third, we should shape our relationship with China in a way that we got the most out of it.'[39]

As Hawke recalled it, the only embarrassment during the visit took place at a parliamentary lunch. Hawke chatted amiably with Zhao via his interpreter, and suggested the outgoing speaker of the House of Representatives, Billy Snedden, might also like to engage with the Chinese premier. 'Prime Minister, I think we should congratulate the Premier on his use of the knife and fork,' Snedden said.[40]

In 1984 Hawke travelled to China. This was a significant visit that also facilitated Hawke's role as a conduit between East and West. He spoke to Zhao on 7 February and had two further lengthy sessions on 8 and 9 February, in Beijing. Zhao said they were now 'old friends' and should have an 'unrestrained exchange of views'.[41] The first session, on 8 February, focused on international issues. Hawke said he despaired about the superpower rivalry between the United States and the Soviet Union, and the prospect for disarmament. He argued the case for the Nuclear

Non-Proliferation Treaty. Zhao said there were many areas of agreement between China and Australia, and where they did not agree they could still have a constructive dialogue. China only had a small nuclear arsenal, Zhao argued, and viewed the NPT as discriminatory.

The second session, on 9 February, began with Zhao confirming China's wish for Hong Kong to be stable and prosperous after the handover from the United Kingdom in 1997. China 'would not interfere in the internal affairs of Hong Kong' but would manage foreign affairs and defence matters, Zhao said. They discussed Japan, with Zhao commenting that China–Japan relations were 'ranked first' in its external outlook. Hawke reiterated Australia's opposition to Vietnam's occupation of Cambodia, and 'deplored' Soviet influence in Vietnam and the presence of Soviet forces at Camranh Bay and Danang. He said Labor's pledge to resume aid to Vietnam was now off the agenda. Zhao emphasised that China did not support the Khmer Rouge returning to power in Cambodia and favoured a coalition government led by Prince Sihanouk.

After a short break, Hawke departed from the agreed topics and suggested they form a 'joint working group' to consider how to increase the supply of Australia's iron ore and coal for China's steel industry. Hawke wanted Australia to be 'a competitive, major supplier of raw materials' and said this could 'fit in well with China's own development plan'. Zhao was enthusiastic and 'responded positively' by suggesting 'multiforms of cooperation', including joint ventures. These talks led to an Australia–China joint mining venture at Mount Channar, in the Pilbara region of Western Australia. The economic relationship between Australia and China expanded rapidly. In just one year, from 1984 to 1985, Australian exports to China rose by more than 70 per cent and exceeded $1 billion in value. China had been Australia's tenth-largest export market but was now the fifth-largest. By 2021, China produced around half the world's steel, and Australia supplied around 60 per cent of China's iron ore.[42]

Between the two sessions, Hawke met with President Li Xiannian in Beijing. Li had visited Australia in 1980. Hawke said that, a decade ago, 'China had been a divisive issue in Australia' but it was now 'a central foundation of Australia's foreign relations'. In discussing China's growth and transformation, Li acknowledged that China had made 'leftist errors'. He said Mao Zedong 'had good intentions' but had put too much emphasis on the 'collective will', and the 'objective conditions' for reform and development had not been right. China was 'learning from experience', Li said. He explained that China would continue to focus on 'opening to the outside world' but would 'preserve stability and unity at home'. And he argued that China did not have territorial ambitions. 'No one would get anywhere if countries tried to swallow each other up,' Li said. 'It was better to learn to live together in peace [and] coexistence.'[43]

During this visit, Hawke also had extensive dialogue with Hu Yaobang, general secretary of the Chinese Communist Party, in Shanghai on 11 February. They discussed Vietnam and Cambodia. Hu said that 'China was for a political settlement – eventually' and he hoped Hawke 'would play a role in helping to resolve this question'. China would support 'an independent, non-aligned, neutral' Cambodia once Vietnam withdraws, Hu said, provided there was a coalition government headed by Prince Sihanouk and friendly relations were maintained with Vietnam and other ASEAN nations. Again, he emphasised that China would welcome Hawke conveying this message to Vietnam. The Chinese saw him as a trusted interlocuter.[44]

In 1985, Hu Yaobang and Hu Qili visited Australia. Hawke found Hu Yaobang's energy and enthusiasm to be infectious. He enjoyed talking with him, and their discussions ranged well beyond Australia–China relations. With Hawke, they visited the joint mining venture at Mount Channar, the first of its kind in the world for the Chinese leadership. Other economic partnerships followed, including Chinese investment in the Portland Aluminium Smelter in Victoria, and a purchase agreement with the BHP steel mill in Whyalla in South Australia. In 1984 there was just one joint venture between Australia and China; by 1986 there were sixteen.

In May 1986, Hawke visited China again. Two-way trade and investment, cultural exchanges and political engagement had expanded rapidly in the previous few years. He had discussions with Hu Yaobang as they visited the outer provinces, including Sichuan, and also with Zhao Ziyang and Deng Xiaoping. Hawke's record of conversation with Zhao on 19 May in Beijing began with the Chinese leader noting that most of Hawke's staff had beards, which might lead some to mistake them for Marxists. Hawke replied that the most famous bearded Australian was Ned Kelly, who believed in the redistribution of income through the most direct means.

Hawke explained his government's focus on disarmament and its commitment to a Comprehensive Test Ban Treaty. He encouraged China's engagement with South Pacific nations. He emphasised that, under ANZUS, Australia and the United States would continue to cooperate in the region, and that this would contribute to global security. On Indochina, Hawke reiterated Australia's support for the withdrawal of Vietnam from Cambodia, preventing Pol Pot from returning to power, and for a negotiated settlement. He encouraged dialogue between North Korea and South Korea.

Zhao's most extensive, and revealing, comments concerned the United States and the Soviet Union. He said both agreed to substantially reduce their nuclear arsenals but sought military superiority through negotiations. He thought the Soviet Union's strategy was to ease tensions to give it more time to address its domestic situation. 'Without reforms and improvements in economic performance it would be very difficult for the Soviet Union to maintain its rivalry with the United States for hegemony,' Zhao said. 'As a consequence, in the next century, the USSR might no longer be able to retain its status as a superpower.'[45]

On 20 May, Hawke met with Deng in Beijing. They spoke for over an hour. Deng outlined to Hawke the rapid economic development taking place in China but conceded that mistakes would be made and these had to be recognised and addressed. He predicted a population for China by the end of the century of about 1.2 billion, with a per-capita income of around US$800–1000. He argued to Hawke that as China grew in economic strength, it could use this power as 'a force for peace'. Deng said the Soviet Union lacked flexibility in its economic policies and therefore it would not be able to develop economically like China.

He emphasised that he did not interfere in policy matters but was concerned with the 'big sweep' of the reform program. Hawke thought it was one of the most interesting hours of his life.[46]

Hawke's most detailed talks on this trip were with Hu Yaobang, late at night in Chengdu (21 May) and Nanjing (22 May). Hu complained to Hawke that the United States did not engage at a deep enough level with China, and there were disagreements, especially over Taiwan. China wanted to boost trade, aviation and mail services with the United States. Hawke undertook to convey to the United States, via George Shultz, that they should invest more time in developing the relationship with China. Hawke was sympathetic to China's view on Taiwan. 'It is an absurdity to maintain in any way,' he said, 'the fallacy that Taiwan is the legitimate government of China.' They had long talks about the Soviet Union and the rise to power the previous year of Mikhail Gorbachev. Hu emphasised that China was on a very different track to the Soviet Union and said they 'will never be allies'. He was concerned about the Soviet Union's belief that it was a hegemonic power, with its own spheres of influence, and its commitment to supporting global communism.[47]

Hawke gained an insight into the tensions within the Chinese leadership about pursuing economic reform alongside political reform. He recalled that Hu believed political and economic liberation were linked – one would follow the other. But this was not a view shared by Deng. Hu told Hawke that 'socialism had been discredited by the Khmer Rouge in Cambodia' and the United Nations would have to eventually play a role in a settlement in Indochina. This, along with other departures from Chinese political orthodoxy, contributed to Hu's removal from power in January 1987. He had a heart attack and died two years later, in April 1989, an event which sparked the Tiananmen Square protests. In June that year, Zhao too was removed from power and placed under house arrest that would last fifteen years. He died in January 2005.

—

As part of his first extensive overseas trip just months after becoming prime minister, Hawke was in London during their election campaign in mid-1983. He had an audience with the

Queen but could not meet Margaret Thatcher. They did, however, have a phone conversation three days before polling day, on 6 June. Hawke was staying at the Savoy Hotel and had met with Labour leader Michael Foot that afternoon. It would be understandable if Thatcher did not know what to make of Hawke, given the briefing she received:

> Hawke is widely respected, though [his] often deliberately abrasive and even arrogant manner offends some. He is intelligent, industrious, shrewd, articulate and a formidable negotiator. He is thought to be more to the centre than his centre-left public image . . . Had a widely known weakness for drink and women, and studiously cultivated an 'ocker' image.[48]

A dispatch from the United Kingdom's high commissioner in Canberra reported 'misgivings about his suitability to be prime minister'. He noted Hawke's 'heavy drinking', his 'violent' outbursts, his 'ludicrous advances to unreceptive ladies', and his general loutish behaviour. Hawke was characterised as 'a façade, obsessed by his media image and his own popularity'. But the high commissioner conceded he might be proved wrong.[49] In a rather perfunctory dialogue, Hawke and Thatcher discussed the recent Williamsburg Economic Summit, the global and Australian economic outlook, and the 'political scenes' in Britain, Europe and America.[50]

Ahead of Hawke's first CHOGM in New Delhi, India, from 23 to 29 November 1983, Thatcher was advised that Hawke would respond positively to 'special attention'. This advice – to treat Hawke like a rookie leader in search of friends – came from Malcolm Fraser.[51] A 'working breakfast' stretching over an hour was held on 23 November. Hawke and Thatcher discussed a range of international issues relating to Grenada, Cyprus and Hong Kong, along with broader topics such as disarmament and uranium mining and export in Australia. They both felt the CHOGM program was too long, the communiqué should be kept as short as possible and further regional meetings were unnecessary. 'While we [do] not agree on all things, our positions on the fundamental issues [are] very close,' Hawke said.[52]

Charles Powell, foreign policy adviser to Thatcher, recalled that she was keen to improve relations with Australia. 'It was not a very happy relationship between Malcolm Fraser and Margaret Thatcher, a grudge which she bore ever thereafter, as he was constantly and unnecessarily difficult,' Powell said. 'Australia was the number one Commonwealth country as far as she was concerned, and there was respect for the way Hawke was running his government in Australia.'[53]

Hawke was still finding his way at CHOGM. He absorbed how CHOGM worked, the bureaucracy behind it and the personalities of the various leaders. He established a personal and professional rapport with most leaders in the plenary sessions and in sideline meetings. However, Hawke did not get on well with Indira Gandhi and they clashed over what he saw as her willingness to criticise some countries, such as Israel, for human rights abuses but not others, such as the Soviet Union. He viewed Gandhi as an apologist for the USSR.

He put down a marker for the future when he said that Australia abhorred apartheid in South Africa and praised the work of his predecessor. Hawke had witnessed the injustice himself when he visited South Africa in 1953 and became an advocate for racial equality in the 1970s. Hawke realised that CHOGM could be a vehicle for 'mobilising world opinion against apartheid' and forcing South Africa to change its policy. 'It was just fundamental to my thinking: the total repugnance of apartheid and so I made it my mission when I became prime minister,' he recalled.[54]

Hawke's second CHOGM was held in Nassau, the Bahamas, from 16 to 22 October 1985. The major issue would be the future of apartheid in South Africa. Thatcher wrote to Hawke on 10 October, stressing they agreed that apartheid should be abhorred and abolished. The question, she said, was how to achieve it. 'I am firmly opposed to additional economic sanctions,' she wrote. 'I believe that such an approach is fundamentally mistaken.' She likened it to 'foreign bullying' and said it would not deliver a political solution. She hoped to avoid 'confrontation' over the issue in Nassau.[55]

Hawke and Thatcher spoke before the first session in Nassau on 17 October. He stressed that it was never the intention to 'embarrass, isolate or attack the United Kingdom'. He too wanted to achieve a free South Africa without sanctions. But, he said, 'there had to be a preparedness to act' on sanctions while dialogue between white and black South Africans continued. Thatcher was relieved and said this was 'a much better route' than what other leaders were proposing. She accepted dialogue alone might 'not be enough' and could 'conceive' of a formulation where dialogue was reviewed within a specified time period. Hawke was open to this.[56]

Hawke sought an agreement within this framework – a preference for dialogue rather than sanctions. He proposed the Eminent Persons Group (EPG), which would engage with South Africa's leaders and benchmark progress. In his speech to the first session of leaders, Hawke sought to unlock the secret of the Commonwealth's strength: understanding the limits of power. South Africa would have to be persuaded by the moral argument that apartheid could not be tolerated, or it would have to face the impact of sanctions. 'The spirit of men and women yearning to be free, to have that right to determine their own destiny, will not be extinguished,' Hawke said. 'It will not be extinguished, however brutally that arsenal is unleashed upon them.'[57]

The leaders retreated to Lyford Cay to hammer out an agreement. Kenneth Kaunda, the president of Zambia, invited Hawke to play golf. Hawke had not played since the 1960s. He rediscovered the game and it became not only a form of exercise and enjoyment, but an arm of his diplomacy with other world leaders. The meeting, however, was not tranquil. Thatcher was in sharp disagreement over the wording of the leaders' agreement. Hawke was exasperated with Thatcher and his exchanges with her were 'acrimonious'. The plenary session was particularly 'virulent' as Thatcher was isolated in her views. Eventually, in return for several concessions, including a statement condemning violence, Thatcher agreed to establish the EPG to engage in dialogue with South Africa alongside a stage-by-stage application of sanctions if these talks did not prove successful.[58]

Powell, who was at the meeting, said Thatcher 'bitterly resented' the way she had been treated, but generally appreciated that Hawke was upfront with his views and was not patronising or condescending as Malcolm Fraser had been. 'Generally, their personal relationship was fine,' Powell recalled. 'They had their battles, but he enjoyed them, she enjoyed them, they were both the sort of people who had battles. This is how they reached their conclusions – by argument.'[59]

A meeting was held to discuss membership of the EPG. Nominations would be sent to Sonny Ramphal, the Commonwealth secretary-general. Hawke nominated Fraser as co-chair of the EPG. Cabinet endorsed Hawke's nomination of Fraser.[60] Thatcher spoke against Fraser's appointment but did not block it. In 1986, Fraser was scheduled to meet Nelson Mandela at Cape Town's Pollsmoor Prison. When they met, Mandela asked: 'Tell me, Mr Fraser, is Donald Bradman still alive?' Fraser replied that the Don was indeed alive. Years later, Alister Drysdale, a former adviser to Fraser, organised for Bradman to sign a cricket bat as a gift for Mandela. He inscribed it: 'To Nelson Mandela in recognition of a great unfinished innings – Don Bradman.'[61]

Bob Hawke was generous to both of his predecessors. In addition to supporting Fraser's appointment to the EPG and as secretary-general of the Commonwealth, he appointed Gough Whitlam as Australia's Ambassador to the United Nations Educational, Scientific and Cultural Organization (UNESCO). During the three-year appointment, made on 13 July 1983, Gough and Margaret Whitlam lived in the Australian Embassy complex in Paris.[62]

During an extensive overseas trip that included the United States, Belgium, Italy, Greece and Singapore in April 1986, Hawke travelled to the United Kingdom for further talks with Thatcher. By now they were well acquainted. 'We had a love/hate relationship,' Hawke recalled. 'I was always fighting with her over apartheid. She was virtually the only one in the whole of CHOGM who supported the South African government. While I was very critical of her positions on issues, I did not question her integrity. I do not think Margaret had a first-class mind, but she was a very hard worker, and you always knew that when you had a meeting with her, she would be right across the brief.'[63]

John Mason, the UK high commissioner to Australia, had changed his tune about Hawke. By the end of Hawke's first year in government, he thought the prime minister had 'not put a foot wrong' during his overseas visits and had 'a very good ministry', and said Australians had found 'a leader in whom she could trust and of whom she could be proud'.[64] A briefing for Thatcher described Hawke as the Australian government's 'strategist, manager and publicist', an 'extremely popular' leader who left the running of departments 'to his highly competent ministry'. He was characterised as having 'centre-right views' on economic management, uranium mining and the ANZUS alliance.[65]

Hawke met Thatcher at 10 Downing Street on 21 April for forty-five minutes ahead of a further session with officials. They discussed the United States' airstrikes against Libya, New Zealand's banning of US ships, the South Pacific Nuclear Free Zone, and South Africa. They agreed on the importance of the EPG. Hawke thought there would be a suspension of violence by the African National Congress if there was a 'positive response' to the EPG. But Thatcher warned about driving state president P.W. Botha 'too hard' on apartheid.[66]

The EPG reported to a special CHOGM meeting in London on 3–5 August 1986. The report was far from encouraging. The South African government would not jettison race classification and group rights, and ruled out a move towards a 'one person, one vote' unitary political system.[67] The communiqué issued after the London meeting endorsed the staged application of sanctions that had been agreed at Nassau, including bans on trade, investment and tourism with South Africa. This was a victory for Hawke, but further battles with Thatcher lay ahead.

From 13 to 17 October 1987, CHOGM met in Vancouver, Canada. Again, South Africa was the main issue. Barend du Plessis, South Africa's finance minister, acknowledged that same month that sanctions were having a devastating impact on the economy. The London communiqué recognised that sanctions could be eased, provided there was a constructive dialogue on dismantling apartheid. Hawke believed that tightening sanctions would force South Africa to confront its destiny as a nation of a free people, without racial segregation, living together in harmony. It was time to tighten the screws. Hawke invited Australian expatriate investment banker Jim Wolfensohn to come from New York to Vancouver to meet with leaders and develop the proposal further. This led to the mobilisation of the international investment community to support financial sanctions.

Powell described the differences between Thatcher and Hawke. 'They had the same starting point that apartheid was abhorrent and must be destroyed, but a completely different view on the strategy for achieving that,' he explained. 'Because sanctions hit the black people of South Africa more than they would hit anyone else, the way to proceed was by relentless pressure on the government. She was the only person they listened to, even the dreadful P.W. Botha, and she spared him not at all and beat him up whenever they met. Over the long term, she got through to him, which explains why she was well placed when F.W. De Klerk came to power to continue a much easier relationship with him, but one which was no less pressing.'[68]

Hawke was exasperated that Thatcher could not understand the intellectual, let alone the moral, argument for the application of trade and investment sanctions on South Africa. Pressed for an explanation why, he simply said: 'Well, she was a grocer's daughter, wasn't she?' He did not regard her as highly intelligent, thought she was intolerant of those who had not climbed the ladder of economic and social improvement as she had, and her dogmatism meant that she rarely changed her positions despite the rationality and persuasiveness of alternative perspectives. 'She just had this very conservative view,' he said.[69]

Ahead of CHOGM in Vancouver, Colonel Sitiveni Rabuka led a series of coups in Fiji to reassert the supremacy of ethnic Fijians over Indo-Fijians with South Asian heritage. The first coup took place on 14 May 1987. A week later, on 21 May 1987, the Australian cabinet decided that it would urge the reinstatement of the deposed government of Timoci Bavadra or encourage new elections. Kim Beazley and Gareth Evans hatched a plan whereby the Royal Australian Navy would fly a helicopter over the New Zealand High Commission, rescue Bavadra and fly him to safety in western Fiji. 'I thought they had been watching too many Rambo movies,' Hawke recalled.[70] After a short-lived government of national unity, Rabuka staged a second coup on 28 September. Cabinet refused to recognise this regime and suspended Australian aid to Fiji. The following month, Fiji was declared a republic.

Hawke spoke to Sir William Heseltine, the Queen's private secretary, before CHOGM leaders met on 13 October. (They were contemporaries at Perth Modern.) The prime minister said the Commonwealth could not pretend the coup had not happened, and they needed to accept that Fiji's link to the British monarchy had been severed. He suggested the governor-general, Sir Penaia Ganilau, should be informed accordingly. Heseltine had been in dialogue with Penaia, who was isolated and looking for advice. 'By the time we got to CHOGM,' Heseltine recalled, 'Penaia was still claiming to be the governor-general and we were still recognising him as the only legal form of authority. But it was becoming more and more obvious to me, and certainly to the Queen, that it was a pointless pretence to suggest on our part that the governor-general was still in charge. But I had not quite come to the decision that we ought to bring the thing to an end when we got to Vancouver.'[71]

Thatcher, however, thought the status quo should prevail and the Governor-General should not stand down. She insisted it was not a matter to be determined at CHOGM. This view was conveyed to the Queen. When Hawke spoke to the Queen, he reiterated what he had said to Heseltine. 'She talked with a number of the other leaders and, as result of her direct intervention, the CHOGM position was made much tougher and it was recognised that the monarchy no longer existed in Fiji,' Hawke recalled. 'She was a real participant in CHOGM and not just a figurehead.'[72] The British monarchy came to an end in Fiji when Penaia resigned on 15 October 1987.

22

ECONOMIC
CRISES

In the wake of the 1984 election, Hawke made several changes to the cabinet and ministry. He was unhappy with Gordon Scholes. Hawke had approached him earlier in the year and asked him to stand aside, but he refused. He found Scholes so exasperating that he once doodled on a pad, rearranging the letters in his first name, and came up with what he thought was a better option: 'Drongo'. Hawke moved Scholes out of the defence portfolio and to the outer ministry by making him the largely irrelevant minister for territories. Gareth Evans, too adventurous as attorney-general, was moved to resources and energy. Lionel Bowen became attorney-general. John Dawkins took trade. Peter Walsh went to finance. Kim Beazley took on defence. And Chris Hurford was moved to immigration.

Early in the second term, there were signs that some MPs felt shut out of decision-making and were uneasy about the pace of market-based economic reform and fiscal consolidation, and the direction of foreign policy. Hawke had already been forced into a retreat on the MX missile. Some MPs were also uncomfortable about his corporatist style of government, which sought to build a bridge between capital and labour. The increasing factionalism within the party meant that disputes were often managed rather than publicly ventilated. This is not to say there were not strong disagreements in cabinet or in caucus, but few dissidents carried the day.

Nevertheless, in response to concerns among Labor MPs, Hawke established a process to improve relations between cabinet, the ministry and caucus. Paul Keating was given the task of leading this process, which became known as the Kirribilli Committee because its first meeting was held at Kirribilli House. It led to a new caucus committee system.[1] Ministers were reminded of the need to undertake 'the maximum possible' consultation with caucus members about policy. Ministerial staff were expected to provide regular briefings to caucus committees. And caucus committee chairs would have regular meetings with Hawke.[2] These were processes aimed at improving party unity, but the government was not going to be derailed from its agenda.

Keating wasted little time after the election in winning cabinet endorsement for continued spending restraint, deficit reduction and wage moderation through the accord process.[3] The 'trilogy' of fiscal commitments pledged by Hawke during the campaign was also formally adopted.[4] On 26 February 1985, cabinet agreed to Keating's proposal to accept sixteen of the forty-two applications from foreign banks to be granted licences to operate in Australia.[5] These enterprises would employ 8000 people and hold aggregate capital of over $1.5 billion. Amid further claims of party heterodoxy, it was reported as 'a big victory for Mr Keating over the left wing of the Labor Party', giving 'a clear signal to the business community that he and Mr Hawke have asserted full control over economic policy'.[6]

While Hawke and Keating saw eye to eye on most things, the prime minister did assert his authority over two appointments to the Reserve Bank board. When vacancies arose in 1983 and 1984, Keating mulled the appointments of ACTU advocate Jan Marsh, secretary Bill Kelty and vice-president Simon Crean. But Hawke had other ideas. He pushed successfully for two of his old mates to be appointed: Charlie Fitzgibbon from the Waterside Workers' Federation (in December 1983) and Sir Peter Abeles from TNT (in August 1984).

Over the summer of 1984–85, Hawke and Keating began preparing for the taxation summit. It was to be an exhaustive policymaking process that would culminate in a draft white paper outlining reforms to be presented to the summit. Keating did not believe that summitry was the best way to make policy. But Hawke felt the process would help to bring key stakeholders and the public along with the government. Consultation with business, unions and community groups began. Submissions were sought. Keating commenced briefing caucus in March, and cabinet's revenue committee started detailed work in April.

Keating became an early advocate for a consumption tax. He was encouraged by Treasury that it could raise enough revenue to replace wholesale sales tax and reduce marginal income tax rates. It would also provide new revenue to fund budget outlays and avoid deeper cuts to spending otherwise needed to consolidate the budget. He was also persuaded about the merits of a fringe benefits tax and a capital gains tax. Hawke was willing to let Keating develop the idea of a consumption tax and subject it to cabinet scrutiny and public debate. Business groups, economic commentators and the opposition were favourable. Kelty and Crean, from the ACTU, were also open to a consumption tax, provided there were exemptions and compensation.

After months of public debate about a consumption tax, cabinet met on 12 May 1985 to debate Keating's white paper.[7] The treasurer proposed a new tax system that prized equity, efficiency and simplicity. He advocated a 12.5 per cent broad-based consumption tax on goods and services. It would be a retail sales tax applied at the final point of sale rather than a value-added tax, which is applied along the supply chain. It would absorb the existing wholesale sales tax system. There would be reductions in marginal income tax rates, the introduction of fringe benefits and capital gains taxes, and tax breaks such as negative gearing would be curbed or abolished.

Several cabinet ministers were persuaded by Keating's advocacy: Gareth Evans, Kim Beazley, Mick Young and Susan Ryan. Ralph Willis argued for a more gradual approach to reform. Peter Walsh and John Dawkins thought there might be too much 'political pain' in adopting a consumption tax and suggested other ideas be considered.[8] The debate was exhaustive. This first meeting began at 3 pm and did not finish until about 1.30 am. There were more long days and nights ahead.

The white paper included three options. Option A was a modest package that included income tax reductions, new capital gains and fringe benefits taxes, and measures to combat tax avoidance.

Option B included most of the first package with a 5 per cent consumption tax, while maintaining a reformed wholesale sales tax system. And Option C, the government's preferred option, included a 12.5 per cent broad-based consumption tax, the abolition of the wholesale sales tax system, significant cuts to marginal income tax rates, new capital gains and fringe benefits taxes, plus tax avoidance measures. Compensation would accompany the introduction of the consumption tax, funded by the increased revenue to government.

The final cabinet debate, on 22 May, was gruelling. Keating passionately argued for Option C, explained each of the proposed changes in detail and answered every question. Only Peter Walsh and Stewart West expressed any significant concerns. Walsh argued that the compensation for low-income individuals and families was so inadequate that it might cost the government the next election.[9] Not surprisingly, Hawke let the cabinet debate run into the early hours of the morning. Eventually, he summed up the discussion and announced the decision: Option C was the government's preferred position. The white paper was endorsed, with some modifications to its language and presentation, and on the proviso that Keating consult further with the ACTU.

Keating travelled the length and breadth of Australia selling his tax package, made public on 4 June, like it was a holy crusade. He spoke to unions and business groups. He accepted almost every media interview request. But there was far from unanimous agreement from business and unions, which meant a compromise was needed. Business groups and the Coalition supported the consumption tax but opposed the fringe benefits and capital gains taxes. Social welfare groups opposed the consumption tax because it was regressive. Unions were not sold but could support the consumption tax, provided there was general agreement and adequate compensation.

Ultimately, Hawke judged that Keating's tax crusade had failed to win consensus. His staff – economic adviser Ross Garnaut and political advisers Peter Barron and Bob Hogg, along with press secretary Geoff Walsh – thought the tax could not be matched with a compensation package that would sufficiently ameliorate the impact on low-income voters. They suggested the consumption tax be dropped. Hawke was spooked by the party's polling, which had been leaked to the media, likely by his staff, showing significant opposition to a consumption tax.[10] Keating viewed Hawke as a weathervane on the consumption tax. It was at this time that Hawke was referred to within government as 'Old Jelly-Back' or 'Silver Bodgie'. It was a nickname thought to have come from Keating or Peter Walsh, but both denied it.[11]

The National Taxation Summit, held in the House of Representatives, opened on 1 July 1985. As the 150 delegates arrived at Parliament House, they were greeted by a large throng of protesters, mostly farmers. It was almost immediately clear that Option C would struggle to win support. Labor premiers Neville Wran, John Cain, John Bannon and Brian Burke provided only qualified support. Bob White, from the Business Council of Australia, shocked Hawke and Keating when he said his organisation could not support any option because it could not countenance a capital gains or fringe benefit tax. Crean and Kelty made it clear they would find it difficult to support a consumption tax if business could not support capital gains and fringe benefits being taxed.

Privately, Crean and Kelty made it clear to Hawke and Keating that the ACTU could accept a consumption tax if food, clothing and housing were exempt. Hawke thought a deal could be struck between government and unions, and perhaps business, on this basis. But Keating wanted all or nothing. He would not deal. Accordingly, Hawke did not see a viable pathway for the consumption tax. That evening, 3 July, Hawke met with Crean and Kelty at the Canberra International Hotel. Hawke had decided to cut Keating loose. He would abandon Option C, embrace Option A with revisions, and consider the ACTU proposal for a new services tax while keeping the existing wholesale sales tax system. The story was leaked to journalist John Short. Keating read it in *The Sydney Morning Herald* the next day. That morning, 4 July, the Labor premiers told Hawke and Keating they could not support Option C. Keating's so-called 'tax cart' was losing wheels as it neared the finish line.

In the final session, which began after 4 pm, Hawke read into the record a eulogy for the consumption tax. He said it had not been possible to achieve broad community support for the government's full tax plan, but an ambitious set of proposals would guide future policy development. An emotional Hawke patted Keating on the arm. 'No prime minister could have asked for better, closer, more effective cooperation than I have enjoyed with Paul Keating,' he said, prompting applause.[12] Keating reciprocated the public display of unity at a later press conference. 'No treasurer, with the best intentions in the world, can get a reform proposal like this through a cabinet without the support of the prime minister,' he said. 'In the time I've been treasurer, that support has been unqualified, and I appreciate it very much.'[13]

The tax summit demonstrated the limits of consensus. The tension between Hawke and Keating was palpable. The optics of having business, union and community leaders, and state premiers outline objections to the government's tax package was far from ideal. The summit, in the end, was close to being a complete debacle, as business leaders baulked at returning to the chamber and being presented with a set of proposals with the implication they had been agreed to. There was, in fact, no agreement, but rather a direction for the government to go in.

Keating had been humbled by Hawke. The prime minister should not have abandoned his treasurer without giving him the courtesy of telling him, let alone explaining why. It was the most significant policy defeat of Keating's career. Their relationship was never the same after the summit. Gareth Evans thought Hawke had subjected Keating to the political equivalent of having 'three quarters of one testicle cut off'.[14] Ralph Willis thought Keating had been subjected to a 'public humiliation'.[15]

But that was not how Hawke saw it. 'I said to him that he could have every opportunity to develop [Option C],' he reflected. 'But it became clear to me before the end of the summit that it wasn't a political goer, and I told him. But he went and produced a very significant reform package.'[16] Hawke realised that a grand bargain on tax policy could not be struck. Keating would not negotiate. And without compromise, there can be no consensus.

Following the summit, Hawke and Keating made a joint submission to cabinet outlining the pathway forward on taxation reform.[17] On 19 September, Keating announced the changes to the parliament. It would be, despite the drama of the summit, the most substantial package of taxation reforms before or since. The top marginal rate of income tax was slashed in two stages from 60 per cent to 49 per cent, and the lowest rate fell from 31 per cent to 21 per cent. The company tax rate increased from 46 per cent to 49 per cent to align with the top marginal income tax rate. (In May 1988, the corporate tax rate would be slashed from 49 per cent to 39 per cent.) Capital gains and fringe benefits taxes were introduced. Full imputation on company dividends to avoid double taxation and foreign tax credits for income earned offshore were introduced. There would not be a services tax but the wholesale sales tax base was broadened.

Hawke insisted the reforms be put to a meeting of the full ministry rather than to cabinet. Keating thought this was unnecessary. On 15 September, during the three-day meeting, Hawke travelled to Papua New Guinea. There was opposition from troglodyte ministers Tom Uren and Arthur Gietzelt, which forced Keating to make several minor changes. Keating thought Hawke had set him up to fail. On a newspaper clipping, Keating wrote of Hawke: 'The envious little bastard did everything to destroy it.'[18] When a poll showed that voters largely approved of the taxation reforms, Keating wrote on another clipping: 'NO THANKS TO HAWKE.'[19]

When I presented these clippings to Hawke in December 2012, he thought it was a perverted version of history. 'That's just absolute bullshit and totally wrong,' he said. 'I just feel sorry for the poor bugger. I paid tribute to him and what he did. If he feels it necessary for some reason to go on like that, poor bugger, I genuinely feel sorry for him. I am about paying tribute to Paul for the good things that he did, I'm not here to knock him. I feel genuinely sorry for a bloke who carries on like that.'[20]

It was evident the taxation summit damaged the Hawke/Keating partnership. In this period, there were several venomous exchanges between them in cabinet on unrelated matters.[21] Hawke found Keating too brusque with colleagues and ill-disciplined in his public comments and disliked that he was not on time for meetings. Keating thought Hawke had showed too much vulnerability with his public tears over Rosslyn's drug addiction, had squandered the chance of a major election victory in 1984, and had deserted him during the taxation summit.

Keating has claimed that Hawke effectively stopped leading the government from 1984. He believed Hawke was racked by inner turmoil and guilt over his family problems. And he thought Hawke lacked the energy, ambition and vision to nourish the cabinet and lead the nation. It is true that Hawke was depressed from around mid-1984 until early 1985. There is also no doubt Keating was the policy innovator and dynamic salesman who provided loco-motive drive to the government. But it is an exaggeration to say that Hawke was missing in action for a prolonged period and no longer fulfilling his prime ministerial duties.

Indeed, no cabinet minister agrees with Keating's assessment. Peter Barron, the brilliant political strategist who advised Hawke and was close to Keating, disagreed strongly with Keating's claim that Hawke spiralled into a deep and lasting funk. 'At all times, even during the fade away times of the 1984 campaign, Bob was the prime minister – full stop,' Barron said in a rare interview. 'That never actually went away, and it is fantasy to think that it did. Bob was the prime minister both in name and in action.'[22]

The issue of leadership succession was a matter, at this stage, not broached between Hawke and Keating. But it was referred to among caucus and cabinet members, and in the media. Prior to the previous election, in December 1984, Hawke said he planned to serve three terms as prime minister. 'I hope to serve this next term after the election on December 1, which will take us to about 1988,' he said. 'I would like to serve another term then. By that stage I would be in my early 60s, and I think by about that time I would probably think about retiring from the leadership.'[23] Keating took this as a positive sign that Hawke would, at some stage, retire and hand over the leadership. It was, after all, in line with what he had said at the Boulevard Hotel in 1980. Then it had been a vague commitment to two terms; now it was three.

Meanwhile, leadership tensions between Andrew Peacock and John Howard surfaced in the Liberal Party. Peacock had flair and panache; Howard was solid and studious. Peacock was an effec-tive communicator; Howard was a policy wonk. Peacock was liberal; Howard was conservative. It was along these lines that they clashed. Peacock felt undermined by Howard, his deputy, and was suspicious about a leadership challenge. 'I was disappointed in not getting full support from my deputy,' Peacock recalled.[24] He asked Howard to declare his loyalty and pledge not to challenge his leadership. Howard refused, rejecting the suggestion that he needed to declare loyalty. So, on 5 September 1985, Peacock asked his party room to dump Howard as deputy leader and replace him with John Moore. The strategy backfired.

Howard stood against Moore in a ballot for deputy leader and won by thirty-eight votes to thirty-one. Peacock had been rebuffed and felt he had no option but to resign. Liberal MPs were stunned. A resignation had not been foreshadowed; if it had, the party room may have voted to make Moore deputy leader. In any event, Peacock was out and a ballot for leader had to be held. Howard nominated and so did Jim Carlton. It was not even close: Howard won fifty-seven votes to Carlton's six. Neil Brown was elected deputy leader, defeating eleven other candidates. Hawke was now facing his third Liberal leader.

—

On 13 May 1986, the monthly trade figures revealed that Australia's current account deficit had increased to $1.48 billion. This was an alarming number. It meant that Australia's terms of trade – the value of exports relative to the value of imports – were in sharp decline. They were the worst figures since the Depression. The next day, while attending a function for Labor MP Neil O'Keefe in his electorate in Melbourne, Keating spoke to John Laws on Sydney radio station 2UE from the kitchen. Keating warned that Australia was at risk of becoming 'a banana republic'. He explained that unless Australia improved its competitiveness and stopped living beyond its means, it would become 'a third-rate economy'.

These comments sent shockwaves through the financial markets. While Keating went on with the breakfast function, the dollar was in freefall. It lost three cents within three hours, and hit a low of 69.30 US cents, and would end the day at 70.03 US cents. Keating's comments were not premeditated. He was simply being frank about the true state of the economy. Keating explained that the value of exports was declining despite the devaluation in the currency, and the only remedy was to reduce spending and make exports more competitive. The alternative was higher interest rates to dampen demand for imports, and that was neither economically nor politically viable.

Hawke was on his way to Japan when Keating made these comments. He was furious when he learnt of what Keating had said. He thought Keating's warning was 'unnecessarily dramatic'.[25] Paul Ellercamp, press secretary to Hawke, recalled the travelling media pack were eager to get Hawke's reaction. The prime minister tried to get in touch with his treasurer but could not reach him by phone for several days. 'The problem was that Hawke appeared not to be in control,' Ellercamp said. 'This was seen as a move by Keating to fill a power vacuum in the leadership of the nation. Our perception was there was a rogue treasurer on the loose in Australia.'[26]

Amid growing calls for action at home, Keating and Ralph Willis met with business and union leaders. This was dubbed a 'mini summit' by the media. But only Hawke called summits. He made it clear there would be no summit, and he rang Lionel Bowen, the deputy prime minister, and told him to take charge. From Tokyo, Hawke eventually spoke to Keating and expressed his incredulity at the 'banana republic' remarks. Now in Beijing, Hawke briefed the travelling media on background about his instructions to Bowen. The next day, as Hawke spoke to ministers by phone, Keating had these articles in front of him as he listened to the prime minister deliver a tongue-lashing and ticked off his words.

Chris Conybeare, Hawke's principal private secretary, recalled the prime minister's staff being astonished by Keating's remarks: 'The overwhelming impression in the travelling party was that the treasurer had gone public in a way that seemed to be calculated to create maximum embarrassment for the prime minister.'[27] Advisers Peter Barron and Bob Hogg urged him to deal with Keating. Barron told Hawke: 'You need to pull Keating into line because he'll pinch your job if you are not careful.'[28] Hogg agreed. 'It was our instinctive interpretation that it was Paul making a play for the leadership,' he recalled. 'The end result was that Keating was put back into his place, but he didn't like it.'[29]

Keating could not attack Hawke, so he focused his guns on Hawke's staff. 'It's the Manchu Court, they sit around like courtiers,' he said.[30] The comments about the Manchu Court – a reference to eunuchs who, despite having no formal authority, exerted power during the Chinese Qing dynasty – made front page news. Hawke thought Keating was referring to the role that Barron, Hogg and Garnaut had played in scuttling his consumption tax proposal a year earlier. 'That more than anything played a large part in his rather colourful description of the Manchu Court,' he thought.[31]

Michelle Grattan, who was on the trip, recalled that the prime minister was 'furious' with the treasurer. 'Hawke's staff took the view that Keating needed to be reined in. There was frustration between Hawke and Keating,' she said.[32] Steve Sedgwick, principal economic adviser to Hawke, said they also understood the policy challenge that confronted them. 'It was thought that if the government could actually address the policy settings and manage the politics of it, then the government would be rewarded,' Sedgwick said. 'There was always a risk, but you had two of the best salesmen in the country explaining what needed to be done.'[33]

On 11 June 1986, Hawke made a televised address to the nation, outlining the economic crisis and the government's response. He sought to reassure voters that the government would be responding with 'restraint' to improve competitiveness but also with 'equity', so the burden of adjustment would be shared. There would be cuts in real wages and reductions in government spending, and those on employment benefits would have to undertake community work to keep receiving payments. Business was asked to taper executive pay increases, keep a lid on prices and invest in new plant and equipment.[34]

Hawke made it clear that he was directing the economic strategy of the government, not Keating. The speech was pre-recorded in a Canberra studio in the early hours of the morning due to a cabinet meeting running over time. There was a lot invested in this speech. It was directed and produced by Peter Faiman, whose showreel included *Crocodile Dundee* and *The Don Lane Show*. Hawke spent two hours getting the presentation exactly right.[35]

The government's economic strategy moved into a new phase in the wake of the 'banana republic' controversy. The fiscal consolidation was unprecedented, and remains unmatched. Cabinet had already agreed to a spending reduction of about $1.4 billion in March, prompted by concerns about the external account and interest rate increases.[36] In May and June, the 1986–87 budget was revisited. A further $1.5 billion would be cut from spending. The Expenditure Review Committee recommended savings across the board: reducing unemployment and sole-parent payments, cutting health spending, deferring pension increases, restricting eligibility for the Pharmaceutical Benefits Scheme, increasing student charges, selling assets, reducing foreign aid and ending the ban on uranium exports to France. In the 1986–87 budget, real growth in total outlays was less than zero. The caucus was in uproar, but the government maintained its course.

Sedgwick attended the ERC from 1985 to 1988. 'It often met all day and into the night,' he recalled. 'Peter Walsh had always read all the paperwork. He was prodigious. He was the detail man. Keating was a lot more strategic, looking at the overall picture, and did not want to chase every rabbit down the hole. Hawke intervened depending on his interests or the importance of the issue. He managed the politics of the group and handled ministers who might be unhappy.'[37]

Walsh, as finance minister, was critical in making these savings. As ministers requested new funding or asked for funding to be continued, he would put their submissions 'through the mincer'. He could be brutal and unsparing in 'chopping up rhetorical humbug' and 'scourging sloppy ministerial arguments', Bill Hayden recalled. 'He took no prisoners, gave no sanctuary, recognised no neutrality.' Keating, who liked and respected the rather dour Walsh, called him 'Sid Vicious'.[38]

Susan Ryan recalled the 'good cop, bad cop' combination of Walsh and Keating. 'Walsh was a terribly aggressive bugger,' Ryan said. 'Anything he saw as middle-class – education, women, special measures for migrants – he'd say, "It's all middle-class rubbish. That's not what we are here for." He was quite abusive and quite effective, and he would sway other cabinet ministers. Keating never, ever had that approach. He would just say, "No, we can't do it. I know you want to do this program, but the money is not there." He'd take you through why we couldn't do it and what the implications would be.'[39]

Barry Jones was another minister who ran the gauntlet of ERC. 'Hawke was obviously very brilliant, he was a very good chairman of cabinet and he had an amazing capacity to master a brief,' Jones recalled. 'Somebody would ask me about some issue and I would come up with an answer but Hawke would say, "Hang on. No, that's not right." He would flick through the pages and say, "Look at page 247, that is inconsistent with what you just said." It was really awful.'[40]

Brian Howe joined the ERC in 1987, and saw it as the 'engine room' of the government. 'It was preoccupied with detail and was not always politically strategic,' he recalled. 'I was trying to look after social policy but had a wider brief to look at decisions that were not ideal from a policy viewpoint or were politically stupid.' Howe, from the Left, conceded he was often in 'ideological pain' during ERC meetings as fiscal prudence became the order of the day.[41]

Between May and June, the dollar continued to fall in value and plunged through the psychological barrier of 60 US cents. When the ERC met on 28 July, the dollar had fallen by 10 per cent over the previous twenty-four hours. Keating provided regular updates to ministers from a portable Reuters screen as they slashed and burned through line items in the budget. Walsh was extremely worried. Eventually, the dollar bottomed out at 57.15 US cents. Walsh recalled being 'closer to despair than I had been even in 1975', during the constitutional crisis over supply.[42]

Treasury now records, using a new method of accounting, that spending fell from 26.9 per cent of GDP in 1986–87 to 23.1 per cent of GDP in 1988–89. Most of the heavy lifting was done by cuts to real spending rather than moderating spending increases or relying on increased revenue and asset sales. The budget returned to surplus in 1987–88, according to Budget Papers at the time, and remained in surplus for four years in a row. No government had achieved a budget surplus since the 1950s.

Through 1986 and 1987, the government, in response to the external account crisis, stepped up its program of microeconomic reform. This work was led by Hawke, Keating and John Button through the Structural Adjustment Committee of cabinet.[43] In addition to decentralising wage bargaining with Accord Mark III, the government moved to corporatise and deregulate govern-ment enterprises in the telecommunications, transport and postal services sectors.

Private industry was also in the frame. Button, the minister for industry, advised cabinet on 9 October 1986 that too many industries were 'addicted to government assistance' and unable to innovate to lift productivity and competitiveness. Following his work with the steel, automotive and heavy-engineering sectors, Button moved to reform the clothing, textile and footwear industries. This was aimed at making industry policy more 'export oriented, more flexible and capable of adapting to changing market conditions and technological developments'. Key tools to achieve this were updating plant and equipment, improving management and removing regulation. A \$32.5-million, seven-year package was developed with unions and industry that included adjustment packages for workers who would be worse off.[44]

John Kerin, the minister for primary industry, led the productivity and competitiveness agenda in the rural sector. The same overarching principles applied: driving innovation with Cooperative Research Centres, developing export markets, updating equipment, improving farming techniques and providing adjustment support. Weaning the sector off protectionism was a tough sell to farmers, most of whom did not vote Labor. It demanded extensive engagement with peak bodies, producer groups and rural communities. 'It was very difficult,' Kerin recalled. 'It required detailed negotiations. But almost all the protection is now gone. The biggest funding from government was into research and development. We emphasised improving market access. And, with any deregulation agenda, transitional arrangements were critical.'[45]

Another industry subject to regulatory change was the media. The government twice decided to merge the ABC and SBS, but retreated each time in the face of opposition, especially from multicultural groups. Cabinet also debated whether to allow SBS to carry commercial advertising and whether the ABC should be permitted to enter into commercial partnerships, but ultimately rejected these proposals. The bigger issue, however, concerned the commercial television networks. There were disagreements between Hawke and Keating on one side and Michael Duffy, the minister for communications, on the other. Ultimately, the government's decisions, which were perceived as favouring media proprietors Rupert Murdoch and Kerry Packer, were controversial.

The debate over television network licensing through 1985–86 was long and rancorous. One of the issues was the 'two-station rule', which held that a proprietor could control a commercial television station in only two markets, no matter how big those markets were. The effect was that Murdoch and Packer, with television stations in Sydney and Melbourne, were in a dominant position. Duffy wanted to allow proprietors to be able to aggregate television stations across multiple markets, provided the combined audience reach did not tip over a certain percentage. Duffy proposed a 43 per cent audience threshold figure, which represented the combined population of Sydney and Melbourne, and he thought was large enough. This would confine Murdoch and Packer to Sydney and Melbourne, and provide an opportunity for television stations in smaller cities and regions run by Alan Bond, Kerry Stokes, Christopher Skase and Robert Holmes à Court to build a larger market foothold. But Hawke wanted to find a way to protect the dominance of Murdoch's Channel Ten and Packer's Channel Nine.[46]

The key issue, Duffy explained, was the 'power' of the moguls. 'There was a view you would be rewarded by giving them want they wanted, and I thought that was extremely naive,' he said. The bottom line was that Hawke, and most other cabinet ministers, did not want a new media policy that alienated Murdoch or Packer. Duffy recalled Peter Barron from Hawke's office dropping off 'an alternative recommendation' for his cabinet submission prior to a cabinet meeting. Duffy's adviser Tom Burton was told this proposal would win cabinet support. 'The problem was the top of the fax showed it had come from Channel Nine,' Duffy said.

The debate bounced between cabinet and caucus for a year. The pivotal cabinet debate took place on 24 November 1986 and ran for four hours. 'It was like a ping-pong match between Bob and myself,' Duffy remembered. 'It was an unpleasant day.' The result? 'I got comprehensively rolled.'[47] Cabinet agreed on a 75 per cent audience reach limit, which was later reduced to 60 per cent. In any event, this guaranteed the development of three major networks, and preserved Packer's television dominance.

A further change came about with a compromise brokered by Keating to introduce new cross-media ownership laws. It meant that media companies could not dominate the print, radio and television markets in one city. This required several proprietors to divest themselves of assets, reducing media concentration and increasing diversity. The big media companies 'could be a queen of the screen, or a prince of print, but not both', Keating said.[48] The deregulated system would enable smaller proprietors to grow their market share, and would protect the television interests of Murdoch and Packer, but without the special treatment that had caused consternation in caucus.

A critical early test was News Limited's $1.8 billion takeover bid for the Herald & Weekly Times newspaper group. It was endorsed by cabinet on 8 December 1986. This decision, which would lead to News Limited acquiring about 60 per cent of Australia's daily newspapers, required it to divest itself of television, radio and print media assets in several states.[49] The big winner, though, was judged to be Packer, who could now build a dominant television network, as his magazine titles were not affected by the cross-media laws. The value of Nine went through the roof. Weeks later, Packer sold Nine to Alan Bond for $1 billion.

Hawke and Keating, and the cabinet, were united in responding to the economic crises with long-term structural reforms. But, like in 1984, Labor's Left faction was spoiling for a fight. Some of the party's rank and file were disillusioned as the party's longstanding policy beliefs were thrown overboard in response to economic necessity. They overlooked the substantial increase in welfare payments to those most in need, the rebirth of universal health insurance in Medicare and the formation of the Prices and Incomes Accord, which represented the high point of the party–union nexus since 1891. Hawke and Keating felt a need to defend the party against claims it had drifted from its historical moorings.

The prime minister and treasurer argued that economic growth was necessary to achieve lasting social change. Labor, they said, had always been a practical and pragmatic party which aimed to 'civilise capitalism' rather than overturn it. The party had to remain relevant and responsive, and not be side-tracked into confusing the 'ends and means' of the party's philosophy.

'The world was changing rapidly,' Hawke recalled. 'We could not go on thinking the attitudes and policies of the past would be appropriate for meeting these challenges. We never wavered from the basic Labor commitment of fairness to all. Our methods, not our values, had to change.'[50]

This was the message to the party's national conference, held in Hobart on 9 July 1986. Hawke asked the party to keep faith with the government. The task for the party was to meet the 'challenges and problems of the present'. The conference, Hawke argued, had to show the Australian people that the party could govern effectively for the modern era.[51] The Left, however, were not convinced. Hawke and Keating had to battle a series of amendments, put by Lindsay Tanner, George Campbell and Frank Walker, which urged increased government spending, easing wage restraint and, astonishingly, reverting to a degree of regulation over the exchange rate. This was not only old Labor thinking, but also utterly delusional about the contemporary economic reality.

Hawke would not have a bar of it. He gave them 'ten out of ten' for 'economic illiteracy' and 'political naivety'. He explained that higher spending meant 'a higher budget deficit' and 'further pressure on interest rates'. He said this burden would be met by the party's core constituency: 'the battlers'. On more financial-market intervention, Hawke was unrestrained: 'Have you ever heard such unadulterated nonsense as is in this motion but, more particularly, as is spelt out by Walker and Tanner, about the float? What they are saying is that we should get back to a situation where the limited resources of the country in terms of monetary management are going to be in there propping up the rate.' The Left wanted to abandon the float.[52]

Keating lashed the Left's position as 'idiocy' and 'nonsense' which would 'shove interest rates up' and 'bring on a recession'. This, he argued, was the consequence of abandoning a floating currency. 'I mean, a little bit of understanding rather than just straight ignorance of the problem would help a great deal,' he said. 'The float of the dollar is perhaps the most fundamental thing the government has done, and in the end, it will be the fundamental saviour of the Australian economy.' He accused the Left of propagating a politics of 'the warm inner glow' and 'feeling good', which he said was divorced from reality. Keating said he took 'no pleasure' in seeing the Left's 'crazy propositions' voted down. He would rather them be part of the reform program than attack it.[53]

Meanwhile, there were significant changes in Hawke's office in 1986. Graham Evans left. So did Peter Barron, Bob Hogg and Geoff Walsh. Chris Conybeare became Hawke's principal private secretary. In 1985, Ross Garnaut had left to take up the appointment as Australia's ambassador to China, and Steve Sedgwick was appointed senior economic adviser. Bob Sorby joined Hawke's staff as senior political adviser. He had worked as a journalist, political adviser and lawyer, and had made Hawke a lot of money running defamation cases for him. Paul Ellercamp had joined the staff in mid-1985 and was appointed press secretary in mid-1986. Ellercamp found it difficult to establish a close relationship with Hawke. 'Hawke liked to be surrounded by educated larrikins and I was neither educated nor a larrikin, and he and I just never really clicked,' he reflected.[54] Barrie Cassidy, who did fit into that mould, was appointed press secretary in November 1986.

Another person Hawke tried to recruit to his staff was journalist Paul Kelly. Graham Evans talked to Kelly about taking on the role of senior political adviser, and Hawke invited Kelly to Kirribilli House to talk it over. 'He didn't do an interview with me, it was as though I was already in the job,' Kelly recalled. Hawke talked to Kelly again about taking the job during a trip to the Philippines in May 1986. 'I was somewhat open to it, but in the end I decided against it,' Kelly said. 'I couldn't leave journalism.'[55]

23

LET'S STICK TOGETHER

Since the December 1984 election, it had been anything but smooth sailing for the Labor government. There was the drama and acrimony over the 1985 taxation summit and Keating's 'banana republic' warning in 1986, which necessitated a dramatic shift in economic policy. This turbulent policymaking was having an impact on the government's standing with voters, who were having to absorb the impact of the reforms.

In August 1985, pollster Rod Cameron warned Hawke that the government was suffering from 'image problems', including a 'perceived indecision and lack of direction and being seen as out of touch'. The problem, though, was not one of 'credibility' but of 'image', which was 'more easily retrievable'. The next election was not lost, but a significant improvement in the government's political standing was needed.[1]

Little had improved by October 1986. Cameron reported that voters were concerned about the trade deficit, the lower dollar and cost-of-living pressures. 'Economic credibility in terms of Labor vs Liberal is in bad shape,' he noted. But politics is a relative contest, and voters were not convinced the opposition was a satisfactory alternative. Cameron reported that Hawke's leadership was still 'a major asset' for the government, but warned that he appeared at times to be 'indecisive' and 'no longer in control' of events.[2]

There were growing tensions between Hawke and Cameron, Margaret Gibbs and Bob McMullan, the party's national secretary. These would continue through the 1987 election and beyond. 'We had a love-hate relationship with Bob,' Cameron acknowledged. 'When we were talking about anything other than politics he was chummy and matey, but he was not great at accepting bad news.' McMullan acknowledged the frictions. 'I was having disagreements with Bob,' he recalled. 'The relationship was becoming more challenging. I didn't feel I had the influence that I once had.'[3] (McMullan would quit in 1988, while Cameron and Gibbs had to be persuaded to stay on for the 1990 election.)

As irritated as Hawke was by bad news, the truth was his government was in trouble. Its economic policies, especially wage restraint, were causing a backlash among blue-collar voters. While they benefited from policies such as Medicare, they were not seeing much improvement in their pay packet. When the dollar collapsed, the remedy was to cut government expenditure and reduce real wages to keep a lid on inflation. Wages would rise in return for productivity gains, not automatically to keep pace with inflation. This was a tough message for traditional Labor voters. By the end of 1986, many Labor MPs and ministers thought the government was doomed.

By early 1987, Hawke thought the government needed more time to convince voters to trust it for a third term. Labor had never won three elections in a row. Hawke told McMullan to begin planning for an early 1988 election. It would coincide with the bicentenary of the establishment of the British penal colony in Sydney. It would be a time of national commemoration, with a tall ships' re-enactment, gala concerts and a nationwide television spectacular.

But Keating began pushing for an election by mid-1987. His idea was to bring down a mini-budget in May, slashing expenditure further and cementing the government's economic reform credentials, and then follow this with a snap election in July. 'Hawke did not want to go to an election, and Keating did, and he was right about that,' recalled Cameron.[4] Hawke told journalists on 1 April 1987 that there would not be an election until late that year or early next. On 14 May, Hawke said he could not envisage any circumstances in which there would be an early election.

Keating's 13 May budget statement reduced spending by $4 billion. This was on top of $1.5 billion in savings already locked into the 1986–87 budget. There were further asset sales, cuts to defence spending and changes to welfare that included abolishing dole payments for sixteen- and seventeen-year-olds and tightening means-testing of family payments. The cuts, Hawke had flagged to caucus members on 24 February, would be 'equitable and responsible'.[5] Support for Labor surged. A poll in *The Age* showed the government with a primary vote of 49 per cent and the opposition with 44 per cent.[6] Newspoll found Hawke's satisfaction rating had jumped to 55 per cent, while Howard's had declined to 31 per cent.[7] Keating saw the May statement as the lynchpin of Labor's election strategy.

Hawke was also being encouraged to consider an early election by his political adviser, Bob Sorby. He had wanted to go the polls earlier, to seize on the 'Joh for PM' campaign. 'You don't get a better opportunity than a mad Queenslander who wants to be prime minister,' Sorby explained. But he could not get Hawke to agree, so Sorby began leaking to the media, hoping they would take up the case. 'I just had to get the debate out there about an early election,' he acknowledged. 'I just couldn't leave it with Hawkey.' Sorby thought Keating's May statement was risky: if it was received poorly, it would rule out an early election.[8]

Speechwriter Graham Freudenberg was also in the early election camp. So was Richard Farmer, who had begun seeing Hawke on weekends at the Lodge to provide an alternative source of political advice. When Hawke ruled out an early election, Freudenberg sent an angry telegram to Jean Sinclair. 'I must place on record my deepest anger about the manner, timing and content of the announcement yesterday,' he said. Sinclair showed it to Hawke.[9]

On 27 May, two weeks after the May statement, Hawke announced an election would be held on 11 July 1987. It would be a six-and-a-half-week campaign, and a double-dissolution election, only the sixth in Australian history, with the trigger being the Australia Card Bill. It was also only the second election held in midwinter, following John Curtin's triumph in August 1943. 'The people of Australia have demonstrated a willingness to shoulder and share burdens and a sense of responsibility in the face of huge difficulties imposed upon us by the changes in our terms of trade,' Hawke argued. The purpose of the election, he said, was to seek 'a renewed mandate' for the government's economic policies.[10]

For the first time since 1983, there were conflicts in the prime minister's office alongside those in the party organisation that were reported in the media. Bob Sorby was the main political adviser during the campaign. Barrie Cassidy and Grant Nihill handled the media. Craig Emerson, who had joined the office a year earlier and had responsibility for environmental policy, also travelled with Hawke. Conybeare described Emerson as 'the kid' in the office and a 'handmaiden' to Hawke.[11] Cassidy said Emerson was a 'surrogate son' for the prime minister.[12] Sorby found Emerson to be irritating and ingratiating.[13] But Hawke respected Emerson's work ethic and enjoyed his youthful energy and enthusiasm, and his company.

Journalist John Lyons wrote about the 'divisions' and 'resentments' among the 'courtiers'.[14] Sorby had strong differences with Cassidy, Nihill and Emerson. He thought they were sycophantic and not prepared to give Hawke tough advice. Sorby refused to place Hawke's bets or fetch his cigars in public and said it was necessary to 'stand up to Hawke'.[15] Emerson rejected the suggestion they did not give Hawke frank advice when warranted. 'There were two styles with Hawke: one that was direct in front of other people and one that was direct enough but with no raised voices or blunt language,' he explained. 'Sorby could be very forceful and direct with Bob, and our view was that that was not very productive. My view was that Bob performed at his best when he was confident. I never thought being a harsh critic would be all that helpful.'[16]

The campaign would be long and hard. In Labor's favour, though, was a divided Coalition. John Howard, facing his first campaign as Liberal leader, declared the economic crisis would deliver him electoral victory. 'The times will suit me,' he said the year before.[17] But in fact they were treacherous times for the Coalition. On the day Hawke called the election, Joh Bjelke-Petersen said he would run for a seat in the House of Representatives. The 'Joh for PM' or 'Joh for Canberra' campaign was in full swing. Bjelke-Petersen was in California when the election was called, and said he planned to visit Disneyland. It was a fitting metaphor. Another breathing down Howard's neck was businessman John Elliott, who had confirmed his political ambitions and was considering nominating for a federal seat.

Bjelke-Petersen's ill-fated campaign was promulgated by Queensland National Party president Robert Sparkes. Bjelke-Petersen undermined Ian Sinclair, the leader of the National Party, and Howard as leader of the Liberal Party. Andrew Peacock toyed with the idea of supporting Bjelke-Petersen's federal ambitions and ruminated on returning to the leadership. On 10 February 1987, a poll showed Howard and Sinclair trailing Bjelke-Petersen and Peacock as preferred Coalition leaders by 23 per cent to 60 per cent.[18] On 23 March, Howard sacked Peacock from the front bench after the former leader's car phone conversation with Victorian Liberal leader Jeff Kennett was leaked. They had both called Howard a 'cunt'. On 28 April, the Coalition was formally dissolved.

Howard thought the 'Joh for PM' campaign made his campaign almost impossible to plan. 'It created a sense of disunity plus it disabled our capacity for proper policy preparation,' he recalled.[19] Ian Sinclair thought the rifts ruined any chance the Coalition had of winning the election. 'If you have divisions in the party, you can't expect people to support you to govern,' Sinclair said.'[20]

Labor's election message was that the work they had begun had not been completed, so it was not the time to change the government. Labor's theme of 'sticking together' and not 'changing horses in midstream' was encapsulated in the words of its jingle:

> We're on our way, we're on the right track,
> Australians have always been good at fighting back.
> With a little more strength, and patience, we'll see Australia right.
> Nothing worth having ever happens overnight.
> Together, let's stick together, Australians together, let's see it through.

The strategy seemed to be working, according to Labor's polling in marginal seats during May. On the key question of who was better able to manage the economy in difficult times, Labor led the Liberals by 50 per cent to 29 per cent. Labor also had a leadership advantage. Hawke was approved by 59 per cent of voters, compared to Howard with 33 per cent.[21] By early June, Coalition disunity was emerging as a vote-switching issue.[22] By mid-June,

Labor had moved ahead of the Coalition in marginal seats, with voters citing the superior economic policies of the government and the conflict in the opposition.[23]

Howard, despite the Coalition difficulties, was focused and disciplined. But his campaign came unstuck on 10 June, in Box Hill in Melbourne, when he outlined his tax policy. Howard pledged $7.3 billion in business and personal tax cuts, abolition of capital gains tax and changes to fringe benefits tax. The government's costing of the policy revealed a $1.6 billion 'double counting' error. Keating savaged Howard, accusing him of 'a desperate grab for votes' with a tax policy that did not add up and would destroy the budget and the economy. Howard acknowledged the error but insisted it was only $540 million.[24] 'That was very damaging,' Howard acknowledged. 'That hurt us badly.[25]

Labor's advertising campaign featured a homemaker called 'Whingeing Wendy', who asked Howard: 'Where's the money coming from?' Labor's polling found that the tax gaffe, disunity in the Coalition and voters having 'no confidence' in Howard were emerging as decisive issues in the campaign.[26] Tony Eggleton, the Liberal Party's campaign director, recalled that Hawke and Keating's 'teamwork and stability' was an essential part of Labor's recovery over the previous year as the government rebuilt its credibility as 'economic managers'.[27]

But Labor knew winning a third term would still be difficult. At the outset of the campaign, Hawke elevated environmental protection as a major issue. The government had green credentials. It stopped the Franklin Dam in Tasmania. Less than 20 per cent of the Great Barrier Reef was incorporated into the Great Barrier Reef Marine Park when it came to office; Labor promised to make it 100 per cent. Stage II of the Kakadu National Park in the Northern Territory had been nominated for World Heritage listing in September 1986, and the boundaries for listing Stage III of the park were decided by cabinet in December 1986. Hawke announced that the wet tropics of North Queensland, including the Daintree rainforest, would also be nominated for the World Heritage List. And he pledged to protect the old-growth forests of Tasmania.

These environmental policy decisions paid a political dividend. The Australian Conservation Foundation broke with tradition and endorsed Labor in the House of Representatives. The Wilderness Society put its name to a television advertisement trumpeting Labor's promise on Tasmanian forests. These advertisements, Richard Farmer revealed, were paid for by Labor. 'The deal was they would put the ads on television supporting Labor but they had no money to pay for it,' Farmer recalled. 'So I organised the money. I don't know where we got it from but we got it.'[28]

Pitching for green votes meant a careful balancing of constituencies that were often pitted against one another: upper-class and middle-class voters motivated by post-materialist concerns such as the environment, and working and middle-class voters who were concerned about employment and the cost of living. 'We were doing this in the national interest, and the world interest, and then the blokes at the workplace were paying the price by losing their jobs,' Hawke acknowledged. 'That is why we always took the view that we had to provide assistance for retraining and relocation.'[29]

Hawke launched Labor's election campaign, for the third time, at the Sydney Opera House on 23 June 1987. It did not get off to a good start. New South Wales Labor secretary Stephen Loosley knew that Hawke often had the Navy send a small boat over to Kirribilli House so he could cross the harbour. 'I thought it would make a nice picture,' Farmer told Loosley.[30] Instead, the Navy sent over the Admiral's Barge. Bob and Hazel were ferried across the water in royal style to the Man O'War Steps. Peace activist Ian Cohen disrupted the arrival and had to be prodded away with a barge pole. And when Hawke alighted, a construction hand yelled out: 'I thought you were for the workers, Bob.' Instead, a presidential style Hawke was arriving on a boat like an Egyptian pharaoh visiting his subjects along the Nile. Former Labor MP Fred Daly joked that the difference between Gough Whitlam and Hawke was that Hawke came by boat while Whitlam would have walked.[31]

Inside, among some 800 Labor faithful, were a mix of television and sporting stars, artists and singers, former premiers (Neville Wran and Don Dunstan) and a prime minister (Whitlam). Three Chopin pieces were conducted by Roger Woodward and the Sydney Symphony Orchestra. Julie Anthony sang 'Advance Australia Fair'. Mick Young, Labor's national president, acted as master of ceremonies. The mood was sober, not triumphal, but television viewers could be forgiven for wondering what had happened to the Labor Party of old.

Hawke delivered a lengthy campaign speech, arguing that no election was more important. 'Are we to continue to unite together in the great task of national renewal, reconstruction and revitalisation, for which we have been working so hard together, and on which the success of our country depends?' he asked. 'Or are we to take the other course, the path of our opponents – inflicting upon the nation itself all their own divisions, all their own disunity, all their own instability?'[32]

The overall message was one of continued belt-tightening and austerity, but there were a modest number of new promises – valued at $303 million in the next financial year – focused on assistance for families with children, the unemployed, pensioners, young people and the elderly. 'Toughness with fairness' was the theme. Hawke emphasised Medicare, which had emerged as a frontline issue, along with the environment. No mention was made of the proposed national identity card that was the reason for the double-dissolution election.

Hawke's speech contained a sentence that would haunt him for the rest of his life: 'By 1990, no Australian child will be living in poverty.' The speech shorthanded the pledge, but the press statement contained the full version: 'By 1990, there will be no need for any child to live in poverty.'[33] The drafting of the speech was a disaster, with different versions – one penned by Graham Freudenberg and Richard Farmer, and another by Stephen Mills – having to be consolidated. Sorby recalled trying to tone down the child poverty promise, but Hawke ignoring him. 'It was my biggest failure when working for Hawke,' Sorby said.[34] Mills said the process was a 'train wreck' and 'we should have handled that better', but he noted that Hawke never complained.[35]

The government had grappled with how best to provide more assistance for low-income families. Labor had increased payments for children in poorer families by 70 per cent, but they remained worse off than they were in the mid-1970s. About 20 per cent of children were in low-income families. Child poverty was on the rise. Improving welfare payments and taxation measures became a priority for cabinet, led by social security minister Brian Howe.

The details of what would become the landmark Family Allowance Supplement were finalised after the election.

During the campaign, some in the press gallery criticised Hawke for not conveying a compelling 'vision' for Australia's future. On a flight from Melbourne to Perth, Hawke put pen to paper himself and outlined his vision. Emerson used it to brief the media, but it was not reported. Hawke wrote:

> For me, for my party, for my government, the vision has
> been clear from day one. [Remember] the central promise:
> National Reconciliation; National Recovery; and NATIONAL
> RECONSTRUCTION. And that reconstruction means not
> only a reconstruction of our economy, but a reconstruction of
> our view of ourselves, our view of our place in the world . . .
> If I can put that vision in a sentence it is this – it is for an
> Australia with a growing, more efficient economy, more relevant
> to an increasingly competitive world, a more compassionate
> Australia targeting its welfare resources to those most in need,
> and an Australia living in a world at peace, a world increasingly
> able to devote more of its resources not to the possible
> obliteration of but to the uplift of mankind.[36]

While the media were sceptical of Hawke's pitch, they also took him to task for refusing to debate Howard. Hawke had lost the debate against Peacock three years earlier. Another debate would risk giving Howard a chance to revitalise his flagging campaign. 'That would be just mad,' Sorby explained.[37] Howard was scathing of Hawke. 'It was an act of monumental cowardice,' he thought.[38]

Hawke, his staff, and family and friends watched the election results from a suite at the Hyatt Hotel in Melbourne. Hawke was confident Labor would be returned to power based on its economic and social policy achievements, and the discord in Coalition ranks.[39] Howard had a moment of excitement early in the night when the Liberal Party picked up a seat in Melbourne and one in Sydney. 'I thought after everything it would be sweet justice served to get a stroke of good luck and win, but it didn't turn out that way,' Howard recalled.[40]

Labor won six seats but lost two, and increased its parliamentary majority to twenty-four seats. In returning to government for a third term, its primary vote fell 1.65 per cent to 45.90 per cent. Despite the divisions in the Coalition, the Liberal Party increased its primary vote slightly to 34.32 per cent, and so did the National Party (excluding the Country Liberal Party), which was up to 11.35 per cent. Nevertheless, the Coalition surrendered four seats to Labor. The two-party vote saw Labor with 50.83 per cent to the Coalition's 49.17 per cent, representing a swing away from the government of 0.94 per cent.

The main element in Labor's victory was the voters' judgement on who was more capable of 'managing the country in tough times', according to McMullan's campaign report. The economic policies, as Keating predicted, paid a political dividend. The two other factors were the disunity in the opposition and Labor's environmental credentials. McMullan reported that Labor's vote in marginal seats actually increased, even though the party's vote declined nationally. The government had steadily rebuilt support from disaffected voters in 1985–86. Labor had a leadership advantage with Hawke, but the 'team' around him was also important.[41]

At the post-election caucus meeting, Hawke did not single out any minister for special mention. Keating was seething. 'I didn't need a mention, but I was entitled to one,' he said.[42] He added that to a long list of grievances with Hawke, which would fracture their relationship in the coming term.

Meanwhile, Howard retained the Liberal leadership after a challenge from Peacock, who was defeated by forty-one votes to twenty-eight. Peacock became deputy leader, and felt it was only a matter of time before he had 'a day of reckoning' with Howard.[43]

—

In embarking upon an unprecedented third term for Labor, Hawke turned his mind to the structure and operations of government. Mike Codd, the head of the Department of Prime Minister and Cabinet, had begun sounding out departmental secretaries during the election campaign. John Button wrote to Hawke on 3 June 1987 suggesting a significant reduction in departments and the introduction of assistant ministers.[44] Hawke set the letter aside but had begun thinking about the structure of government before voters went to the polls.

Codd recalled seeing Hawke on the Sunday after the election and presenting his plan to shake up departments and ministries. Hawke needed little persuading. 'The hardest thing for him was the arrangement of senior and junior ministers, and dealing with the Labor tradition that all ministers are equal,' Codd recalled.[45] The establishment of the inner and outer ministry in March 1983 had helped, but the issue was not just who was in or out of cabinet. Hawke wanted a ministerial structure where there were several ministers in the same department effectively reporting to senior ministers.

A fortnight after the election, Hawke unveiled a significant restructure of government departments. Cabinet ministers would now oversee major departments, with junior ministers, outside cabinet, assisting them.[46] The result was the overall ministry was increased from twenty-seven to thirty, with seventeen in cabinet. The number of departments was reduced from twenty-one to eighteen. This represented a significant change to the machinery of government and was intended to make the public service more responsive and efficient, and to allow ministers to focus on 'strategic directions and government priorities'.[47]

Hawke won support from faction leaders for his rearrangement of departments in return for agreeing to their wish to expand the ministry. He first spoke to Keating, Richardson, Ray and Evans about this, and they agreed. Hawke met with faction leaders from the Right, Centre Left and Left on 21 July. The negotiations resulted in the ACT's Ros Kelly (Right) joining the ministry, saving Tasmanian Michael Tate (Centre Left) and securing the elevation of Queenslander Margaret Reynolds (Left). This was Hawke's most significant intervention in the shaping of the ministry since becoming prime minister.

During the government's third term, there were further changes to Hawke's personal office. Sandy Hollway succeeded Chris Conybeare as principal private secretary in 1988. Steve Sedgwick departed as senior economic adviser. Bob Sorby also left. Geoff Walsh returned as senior political adviser. The animosity between some staff continued after the election. Craig Emerson wrote to Hawke on 28 March 1988 about 'disturbing developments' in the office, noting the 'differences' between Cassidy and Sorby. 'What we need to achieve is a team of advisers which get on, respects each other and whose interests coincide totally with yours,' he wrote. Emerson added that he did not have 'prime responsibility' for anything and wanted to be appointed the senior economic adviser and also as a political adviser.[48] Hawke ignored the infighting. Rod Sims was appointed senior economic adviser with responsibility for all the major economic issues in the office.[49] Emerson continued to play a valuable role on environmental policy.

The thorny issue of the Australia Card proposal, although hardly mentioned during the election campaign, had to be dealt with. The idea was to establish a national identity system which could be used to crack down on taxation and welfare fraud. The card was to be developed by the Health Insurance Commission and the Australian Taxation Office, and was announced in Keating's taxation reform statement on 19 September 1985. Legislation was first introduced in 1986. After widespread community opposition, and the realisation that flaws in the legislation meant it could be disallowed in the Senate, the Australia Card was dumped in 1987. However, some of its features lived on with the introduction of the tax file number system in 1988.

The cost of meeting Hawke's child poverty pledge was initially budgeted at more than $1 billion over three years. On 7 August 1987, Brian Howe sought approval to introduce a Family Allowance Supplement, uniform rent assistance and a child disability allowance. 'The proposals are the cornerstone of our commitment to abolish child poverty by 1990,' he informed the cabinet.[50] The FAS boosted total payments made to families by $400 million each year. The government also set up a Child Support Agency to collect maintenance payments because of the chronically low levels of support provided by separated and divorced parents, and the inadequate enforcement mechanisms.

By 1990, Hawke's child poverty promise had become an albatross. In June that year, Archbishop Peter Hollingworth presented 26,000 postcards from children expressing concerns about poverty to the government. The postcards said 'politicians will only do something if they feel they have to' at election time. Hawke rounded on Hollingworth, saying: 'You ought to be ashamed of yourself.'[51] Over the decade, the increase in financial support

to low-income families had been substantial. The Australian
Council of Social Service said Hawke's child poverty pledge had
led to an 'extraordinary' 30 per cent reduction in child poverty as
spending per child in low-income families significantly increased.
The reform package included additional financial assistance along
with other housing, education, training, childcare and taxation
benefits.[52] Hawke regarded the FAS as his government's 'greatest
social reform'.[53]

While fiscal consolidation would continue through 1987 and
1988, with deep cuts in outlays, microeconomic reform stepped
up a gear. On 25 May 1988 it was announced that tariffs for most
sectors would be reduced to 15 per cent or 10 per cent, additional
public enterprises would be corporatised ahead of eventual privatisation, the shipping and airline sectors would be deregulated, and
there would be reforms to the waterfront. The purpose was to
boost industry productivity and competitiveness in order to lift
export performance.

Tourism had become one of Australia's largest industries by the
mid-1980s. When John Brown presented cabinet with a plan to
overhaul international tourism promotion in October 1983, there
was not much support. Brown went to Hawke and got permission
to make his case to the Expenditure Review Committee. This
time, Brown enlisted comedian and actor Paul Hogan to better
sell Australia to the world. With the help of Alan Johnson from
advertising agency Mojo, a videotape of Hogan appealing for
the money was played to the ERC. A television was wheeled
into the cabinet room. 'Listen, you blokes, give Brownie the
money,' Hogan said. 'We can sell Australia, he and I. You can't sit
round the woolsheds forever waiting for cardigans to come back
into fashion.'[54]

Hawke was immediately enthusiastic. The victory of *Australia II*
had put the international spotlight on Australia, he believed, and
should be capitalised on. The tourist potential stemming from
the America's Cup win had been noted by cabinet on 27 September 1983.[55] However, many in cabinet were sceptical. The budget
for tourism promotion was then $10 million a year. A 10 per cent
increase to $11 million was suggested. But Brown asked for
$20 million to spend on overseas advertising focused on luring

American tourists to Australia. With Hawke's support, Brown got it. 'I walked out of there with $20 million,' he recalled. 'Five years later, we became the tourism success of the world.'[56]

The campaign, which ran from 1984 to 1990, was called 'Come and Say G'day'. The first commercial was shown in the United States in January 1984. Hogan showcased Australia's beaches, bush, outback, cities and wildlife. 'I'll slip an extra shrimp on the barbie for you,' he told Americans. It was an instant classic. Australia leapt from seventy-eighth on Americans' list of most-desired holiday destinations to seventh in just a few months. Applications for holiday visas increased by 54 per cent by 1985. Australia's tourism industry was turning over $20 billion a year and generating more than 20,000 new jobs each year by 1987. A huge increase in visitors from Japan, the United Kingdom and Europe followed. Australia's tourist numbers rose from about 900,000 people to about 2.4 million each year between 1983 and 1988. It was one of the great achievements of the Hawke government.[57]

By the third term of the government, ministers agreed it was time to address the sustainability of funding for higher education and the contribution of students to their own learning. In the August 1986 budget, the government had introduced a $250 administration charge for students. Now they wanted to go further. The Whitlam government had abolished full fees for higher education in 1974. It was estimated that before this time, about 60 per cent of students were financially assisted with Commonwealth or state scholarships. This enabled bright students from low socio-economic backgrounds to attend university with their fees fully or partly paid. The abolition of fees had not significantly changed the proportion of students from low socio-economic backgrounds attending university or college.

The government considered means-tested fee relief, scholarships and student loans through 1985–86. A subsidised loan scheme with the Commonwealth as guarantor, running alongside AUSTUDY and providing a means-tested living allowance, was the government's preferred option. A paper prepared for Hawke argued that because education afforded students an opportunity to improve their income-earning capacity, the burden of funding should be placed on those who benefited most from it, and that paying back the cost of their degree provided a stimulus for students to finish their education and maximise its benefits. A subsidised loan scheme would break the nexus between government funding and the availability of student places, and would also improve equity and efficiency.[58] The Wran Committee, chaired by Neville Wran, further developed the user-pays principle and came up with the basis for a new funding model for higher education. The Higher Education Contribution Scheme (HECS), which replaced the administration charge, was announced in the 1988–89 budget and commenced on 1 January 1989.

Susan Ryan vigorously resisted the abolition of free university education. But most ministers had the view that affluent middle-class kids went to university and then went on to earn above-average incomes, so why should working-class kids be taxed to pay for it? Ryan found it hard to push back against these arguments. 'I should have had a more cooperative attitude,' Ryan conceded. But she went around cabinet and appealed directly to Hawke and to the caucus education committee. This irritated her colleagues and sealed her fate – she lost the education portfolio after the 1987 election. 'I was fighting a losing battle,' she recalled.[59] Hawke regarded HECS as a critical reform. 'There is no such thing as free education; it's a question of who pays,' he said. 'HECS opened up the opportunity of tertiary education to all who wanted it. If students received the advantage of an education, when they reach a certain level of income they should start to repay the community for what the community has paid them.'[60]

HECS was part of a larger suite of controversial reforms introduced by John Dawkins, who succeeded Ryan as minister for education. The 'Dawkins Revolution', as it became known, was foreshadowed in a ministerial statement on 22 September 1987. The goal was to continue to improve quality, equity and diversity, and to make the sector more efficient and internationally competitive. 'There was a lot of opposition within the party and within the sector,' Dawkins acknowledged. The methodical policymaking process included a green paper in December 1987 and a white paper in July 1988. The changes resulted in a number of amalgamations between universities and colleges of advanced education and other colleges becoming universities; overhauling university management, employment and decision-making processes; centralising access to research funding through the Australian Research Council; and transferring bureaucratic power from statutory bodies to the new Department of Employment, Education and Training. 'The result was that we significantly improved the quality of education and expanded access, enrolments and graduates increased massively, and the sector became a big export earner,' said Dawkins.[61] Barry Jones thought the reforms were a huge mistake and 'turned universities into corporations', 'knowledge into a commodity', and 'expertise and differentiation' was lost.[62]

In September 1988, four referendum proposals were put to voters that provided for four-year parliamentary terms for both houses of parliament, fair and democratic parliamentary elections, recognising local government in the Constitution and extending and ensuring certain rights and freedoms. All proposals were rejected. This was the second time the government had tried and failed to amend the Constitution. Attorney-General Lionel Bowen pushed hard for the referendums. This was Hawke's gift to Bowen for being a loyal deputy. Hawke talked to Howard about the referendums, hoping to win the opposition's support. But the Liberal leader could only support the Senate being two House terms, whether fixed or not. It was a deal breaker. Hawke revisited the idea of four-year terms with John Hewson when he became Liberal leader after the 1990 election, and they agreed it would be put to the voters in a referendum at the 1993 election.[63]

The Hawke government had promised to protect the Lemonthyme and Southern forests of Tasmania prior to the 1987 election. An inquiry into the heritage value of the forests, headed by former New South Wales Supreme Court justice Michael Helsham, reported to the government on 17 May 1988. It recommended, astonishingly, that most could be logged. Graham Richardson, who had become a crusading minister for the environment, urged ministers to ignore the report. But he faced strong opposition from key economic ministers – Peter Cook, John Kerin, Peter Walsh, John Button, John Dawkins and Gareth Evans – who took a pro-development stance, concerned about the impact that ending logging would have on blue-collar workers, their families and communities.

Hawke recalled there were four separate cabinet meetings, or about fifteen hours of debate, over a six-week period concerning the Helsham report. Richardson won the support of Michael Duffy and Kim Beazley. The surprise to all in cabinet was that Paul Keating joined the pro-environment side of the table, not because of any factional allegiance to Richardson but because he believed a compelling argument had been made to protect the forests, which included the tallest trees on the planet. Hawke, having allowed extensive debate, came down on that side too. If he had gone the other way, Richardson would have lost and the forests would have been logged. 'I had to convince Hawke,' Richardson recalled. 'He wasn't doing it because it was a Right faction thing or because he was my mate, he had to be convinced. That was the way cabinet operated.'[64]

The result was that cabinet torpedoed the report, and areas banned from logging increased from about 8 per cent to 70 per cent of that part of Tasmania. It constituted around one-third of all forests in Tasmania. The decision was coupled with an adjustment and compensation plan for forestry workers. It represented a victory for the environment but another blow for Labor's traditional working-class constituency.

Hawke regarded the prohibition of mining in Antarctica as his signature environmental achievement. In May 1989, a submission came to cabinet that would permit mining in Antarctica in accordance with the proposed Convention on the Regulation of Antarctic Mineral Resource Activities (CRAMRA). The submission was proposed by Evans and Richardson. Hawke read it on a Sunday afternoon at the Lodge. 'I just couldn't believe it,' he recalled. 'Here was a recommendation saying we should sign this agreement which is going to regulate mining in the Antarctic.'[65] Hawke told Evans and Richardson that this was not on. Hawke insisted that a new agreement be negotiated, one that protected the unspoiled wilderness. When the matter was argued in cabinet, Hawke was 'clearly in the minority' but exercised his authority to carry the debate.[66]

'I think I got Antarctica wrong,' Richardson later conceded. 'I took the view that inevitably someone would mine there, and if that's the case we should have a regime to make sure we didn't stuff up the place too badly.'[67] Evans was not particularly troubled by Hawke taking a different view. 'It was critical to stay in harmony with the prime minister on foreign policy issues,' he recalled. 'Antarctica is unequivocally a Hawke triumph.'[68]

Hawke personally led a diplomatic effort to overturn the agreement. In June 1989 he met with President François Mitterrand and Prime Minister Michel Rocard of France, and enlisted the support of explorer and conservationist Jacques Cousteau. Hawke made the case to Margaret Thatcher and to George H.W. Bush, as Antarctic Treaty partners, but they were not persuaded. Eventually, Hawke's diplomacy won them over. The US Congress backed what was regarded as an Australia/France initiative the following year.

Craig Emerson, environmental policy adviser to Hawke, recalled the international campaign. 'All the difficult things we had [achieved] on the environment could all come crashing to the ground if we did not take a lead on Antarctica,' he recalled. 'There were people saying it would be disastrous if there was unregulated mining in Antarctica. They argued regulated mining was better than unregulated mining. But Hawke took the view that no mining was better than regulated mining.'[69]

However, the issue would become another front in the history wars between Hawke and Keating. Hawke had not stated a view on the treaty prior to the cabinet debate. But Keating wrote to Hawke on 27 April 1989, ahead of the cabinet meeting, to advocate Australia taking 'a leading role' in ensuring that Antarctica was protected for future generations. 'The Antarctic is of enormous ecological importance,' the treasurer wrote. 'It is perhaps the last area on earth that remains untouched by development.'[70] A year earlier, Keating had written to ministers criticising CRAMRA on economic and environmental grounds.[71] New Scientist reported that Keating 'has turned a distinct shade of green', given his support for banning minerals exploration.[72] Keating met with Rocard in Paris on 30 September 1988, seven months before the cabinet debate, and advocated that Antarctica be reserved as 'an environmentally protected zone'.[73]

Keating argued that he in fact 'saved' Antarctica.[74] Hawke was furious about this claim. 'It was my initiative absolutely,' he insisted.[75] Keating did have strong views about Antarctica before the cabinet debate, and he had advocated them directly to Rocard. It is also true that only Hawke, as head of government, could negotiate with other world leaders to put the ban in place. He did engage in shuttle diplomacy to ensure the treaty partners saved Antarctica from mining. In the final analysis, Antarctica is a good example of Hawke and Keating being likeminded on policy and working together – although not in concert – towards the same goal.

In any event, the landmark Protocol on Environmental Protection to the Antarctic Treaty – known as the Madrid Protocol – was agreed by the parties in July 1991 and signed in October 1991, banning mining in Antarctica for the next fifty years.

—

While there were tensions in cabinet and among Hawke's staff and the party office through 1987 and 1988, the Hawke office still worked effectively and efficiently, under the leadership of Conybeare and Hollway. The 'Glee Club' on Friday evenings was instituted. Drinks would be served in the prime minister's office. Sometimes songs would be sung. And there would be putting competitions on the plush carpet of the Parliament House lobbies. Some staff played golf in the morning with Hawke before beginning the workday, and on weekends were invited to the Lodge for games of snooker and tennis.

Sometimes Hawke's bad back played havoc with his golf or tennis. He would often see a Chinese acupuncturist when in Melbourne. Sorby recalled going to the golf driving range in Canberra early one evening in April 1987. 'Hawke was belting the balls off the block and getting all hot and sweaty,' he recalled. 'Then he asked for sixty more balls to hit. I thought, "Oh, mate, you don't need this." And, of course, in the cold weather his back went into a spasm.' Hawke was temporarily crippled. They had to get him into the car and back to his Parliament House office without anyone noticing. Sorby spoke to Ossie, the butler, and organised a few hot-water bottles, some aspirin and a cigar, and propped Hawke up in his chair. He thought it would soon be fixed.

Half an hour later, Sorby looked through the peephole and was startled by what he witnessed. 'I saw a head going up and down behind the desk and I thought, "Jesus Christ, what is going on here?"' he recalled. 'I knew Bob had signed up for a few things so I thought I would go in discreetly. Ossie had convinced Bob to lie down on the floor with his shirt off and Ossie gave him a special back massage.' Sorby got Hawke dressed and back into his chair and thanked Ossie for his service. Ossie would do anything for Hawke.[76]

Media adviser Grant Nihill recalled that Hawke was sometimes lonely in the evenings at the Lodge. He would phone the barman at the National Press Club on a Friday night to track down his staff and invite them and a few journalists over for a game of snooker. Hawke would hand out the cigars, drinks would be served, and pies and sausage rolls would be offered around. 'People at the bar thought we must be important, being called to the Lodge to discuss political strategy or policy issues,' Nihill said. 'But he just wanted the company.'[77]

Late Friday afternoons were usually reserved for Hawke to read *The Sportsman* and mark up the form guide. He would hoover up intelligence from friends, trainers and jockeys during the week, and place his bets – usually no more than $200 – directly or through friends. This was, above all, an intellectual exercise. It provided a release from the demanding workload and pressures of the prime ministership, and previously the ACTU, and was essential to his mental wellbeing.

Roger Martindale, the head of Hawke's security detail, recalled a trip to Fremantle in June 1987 that demonstrated the prime minister's commitment to punting. A brick-sized phone with a thick aerial had just been installed in the car. Hawke asked if he could use it. Martindale told him to press a particular button to get a line, and when he was finished to press another button to hang up. They went to a function and then drove back to Perth. Four hours later, Martindale picked up the phone and heard, 'Race two at Mooney Valley . . .' Hawke had not hung it up, and the bill ran into the thousands.[78]

Barrie Cassidy recalled taking a long flight to Perth with Hawke on his first day as press secretary in November 1986. Hawke spent the trip with his head buried in newspapers, marking them up. When he got off the plane, the papers were handed to Cassidy.[79]

At the hotel, Hawke asked Martindale to bring him his papers. But Cassidy, not realising it was Hawke's marked-up form guide, had put them in a rubbish bin. 'I've fucked up,' Cassidy said. 'I don't want to get sacked. Can you tell him?' Martindale went to Hawke's suite. 'He came to the door with absolutely nothing on, with his pendulum swinging in the breeze,' Martindale said. Hawke was irate. They tried to retrieve the papers at the airport but had no luck. The hotel manager offered to hire a plane to pick up another copy of *The Sportsman* in Sydney, but it was too late.[80]

Hawke loved going to racetracks whenever he could. He would be feted in the VIP areas and committee rooms, but would zip in and out to talk to trainers, jockeys and bookmakers. 'There's no microcosm of Australia like the racecourse,' Hawke argued. 'You get the battler, the multi-millionaire, the professional people, the housewife. I stop and talk with them, a whole cross-section of them.'[81]

Bob Carr, then opposition leader in New South Wales, observed Hawke at Randwick Racecourse in 1989. 'There was the prime minister in the Australian Jockey Club rooms: a radiant of super-abundant grey-to-white hair; his tanned masculine face; neat, compact figure in his grey John Cutler suit,' he diarised. 'He was even leaving the luncheon table to place bets or listen to interstate races. I saw him watching races through binoculars, studying a heavily annotated form guide.' Carr's conclusion? 'This was a very Australian setting: lazy informality among well-dressed leading name businessmen and wives, a judge or two, a few politicians [and] a prime minister darting in and out to lay bets.'[82]

Along with cigars, women and horseracing, Hawke loved casinos. Richard Farmer, who worked as a campaign consultant, recalled that during the 1990 election, Hawke would ask to stay at the Wrest Point Hotel Casino when in Hobart, at Burswood Casino in Perth or at Jupiter's Casino on the Gold Coast. 'We tried everything we could to avoid it but did not have much luck,' recalled Farmer. 'In those days he would do anything to be at the blackjack table, smoking cigars, and then have a root somewhere afterwards.'[83]

Hawke was also a regular at Aspinall's, a private casino in London. In August 1986, Sorby accompanied him there to play blackjack one evening at about 10 pm. He watched the prime minister play until about 4 am. 'I just kept him company,' Sorby recalled. 'When he had lost a fair a bit of money, I said, "We really should go, Bob."' So they left.

After dinner the following night, Hawke said he was going back to win the money he had lost. 'No, Bob, you don't want to lose anymore,' Sorby told him. But they went. Luck often ran with Hawke, and he left with £25,000. Sorby said he had better take the money back to Australia.

A few days later, Hazel walked into Sorby's office. 'Where is it?' she said.

'What?' Sorby replied.

'Where is the money? I want it now.'

Sorby collected the money and gave it to her. 'It was quite fucking extraordinary,' he reflected.[84]

24

BOB
AND PAUL

B ob Hawke often said that he and Paul Keating comprised
the greatest duo in Australian politics since John Curtin
and Ben Chifley in the 1940s. While they had disagreements on
policy and political strategy, they remained an effective partnership and were almost always on the same side in caucus and
cabinet debates. They were, however, very different in their
personalities. And they differed in how they approached the
task of advocacy. Barry Jones, the minister for science between
1983 and 1990, admired how Hawke and Keating were able to
persuade voters. 'They could transform how voters perceived
issues,' he said. 'They understood that we can change the political culture and change the way people react if they got out and
argued a case. Well, that doesn't happen anymore. We are in an
era now of political minimalism with an ultra-cautious and short-
term view.'[1]

Hawke never believed parliament was essential for communicating the government's agenda; with its outcomes predetermined,
he saw it as a waste of time. He focused his efforts on television
and radio, plus occasional print media interviews, press conferences and set-piece speeches. Keating, however, saw parliament
as essential to gaining political ascendancy over the opposition.
If you won debates in the parliament, he believed, you would win
debates in the electorate. Keating viewed Question Time like a
gladiator viewed the colosseum: blood sport. He marshalled facts
and figures, charm and humour, as well as bullying and abuse.

The press gallery gave Keating rave reviews, and his performances lifted the spirits of Labor MPs.

Hawke saw speeches as part of the 'educative process' that was essential to winning support for reform. 'Speeches by leaders of reformist governments, which is what Labor governments should be, need to be educative in making the electorate understand the need for change,' he said.[2] Keating could deliver an effective set-piece speech, such as when presenting the budget, but was much more impressive when speaking extemporaneously. He struggled to bring the prepared text alive like he could in parliament or at a press conference.

Graham Freudenberg recalled that Hawke would not often change the text of a speech that was drafted for him. He would underline words and sentences that he wanted to emphasise and make minor additions with a pen. Freudenberg referred to Hawke as 'the passionate persuader'.[3] Stephen Mills, also a gifted speech-writer, said Hawke was largely happy with the speech drafts that he received and often he added an opening or closing paragraph to sharpen an argument. 'His style was to be very logical and try to persuade people with an accumulation of facts,' Mills said. 'This approach could win an argument but was not always persua-sive. Hawke was at his best when something offended his sense of decency and equality.'[4]

Hawke had been the darling of the industrial round in Melbourne and developed close relationships with journalists. The press gallery in the national capital was different. There Hawke was viewed with scepticism: he was an outsider when he arrived in Canberra. He did not walk the corridors of the press gallery very often or cultivate relationships with journalists. Keating had done this since his arrival in Canberra in 1969. Partly as a result, he received broadly favourable press coverage and commentary from leading journalists.

Hawke generally had a positive relationship with gallery leaders such as Laurie Oakes, Michelle Grattan and Paul Kelly. He did not often ring journalists directly, relying on his press secretaries to do this, but Keating did it all the time. Hawke also looked for radio and television opportunities outside Canberra, which some-times irritated the press gallery. Colin Parks said Hawke would sometimes instruct press secretaries to ring up a journalist if he was unhappy with their story and 'give them heaps'. He would later ask how it went. 'Oh yeah, we gave them heaps, Bob,' they would say. Seldom did Hawke ask for details. They never had any intention of giving a journalist a blistering tirade.[5]

Hawke began each day by ringing one of his press secretaries at 5.30 am or 6 am. 'G'day, Grunter, what's in the papers?' he would say. Nihill recalled that sometimes he got caught out while still in bed, and would gesture to his wife to quickly scoop up the newspapers from the front lawn; they would be unwrapping them as he briefed Hawke. He was always interested in what gallery journalists were writing and how particular issues had been reported. 'Good onya, mate,' Hawke would say when Nihill was done with the briefing. 'I'm off to play golf.'[6] Cassidy recalled that he sometimes went over to the Lodge on Saturday mornings to review the newspapers. 'Send him up,' Hawke would say to one of the staff. Cassidy would walk into Bob and Hazel's bedroom with an arm full of papers. 'Take a chair, Butch,' Hawke would say. He would run through the papers while they remained under the covers.[7]

Hawke avoided doorstops while travelling but did offer the occasional comment to journalists when arriving at Parliament House. He held press conferences fairly regularly, although not as often as the gallery wanted. Hawke would occasionally go to the Non-Members' Bar at Parliament House and talk to journalists, and his staff would flag with selected journalists that he would be available for an off-the-record conversation. 'I thought he had a really good relationship with the gallery,' recalled Cassidy.[8] He remembered organising dinners for groups of journalists at the Lodge. Hawke would also occasionally have journalists into his office for a one-on-one briefing or interview. He always engaged with the media while travelling, especially on planes, which underscored the importance he placed on foreign policy.

Hawke would use speeches to the party faithful, especially conferences, to call for unity during a time of profound change. On 8 June 1988, at the party's national conference in Hobart, he said Labor must remain a party of contemporary relevance, with its focus on the future and not the past. Labor must be mindful of its role as 'the party of progress and reform'. Hawke argued that 'the meaning of reform' was 'not about soft options' and 'not a matter of invoking some dogmatic formula'. It was the same message he had given in 1986 and 1984: Labor had to demonstrate that it could meet the challenges of the present rather than wallow in the past with outdated and unworkable policies from a bygone era.[9]

Left faction leaders Peter Baldwin and Frank Walker, however, urged the party to change its economic platform to refocus on redistributing income, wealth and power. They advocated new industry assistance, re-regulation of the financial sector and the reintroduction of exchange controls to regulate the currency. The government's policies only prevailed because of the alliance between the Right and Centre Left factions. Peter Beattie, as Queensland Labor secretary, was a delegate to national conference and attended national executive meetings. 'These were very tough conferences for the party,' he recalled. 'They were about confirming the major reforms. There was always a brawl. It was a huge period of turmoil. The votes were always close. It was about the power of the conference deciding who runs the party. And it was part of educating Australia about the modern world.'[10]

Hawke explained how he approached these debates, which were often traumatic for the party and the unions. 'I tried to blend the continuity of our existence as a labour movement with the need for accommodation to changing circumstances,' he said. 'There were certain fundamental principles that were unchangeable and which defined the movement. But there were a lot of historical sacred cows that needed to be slaughtered. And so, it was a process of culling the herd. We just had to face up to new realities.'[11]

—

Although they were a great team, Keating believed he was the driving force of the government. He thought Hawke had been in a funk from the time of the 1984 election, but the 1987 election victory temporarily quelled his criticism of the prime minister's performance. It began to surface again at the end of 1987 and into 1988, though. On 14 March 1988, journalist Geoff Kitney noted Hawke's 'fundamental loss of direction' and the 'deep disquiet' among ministers over his 'political judgement'.[12]

Bill Hayden viewed Hawke as 'the prime minister' but thought Keating was 'the leader'.[13] Graham Richardson agreed Keating was the driving force: 'The prime minister was out there being loved and loving it, the treasurer was guiding the hard but necessary policy shifts that kept us in business.'[14] Gareth Evans acknowledged 'a degree of disaffection with aspects of Bob's leadership' and that MPs 'were anxious that Bob lift his game'.[15] Button characterised the Hawke–Keating relationship as a 'working alliance', which would continue 'like an exhausted marriage of convenience' for the rest of the third term.[16]

But that is not how Keating saw it. When he delivered the budget on 15 September 1987, he stunned the parliament by revealing it was in balance. The deficit was projected to be just $27 million. It had been achieved by continued spending restraint, a lift in tax revenue due to the growing economy, and $1 billion in privatisation of government assets. Keating's sixth budget, delivered on 23 August 1988, represented the high point in his management of the nation's finances. A $5.46 billion budget surplus was unveiled.[17] 'This is the one that brings home the bacon,' he said. Keating thought he had earned the prime ministership. Bob Carr recorded a conversation with Keating in his diary a month before: 'He's furious that Hawke won't give way for him, and the party won't make Hawke go. "It's Labor making another fucking tragic error of judgement, like sticking with Evatt and sticking with Calwell," he says.'[18]

At a business function in August the previous year, Hawke said that Keating was 'the frontrunner' to succeed him as prime minister, but also mentioned Mick Young and Kim Beazley as future leaders of the party.[19] The following year, in June 1988, it was reported that if Hawke quit, the person he wanted to replace him was not Keating but Beazley.[20] These interventions were calculated to assert Hawke's authority over Keating.

Bob Sorby planted these stories. 'Something had to be done with Paul,' he revealed. 'Paul felt his time was running out to be prime minister. I used to see Keating a lot, and I would go down to his office to keep an eye on him.' During 1988, Keating told Sorby that Hawke should step aside for him. Sorby tested Keating's support in caucus. 'I made a few phone calls and I couldn't find any mood against Hawke anywhere,' he said. So he told Keating to put his leadership baton back in his knapsack. 'You are going to be prime minister one day, Paul,' he said. 'But not yet. Your time will come.' This conversation destroyed their relationship. Sorby, who had worked on Keating's staff in opposition, never spoke to him again.[21]

Keating had pressed Hawke about a leadership transition on New Year's Eve 1987. During drinks at Kirribilli House, he asked the prime minister if they could have a private word. They retreated to the study. Was Hawke thinking about quitting during 1988? Hawke demurred. Keating returned to the subject again, in January 1988. No, Hawke was not leaving. Keating was impatient. 'I told him then that I intended to continue,' Hawke said. During this conversation, Keating apparently canvassed quitting politics and going to live in Paris – the so-called 'Paris option'.[22]

The third term in government was Keating's preferred time-table for a leadership transition. The 1988 budget, recalled his adviser Seumas Dawes, was expected to be his last.[23] He was fatigued by the workload. He was tired of tussling with journal-ists. He could be irritable with ministers and caucus colleagues. He wanted Hawke's job, which he thought he had earned, and he wanted it in 1988. But there was no chance of that happen-ing. While Keating was recognised by ministers as the likely, and indeed only, person to succeed Hawke, almost nobody wanted to push the prime minister out.

On 24 August, the day after the presentation of the 1988 budget, Hawke entertained the idea that Keating might quit politics. He told Paul Lyneham on the ABC's *7.30 Report* that if Keating did go, there would be no trouble replacing him. 'We would miss him,' Hawke said. 'He has been an outstanding treasurer, not just by Australian standards but by international standards.' Pressed by Lyneham, he added: 'I want him to stay. I think he will. But being hypothetical about it, if he were to go, there are people of very considerable talent in the ministry, and the position would be filled.'[24]

Keating was enraged. At 1.45 pm the following afternoon, just before Question Time, he walked around to Hawke's office. 'You think I'm dispensable,' Keating snarled. 'What you're really saying is the relationship between you and me is finished. I'm telling you, you're dead right. As far as I'm concerned, you and I are finished. The relationship is over, dead and buried.'[25] Hawke was taken aback but not surprised to be subjected to this sort of language. 'I'm not going to be someone else you can walk over,' Keating said. 'When I decide to come at you, mate, I'll take your head right off!'[26]

Hawke regarded Keating's reaction as 'hysterical', 'illogical' and 'self-deluding'. Hawke recalled: 'I explained that he was being stupid in his interpretation and that I thought he would come to see things differently. I told him he was being immature and to grow up.'[27] But Hawke should not have been led by Lyneham into speculating about Keating's future. It was unnecessary and it distracted from the government's surplus achievement.

The prime minister's staff thought that a leadership challenge from the treasurer was likely. This would be damaging for the government, even though Hawke would prevail. Hawke's staff discussed edging Keating out of politics. 'Advice was given to Hawke that it would be in his own best interests if Keating could be persuaded to move on,' Cassidy recalled.[28] This may have been what was behind Hawke's loose talk.

But having pushed too hard, Hawke had to ease back. Richardson told him to go back on television and calm the situation down. That evening, 25 August, Hawke spoke to Ray Martin on *A Current Affair*. 'I don't want Paul Keating to leave,' Hawke said. 'I want him there, because it's very much in many respects a Hawke–Keating government.' Hawke added that he recognised Keating had 'a totally legitimate ambition' to become prime minister one day.[29] Richardson encouraged Keating to see Hawke and repair the relationship, but he was still too angry.

Just how angry Keating was with Hawke soon became apparent. Richardson phoned Keating from his car. The conversation was picked up on a phone scanner and recorded, and a transcript circulated through the press gallery. Keating had unleashed a stream of invective towards Hawke. 'He is an envious little cunt,' Keating said. After the trash talk had gone on for a while, Keating asked where Richardson was calling from. 'The car,' he said. 'You must be mad,' replied Keating, and promptly hung up.

Hawke read the transcript a few days later, on his way to a party function at Parliament House in Sydney. He was furious. Hawke phoned Keating from the office of Johno Johnson, the president of the New South Wales Legislative Council, and gave him both barrels. 'The language that Hawke used would have cleared the bar in the John Curtin Hotel in Hawke's heyday,' Cassidy recalled.[30]

Hawke and Keating spoke later that night while Hawke was at Kirribilli House. They agreed to meet at the Lodge at 3.15 pm on Sunday, 28 August. John Button said on Ten's *Face to Face* program that it was time to set a timetable for a leadership transition from Hawke to Keating.[31] The caucus was on edge. Kim Beazley phoned both Hawke and Keating before their sit-down and urged them to keep it cool, calm and collected.

Keating made a record of this discussion.[32] He said there was no guarantee the government would win a fourth, let alone a fifth election. He wanted a leadership transition before the next election. Hawke refused. 'I am asking for one election – you are asking for four,' Keating said. '[You] must acknowledge that governments have a finite lifespan . . . If you, RJH, say you want 8½ – I say I don't agree.' Hawke doubted Keating understood what the job of prime minister truly entailed. Keating rejected this and said he had thought about how to reorganise the government. He might even combine the roles of prime minister and treasurer, as Ben Chifley had done. Hawke laughed and said that was an absurd idea.[33]

Hawke tried to refocus the discussion. He said he remained the best person to lead the government to the 1990 election. He thought Labor would win. But Hawke gave Keating some hope: he said that it might be possible to facilitate a leadership change sometime in the fourth term, perhaps December 1990. Keating replied that this was still more than two years away. It was intolerable to think he would have to wait for this length of time. Keating left Hawke with a warning. '[It is] a big decision for you, Bob,' he said. 'Malcolm Fraser was a leader who went out a loser.'[34]

That evening, Hawke spoke at a conference at the National Gallery. Keating had dinner with Button and John Dawkins. They talked about the leadership. Button and Dawkins agreed to talk to Peter Walsh, and the three of them would urge Hawke to hand over to Keating before the next election. Button and Walsh chickened out, so Dawkins saw Hawke alone, on 29 August. Dawkins gingerly raised the leadership issue. 'Oh, sit down, mate, and I'll tell you why I'm not going and why I don't think Paul is up to it,' Hawke responded.[35] It was courteous and convivial, but Hawke told Dawkins he was 'wasting his time'.[36] Having shown Dawkins the door, Hawke thought that was the end of that.

Dawkins had dinner with Paul Kelly at the Tang Dynasty in Kingston. Kelly revealed the Hawke–Dawkins meeting in *The Australian*. Dawkins thought it was an off-the-record discussion over dinner.[37] But Kelly already knew about the meeting and felt no concern about writing it.[38] The opposition made much of the story in Question Time. National Party leader Ian Sinclair said it was not so much a question of 'Hi ho, Silver', but 'Heave ho, Silver'. Hawke sat next to Dawkins and put his arm around him.[39] It had been a rocky week for the government. Hawke told caucus on 30 August that Keating was Australia's best ever treasurer, and their relationship was 'strong and would continue to be so'.[40]

Keating contemplated a leadership challenge, but Richardson advised that he would win only a 'handful of votes'.[41] The party wanted the duo to continue. Keating had to cool it. He went overseas for meetings, and when he returned, having discussed his future with staff, he told the parliament on 17 October: 'My friend and colleague will remain prime minister as long as he chooses.'[42] It was a message Keating confirmed to Hawke in private. But Keating was not done with the leadership. He asked Hawke for a meeting, with witnesses, to discuss the leadership. Hawke agreed. He offered businessman Sir Peter Abeles. Keating said he wanted Richardson. Hawke said nobody from caucus. Keating suggested ACTU secretary Bill Kelty. Hawke agreed.

Kelty and Abeles knew one another well: both sat on the Reserve Bank board. Kelty took responsibility for organising the meeting's time, date and venue. It was to be top-secret. 'I desperately wanted them to meet,' Kelty recalled. 'Paul is no longer himself. Bob is no longer himself. The economy is starting to drift. The government is starting to drift.' Keating would tell him: 'It's fucking Bob.' Hawke would tell him: 'It's fucking Paul.' He thought it was time they got their act together.

The meeting would take place at Kirribilli House on Friday, 25 November 1988. Hawke was already there, having flown from Canberra that afternoon. Keating came alone, arriving at about 7.30 pm. Kelty had flown from Melbourne that morning, and met Abeles at his hotel. They hopped into Abeles' car and drove through the city and across the harbour. 'He kept running into the kerb,' Kelty recalled of Abeles' driving. He told him to keep the car on the road or somebody was going to get killed. Was Abeles nervous about the meeting? 'No, he was just a bad driver,' Kelty recalled.[43]

The sun was setting when the four men came face to face. After shaking hands, they relaxed into the sofas in the drawing room. Tea, coffee and biscuits were brought in. Kelty and Abeles thought they would be there for a while, so both asked for the tea to be poured. Kelty thought it was cold. Before Abeles could take a sip, Hawke launched straight in and put an offer on the table: he would lead Labor to the next election, in 1990, and relinquish the leadership to Keating after one or two years. Keating immediately accepted.

Hawke then leaned back and offered a brief tutorial to Keating on 'what leadership entailed'. He noted Keating's 'unpopularity' and 'unacceptability' to many voters, and said he needed to improve his relations with caucus members and ministers. 'If you're going to be a successful leader, you've got to have your people around you feeling that you don't treat them with contempt,' Hawke said.[44]

'Don't be too hard on me,' Keating replied. 'I've had to carry the can for so much of these changes, which has left you, Bob, free to, look, you know, preen yourself as best you could.' Keating was not going to argue with Hawke. He was happy to let the free advice come his way. 'I took those bon mots with a grain of salt,' Keating said.[45]

There was one more thing, said Hawke: if the meeting leaked, the deal was off. After about ten minutes, it was over.

When they left, Keating asked Kelty if he thought Hawke would keep his word. 'I doubt it,' Kelty replied. 'Hawke's a negotiator. You actually keep agreements out of a negotiated settlement. But this wasn't negotiated. It was almost given flippantly as a statement.'[46]

What did Abeles think? 'That was a good meeting,' he told Kelty in the car. But its significance did not immediately register. 'I didn't even concentrate when they discussed some of their own issues,' Abeles recalled. 'Three years later, I came home from overseas and I read in the paper that I was at a very fateful meeting.'[47]

Hawke did not tell anybody on his staff about the so-called Kirribilli Agreement. He did not tell his principal private secretary, Sandy Hollway, or his successor, Dennis Richardson. He did not tell Geoff Walsh, his political adviser, or his two press secretaries, Barrie Cassidy and Grant Nihill. In contrast, Keating soon informed his senior staff – Don Russell, Tom Mockridge, Seumas Dawes and, later, Mark Ryan.

The Kirribilli Agreement represented a victory for Hawke over Keating. The prime minister had outwitted his treasurer. It meant Hawke had a guaranteed two or three more years as prime minister. He would lead Labor to a fourth election. Keating could not challenge him or undermine him, because he had effectively agreed not to in front of Kelty and Abeles. Hawke would then be able to say that Keating broke their agreement.

Hawke envisaged an unchallenged ten-year term. A year later, he said in an interview that he would lead Labor to the next election and the one after that, and would 'think' about retiring in 1994 or 1996 at age sixty-five.[48] No wonder Keating came to believe Hawke never had any intention of honouring the Kirribilli Agreement.[49]

25

IN BED
WITH BOB

Bob Hawke went off the grog when he entered parliament, and did not drink alcohol during his prime ministership, but he did not relinquish his insatiable appetite for sex with women he was not married to. He maintained relationships with several women in different cities. When Hawke rolled into a capital or regional city, some women would ring his office to let him know they were available. Sometimes, but not often, Hawke would proposition women, or they would proposition him. But he had a steady group of women who satisfied his sexual needs. 'While he was prime minister, there were about four women he was having serious affairs with,' acknowledged Blanche d'Alpuget. And he had affairs at the Lodge.[1]

Hawke is not the only prime minister to risk his integrity with dangerous liaisons. Australian politics in the 1960s and 1970s sizzled with stories of extramarital affairs, sexism and harassment. John Gorton had multiple affairs, escaped from the Lodge to go to late-night parties and drank too much. Harold Holt disappeared in the surf at Cheviot Beach off Portsea while his secret lover, Marjorie Gillespie, watched from the shore. Ben Chifley is said to have had an affair with his secretary, Phyllis Donnelly, and her sister, Nell. It has been suggested that John Curtin and Robert Menzies also strayed from the marital bed.[2]

But Hawke is the only prime minister to admit his infidelity while prime minister. On 21 March 1989, he was interviewed by Clive Robertson on his *Newsworld* program. Asked about his womanising, Hawke said: 'I was unfaithful to my wife.' Robertson followed up: 'Did you stop that?' Hawke replied: 'Yes.' This was, however, not true. Hawke explained that Hazel knew about the infidelity. 'She understood that it was part of a pretty volatile, exuberant character, and she knew my love for her had never changed,' he said. Hawke's eyes filled with tears. 'I have always loved Hazel, and always will,' he said.[3]

John Brown, the minister for tourism between 1983 and 1987, spent a lot of time with Hawke. 'When he was prime minister, he was terribly indiscreet, and how he got away with it I don't know,' said Brown. 'He always wanted to talk to me about girls.' They were made for each other. Brown was known as the 'Minister for Good Times': he famously had sex with his wife, Jan, on his ministerial desk in West Block in March 1983. She left her 'black lace perfumed knickers' in his departmental head's ashtray on the way out.[4] When the Sydney *Sun* revealed the story ahead of a *60 Minutes* interview on 26 April 1987, Hawke rang Brown. 'Mate, what would you have done if you had fallen off the desk?' he asked, laughing hysterically. 'This is the funniest thing I've ever seen.'[5] A satirical note was circulated among ministerial offices warning of the dangers of having sex at desk level, and suggested such activities be kept strictly at ground level.

There was plenty of sex going on between politicians, public servants, political staff and journalists. In fact, Parliament House was heaving with conduct that would not be tolerated today – and nor should it have been tolerated then. Brown and Hawke were not the only ministers treating Canberra like a sexual smorgasbord. Several ministers were busted having sex with staff in the back of ministerial cars. Another minister had sex with a woman on the cabinet table, it was reported. The headline was 'Yes, yes, oh yes Minister'.[6] The only minister with access to the cabinet room was Hawke. The code among journalists was that the private lives of politicians were strictly off limits. Such things were not reported unless they impacted on their public duties.

Hawke's principal private secretary, Graham Evans, was aware of Hawke's past and took steps to ensure the government's integrity was not at risk. 'One of the potential issues for the prime minister after his election was whether he was still having any affairs and whether this could compromise him, particularly on security matters,' Evans said. 'I discussed the matter with Geoff Yeend and then, at his suggestion, with the security personnel attached to the prime minister. This was a matter I subsequently checked. There was no risk of compromise.'[7]

Brown recalled taking Hawke to Jupiter's Casino on the Gold Coast after it opened in November 1985. 'There was a woman who was all over Bob and he wanted to get away with her,' Brown recalled. 'Everybody was watching. I had to drag him out of there.' In April 1986, Hawke was in London. Brown had been having an affair with a young woman who had worked in Parliament House, and Hawke knew she had returned to England. 'I'm here on my own,' Hawke said by phone from London. 'Have you got her number?' Brown said he would try to find it, but he had no intention of passing it on to Hawke, and rang back to say she had gone on holiday to the Canary Islands.

In February 1988, Hawke and Brown attended the Australian Wool Corporation's showcase of bicentennial designs at the Sydney Opera House. 'He fell in love with this Irish model,' Brown recalled. The next day Hawke and Brown played eighteen holes at Royal Sydney Golf Club, and Hawke pestered Brown to track her down. He eventually got her on the phone in the clubhouse, but she told Hawke she was heading back to Ireland so could not meet up. 'He was the keenest chaser of women I've ever seen,' Brown said.[8]

Hawke's dangerous liaisons were known to his security detail. They had little option but to acquiesce, because they needed to know where he was at all times, and that he was safe. Roger Martindale, who headed Hawke's security team from 1983 to 1990, said they sometimes drove him to meet lovers because they did not want him using a Commonwealth car with a flag on the bonnet that would draw attention. 'We were all adults,' Martindale explained. 'He never asked anything of us. He just expected discretion from everybody.'[9]

Not all of Hawke's staff were aware of what was going on. Barrie Cassidy, press secretary from 1986 to 1991, realised only later that Hawke had been having affairs. 'It went on but I wasn't aware of it,' he said. But he thought something was odd when the prime ministerial entourage would arrive at Sydney airport and the staff would file into cars. 'Often we would get to a roundabout at the Sydney Cricket Ground and [his car] would go right and the rest of the convoy would keep going,' he said. 'He did have this habit of calling on Peter Abeles quite often in Sydney, but I discovered later that it wasn't always Peter.'[10]

Hawke's longest on-and-off affair was with Jean Sinclair, who had become his personal assistant at the ACTU in 1973. It continued during the prime ministership. She was married to Angus Sinclair, later the dean of the Faculty of Economics at Monash University, but they lived in different cities during the period of the Hawke government. She knew how to handle Hawke. She did not flinch when giving tough advice, and he trusted her implicitly. She had a calming influence and a warm smile, was a shrewd judge of character and generous towards others.

Bob Sorby recalled Hawke 'would talk about women in a way that would not be acceptable today' and acknowledged 'he did have affairs' while he was prime minister. Sorby, who was on staff from 1986 to 1988, recalled 'a brief relationship' with 'a woman from another office in Parliament House'. But the main relationship was with Sinclair. 'She had a flat and once or twice a month Bob would go off and then he would be back,' Sorby said. 'Very discreet.'[11] Bob Hogg, who worked for Hawke from 1983 to 1986, was also aware of Hawke's relationship with Sinclair. 'He had a long-term relationship with Jean,' he said. Asked if it continued while he was prime minister, Hogg said: 'It's very likely but it would only have been sporadic.'[12] Martindale was aware of the Hawke-Sinclair relationship. 'It was generally known that he and Jean had been having an affair for some time,' he said.[13]

Sinclair died after a long battle with cancer at Melbourne's Freemasons Hospital on 9 September 1991. She was fifty-one. Hawke visited her several times in the months before she died. Graham Freudenberg, who was close to Sinclair, described her as Hawke's 'right arm'.[14] Hawke was too distressed to speak at her funeral at St Peter's Anglican Church, in East Melbourne. He had lost more than just a trusted colleague and confidante. He had lost a lover.

D'Alpuget's affair with Hawke resumed when he was a shadow minister and continued until around the time he became Labor leader. It ended when she went to Israel to begin writing a new book, then restarted around mid-1984, when Rosslyn's heroin addiction became public. They met at the Lodge. 'I knew something was terribly wrong because he was in an absolute state for weeks beforehand, and he was again being very secretive and not telling me what the problem was,' D'Alpuget recalled. 'He was surrounded by people, police guards and so on and so forth, so getting in to see him at the Lodge was the only place that we could meet.'[15] With Hawke in emotional turmoil, facing an election campaign and unwilling to share his innermost thoughts, the affair broke off. D'Alpuget thought it was over for good. At this point in his life, Bob needed Hazel, not Blanche.

But in March 1986, Blanche was back. Hawke had agreed to an interview with Blanche for *The Age*. It caused a stir among the staff, who lined up to look through the peephole from the principal private secretary's office into the prime minister's office. 'The chemistry between them was extraordinary,' recalled deputy press secretary Paul Ellercamp.[16] But in her article, Blanche wrote that she was shocked by what she saw. 'There was a deep loneliness in him,' she thought.[17] The prime minister's biographer reported that he was a vastly diminished figure. D'Alpuget described Hawke as drained of the energy he had had when she first met him in the early 1970s. 'My overwhelming impression was a lack of vitality, that he was vanishing, and I kept thinking of the remark around Canberra attributed to Paul Keating: "Old Silver will die in office."'[18]

This two-part interview was political dynamite. Here was Hawke's biographer – and, many assumed, lover – saying he had lost his mojo. It was seized upon by Keating to argue that Hawke should hand over the prime ministership. The affair did not resume then, however. D'Alpuget wrote that Hawke was 'formal', 'friendly' and 'conventional'. 'The room was quiet and felt empty,' she said. 'Hawke felt distant.' And more: 'The atmosphere felt like lead.' If that was not enough, D'Alpuget said that Hawke, as prime minister, had 'never allowed himself to embrace the hedonism that had been half his joy in life'. This was an extraordinary article. It was D'Alpuget talking to Hawke as a secret lover but disguised as journalism. This was projection, she acknowledged; it was not about him but about them.[19]

D'Alpuget divorced her husband that same year. After the Kirribilli Agreement was made in November 1988, Hawke felt secure in his leadership and decided to take more risks. '[Hawke] had called Keating's bluff and won,' D'Alpuget later wrote. 'He had a leg-rope on his treasurer and his treasurer's supporters for the next two to three years.'[20] Hawke resumed his affair with D'Alpuget. He tracked her down via Susan Ryan and they met at a mutual friend's house in Sydney. D'Alpuget wore a red wig and a Stetson hat. '[We] rushed into each other's arms, laughing,' she recalled. 'We laughed at ourselves, and with delight and relief that we still loved each other.'[21] The great love affair soon regained its old rhythm. They often met clandestinely, arranged by a go-between, at her apartment or that of a mutual friend in Sydney. The secrecy intensified the romance. The affair would continue for the rest of Hawke's prime ministership, and beyond.

Hawke was still seeing other women at this time, while D'Alpuget had two other boyfriends, including one she was particularly keen on. Hawke knew one of the boyfriends because he had come onto ASIO's radar. 'He knew he had a rival,' D'Alpuget said. The idea of a longer-term commitment – marriage – was not mentioned.[22]

Press secretary Grant Nihill often helped 'facilitate' Hawke's secret rendezvous. '[He was] genuinely in love with Hazel and genuinely in love with Blanche,' Nihill said. Hawke would tell Nihill that he was seeing Blanche, often in Sydney, and asked him to come along. 'Bob and I were close,' Nihill said. 'Someone always had to be with him, and that someone was me in those final years. He wouldn't go anywhere on his own.' Nihill would wait in another room while they had sex.[23]

As Bob and Hazel were telling the world that they had never been happier in their marriage, he sat down for another interview with D'Alpuget to mark his sixtieth birthday in late 1989. She was happy to report that this time, almost four years later, he was back. 'He's found a way of being prime minister and himself at the same time,' she wrote. 'He seems, and he says he is, happier than ever before in his life.'[24] Of course he was. Hawke had secured several more years as prime minister. Hazel was happy in the marriage. And the affair with D'Alpuget had resumed.

Hawke did not believe he had an addictive personality. He refused to accept that he was an alcoholic, and would never have accepted that he had an addiction to sex, but D'Alpuget believed he did. The World Health Organisation has diagnosed this as Compulsive Sexual Behaviour Disorder. Unusual genetic activity which leads to high levels of oxytocin, known as the 'love hormone', seems to compel certain people to lose control and perform risky sexual activities.[25] Asked if Hawke had a sex addiction, D'Alpuget responded: 'I think so. Because sex will calm people down, and he was a very highly strung man. At the end of a day of intense activity, he somehow had to let off steam, as it were, and there's nothing like a roll in the hay or five to do that.'[26]

Hazel knew about Jean and Blanche, and probably others. 'The affairs were, in a way, the least of the worries,' her close friend Wendy McCarthy said. 'The alcohol mattered more than the affairs. She would not have been happy about it but there was nothing she could do about it. She was resigned to it.'[27]

Several of Hawke's ministers were aware of his extramarital relationships. Some witnessed women arriving and leaving the Lodge. They could not have cared less about Hawke's private life, and none thought it impacted on his judgement as prime minister or on the carrying out of his public duties and responsibilities, but many were appalled by his treatment of Hazel. Gareth Evans said: 'Hazel was salt of the earth and Hawkey just didn't recognise what a treasure he had in terms of the support she had given him, the personal loyalty she had given him and the way she brought up the kids.'[28] Brian Howe also took a dim view. 'His treatment of Hazel was abominable,' he said. 'And not just in the early days. I mean, over a very long period of time. Hazel was a fantastic person.'[29]

Hawke demanded the highest standards of public accountability from his ministers, but never questioned their personal morality. There was no double standard. But he was determined to act on anything that risked the integrity of his government, whether it was excommunicating David Combe for drunken fantasies about getting rich from lobbying, sacking Mick Young for not declaring a Paddington Bear, or demanding that John Brown resign over allegations he had misled parliament over contracts for Expo '88. But Hawke did turn a blind eye to his own personal indiscretions, which risked the moral integrity of his government. 'Anything that had a whiff of overt lack of integrity, mates were disposable,' Evans said. 'But getting pissed and gambling, and fucking other women, was not something that troubled him.'[30]

It is a damning judgement.

26

COLD WAR
CONCILIATOR

The final decade of the Cold War witnessed the fall of the
Berlin Wall, the end of the Soviet–Afghan War, the collapse
of the USSR, the reunification of Germany and the defeat of
Iraq in the Gulf War. The 1980s and early 1990s represented
the zenith of collective post–World War II leadership: Ronald
Reagan, George H.W. Bush, Margaret Thatcher, John Major,
Brian Mulroney, François Mitterrand, Helmut Kohl, Yasuhiro
Nakasone, Deng Xiaoping, Nelson Mandela and Bob Hawke.

Mulroney, the conservative Canadian prime minister from
1984 to 1993, is the last of the West's Cold War warriors.[1] 'The
Soviet Union had nuclear weapons directed at New York, Washington, London, Paris and Ottawa,' recalled Mulroney. 'So this
was life or death, and that's why the Cold War leadership on our
side was so vital. At the end of the day, we all believed in the same
thing – freedom, democracy and liberty for our citizens – and
pushed on with those as our major objectives, and they were all, if
I can say, successful.'

Mulroney regarded Hawke as one of the significant leaders of
the 1980s. Hawke not only forged effective relations with Reagan
and Bush, but was also seen by others in the West as a leading voice
on how to deal with the Soviet Union and China. 'As a man he was
a good, loyal, supportive friend, and as a politician he was unique
in his approach and his attitudes towards people and towards challenges. I thought he was a highly successful leader and a delight to
be with,' Mulroney said.[2]

By the late 1980s, Hawke had become one of Australia's best-travelled prime ministers. He had visited most capitals in Asia and the Pacific.[3] He had been to the United States, the United Kingdom and Europe.[4] He had visited the Soviet Union and the Middle East. He had met with presidents and prime ministers, dined with kings and queens, and had an audience with Pope John Paul II (his second). He had an excellent relationship with Israeli leaders, forged during multiple visits in the 1970s. In January–February 1989, Hawke visited India to meet with Prime Minister Rajiv Gandhi, and then Pakistan to meet with Prime Minister Benazir Bhutto.

Hawke saw an opportunity to parlay his relationships with world leaders into a role as an East–West mediator. This was an audacious idea, and one that would naturally be met with scepticism, given Australia's relatively small economic size and diplomatic clout, but documents and testimony confirm that Hawke did help in building a bridge between British and American leaders with their Chinese and Soviet counterparts. He also played a broader role on the world stage as one of the leaders in the campaign to end apartheid in South Africa, and to ban mining in Antarctica.

He used two mechanisms in his quest to be a global conciliator: bilateral relations and multilateral institutions. Hawke placed great emphasis on building personal connections with world leaders. He also saw institutions as a vehicle for change: CHOGM, the South Pacific Forum, the United Nations and, later, APEC. George Shultz, the US secretary of state, acknowledged that Hawke was an important conduit of information. 'I remember discussing these issues with Bob,' Shultz said. 'He was very much of the same view that we were – that there was a breakthrough in the Cold War that was coming, and we must make sure we handle it right. His views were always welcomed because he was a sensible guy who did a lot of homework, and so you listened to him.'[5]

In his first three years as prime minister, Hawke visited China twice, and twice hosted senior Chinese leaders in Australia. A third visit by a Chinese leader – Li Peng – would take place in 1988. He had extensive dialogue with them. Reagan, Bush and Thatcher – the foremost Western leaders – were interested in Hawke's assessments, which he provided in writing, by phone and in person. The initiative, however, had come from the Chinese, not the British or Americans. 'The Chinese asked me to act as an intermediary between them and the United States.' Hawke explained. 'They were worried that the United States was thinking that China was getting too close a relationship with the USSR, and they asked me if I would talk to Reagan and explain that this was purely economic.'[6] After Hawke's meeting with Hu Yaobang in Shanghai in 1984, he wrote to Reagan to pass on the message that there was no grand Sino-Soviet alliance.

Hawke also engaged Thatcher and Major on the future of Hong Kong, which the United Kingdom was to hand back to China in 1997. Thatcher's government was in negotiations with China when she first discussed Hong Kong with Hawke in New Delhi in November 1983. After Hawke travelled to China in February 1984, he raised the issue of Hong Kong with Premier Zhao, and then conveyed the response directly to Thatcher. '[Zhao] expressed satisfaction at the way the talks were proceeding,' Hawke wrote to Thatcher on 10 February 1984. 'He emphasised that the Chinese objective was to preserve Hong Kong's stability and prosperity while at the same time resuming Chinese sovereignty after 1997.'[7] Thatcher wrote to Hawke thanking him for the letter and saying she was 'encouraged' by his talk with Zhao.[8] She wrote again on 25 September to brief Hawke on the draft agreement with China on the future of Hong Kong regarding the future social, legal and economic systems, and noted his 'close interest' in the territory.[9]

—

A visit to the Soviet Union was a further opportunity for Hawke to enhance his role as an East–West mediator. Reagan had proclaimed the Soviet Union to be an 'evil empire'. There had been no high-level summit dialogue during his first presidential term (1981–85), but relations began to thaw when Mikhail Gorbachev came to power on 11 March 1985. Reagan met Gorbachev in November 1985 in Geneva, Switzerland. A second summit was held in October 1986 in Reykjavik, Iceland. These talks improved relations significantly but did not lead to any breakthrough agreements on disarmament. Hawke watched developments closely and talked to Shultz – the architect of a renewed détente – about it extensively.

The West viewed Gorbachev as a different kind of Soviet leader. The Soviet Union had been through an unstable period, with a number of rulers dying after short periods in power: Leonid Brezhnev (1982), Yuri Andropov (1984) and Konstantin Chernenko (1985). Hawke visited the Soviet Union from 29 November to 2 December 1987. It would be the first visit by an Australian prime minister since Gough Whitlam's in 1975. Hawke's trip took place after the first two Reagan summits, and after Soviet foreign minister Eduard Shevardnadze's visit to Australia in March that year. Bill Hayden, as minister for foreign affairs, travelled with Hawke.

Hawke's confidential briefing for the visit – his fifth to the USSR – described Gorbachev as having 'the most formidable array of qualities in a Soviet leader' in many years.[10] He was 'shrewd, resolute and charismatic', with an ability to seduce people with 'charm and guile'. He had a 'folksy populism' and 'cultivated' an 'image of modesty' but was smarter than any leader since Vladimir Lenin. He was known for his ability to 'develop a rapport' with individuals. He liked to discuss East–West relations, the differences between socialism and capitalism, and philosophy. He did not like to discuss human rights or Soviet expansionism.

Hawke wished to gain an understanding of the changes underway in the Soviet Union; to develop the bilateral relationship with enhanced political and diplomatic links, trade and investment, culture and educational exchanges; and to discuss geopolitical issues. The Soviet Union was under no illusion about Australia's membership of the Western alliance, and knew it would share intelligence with the United States, but Hawke's briefing note said its leaders also viewed Australia 'as a significant country in the Asian/Pacific region' and saw an opportunity to influence Australia's views on issues such as arms control.[11]

On arrival, Hawke addressed a lunch in Leningrad, and spoke of the opportunity that Gorbachev's policies of *perestroika* and *glasnost* held, not only for the Soviet Union but for the world. 'They contain the promise of fundamental and sustained improvement in relations between East and West,' Hawke said. 'Much can be done to replace hostility with trust by promoting a freer exchange of ideas and freer contacts between peoples.'[12]

Hawke met several Soviet leaders, but the highlight was his meeting with Gorbachev. Scheduled to last just fifteen minutes, it stretched to two and a half hours. When they met, Hawke smiled and looked into Gorbachev's eyes, shook his right hand and then placed his left on Gorbachev's forearm. They met in a room at the end of the St Catherine Hall in the Kremlin. No other person was present, apart from the translator. Hawke thought this was one of the most important and fascinating meetings of his prime ministership. Together, they conducted a *tour d'horizon* of geopolitics. 'I liked him,' Hawke recalled. 'I thought he was a genuine man and clearly a decent man. He was aware of the inadequacies in the Soviet Union.'[13]

Hawke found Gorbachev warm, easy to converse with and well-briefed. They discussed the Soviet presence in Afghanistan and Indochina, and Gorbachev suggested there was a change in attitude underway. Hawke explained his support for Israel's right to exist safely behind recognised borders, and the right of Palestinians to their own state as part of an overall settlement. They talked about the campaign through the Commonwealth to end apartheid in South Africa. Gorbachev asked Hawke for his impressions of China, then undergoing major economic reform and opening itself up to the world. Hawke was blunt in his assessment: 'Mr Secretary, I think China has got it right and you have got it wrong.' Hawke argued that economic reform should precede political reform.[14]

Most interesting was Gorbachev's acknowledgement to Hawke that he understood the flaws in the Marxist-Leninist economic model, and the error of allocating scarce resources to military expenditure in the hope that the Soviet Union could somehow match the United States. In other words, Hawke felt that Gorbachev knew the much-vaunted Soviet model over which he was presiding was crumbling. The policies of *glasnost* and *perestroika* aimed to address these weaknesses, but they were unlikely to be enough.

Hawke made the case for nuclear disarmament, consistent with Australia's leadership on the issue. Gorbachev's third summit with Reagan, in December in Washington, DC, would include signing the Intermediate-Range Nuclear Forces Treaty, which limited nuclear weapons. Fears of a nuclear war between the United States and the Soviet Union, with much of the rest of the world as collateral damage, were at the front of his mind during these talks. 'I was convinced that with hard work on all our parts, and in speaking honestly with Gorbachev, we could avoid it,' he said.[15]

Gorbachev wanted Hawke to convey a message to the Americans. The Soviet leader said he had established a good relationship with Reagan and Shultz. Their talks on nuclear weapons were making progress. But he was concerned about several politicians and thought leaders in the United States who did not want a lessening of tensions with the Soviet Union, thinking it was a form of appeasement, and who were sceptical of commitments being made in the summit processes. Gorbachev thought this 'influence' in American politics, and specifically in the Republican Party, was acting as a handbrake on his talks with Reagan.[16]

Hawke wrote a five-page letter to Reagan on 4 December 1987 about his talks with Gorbachev. He conveyed the Soviet leader's 'apprehension' about the 'motives' of those with more 'extreme' views influencing his administration. Gorbachev had 'seriousness of intent' in proceeding with reforms to the Soviet economy. 'Restructuring, openness and new thinking have a long way to go in practice,' Hawke cautioned. 'Clearly therefore we must not be naïve or complacent. But, on the whole, my talks leave me with a sense of cautious hope for the long term.' Hawke also mentioned the differences of opinion between Australia and the Soviet Union on human rights, Soviet Jewry, Afghanistan and Cambodia.

Hawke encouraged Reagan to continue talking with Gorbachev about reducing their nuclear arsenals. Hawke said he found the Soviet leader to be 'intelligent, astute, quick, charming but liberally endowed with skepticism about the West'. He concluded on a personal note:

> I believe, Ron, that we are privileged to be leaders of our nations at a point in history which offers unparalleled opportunities for a meaningful and constructive peace between nations in which our resources may be directed more to meeting the material needs of a troubled world. You have played an important role in making this possible.[17]

As the hours ticked by in the Kremlin, Hayden cooled his heels with Australia's ambassador to the Soviet Union, Robin Ashwin. When Hayden was eventually invited to join Hawke and Gorbachev, he found the Soviet leader to be impressive but also naive about the economic implications of his reform program. 'It was like the Revolution in 1917 – they didn't think through the consequences,' Hayden recalled. 'Hawke got on with Gorbachev very well. I think they both saw themselves as men in history.'[18]

The status and freedom of the Jewish Refuseniks had caused Hawke pain in 1979. Now he wanted to make amends. He asked Gorbachev to consider their inalienable human rights and asked that those Jews who wished to leave the Soviet Union be permitted to do so. Hawke sought to persuade Gorbachev of the justness of their cause, and Gorbachev agreed to consider it. Hawke presented him with a list of six Refuseniks and asked that they be released. Gorbachev resorted to the arguments Hawke had heard a decade earlier: that they had benefited from education and training and would now take those skills to another country. Days later, though, as Hawke was preparing to leave Moscow, Gorbachev's interpreter presented him with the news that they would be released.

For Hawke's friend Isi Leibler, who felt Hawke had been seduced and manipulated by the KGB when negotiating for the Refuseniks in 1979, it was another atonement. 'He felt a moral responsibility towards the Refuseniks,' Leibler said. 'This manifested itself in the release of a number of Refuseniks as a gesture by Gorbachev to Hawke when he visited as prime minister. As a friend to those who were released, I was obviously delighted. But the true significance only became apparent later, when this led to much wider progress with Soviet Jews, including religious freedom and the right to emigrate.'[19]

Hawke shared his assessment of Gorbachev with other members of the Western alliance. They, in turn, shared their assessments with him. John Major wrote to Hawke about his meeting with Gorbachev in March 1991, as the Soviet Union was on the verge of collapse. Hawke replied to Major:

[We] need to show support for Gorbachev as one man with the vision and strength to press for reform, while keeping threats at bay. I therefore agree entirely with your assessment that at this stage the West should maintain its support for Gorbachev, while recognising the reality that other forces are also at work in shaping the future of the Soviet Union.[20]

On 10 May 1991, Hawke shared his private views about Gorbachev while meeting the ambassador designate to the Soviet Union, Cavan Hogue. He was less admiring than he had been a few years earlier. 'Gorbachev had had the chance to take the tough decisions, but had not done so,' Hawke said. 'Now his political stature was diminished and eroded; the essential capacity to get people to accept change had been reduced . . . if Gorbachev had managed to get significant economic reform in train, there might have been a better chance of containing the current tendency towards a breakup of the Soviet Union.' But Hawke thought Gorbachev was a brave and courageous leader, and it was in the interests of the Soviet Union that he remained in power. Hawke instructed Hogue to convey his 'great respect and affection' for Gorbachev.[21]

The break-up of the Soviet Union was inevitable. Hawke kept in touch with Gorbachev, reassuring him that he had the backing of Western nations, and spoke to him directly after the attempted coup in August 1991, which was put down by Boris Yeltsin. On the phone, Hawke said he was relieved that Gorbachev was safe and had 'returned to power'. Gorbachev thanked Hawke and said he was 'pleased to have Australia's support over the past difficult days'. Gorbachev said the coup leaders had been defeated. Hawke pledged Australia's continued support. In the days ahead, the Soviet Union faced 'grave challenges', Gorbachev replied.[22]

Two days later, Gorbachev stood down as general secretary of the Communist Party. Four months later, on 25 December 1991, Gorbachev relinquished his position as president of the Soviet Union. The next day, the Supreme Soviet voted itself out of existence. It was the end of an era. Hawke was out of office too, having lost a caucus leadership ballot, and relinquished his power just five days earlier.

—

In January and February 1987, Hawke travelled to Jordan, Israel and Egypt. The Middle East had been Hawke's foreign policy preoccupation during the 1970s: he dreamed of playing peace-maker. After the March 1983 election, Hawke said his personal relationships with leaders in the region might be helpful in bringing peace. But his staff knew this was a fantasy. 'One of my major unstated jobs was to make sure he didn't visit the Middle East,' foreign policy adviser John Bowan recalled. 'There was a feeling that this was way outside our real sphere of interest, and it would just be satisfying a personal interest.'[23] Finally, after four years in government, it was decided to let Hawke go.

In Israel, he met with Prime Minister Yitzhak Shamir and Vice Premier Shimon Peres. In Jordan, he met with King Hussein, Crown Prince Hassan bin Talal and Prime Minister Zaid al-Rifai. In Egypt, Hawke met with President Hosni Mubarak and Prime Minister Atef Sedky.

Hawke's big idea was that peace could be brokered if the Palestinians formed a separate state that became part of a 'confederation' with Jordan. Bowan thought this was bonkers, and told Hawke so. 'When we were in Egypt, Bob had this private meeting with Mubarak, and a couple of us were called in so Mubarak could explain why this confederation with Jordan was not such a bad idea,' recalled Bowan. 'He used the president of Egypt to put a couple of staffers in their place. It was quite funny.'[24] Hawke canvassed this idea of a confederation publicly on the trip, and again on his return to Australia.

Hawke often had tough exchanges with Isi Leibler, the president of the Executive Council of Australian Jewry. Leibler was concerned about Hayden and Evans meeting with Palestine Liberation Organization leaders. Relations with the PLO were downgraded at the time of the Gulf War. But Hawke told Leibler he would not break off all contact with the PLO, even though he agreed their credibility was vastly diminished. 'The Palestinian voice must be heard,' Hawke told Leibler in March 1991. 'The real difficulty [is] that the Palestinians seemed committed to the PLO as their voice.' Hawke also made it clear that 'there would not be peace' without resolving 'the Palestinian problem' – that is, a Palestinian state – and he encouraged dialogue towards that end.[25]

In these years, Leibler never doubted Hawke's essential commitment to Israel and recognised that he had supported Israel often at great personal and political risk. In his post–prime ministerial years, Hawke spoke strongly in support of Palestinian statehood. His views, which continued to shift during his prime ministership, upset and annoyed many of his friends in the Jewish community. When accepting a World Jewish Congress award on 17 May 1988, Hawke compared Palestinians in the occupied territories to Jews in the Soviet Union and blacks in South Africa. 'I was deeply angered with him,' Leibler recalled. 'After addressing the Refuseniks, he stunned the audience by comparing their plight to that of the Palestinians. From that time onwards, our relationship was still close but never the same.'[26]

In the years before his death, Hawke supported Australia providing diplomatic recognition to Palestine without a 'two-state solution' as a precondition. It was a policy that won support within Labor and internationally, with more than 130 other nations endorsing a Palestinian state. Among the many factors which help to explain this shift were the growing global backlash against Israel's settlement policy in the West Bank and East Jerusalem; the stalled Middle East peace process; the stridently right-wing government of Benjamin Netanyahu; and changing ethnic demographics in Labor seats which found little support for Israel.

—

In Ronald Reagan's final year in office, he met with Hawke for a fourth time, on 23 June 1988. The routine for these White House visits was now set. They had an 11.30 am meeting in the Oval Office, followed by larger talks in the Cabinet Room, then refreshments in the State Dining Room and a working lunch next door in the Family Dining Room. Departure statements were made in the East Room. Reagan wrote in his diary:

> It was Hawke time. He's been here 4 times. We had a good meeting & lunch at the W.H. We have a great relationship between our 2 countries. I think I reassured him that our summit negotiations weren't going to affect their wheat exports. Lunch turned into a story telling session. We did departure statements in East Room – it was 100° on the S. Lawn.[27]

As a testament to the Hawke–Reagan relationship, and the strengthening of Australia–United States relations over the previous five years, Hawke became the first Australian prime minister to address a Joint Session of the United States Congress, on 23 June 1988.[28] As Reagan prepared to depart the White House, he wrote Hawke a generous and warm letter, reflecting on 'the road we have walked together':

> Your counsel, friendship, and Australian support have brought us closer to achieving our common goals. I take considerable pride, as does George Shultz, in the vitality of our security relationship with Australia and in the fact that overall relations between the United States and Australia have never been better. I know that George Bush will continue to value your counsel, friendship, and Australia's contribution to the Western alliance.[29]

Hawke's strategy with Reagan had been vindicated. The country-to-country relationship, as Reagan said, had never been stronger. Hawke's relationship with the US president would only deepen with the next occupant of the Oval Office.

George H.W. Bush was sworn in as the forty-first president of the United States on 20 January 1989. He was a moderate Republican who was more pragmatic and less ideological than Reagan. Bush and Hawke were friends. In Bush's diary, the president-elect surveyed his relationships with world leaders a few weeks before taking office. 'Bob Hawke of Australia and I have what I think is a special rela-tionship,' he wrote.[30] Bush had attended all Hawke's meetings with Reagan, and the two had met separately for policy talks, meals and golf. Hawke had wanted and expected Bush to win the November 1988 presidential election. This relationship was both professional and personal. Hawke got on very well with Reagan, but with Bush he said he had 'both an official and a social relationship'.[31]

Bush recalled his relationship with Hawke in equally warm terms. 'It has been a close personal relationship grounded in respect, and trust,' Bush said in 2018. 'Start with the fact that I like Bob Hawke, and have always enjoyed his company. I always respected his devotion to Australia and its welfare. And of course, his skill as a political figure makes him unique in Australian history. So he's a great friend in addition to being a great man.'[32]

James Baker had an unrivalled view of the Bush–Hawke relationship. Baker was secretary of state and White House chief of staff under Bush. They had been friends for 60 years. So what did Baker observe of Bush's relationship with Hawke? 'They were very, very close', he said. 'We had no better friends than our Australian allies.'[33]

The Hawke–Bush relationship was inimitable. No previous Australian prime minister and United States president enjoyed such close and regular contact. It did not mean, though, that Hawke pulled his punches, especially when seeking a fairer deal for Australian farmers caught in a cross-subsidy war between the United States and Europe. 'I recall that Bob never – ever – hesitated to make his case for Australia and its interests,' Bush said.[34]

Hawke made a state visit to the United States in June 1989. Before the official talks, Bob and Hazel were invited to Camp David, the presidential retreat in Maryland. On 25 June, Bush noted in his diary that Hawke seemed 'a little nervous' during the stay:

> He wants me to mention his Pacific Rim Initiative, and the chemical weapons in the arrival statement. I think he's worried about his standing at home, but we're going all out to make him welcome. I told him to talk about the agricultural enhancement program in Congress. We differ with him on that, he knows that we're aiming at Europe, but it's very unpopular in Australia, so I told him this visit isn't going to hinge on the differences we have on that, and he agrees. He also has this environmental treaty having to do with the Antarctic, where our environmentalists are for the treaty, but he is opposed [to] the treaty, but we can work all of that out, too.[35]

On 27 June, George and Barbara Bush met Bob and Hazel on the South Lawn of the White House. There were marching bands, anthems played and a ceremonial viewing of the guard. Hawke was also given a lavish dinner in the State Dining Room, where they feasted on Alaskan salmon in champagne jelly, a roasted saddle of veal with rosette potatoes, and summer bombe with fresh cherries for dessert. The red carpet was well and truly laid out, and in their speeches the leaders laid on the mutual affection with a trowel.

Hawke had met with Bush for an hour earlier that day, first in the Oval Office and then in the Cabinet Room. They had a large agenda. They discussed China, with Bush noting that Australia had been ahead of the United States in developing relations with the world's most populous country, the future of United States military bases in the Philippines, and the chance of a peace settlement in Cambodia. They talked about the Soviet Union and Gorbachev's commitment to arms reduction. They briefly considered the Middle East. And they debated trade policy, with Hawke arguing that Australia had been disadvantaged by the trade war with Europe, but he hoped the Uruguay Round of multinational trade negotiations would level the playing field.[36]

Hawke continued to push Bush via phone and letter about the Export Enhancement Program and the 'damaging' impact on Australian farmers. 'The current adverse effects of the EEP expenditure are clear: over the past twelve months, every four dollars per tonne spent under the EEP cost Australia's wheat growers one dollar,' he wrote to Bush on 5 March 1991. 'As a direct result of the EEP, next year our production will be down by half a million tonnes.' Hawke called for the elimination of subsidies.[37] Much depended on the Uruguay Round. Reagan had made a firm pledge to Hawke that Australia's trade interests would be considered when implementing the EEP. Although little changed, Bush renewed that pledge and continued to emphasise that the United States supported freer agricultural trade.[38]

Hawke's conception of himself as bridge between East and West intensified during the Bush presidency. On 5 July 1989, Bush returned Hawke's call from the Executive Residence of the White House to discuss the prime minister's visit to Hungary. Hawke provided Bush with pen portraits of political figures, spoke about the prospect for democratic elections after the end of socialist rule, and urged the United States to contribute to Hungary's economic development.[39] A fortnight later, Bush phoned Hawke to talk about his trip to Poland and Hungary, expressing his optimism about the transformation in Eastern Europe and thanking Hawke for his earlier intelligence. Bush said they should continue 'working together on these matters'.[40]

When the United States invaded Panama in December 1989 – its most significant military action since the Vietnam War – Bush phoned Hawke to brief him. He explained that the United States wanted to 'restore democracy in Panama' after General Manuel Noriega tried to overturn recent election results. The invasion was controversial and would later be condemned by the United Nations General Assembly. Hawke told Bush that 'we don't like to use force to achieve our objectives', but added that he would 'have no cause for concern' with regard to anything Australia might say about it.[41]

When Bush phoned to congratulate Hawke on winning a fourth term in March 1990, he took the opportunity to tell the president that the West should support Gorbachev, given there were 'so many sinister forces arrayed against him' as the Soviet Union was crumbling.[42]

—

To mark the Bicentennial, Margaret Thatcher visited Australia from 1 August to 6 August 1988. It was the most substantial visit by a British prime minister since 1957. It was Thatcher's fifth visit to Australia. She was invited by Hawke, and travelled to Perth, Alice Springs, Canberra, Melbourne, Sydney and Brisbane. The visit was hugely successful. It prompted both countries to recognise the need to elevate United Kingdom–Australia relations.

In their talks, Hawke and Thatcher discussed how to substantially boost the two-way trade and investment relationship. They were united in wanting to see an end to agricultural protection, and would work together to ensure the Uruguay Round negotiations were successful. They also discussed East–West relations, with a focus on the Soviet Union and the prospects for change under Gorbachev. Hawke recognised Thatcher's foresight in seeing that the West 'could do business with him', but both were cautious about whether his 'words were matched by deeds'. They did not, oddly, discuss South Africa.[43]

Hawke had been pressing Thatcher for years for a permanent loan of one of two copies of the *Commonwealth of Australia Constitution Act 1900*. She was personally supportive but faced resistance in Whitehall – which she eventually overcame. 'The birth of a nation was a remarkable event and not to have it legitimised by a birth certificate must be galling, especially when the foster parents had two,' she told the lord chancellor and foreign secretary. Thatcher said they were being 'selfish', and asked them to imagine how they might feel if another country had two copies of the Magna Carta while the United Kingdom had none.[44]

Ahead of Hawke's visit to London the following year, his briefing notes recognised that Thatcher's ten-year government was in trouble: 'Her radical conservative program which, until now, has received widespread support in the United Kingdom, is reaching a difficult stage of implementation.' Thatcher's 'energy remains unflagging', but her 'stubborn determination' and 'abrasive style' was increasing the hostility towards her at home and abroad.[45] Hawke found his one-on-one meetings with Thatcher, apart from those on the issue of apartheid, to be focused, efficient and productive. 'She by nature was a very strong right-wing person,' he recalled. 'While she didn't have an absolutely first-class mind, she had a good mind, and she worked very hard.'[46]

Hawke made a four-day visit to London in June 1989. The highlight was a British–Australian Summit held at 10 Downing Street on 21 June with senior ministers and officials. While they discussed trade and investment, education and cultural issues, and defence cooperation, it was the broad sweep of foreign policy that was especially rewarding for both sides. Hawke expressed to Thatcher his 'dismay' and sadness over the Tiananmen Square crackdown, and his fear that Zhao Ziyang would be executed. He asked whether she still had confidence in Gorbachev, and she affirmed that she did. They discussed progress in South Africa. And Hawke tried to persuade Thatcher to support banning mining in Antarctica.[47] Hawke enjoyed the talks. 'We both have lively interests in various parts of the world and it was valuable to have an opportunity to consider these at length,' he wrote after.[48]

Hawke had met British Labour leader Neil Kinnock on previous visits. The leaders of the fraternal parties got on well. Kinnock admired Hawke's delivery of 'practical, progressive, constructive and substantial' reforms. They both agreed that principle in politics mattered for little without power. They had both dragged their parties into the modern era. Kinnock thought there was much for British Labour to learn from Australian Labor, and the following year he sent two of his up-and-coming MPs on a fact-finding mission to Australia: Tony Blair and

Gordon Brown. Blair and Brown met with Hawke for several hours.[49]

Kinnock was invited to the official dinner for Hawke at 10 Downing Street on 22 June 1989. Kinnock watched Hawke and Thatcher as they chatted throughout the meal. He was a little uneasy about how well they were getting on, and expressed this to Hawke's principal private secretary, Sandy Hollway. Moreover, Kinnock thought Thatcher was flirting with Hawke. In their banquet speeches, Thatcher and Hawke offered high praise to one another that made Kinnock especially uncomfortable. 'Steady on, Bob,' he said. 'I mean, you can praise your enemies from above but never from the side, and certainly not from below.'[50]

In 1987, Hawke posted former Labor minister Doug McClelland to London as Australia's high commissioner. Hawke briefed McClelland on the importance of the relationship with Thatcher. 'They had different points of view but they got on very well together and had a high regard for each other,' McClelland recalled. This bridge-building exercise would see McClelland and Hawke play a minor role in the restoration of diplomatic relations between Argentina and United Kingdom in 1989, following the Falklands War. To reach an agreement which set aside the issue of sovereignty, known as the 'sovereignty umbrella', the framework had to address the issue of fighter jets on the islands.[51]

McClelland recalled being summoned to see Thatcher. 'I think you are the person who might be able to solve an enormous problem for me,' she said. 'We have been at war with the Argentinians over the Falklands. We have Harrier Jets on the Falkland Islands and you people are flogging second-hand Mirages to Argentina. I want you to speak to Bob and stop the sale of the Mirages to Argentina.'

McClelland spoke to Hawke and to Beazley, who asked for forty-eight hours. 'Mate, we can fix that,' Beazley said to McClelland. After a day or two, Beazley phoned McClelland in London. 'Tell her everything is okay,' he said. 'We are going to sell the Mirages to the Pakistanis.' Australia began selling the Mirage III – which had been withdrawn from service in 1988 – to Pakistan in 1990. This was a strict backchannel negotiation.[52]

The CHOGM in Kuala Lumpur from 18 October to 24 October 1989 once again witnessed Hawke and Thatcher in disagreement over apartheid. The leaders agreed to tighten financial sanctions on South Africa. The proposed communiqué invited the International Monetary Fund to consider how to channel funding to South Africa if there was progress towards dismantling apartheid. At the leaders retreat at Langkawi, Hawke was surprised that Thatcher was willing to agree to the draft. However, when the leaders returned to Kuala Lumpur to endorse the communiqué, Thatcher was having none of it. She disassociated the United Kingdom from the Langkawi Accord. Hawke was furious and, along with Rajiv Gandhi, Kenneth Kaunda and Robert Mugabe, condemned her stance.

Brian Mulroney recalled the bust-up. 'We thought we had an agreement, and in the middle of the night she baulked [and] changed her position,' he recalled. 'The next morning, when Bob and I walked in together, Margaret said to us, "Now, what have you two been up to?" And I said, "Margaret, that is not the question. The question is: what have you been up to?" Bob proceeded to launch an attack on her for what he considered as the deceitful British position, and I got into her very strongly myself.'[53]

Charles Powell, foreign policy adviser to Thatcher, thought it was naive to expect she was ever going to change her view. The problem was that she believed that when foreign ministers – in this case, John Major – were drafting the communiqué, it would state 'Britain's divergent opinion'. It did not. 'She thought there was agreement that the British view would be stated, and when it wasn't she felt we had to state it separately,' Powell explained.[54]

Bernard Ingham, Thatcher's press secretary, recalled that she felt ganged up on and misled.[55] 'Thatcher thought that sanctions wouldn't work,' he said. 'You had to go and encourage South Africa to change. The problem was that [when] Hawke came to see her for breakfast, he never mentioned once the idea that the financial sanctions were being cooked up, and then suddenly in the meeting she was confronted with this and she thought that was a bit off. He ought to have told her.'[56]

Meanwhile, Malcolm Fraser's bid to become secretary-general of the Commonwealth failed. Instead, Chief Emeka Anyaoku from Nigeria was chosen. Hawke had backed Fraser's candidacy and invested significant time and resources to help him. Fraser wrote a gracious letter to Hawke thanking him for his strong support.[57] Hawke respected Fraser's impeccable record on racial issues. Tamie Fraser judged that while they had political differences, there was a mutual regard between the two men that developed in the 1970s. 'Perhaps during this time there was an unacknowledged respect for each other's ability in the political arena, which led to Hawke's support later for international appointments,' she said.[58]

It was Thatcher's last CHOGM, as she would be out of office the following year. She had been prime minister since 1979, governing through a period of domestic and global upheaval. She decided not to recontest a second-round leadership ballot after being challenged by Michael Heseltine, and resigned. When the end came, she felt hurt and betrayed by her party. Thatcher wrote to Hawke thanking him for 'the great cooperation and friendship which you have shown me during our time together in office'.[59] Hawke replied, extending his 'great appreciation' for the contribution she had made to international affairs and to developing the United Kingdom–Australia relationship. 'I have always appreciated your direct and straightforward approach,' he wrote.[60]

On 15 August 1989, F.W. de Klerk became prime minister of South Africa. On 2 February 1990, while outlining sweeping reforms to begin dismantling apartheid, he announced that Nelson Mandela would be released from prison after twenty-seven years. On 11 February, Mandela walked free. Hawke had been part of the trio of leaders, with Brian Mulroney and Rajiv Gandhi, who led the international fight against apartheid in the Commonwealth. It was investment sanctions, more than anything else, that hastened its demise. In 1990, Barend du Plessis, South Africa's finance minister under presidents Botha and De Klerk, said investment sanctions were 'the dagger that finally immobilised apartheid'.[61]

Mulroney lauded Hawke's role in ending apartheid. 'Hawke and I began working hand in glove until Mandela was freed, all over those years, various meetings around the world, be it at Buckingham Palace, the Bahamas, the United Nations, in Kuala Lumpur and various bilateral and international conferences,' he reflected. 'Hawke emerged as one of the great leaders in the Commonwealth.'[62]

However, Powell believed Thatcher's position was ultimately vindicated. 'I don't believe sanctions had any decisive effect,' he said. 'She was the only one they listened to in South Africa. They knew she was opposed to apartheid, and she gave them a hard time in private, but she wasn't going to be involved in imposing sanctions.' He noted that Mandela got on well with Thatcher and thanked her for the role she had played in ending apartheid.[63] John Howard, like Thatcher, condemned apartheid but did not support sanctions.[64] He conveyed this to Thatcher when he met her at 10 Downing Street on 26 July 1988.[65]

Hawke's final CHOGM, from 16 October to 21 October 1991, was held in Harare, Zimbabwe. Hawke worked with new British prime minister John Major and other leaders to turn the Commonwealth in a new direction. For his part, Major was in no doubt that economic sanctions had delivered the decisive blow against apartheid in South Africa. 'Apartheid was unforgiveable in every way,' Major said. 'I accepted the argument that sanctions would weaken and destroy it.'

The CHOGM leaders agreed to the landmark Harare Declaration, which set the Commonwealth's values and priorities for a new age. 'Governance in some countries of the Commonwealth was unacceptable,' Major recalled. '[The] Harare Declaration set out the standards of good government expected of Commonwealth members. Bob was vocal about its importance – as was I. As a result of the declaration, nearly every Commonwealth country had an elected government within six years.'

During a break in official talks, Hawke and Major opened the batting in a charity cricket match at the Wanderers ground. Major noticed that at the end of most overs, Hawke took a crafty single to retain the strike. 'I was entirely relaxed about this until, after a few overs, we were invited to retire and make way for "the real cricketers",' Major recalled. 'By that time, I had scored about ten runs and Bob over twenty. Bob had known our tenure at the crease was limited, but had somehow omitted to tell me. Australians always play hard, and he certainly did on that occasion. "Geez, John," he said, "didn't I mention it?" No – he did not.'[66]

Hawke and Major had a bilateral meeting while in Harare. Hawke's brief characterised Major as more 'consultative' and 'team-oriented' than Thatcher, but said he was not 'perceived as a strong leader' and his public manner appeared 'overly formal'. Yet his low-key but firm approach to the Gulf War and the Soviet Union won him plaudits. He revived the Conservative Party's fortunes and made it competitive in the polls after it looked certain to be headed to defeat if Thatcher stayed at the helm.[67]

The most important part of the Hawke–Major dialogue concerned East–West issues. Major viewed Hawke as likeminded on the future of China and the Soviet Union, and was happy to share his assessments and receive Hawke's. At the time of the attempted coup in the Soviet Union in August 1991, Hawke spoke on the phone to Major, who had been in direct contact with Boris Yeltsin. It was a highly volatile and unpredictable situation, but it seemed the coup attempt was 'crumbling fast', Major said. Even so, it was evident to both prime ministers that the Soviet Union would not survive.[68]

On 11 September 1991, Major wrote to Hawke about his recent visits to Moscow and Peking, where the contrast was stark. 'In Moscow the place is humming politically but in dire straits economically,' he wrote. 'Peking is the reverse and [the] Chinese set some store by their thriving market economy as one reason why China is different from the Soviet Union.' Major also briefed Hawke on Hong Kong. 'It would be enormously helpful if you were able to go on telling the Chinese leaders that the whole world has a continuing interest in Hong Kong's stability, prosperity and freedoms after 1997 and that Chinese behaviour in that respect will be one touchstone of her growing relationship with the West,' Major suggested. He urged Hawke to re-engage with China at a personal diplomatic level, because they could not be influenced 'by long-distance loudhailer'.[69]

Major continued to get to know Hawke in their post–prime ministerial lives. 'We both travelled the world a great deal, and often found each other in the same place at the same time,' Major recalled. 'It was invariably a cause for celebration, a very good lunch or dinner, an exchange about politics in whichever part of the world we found ourselves and – above all – an enjoyable, but often disputatious, conversation about our joint obsession with cricket.'[70]

—

Nelson Mandela visited Australia from 22 October to 27 October 1990, just eight months after his release from prison. The government agreed to fund all internal costs for Mandela and his party of twelve. This included the use of two VIP jets. Public servants stressed that he should be treated as a 'guest of government' rather than as a 'head of government', which would breach protocol. He was, they argued, 'only the deputy president' of the African National Congress.[71] A profile of Mandela prepared by the Australian High Commission in Pretoria described him as busy negotiating with government, attending political rallies, giving interviews, meeting international figures and managing conflicts within the ANC. It offered this insight:

> Mandela displays consummate political sensitivity and skill. His statements are thoughtful and display a depth of knowledge of world events which completely belies his 27 years in prison. He has lost none of the forensic ability he showed in the fifties as one of the most successful lawyers in Johannesburg. His manner is courtly and he has great charm. Above all, he shows no bitterness either for himself or for his cause and demonstrates an extraordinary empathy for the political difficulties of his opponents.[72]

Hawke had not met Mandela before, and was considering a visit to South Africa to meet him at the time of the upcoming CHOGM in Harare. Mandela had not initially included Australia on the schedule of his visit to the Asia-Pacific, which included stops in Indonesia, Japan and India. This led to Gareth Evans – who had worked determinedly at ministerial level to see apartheid abolished – writing a cranky letter to Mandela on 5 September 1990:

> I hope you will understand the potential difficulties we would face in Australia in explaining to a domestic constituency, whose support it has not always been easy to maintain for our Southern African policies, if you were seen to visit, long before us, countries in our region who had been less in the forefront of the struggle against apartheid.'[73]

Mandela promptly reconsidered, and his visit was announced by Hawke on 27 September.[74]

Ahead of the Hawke–Mandela meeting, a briefing paper described his approach: 'Mandela is confident, commands attention and is softly spoken. He speaks well in public. In private meetings he often speaks without reference to notes, building a logical (if not always concise) argument. He often leaves little opportunity for dialogue or questions.' This brief included Mandela's 'habits', which included rising every morning at 6 am; liking short early-morning walks; preferring to have 'familiar faces' around all the time; having two hours' rest every afternoon; and not enjoying late nights.[75]

Mandela arrived at Parliament House just before 10 am on 23 October 1990. He had a one-hour meeting with Hawke. Mandela expressed his 'deep appreciation for the moral, political and material support which Australia had given the ANC'. The application of sanctions 'had been particularly effective' in the campaign against apartheid, and gave the ANC 'strength' to continue their fight. Mandela said the ANC needed aid for political campaigning and the resettlement of South Africans returning from exile. Australia provided $15 million in development and humanitarian aid. Hawke recounted his own involvement in the anti-apartheid movement, as ACTU president and as prime minister. He said sanctions should remain until there was change, but added that they should 'not be kept on longer than is necessary'. Mandela agreed, but stressed that the 'pillars of apartheid' had to be dismantled before sanctions could be lifted to 'get the economy working'.[76]

Hawke and Mandela joined the cabinet for further talks. Mandela briefed ministers on violence in townships, political negotiations between the ANC and the government, and the need to ensure the economic reforms secured a fair redistribution of wealth or 'the peace process would be valueless'. In response to a question from John Button about pressure on De Klerk from right-wing white South Africans, Mandela said the president was in danger of losing electoral support. 'The peace process depended on the ANC and President de Klerk working together,' he emphasised. 'It [is] in the ANC's interest to retain him in power and [we] are trying to help him.'[77]

A lunch was held in Mandela's honour in the Great Hall of Parliament House. Mandela left nobody in doubt about the contribution Australia had made to ending apartheid and said economic sanctions had played 'a major role':

> We have come here to thank the government and the people of Australia. Your inestimable support of our organisation, the African National Congress, and the struggling people of South Africa continues to be a source of strength and inspiration to us.
> Without your contribution to the international movement against apartheid we would not have reached so close to the achievement of a non-racial, democratic, united, non-sexist South Africa.[78]

Mandela spoke at a fundraising dinner at the Hilton Hotel in Sydney the next day, joined a prayer service at St Mary's Cathedral, and addressed a rally on the forecourt of the Sydney Opera House. The visit was a triumph.[79]

Hawke was thrilled to meet Mandela. 'He is the most impressive individual I met in the time I was in politics,' he recalled. Mandela told him that he would not forget but had to forgive those who were responsible for apartheid and his imprisonment.[80] The respect and admiration was mutual.[81] Dennis Richardson attended the Hawke–Mandela meeting. 'I had never known the meaning of the word "charisma" until I met Mandela, and I have not experienced it since,' he said. 'The other thing that stood out was his warmth for Hawke.'[82]

—

Engagement with the Asia-Pacific was another focus of Hawke's prime ministership, although he preferred to label it 'enmeshment'. As economic power shifted from West to East, there would be enormous opportunities for Australia. In 1970, East Asia accounted for 12.3 per cent of global economic growth. By 1991, it had increased to 21.3 per cent. Hawke travelled to almost every country in the Asia-Pacific region, with his priorities being to expand economic opportunities, strengthen diplomatic ties, facilitate cultural exchanges and encourage study at Australian universities. Hawke did not neglect the South Pacific, making several visits to Papua New Guinea and other nations.[83]

In October 1989, Ross Garnaut completed his report *Australia and the North East Asian Ascendancy*, which identified the opportunities for Australia in North Asia. It reaffirmed Hawke's belief that Australia's capacity to influence the region would continue to depend on creative middle-power diplomacy and leading by example.

Hawke made four visits over nine years to Japan, then Australia's most important economic partner in the region. He got on well with Prime Minister Yasu Nakasone when he visited in 1984, and later found him a willing ally in making agriculture a focus of the Uruguay Round. Hawke sought to shift Australia's trade balance with Japan. While Australia had a prosperous iron-ore and coal trade, Hawke sought greater market access for manufactured goods and services, including education and tourism. He also encouraged Japanese investment in Australia. The transformation was remarkable. Manufactured exports to Japan increased in value from $6.3 billion in 1983 to $14.8 billion in 1991, and the share of these exports as a proportion of Australia's total manufactured exports over the same period increased from 5.1 per cent to 14 per cent.

The Hawke government opened Australia to the world by removing trade barriers, and sought to influence other countries to do the same. On 25 August 1986, Australia formed the Cairns Group of fourteen nations aimed at liberalising trade in agriculture. It represented 560 million people and 25 per cent of the world's agricultural exports. The Cairns Group – which took its name from the location of the first meeting – hoped to influence the new multinational trade negotiations round within the General Agreement of Tariffs and Trade (GATT) beginning that year. The European Community's Common Agricultural Policy (CAP) and the United States' Export Enhancement Program (EEP) were distorting global agricultural markets, with Australia being collateral damage. It was estimated the CAP cost Australia $1 billion a year in lost markets and reduced prices, while the EEP cost wheat farmers $600 million a year. John Dawkins was Australia's trade minister. 'We wanted to create a new force in trade negotiations with a cohesive group that could work together,' he reflected.[84]

Hawke advocated a better deal for Australian farmers to the Reagan and Bush administrations. He was also a public advocate for freer trade. Hawke told the Americans that Australia's continued support for the joint defence facilities were a matter of public debate, and farmers were threatening to march on Pine Gap. Hawke never used the joint defence facilities as a bargaining chip, but he did use them to emphasise the anger that many Australians felt towards their administrations. While discussions were frank and comprehensive, and the Americans recognised Australia's concerns, the EEP remained a policy tool to influence the trade practices of other nations, especially those in Europe.

The only way Australia was going to make significant headway with the Americans and Europeans on trade was through a larger multilateral forum with a clear purpose to tackle trade liberalisation. On 31 January 1989, in an address to the Korean Business Associations in Seoul, Hawke proposed the establishment of the Asia-Pacific Economic Cooperation forum (APEC). The purpose would be to lower trade barriers and expand regional cooperation, including regular meetings at ministerial level. He referred to the Organisation for Economic Co-operation and Development (OECD) as a model, but his ambitions were larger: a new intergovernmental vehicle for regional economic cooperation.

'Our economic futures are interlinked,' Hawke argued in Seoul. 'The Asia-Pacific region is at a pivotal point in history. And the region is located at a pivotal point in the global economy. We have much to offer each other ... Cooperation offers the region the opportunity to influence the course of multilateral trade liberalisation, avoid alternative approaches which would undermine this objective and enable us to enter the next century with confidence that our potential will be fulfilled.'[85]

This was a major initiative. It underlined Hawke's beliefs in institution building and consensus policymaking. But it got off to a rocky start. There were concerns that Hawke was proposing a Pacific trade bloc to counter the Americans and Europeans. This was not his intention, and ran counter to the purpose of freer trade. The Americans were angry about not being informed of APEC in advance. Hawke recalled that Malaysia did not want the United States to be part of APEC. When cabinet discussed the idea on 6 March 1989, it was clear that Australia was 'open to the inclusion of the United States and Canada' but was not advocating it.[86] Mike Codd explained: 'Including the United States had to be an idea that came from the ASEAN countries, not from us, even though we felt they had to be in this body eventually.'[87]

'Bob came to us and laid out the idea for the APEC forum,' James Baker recalled. 'I know that we embraced it fully because I was secretary of state at the time and we worked closely with the Australians to get that done. We didn't have any concerns about the fact that the idea originated with Bob.'[88] Gareth Evans recalled a more colourful conversation with Baker when the Americans thought they may not be included. 'If you think you can screw us around like this, you don't know what an alliance relationship is all about,' Baker told Evans.[89]

Richard Woolcott was appointed as Hawke's special envoy to sell the idea of APEC to a sceptical region and assuage the Americans. 'After Hawke's speech in Korea, everybody was ringing up to ask, "What the hell does this mean – an Asia-Pacific community?"' Woolcott recalled. 'He asked me to go to all the major countries in the region and assess their views. He wanted to know who thought who should be in and who should be out. So I did that, and the only country that was rather questioning of it was Malaysia. It was remarkable that APEC was proposed in January and came into existence at the ministerial level in November. It was quite an achievement.'[90]

The initial focus of APEC would be to accelerate the Uruguay Round. The APEC forum would also bring a new focus and energy to economic discussions in the Asia-Pacific. APEC would be a forum of regional economies, rather than countries, which would enable ministers from China, Taiwan and Hong Kong to sit at the same table. The first APEC ministerial meeting convened in Canberra on 6–7 November 1989. The initial twelve-member economies were: Australia, New Zealand, Japan, South Korea, Indonesia, Thailand, the Philippines, Singapore, Malaysia, Brunei, the United States and Canada. China, Hong Kong and Taiwan would join a year later. 'No international organisation has had such a brief period of gestation,' Hawke recalled.[91]

—

The biggest investment Hawke made in building the relationship with another nation in the Asia-Pacific region was China. The premier of China, Li Peng, visited Australia from 14 November to 20 November 1988. He had succeeded Zhao Ziyang in March that year. For Hawke, this visit underlined the close relationships he had formed with Chinese leaders since April 1983. It also built upon the work of the Whitlam and Fraser governments. Between 1973 and 1988, two-way trade between Australia and China increased fourteen-fold. Chinese students began studying at Australian universities, cultural exchanges expanded and scientific cooperation was developing. Hawke had two days of talks with Li on 17 and 18 November. Less than a year later, Australia–China relations went into a temporary freeze.

It is one of the iconic images of the twentieth century. A lone man, dressed in black pants and white shirt, holding plastic bags, standing defiant in front of a phalanx of tanks in Beijing's Tiananmen Square in June 1989. When the tanks try to get around him, he stands in their way and climbs on top. Eventually, he is hurried away by two men. The Chinese government's brutal response to the student-led pro-democracy protests sent shockwaves around the world. It was the culmination of a series of protests that challenged the authority of China's leaders, including Deng Xiaoping. Hundreds, perhaps thousands of protesters were murdered or maimed. Dead bodies, machine-gunned by soldiers and police, lined Beijing's streets.[92]

Hawke was shocked and sickened by what had happened. 'When I received a message from the embassy telling me of the incidents of the tanks rolling over the students, it broke my heart for China,' Hawke recalled.[93] Richard Woolcott, the secretary of the Department of Foreign Affairs and Trade, had been informed by Li Peng that the Chinese government would not accept 'chaos' and would take whatever steps were necessary to bring about 'social order'. Hawke spoke to Woolcott about condemning the violence in Beijing. 'He was quite determined to do it,' Woolcott recalled. 'He felt strongly about it. He understood there would be quite a negative reaction in China.'[94]

Hawke had read a cable from the Australian ambassador, David Sadleir, describing in striking detail what had happened in and around Tiananmen Square on the evening of 3 June. The cable, informed by sources in the Chinese government, said 'it is evident that atrocities have been committed on a massive scale' but also noted that 'certain details may eventually prove to be inaccurate'.[95] Sandy Hollway and John Bowan tried to talk Hawke out of reading from it at a memorial service for the victims. Their concerns about the accuracy of aspects of the cable – such as tanks 'crushing everyone in their path' and bodies being 'incinerated' by flamethrowers – would later prove justified.[96]

Bowan phoned Dennis Richardson in the Department of Prime Minister and Cabinet to see if he could persuade Hawke not to read the cable. Richardson told Hawke it was classified and he could not read from it. Hawke rejected that. Richardson then said the details had to be confirmed. That did not work either. Richardson tried another tactic. 'There is also the possibility that you become emotional,' he said. Hawke bristled. 'That is for me to worry about, not you.'[97] Hawke's staff referred to his tears as the 'optic nerve'.[98]

At 1 pm on 9 June 1989, Hawke addressed the service in the Great Hall at Parliament House. It was estimated that 4500 members of the public and staff were present, with hundreds more in the entrance foyer, stairs, balconies and outside. Hawke read from the cable, which graphically catalogued how the demonstrators had been killed. As he spoke, tears streamed down his face and he had to stop several times to compose himself.

'We meet here to mourn this tragedy and to share the grief of those who have lost members of their families, their loved ones and their friends, and to express our profound sympathy to the Chinese-Australian community that has expressed its outrage at the massacre in Beijing,' he said as he wept. 'We meet here to show our support for the Chinese people and to reaffirm our commitment to the ideals of democracy and freedom of expression that they have so eloquently espoused.' He added: 'To crush the spirit and body of youth is to crush the very future of China itself.'

Hawke condemned the Chinese government for the ruthless repression of its people. He instructed Sadleir to convey this view to the Chinese government. China was condemned in international forums for its breach of human rights. Hawke cancelled a planned visit to China later that year, and suspended other government-to-government exchanges, including a visit by HMAS *Parramatta* to Shanghai. Hawke would not have any significant contact with Chinese leaders for the next three years, and a ban on ministerial visits remained in place until January 1990.[99]

In response to the crackdown, Hawke extended the temporary entry visas of Chinese nationals in Australia who did not want to return. He faced opposition from within the public service to the idea of granting temporary humanitarian protection. 'You can't do that, prime minister,' Hawke was told. 'I've just done it,' he replied.[100] It was, however, a decision for cabinet. That decision noted that the extension of visas had 'serious implications' for Australia's migration program.[101] Eventually, about 42,000 permanent residency visas would be granted to Chinese nationals living in Australia.

John Bowan recalled that Hawke's speech was a 'watershed' moment in Australia–China relations. 'Bob had developed a very good personal relationship with Zhao Ziyang, who was one of the great losses out of Tiananmen,' he said. 'He really did see the importance of China to Australia. He was very moved by what had happened. We had a visit by Li Peng the year before. During a lunch at the Lodge, Ross Garnaut mentioned that he had played tennis with a few Chinese leaders. Li said, "You shouldn't play with them." The temperature in the room dropped. That would have convinced Bob that Zhao was the right guy.'[102]

The events in Tiananmen Square cast a long shadow over China. The Chinese government has whitewashed the incident from history. The notion that economic reform would lead to political reform has been misplaced. This was the great hope in the 1980s and 1990s, and beyond. Some of China's senior leaders at the time, including Zhao Ziyang and Hu Yaobang, believed that economic and political liberalisation were two sides of the same coin. Hawke was close to Zhao and Hu, and hoped they would succeed. But he also understood that Deng's economic reforms, which lifted millions out of poverty and transformed China into a leading economy, could be set back by a push for political reform. Hawke described Deng as a 'pragmatic strategist'. But he still held out hope that, over time, China would continue to embrace political reform.[103]

In 1993, Hawke was invited back to China. He was now an ex-prime minister. He recalled meeting Jiang Zemin. The Chinese president extended his hand. 'There is something I've got to say to you,' he said. 'China regards you as one of their best friends.'[104] Hawke was moved by the gesture. No Australian prime minister has condemned Chinese leaders in such strong terms since. But the Chinese government respected Hawke because he had demonstrated a long-term commitment to the relationship. Hawke understood the need to speak truth to power, and stand up for Australia's values, while being pragmatic about the importance of maintaining bilateral relations.

27

FOURTH TERM

When the global stock market crashed in October 1987, there were fears of a depression. It was seen as 'the tremor before the big earthquake' and put the Hawke government on edge.[1] By January 1988, however, there was little sign of the economy slowing. In fact, the Australian economy was booming – there were concerns it was overheating. Keating pushed the Reserve Bank to raise the official cash rate to slow the economy, but it was not until March/April 1988 that it acted. Official interest rates rose from 10 per cent to a peak of 18 per cent in November 1989. The standard variable mortgage rate reached 17 per cent, and many business loans were over 20 per cent. A boom followed by a bust was feared.

The Treasury, the Department of Finance and the Reserve Bank all misread the economy, and the Reserve Bank was slow to reduce rates as the economy cooled. Official interest rates did not begin to fall until January 1990, and then only slowly. Many Australians defaulted on their home loans, saw their businesses go bust or lost their jobs. The economy plunged into a recession that was longer than any since the Great Depression of the 1930s. Unemployment climbed to over 10 per cent during 1991. The recession tarnished the economic legacy of the Hawke government. It would not be until a decade or more later that its landmark economic reforms were almost universally regarded as having been primarily responsible for the sustained economic growth, productivity gains and higher standards of living that followed the recession.

The Hawke government reached a milestone by early 1988. It had turned around the current account deficit and returned the budget to surplus, the economy was growing, business investment and confidence was up, unemployment had fallen significantly, inflation had been contained, real wages were increasing, and industrial disputation was at its lowest level in decades. These things had been difficult to achieve, asking much of voters as the economy restructured and transitioned, and required the acceptance of a somewhat sceptical party and union movement. But now the policy task was more challenging.

Hawke recognised the government did not fully understand what was happening to the economy, nor did it have the right policy response. 'Like most economists around the world, we underestimated the resilience of the market economy,' Hawke conceded. 'We kept interest rates too low for too long, and then when we did have to move them up, we moved them up too fast. That caused problems for a lot of people, including blue-collar workers. If we had acted earlier, we would have mitigated some of the impact from the recession.'[2]

With the economy buoyant in early 1989, the cabinet reaffirmed its strategy of fiscal restraint, flexible monetary policy and continued structural adjustment. Keating told ministers on 1 March that the existing economic policy framework was appropriate for continuing to dampen demand.[3] By the time of Keating's seventh budget, on 15 August, the government's confidence was diminishing. Again, the task was to put downward pressure on demand to reduce inflation and interest rates. There was an increase to pensions and relief for taxpayers and home owners. A $9.12 billion surplus was lauded but masked the underlying economic problems.

As the government faced new economic challenges, the decision-making process to determine the right policy settings was fundamental. Rod Sims, who joined the prime minister's office as principal economic adviser in September 1988, said he had never seen anybody assess issues like Hawke. 'If an issue was really complex, he would listen to different views and take the time before making a decision,' Sims said. 'He was always relaxed, never rushed or panicked. He was intelligent, wise and stunningly well organised. You could see his mind whirring as he reflected on issues. Then, once he had dealt with it, his mind was freed and he moved on to the next thing.'[4]

The government and the unions struck a new wage–tax trade-off in the 12 April 1989 economic statement, which stopped a wages blowout and spiralling inflation. This agreement effectively saved the Prices and Incomes Accord. It was seen as a bridge between Accord Mark IV, inked in September 1988, which provided for a 3 per cent wage increase coupled with award restructuring, and Accord Mark V, signed in August 1989, which provided two-tier wage increases based on productivity and further award restructuring.

But not every union was onboard with the principle of wage restraint. When the Australian Federation of Air Pilots sought a 30 per cent pay increase in August 1989, it threatened the survival of the accord and undermined the government's economic strategy. This union, aloof from the rest of the industrial movement and supremely arrogant in its approach to bargaining, held the nation to ransom. It benefited from the two-airline duopoly – which the government announced would be abolished that same year – and pressured Australian Airlines and Ansett to bow to its demands. Hawke led the government's response to the pilots' strike and provided regular updates to cabinet.[5]

The pilots' union refused to give in, would not fly planes and advised its members to quit their jobs. Sims met with the pilots' union and went to a meeting with their members. 'These pilots felt they had the whip hand against the government and believed if they just remained united then the government would give in to their demands,' he recalled. 'They were telling their members that Hawke was about to crumble. When the pilots resigned from their jobs that was a critical mistake. The pilots' strike represented a threat to the entire wages system.'[6]

The government refused to give in. The Royal Australian Air Force and Royal Australian Navy were used to fly and crew planes, and recruitment of new flight crews at home and abroad was under-taken. These decisions would normally have been extremely difficult for a Labor government, but the pilots' union was not affiliated to the ACTU, and the ACTU was committed to the accord and could not countenance a rogue union jeopardising all it had worked for. Hawke met with the pilots' union leadership several times and urged them to come to their senses. Decisions in the industrial tribunal and legal action in civil courts effectively destroyed the union and resolved the dispute after more than six months.

Hawke saw the pilots' dispute as a critical moment in the life of his government. 'Wage restraint was an intrinsic part of the economic reforms,' he said. 'It was why I took such an intransigent stand against the pilots. Because if we had allowed them to have their 30 per cent increase, or anywhere near that, it would have shattered the basis of the accord. I had them in and I said, "All the unions are supportive. They are doing the right thing, you have to do the right thing. I'm not going to budge from this, if I have to break you I will." But they didn't listen.'[7]

—

With the Kirribilli Agreement behind them, Hawke and Keating returned to being the government's premier salesmen. A new round of publicity was organised to sell the August 1989 budget and reaffirm the government's economic credentials ahead of an election expected in the first half of 1990. In shirtsleeves and with their arms around each other, the two were pictured on the front page of *The Sunday Age* on 20 August 1989. 'And they said it wouldn't last,' was the headline. The message was that the 'double act' was still together. Michael Gordon quoted Hawke and Keating saying they were 'closer than ever' and were keen to campaign together at the next election.[8]

The next day they appeared together on *The Midday Show*, hosted by Ray Martin. The audience of stay-at-home mums, pensioners and small children witnessed Hawke and Keating trade banter with Martin about economic and social policy as well as their relative sex appeal. Hawke said they were 'a couple of good mates', while Keating reassured the audience of around 2 million that they were 'a long-term team'.

Martin, however, was unconvinced. 'Their body language was brutal, like that of a couple at the marriage counsellor's clinic with irreconcilable differences,' he recalled. In an awkward moment, Martin presented them both with a box of silk pyjamas as a memento; one of his producers thought it looked like they had each been handed a 'steaming turd'.[9]

While Hawke and Keating presented an image of unity, all was not well in the Liberal Party. On 9 May 1989, there had been another bizarre leadership change. This time, Andrew Peacock toppled John Howard in a surprise coup organised by his supporters, who dubbed themselves 'cardinals'. Peacock defeated Howard by forty-four votes to twenty-seven in the party-room ballot. Fred Cheney defeated Peter Reith by the same margin to become deputy Liberal leader. Then, on the same day, Ian Sinclair was the victim of another coup when Charles Blunt toppled him as leader of the National Party. Hawke and Keating were not surprised to find themselves facing Peacock again. It prompted Keating to ask: 'Can a soufflé rise twice?'

Howard's leadership had been faltering for some time. He had tried to revive his fortunes in December 1988 with a comprehensive policy manifesto, *Future Directions*, that gave voice to his conservative values. The 109-page document put the family, enterprise and individual liberty at the heart of the Coalition's policy framework. Voters were not impressed. *The Bulletin* ran a cover story, showing Howard next to the headline 'Mr 18% – Why on earth does this man bother?' According to Morgan Gallup, Hawke led Howard as preferred prime minister by 69–18 per cent.[10] Polls showed voters favoured Peacock over Howard as Liberal leader by 79–15 per cent. Peacock's return lifted support for the Coalition, but Hawke still maintained a comfortable lead as preferred prime minister, by 52–38 per cent.[11] The media declared Howard dead and buried.

In reflecting on his time as Liberal leader in the 1980s, Howard said he had tried to offer constructive support to Labor on economic reform. 'Most of the reforms they undertook, I supported, [such as] tariff reform, financial deregulation, and most of Labor's fiscal consolidation,' he said. 'I did argue that Hawke should have gone further on reform in some areas. So, politically, adopting that position made it easier for the government of the day.'[12] This claim would become an article of faith in the Liberal and National parties. However, the Coalition did not support the Prices and Incomes Accord, the assets test on pensions, the introduction of a capital gains tax and a fringe benefits tax, or superannuation.

Only Howard strongly supported the float of the dollar. There was no support from the Coalition for the seminal social policy reform of the decade, Medicare.

Hawke never believed Howard or Peacock deserved any credit for Labor's reforms. Many of the government's policies, including budget initiatives, were negotiated through the Senate with support from the Australian Democrats. 'The fact is John Howard should have done these things when he was treasurer, but of course he had a prime minister who was just economically inept and not interested,' Hawke said. 'I welcomed the support we did get but we were determined to do it anyway and we had the support from the electorate.'[13]

As the government looked towards 1990, there was no guarantee of winning a fourth election. After the 1983, 1984 and 1987 elections, the government had at times lagged the opposition in the polls, only to consolidate, rebuild and win again. The 1990 election would, however, be the most challenging.

Geoff Walsh returned to Hawke's office in late 1988. In a series of notes to Hawke, he chronicled the increasing cynicism of the electorate, and the feeling that the government was out of touch and not in command of the economy.[14] Walsh encouraged Hawke and Keating to 'take control of the economy debate', develop a more 'coherent' message and sell it 'aggressively' to voters. 'The electorate believes our policies have failed and that the burden of them is unfairly distributed,' he wrote.[15] He argued the government needed a clear strategy to win back blue-collar voters while emphasising its environmental achievements, and could improve the image of the government with 'sympathetic and understanding language'.[16] When Hawke called a pensioner a 'silly old bugger' during a visit to a shopping centre in Whyalla in September 1989, it underscored the problem.[17]

Rod Cameron's polling showed Labor behind in marginal seats in Sydney, Melbourne, Brisbane and Adelaide over the summer of 1989–90. There was, however, recognition that the government's economic policies were seen to be working. Labor enjoyed a negligible lead over the Coalition (42 per cent versus 41 per cent) on who was most trusted on economic policy. But this question of 'economic confidence' would widen to a 46–34 lead for Labor by

February 1990. Voters found Peacock to be less convincing than they first thought. There was 'disillusion' with his performance which was stopping voters switching parties. Hawke still had a leadership edge.[18] But would it last?

The year ended on a sad note for Hawke with the death of his father, Clem, after he suffered a stroke at the Resthaven nursing home in Adelaide on 23 December 1989. He was ninety-one years old. Hawke penned his death notice to be published in the *The Advertiser*. Clem had been the loving husband of Ellie, the father of Bob and Neil, and father-in-law of Hazel. He was grandfather to Susan, Stephen and Rosslyn. And great-grandfather to David, Kel, Paul, Sophie, Sam and Ben. 'A good and gentle man whose life reflected his deep conviction that a belief in the father-hood of God involved a commitment to the brotherhood of man,' Hawke wrote. 'Dad – thank you for everything.'[19]

The funeral was held on 27 December 1989 at Hawthorn Uniting Church. Around 200 mourners attended, including Hawke's colleagues Lionel Bowen, Paul Keating, Neal Blewett, Nick Bolkus and South Australian premier John Bannon. Hawke worked through matters arising from his father's estate over the next few months. Clem's unit at 10 Clifton Street, Hawthorn, was sold for $93,000. The remainder of his estate was valued at over $73,000. Hawke organised for his mother's cremated remains to be transferred from Karrakatta Cemetery in Perth to Centennial Park in Adelaide so Clem and Ellie could be together again. He visited the dual memorial to say a final farewell on 23 June 1990.[20]

—

On 16 February 1990, Hawke announced that an election would be held on 24 March. It would be the fourth time he had sought a mandate to govern. And it would be the second Hawke–Peacock match-up. The leadership of the Labor Party was a campaign issue. Nine days before Hawke announced the election, he had to douse speculation that he might not serve a full term as prime minister if re-elected. The mercurial John Button suggested he might quit, and he hoped Hawke and Keating had reached an agreement on the leadership. 'I suspect, incidentally, that they have,' he said. Hawke said this was 'gratuitous and incorrect'.[21]

The economy, though, was the central election issue. Keating promised voters there would be 'a soft landing'. But Australians were already doing it tough under high interest rates. Hawke characterised the choice for voters as going 'forward as a community, creating a fair society, an efficient and productive economy and a healthy environment for ourselves and our children' or turning 'the clock back to the days of entrenched privilege, lost opportunities and environmental degradation'. Peacock said the choice for voters was between 'a government of the special deal and the quick fix' and the Coalition's 'programs for people in the public interest and well thought out policies to turn the Australian economy around'.[22]

A strategy note prepared by Rod Cameron revealed that, after seven years, the electorate was feeling reform fatigue. Swinging voters, who would determine the election, were 'disillusioned, despondent and cynical'. It was the same position the government had been in prior to the 1987 election. The danger now was that most voters felt it was time for 'a change in government'. The silver lining in this dark cloud was that the same voters had little 'confidence' in Peacock and the Coalition, which lacked 'credibility'. There was also a feeling by voters that the government's economic policies 'are starting to work'. The upshot was that it would not be enough for Labor to just attack the Coalition – it needed to demonstrate it had the best ideas, policies and vision for the future.[23]

Cameron and Gibbs identified a residual respect for Hawke and Keating, on which the party could draw to win a fourth term. 'They educated an apathetic and economically uninterested electorate about the need for reform,' Cameron said. 'Swinging voters, the least politically informed, accepted to some extent the need for reform. Hawke could unify and bring the nation together. The electorate believed that he genuinely had the nation's interests at heart and was not motivated by partisan politics or self-interest.' Gibbs said the research was used to help explain policy. 'Our research was never designed to change the policy but to show the selling points and recognise the fears and how to address them,' she said.[24]

On 21 February 1990, Labor announced the Accord Mark VI. The aim was to reduce inflationary pressures with another wage–tax trade-off. Unions were encouraged to continue to restructure basic awards, accept over-award enterprise bargaining and push ahead with amalgamations. Superannuation would increase from 3 per cent to 6 per cent of wages. But the continuing pilots' strike undermined the government's claim to have reduced industrial disputation and a cooperative relationship with unions.

The Hawke government had by now acquired a permanent shade of green. Its environmental achievements included stopping the Franklin Dam in Tasmania, protecting the Lemonthyme and Southern forests in Tasmania and the wet tropics of North Queensland, safeguarding the Great Barrier Reef, prohibiting sandmining at Shelburne Bay at Cape York, and launching a campaign to protect Antarctica from mining. Now, a new phase in the government's approach to the environment was needed. It would be less about iconic conservation initiatives and more about environmental sustainability.

On 20 July 1989, Hawke affirmed the government's environment credentials with the *Our Country, Our Future* statement. It addressed biological diversity, species protection, waste management, fisheries, the ozone layer and greenhouse gasses. It included a commitment to planting One Billion Trees by 2000. Some $350 million was set aside to establish the National Landcare Program, a grassroots movement that brought together conservationists and farmers that was proposed by the Australian Conservation Foundation and the National Farmers' Federation.

The brains behind the new environmental strategy was Simon Balderstone, then working as a consultant in Graham Richardson's office. The idea was to develop a strategy that was both good policy and good politics. On 2 November 1988, Balderstone faxed ALP national secretary Bob Hogg the nuts and bolts of his proposal. The theme was 'think globally, act nationally'. He identified issues to do with air, water and land: forests, greenhouse gases, the ozone layer, soil, species and ecosystems, and conservation of iconic sites. Action needed to be across four tiers: local government, state government, federal government and by international cooperation.

'Rather than having each issue, or action, publicly dealt with in isolation, we must be projecting them as part of an overall strategy,' Balderstone wrote:

Inter-connected reasons for actions have to be pushed e.g. saving rainforests helps reduce the greenhouse effect and stops land degradation and preserves habitat, etc. 'End of world' issues such as pollution, greenhouse, ozone, soil will continue to increase in profile and importance. To that extent, government action on those fronts must be concrete, as the differences between party policies have to be accentuated. In 'specific area' policies, such as wet tropics world heritage, the differences are demonstrably large. But in 'end of world' issues, these differences will remove that problem.[25]

This was the genesis of the *Our Country, Our Future* statement.

The issue of climate change – known then as 'the greenhouse effect' – was emerging as a political issue. Tackling climate change was seen as building on the successful global strategy to eliminate chlorofluorocarbons (CFCs) in household products as these depleted the Earth's ozone layer. Cabinet supported the goal of a 20 per cent reduction in carbon emissions by 2005, following the Toronto Conference on the Changing Atmosphere held in June 1988. The following year, cabinet made 'a strong commitment to address' climate change with 'a comprehensive strategy', but acknowledged that more work had to be done to mitigate the impact on local industry and understand the science. A National Greenhouse Advisory Committee was established.[26]

On 9 July 1990, Hawke wrote to Keating urging that work continue on identifying 'possible courses of action' to reduce greenhouse gases as a whole-of-government effort.[27] On 11 October that year, cabinet confirmed an interim planning target to stabilise emissions at 1988 levels by 2000, and then to reduce emissions by 20 per cent (on 1988 levels) by 2005. The following year, on 16 December 1991, cabinet resolved to reduce emissions via an 'effective and equitable' international treaty, but was uncertain whether other nations would willingly do the same, and resolved not to adopt measures which had 'net adverse economic impacts nationally or on Australia's trade competitiveness'.[28] Ros Kelly, the minister for the environment, said this was a necessary compromise. 'That was how I got it through,' she recalled.[29] It was one of the final matters considered by the Hawke government.

Labor strategists knew the party's primary vote would fall at the March 1990 election, but hoped to win some of this back via preferences. The most important issue in the campaign, after the economy, was the environment. Hawke made a direct appeal for the preference votes of those who were motivated by the environment and likely to vote for the Greens or the Australian Democrats. In radio and television commercials, Hawke asked: 'If you care about the environment, if you care about the future of Australia, your preference choice must be Labor.'

Bob Brown, the Tasmanian Greens MP, had met and talked with Hawke about a range of environmental issues over the previous seven years. 'Hawke did understand that the environment was a rising issue of concern to all Australians,' he recalled. Brown acknowledged there was 'a quid pro quo' between the government and environmental groups: if the government delivered on their concerns, they responded with political support. Brown summed up Hawke's environmental legacy: 'Hawke led the champion environmental government that Australia has seen since Federation.'[30]

Hawke and Keating had fun with the Liberal campaign. The Liberals tested the slogan 'A vote for Bob Hawke is a vote for Paul Keating'. It was designed to make the Labor leadership an issue and reinforce some antagonism towards Keating over his economic management. Hawke turned the tables by tapping into voter doubts about Peacock: 'A vote for Andrew Peacock is a vote for Andrew Peacock,' he replied. The official Liberal Party slogan was 'The Answer Is Liberal'. This made the opposition the focus, rather than the government. Keating countered: 'If the answer's Liberal, it must have been one hell of a question.'

Hawke was energetic, disciplined and on-message. But there was always a risk that he would turn grumpy or get cranky. Alarm bells rang when, at the start of the campaign, Hawke arrived at a press conference and, finding there was no space to put down his papers, stretched out his arm and cleared the microphones with a large sweep. But Barrie Cassidy thought Hawke was soon back at 'the top of his game'. In his view, Labor's strategy of maximum media coverage – long press conferences and interviews on radio and television, and some in print – put Peacock on the back foot and showed that Hawke had command of the issues.[31]

Peacock knew this was his last chance to become prime minister. He had nothing to lose and ran a highly opportunistic campaign. However, voter uncertainty about Peacock's capacity to lead was underlined by an unfunded health policy and opposition to the Australia-Japan Multifunction Polis, a planned high-technology city of the future in Adelaide. The Coalition stoked racism when it raised concerns about a Japanese enclave in Australia and questioned foreign investment. Journalist Paul Kelly lashed the opposition leader for his ignorance and misrepresentation, and charged him with prejudicing the national interest 'in a way that should eliminate him from the prime ministership'.[32] This led to a tense exchange caught on television at the National Press Club, where Peacock called Kelly 'a bastard'. Peacock later called Kelly from his plane to apologise and they patched up the relationship.[33]

Hawke and Peacock went head to head again in a one-hour election debate on 25 February. Hawke had refused to debate Howard but felt he had Peacock's measure. Moreover, this was going to be a closer election than in July 1987. Labor insisted the debate be held at the outset of the campaign, in case it did not go well. Peacock, eager to repeat his performance of six years earlier, agreed. On the night, Hawke appeared confident and relaxed while Peacock seemed overwhelmed and anxious. The economy was the key issue, yet Peacock failed to articulate how he would address inflation and stumbled over his policy to abolish capital gains tax, which would benefit the wealthy. Polls judged Hawke the clear winner.

On 8 March, Hawke launched Labor's election campaign at the Performing Arts Centre in Brisbane. The extravagant style of the previous election campaign launch was gone. This was a back-to-basics launch in front of 1500 supporters. The message of Hawke's policy speech was that voters should have confidence in Australia's future, as Labor would deliver 'stronger prosperity from a world-competitive economy, greater financial security for families, a ladder of opportunity for all Australians and unshakable protection of the natural environment'. He promised funds to establish Cooperative Research Centres to drive innovation, boost subsidised childcare places and provide additional financial support for families and students.[34]

Margaret Gibbs' focus groups were essential in coming up with the right lines for Hawke to use. In concept testing in December 1989, this statement was found to be the most effective: 'We know it's been hard but if there was an easy way we'd have done it long ago.' It worked because it positioned Hawke as sincere and believable, and not too gloomy or negative.[35] By the time of the election, voters were disillusioned with both major parties. However, Hawke's 'leadership advantage' strengthened by the end of the campaign. The 'better the devil you know' sentiment gave Gibbs 'some cause for optimism'.[36]

On the eve of the election, Keating telegrammed Hawke: 'Best of luck tomorrow. Confident of Labor victory.'[37] They both had much riding on the result. Hawke watched the election results from a suite on the thirty-third floor of the Hyatt Hotel in Melbourne. When the votes started to come in, the outcome was not immediately clear. The election would be a cliffhanger. By midnight it looked like Labor would win, but it would take days until the result was certain. Labor's primary vote fell by 6.46 per cent to 39.44 per cent. The Coalition won 50.10 per cent of the two-party vote to Labor's 49.90 per cent. Eight seats were lost. Preferences from the Greens and Australian Democrats helped Labor secure more than ten seats. In the end, Labor had a majority of eight seats. It had won the election.

Peacock had been supremely confident of victory. 'I thought we would win,' he recalled. Although the Coalition won the two-party vote, Peacock accepted the result. 'You have to win the seats – that's the system,' he said. 'I never complained about losing the election and I didn't think I was robbed.'[38] Tony Eggleton, running his last campaign for the Liberal Party, also expected to win. He thought their campaign planning, the longevity of the Labor government and high interest rates would be enough to return the Coalition to power.[39]

Bob Hogg, in his report to Labor's national executive, pinpointed three factors that explained Labor's victory: leadership, the environment and Medicare. Doubts about Peacock's leadership, underscored by how he had returned to the job, and his failure to produce a funded health policy were additional factors. But the campaign itself was 'critical' to the outcome.[40]

Cameron recognised the partnership of Hawke and Keating as being important in Labor's victory, but much was due to Hawke. 'The simple equation was: a still-credible and reasonably popular Hawke versus a low-credibility Peacock,' he explained. 'Hawke, personally, was the major factor in the election win.'[41]

—

Having returned to government for a fourth term, Hawke reshuffled ministerial portfolios and made several new appointments. Keating became deputy prime minister following the retirement of Lionel Bowen. John Button continued as Senate leader and Gareth Evans was elected as Senate deputy leader.[42] But, despite his authority from the election result, Hawke made a mess of appointing the rest of the ministry.

Graham Richardson desperately wanted to have the transport and communications portfolio, and expected Hawke to give it to him. Hawke denied this request. It was commonly thought that Richardson's closeness to Kerry Packer, who owned Channel Nine, was the reason. But Packer would not reacquire Channel Nine from Alan Bond until July 1990. Still, Richardson insisted Packer was the reason. '[Hawke] was referring to Kerry Packer, no question about it, because Kerry was a friend of mine,' he said.[43]

In fact, it was the transport portfolio that concerned Hawke. He claimed Richardson had a meeting with Peter Abeles, who owned TNT, before the election and made a request which stretched the limits of propriety. 'Peter Abeles told me something concerning Graham which in my judgement precluded him from properly being in that position,' Hawke claimed. He implied that it was a shakedown. Appointing Richardson would risk the government's reputation.[44] Richardson later 'utterly and totally' rejected the allegation.[45] But he accepted that Abeles had it in for him. 'Abeles hated me, so who knows what Abeles said,' Richardson commented.[46]

In any event, Richardson was enraged with Hawke. He felt he was owed the portfolio given his support for Hawke and his work in crafting the environment strategy which helped Labor win a fourth term. Hawke offered Richardson the social security portfolio. Then, he suggested he take the defence portfolio. But

Robert Ray had already been told that he would become defence minister and was not going to shift to accommodate Richardson. And then, now floundering, Hawke suggested Richardson might like a diplomatic appointment as high commissioner to London.

Richardson was furious. 'Nothing in politics, or indeed any facet of my life, has ever made me as angry,' Richardson said. He vowed to seek 'revenge' against Hawke and was now 'completely won over to Keating's side'.[47] Bob Carr, then New South Wales Labor leader, wrote in his diary about a conversation with Laurie Brereton. 'Hawke's split with Richardson,' Carr wrote. 'He dumped him in Social Security which he didn't want. Now, Laurie said, Richardson is of the view Hawke has to go this term.'[48] The consequence of not appointing Richardson to the transport and communications portfolio, Hawke recognised, was that he was 'almost certain' to face a leadership challenge.[49]

Richardson was not the only minister Hawke mismanaged. There was pressure from the New South Wales Right faction to move Ralph Willis on from cabinet. Willis recalled Hawke asking if he wanted to be Australia's high commissioner in London – he promptly declined.[50] Ray was informed that he was going to be finance minister, then social security minister, before he got what he wanted: defence.[51] John Kerin recalled Hawke offering him the defence portfolio at one stage, and also environment.[52]

Meanwhile, there was yet another change in the opposition when Andrew Peacock resigned as Liberal leader. He was philosophical. 'I didn't have this obsession with being prime minister,' Peacock recalled. 'I wanted to do a good job in politics, but being prime minister was not the be all and end all for me like it was for others.' He remained on the front bench and became a backroom powerbroker, but would quit parliament four years later.[53]

John Hewson had been shadow treasurer and performed well during the 1990 election campaign. On 3 April, he succeeded Peacock as Liberal leader. He secured the leadership with sixty-two votes to Peter Reith's thirteen and Alasdair Webster's five in the party-room ballot. Hewson was a very different leader than Howard, Peacock or Fraser. The young, Ferrari-driving economist with four university degrees had risen rapidly through Liberal ranks. He won the seat of Wentworth in 1987, joined the front bench in 1989 and was leader by 1990. He pitched himself as an anti-politician, a straight talker and a reformer. He promised to be a positive politician and to eschew negative campaigning.

—

Labor's fourth term was about 'making history' with an ambitious microeconomic reform agenda, argued Hawke.[54] The changes underway were already revolutionary, such as reducing general tariffs, phasing out agricultural levies, abolishing the two-airlines policy, corporatising business enterprises, reforming the waterfront and shipping industries, and restructuring the award and enterprise bargaining system. This was not a government flagging as it began its eighth year in power. Now Hawke wanted to further energise economic growth, boost productivity and improve competitiveness. This reform push was to be known as 'New Federalism'. Hawke sought a fresh compact between state and federal governments on roles and responsibilities, on areas for cooperation and possibly on revenue and taxation reforms.

The idea came from Mike Codd, secretary of the Department of Prime Minister and Cabinet, who had presented Hawke with a detailed paper after the previous election. The suggested focus for microeconomic reform was education, health and housing. 'The purpose of realigning Commonwealth and State responsibilities would be to seek to simplify government roles and responsibilities and their administration, and thus lead to substantially greater efficiency in the long term for both levels of government,' he had written in 1987.[55] He presented it to Hawke again on 20 April 1990. Codd thought it could be linked to the centenary of federation and include 'sensible constitutional change'.[56] Cabinet endorsed the initiative on 2 June 1990. The strategy agreed was to use 'a mix of fiscal and non-fiscal levers' to encourage the states to embrace microeconomic reform.[57] In a speech at the National Press Club on 19 July, Hawke unveiled the New Federalism proposal.

Hawke had once advocated abolishing the states; now he was seeking to work with them to deliver the greatest change to federal–state relations since World War II. While public servants and ministers worked behind the scenes, Hawke used two Special Premiers' Conferences – in Brisbane on 30–31 October 1990 and in Sydney on 30 July 1991 – to try to secure a landmark agreement. These conferences were successful in leading to a raft of reforms: a national electricity market, uniform food standards, a single-gauge rail system, a national rail freight corporation, national heavy road vehicle regulations, mutual recognition of training qualifications and occupational licensing, and streamlining federal–state environmental assessments.

The first Premiers' Conference was critical to the success of the overall program. 'The only way I thought we could get this through was to actually draft the communiqué before the meeting,' recalled Codd. 'So I took Hawke through it and suggested he pass it around the table at a private dinner with the premiers before the meeting and see if they would agree to it.' Hawke took up Codd's suggestion and reached agreement over dinner. The Council of Australian Governments was born.[58]

Nick Greiner, the New South Wales Liberal premier, admired Hawke for getting the premiers to sit down together. 'Hawke was good at bringing conflicting forces together, at crafting outcomes and working out solutions,' he said. 'I got on well with Hawke because we both saw an opportunity to fix what was wrong with Australian governance, and how the three levels of government overlapped on most things.'[59]

One idea Hawke flagged that did not get off the ground was to give the states a share of income tax. This idea was shelved after a lack of support from premiers and after criticism from Keating, who by then was on the back bench. Hawke wanted to address the vertical fiscal imbalance, and to that end agreement was reached on a review of financial arrangements and taxation powers. This became a matter of conflict between Hawke and Keating. In this maelstrom of competing egos and sabotage, the third Special Premiers' Conference planned for November 1991 was shelved.

Rod Sims, who worked on the New Federalism agenda, said the reforms achieved then, and those that followed, had a long-run positive impact on growth. 'These things unlocked productivity growth in so many sectors,' he said. 'It drove dynamism throughout the economy. It also brought Commonwealth public servants together with state public servants in ways they had not before.'[60] The New Federalism agenda laid the building blocks for the National Competition Policy reforms, which turbocharged productivity and competitiveness in the 1990s and 2000s.

In the lead-up to the 1990 election, Hawke pledged to establish a national program for the early detection of breast cancer. Wendy Fatin, who became the minister assisting the prime minister for the status of women after the election, appealed to Hawke to fund an initiative that would enable women to be diagnosed via mobile vans. 'It was becoming difficult to get this on the cabinet agenda because it was going to cost money and there was bureaucratic resistance,' recalled Fatin. She organised to see Hawke alone, without officials or advisers, and outlined the initiative. 'You reckon it would be a good idea, do you?' he asked. Fatin answered Hawke's questions about how it would work, who would run it and how much it would cost. She encouraged him to think about his mother, wife and daughters. 'Yes, we'll do it,' he said. Fatin said it showed that Hawke could be persuaded if an idea both satisfied a sound policy objective and was good politically.[61]

There was more to do on microeconomic reform. On 12 March 1991, Hawke delivered the landmark *Building a Competitive Australia* statement to parliament. This marked the death knell for Australian protectionism. It outlined a second round of tariff cuts, the first round being in the 1988 May statement, to a general level of 5 per cent by 1996. The government was to push further on industry deregulation and privatisation, including the sale of Australian Airlines and the part-privatisation of Qantas. Wholesale sales taxes for business would be cut, depreciation of assets would be simplified, research and development would be prioritised via Cooperative Research Centres, and training and apprenticeships would be overhauled. It was about making Australia the 'clever country', Hawke said.

Hawke had taken the lead in developing the statement with Keating and Button. In presenting it to parliament, he appealed to higher principles, arguing that it was a nation-building plan in which every citizen had a stake. 'These measures continue and intensify the far-reaching reforms my government has initiated over the past eight years,' he said. 'Ultimately, they sharpen our ability to reduce the current account deficit and stabilise foreign debt. I emphasise that they share one overriding objective: building a competitive Australia.' He tried to strip the statement of economic jargon. 'I want all my fellow Australians to understand where the nation is moving and to understand how all of us workers, employers and government have complementary roles to play in achieving our common goals. I say it again: in the final analysis the challenges ahead demand the involvement of all Australians.'[62]

The most spirited debate in cabinet over microeconomic reform had taken place six months earlier, between Keating and Beazley over the future of Australia's telecommunications sector. In the end, cabinet essentially backed Beazley's plan for limited competition in a duopoly structure: merging Telecom with the Overseas Telecommunications Commission (OTC) – renamed Telstra in 1994 – which would then compete for local telephony services against a new entrant, which eventually became Optus. Keating advocated a more competitive structure whereby Telecom would compete with several companies for general phone services.

The final policy was signed off by cabinet on 10 September 1990.[63] However, debate was vigorous, often bitter, and ranged from the cabinet room to the caucus and even public forums. Hawke, as was his style, let the debate play out for months. At the final meeting, Keating lost it. He gathered up his papers, threw a pencil on the table and stormed out. 'This is a fucking second-rate decision from a second-rate government,' he said.[64] Robert Ray gave Keating both barrels. 'Take your bat and ball and go home, you little bastard,' he said.[65] It was Keating's most significant defeat on policy since the taxation summit. His anger made some ministers, including Richardson, question whether he had the temperament to be prime minister.[66]

As in 1984, 1986 and 1988, the Left faction were determined to torpedo an important cabinet decision on economic reform. On 24 September 1990, a special national conference of the Labor Party was held in Canberra. Hawke said the conference was about whether 'this party and this government can maintain its relevance to the needs of the Australian people'. Again, the debate came down to what the party stood for. 'This conference is not a conference about ends,' Hawke said. 'It is a conference about means.' Market competition was not antithetical to Labor tradition but firmly within it, he said. A competitive industry would deliver Labor's goal of improving the lives of everyday Australians.[67]

The Left supported the Telecom/OTC merger but wanted the entity to remain in government ownership, with no competition for phone services. The key motion was defeated by fifty-eight votes to forty-three. The Left also opposed the privatisation of 49 per cent of Qantas and 100 per cent of Australian Airlines. The rebel faction wanted Qantas and Australian Airlines to merge and remain in public ownership. This motion was rejected by sixty votes to thirty-nine. These votes were worryingly close – a shift of a dozen delegates would have spelled defeat for the government. Again, the alliance between the Right and Centre Left prevailed.

The 1980s witnessed significant changes in Australia's immigration program. Chris Hurford, who became minister for immigration after the 1984 election, encouraged skilled migration. His aim was to make 'settlement easier and achieving social harmony for those already here and those arriving', he recalled.[68] Robert Ray, as minister for immigration, continued this emphasis but made further changes to the policy framework, emphasising skilled migrants over family reunions. Ray made a landmark change with the *Migration Amendment Act 1989*, effectively ending the process of lobbying by MPs to support family reunion claims backed by influential ethnic groups. Immigration policy would now be mostly based on regulations rather than on ministerial discretion.

Immigration and multiculturalism became hot-button political issues in the 1980s. The post-war immigration program was one of the reasons Hawke had joined the Labor Party. He had a passionate commitment to multiculturalism. In 1988, John Howard called for Asian immigration to be 'slowed down a little'. Hawke took Howard head on in a spirited parliamentary debate. A motion was moved supporting Australia's immigration policy. In Hawke's speech he highlighted the political unity that had underpinned the migration program. It was a policy which expressed a 'triumph of compassion over prejudice, of reason over fear, and of statesmanship over politics', he argued. The motion was carried eighty-one votes to fifty-three. Three of Howard's Liberal Party colleagues crossed the floor to vote with the government, including former immigration minister Ian Macphee and a future immigration minister, Philip Ruddock. In the Senate, Peter Baume crossed the floor to vote with the government.[69]

Gerry Hand, who became minister for immigration after the 1990 election, continued the focus on attracting young skilled migrants to Australia. However, schemes such as the English Language Intensive Courses for Overseas Students (ELICOS) and the Business Migration Program (BMP) were riddled with fraudulent claims, and the government struggled to maintain the integrity of the overall immigration program.[70] While extending visas to Chinese nationals living in Australia after the Tiananmen Square massacre showed flexibility and humanity in the government's policy settings, Hand became increasingly concerned about the number of illegal, or unauthorised, refugees, which threatened the integrity of Australia's borders. The number of refugees arriving by boat increased from twenty-six in 1989 to 198 in 1990, and to 214 in 1991. Moreover, these refugees were deemed to have taken the places of those waiting in refugee camps abroad for their asylum claims to be assessed.

Using his ministerial powers over discretionary detention for illegal refugees, Hand established a refugee processing centre at Port Hedland, Western Australia, in 1991. The government was moving towards a formal system of detaining unauthorised arrivals for processing before they were settled in the community or deported. 'It was the right thing to do,' Hand reflected. 'We found people were claiming to have come from parts of the globe and they were not from there at all.' In 1992, the Keating government introduced mandatory detention for all illegal immigrants. Yet the Hawke/Keating policies were 'never intended to keep people in detention for indefinite periods', Hand insisted.[71]

Hawke wanted to make improving the lives of Aboriginal and Torres Strait Islander peoples a focus of his government. There were important initiatives during these years. In October 1984, Uluru (Ayers Rock) was handed back to its traditional owners. In August 1987, the Royal Commission into Aboriginal Deaths in Custody was established. In March 1990, the Aboriginal and Torres Strait Islander Commission (ATSIC) replaced the Department of Aboriginal Affairs and the Aboriginal Development Commission. The concept was designed to give Indigenous Australians a voice in decision-making, with the involvement of regional councils and a board of commissioners led initially by Lowitja O'Donoghue. In September 1991, the Council for Aboriginal Reconciliation was formed, with Patrick Dodson as the first chairperson. But these initiatives fell well short of what Labor hoped to deliver for the First Australians.

In the early years of the government, Hawke pledged that land rights for Aboriginal and Torres Strait Islander peoples would ensure that sacred sites were protected, that mining could be prohibited on certain lands, and that royalties and compensation would be payable. But facing opposition from Brian Burke's West Australian Labor government and the mining industry, land rights were shelved. On 19 October 1984, during the election campaign, Hawke said his government would not override Burke's state legislation, which limited native title rights to Crown land that was not designated for any public purpose.

Dodson was director of the Central Land Council when Hawke promised to deliver national land rights. He had met Hawke when he was ACTU president during the Noonkanbah dispute. 'He had an interest in Aboriginal people, but I don't know if he fully understood us at that point or whether he came to fully understand us, but he was at least open to a decent and respectful discussion,' Dodson recalled. He, like other Indigenous leaders, saw the retreat on land rights as 'a cop out to Burke' and the mining industry in Western Australia. 'It was a huge setback to the demand for land rights justice,' Dodson said.[72]

Aboriginal affairs minister Clyde Holding developed a national model for land rights, with no right of veto over mining, but by mid-1985 it had run into opposition from the states, the mining industry and Indigenous groups. The federal government preferred the states to develop land rights legislation based on the national model, rather than take the lead and implement laws that would override those of the states. Gerry Hand became minister for Aboriginal affairs after the 1987 election. 'I was extremely disappointed about land rights,' he recalled. 'The party let the Aboriginal community down. I doubt whether they will ever forgive us for it.'[73]

On 12 June 1988, Hawke and Hand travelled to the Northern Territory to participate in a celebration of Indigenous culture and heritage at Barunga. Thousands of Indigenous Australians from all over Australia attended. Hawke promised a 'treaty' or 'compact' to advance reconciliation. 'We thought it was marvellous,' recalled Dodson.[74] But, again, hopes were dashed, and it never eventuated.

On his last day as prime minister, 20 December 1991, Hawke spoke at the unveiling of the Barunga Statement – a message-painting with panels surrounding a petition calling for self-determination and respect for their identity – at Parliament House. Through tears, Hawke expressed his regret that more had not been done, but said the statement 'symbolised the commitment of the Hawke government to the Indigenous people of Australia'. Galarrwuy Yunupingu said that Hawke's task, in keeping with Indigenous tradition, was to pass it on to a new leader who, in turn, would pass it on again.[75] It was a fitting statement.

Hawke's adviser, Simon Balderstone, watched the outgoing prime minister deliver the speech. 'He was emotional and deflated,' Balderstone recalled. 'Here was a bloke on the prime ministerial deathbed. He was resilient and stoic, and said this was important and we had to get it done.'[76] But it was too much for Charles Perkins, the former head of the Department of Aboriginal Affairs, who was appalled.[77] 'I thought to myself, "What a sad scene for Aboriginal affairs,"' he recalled. 'Here's the prime minister crying over what he should have done or could have done in Aboriginal affairs and didn't do it. It was only his fault. He was the prime minister.'[78]

Hawke was better placed to advance Indigenous land rights than any prime minister before him. He had authority within government, was respected by Indigenous leaders and popular with voters. Hawke was a master communicator, but he failed to use these skills towards a cause which he empathised with and knew was right. 'There was one person who could have pulled it off and that was him,' Hand said.[79] 'He was a great orator, very influential, very popular,' reflected Dodson. 'He could have achieved what he had set out to if he had a clear vision and commitment to what Aboriginal people were telling him they wanted to see done.'[80]

Failing to deliver national land rights was one of Hawke's regrets. 'While we got up a model which said this is the way we should go, we were not able to get agreement because in Western

Australia they found it to be a very difficult political issue that was being used against them by conservatives,' Hawke said. 'While every government, looking back, could have done more than it did, including my government, I am still proud of what we did do.'[81]

—

Through 1990, Treasury was advising the government there would be a 'strong pick-up' in growth by midyear. Keating was not so confident. 'My own view is that the slowdown will be longer and deeper than suggested by the forecasts,' he advised cabinet on 11 May 1990.[82] A few months later, on 21 August 1990, he presented the budget with a forecast surplus of $8.1 billion, with outlays and revenue as a proportion of GDP continuing to fall. The government would reap $1 billion by curbing middle-class welfare via an assets test for family welfare payments, and stricter eligibility requirements for pensions, unemployment and student benefits.

Ralph Willis, the minister for finance, was also concerned about the economy and felt Treasury failed to see the danger signs. 'The economy seemed to be going okay, according to the figures, but we were hearing and seeing different things in our electorates,' he recalled. 'I became more worried about it as the year went on. John Fraser, the deputy secretary of the Treasury, came to see me and said everything is fine. We were told not to worry about a recession.'[83]

Meanwhile, the State Bank of Victoria was on the brink of collapse. It was the fifth-largest bank in Australia, with $25 billion held in deposits. It had made several bad financial decisions, including buying into Tricontinental Bank to give it a merchant arm. Cabinet approved Keating's proposal for the Commonwealth Bank to take it over with a bid of $1.6 billion on 23 August. As the Victorian government was unable to inject capital into the bank, there was no other option but for the Commonwealth Bank to step in. The future of the State Bank led to considerable debate in cabinet and in caucus, with Keating and Hawke having to reassure the party that the decision was in the best interests of the country.[84]

On 29 November 1990, the government's worst fears were realised: Australia was in recession. In the June quarter, growth declined by 0.4 per cent. In the September quarter, growth declined by 1.6 per cent. This met the technical definition of a recession: two consecutive quarters of negative growth. There had been no soft landing; the economy had fallen through the floor. Keating presented the grim news at a press conference. 'The national accounts do show that Australia is in a recession,' he said. 'The most important thing about that is that this is a recession that Australia had to have.' These words would haunt Keating for the rest of his life. They implied that the government had tried to engineer the recession. He tried to explain that high interest rates had undermined exports and production, which had induced the recession. But his phrase was a major error of judgement, devoid of empathy for those who had lost their jobs, homes and businesses.

Keating later claimed that Hawke was consulted about the form of words he used, and that he had not protested. Two of Keating's staff – Don Russell (principal private secretary) and Mark Ryan (press secretary) – had run the statement by Hawke. 'It was in a press release,' Ryan recalled. 'Russell and I walked it around to the prime minister's office, and Hawkey looked at it and gave it his tick of approval.'[85] Hawke said this was completely false. 'Any claim that I was consulted about that phrase beforehand is an absolute lie,' he said.[86] Hawke and Keating accepted that policy settings had been defective through 1988–90, and regretted the recession, but added that they were guided by Treasury and the Reserve Bank, which had also misread the economy.

The recession, along with high interest rates, blighted the economic record of the Hawke government. Australia's recession was replicated in almost all the major OECD countries during the period. There had also been recessions during the Menzies, McMahon, Whitlam and Fraser governments. While the Hawke/Keating recession was the longest, the Fraser/Howard recession was the deepest. Interest rates reached 18 per cent in November 1989, but they had reached 21.4 per cent in April 1982, during the Fraser government, and 23 per cent in May 1974, under the Whitlam government. By 1990, however, none of this mattered to voters who had borne the brunt of the most significant economic transformation in Australian history and now had to endure a recession. The benefits of the economic changes would be felt in the long-term, not the short-term.

—

On 9 December 1989, Hawke turned sixty. Bob and Hazel had a joint sixtieth birthday party at the Lodge, inviting several ministerial colleagues, staff, old friends and family, including Susan, Rosslyn and Stephen and their children. It was a happy time.

Bob and Hazel, who had been very worried about their children when they were in their teens and twenties, recognised that 'things seem to be working out for them', even if they had 'done it their way'. They were delighted that Ros was healthier and happier, and was living in Canberra with her two boys. They were proud of Stephen's book, *Noonkanbah: Whose Land, Whose Law*, published that year. Hazel would spend several weeks every year with Stephen and Lesley and their boys in Derby. Bob and Hazel enjoyed seeing Susan and her two children when in Sydney.

The end of the decade marked a transformation for the Hawke family. Bob and Hazel told *The Australian Women's Weekly* that they had never been happier. In a rare joint interview, Bob acknowledged that Hazel had pulled him back from the depths of despair five years earlier, when he had to be talked out of resigning after Rosslyn's drug addiction became public. He was depressed and overwhelmed by personal and public pressures, but now he looked forward to more years as prime minister. [87]

Bob and Hazel were doting grandparents to six children aged between seven and two: Kel and Sam in Western Australia, David and Paul in Canberra, and Sophie and Ben in Sydney. To the six they were known as Pop and Nana. Hawke reflected on being a father and grandfather for *New Idea* in July 1987. 'I'm a better grandfather than I was a father,' he acknowledged. 'I know what mine missed through my not being available. I should have, at times, made more effort about it, even though I was desperately busy a lot of the time.'[88]

Hazel, meanwhile, was continuing to use her voice to raise awareness of women's rights, poverty and Indigenous issues. She supported charitable organisations such as Ted Noff's Life Education Centres. In 1988, to mark the Bicentenary, she led the Sydney

Symphony Orchestra on a ten-day tour of the United States. It was a triumph. Hazel also took to the stage to play piano to support the arts and young performers. In March 1989, she had a well-publicised facelift. She was happy to talk about how women should not be afraid to do whatever made them happier as they got older. In February 1990, journalist Glenn Milne said Hazel was 'a rolled gold asset' for Hawke. 'If Hazel has stuck by him, the rationale goes, there must be some good in him.'[89]

In June 1991, Bob and Hazel purchased a three-bedroom home perched on a hill at Northbridge, in Sydney, overlooking the harbour. They paid $1.23 million and planned a renovation. The family home in Sandringham had been sold for $430,000 in 1986. The Hawkes also owned a four-bedroom home in Deakin, Canberra, which had been purchased in 1987. It was now where Rosslyn lived with her two sons. It was put up for sale when the Northbridge home was purchased. Hazel expected the next phase of their lives together, after the prime ministership, would be a continuation of the happiness they had rediscovered.

28

THE VIEW FROM
YARRALUMLA

The opening of the new Parliament House on Capital Hill on
9 May 1988 marked the end of an era in Australian politics.
Old Parliament House, opened in May 1927, was only meant to
be temporary. Its crowded conditions and rundown edifice meant
a new building was in the planning since the 1970s. New Parliament House was a mammoth project. It was plagued with delays,
disputes with contractors and unions, and cost overruns through
the 1980s. On 7 November 1988, after the building had been
occupied, cabinet was informed that the budget had blown out to
$904.36 million.[1] The cost would continue to rise, and would ulti-
mately exceed $1 billion. Malcolm Fraser, the prime minister who
approved the design and construction, later said it was one of his
greatest regrets. He saw the new building as too grand and extravagant, and lamented that it changed the character of politics, which
became more tribal as politicians became more isolated from each
other and from citizens.

Bob Hawke had spent eight years in Old Parliament House,
including five as prime minister. He was thrilled when he moved
into the larger and more modern prime ministerial office. 'There
was just so much bullshit talked about how terrible it was that we
were moving from the old place,' Hawke recalled. 'The working
conditions in that Old Parliament House would not have passed
the conditions of the *Factories and Shops Act* in any state. The
working conditions were appalling. As far as I was concerned it
could not happen quickly enough.'[2]

The geography of power changed in the new prime ministerial suite. While Sandy Hollway had been in the office next door to Hawke, he was now located across the corridor, near the entrance to the suite. The overall office was much larger, with a rabbit-warren of corridors leading to smaller offices with an open-plan area and media room in the rear. Hawke walked around the office less and saw his staff less often, simply because of the size. Instead of being monitored via a peephole, there was now a closed-circuit television camera, which was accessible from Hollway's office. Hawke's office was fitted out with custom-made furniture and a private bathroom. He now arrived by car at the rear of the building and was driven into a courtyard that would be used for visiting dignitaries and media conferences.

Hollway thought the new suite was a huge improvement. 'I regarded Old Parliament House as a cluttered relic,' he said. 'It was inimical to the good reign of government. The old office was crowded and noisy. Advisers could now have quiet time if they needed it. There was somewhere to go for a meeting. They could focus on their jobs with more space and uninterrupted time. I thought it made a big difference.'[3]

In his speech on 9 May at the opening of the new Parliament House, Hawke said the building stood as 'an enduring statement of our nation's profound commitment to the principles and practices of democratic government'. He had laid the foundation stone for the building on 4 October 1983. Queen Elizabeth II formally opened Parliament House, ahead of the House of Representatives and the Senate meeting in the new building for the first time in August 1988. Her father, the Duke of York (later King George VI), had opened Old Parliament House on 9 May 1927.

Hawke admired the Queen. 'She had a marvellous commitment to the Commonwealth,' he recalled. 'There were fifty-one members of the Commonwealth then and you could talk to her in detail about the politics and economics of any member country.'[4] Sir William Heseltine, the Queen's private secretary, noted that Hawke was the eighth Australian prime minister with whom she had dealt as monarch. 'They got on well together and had a common interest in horse racing,' he said. 'Hawke was a republican, but he did not let that affect the very proper relationship.'[5]

The Queen's vice-regal representative was Sir Ninian Stephen, who had been governor-general since July 1982. He had previously served on the High Court. Hawke and Stephen respected one another, but it was not an especially close or confiding relationship on government matters. Hawke was more often a visitor to Government House for official functions, such as lunches and dinners, and for the swearing-in of ministers, than he was for talks with Stephen.

Hawke reflected fondly on Stephen. 'I could not have asked for a better appointment to be made by my predecessor,' he said. 'There was the formal part of the job, but we also developed a personal friendship.' Stephen invited the Hawkes to dine at Government House shortly after the March 1983 election. Hawke recalled asking Stephen why he had accepted the job of governor-general. 'Well, I never really liked the law that much,' he replied.[6] Hawke extended Stephen's tenure through the Bicentennial year, 1988, so he could host the five royal tours that were to take place. He then appointed him as Australia's ambassador for the environment, with a roving international brief.

Stephen wrote to Hawke about his overseas trips, his meetings with other heads of state, and his assessment of events and issues. On 9 March 1989, having retired, Stephen wrote a final letter to Hawke. 'I wanted to say how much I have appreciated our relationship,' he said. 'During my years as Governor-General, with you as prime minister, I believe that the role of Governor-General did undergo changes, all of them, I thought, for the better and none of which would have happened without your support and goodwill.'[7]

———

A few months after Hawke moved into his new office in Parliament House, there was a new occupant at Government House: Bill Hayden. The former Labor leader had raised the appointment with Hawke in early 1987. Hawke recalled the discussion as 'an emotional moment' with Hayden, as tears welled in their eyes and they warmly embraced one another. 'My family have the view that I've been judged not worthy of high office,' Hawke remembered Hayden telling him. 'The one thing that would fix that is if I was appointed governor-general.' Hawke immediately said: 'You've got it.' The appointment was widely interpreted as a healing of past political wounds, but Hawke did not entirely see it that way. 'He had done a good job as foreign minister,' Hawke said. 'It pleased me that I was able to make him happy.'[8]

Hayden said the meeting was 'relaxed' and 'good-humoured', and recalled the conversation a little differently. He said the appointment was because his hearing was 'deteriorating' and, recognising that his career in politics had 'peaked' as minister for foreign affairs, he still wished to contribute to public life. 'Bob was quite receptive to the suggestion by me that I become governor-general,' he said. 'I don't recall any emotionalism on either Bob's or my part.'[9] Hayden did add, though, that he wanted his wife and daughters to 'feel some pride' in his life of public service, and becoming governor-general would achieve that.[10]

John Howard, the opposition leader, opposed Hayden's appointment as governor-general. He said it was wrong for a republican to be appointed to the vice-regal post, and questioned Hawke's motivations. 'It's no more than a massive attempt by the prime minister to wipe some blood off his hands on to the carpet of Yarralumla,' Howard said.[11] When Hawke privately broached the Hayden appointment with Howard in June 1988, he replied that Hayden was totally unacceptable.[12]

Hawke discussed Hayden's appointment with Heseltine during the royal visit. The Queen's private secretary made this entry in his diary, revealing the political sensitivity of the appointment was a consideration for Buckingham Palace:

> He told me, without too much beating about the bush, that he was intending to appoint H., - & asked if this wd. cause any difficulty to HM. I said there were only 2 difficulties we were worried about – an apptmt which wd. not be acceptable to Oppn, wh wd cause such a political furore as to bring the post into disrepute – or a person being apptd who by virtue of his views or reputation as an aggressive republican wd. cause embarrassment to the Q personally, & who wd. again bring the office into disrepute. He said I wd. know he himself believed Aust wd. ultimately become a republic but it was not a live issue – Hayden

similarly – but I cd. give his personal assurance to Q he wd. never appoint anyone whose apptmt wd. embarrass her, or bring the office into disrepute. He had too much affection, admiration & respect for her ever to do that. His relationship to Hayden was much warmer & closer since the unfortunate events of 83 & he was confident that Hayden as GG wd. never do anything to embarrass Q. There were plenty of precedents for a political apptmt & he wasn't going to be dictated to in this matter by the Oppn who were 'cretins'. They thought they had a hereditary right to govern, but they hadn't the capacity to do so.[13]

Hayden was officially endorsed as governor-general by the full ministry on 17 August 1988.[14] The appointment would take effect on 15 February 1989. Hayden would serve seven years in the role, through two prime ministers, making him the longest-serving governor-general since Lord Gowrie, who retired in January 1945.

Heseltine thought Hayden was a fine governor-general. 'Hawke got it right about Hayden, who after a few months in the office seemed to have adopted the role of convinced monarchist, and wrote quite frequent reports to Her Majesty of activity in the "Canberra Bubble", on which he was of course a great authority,' he recalled.[15]

Such letters are not unusual or improper, yet they are a relic of a bygone age. Modern governors-general do not write letters that ruminate so extensively on political events. Hayden said the Queen and the royal household had never sought to interfere in Australian politics, but welcomed being kept informed of political events and personalities.[16] Hayden's 'periodic reports to the Queen', as he termed them, are revealed here for the first time.[17]

—

Bill Hayden wrote his first letter to Queen Elizabeth II on 6 October 1989. These letters were invariably addressed to 'Your Majesty, Madam' and signed off in this manner: 'I have the honour to remain, Madam, your Majesty's most obedient, humble, servant, Bill Hayden'. In his first eight-page letter, he surveyed the political scene and the state of the economy. He thought the Hawke government faced 'a very real prospect' of 'being defeated' at the

next election. While his 'political instincts and experience' led him
to believe the government was facing 'an electoral disaster', the
polls seesawed, which showed the government was 'still in the race
with a fighting chance'. The biggest thing going for the government was the opposition. 'Andrew Peacock, according to the polls
is lacking gravitas,' Hayden told the Queen. He described the
opposition as 'disorganised', 'confused' and in 'conflict'. Peacock
was often upstaged by Howard. And the 'bright star' emerging in
opposition ranks was John Hewson.

The most perceptive aspect of this letter was Hayden's assessment of Hawke and his still considerable electoral appeal:

> The prime minister maintains his extraordinary popularity
> with the general public. This popularity defies reasoned
> understanding. The prime minister is not a good parliamentary
> performer, he rigorously eschews any use of subtlety or
> understatement in debate. He had a crackly Australian accent,
> loves the popular sports of ordinary people and evidences no
> interest in the finer qualities of modern lifestyle. For all of that
> the people love him.

Hayden recounted watching 'almost in disbelief' the television
news, which showed Hawke visiting a shopping centre in Sydney.
'He was being literally mobbed by hundreds of "mums" most of
whom seemed to be in their mid-20s to late 30s-early 40s. Many of
them were holding infants aloft – youngsters too small to comprehend what was going on – to see the great man.' Hawke's 'great
skill', Hayden told the Queen, was that he could communicate
with 'ordinary' people who trusted him. He said treasurer Paul
Keating and finance minister Peter Walsh, who were both 'unpopular' with voters, were nevertheless 'the two great strengths and
lynchpins of the government'.

The economy, though, was 'overheated', and the government
was 'desperate' to dampen demand. In a lengthy analysis, Hayden
explained the government was using a mix of policy levers to try
to avoid the economy 'skidding along towards a crash landing'. He
was concerned about voters resenting wage restraint while seeing
the privileged flaunt their wealth. On the bright side, Hayden
said, employment had grown strongly, industrial relations were

more harmonious than at any time since the end of World War II, and there was a great deal of 'community cohesion' behind the government's direction. He also noted that social welfare benefits were now much better targeted towards those in need, and middle-class welfare had been reduced.[18]

Heseltine replied on the Queen's behalf on 23 October. She was 'most grateful' to receive the letter. 'Her Majesty follows developments in Australia, both political and economic, with the closest attention,' he wrote. Heseltine noted that when Hawke had met the Queen in June, he was tight-lipped about any election plans. The economy, he said, must be 'a considerable worry' in this context. There were economic challenges in Britain, too. As an aside, he noted that 'Thatcherism' was no longer 'universally recognised as the success which it was a year or so ago'.[19]

Hayden's next letter focused, extraordinarily, on corruption and criminality in several state governments, and offered an assessment of the politics around Australia. 'Scarcely a week goes by without some new disclosure of official corruption,' he lamented to the Queen, in politics, the courts and policing. 'In this culture, ethics are a hindrance,' Hayden wrote. 'In it everything has a price and can be bought, including favours. The smart operators prosper, only mugs get caught.' He reported conversations with business leaders who were cautiously optimistic about the economy. He argued that the major parties should be talking more about their values and visions for the future. In the Liberals, there were calls to heed how Robert Menzies 'gave philosophical meaning' to what the party stood for. In Labor, there was 'growing disquiet' about 'the retreat from ideals'.[20]

Australia went to the polls on 24 March 1990. Hayden told the Queen that he expected the Hawke government to be defeated. He was wrong, and acknowledged this in a further letter to the Queen on 10 April, explaining that he thought high interest rates would doom the government. He judged Labor's campaign as 'lacklustre', but assessed the Liberal campaign to be 'awful', while the Nationals were 'invisible'. He noted the impact of Green preferences going to Labor. He thought Labor's new team of ministers were of varying quality, and reported the election of new Liberal leader John Hewson, his deputy, Peter Reith, and the new Nationals leader Tim Fischer.[21]

Hayden's predictive powers may have been redeemed in a remarkable letter he wrote to the Queen on 25 July, when he prophesied that Keating would challenge Hawke for the leadership:

> There is a movement underway, masterminded by Senator Graham Richardson of NSW, to have Prime Minister Hawke replaced by Mr Keating before the next election, and on his hopeful timetable, sometime before the end of next calendar year. I should record here that Senator Richardson has a strong track record for 'getting the numbers up' when he decides to 'king make'.

In a wry aside, Hayden added: 'Prime Minister Hawke's ascendancy to the leadership of the Labor Party in 1983 owes much to Senator Richardson's organising drive, although the unspectacular performance of the then leader of that party would have assisted Senator Richardson.'

Hayden was, however, 'sceptical' about this 'grand strategy'. He concluded this part of his dispatch with another self-deprecating aside: 'On the other hand, I seem to recall being sceptical several years ago when Senator, then plain Mr Richardson, advised me he was going to "roll" the then Labor Leader of the Opposition. I could be wrong again, but if so, not so painfully wrong as last time.' Hayden was enjoying these letters rather too much.[22]

On 19 August 1990, David Smith, the governor-general's official secretary, was made a Knight Commander in the Royal Victorian Order by the Queen at Balmoral Castle. It was a fortnight before his retirement. Hawke was furious. He opposed knighthoods being awarded to Australians and had abolished them from the Order of Australia in 1986. Heseltine wrote to Hayden about Smith's impending retirement on 12 January 1990. He noted that Smith had been very much respected at Buckingham Palace for his service to successive governors-general and to the monarchy.

Heseltine told Hayden that Hawke was 'sounded out' about bestowing a knighthood on Smith within the Queen's personal order as a 'mark of esteem and gratitude'; the prime minister was not supportive. Heseltine had spoken to Mike Codd, the head of Hawke's department, who made this view known. Heseltine wondered if Hawke's view might change if it were made at the time of Smith's retirement. 'You could remind him that this Order is in The Queen's personal gift and no recommendation from him is required,' Heseltine wrote to Hayden.[23]

Hayden replied on 15 February giving his support to the idea, saying the knighthood would be 'richly deserved'. He noted his general disapproval of imperial honours, but this was a personal award of the Queen. He would raise it with Hawke but suggested waiting until after the election.[24] On 18 April, Hayden reported to Heseltine that Hawke had gone from 'distinctly unenthusiastic' to now being 'totally opposed'. Hawke was, however, supportive of the suggestion that Smith be made a Companion of the Order of Australia.[25] But it had been decided. The Queen and Hayden agreed that Smith would be bestowed the KCVO.

The vast social, economic and environmental policy changes taking place in Australia were reflected in the correspondence. Hayden was distressed by those Australians who had lost their savings when building societies had gone bust. He worried about rural communities impacted by commodity price falls and farm failures. He was concerned about urban Australia thrashing about in a 'sea of political discontent' as the economy headed for a 'hard' landing. He fretted about high levels of unskilled migration under family reunion programs, the ability of communities to absorb so many people and the tendency of some ethnic groups not to integrate into a truly multicultural Australia. Hayden also wrote about tensions between 'noisy advocates' of green causes and their 'demands on the community'.[26]

In a reply to Hayden's bleak letters, Robert Fellowes – who had succeeded Heseltine as private secretary – said the Queen found them 'interesting and comprehensive', even though they did not always make for 'cheerful reading'. On 20 November, Fellowes said the diagnosis of problems in Australia were mirrored in the United Kingdom. 'Here we have disaffected farmers, government in disarray, and what promises to be a deep recession, although probably not as deep as yours,' he wrote.[27]

By the new year, the view from Yarralumla continued to be miserable. On 5 March 1991, Hayden wrote to the Queen about the continued deterioration of the economy. For Hawke, there had been a reprieve in his personal standing in the polls due to the Gulf War. Hayden noted that Hewson had more support in the polls than Hawke, but there were voter doubts about his 'half-baked' policy ideas. The good news was that Australia had beaten England in the Ashes cricket series.[28]

In June, Hayden reported that Keating had indeed challenged Hawke's leadership. He argued the disclosure of the Kirribilli Agreement had damaged Hawke. 'The prime minister lied to the Parliament and to the community by denying that he intended to stand down in favour of Keating,' Hayden wrote. He reported that aides were looking at 'face saving' ways for Hawke to quit, while Keating awaited a move to 'draft him into the leadership' from the backbench.[29]

At Labor's national conference in June 1991, the party carried a resolution to support Australia becoming a republic. On 8 July, Hayden informed the Queen. He included opinion polls, which showed support for a republic increasing. He noted that the Australian Republican Movement had been formed in Sydney. Hayden had spoken to one of the conveners, Donald Horne, who wanted him to reassure the Queen that 'no disrespect' was intended. Hayden judged the republic to be 'a low priority for most people'.[30] Fellowes responded on 23 July, noting that they were aware of the publicity around the republic issue and 'it is quite clear that The Queen and her family must nurture their links with Australia'. She would welcome 'suggestions' about 'future moves'.[31]

On 13 September, Hayden advised the Queen that Hawke thought Keating's challenge was 'stagnating'.[32] But on 19 December, Keating defeated Hawke in a second leadership ballot. Hayden wrote to the Queen on 24 December. Keating, he wrote, had been 'relentlessly stalking' Hawke and had 'finally pounced on his quarry'. Hayden thought what finished Hawke was his failure to tear apart Hewson's *Fightback!* manifesto. Furthermore, the economic recovery never came. John Kerin, as treasurer, was not an effective replacement for Keating. And the media was strongly against Hawke continuing as prime minister.[33]

—

Bill Hayden's autobiography, published in April 1996, provided frank assessments and interesting observations about Hawke. One involved being summoned to Hawke's suite at the Wrest Point

Hotel Casino in Hobart during Labor's national conference in 1988. The door opened and Hawke stood there 'stark naked':

> He was briskly rubbing his back with a towel held by one hand high above his shoulders and the other somewhere near his waist. He had evidently just showered. He looked reasonably fit, springing into the room with all of the bounce and confidence of a boxer from one of the lighter weight divisions. I suspected he harboured visions of himself as a Greek god, I saw only an extroverted quinquagenarian flasher. While his important appendage was dingling and dangling as he moved, I kept a straight face, trying to ignore the entertaining idiocy of the act, and talked about my recent trip; he meanwhile settled back, indolently, on a long sofa to listen. As I talked, I couldn't help thinking how far from impressive were the dimensions of the apparatus which he displayed with such evident pride and satisfaction and him supposed to be such a lady-killer.[34]

Hayden's less than flattering assessment of Hawke's penis led to a confrontation between the two men at a function in Parliament House shortly after the book was published. 'Hawke was sauntering up the aisles between the tables,' Hayden recalled. 'He came over and gave me a punch in the solar plexus and I fell back in my chair. The people around me fell into laughter, thinking it was a joke.' But Hayden was startled and thought about hitting him back. Hawke leaned in and said, 'What you wrote about me coming out of the bathroom at the conference in Hobart was dreadful, cheap and nasty. If you say that again you will be hearing from my lawyer.'

Hayden was perplexed. 'I didn't know that the size of his dick was that important to him,' he reflected. 'In my old job, I would have nabbed him for flashing.' As Bill and Dallas left the Great Hall, they spotted Blanche d'Alpuget. 'What's wrong with Bob today?' Hayden asked. 'He punched me in the tummy.' She replied, 'Oh it was just a playful push.' The Haydens went to their car. 'I had not realised that in writing those words,' Hayden recalled, 'I had, metaphorically, hit Hawke where it hurts.'[35]

29

HAWKE
AT WAR

On 25 April 1990, Bob Hawke stood on the shores of Gallipoli and paid tribute to the Australians who had fought and died there. Exactly seventy-five years earlier, in the pre-dawn hours, Australian soldiers had run ashore on the rocky sands and scaled the craggy cliffs. Anzac Day had long been vested with significance for Australians. The anniversary elevated it to a higher level. Hawke understood that most Australians had parents and grandparents, aunties and uncles, brothers and sisters, sons and daughters who had served in one or more of the many conflicts in which Australians had fought since before Federation. Anzac Day spoke to the values that defined what it meant to be Australian: courage in adversity, mateship and community, service and responsibility. It was the first time that an Australian prime minister had been to Gallipoli since the end of World War I. Veterans joined Hawke for the special journey. Hawke also invited opposition leader John Hewson to join him.

Margaret Thatcher also participated in the commemorations. Hawke had asked her several times to come and was delighted when she did. Bernard Ingham, Thatcher's press secretary, thought it was the high point of their personal relations. 'They did get on well,' he said. 'I particularly remember the visit to Gallipoli and the Dardanelles for the seventy-fifth Anzac anniversary, and they got on extremely well. I would add that they got on well when they decided not to discuss South Africa.'[1]

Hawke gave two speeches on the anniversary. 'Because of

the courage with which they fought, because of their devotion to duty and their comradeship, because of their ingenuity, their good humour and their endurance, because these hills rang with their voices and ran with their blood, this place Gallipoli is, in one sense, part of Australia,' Hawke said. The message he wanted most of all to convey was not of war but of peace. 'As the dawn emerges from the blackness of night, let us hope that the nations of the earth are emerging from the self-destructive practices of enmity and will build, in sunlight, a world of peace,' he said.[2]

It was, Hawke recalled, one of the most moving and poignant experiences of his prime ministership. At the dawn service, young Australian backpackers came face to face with the Australian veterans, and they 'embraced one another'. At a morning tea reception, the Australian veterans met the Turkish veterans and they too 'embraced one another'. Hawke had tears in his eyes as he remembered the day. 'Oh, it was marvellous,' he said.[3]

—

Bob Hawke would soon send troops to another war abroad. On 2 August 1990, Iraqi dictator Saddam Hussein invaded his oil-rich neighbour Kuwait. The United Nations Security Council immediately passed Resolution 660, which condemned the invasion of Kuwait and demanded that Iraq withdraw its forces immediately and unconditionally. On 6 August, the Security Council imposed sanctions on Iraq. The Australian government, which had a lucrative wheat trade with Iraq, supported this decision. On 9 August, Hawke met with foreign minister Gareth Evans and defence minister Robert Ray, along with deputy prime minister Paul Keating, Senate leader John Button and attorney-general Michael Duffy (Evans, Ray and Button were on the telephone), to consider what possible future courses of action were open to Australia. To help enforce sanctions, Ray advised that the Australian Defence Force could send two frigates – HMAS *Adelaide* and HMAS *Darwin* – and replenishment oiler HMAS *Success* to the Persian Gulf within a few days.

Hawke spoke to President George H.W. Bush by phone on 10 August. Hawke said 'there have been some raisings by your people to join this naval multinational task force' and he was eager to 'decide' how best Australia could 'contribute'. Bush replied:

'I think there would be great interest in your participating.' No formal request had been made for Australian participation, but there had been some informal discussions at a diplomatic level and Bush saw merit in having a broad coalition of countries to enforce the UN sanctions.

'If the request comes, we are prepared to send three ships,' Hawke said. He added that Australia preferred a United Nations 'flag over all this', and wanted to discuss 'the status, membership, command and purpose of the task force'. Hawke was moving fast.

'Bob, I am advised it is very hard to get the UN flag over the interdiction effort,' Bush replied.

Hawke said it would be ideal if Japan and Canada could join the blockade too, and suggested a simultaneous announcement. Bush was supportive and said it could be arranged. 'This is a timely and very important call,' the president said. Hawke, steering the call, wanted to close the deal. He had two issues. First, a guarantee that Australia will be consulted rather than just compliant. And second, that the invitation to contribute to the naval force came specifically from the United States.

> HAWKE: At the press conference, I can say you will have your people talking with us on a more definite basis as, I understand, participation is concerned. For presentation, you called me, we had a yarn, we will be working [out] participation. We indicated our willingness to be a part of it.
> BUSH: Is it alright to say that now?
> HAWKE: I think it will be within 7 hours from now.

Hawke wanted to confirm that Bush would say Australia was asked to participate, not that Australia asked to participate. Bush got the message. 'We will say that I called you to request if Australians could participate. You were positive,' the president replied. 'Details will be worked out by others. We will, in seven hours, watch for the take, then we'll make a positive suggestion.'

Hawke said they could in fact make an announcement within two and a half hours. He suggested Bush call Canadian prime minister Brian Mulroney, and then Hawke would phone Mulroney to seal the deal on Canadian participation. 'Ring Mulroney and get it going,' Hawke said.

'I will call right now,' Bush replied. 'Thank you, you are a good friend.'[4]

There is no other conclusion: Australia invited itself to the Gulf War. No formal request was made by the United States. In fact, Hawke asked Bush to say that he had requested Australian involvement.[5]

At a press conference later that day, Hawke misled Australians about his conversation with Bush. 'President Bush called me this morning,' Hawke said. 'I had a lengthy conversation with him, and out of that conversation we agreed that Australia would contribute to a multinational task force in the gulf.' But some in the press gallery had heard a different version of events:

> JOURNALIST: US television networks have reported that you at some stage actually phoned President Bush – was there an earlier conversation?
> HAWKE: No. I didn't phone President Bush. But as I said quite straightforwardly, there had been earlier discussions at officials levels initiated in the first place by the United States, but the only contact between President Bush and myself was the phone call from him to me this morning.[6]

At the press conference, Hawke announced that Australia would send three ships to the Persian Gulf. Australia's naval contingent departed from Garden Island in Sydney on 13 August.[7] It was not until 14 August, however, that cabinet formally 'noted' the deployment of two guided missile frigates and one replenishment tanker.[8]

Hawke, when presented with the transcripts of his phone calls with Bush, was not concerned about being seen to be too eager to go to war. 'You had a sovereign independent state invaded without cause by a neighbour,' Hawke said. 'If that had been allowed to stand then the rules of international behaviour would have changed forever, and you could not allow it to happen.'[9]

Bush, also reminded of these phone conversations, recalled the 'strong' and 'unwavering' support from Australia. 'The invasion of Kuwait was one of those "put up or shut up" moments for the global community – either you were for the rule of international law, for the defence of a fellow member of the United Nations and a sovereign nation, or you were not,' Bush recalled. 'Bob Hawke made a strong, principled stand with the civilised world, and followed through to help right a historic wrong. It meant a great deal to me personally.'[10]

Hugh White, foreign policy adviser to Hawke, recalled the context of the invasion. 'It was a direct test of whether or not the United Nations really could work the way it was meant to, and whether the new post–Cold War order was going to be rules-based or fucking chaos,' White said. 'Hawke happened to be reading William Manchester's biography of Winston Churchill at the time, and although he wasn't by nature a Churchillian, he did have that towards the front of his mind. He also understood that this was a test of our credentials as a United States ally. The cause itself was just and legitimate. Those imperatives sat alongside one another.'[11]

Keating recalled a meeting in Hawke's office to discuss the Australian response to any request to join a coalition force in the Gulf. 'Hawke was expecting a call from the president and we discussed what we would say if the president called,' he said. The deputy prime minister was supportive of Australia playing a role, but a limited one. 'An early yes from us is a minimum contribution from us,' he suggested. Keating said ministers were not told that the prime minister had in fact made the call himself and offered Australia's support, pre-empting a request from Bush. Keating said Hawke was 'a classic mug in dealing with these sorts of issues'.[12]

Hawke often claimed that Mulroney was reluctant to join the coalition forces because he was concerned about Canada's wheat trade with Iraq. He said Bush had phoned him to see if he could help to persuade Mulroney to join the coalition. Hawke talked to Mulroney. 'What's this bloody nonsense that you have got a bloody big wheat market,' Hawke apparently said. 'So have we.' He said Canada quickly followed Australia's lead.[13]

The evidence, however, does not support this. Records of Mulroney's phone calls with Bush show they spoke on 9 August 1990. Mulroney had actually spoken to Hawke before Bush called about a Canadian commitment to the Gulf. '[Hawke] wanted to know, if he were invited by the Saudis or the United Nations, what our reaction would be,' Mulroney told Bush. 'I said, "Bob, we are by no means a superpower, but I could understand the benefit to the president of the United States." I said we will join in and support the effort.' Mulroney, who had a close relationship with Bush, needed little arm-twisting.[14]

According to Mulroney, Hawke's recollection was faulty. In fact, he had already talked to Bush about the situation in the Persian Gulf, and they had arranged to have dinner at the White House. 'I committed to Bush on 6 August and Canada was the chairman of the [UN] Security Council during that period,' Mulroney said. 'Nobody had to talk me into anything.'[15]

On 21 August, Hawke made a detailed statement to parliament about the deployment of Australian vessels to the Persian Gulf as part of Operation Desert Shield. Of particular concern was the fate of about 150 Australians in Iraq and Kuwait who could not leave and might be targeted by Hussein's forces.

Audaciously, having played the role of East–West conduit, Hawke thought he could resolve the Iraq–Kuwait conflict. He phoned Hugh White at about 3 am one morning. 'Hughie, Bob here. Sorry to pull this fucking Fraser stunt on you but can you come over to the Lodge?' Hawke's idea was that he would contact the Crown Prince of Jordan and try to persuade him to contact Hussein and encourage him to withdraw from Kuwait. If Iraq withdrew from Kuwait and released its hostages, Hawke thought, it could have its territorial issues arbitrated by an independent tribunal. He even floated sending White as his personal envoy to begin the talks.

'It was a sign of Hawke's anxiety about where conflict in the Middle East might lead,' White recalled. 'He was convinced that Hussein could be brought to understand that his best interests were going to be to accept a settlement. I told him I did not think it was a good idea.' Hawke was not persuaded. He made a call to Bush. 'Okay, Bob, well, that is an interesting idea,' White recalled Bush saying to Hawke. It was hardly an endorsement. On 24 August, Hawke talked to the Crown Prince. But his global peacemaker role was short-lived: after about twelve hours of phone calls and meetings, he let the idea go. According to White, Hawke's ego led him to think 'he could save the world'.[16]

Hawke continued to talk to Bush about Iraq's occupation of Kuwait. On 15 November, following a discussion about the Uruguay

Round with respect to agricultural trade, Hawke asked Bush for an update. Bush said the 'sanctions appear to be working' and they wanted 'a peaceful solution', but were nevertheless readying for war. 'We continue to build our forces so that if we need to use force we will prevail and prevail rapidly,' Bush said. 'We remain supportive of what you are doing,' Hawke replied. 'There can be no conditionality on anything, including the release of the hostages. We share the hope that this will be resolved peacefully as a rational judgment by Saddam Hussein in the interest of his own people.'[17]

On 29 November, the UN Security Council passed Resolution 678, issuing a warning to Hussein that his forces must exit Kuwait by 15 January 1991 or member states were authorised to use 'all necessary means' to force his withdrawal. Australia's ships had been deployed to enforce sanctions. Now Hawke thought they should move into the Persian Gulf and be deployed in concert with US and other allied forces. That same day, senior ministers Hawke, Keating, Button, Ray and Evans met to formulate a policy recommendation to cabinet.[18] They agreed to deploy forces into combat, but not to expand Australia's contribution.

Hawke claimed Keating was reluctant to commit Australian forces to combat. 'What has the US done for us?' Keating purportedly said.[19] This claim, which led to a public spat when *The Hawke Memoirs* were published in 1994, did not stack up. Keating said it was false, and Evans and Ray backed him.[20] In response, Hawke said Keating was a 'liar'.[21] Button, by then in retirement, issued a statement revealing he had questioned Australian ships being moved into the war zone. 'I asked the rhetorical question, "What has the United States done for us?"' Button said. 'No one else used these words.'[22] A newspaper article published at the time of the meeting described Keating as being 'gung-ho' and referring to Hussein as 'that turd'.[23] Hawke relied on a note of the meeting taken by White. That handwritten note shows that Keating did make this remark.[24] However, White said it was a mistake to attribute the remark to Keating.[25]

On 3 December, Hawke consulted cabinet ministers and faction leaders, and secured their support. This was not a formality. Labor had a deeply ingrained anti-war sentiment, and a degree of hostility towards the United States. Labor had vigorously opposed the

Vietnam War, at great political cost at the time, but was subsequently vindicated. Hawke had to tread carefully or he risked a party revolt. He argued, correctly, that there was no parallel with the Vietnam War. This action was being taken with the endorsement of the United Nations. Australia could not stand by while one country illegally occupied another; this was how world wars had begun. On 4 December, in a second major address to parliament, Hawke announced that Australia would commit forces to operations against Iraq in accordance with Resolution 678.

As the withdrawal deadline of 15 January 1991 approached (4 pm on 16 January, AEST), it was clear that attempts to prevent a war had failed. On 10 January, Bush had phoned Hawke to inform him that talks between James Baker and Tariq Aziz, Iraq's deputy prime minister, had been 'unproductive'. Hawke asked Bush about the odds of going to war: 'Will the balloon go up?' Bush said he could not say publicly what he told Hawke: 'I have to tell you, as a friend, yes.' Hawke pressed Bush for 'a further talk' before any action was taken. Bush baulked a little but acknowledged that Hawke had been 'side by side with me on this', so he would 'be glad to do it' if it could be arranged without jeopardising 'the element of surprise'.[26]

Bush confided to his diary that, if war could not be avoided, he hoped that the devastating attack to be unleashed would prompt Hussein, a man he described as evil and mad, to quickly surrender. The president was tired, had not slept and was a bundle of mixed emotions. As the clock wound down, Bush phoned former presidents Ronald Reagan, Jimmy Carter, Gerald Ford and Richard Nixon, along with congressional leaders and alliance partners, including Hawke. Hawke was desperate to know in advance when combat operations would commence. 'Hawke was very understanding and appreciative, telling me that a call just an hour before would help him with his [parliament],' Bush noted in his diary.[27] Hawke was notified by Bush at 9.49 am on 17 January, within an hour of the war beginning. They spoke for four minutes.[28]

Gareth Evans had been asking James Baker for maximum possible consultation about the war. Baker acknowledged some 'tension' with Evans. 'Australia was a coalition partner and we counted them as an important part of the coalition to liberate Kuwait,' he said. 'Gareth wanted me to tell him exactly when the balloon was going to go up to start the war. And, of course, we hadn't given anybody that information because we were dreadfully fearful that that would cost lives if that ever got out. He and I had a few words over that, but I enjoyed working with Gareth and I found him to be a very effective foreign minister.'[29]

Evans had a different recollection of this conversation. 'Well, Jim, we really would appreciate being consulted about when the war starts,' Evans recalled telling Baker.

'Who's running this fucking war?' Baker replied. 'We appreciate your support but we are running this war. We have the military leadership. You guys will cooperate.'[30]

Robert Ray thought the level of consultation was proportionate to Australia's commitment. 'How many chips you put on the table reflects how often you are consulted,' he said. 'We put a few chips on the table but not enough to be constantly consulted.'[31]

On 17 January, Operation Desert Storm began, with the United States leading a coalition of thirty-five nations to liberate Kuwait. Following his short phone call with Bush, Hawke briefed Keating, Evans, Ray, Button and Duffy. He spoke to General Peter Gration, Chief of the Defence Force, and authorised a signal being sent to Australian forces in the Persian Gulf. Hawke then held a press conference to announce that Desert Storm had commenced. He reiterated the reason for the commitment, accepted there was uncertainty about the fate of Australian soldiers and the outcome of the war, but was assured by their capabilities and their bravery, and hoped they would return home safely. As Australian Navy vessels faced the risk of landmines and air attacks, Hawke later authorised a specialised team of twenty-three Navy mine-clearance divers to assist the fleet.

Parliament was recalled for a special sitting on 21 and 22 January for the purposes of providing MPs with an update on the war and to facilitate debate. Hawke moved a resolution in the House of Representatives supporting the United Nations–sponsored but United States–led coalition, including Australia's commitment of three Navy vessels and 750 personnel. In a charged atmosphere, Gerry Hand reluctantly supported the resolution but broke down and could not complete his speech. 'I was quite traumatised,' he recalled. 'But I took the view that Iraq had invaded a sovereign country, Kuwait, and it had the backing of the United Nations.'[32] The House carried the resolution in support of the war and the deployment on the voices, rather than with a division.

However, ten Labor backbenchers refused to support the deployment. In the House, these were: Peter Duncan, Stewart West, Frank Walker, Carolyn Jakobsen, Elaine Darling, Jeanette McHugh and John Scott. In the Senate, three Labor backbenchers abstained from the vote: Bruce Childs, John Coates and Margaret Reynolds.[33] The Labor MPs who did not maintain caucus solidarity and support the decision were censured by the party's national executive on 8 February 1991.[34] All were from the Left faction, apart from Darling, who was of the Centre Left.

It was a quick war. The opening weeks saw enormous aerial firepower directed at Iraq's military installations. On 7 February, Bush phoned Hawke to tell him 'things are going well'. Hawke asked about the prospect of ending the conflict without a 'ground war'. Bush was doubtful this could be achieved but hoped it would be. 'I do not want a prolongation of the war,' he said.[35] Bush diarised that he had spoken to Hawke again, this time about reports from Baghdad that civilians were being bombed. '[Hawke] knows that's not the case,' Bush noted. 'In fact, most people know it's not the case. I was pleased with his support last night.' Bush was highly critical of media coverage of the war. So was Hawke, who thought the ABC's reportage was also biased.[36]

On 24 February, the ground assault began. Bush, at Camp David, phoned Hawke four hours before he announced that an order had been given to General Norman Schwarzkopf 'to intensify the ground war to liberate Iraq'. Bush confided his concerns to Hawke. 'I wanted you to know ahead of time,' he said. 'I have worried about it. The loss of ground troops is on my mind. I hope it will be quicker than people's predictions, with fewer casualties.' Hawke had earlier spoken to National Security Adviser Brent Scowcroft and reiterated that the conclusion of the war must not only be Iraq being removed from Kuwait; Hussein must also be made to 'repudiate his claim to Kuwait'. Hawke urged Bush to 'nail this bastard on the horns of a dilemma'. Bush agreed. 'Do not just bugger around the edges – put him to it,' Hawke said.[37]

Within 100 hours, a ceasefire was declared after Iraq was expelled from Kuwait's borders. By 28 February, combat operations were halted. Hawke spoke to Bush. 'Congratulations, my friend, on a magnificent effort,' Hawke said. They discussed the ceasefire, the broader impact on the Middle East and the future for Hussein. 'There is a feeling here in the analytical community that the man will not be able to survive this,' Bush said. Hawke said he had appreciated his talks with Bush over the previous months. 'It has been a pleasure to be side by side,' Bush responded.[38]

The Gulf War elevated the risk of terrorist activity in Australia. ASIO briefings provided to Hawke during the conflict show that the counter-terrorism alert was raised to level 2 – 'Special CT Risk'. ASIO interviewed and monitored 'radical elements within the Australian Arab community to determine the likelihood of retaliatory violence', Hawke was told. Possible terrorist targets were identified. Cooperation with federal and state law-enforcement agencies was increased, and security measures were stepped up at airports.[39]

Hawke often claimed that Bush had confided that he was being pressured to send the coalition forces to Baghdad and remove Hussein from power. 'Bob, I'm being pressed very hard by a lot of my colleagues to go into Iraq,' Bush apparently told Hawke. 'You can't possibly do that,' Hawke replied. 'You've got together a strong coalition including Arab states and you did that to get these people out of Kuwait. It would be a break in confidence, a break in trust, if you were to do that.' Bush agreed.[40]

It is another great story, but the evidence does not support it. None of Bush's declassified phone records with Hawke backs it up. Nor does his diary. 'I was always committed to ejecting Saddam's troops from Kuwait,' Bush recalled. 'The idea of going to Baghdad in that situation was not on my mind.'[41] Baker also rejected Hawke's claim. 'There was no such debate,' he said. 'Not one of President Bush's aides [or] top people – secretary of state, defense, CIA – argued that we should go to Baghdad. I think Bob was wrong if he thinks there was a debate within the United States administration at the time about going to Baghdad.'[42]

There was one person who thought the coalition forces should consider going on to Baghdad and remove Hussein from power:

Keating. 'Desert Shield and Desert Storm had such enormous military superiority that they were able to take out Saddam's regime,' Keating said. 'But I was never an unqualified runner into Baghdad. It was only on the basis that we could have a provisional Iraqi government that could take over.'[43] Years later, in September 2002, Keating reminded Hawke of the view he had expressed at the time of the First Gulf War. 'I was for pressing on to Baghdad when Desert Shield was effectively unstoppable,' he wrote.[44]

Hawke was immersed in the war. 'The Gulf War was in many ways the most demanding single challenge I dealt with in my public life,' he later recalled.[45] He was thrilled to be talking to Bush during the war. There is no doubt, given the extent of their talks, that Hawke enjoyed a close relationship with Bush. This was to Australia's benefit. He also organised to be given daily briefings by intelligence and defence officials. He monitored events closely and kept Australians informed of developments.

General Peter Gration, the Chief of the Defence Force, wrote a personal letter to Hawke on 5 March 1991:

> I would like to take this opportunity to express to you my personal congratulations and those of the ADF on your outstanding national leadership throughout the crisis, and on the very clear way you kept the nation briefed on developments at critical points. Your briefings were a major factor – probably the major factor – in the overwhelming support of the majority of Australians for a national effort.[46]

Meanwhile, Keating's leadership ambitions were on hold. He stewed as Hawke's approval rating was boosted by the war. By February 1991, Hawke's satisfaction rating had lifted from 31 per cent to 40 per cent in Newspoll. However, the Coalition remained in a dominant position, leading Labor by 49 per cent to 35 per cent on the primary vote.[47] In November 1990, Hewson had become the first opposition leader to overtake Hawke as preferred prime minister, leading 43–41 in the Morgan Gallup poll. (Hawke led as preferred prime minister in the Newspoll.)[48] Keating knew he could not force Hawke to resign during the Gulf War. Australia was at war, and Hawke was loving every minute of it. Keating privately referred to Hawke as 'Napoleon without the hat'.

30

KEATING
STRIKES

On 10 July 1990, Bob Hawke became Australia's second-longest-serving prime minister, surpassing Malcolm Fraser. The Hawke office was focused on the milestone, even drawing up a chart to count down the days.[1] It was a moment of satisfaction for Hawke, who had also chalked up four election victories in a row, more than any other Labor leader, and more than any Liberal leader since Robert Menzies.

With the looming conflict in the Middle East occupying much of Hawke's time, Paul Keating became concerned that the prime minister was crab-walking away from the Kirribilli Agreement. In the afternoon of 9 October 1990, in the prime minister's office, Keating asked Hawke to establish a timeline for the leadership transition. Hawke baulked. He said that he wanted to remain prime minister for at least the following year. Hawke had two projects he wanted to 'see through': the New Federalism initiative with the states and CHOGM in Harare in October 1991.[2] This was in keeping with the Kirribilli Agreement, but it was pushing the timetable to the limit.

Keating went to see Gareth Evans. 'What's all this fucking CHOGM shit about? Is the next one important?' he asked Evans.

'Well, basically, it's bullshit,' Evans replied.[3]

Hawke's rationalisations for not quitting left Keating unconvinced. He thought Hawke was stringing him along. He had insurance and he decided to call it in.

On 28 November 1990, Keating told Richardson about the Kirribilli Agreement.[4] They decided to ask Hawke for a second meeting with Abeles and Kelty. Hawke refused. 'Bob was not prepared to be held to account by Abeles and Kelty because he never intended to go,' Keating thought.[5] So, Richardson and Keating agreed that a leadership challenge should be mounted on the basis that Hawke had reneged on an agreement about the leadership. Keating said he would ask Hawke to resign by March 1991. If he did not, Keating would resign as treasurer by June 1991. There was now a plan and a timetable.

The following week, Keating gave the end-of-year off-the-record address to journalists at the National Press Club in Canberra. This speech, delivered at 9.15 pm on Friday, 7 December 1990, would plunge the government into a full-blown leadership crisis. 'We've got to be led, and politics is about leading people,' Keating said. 'Politicians change the world, and politics and politicians are about leadership, and our problem is – if you look at some of the great countries, of the great societies, like the United States – we've never had one leader like they've had. The United States has had three great leaders: [George] Washington, [Abraham] Lincoln and [Franklin] Roosevelt. And at times in their history that leadership pushed them on to become the great country they are. We've never had such a person, not one.'[6]

The speech was dynamite. It was obvious to everyone who heard it that Keating was critiquing Hawke's leadership. That is how Hawke saw it. But Keating claimed he was not speaking about Hawke. Keating's staff have differing interpretations of the speech.[7] Michelle Grattan was sitting next to Keating at the dinner and introduced him to speak. 'He was making notes on a drink coaster,' she recalled. 'It was getting quite late, and he finally made the speech and people started talking about it immediately. He didn't seem to comprehend how people would see it. He was in a very emotional state. It was less than premeditated, but he took the opportunity to vent.'[8]

The night before the speech, Treasury secretary Chris Higgins had dropped dead on a running track in Canberra. Keating was close to Higgins and devastated about his sudden death. He thought about Higgins as he ruminated on the purpose of public life. Keating described John Curtin as 'a trier'. He then said: 'Leadership is not about being popular. It's about being right and about being strong. And it's not whether you go through some shopping centre, tripping over the TV crews' cords.' In the most memorable part of the speech, Keating referred to himself as the Plácido Domingo of Australian politics.[9]

Hawke learnt about the speech the following morning from his press secretary Grant Nihill, who had been phoned by journalist Peter Logue with an account of Keating's speech. 'Silly boy,' Hawke told Nihill.[10] He was furious and interpreted it as an attack on his leadership. Hawke thought it was the start of a campaign to wrest the prime ministership from him. 'It was quite clear that this man's naked ambition and arrogance was leading him to a total perversion of the history of the labour movement,' Hawke said.[11] He phoned Keating, reaching him in Blackall, in central Queensland, and expressed his anger. They agreed to meet on Monday afternoon.

The speech was conveyed to Richard Farmer and Alex Mitchell, who were not at the dinner, and their accounts of the speech were splashed over the front pages of the Sunday newspapers in Sydney and Melbourne.

Hawke was in Sydney on the morning of Monday, 10 December. He spoke briefly to journalists outside the Commonwealth Parliamentary Offices on Phillip Street.

> HAWKE: All I want to say is this. I will be seeing the treasurer later today in Canberra, and that's all I've got to say at this stage.
> JOURNALIST: Is it time to cut Plácido Domingo's vocal cords?
> HAWKE: Good question. I've got nothing to add to what I've said. I expect to be seeing Mr Keating later in Canberra today.
> JOURNALIST: You look very relaxed.
> HAWKE: Yes, I feel very relaxed.[12]

At 4.15 pm, Hawke and Keating met in the prime minister's office in Parliament House. The meeting, which stretched for almost four hours, was the most bitter confrontation the two men had ever had. Across the hallway, Hawke's staff watched it unfold on a small, soundless, black-and-white, closed-circuit television. 'Hawke had his coat off, smoking a cigar, leaning back in his chair and looking relaxed,' Barrie Cassidy recalled. 'Keating kept his coat and tie on, he would throw his arms up in the air or lean over the desk, did most of the talking and was aggressive.'[13]

A large part of the discussion was a battle over history. Hawke was incensed about Keating's critique of Curtin. He thought Keating was channelling Jack Lang's attacks on Curtin decades earlier. Keating was an admirer and a friend of Lang, the former New South Wales premier, who helped destroy Jim Scullin's Labor government in 1931 during the Great Depression. 'The mouth was the mouth of Paul Keating, but the words were the words of Jack Lang,' Hawke said. He thought it demonstrated that Keating was not ready for leadership. Although they agreed to meet again the following month, Hawke told Keating that the Kirribilli Agreement 'was now very much in issue'.[14]

It was 8.15 pm. The prime minister's staff had no doubt that a leadership challenge would soon follow.[15] Meanwhile, word had spread through Parliament House that Hawke and Keating's meeting had gone for hours and hours. They issued a joint statement. 'We have today had a long and constructive conversation in which Paul conveyed he had intended no offence nor implied any challenge to me in his remarks last Friday night,' it said. 'I said to him that I intended to remain through this term as leader of the party and wished to see him continue as deputy prime minister and treasurer. Paul confirmed that he totally concurred with this course.'[16] At a frenzied and lengthy press conference the following day, Hawke declared: 'I will lead the party to the next election and with the intention of going through that term.'[17]

The two met again on 31 January in Hawke's office.[18] During the three-hour conversation, Hawke informed Keating that he had decided to 'go on' as prime minister. His argument was twofold: there were things that he wanted to complete in domestic and international affairs, and he thought he was the best person to lead the party to a fifth election. For Hawke, the critical factor in deciding to renege on the Kirribilli Agreement was the 'Plácido Domingo' speech, which he regarded as grossly disloyal. But Keating thought this was just an excuse not to vacate the prime ministerial office. He pressed Hawke to honour the Kirribilli Agreement. 'I require nothing of you other than you keep your word,' Keating said.[19]

But Hawke had decided not to resign. He also had grave reservations about Keating's suitability for the prime ministership.

Hawke claimed that Keating said he would quit politics, and leave Australia, if he did not get to be prime minister. 'We'll be off to Europe,' Keating said. 'We won't be staying here – this is the arse-end of the world.'[20] Keating insisted he never uttered those words while discussing the prime ministership. But he did say to journalists that, one day, he might go and live in Paris.[21] He also said it to his ministerial colleagues.[22]

Hawke said it was those words that confirmed in his mind that he could not hand over the prime ministership for Keating. 'That was the end for me,' Hawke recalled. 'Any bloke who describes his country as the arse-end of the world, and who is going to piss off to Paris, is not fit to lead and be prime minister. I thought, "Fuck me, how can you have a bloke who thinks that about the country and have him as prime minister?"'[23]

Keating continued to press for the Kirribilli Agreement to be honoured and raised the prospect of a leadership change once the Gulf War was over, but nothing was agreed. Hawke would not go.[24] Keating was furious. 'The agreement was unconditional,' he said. 'Other than that it did not leak – and it did not leak.'[25]

Hawke readied for a leadership challenge. When Colin Parks, known as 'Curly', returned to Hawke's office as political adviser in early 1991, he bumped into Keating as he was heading to the House of Representatives for Question Time with Hawke. He pulled back to chat to Keating. 'Hi, Paul,' he said. 'Just so you know, I'm back working in Bob's office.'

Keating replied: 'Yeah, mate, I know. It's not him you have to worry about but me.'

For Parks, that set the tone for the rest of the year.[26]

By 1991, both Hawke and Keating were unpopular. The recession had hurt their standing in the electorate. They were also approaching eight years in power – by May Labor had been in government longer than ever before – and were often portrayed by the media as tired and out of ideas. Hawke's approval rating was just 40 per cent at the start of 1991. But he maintained an edge over opposition leader John Hewson as preferred prime minister in the Newspoll. If Hawke went, voters preferred Kim Beazley to Keating as prime minister.[27] While Keating was regarded by most in caucus as Hawke's successor, he looked like a weak challenger in the summer of 1990–91. But Keating had a trump card: the Kirribilli Agreement.

There were glimmers of hope that the economy was finally showing signs of recovery from recession. On 30 May, the national accounts revealed growth of 0.1 per cent in the March quarter. Interest rates fell to 10.5 per cent that month. The annual inflation rate had fallen to 4.9 per cent, in large part a testament to the Prices and Incomes Accord. Unemployment, however, was approaching 10 per cent.

Leadership speculation was rife in the first half of 1991. Hawke continued to tell journalists that he would remain prime minister and lead Labor to the next election, due in early 1993. Keating was being profiled by journalists who asked what kind of prime minister he would be. By March, Hawke's lift in the polls after the Gulf War had proved fleeting: Newspoll showed his net satisfaction rating to be minus 18 per cent.[28] Keating, however, saw his net satisfaction rating sink to minus 44 per cent.[29]

The parliamentary contest became a showring in which Hawke and Keating paraded their respective leadership styles. Hawke had come under sustained attack in April after it was revealed he attended a $950,000 fundraising lunch in Perth which embroiled him in the 'WA Inc.' scandal. It was claimed by the opposition that Hawke had agreed to changes to the gold tax in return for donations. During explanations to parliament, Hawke got dates wrong and had to correct the record. Keating came to Hawke's defence with a counterattack that made the press gallery take notice. 'Since Keating's parliamentary dominance is about all that keeps Labor in the fight at the moment, caucus members would be forced to think very carefully about life without him,' wrote Laurie Oakes in *The Bulletin*.[30]

Robert Ray was informed about the Kirribilli Agreement by Graham Richardson in early May 1991. It did not persuade him to switch sides, but he thought making the agreement was a bad idea. He did not believe Hawke had a compelling reason to break it. 'The Labor Party determines the leadership, not two pricks meeting with two total turds in Kirribilli,' he thought.[31]

Kim Beazley was told about the Kirribilli Agreement by Keating a few days before it became public. 'I don't think they should have made it,' he reflected. 'They don't dispose of the Labor Party leadership, either of them, it is disposed of by the caucus.'[32]

Gareth Evans thought Hawke should have stuck to the Kirribilli Agreement. 'I thought it should have been honoured,' he said. 'To go out on a total high would have been a graceful and sensible thing to do.'[33]

In December 1990, following Keating's 'Plácido Domingo' speech, Bob Hogg, Labor's national secretary, had met with Hawke to talk about the leadership. He advised Hawke to reach an understanding with Keating with a view to a handover, perhaps at the party's centenary conference in June 1991. Now, it was too late. Hogg told Hawke on 24 May that he should resign and pass the reins to Keating. Unmoved, Hogg put pen to paper and presented Hawke with three options: retire on his own terms and hand over to Keating; face a leadership challenge that, if defeated, would likely lead to a second challenge; or win a challenge and force Keating to leave parliament. Hogg made it clear that he favoured the first option – an orderly transition. 'I'm not suggesting that you duck a fight for the sake of it, but rather you should consider what is the point of such a fight,' Hogg wrote.[34]

On the evening of 29 May, Richardson met with Hawke and encouraged him to resign. He said he knew about the Kirribilli Agreement. 'You made a promise and you broke your promise,' Richardson said. 'He's coming for you.'[35] Hawke said he would not resign. Richardson asked if he would make way for Keating by the end of the year, still in keeping with the Kirribilli Agreement. Hawke replied that he would think about it when he was overseas in June. Richardson wanted an answer now. Hawke agreed to think about it; they would discuss it the following day. They met the next day, on 30 May, at 12.30 pm. Hawke reverted: he would not resign but would think about it when overseas. Richardson told Hawke to expect a motion to vacate the leadership at the caucus meeting the following week. He said the Kirribilli Agreement would no longer be kept secret. The battle lines were drawn.

That afternoon, at around 5 pm, Keating walked around to Hawke's suite.[36] He was there to inform the prime minister that there would be a leadership challenge. Keating nodded to Dennis

Richardson, Hawke's principal private secretary, as he motioned towards the door and said, 'Okay to go in?'

Richardson stopped him. 'Excuse me, Mr Keating, but the PM has got people with him,' he said.

'Who's he got with him?' Keating asked.

Hawke was meeting with Queensland premier Wayne Goss, his chief of staff Kevin Rudd and the Australian Workers' Union boss Bill Ludwig. Colin Parks was also in the room. Hawke was seated at his desk and the others were in chairs in front of him. They were discussing compensation for ending mining on Fraser Island. It was suggested the treasurer come back in ten minutes. 'Keating was very agitated,' recalled Richardson.

Keating returned and said, 'I've got to go in. I've got to go in.'

Richardson interrupted the meeting: 'Sorry, PM, the treasurer wants to see you urgently.' Keating went in.[37]

'I need to talk to Bob,' Keating said. Hawke adjourned the meeting with Goss, Rudd, Ludwig and Parks.

Parks recalled seeing Kim Beazley in Richardson's office. 'What's going on?' he asked.

'Paul is upset and talking about a challenge,' Richardson replied. He told Parks that Keating had been around earlier in an emotional state and reluctantly left when told Hawke was in a meeting.[38]

Hawke spoke to Keating alone for five to ten minutes.[39] Keating said that given Hawke would not honour the Kirribilli Agreement, he would challenge for the leadership. 'I told you when you made the commitment you've now broken that I'd come after you and you'd be the first to know,' Keating said.[40]

'Alright, that's the way it's going to be,' Hawke replied.[41] Keating left.

Hawke invited Goss, Rudd, Ludwig and Parks to resume the meeting. Hawke made no comment about what they had discussed. A short time later, Keating rang Hawke. Hawke ducked down and had a whispered conversation. 'Paul, I told you we would discuss this when I got back from London,' Parks heard Hawke say. The prime minister was scheduled to go to the United Kingdom for an official visit the following week.[42]

'I looked at Parks and Parks looked at me, and our eyebrows went up,' recalled Rudd. 'We knew it was on.'[43]

Parks whispered to Rudd: 'He's challenging.' After a minute or so, the discussion about Fraser Island continued.

When the meeting in the prime minister's office concluded, and the Queenslanders left, Parks asked Hawke: 'What's going on?'

'I'll tell you later,' he replied.[44]

Before heading to a cabinet meeting, Hawke phoned Keating and asked him to keep the Kirribilli Agreement secret. That was not possible, Keating replied.[45] Hawke did not know that at 5 pm, Graham Richardson had informed Laurie Oakes about the Kirribilli Agreement, so it would lead the 6 pm news on Channel Nine.

'I knew exactly that I was being used to fire the starter's gun for Keating's first challenge against Hawke,' Oakes recalled. 'It gave Keating a justification for moving against a successful prime minister.'[46] Breaking the Kirribilli Agreement gave legitimacy to the leadership challenge.

Oakes' bombshell revelation about a secret deal on the leadership that had been broken by Hawke went to air just after 6 pm in the east coast capital cities – he did not have time to make it the lead story – and at 6.30 pm in Canberra (where Channel Nine ran a local news bulletin at 6 pm). The cabinet continued meeting while all hell was breaking loose in the lobbies.

Keating made two notes about the Kirribilli Agreement which were used by Richardson to brief Oakes. The first detailed the discussion at Kirribilli House and noted the agreement followed a commitment given by Hawke to Keating in 1988 to 'resign at a suitable time' after the 1990 election. The meeting with Kelty and Abeles was to give this understanding a 'formality':

> The meeting had only one item under discussion, namely the leadership, which the prime minister came to directly.
>
> He said he wished to lead the party to a fourth election and if won would serve some suitable time thereafter, and then resign in favour of the treasurer, giving the treasurer the time and opportunity to establish himself.
>
> In return it was understood the treasurer would serve and fight the election with him. It was agreed by all that it would be important to the government's prospects for the prime minister and the treasurer to go to the election as a fighting unit.

The prime minister's promise to resign during the fourth term was unconditional, save for the fact that he said that if the details of the agreement leaked, his commitment to the arrangement would terminate.[47]

The second note comprised several points for Richardson to make to Oakes, which included:

Given that the prime minister has failed to keep his promise
to the treasurer to retire at an opportune time during the
government's fourth term of office, he was either telling the
treasurer what he knew at the time to be a monstrous lie, or he
was subsequently and consistently lying to the Australian people
when he said he would see the fourth term out.[48]

Dennis Richardson, Barrie Cassidy and Grant Nihill found out about the Kirribilli Agreement when it was revealed on television. Parks had been told a week earlier by Robert Ray. 'Bob's failure to tell us immediately what the Keating meeting was about may have been because he was hoping to keep it a secret,' Parks reflected. 'Hawke may have thought he could negotiate with Keating when he returned from London. Of course, that pipe dream was smashed at 6 pm when Oakes broke the Kirribilli Agreement story.'[49]

During a cabinet break, Hawke called Richardson, Parks, Cassidy and Nihill to his office. They were soon joined by senior ministers. As the news about the agreement and a leadership challenge spread through the building, the momentum seemed to be running with Keating, so Hawke decided to act quickly. At 10.30 pm, Hawke called an immediate caucus meeting for the next day, Friday, 31 May, at 8 am. This was communicated to Labor MPs by phone and fax machine. Keating would have little time to persuade MPs to elect him leader.

Bill Kelty was in Parliament House that afternoon and was scheduled to meet Hawke. The ACTU secretary was close to Keating, having bonded over the accord, and retained affection and respect for Hawke. Kelty loved Hawke and he loved Keating. It was a difficult conversation.

'Don't think that I didn't create for myself a real problem in allowing you and Paul to get close,' Hawke said.

'I knew that,' Kelty replied. He told Hawke he should make way for Keating. 'You made the Kirribilli agreement, mate,' Kelty said. 'You keep agreements. That's my view. You keep agreements.'[50]

The conversation got heated and emotional. Kelty urged Hawke to run for the position of director-general of the International Labour Organization in 1993. From there, he could launch a bid to become secretary-general of the United Nations. 'You will be head of the ILO and head of the United Nations,' Kelty said. 'We can organise it. We can make it happen. You will be the most significant person in world leadership because you have the skills and capacity.'

Hawke was not interested. 'I'll beat Paul,' he said to Kelty. 'I tell you, I'll beat Paul.'

Kelty prepared to leave. 'I think it is going to be a bad decision you are making, mate,' he said. 'It is a bad decision for the ILO and a bad fucking decision for the world.'[51]

Hawke rang Simon Crean before news of the Kirribilli Agreement broke. Crean, the former ACTU president, was minister for science and technology. 'You're alright, mate?' Hawke asked.

'What are you talking about?' Crean replied.

'I think there is going to be a leadership challenge – have you heard anything?' Hawke asked.

Crean said he had not.

'But you're with me?' Hawke inquired.

'Yes,' Crean replied. Crean supported Hawke. But when he learned about the Kirribilli Agreement, he felt some disquiet. 'He should have honoured the agreement,' Crean later reflected. 'There should have been a leadership transition, and the foundation of it was there.'[52]

It was time to count numbers. Hawke met with Robert Ray, Kim Beazley, Gareth Evans and Simon Crean (Right); Gerry Hand, Nick Bolkus and Peter Staples (Left); Michael Duffy (independent); and Neil O'Keefe (unaligned). They began assessing the caucus and phoning MPs. Hawke went to bed at 4 am the following morning. Ray and Bolkus thought Hawke could expect about seventy votes to Keating's forty. Hawke's defence was better organised than Keating's attack. Hawke could rely on the Victorian Right and most of the Queensland Right (about twenty-four MPs), almost all of the national Left (about thirty-two) and most of those who were unaligned (about eleven). Hawke's support was more broadly based across factions and states. Keating had almost all of the New South Wales Right (about twenty-one MPs), plus the ACT's Ros Kelly, about two-thirds of the Centre Left (about twenty-one) and a few MPs from the Left (Frank Walker, Peter Duncan and Stewart West).

Of the other fifteen members of cabinet, Hawke had the solid support of nine ministers: Gareth Evans, Ralph Willis, Michael Duffy, Kim Beazley, John Kerin, Brian Howe, Robert Ray, Gerry Hand and Nick Bolkus. Keating had six cabinet ministers supporting him: John Button, John Dawkins, Graham Richardson, Neal Blewett, Ros Kelly and Peter Cook.

The caucus meeting began at 8.05 am on 31 May. Hawke was invited to address MPs. He walked to a microphone at the front of the room. In his hand was a statement he had written himself. 'Yesterday afternoon at about 5 pm, Paul came to my office and informed me he intended to challenge me for the leadership,' Hawke said. 'This has created a situation which obviously in the interests of the party cannot be allowed to continue and must be resolved immediately.' He then directed his remarks to Keating. 'Paul, as you have indicated, you wish to challenge me for the leadership, I now give you the opportunity to move that the position of leader be declared vacant.'[53] MPs were puzzled. Hawke would not resign to facilitate a ballot. It would require a show of hands for a spill motion. As Hawke returned to his seat, Peter Walsh interjected: 'At least Hayden had the decency to resign in 1982.'[54]

Keating then responded, from the microphone at the front of the room, by emphasising what had happened in July 1982. 'Bill had declared his position vacant and there had been a secret ballot,' he said. Accordingly, Keating wanted Hawke 'to resign to enable a ballot' and would not move a spill motion or support one. Hawke 'repudiated' the suggestion that he vacate the leadership and said there was no comparison with his challenge to Hayden. The difference, he argued, was that the incumbent had initiated the ballot in 1982, whereas the challenger was calling for it in 1991.[55]

The meeting descended into high farce. Graeme Campbell called for all leadership positions to be declared vacant. Chris Schacht asked for clarification about the rules. Gordon Scholes said if Hawke did not resign, the meeting could only accept his report. Alan Morris also asked about the rules. Beazley said there could only be a ballot if positions were vacant. He said to Keating: 'You brought this situation on. You move for the leadership to be vacated.'[56] Keating said if there was to be a spill motion moved, then it should happen at the usual weekly caucus meeting. Russ Gorman, wanting to discuss media reports about the leadership, was ruled out of order. Michael Lee then asked: 'Is there any further business?'[57] Richardson replied: 'Let's get out of here.'[58] After fifteen minutes, the meeting was over.

This was a major miscalculation by Hawke. He could have resigned the leadership and easily defeated Keating in a ballot. Instead, he gave Keating time to win over caucus members. The Keating camp called Hawke weak. Realising the blunder, Hawke phoned Keating at 9 am and said he would authorise another special caucus meeting for 10 am. Keating said, stretching the truth, that too many MPs had already left Canberra. Keating circulated a statement to caucus members saying he had not asked for the meeting at that time but would challenge for the leadership. He said there was no need for a show-and-tell spill vote and urged Hawke to facilitate 'a secret ballot' for leader.[59]

The second meeting went ahead. Around seventy MPs, mostly Hawke supporters, attended. At 10.05 am, Hawke said it was 'in the party's best interests for the leadership question to be resolved', and that he would resign to facilitate a secret ballot. The problem was that Keating was not there, and nor were around forty other caucus members. There was 'a boycott', Hawke said. He asked for the meeting to be adjourned until 10 am on Monday, 3 June. After just two minutes, the meeting concluded.[60] The Hawke camp thought Keating was gutless.

In truth, Keating won a tactical victory: he now had time to persuade more caucus members to back him. Gary Punch assessed Keating's support at that stage to be about twenty-six MPs. This meant that Hawke would have crushed Keating if a ballot had been held then.[61] Hawke would have won over eighty votes, and would have killed any chance of a second leadership challenge by Keating. Hawke, however, assessed his support at closer to seventy MPs on the Friday morning.[62]

The opposition could not believe their luck. John Hewson, though, doubted Labor would dump Hawke. 'I thought he would probably stay because he was always forgiven by the electorate,' Hewson said.[63] Andrew Peacock was not surprised. 'Bob had been prime minister for a while and had some great achievements, but he was starting to look like a spent force,' he said.[64] John Howard was appalled by the Kirribilli Agreement. 'They don't own the leadership of their party; it is a gift of the caucus,' he said. 'I was vaguely offended that it was done in the presence of a corporate representative and a union leader. It was the apogee of the corporate state.'[65]

Hawke and Keating, incredibly, attended a premiers' conference later in the day. The caucus ballot would be held in three days' time. Hawke rang MPs directly from the Lodge that weekend. He refused media requests, including one from Oakes to appear on the *Sunday* program on Channel Nine. Hawke did not want to look panicked or be seen to be trawling for votes. Keating took up the opportunity.

Hawke did not win the backing of any major masthead. *The Sydney Morning Herald* editorialised: 'Mr Hawke should stand aside for Mr Keating now.'[66] *The Age* said: 'Keating is the best bet for the future given Labor's grim electoral prospects.'[67] *The Australian Financial Review* declared it was 'time for a change in leadership'.[68] *The Australian* argued: 'Labor would be better placed to provide firm government over the next two years under Mr Keating.'[69] *The Telegraph Mirror* said Labor 'must bite the bullet and replace [Hawke] with Mr Keating'.[70] *The Courier-Mail* pronounced Hawke 'finished' no matter the outcome of the ballot, whereas Keating was 'the chief star in Labor's parliamentary firmament'.[71]

Hawke had been a media favourite for two decades before entering parliament. Now, after eight years as prime minister, they turned on him with a vengeance. Keating's concerted courting of the press gallery had paid a dividend. But Hawke had the voters onside. Newspoll showed Hawke to be preferred as prime minister over Keating by a whopping 61 per cent to 14 per cent. The gap was wider among Labor supporters, with Hawke leading Keating 77–17.[72] The Saulwick Poll had Hawke leading Keating by 66–18 per cent on the question of who would be the better prime minister.[73]

Hawke, as in 1982, argued that he was the more likely to lead Labor to victory at the next election. The polls, he argued, showed this – and this, more than anything else, was what mattered. He played down the Kirribilli Agreement. He asked MPs to trust him to save their seats. Keating, he argued, would be toxic to the electorate and was unworthy of the prime ministership.

Keating asserted that new leadership was needed to take the fight up to Hewson and defeat the Coalition. Hawke had agreed to hand over the leadership, he said, but welshed on that deal. Hawke had run out of ideas and could not rejuvenate the government. Moreover, Hawke had agreed with all his economic policy decisions, and the recession was a collective responsibility of cabinet.

The caucus meeting began at 10.05 am on 3 June. Hawke immediately vacated the leadership. Jim McKiernan, the returning officer, called for nominations for leader. Hawke and Keating nominated, and 110 ballot papers were prepared and issued to MPs in a cordoned-off section of the room. (Hawke had won a draw to have his name placed in the top position.) After all the votes were lodged, the ballot box was emptied onto a table and the ballots were tallied. This took about thirty minutes. Hawke won, receiving sixty-six votes, and Keating forty-four.

Hawke thanked MPs for 'the vote of confidence'. He said there must now be 'a healing process' and the government 'had to come together' to win the next election. He paid tribute to Keating for his service as treasurer. Keating congratulated Hawke. He was honoured to be treasurer, and said the economic reforms would deliver results in the 1990s. Keating pledged that he 'would not do one thing to damage the government or the party' in the lead-up to the next election.[74]

Hawke addressed the media later that afternoon. He began by again thanking the MPs who had voted for him and praised Keating's record as treasurer. He said their partnership was one of the most 'outstanding' in post-war politics. The media was feverish in their questioning, and Hawke was irritated and combative in his replies. Journalists accused Hawke of deceiving voters by promising he would serve a full term as prime minister if Labor won the March 1990 election, when in fact he had promised to hand the job over to Keating. Hawke said he had only made the Kirribilli

Agreement because he thought Keating might quit politics and it was necessary to persuade him to remain treasurer. But the events of late 1990 and early 1991 meant the 'undertaking was off'. Moreover, Hawke hoped Keating would come to see that 'the best outcome' after the last election was 'that I should go on'.[75] These statements were a poor justification for failing to honour the deal.

Hawke outlined the framework for the Kirribilli Agreement in a rough handwritten note he made in 1991:

1. Peter A[beles] and [Kelty] believed independently of any H[awke]/K[eating] discussions there should be a meeting of friends to resolve the tensions.
2. PK independently asked whether Kelty would attend a meeting all [had] been talking about [as a witness].
   - PK had spoken to Peter & BK & Peter himself [had] spoken to PK and me
   - Series of discussions
3. Meeting not to witness some arrangement.
4. BK initiated meeting [they had] been talking about.
5. Never was [it] a question of Abeles being there for me and Kelty for Paul
   - always 4 mutual friends.
6. Nothing I've said does he dispute.[76]

Keating rejects this interpretation of the Kirribilli Agreement. He said the 'purpose' of the meeting was indeed to 'witness' an 'arrangement'. Keating added that Kelty was invited as his nominee, and Abeles was there for Hawke.[77]

At 11.30 am, the caucus met again to elect a new deputy leader and a minister to replace Keating, who resigned both positions. Brian Howe and Graeme Campbell stood for deputy leader. Howe received eighty-one votes and Campbell eighteen; a further ten votes were informal.[78] Howe became deputy leader and therefore deputy prime minister. Howe's elevation was recognition of his policy contributions in cabinet and his leadership in the Left faction. Ross Free filled the vacancy in the ministry. Hawke was appointed treasurer – a position he held from 3 June to 4 June.[79] Hawke then appointed John Kerin as treasurer, Simon Crean joined cabinet and became minister for primary industries and energy, and Free took the science and technology portfolio. Roger Price – as reward for deserting the New South Wales Right faction – became parliamentary secretary to the prime minister. The new ministers were sworn in at 9 am on 4 June.

The most obvious person to appoint as treasurer was Ralph Willis. 'I was incredibly disappointed,' Willis recalled. 'I quite liked John. But I just could not see him in the role of treasurer.'[80] Hawke had wanted to appoint Willis but felt he could not because all the other leadership figures in the government were Victorians: deputy prime minister Brian Howe, Senate leader John Button and deputy Senate leader Gareth Evans. Hawke himself held the Victorian seat of Wills. It was an understandable judgement but it was, in hindsight, wrong.

At 12.30 pm, Keating addressed the media. He congratulated Hawke and said he would not make any future leadership challenge, nor would he destabilise the government. 'I had only one shot in the locker, and I fired it,' he said. Keating was in good spirits. He parried questions with ease. The contrast with Hawke was total. Keating then sat on the back bench during Question Time. That evening, a party was held in Keating's office. While many at the party could be forgiven for thinking this was just the opening salvo in a long battle ahead, the challenger himself insisted there was no such strategy. 'I thought it was all over,' Keating said.[81]

Barrie Cassidy, who would soon leave Hawke's office to return to journalism, told Hawke after the first leadership challenge that he should quit and hand over to Keating.

'I am strongly of the view that to protect your own legacy, and after having had eight years as prime minister, you would be better off leaving,' Cassidy said.

'I think you're just tired, Butch,' Hawke replied.

'Well, you are right about that, but it is still my view,' Cassidy said.[82]

But Hawke was never going to quit.

31

END OF
DAYS

Bob Hawke now sought to stabilise and refocus the government, reunite the party and rally the faithful. This was the message of Hawke's opening speech to Labor's centenary national conference on 26 June 1991. 'We meet as the representatives of Australia's most important and enduring force for change and progress – an institution uniquely Australian in its creation and character, uniquely Australian in its values and in its achievement – the Australian Labor Party.' Hawke tied the story of Labor to the story of Australia, describing the party as 'the engine room of national renewal, the generators of change, the pioneers of reform'.[1]

But within days of the leadership challenge, the cabinet and caucus were enveloped in a major dispute over whether mining should be allowed at Coronation Hill in the Kakadu National Park, in the Northern Territory. This was the most impassioned and acrimonious debate in cabinet during Hawke's prime ministership. In 1987, the government proclaimed Stage III of the park and excluded a large mining exploration zone, but it had given a commitment to BHP that it could continue its plans to mine gold, platinum and palladium at Coronation Hill, which was within this excluded zone.

The government received two reports by Justice Don Stewart. The first was presented in his capacity as chairman of the Resource Assessment Commission. The second considered the protection of Indigenous areas within the zone under the subsection 10(4) of the *Aboriginal and Torres Strait Islander Heritage Protection Act 1984*. The RAC found that mining would have a small, though manageable, impact on the ecological integrity of the area but would damage the Jawoyn people's ability to sustain their cultural and religious values, beliefs and practices. The s.10(4) report was unequivocal in its conclusion that the zone was a significant Indigenous site and should be protected from mining.

Hawke, who had met with Jawoyn leaders and studied the reports, was convinced that mining should not proceed because it would fundamentally undermine their sacred site. The Jawoyn believed that the serpent god Bula lived under the ground, and mining this area would bring dreadful consequences to their community. It was known as the Sickness Country. Hawke felt strongly that their beliefs should be respected and mining should therefore be prohibited. In accordance with Hawke's instructions, four ministers – Nick Bolkus, Ros Kelly, Robert Tickner and Alan Griffiths – presented a submission outlining the issues, with options for cabinet on how to proceed.[2]

Simon Balderstone, environment adviser to Hawke, recalled that this was first and foremost an Indigenous issue. 'There was a view that this was an environment issue and by this stage Hawke had gone too far and was too green,' he said. 'But it was never about that. It was about the Indigenous community and their beliefs. I told Hawkey that this was the one that we really cannot lose. This is a totem issue.' Hawke needed little convincing. 'Hawke felt he had earnt the political capital to be able to make the call on this one,' Balderstone said.[3]

The critical cabinet debate took place on 18 June and ran for almost five hours. 'This was a debate where very few people were undecided,' Bolkus recalled. 'It was a debate that brought out the worst of Australian prejudice and racism. No mining was a hard proposition to sell. One should remember that Hawke was the son of a preacher man and that was probably more important than people may think.'[4] Kelly, the minister for the environment, argued that mining should be banned on environmental grounds. 'If you allowed any mining, the whole area would end up being destroyed so you had to draw the line somewhere,' she recalled.

'I had to have Hawke with me or I was never going to get it through. It was the right decision.'[5]

Hawke's cabinet room notes show there was a variety of views. After the submission was presented, Hawke, unusually, led the debate by stating his view upfront: that mining should be disallowed because the Indigenous people's beliefs should be respected. Hawke was forceful and passionate. He referred to the 'monumental hypocrisy' of those who professed to believe in the mysteries of Christianity, including the Holy Trinity, but could not fathom the ancient religious beliefs of the local Indigenous people. He accused ministers of arguing 'a miscellany of misrepresentation, intimidation and thinly veiled supremacist discrimination'. It was strong stuff.[6]

Griffiths, the minister for resources, predicted a 'political holocaust' if mining was not allowed and said it would be 'enormously damaging' to Australia. He spoke for nineteen minutes. Bob Collins, the minister assisting the prime minister for northern Australia, argued that allowing mining was 'the only tenable political option and also a principled position' for the cabinet to take. He spoke for thirty-one minutes. They were backed by Treasury analysis showing that prohibiting mining would expose Australia to perceptions of sovereign risk for investors. Hawke spoke again, rebutting these claims, for a further half-hour. Kelly recalled Hawke had tears in his eyes as he urged cabinet to respect the sacred beliefs of the Jawoyn people.[7] The only strong support for his position came from Bolkus, Kelly and Robert Tickner, the minister for Aboriginal affairs. In the end, most cabinet ministers, perhaps three-quarters, supported mining.

Hawke had clearly lost the debate. Indeed, Robert Ray thought he had 'argued the case atrociously'.[8] Hawke suggested cabinet debate it further. But Kim Beazley told Hawke the debate had gone on long enough and it was time to 'make a decision'.[9] Hawke said cabinet's decision would be to prohibit mining at Coronation Hill and incorporate the Kakadu Conservation Zone into the Kakadu National Park. Collins recalled ministers being appalled – they 'just started walking out of the room'.[10] Hawke had got his way.[11] 'I did not have the numbers around the cabinet table but I did have the authority of the prime ministership,' he reflected.[12] But the cost was high. 'Hawke's leadership ended there in the cabinet room,' thought Brian Howe.[13]

The debate spilled over into caucus two days later. Hawke faced an open revolt in the party room – the most significant of his prime ministership – with an attempt to overturn the cabinet decision. A motion proposed by Gary Johns and seconded by Michael Lee wanted the decision reviewed. Hawke accepted there was a difference of views and said 'it was a difficult decision' but it must hold. The caucus debate went for more than an hour, with most MPs opposed to Hawke. Hawke's caucus notes reveal he thought Johns was speaking 'crap' and Lee was guilty of a 'tortuous analogy' with other mining decisions.[14] But they could not deliver a rebuff to Hawke. To do so would not only be humiliating, it would also doom his prime ministership. So, caucus upheld the cabinet decision.[15]

Meanwhile, Keating remained the 'world's greatest backbencher', as one cartoonist characterised him. He was not quitting parliament and instead had become a roving policy think tank. He gave speeches and interviews on superannuation, cities, federalism and the economy. He supported Australia becoming a republic and changing the flag. He told Ray Martin on *The Midday Show* on 17 July that he would like to be prime minister 'at some stage'.[16] He was profiled by *Four Corners*, who trailed him on a visit to his alma mater, De La Salle College in Bankstown, Western Sydney.[17] The press gallery viewed everything Keating said through the lens of leadership. Keating, stripped of power, was now climbing in the polls. At the end of May 1991, Hawke led Keating as better prime minister by 66 per cent to 18 per cent.[18] By August, Hawke had 51.6 per cent to Keating's 30.3 per cent.[19]

Hawke viewed each one of these forays as an act of political treachery and sabotage. Keating, even though he ruled out a further leadership challenge, was a permanent distraction. With the former treasurer second-guessing policy and advocating his own agenda, it smacked of disunity. Indeed, Keating was coming on so strong that he was advised to ease back; Glenn Milne reported that his supporters believed 'a shift will come only through a judgement on Mr Hawke's performance without internally generated pressure'. Keating did not give any interviews or make any speeches after mid-November. On 8 November, he declared on ABC Radio's *PM* program that he would not be challenging Hawke.[20]

This strategy would prove to be the right one. Hawke was struggling to maintain his authority, regain political momentum and win ascendancy over Hewson. When he had become opposition leader after the 1990 election, Hewson told his party room that it had 'zero policy credibility' and would have to develop a new policy agenda. He thought it would likely take two elections to regain government. On 21 November, Hewson unveiled the most sweeping policy manifesto seen in two decades: *Fightback!* The media was spellbound by the policy document. It looked audacious and impressive. Newspapers printed pages and pages of explanation and analysis, as they would for a budget. It looked like the opposition had a young leader with a bold blueprint to lift Australia out of recession and carry it into the twenty-first century.

There were a mix of carrots and sticks in the 600-plus-page policy document. The flagship idea was a 15 per cent goods and services tax. Government spending was to be slashed by $10 billion. Bulk-billing by GPs would end for most Australians. Awards were to be abolished and dole payments restricted. More government enterprises were to be privatised. The sweeteners included $20 billion in business and personal tax cuts; increases to pensions, family and student allowances; and the promise of 2 million new jobs by 2000. *Fightback!* called for a cut in greenhouse gas emissions by 20 per cent, on 1990 levels, by 2000. A new fund would invest in infrastructure. 'It was a pretty hard-line, dry and rational response to the economic circumstances,' Hewson said. 'But at the same time, it was small-l liberal in social policy.'[21]

Hawke's approach to *Fightback!* was to deconstruct it by pointing out detailed policy flaws. The mistake was not to launch an immediate political attack and characterise it as a threat to Medicare, the Prices and Incomes Accord and the social welfare system. This was the critique caucus members were looking for, and Keating supporters were only too happy to point out what was lacking. Hawke was slow off the mark, a point he conceded when questioned in caucus five days after *Fightback!* was released.

'The "Hewson package" was still being subjected to political and technical analysis,' he said.[22]

Not surprisingly, the Coalition surged in the polls to lead Labor by 53 per cent to 30 per cent on the primary vote.[23] The Liberal Party's federal director, Andrew Robb, was stunned by the positive reception to *Fightback!*. He said Hawke looked like 'a rabbit caught in a spotlight'.[24] Hewson had united the Coalition and initially presented as a formidable opponent. Hewson was surprised by the headway he was making over Hawke. '*Fightback!*, for its strengths and weaknesses, just killed Hawke,' Hewson thought. 'It allowed Keating to argue that you needed to dump Hawke to destroy the policy and kill me.'[25]

John Kerin, the new treasurer, had a tough act to follow. So, Kerin promised a different style to Keating: he would be more inclusive and consultative, with less razzmatazz and vituperation. He had been an effective and respected minister for primary industries. He had university qualifications in economics, had worked as an economist for the Bureau of Agricultural Economics, and been a farmer and businessman. He was intelligent and shrewd, with a self-deprecatory sense of humour. The press gallery loved that he could hypnotise chooks.

Kerin's immediate task was to complete the budget and present it to parliament on 20 August. The budget strategy had been developed by Keating and approved by cabinet on 22 May. Its principal focus was to reduce unemployment and inflation, but there were no significant stimulus measures. A deficit of $4.7 billion was projected.[26] There were two other notable initiatives in the budget: a $3.50 charge for GP visits and the introduction of the Superannuation Guarantee, which required employers to make superannuation contributions on behalf of employees, to commence on 1 July 1992.

Kerin had doubts about the overall economic strategy and conveyed his concerns to Hawke. He spoke to Treasury secretary Tony Cole, who reassured him that the 'automatic stabilisers would do the trick'. Cole also suggested Kerin 'announce a cut in interest rates' in the budget speech. Kerin thought this idea was bonkers. He spoke to Bernie Fraser, the Reserve Bank's governor, who advised that they might as well 'give the game away' if he did that. The upshot? 'I had to deliver a budget I did not believe in,' Kerin said. In hindsight, he thought the budget made the recession worse.[27]

Kerin upset the press gallery when he broke with tradition and cancelled the embargoed briefing – known as the lock-up – for journalists prior to the budget's presentation. He also abandoned the night-time address and delivered the budget at 3 pm, after Question Time. It was a disaster. The press gallery was offside. The government lost a primetime audience. These proposals were advocated by Treasury's John Fraser, who wrote to Kerin on 25 July 1991:

> The speech will be televised in mid-afternoon rather than prime-time but, against that, it will allow for more exposure on the evening news and news commentary programs. The so-called sophisticated audience should have the wit to turn their television sets on mid-afternoon just as much as in the evening, but you may lose some of the broader community (to the extent that they watch budget speeches).

Journalists revolted. Michelle Grattan, then president of the press gallery, raised the complaints with Kerin's office. The treasurer decided to give a little, and some radio, television and wire journalists were given 'read-only' access to the budget papers at 2 pm. The newspapers were allowed to send one representative each. It was a bold idea, but one never repeated.[28]

The caucus was also up in arms. The $3.50 GP co-payment attracted considerable opposition. (Brian Howe had proposed a $2 GP co-payment in August 1990, but this was rejected.) Hawke told MPs the co-payment was aimed at dealing with escalating health costs but said he was prepared to consider modifications.[29] Hawke later agreed to reduce it to $2.50. Keating privately told MPs he would abolish it if he became prime minister. Howe conceded it was politically damaging. 'It may have been important in eroding Hawke's standing in caucus, but Keating was out there actively eroding Hawke's support on whatever issue he could find,' Howe recalled.[30] After defending the co-payment at a press conference, Howe tried to exit via a cupboard. In such a highly febrile environment, any divisions and any mistakes were magnified by the media and energised the Keating camp.

Kerin continued to have doubts about the government's economic strategy. By October, unemployment had climbed to 10 per cent. It was Hawke, not Kerin, who delivered a Statement on the Economy and Employment on 14 November 1991.[31] The $313 million package of initiatives seemed like more of the same: boosting training, expanding labour market programs, accelerating infrastructure investment, and facilitating industry restructuring and the development of new industries. It was a worthwhile statement but the response in caucus, and in the media, was underwhelming. Hawke could not gain traction.

Not surprisingly, the under-siege Kerin lost confidence. This was evident when he confused gross operating surplus with gross profit share during a press conference on the national accounts on Thursday, 5 December. 'What's GOS?' he asked journalists. Kerin had 'a memory loss' and simply froze when he could not remember if the 's' in 'GOS' stood for 'share' or 'surplus'. Hawke felt he had no other option but to shift Kerin to a new portfolio. When Hawke delivered the news to Kerin that he was being sacked, they both cried.[32] Kerin was relieved. 'The pressure was just too great and I just couldn't see my way out of the problems,' he recalled.[33]

Kerin is highly self-critical of his six months as treasurer. 'I failed as treasurer and let Hawke down,' he said. 'I did not aspire to be treasurer at all – [it was] beyond my pay scale. I was mad to accept, but I thought that the economy may be on the turn, as Keating had convinced us.' He added: 'It was impossibly difficult being in Keating's shadow, mainly because of my own inadequacies and lack of any preparation for the role.' It is a sad but honest reflection.[34]

The government looked like it was struggling without Keating. On Friday, 6 December, Hawke announced that Ralph Willis would be appointed treasurer. Kim Beazley became minister for finance. Kerin was moved to transport and communications. All four parliamentary leaders – Hawke, Howe, Button and Evans – plus the treasurer, were from Melbourne. Hawke had resisted this in June.

As deputy prime minister, Howe did not feel particularly close to Hawke. On one occasion he spent a night at Kirribilli House and then had breakfast with Hawke the next day. He saw an opportunity to revitalise the government with a major package that addressed employment, education and training. He had consulted several academics and worked up a detailed proposal to discuss with Hawke. 'I thought the government needed a new lease of life and the way to do that was to come up with a program that really addressed what was the issue on everyone's minds,' Howe recalled. 'But Bob wasn't really responsive.'[35]

The Hawke government seemed in a death spiral. On Sunday, 8 December, Hawke addressed the New South Wales Labor Party's annual conference at the Sydney Town Hall. This was Keating territory. Terry Sheahan, the state party president, told delegates that Labor could 'ill afford to go into the next federal election with the dual folly of having one of our most potent batsman sitting in the grandstand'. It was a thinly veiled reference to Keating. Sheahan was hoping to precipitate another leadership challenge.[36] When Hawke spoke the next day, he did so in the lion's den. Graham Freudenberg thought New South Wales Labor should have been 'ashamed' of the way they treated Hawke.[37] Bob Carr said the force of Keating's personality drove his leadership campaign. It was not about policy. 'It was like Cicero remarking of Caesar's march on Rome that "this cause lacks nothing but a cause".'[38]

Amid the destabilisation and the undermining, the polls were diabolical. The Hawke government was circling the drain. The Morgan Gallup poll, to be published in *The Bulletin* on Wednesday, 11 December, was known at the start of the week as parliament resumed. The Coalition was ahead of Labor on the primary vote by 51 per cent to 33 per cent. Hawke's approval rating had plummeted to 31 per cent, and his disapproval rating had risen to 59 per cent. Hewson's approval rating was up to 56 per cent and his disapproval was down to 30 per cent. Hewson led Hawke as preferred prime minister by 46 per cent to 39 per cent.[39] Hawke had now lost his trump card: the polls. While he remained more popular than Keating, and was the preferred Labor prime minster, he could no longer convincingly claim that he would lead Labor to another election victory.

On Monday, 9 December, Geoff Kitney reported in *The Australian Financial Review* that the government was mired in a full-blown 'leadership crisis', as the cabinet reshuffle had done little to boost confidence.[40] The next day, Tuesday, 10 December, Parliament House swirled with speculation that Hawke's support was collapsing. It was reported that 'private pressure' on Hawke from his closest backers could force him to stand down.[41] By Wednesday, 11 December, Alan Ramsey said that Hawke was no longer the Messiah but rather Caesar, who also did not know when to go, and it was inevitable he too would be brought down.[42]

Events gathered pace. That evening, Hawke was at Government House with Bill Hayden, who was hosting a dinner in honour of Cypriot president George Vassiliou. At 10.10 pm, Hawke left and returned to the Lodge. At 11 pm, Hawke's key supporters – Kim Beazley, Robert Ray, Gareth Evans, Michael Duffy, Gerry Hand and Nick Bolkus – met at Ray's home in Yarralumla to discuss the leadership. This group – known as 'The Gang of Six' or 'The Big Six' – agreed the situation was bleak. Ray phoned Colin Parks to let him know they were meeting, and he passed this on to Hawke. The prime minister agreed to see them in the morning. At 1.15 am the meeting of six ministers broke up. They had decided to tell Hawke he could not defeat Keating in a second leadership ballot. Beazley, however, phoned Hawke later that night at the Lodge and told him precisely why they were coming and what they would say. Hawke was ready.

Hawke arrived at Parliament House at 8.05 am the next day, Thursday, 12 December. At 8.10 am, Hawke met with the six ministers in his office. Hawke was told he was unlikely to prevail against Keating and should resign to facilitate a transfer of power. It led to an animated discussion. Ray was reluctant to give in to 'political blackmail' but told Hawke that it 'was better to get out then and get out on top'.[43] Beazley told Hawke: 'Mate, this can't stand. You've got to go.'[44] Duffy said: 'Bob, why are you going on with this, because no matter which way you do the numbers, you can't win.'[45] Hand argued: 'Bob, we don't want you to be humiliated. We know the way the vote is going to go.'[46] Bolkus said: 'Bob, we will back you but we do not think you can win.'[47] Evans summed up the situation. 'Pull out, digger, the dogs are pissing on your swag,' he said. 'The dignified thing to do is to bow to that inevitability and to retire gracefully.'[48]

They presented Hawke with two options: resign now or tell Keating he would resign in the New Year, after the visit of President George H.W. Bush. Hawke was not persuaded. He insisted he had the best chance of leading the party to victory at the next election, and reiterated his view that Keating was unworthy of the prime ministership. 'If the party believes that there should be a change of leadership, then that is something the party has to decide,' he said.[49] At 9.50 am, the meeting broke up and the ministers continued talking in smaller groups.

At 10 am, Hawke officially welcomed the Cypriot president to Parliament House. Hawke and Vassiliou attended a meeting of the cabinet and an official lunch. Hawke reconvened with the six ministers at 3.45 pm. Hawke was insistent that he would not resign. 'He just didn't listen,' Ray recalled. 'He didn't resign because he loved the job and was obsessed with being prime minister. By then he probably hated Paul substantially and had just gone through six months of treachery, and he saw resigning as giving in to terrorism.'[50] The six ministers felt they had no other option but to endorse this decision, and resolved to help him in the caucus ballot.

At 5.05 pm, Beazley fronted a media crush to say that Hawke had their support. 'All conceivable options were considered during the course of those discussions,' he said. 'At the end of the day the prime minister made the decision that was endorsed by them,' he said.[51] In other words, the six ministers had told Hawke he should resign but supported his decision to stay. Hawke could not recover. 'The moment we decided we would go and see him, we knew we had marked his card,' recalled Ray.[52] Bolkus agreed. 'The open verbal conversation was "we are here to back you", [but] the underwritten text was "we are probably going to fail",' he said.[53]

At 6.30 pm, Hawke hosted the press gallery for the annual end-of-year drinks at the Lodge. He was in a cheerful mood as he mingled with journalists beneath the backyard marquee. He ate sandwiches, drank a tankard of non-alcoholic beer and puffed on a cigar. Hazel and Rosslyn were also there. In brief remarks, Hawke said that his political obituary should not be written just yet. 'Any contest next week I'm going to win,' he said.[54] At 8.30 pm, the function ended and Hawke retreated into the Lodge.

Meanwhile, Keating was preparing to quit parliament in January 1992. He had made a financial investment in a piggery – not something you would do if you were hoping to become prime minister. Keating's closest caucus colleagues and staff agree that he was planning to leave parliament, thinking he would never become prime minister, but nevertheless was not ruling anything out. Keating made it clear he was available. But his ambition would be tied to Hawke's performance. There would be no chance of a second challenge if the Hawke government was performing strongly.

While Hawke was under immense pressure, the parliamentary sitting week had ended and he remained prime minister. The problem, though, was that parliament was planning to resume for a special one-day sitting to deal with legislation concerning political advertising. The caucus was scheduled to meet on Thursday, 19 December. 'If the bill had not come back to the House of Representatives, there would have been no occasion for a caucus ballot,' Keating explained. 'The Labor Party would not have met until the first week of February 1992, by which time I would have resigned as member for Blaxland.'[55] Political fates can be tied to such seemingly trivial things.

Beazley was troubled. At 11 pm on Monday, 16 December, he went to the Lodge to talk to Hawke. They sat in the small, book-lined study, and each blazed a cigar. 'Bob, this is hard for me to say, but I really do think you should give it away to preserve your reputation and your legacy,' Beazley said. 'You deserve to go out on top, not voted out by caucus, and I've got to tell you that I think that the numbers in caucus are against you.' Hawke said he could never give into 'terrorism' and that caucus should decide who the leader of the party is. Beazley was holding a losing hand. Hoping to play a trump card, he said he was sure that Hazel agreed with him. 'That's not what I heard,' Hawke replied. He marched upstairs and roused Hazel from her sleep and brought her to the study. In her nightgown, Hazel told Beazley she supported her husband and 'deferred to his judgement'.[56]

John Button was also thinking about the leadership. Nine years earlier he had urged Hayden to resign; now he urged Hawke to resign. On Tuesday, 17 December, Button met Hawke in his office.

'The problem we now have is that the government is stuffed, and the leadership issue has to be resolved,' he told Hawke. 'I don't think the Labor Party can win the next election under Keating, or you. It has gone too far. If that is so, why do you want to remain leader? You have had eight good years in the job.' Hawke insisted he was best placed to lead the government to the election. 'It is my task to win the next election, and I, and only I, can do that,' Hawke said. Button was not persuaded. And Hawke would not bend like Hayden. He would fight to the bitter end.[57]

On Wednesday, 18 December, the Left faction decided it would no longer bind its members behind Hawke; they would have a free vote in any leadership contest. The key to Hawke's victory over Keating in June was that he had most of the Left behind him. That was now weakening. But several Left faction members, such as Peter Duncan, Frank Walker and Stewart West, were going to vote for Keating no matter what the faction's leaders decided.

At 6.30 pm that evening, the caucus Christmas party was held at the Lodge. Caucus was due to meet the following day. The outlook was looking bleaker for Hawke by the hour. Beazley said to Ray, 'Why don't we have another crack?' They met Hawke at about 9.30 pm in his office. They again told Hawke he would lose a leadership ballot against Keating, so he should consider resigning. But Hawke's view was unchanged – he would not resign.[58]

Beazley and Ray left Hawke and continued the discussion in Ray's office. The phone rang; it was Graham Richardson. He said Bob McMullan had prepared a petition of Labor MPs to force a ballot at the next caucus meeting. McMullan wanted to end the stalemate and resolve the leadership. 'I thought the idea that we weren't going to have a second ballot was just crazy,' he recalled.[59] To petition a caucus ballot, they would need the signatures of thirty-seven MPs, one-third of caucus.

Meanwhile, Gerry Hand and Nick Bolkus were informing Hawke of the Left's decision to allow its members a free vote if there was another leadership ballot. At about 11 pm, Bolkus rang Ray and Beazley, and asked them to join the meeting in Hawke's office. They talked for another two or three hours. Sometime after 1 am, Ray told Hawke, 'You could, of course, do this another way. You could call the meeting yourself, release everyone from

their pledges, no show-and-tell ballot. You could do it cleanly.'[60]
Hawke agreed.

Hawke then went back to the Lodge with Grant Nihill. They continued talking while Hawke smoked a cigar and Nihill had another beer. It was the early hours of the morning. At about 4 am, Hawke decided to go up to the bedroom and tell Hazel the grim news. She was woken up. Nihill sat on the edge of the bed. 'It's all over, darling,' Hawke said. 'We don't have the numbers.' Hazel was calm; Bob was resigned to his fate.[61]

The caucus was scheduled to meet at 9 am on Thursday, 19 December. After a few hours' sleep at the Lodge, Hawke arrived at Parliament House at 8.35 am. At 8.55 am, Hawke spoke to Ray, and also to Hand and Duffy, to confirm that he would proceed with a ballot later that day. At 9 am, Hawke gave caucus secretary Carolyn Jakobsen a four-paragraph letter in which he exercised his authority as leader to call a caucus meeting at 6.30 pm. The letter was circulated to Labor MPs. Hawke would resign as leader and offer himself for re-election via a secret ballot. At 10.30 am, Keating confirmed that he would be a candidate for the leadership. The final showdown was now hours away.

Before and after Question Time, Hawke phoned several Labor MPs to reassure them that Labor could win the next election. His tool, as ever, was the polls. The Morgan Gallup poll, published in *The Bulletin*, showed his approval rating had sunk to an all-time low of 31 per cent, whereas Hewson's was 56 per cent. Hawke lagged Hewson as preferred prime minister by 39 per cent to 46 per cent. Labor's primary vote was 33 per cent, compared to the Coalition's 51 per cent.[62] Hawke, though, was not fighting Hewson – he was fighting Keating. A Saulwick Poll published days earlier showed Hawke leading Keating as preferred prime minister by 53 per cent to 34 per cent.[63]

Hawke's key numbers men were Ray, Beazley, Bolkus and Hand. Keating's were Richardson, Laurie Brereton, Leo McLeay and Gary Punch. They would report back to Keating the MPs who could be persuaded or needed to be confirmed as voting for him, and he would then ring them personally. Hawke, it seems, left much of the canvassing to others. Hawke was losing votes. He lost Ben Humphreys, who was promised a cabinet post by Keating supporters.[64] Wendy Fatin, from the Left, voted for Hawke in June but never received a call from him or his supporters in December.[65] Peter Baldwin, also from the Left, voted for Hawke in June but did not hear from him in December – he too voted for Keating.[66] The most significant – and unknown – defection was John Kerin. He was the only cabinet minister to switch between June and December. Kerin thought voting for Keating was the only way to end the destabilisation. He did not tell Hawke.[67]

For the second leadership ballot, Hawke could count on the support of nine cabinet ministers (not including himself): Gareth Evans, Ralph Willis, Michael Duffy, Kim Beazley, Brian Howe, Robert Ray, Gerry Hand, Nick Bolkus and Simon Crean. Keating now had seven cabinet members supporting him: John Button, John Dawkins, Graham Richardson, Neal Blewett, Ros Kelly, Peter Cook and Kerin.

The leadership challenge divided the industrial wing of the labour movement. Jennie George, then the ACTU's assistant secretary, recalled that secretary Bill Kelty was in the Keating camp and president Martin Ferguson was in the Hawke camp. 'Martin was directly lobbying on Hawke's behalf,' she said. 'I was contacted by Pat Staunton from the nurses' union, who happened to be in parliament that day. She complained that the ACTU president was lobbying MPs and that this was inappropriate. I raised my concerns with Martin, with whom I didn't have a close relationship.'[68]

Ferguson recalled Kelty telling him in the summer of 1990–91 that the party would have to 'start thinking about a change' of leader. But Ferguson thought the ACTU should play no role in the party's leadership. He said he did not lobby MPs. 'I was not prepared to be involved in pulling down a Labor prime minister. It was inappropriate for the institution to be involved in such an exercise. Friends of mine in the caucus talked to me about what was going on, but I was not advising them what to do. It was up to them. Bob was appreciative of my support but never asked me to lobby on his behalf.'[69]

Hawke's staff had felt under siege over the previous six months. There was a mix of sadness, disappointment and anger. 'From the first challenge to the second, it was guerrilla warfare day in and day out,' recalled Dennis Richardson. 'The chance to focus on policy in that period was pretty limited.'[70] Around lunchtime, Hawke called the staff into his office. As they stood around the desk, he said: 'I don't think I'm going to win this.' The end was near. There were tears.[71]

Hawke attended Question Time. Keating, a backbencher, stayed in his office. Most questions from Hewson were directed at Hawke and concerned the leadership. Asked whether it was true that no Labor prime minister had ever been rejected by his own party in a caucus ballot, Hawke replied: 'All I can say is that I hope history will repeat itself.'[72]

The caucus meeting began at 6.36 pm on Thursday, 19 December. Hawke walked to the lectern at the front of the room. He announced his resignation as leader and said he would renominate for the position. He told MPs that 'the 1993 election would be a most important one and his leadership gave the best chance for a Labor victory'. If he was successful, he would seek to unite the party, with no recriminations, and put 'the trauma' of the past year behind them. His key pitch was based on 'two indisputable facts'. First, that the media wanted Keating to become prime minister. But, second, the party wanted Hawke. He said the party's will should prevail.[73]

The returning officer, Jim McKiernan, called for further nominations. Keating nominated himself. The meeting was then adjourned to prepare ballot papers. At 6.50 pm, caucus members were asked to make their way to the cordoned-off section of the room and cast their votes. The air was filled with anticipation, uncertainty and tension. In a moment of light relief, Hawke showed Keating his ballot paper, and Keating showed Hawke his.

The ballots were counted. The scrutineers gave their signals. Ray leaned over to Hawke. 'Prepare yourself,' he whispered in Hawke's ear. 'You've lost.'[74] At the same time, Punch gave Keating a nod and seconds later walked over to tell him the result. 'You've won,' he said.[75] Just moments later, at 7.06 pm, McKiernan announced the result of the ballot: Keating received fifty-six votes and Hawke received fifty-one. Keating had won a narrow victory. Hawke congratulated Keating. They shook hands.

Keating paid tribute to Hawke's leadership and described him as a political icon. '[His] electoral record [was] unequalled and we all owed him an enormous debt,' Keating said. Caucus members stood and applauded. Tears welled in Hawke's eyes and dripped down his cheeks. 'There was now a need for consensus and reconciliation within the party,' Keating said. 'This had been the hallmark of Bob Hawke's government and had helped the party and government to make changes to Australia.'[76]

Hawke was invited to address the caucus. He offered his congratulations to Keating and thanked the MPs who had voted for him. Looking to the future, he 'pledged complete support to the party and the government'. He promised not to 'utter one word to harm Paul or his government'. He finished by saying that 'it had been a privilege to lead the party for nine years and his reward was to be able to leave Australia a better place'.[77]

The meeting closed at 7.21 pm. There was a mix of sadness and exhilaration, energy and exhaustion, quiet contemplation and joyous celebration. Two lines quickly formed, one in front of Keating and another in front of Hawke. The victor was congratulated, and the vanquished was commiserated with. McKiernan announced the result to the waiting media in the corridor outside the caucus room. Keating left the meeting at 7.24 pm, and said to journalists that it was a great honour to have been elected leader. Hawke was overwhelmed with emotion and needed a few moments to compose himself. He left the meeting and walked down the corridor, waving and smiling to the media, and went back to his office.

Hawke was devastated and thought caucus had made a mistake it would regret. 'I was terribly disappointed,' he recalled.[78] He returned to his office and was greeted by staff in tears. 'It was stunned and sad silence,' Nihill recalled.[79] 'Everyone was crying,' said Parks.[80] Several ministers were choking up. Mike Codd had tears in his eyes. Later that evening, there were more tears amid much drinking and a few speeches in the cabinet anteroom. Hawke was not especially emotional. 'He was fine,' recalled Dennis Richardson. 'By then he was resigned to it.'[81]

John Howard was the first opposition MP to visit Hawke's office to commiserate. 'I thought Hawke's prospects about a year out from an election were very poor, but I thought at the time that it was a mistake for the Labor Party to get rid of him,' Howard recalled. 'Although his popularity had certainly faded, I still thought he had done quite well.' But Howard did not think Hawke would have won the 1993 election.[82]

At 7.50 pm, just a short time after arriving back at his office, Hawke fronted the press gallery. The press conference was carried live on radio and television. He explained why he did not resign. 'I believe . . . I had the best chance of leading the Labor Party to victory in what I regard as one of the most important post-war elections,' Hawke said. 'Secondly, and very importantly, I took the view that you could not have any more important decision than this for the party, and it was a decision that the party would have to take.' He reflected on the privilege of being prime minister, noted his achievements and expressed his regret that unemployment remained high. He thanked Hazel, his family, his staff, and the MPs who voted for him.

Asked about plans for the future, Hawke joked, 'If it were eleven years ago I'd be getting pretty thoroughly drunk.' That was behind him. 'I'm now a considerably poorer man. My income stream has been diminished. I have considerable debts and I'll have to start thinking about how I'm going to meet those.' He wanted to be remembered as 'a bloke who loved his country', 'loves Australians' and was not changed by the prime ministership. 'I hope they still will think of me as the Bob Hawke that they got to know, the larrikin trade union leader who perhaps had sufficient common sense and intelligence to tone down his larrikinism to some extent and behave in a way that a prime minister should if he's going to be a proper representative of his people, but who in the end is essentially a dinky-di Australian.'[83]

A short time later, Hawke was driven out to Government House. The irony of Hawke's final day was that he had to resign to the man he had replaced as Labor leader: Bill Hayden. In the governor-general's study, Hawke returned his prime ministerial commission and advised Hayden to call Paul Keating. Hayden knew all too well how Hawke had argued the leadership should be determined by the polls. Now Hawke was behind in the polls and had lost the leadership. 'It is thoroughly understandable that those who live by the polls can die by the polls, as Bob's experience has proved,' Hayden thought.[84]

Hayden subsequently wrote to the Queen about his conversation with Hawke. He thought Hawke had reduced Keating's 'promised vote' from sixty-three to fifty-six. 'If I'd only had another twenty-four hours I would have talked the rest around,' Hawke told Hayden. Hayden believed him. But he also thought this would not have bought him a full reprieve, as he wrote to the Queen:

> It would have solved nothing for him if he had turned the vote around. It would have been like a condemned man escaping the gallows because the rope broke. A new rope would quickly be found. Hawke had to win and win well if he was going to destroy the Keating challenge for good.[85]

Indeed, Hawke had two votes that were not cast. Gareth Evans was in Jakarta and Con Sciacca was with his sick son. On the other side, Jim Snow, a vote for Keating, was absent with his sick daughter. If they had been present, it would have been fifty-three votes for Hawke and fifty-seven for Keating. Sciacca and Snow were paired, so their votes can be excluded. The more likely outcome was that if Evans was prevailed upon to return, the result would have been fifty-two votes for Hawke and fifty-six for Keating. The upshot is that a change of just three votes would have made it a 55–53 result in Hawke's favour. A change of two votes would have produced a tie.

Beazley was shocked by the result. 'If I had known it was going to be that close, we would have moved heaven and earth to win the ballot,' he said. 'We could have won.' He thought Humphreys' vote was winnable, along with Fatin's.[86] Add Kerin and Evans, and Hawke would have remained prime minister. Ray was less certain. 'I'm not sure I could have shifted any other vote,' he said. 'They were all pretty much entrenched by then. Two or three people that were very loyal to me were voting for Keating.'[87]

But even a narrow victory for Hawke would have made re-establishing his political authority difficult. Keating would have quit parliament. Richardson and Dawkins would have resigned from cabinet. Bob Collins may have quit the outer ministry. But that was probably it. Blewett would not have resigned from cabinet, and it is unlikely Button or Cook would have either.[88] Kelly would not have resigned.[89] Moreover, Beazley, Evans, Ray, Duffy, Hand

and Bolkus would have remained cabinet ministers. Nevertheless, Hawke would still have faced an enormous challenge to stabilise and rebuild the government, and mount an effective campaign against a popular opposition leader in John Hewson.

Graham Freudenberg, who had worked for Arthur Calwell and Gough Whitlam, was deeply disappointed by Hawke's demise. It was the first and only time a Labor prime minister had been challenged and defeated in a caucus leadership ballot. He saw the defection of cabinet ministers, rather than a caucus rebellion, as the critical factor. 'Just as Whitlam saw the potential of parliament, Hawke saw the potential of cabinet,' he reflected. 'The supreme irony was that Whitlam was a great parliament man and Hawke was a great cabinet man, and these institutions that they both flourished in was what brought them down.'[90]

Hawke had said Keating was his preferred successor. But privately he wanted Kim Beazley to succeed him. If Hawke had retained the leadership and Keating had quit parliament, and Labor won the 1993 election, this would have been likely. Hawke and Beazley talked about it. 'He was the one I wanted to succeed me,' Hawke said. 'I think he would have been a great prime minister.' Hawke also raised with Beazley the idea that he could stand against Keating in a leadership ballot. But Beazley always viewed Keating as Hawke's successor.

Nonetheless, Hawke had no regrets about deciding to contest the second leadership ballot. 'Paul did a lot of good things as treasurer,' Hawke reflected. 'But I had the view, and still have the view, that I was the best person suited to lead the government to the 1993 election and remain as prime minister.' Is Hawke sure he would have won the next election? 'Yes,' he said. 'I'd beaten Fraser. I'd beaten Howard. I'd beaten Peacock twice. And I don't think Hewson would have been better than any of them.'[91]

Keating, however, did have regrets. 'I did not rejoice in his defeat,' Keating reflected. 'I felt very sad about it. Bob and I had a long friendship, a long professional and personal friendship. I didn't want to have to fight Bob for the leadership; I wanted him to pass it over as he said he would.'[92]

Keating emphasised that he was almost always likeminded with Hawke on the direction of public policy. 'We had a similar view

about the way Australia had to go,' he explained. 'My job as treasurer was to dismantle the Deakin legacy. That was a big technical
and persuasive job. But I had the intellectual support of the prime
minister.' Keating added that his relationship with Hawke was
underscored by a personal bond. 'There was a high level of cooperation and friendship right throughout until those last months,'
he said.[93]

Just after 10.30 pm that evening, Hawke addressed the House
of Representatives for the final time. 'I do not think anyone would
gainsay me if at this point I said that it has been an eventful year,'
he said. Hawke thanked members of parliament, the parliamentary
and personal staff, and wished everyone a merry Christmas and a
happy new year. He paid tribute to Kim Beazley, the Leader of the
House, and then bade farewell. 'As this will be my last speech in
this chamber as prime minister,' he said, 'I would sincerely like to
thank all my ministerial colleagues and those of my party who have
accorded me the privilege of leading this party, this government
and this great country over the last nine years. It is impossible to tell
you what pride I feel that you have given me that opportunity.' MPs
from both sides of the parliament stood and applauded.[94]

Hewson, sitting opposite Hawke, felt sorry for him. 'I always had
respect for Hawke and what he had achieved,' Hewson reflected.
'I didn't like the idea that you had to hate the other side.' What did
he think about a Hawke-Hewson match-up at the 1993 election?
'My honest view is that the Coalition probably would not have
won in 1993.'[95]

Hawke and his staff vacated the prime minister's office three
days later, on Sunday, 22 December 1991. It had been made clear
by Keating's staff that they wanted Hawke gone within days.[96] The
staff formed a line from the office stretching out into the courtyard, a kind of guard of honour, to say their farewells. Hawke went
down the line, shaking hands and hugging the staff. He hopped
into a car and was whisked away from Parliament House, and into
history.

—

Bob Hawke's ambition was to reconcile and heal the nation after
years of division and confrontation with the promise of consensus.

He wanted to end the policy stagnation and transform Australia's economic, social, environmental and foreign policy settings for a new age. This policy legacy continues to shape modern Australia. Medicare. The float of the dollar, the Prices and Incomes Accord, dismantling the tariff wall, privatisation. The Daintree, Kakadu, the Gordon and Franklin rivers. And his leadership on Antarctica, apartheid and establishing APEC saw him play an important role on the world stage.

Hawke managed the machinery of government with great skill. He assembled a talented staff and welcomed frank and fearless advice from public servants. Ministers regarded him as a 'chairman of the board' who was a good manager of cabinet business and provided strategic direction for the government. He was an effective communicator and often a powerful persuader. He had a strong work ethic, energy and drive. While luck often ran his way – such as facing a divided opposition – he also showed courage and took policy and political risks.

He had what the English journalist Walter Bagehot described were the essential elements of a statesman: someone of 'common opinions and uncommon abilities' who 'most felicitously expresses the creed of the moment, who administers it, who embodies it in laws and institutions, who gives it the highest life it is capable of'.[97] Voters accepted Hawke's faults and appreciated his virtues. He had authenticity and credibility. Voters knew that he loved them and loved the country. For many Australians, he seemed to understand and share their ambitions and aspirations for themselves and for their country.

It helps explain why, for most of nearly nine years, Hawke was a popular, respected and trusted leader. He had a profound belief in the capacity of the Australian people to come together to resolve their differences in good faith, putting the nation before self-interest and partisanship. It is why he saw political opponents as adversaries not enemies, and never exploited divisions along class, gender and religious lines – it was inimical to his belief in Australians as one people.

He also fundamentally changed the Labor Party by retuning its philosophy, transforming its governing culture and making it electorally dominant. In other words, he made the party fit for purpose: winning elections and staying in power. He achieved his goal of leading a Labor government of longevity. He took Labor to four election victories and is the party's most successful leader.

No other prime minister in the past half-century has been more popular, won more elections or so fundamentally shaped the future of the country.

PART IV

STATESMAN
1991–2019

32

HAWKE
IN HELL

In the immediate years after Bob Hawke exited the prime minis-tership, he experienced something which he never had before: he was shunned by his party and the unions, and his standing in the eyes of voters hit rock bottom. He moved to Sydney. His marriage to Hazel collapsed. He married Blanche d'Alpuget. He became estranged from his children. He became a critic of Paul Keating and predicted that he would lose the 1993 election. He wrote a memoir that was widely panned, including by his closest supporters and friends. He resumed drinking. He gambled exces-sively and often recklessly. He was unloved and unwanted by many in the party he had led to four election victories. His final approval rating as prime minister, according to Newspoll, was 27 per cent. It was a long way from 78 per cent in 1984. Hawke was in hell.

There were two phases to Hawke's post–prime ministerial life. The first, from 1991 to 2003, was a period in which he was mostly unhappy in his public life but found happiness in his private life. The second, from 2003 until his death in 2019, was a time of almost unalloyed public and private joy, as Hawke became an elder statesman, enjoyed business success and basked in the adulation of Australians. The turning point, Hawke thought, was the twenti-eth anniversary of his government's coming to power. The party did nothing to mark the tenth anniversary in 1993, but the twen-tieth was a time of celebration, public recognition, anniversary interviews and retrospectives. By 2003, Hawke was a historical figure, a revered one, and his contemporary views were still in demand. But this was in the future.

Hawke remained in Canberra after losing the prime minister-ship, and was still living at the Lodge. He phoned several former cabinet ministers to wish them a merry Christmas. When Nick Bolkus said that he was in the capital with his son, Hawke invited them to the Lodge for Christmas Day lunch. Bolkus arrived to find the former PM angry and upset. He reassured Hawke that things would be okay. 'It won't be that long before you'll find things to do and create a new life,' Bolkus said.

'That's bloody bullshit,' Hawke replied.

'He obviously felt he had more to contribute,' Bolkus reflected. 'He felt he had been prematurely tossed out.'[1]

Hawke spoke to Keating the day after the leadership ballot. He asked the new prime minister if he could stay at the Lodge for a few weeks. Keating agreed, and it was on 4 January that Bob and Hazel moved out. They were initially put up by John Single-ton in his Birchgrove mansion, with a harbour view in Sydney's Inner West, as their new home in Northbridge on the Lower North Shore would not be ready for almost two years, but soon moved into the Ritz-Carlton Hotel in Double Bay. The suite was provided for free but the Hawkes picked up the tab for their food, drinks and phone use.[2] There were rumours Hawke had initially sought a free suite at the Boulevard Hotel for six months in return for speaking at functions and attending a charity golf day.[3]

Before Hawke left Canberra, he sat on the back bench on 2 January 1992, when George H.W. Bush addressed the parlia-ment. Hawke had repeatedly urged Bush to visit Australia and his trip was a testament to their friendship. It was the first visit by a US president since Lyndon Johnson's in December 1967. Bush noted in his diary that Hawke had been 'thrown out' and Keating seemed 'a little conscious of the change' so Bush tried to 'put him at ease'. The president described the 'warmth of the greeting' he got from Australians in Sydney, Melbourne and Canberra. 'The people are so damn friendly,' he thought. But he regarded the Australian press as 'damn rude'. When Bush finished his address to the parliament, he turned to Hawke and waved. Later that day, Bob and Hazel met with George and Barbara Bush at the US

Embassy. It was emotional for both men. Bush described seeing Hawke in parliament:

> I looked over and saw Bob Hawke and I choked up. He looked smaller and it was because of him that we undertook the visit in the first place and he looked a little bit saddened by alla' this change, but later he came over to the house and I gave him a big abraso [Spanish for 'embrace'] and that played on the front page of the papers.

Bush got on well with Keating. The feeling was mutual. 'Keating told me as I left, of his keen interest and commitment to seeing me re-elected,' Bush recalled. But he did not warm to opposition leader John Hewson, who gave a 'politically over-toned' speech at the formal dinner and then 'got into lecturing' Bush about agricultural subsidies.[4]

Hawke resigned as the member for Wills on 20 February 1992. His letter of resignation was hand-delivered by long-time personal secretary Jill Saunders to the office of the speaker, Leo McLeay, at 4 pm. Keating paid Hawke a generous tribute. 'Bob Hawke and I served together as a team for eight years,' the prime minister said. 'It was a privilege to serve with him. We shared beliefs and goals and worked together to achieve them. It is clear that the past year has been a difficult one for both of us but that does not diminish the camaraderie we shared or the pride in our achievements together.'[5]

It was galling, though, for Labor supporters to see Hawke take a $10,000 fee to announce that he was leaving parliament on Jana Wendt's *A Current Affair* on Channel Nine that evening.[6] Mimi Tamburrino, who had worked for Hawke in Wills since 1980, begged him to stay in parliament. So did several community leaders in Wills, who met him in the electorate office and urged him to remain their local champion. 'Nup, I'm leaving,' Hawke replied. 'I'm not sitting on the back bench.'[7]

Hawke initially had an office at the Commonwealth Parliamentary Offices on Phillip Street in Sydney. Soon he moved into an office on the thirteenth floor of Westfield Towers at 100 William Street. Saunders would run the office. Gough Whitlam had an office on a higher floor in the same building. The two former Labor prime ministers and their staff would bump into each other in the lift, and occasionally catch up for birthdays and end-of-year drinks. Aaron Rule, the manager of Whitlam's office, recalled the relationship between the two former prime ministers. 'I remember Bob coming up to the office with a cake and singing happy birthday to Gough,' he said. 'They may have enjoyed a glass of Passiona. It was lovely to see these two former prime ministers, two Labor icons, very respectful towards each other in the final years. The two offices got on very well and Gough and Bob were always very amicable when seeing each other.'[8]

Hawke took a lump sum payout of $488,250 from his parliamentary superannuation, and initially received a pension of $48,825 a year.[9] He asked Keating for four staff rather than the standard entitlement of two. Keating granted Hawke the two additional staff members for a one-year transitional period. He also provided Hawke with a private-plated vehicle and increased remuneration for staff. These arrangements were extended to all former prime ministers. Keating also had the Commonwealth pick up the bill for Hawke's personal belongings to remain in storage while he arranged his permanent residential accommodation.[10]

A by-election for Wills was held on 11 April 1992. Independent Phil Cleary won the seat, with a huge swing of 19.3 per cent against Labor on the primary vote. It was another reason for party members to vent their anger at Hawke.

—

Now living in Sydney, Hawke's priority was to make money. Peter Abeles told Hawke he needed assistance beyond his personal office and engaged International Management Group. James Erskine, who headed up the Australian office of IMG, met with Abeles and then with Hawke. The IMG strategy was to cash in on Hawke's status as 'a senior statesman' in Australia and abroad. 'He was a superstar,' Erskine recalled. 'He was recognisable by everybody. But he needed to make some serious money. He had left power, really, with nothing. He did not even own a cutlery set.' Erskine had a 'handshake deal' with Hawke whereby IMG would take 20 per cent for any deals negotiated.

Erskine liked working with the former prime minister. 'He was a gregarious guy,' Erskine recalled. 'He enjoyed being Bob

Hawke. He started drinking again, and occasionally had too many sherbets, but I really respected and liked him. He worked hard. He would ring me up at 9.30 pm at night or 6.30 am in the morning. He was prodigious in his work ethic.' IMG negotiated almost everything from the Ritz-Carlton Hotel accommodation and a clothing deal with a men's retailer to corporate appearances and media interviews. IMG also began negotiations to publish Hawke's memoirs. IMG's initial focus was establishing Hawke's new career in the media as an interviewer and commentator.[11]

The idea of becoming a television interviewer fascinated Hawke. He had often said this was what he would do after the prime ministership. IMG helped him put together a program of interviews with leading world figures. The series was to be titled *Profiles of Power.* He wrote letters to George H.W. Bush, John Major, Mikhail Gorbachev, Boris Yeltsin, Michel Rocard, Helmut Kohl, Yasuhiro Nakasone, Hosni Mubarak, King Hussein, Nelson Mandela, Henry Kissinger and George Shultz, asking them to be part of his television venture. They all agreed. However, the interview series did not eventuate. Hawke reportedly wanted all his expenses paid, plus a fee as high as $100,000 for each hour-long interview. No television network took up the offer.[12]

Hawke did work as a highly paid guest reporter for Channel Nine's *60 Minutes* and the BBC. In 1992, Hawke travelled to London to interview John Major, Neil Kinnock and Paddy Ashdown for a report on the British election. He flew to Palm Beach to interview golfer Greg Norman. And he covered the famine in Somalia. Each of these *60 Minutes* interviews earned Hawke $35,000.[13] In 1993, Hawke made a program for the BBC on Australia becoming a republic, which was also shown on *Four Corners.* 'Republic of Oz' saw Hawke interview his old colleagues Paul Keating, Bill Hayden and Gough Whitlam, among others. He was paid $30,000 by the BBC, which also picked up his expenses.[14]

There was one big name, however, whom Hawke tried to land but failed: Don Bradman. He was the most famous living Australian but rarely spoke in public. In October 1992, Hawke visited Don and Jessie Bradman at their home in South Australia. He outlined his vision for the program: it would focus on Bradman's playing career and impact on the game; how cricket had shaped his life and his role as an administrator; and his assessment of how cricket had changed in the twentieth century. Hawke believed they could strike up 'a natural, entertaining and informative dialogue' that would be in the public interest and beneficial for history.[15]

Hawke thought he was on the verge of securing Bradman's agreement for a landmark interview. But Bradman had a few stipulations: a one-hour interview, broadcast in segments of fifteen to thirty minutes, which would be recorded rather than live. Anything he was not happy with would not go to air. And his preference was for Channel Nine.[16] 'I see myself as an old man who has nothing to gain from such an exercise and possibly quite a lot to lose in terms of public opinion,' he wrote to Hawke. To seal the deal, Hawke promised a $50,000 donation to the Bradman Museum Trust from the broadcaster. But Bradman drove a hard bargain: he wanted Hawke to match this with his own personal funds.[17]

But there was another problem. Bradman explained that if he ever did a television special, he had committed to doing it with Ray Martin for Channel Nine. He was reluctant to go back on his word. Hawke assured Bradman that Martin would understand if he did not get the scoop. He was mistaken. Martin made it clear that he expected Bradman to keep his word. Moreover, Martin would match the donation to the Trust.[18] The death knell for Hawke's television special came in a letter from Bradman on Christmas Day 1992: the interview would go to Martin.[19] But then Bradman went cool on the idea, and it was not until 1996 that he sat for the interview with Martin. Kerry Packer, owner of Channel Nine, sealed the deal over lunch with Bradman. He apparently paid $1 million to the Trust.[20]

Hawke was regularly in the media. He wrote columns for *The Sunday Age* for a fee, reflecting on his time in office, ruminating on policy and political issues, and often included criticisms of Keating. He accepted paid interviews on television programs. He also returned to what had made him good money in the 1970s: election night commentary. Hawke was part of Channel Nine's election coverage in March 1993. He joined Channel Seven for the March 1996 election, and was paid $12,000 plus first-class accommodation and transport.[21] Hawke negotiated similar arrangements with different television outlets in subsequent years.

In February 1992, Hawke signed a deal with publishing house William Heinemann to write his memoirs. He was paid an advance of $355,000.[22] Hawke's lawyer, Ian Robertson of Holding Redlich, had introduced Erskine to Heinemann managing director Sandy Grant and handled the legal aspects of the deal. Louise Adler was the publisher and oversaw the project. Hawke wrote sections of the text in longhand, focusing on chapters that dealt with his early life, student years and his time at the ACTU. He was assisted by Garry Sturgess, who researched and drafted large slabs of the prime ministerial years, and by his personal staff (led by Jill Saunders), while Blanche d'Alpuget edited the manuscript.

Hawke called on ministerial colleagues, public servants and former staff to assist, even asking them to write certain chapters. Not all of them obliged. Some dodged the requests; others were happy to help. Craig Emerson wrote to Hawke noting it would be 'extremely valuable' for him 'politically' and 'personally grat-ifying' to be given 'some recognition' of his role in the office.[23] Some former staff were given drafts to review. Ross Garnaut encouraged Hawke to make more of his role in leading public debate about 'enmeshment' with Asia and said he had 'underval-ued Keating's role' in the economic reforms, especially how they were communicated to the party and to voters. 'My concern is that you will be seen as being, like him in relation to you, mean,' Garnaut advised.[24]

The book was intended to be published in mid-1993 but the writing took longer than Hawke expected, and he repeatedly missed delivery deadlines. 'That process was really difficult,' recalled Saunders. 'The publishers kept asking: when is he going to put pen to paper? If I got the chance to read a chapter, I would say, "You can't write that!" And I think he got sick of me. It was so rushed in the end that I could not keep up with all the drafts. It was a relief when it was done.'[25] Hawke had agreed to a second book, on horseracing; it was to be ghostwritten, but his struggle to complete the memoir made it impossible. The *Profiles in Power* television series was going to be turned into a book. And he considered writing a book with his reflections on contemporary policy and politics after the March 1996 election, but that did not eventuate either.

Hawke took up several appointments. He became an adjunct professor at the Australian National University and a visiting professor at the University of Sydney. He joined the advisory council for the Institute of International Studies at Stanford University. He chaired the committee of experts of Education International, headquartered in Brussels, dedicated to improving the quality of, and access to, education. He helped establish the Boao Forum for Asia, which hosted an annual conference of government, business, academic and cultural leaders in China, beginning in April 2002. He was awarded a slew of honorary doctorates, fellowships, awards and honours from all over the world. A memorandum of understanding to establish the Bob Hawke Prime Ministerial Centre (The Hawke Centre) and the Bob Hawke Prime Ministerial Library at the University of South Australia, where he gifted his personal papers, was signed in December 1997.

Meanwhile, Hawke's handshake contract with IMG had come to an end. In 1992, Hawke made about US$500,000 via IMG publicity and media deals. But Hawke realised he could make more money doing business deals. 'We sort of drifted,' recalled Erskine. 'He started making serious money with consultancy deals out of China. He was now making millions of dollars rather than hundreds of thousands of dollars, and he was very successful at it.'[26] Erskine remained friendly with Hawke but Mark McCormack, the overseas founder and owner of IMG, was irate with the former prime minister. Memos from McCormack to Erskine in 1993 reveal that he wanted to sue Hawke for unpaid commissions. Hawke, in turn, threatened to sue IMG.[27] 'I tried to make sure that for all the deals the money came to us and then we paid him 80 per cent but it did not always happen like that,' Erskine said. 'Hawke had a mean streak in him and he didn't like paying for things. But I told Mark we were not going to take legal action against a former prime minister.'[28]

———

There were hopes that Hawke and Keating might campaign together in the lead-up to the March 1993 election. They did not. But Hawke did attend Labor's campaign launch, held at the Bankstown Town Hall, in Keating's electorate. On the eve of the election, Hawke made a prediction: Labor would lose. It was a bad judgement, although one he shared with Malcolm Fraser and John Gorton.[29] Keating's stunning victory damaged Hawke, who had repeatedly said that only he could lead Labor to a fifth election victory. He was wrong, and Keating's election triumph validated the leadership coup.

Ten days after the election, Labor held a 'True Believers' dinner in the Great Hall at Parliament House. It was a lavish event. Keating tried to bury the hatchet with Hawke. 'You can't have a fifth victory without a fourth,' he said. 'Thanks for coming, Bob.' The audience clapped and cheered. Hawke acknowledged the tribute and went to Keating's table and shook his hand. The public reconciliation did not last.

In June and July 1993, the documentary *Labor in Power* was shown on ABC TV. The five-part series had been devised by journalist Philip Chubb. The idea – at least, so Hawke thought – was to document the story of his government. The idea was first pitched in 1989, more as a first-person narrative, with the working title *Hawke Diaries*. During his prime ministership, Hawke had intermittently given tape-recorded interviews to Chubb and solicitor Peter Redlich on the proviso that they were not to be revealed until after he had left office. This was the genesis of the documentary series. However, these earlier interviews were not used in the television documentary. Chubb also planned to write an 'authorised biography' of Hawke, or to ghostwrite his autobiography. The project was not greenlit by the ABC until October 1991, and interviews with Hawke began the following month.[30]

Hawke encouraged ministers, public servants and staff to also be interviewed. They were unusually candid because most of the interviews took place before the March 1993 election, a contest many thought Labor would lose. The result was a compelling documentary about the power struggle between Hawke and Keating. While the series covered the highs and lows of the Hawke government, it was far from comprehensive – it did not mention Medicare, for example – and focused on the disagreements between ministers. It made for gripping television, but relitigated the Hawke–Keating leadership battle and so was unhelpful to the Keating government. Hawke was disappointed with the series.[31]

In June 1994, Hawke was spotted playing blackjack, drinking spirits and smoking a cigar at the Canberra Casino. No longer off the booze, it was ugly, and he had a confrontation with casino staff over his loud swearing. Hawke confidently predicted that Alexander Downer would be the next prime minster.[32] The following month, Hawke was in South Africa for Nelson Mandela's inauguration as South Africa's president. At the Australian ambassador's residence in Pretoria, Hawke was 'embroiled in a shouting match' with Fraser.[33] Hawke was struggling to adjust to life after the prime ministership. He could not come to terms with being dumped by the caucus. He mourned the end of the love affair he had had with the Australian people since the 1960s.

Then came *The Hawke Memoirs*, published in the winter of 1994. This did more damage to Hawke's standing within the Labor Party than anything else. The book was launched by Sir Ninian Stephen at the Museum of Contemporary Art in Sydney on 16 August. Hawke had an extensive round of media events to promote the book, which ranged from *60 Minutes* and *Four Corners* to *The 7.30 Report* and *A Current Affair*. He signed books in shopping centres, appeared at literary lunches and spoke at the National Press Club. Australians rushed to get their copies signed, shake Hawke's hand and pose for photos. But almost every encounter with the media was hostile. Hawke clashed repeatedly with journalists about claims he had made in the book, and became indignant when challenged on his recall of events. Gough Whitlam called it a 'piss and tell' memoir.[34] *The Australian* ran extracts from the book, which Hawke promoted in a television commercial ahead of publication. But parts of the book that were highly critical of Keating were obtained by rival media outlets months earlier, in mid-June.

In the book, Hawke claimed that Keating had said during the leadership battle: 'We'll be off to Europe. We won't be staying here. This is the arse-end of the world.' The gloves were off. Keating savaged Hawke, saying that he was not only wrong but 'deeply offensive' and his claim was 'defamatory'. The memoir, Keating said, was 'intended to personally vilify and politically damage me'.[35] Hawke offered to take 'a lie-detector test' to verify his truthfulness.[36] Hawke also claimed Keating opposed the Gulf War deployment, that he regarded Asia as the place you fly over on the way to Paris, and that his 'banana republic' comment was a result of physical and mental exhaustion. That was just for starters. Now even Hawke's strongest supporters in cabinet – including Kim Beazley, Robert Ray and Gareth Evans – backed Keating and lashed Hawke.[37]

The Hawke Memoirs was a publishing sensation, selling over 80,000 copies and earning Hawke over $650,000 in Australia alone.[38] James Erskine recalled that when added to local and overseas serialisation rights, a paid interview with *60 Minutes*, and sales and events abroad, Hawke earned at least $1 million from his memoirs.[39,] When Hawke signed Sandy Grant's copy of *The Hawke Memoirs*, he wrote: 'Thanks, Sandy. This book better make me lots of money!'[40] It did. But these riches came at a cost to Hawke's standing.

—

Hazel expected to continue the happy phase in the marriage that had begun around the time of their sixtieth birthdays. She and Bob were building a new home and a new life in Sydney – what Hazel referred to as their 'little bit of magic'.[41] But Blanche d'Alpuget claimed that when the 'dream' of the prime ministership was over, so was Bob and Hazel's 'sham' marriage.[42] D'Alpuget thought Hazel 'felt a great liberation from the marriage' when it was over.[43] This was not how Hazel saw it. 'Hazel knew that Bob was always off with someone, but he always came back to her,' said Wendy McCarthy. 'Except this time, he didn't. Hazel believed in marriage and she wanted to stay married.'[44] Hazel was suspicious about Bob's pledges of fidelity during this time. He had reassured her that his affair with Blanche had not resumed; she was only back on the scene to help edit his memoirs. Bob lied to Hazel, and to their children, about his affair with Blanche.[45]

Bob had no intention of remaining married to Hazel; he wanted to be with Blanche. He confided this to his daughter in late 1992. 'He loved Mum, but he no longer felt in love with her,' Susan recalled her father saying.[46] Nevertheless, the façade was kept up for several years. On 2 November 1992, Bob joined Hazel for the launch of her memoir, *My Own Life*, at Bennelong Restaurant in the Sydney Opera House. A few months later, on 24 June 1993, Blanche was in a plane crash in North Queensland while on assignment for *The New York Times*. When Bob found out, he feared the worst. It was then he decided to take the next step to divorce Hazel and marry Blanche. Bob proposed while in bed with Blanche one evening.

On 29 November 1994, Bob and Hazel announced their separation. 'After 38 years together, we have ended our marriage,' they said in a statement. 'Our decision to separate has been one taken mutually and we remain good friends. We have amicably resolved all issues regarding our children and financial affairs and a full settlement has been agreed.'[47] Susan referred to this as 'the Hollywood statement'. There had in fact been many arguments and the break-up was difficult. 'It reflected an intent on both their parts to be amicable into the future, but it didn't reflect the preceding year,' Susan said.[48] Bob moved back to the Ritz-Carlton Hotel. The next day, he choked back tears when he launched the Sydney City Mission's Christmas Appeal. 'Hazel and I remain very, very good friends,' he said. Blanche was asked to respond to rumours of a relationship between her and Bob. 'Absolute nonsense,' she said.[49]

Australia's worst-kept secret was revealed weeks later by the *Illawarra Mercury*, which reported Bob and Blanche were finally together – in public.[50] They had escaped to Berrara Beach, on the South Coast of New South Wales, on Boxing Day to spend a week with Sir Richard Kirby. They were spotted taking romantic walks on the beach, swimming in the surf and shopping. It was a month since Bob had split from Hazel. Then came the news that Bob and Blanche had agreed to sell the story of their impending nuptials to *60 Minutes* and *Woman's Day* for $200,000. The deal, negotiated by Max Markson, would see the couple in swimming costumes and matching white robes as Blanche rubbed suntan lotion on Bob.[51]

To see Bob divorce Hazel, one of the most loved, respected and admired women in the country, did not shock most Australians, but it did appal them. She had, after all, stood by her husband through the ups and downs of his union and political career, put up with the drinking and the womanising, and raised their three children almost by herself. Hawke wanted people to understand how happy D'Alpuget made him. But, for many Australians, this was unforgivable. Hazel moved to a modest house at Middle Cove on Sydney's Lower North Shore and rebuilt her life.

Bob and Blanche were married in the Bay Room at the Ritz-Carlton Hotel in Double Bay at midday on 23 July 1995. The ceremony was performed by Mario Schoenmaker from the Independent Church of Australia. The reception was held at the restaurant Botticelli, where guests drank champagne and dined on oysters, prawns and crumbed john dory, followed by Italian pastries and wedding cake. They included Richard Pratt, Richard Kirby, Rene Rivkin and Peter Abeles, Hawke's former colleagues Kim Beazley, Lionel Bowen and Susan Ryan, along with John Singleton, Bob Ingham, and Robbie and Gai Waterhouse. The newlyweds moved into the four-storey waterfront home at Northbridge. Susan, Stephen and Rosslyn attended the wedding – Susan and Rosslyn wore funereal black – but the children also attended Hazel's 'freedom party' at Northbridge the same day.

—

Hawke made a lot of money in the 1990s and 2000s, enough to live a very comfortable life, but the media often exaggerated how wealthy he became. He raked up fees for speeches, appearances and consultancies. He invested in property and established business partnerships with old friends Peter Abeles and Richard Super. Lawyer Ian Robertson handled Hawke's consultancy and business agreements until his death. Hawke formed several companies, including RJL Hawke & Associates, to open doors and negotiate business deals. Josh Klenbort, an American who spoke fluent Mandarin, and a director of the company like Blanche, handled the detailed business negotiations. Hawke and Klenbort formed a close and successful business relationship.

Hawke would spend almost half the year, with Blanche, travelling to and from Asia, Europe, the United States and Africa. The focus, though, was China, where he would make half a dozen visits each year. He advised Australians eager to do business deals in China and Chinese entrepreneurs looking for investment opportunities in Australia. In 1998, Hawke found himself in competition with Keating. Hawke represented National Mutual and Keating represented Colonial Mutual, both insurance companies eager to expand into China. Hawke's interest in China was not just about money making; he had a deep regard for the country and its people. He also enjoyed the intellectual stimulation and challenge of business negotiations, and meeting a range of people.

After just two and a half years as a businessman, Hawke's companies had grossed almost $2 million before tax.[52] Not all of Hawke's ventures were successful, though, and some were highly controversial. His involvement in the Vitab offshore betting agency in Vanuatu, as well as commercial opportunities he considered in Burma and a proposed casino deal in Pakistan, raised questions about the propriety of his business dealings. Hawke was often too trusting of people, did not do enough vetting, was easily attracted to riches and some people took advantage of this.

Some of Hawke's relationships, especially with Chinese entrepreneurs, troubled his former parliamentary and union colleagues. Labor premiers in the 1990s and 2000s were less than thrilled when they received a phone call from Hawke or he sauntered into their office asking for a meeting and a boardroom lunch on behalf of his clients. They loathed the moment when he would push the cause of a shadowy Chinese businessman. 'Because it was Bob, I always took his call, and he would be talking about some fucking Chinese guy,' recalled former Queensland premier Peter Beattie. 'I never felt comfortable about that. I made sure the company was treated the same as every other company and it was transparent. It didn't mean that I lost respect for Bob, I just didn't like what he did.'[53]

None of this helped to rebuild Hawke's public standing. 'Hawke's post-prime ministerial activities tarnished his reputation,' argued Neal Blewett. 'His rancour against his successor, which mars his impressive memoirs, his sometimes tawdry parlaying of his status, experience and connections into commercial coinage, and above all, his repudiation of his wife of forty years, Hazel, for the younger Blanche d'Alpuget, ended forever his love affair with the Australian people.'[54]

Bill Kelty felt that he had to do something. He was deeply troubled by the extent to which Australians were dismayed and disgusted by Hawke's behaviour: attacking Keating, going back on the grog, the gambling, the divorce, and the money-making and influence-peddling. 'He was effectively black banned,' Kelty recalled. 'The unions didn't want him, the Labor Party didn't want him, he was seen as a pariah for undermining Labor's chances of victory in 1993. He was not a happy man. What really hurt him was that Labor won in 1993.'[55]

Kelty devised a strategy to rehabilitate Hawke. In November 1995, unions were involved in a protracted dispute with mining company CRA (now Rio Tinto) over individual contracts at Weipa in Far North Queensland. While Keating was in Japan for an APEC meeting, Kelty phoned Hawke and asked him to act as the ACTU's advocate in the dispute. Hawke was enthusiastic. He resumed his union advocacy role, appearing before the full bench of the Australian Industrial Relations Commission, and won the claim for equal pay. It was a triumph.

Jennie George, then the ACTU president-elect, said Kelty's primary purpose was to put Hawke back on the path to becoming an elder statesman, not because he was needed to resolve the dispute. 'Bill was keen to re-embrace Hawke,' she recalled. 'We could have handled it internally. But to Bill this was a chance at reconciliation with Bob, with whom he had been very close in ACTU days. He wanted Bob's links to be restored and to be a union hero again.'[56]

Keating was furious with Kelty. 'He had the choice between asking the present prime minister and the former prime minister for help, and he chose the former one,' he said.[57] On a newspaper clipping, Keating wrote: 'This is Bill at his silliest.'[58] Keating thought Hawke was just window-dressing and the ACTU would have won the case without him. 'Marcel Marceau could almost get this one through,' he said.[59]

'Paul hated me,' Kelty recalled. 'He was in Japan, and I was in Sydney, and he rang me up at bloody 2 am and yelled at me for an hour.' Kelty said he would do the same for Keating if he needed help. 'Do you think I wouldn't try to help you if you were in the same circumstances, if you were at the bottom of the Labor Party heap, and your place in history was at stake?' he told Keating.[60]

Hawke's rehabilitation had begun.

33

THE MANY LIVES
OF BOB HAWKE

The defeat of Paul Keating's government in March 1996 marked another turning point in Bob Hawke's life. Kim Beazley was elected Labor leader and, close to Hawke, often called on him for advice. Hawke, now sixty-six, was increasingly invited to appear at party fundraisers and campaign with candidates. The voters were also forgiving. In November 1997, Hawke was rated the best modern prime minister, with 66 per cent of voters judging his performance as 'good'. The admiration for Hawke exceeded that for Keating (54 per cent), Malcolm Fraser (54 per cent), Gough Whitlam (44 per cent) and Robert Menzies (46 per cent). It was indeed, as *The Australian* said, a case of 'all is forgiven'.[1]

While voters judged Hawke's prime ministership favourably, Labor for a time distanced itself from the Hawke/Keating years. 'The Labor Party got a majority of votes in 1998 but couldn't get a majority of seats because the then opposition had given up on the model that Hawke and I had created,' Keating argued.[2] The party felt it had to redefine itself in opposition. In March 1997, the leadership team of Beazley, Gareth Evans and Simon Crean backed a tariff freeze, re-regulation of the labour market and interventionist industry policy.[3] Labor was turning back the clock to a pre-Hawke/Keating era, although Beazley argued it was more about contrasting his style of leadership with Keating's, not Hawke's.[4]

But Hawke saw a difference between the Labor Party that he had led and the Labor Party post-1996. Hawke believed Labor had drifted from the centre ground of politics and away from the model of governance that he and Keating had developed, which had attracted broad voter support. 'We were able to call on all sections of Australia, and did successfully, and that is not happening now,' he said in 2018.[5] Keating agreed, arguing that Labor had jettisoned the Hawke/Keating model. 'It's never been back there since we left,' he said.[6]

After Beazley failed to lead Labor to victory at the October 1998 and November 2001 elections, the party elected Simon Crean as leader. He too was close to Hawke and welcomed his advice, but he was disappointed when Hawke supported a leadership challenge by Beazley in June 2003. When Mark Latham was elected Labor leader in December 2003, Hawke was also willing to offer his counsel, even though he was frustrated Beazley had not returned to the top job. Labor did, however, install Beazley again in January 2005, when Latham resigned after the disastrous October 2004 election.

Hawke thought the Beazley-led opposition would have defeated John Howard's government. He was unhappy when Kevin Rudd challenged and defeated Beazley in December 2006. But he set that aside and campaigned vigorously for the new leadership team of Rudd and Julia Gillard at the November 2007 election, which Labor won. The previous eleven and a half years had been difficult for the party, as it cycled through leaders, lost four elections and wrestled with its future direction. Hawke was thrilled by Labor's victory, but his elation soon turned to despondency.

The Rudd/Gillard government failed to heed many of the lessons that made the Hawke/Keating government successful, whether it was managing internal divisions, the methodical cabinet and policy-making process, respecting the public service and accepting candid advice, developing a cooperative relationship with unions that put the national interest first, or communicating policies persuasively. Hawke criticised the propagation of class warfare, arguing that governments need to have good relations with employers and employees. Labor lost its parliamentary majority at the August 2010 election. Hawke's judgement of the government led first by Rudd and then by Gillard, and then by Rudd again, was that even though it 'achieved a lot of good Labor things', the party needed to be 'brutal' in its assessment and accept that it 'didn't deserve to win' the September 2013 election.[7]

Hawke had hoped the party would turn to Greg Combet as its leader in government or opposition. Hawke regarded Combet as Labor's most outstanding potential prime minister since Beazley, often describing his character as 'pure crystal'. Combet was in frequent contact with Hawke while ACTU secretary (1999–2007) and as a parliamentarian and minister (2007–13). Leadership was a theme of their discussions. But it was not to be, as Combet retired from parliament in 2013.

As Labor cascaded to defeat, Hawke talked to Tanya Plibersek about leading the party in opposition. They had often discussed politics and policy over a meal or over the phone since Plibersek's election to parliament in 1998. Plibersek explained that, at that stage, managing her family responsibilities while leading the party would be too difficult and ruled it out. But Hawke thought Plibersek was the best candidate to lead Labor after the 2013 election.

The contest was between Bill Shorten and Anthony Albanese. It was to be conducted under new rules, whereby caucus and party members voted in equal proportion. Hawke cast his vote for Shorten. He campaigned for Shorten at the July 2016 election, including appearing in a television commercial warning that the Coalition had plans to privatise Medicare. Although Labor was defeated, Hawke hoped and expected that Shorten would lead the party into office in May 2019. But he did not live to see the outcome of that election, nor even to vote.

After the 2001 election, Hawke and Neville Wran had been appointed to review the party. They produced a landmark report that recommended refreshing the party's purpose, revitalising its policymaking and modernising its organisational structure. While some reforms were adopted, much of the report was ignored. On 1 August 2009, Hawke proudly accepted national life membership of the Labor Party from Rudd and Gillard, declaring that the labour movement had been 'an enduring love of my life'.[8] But in his final years, Hawke worried about a party that had become too factionalised, dominated by unions, with falling membership, and candidates and MPs that no longer reflected the broader community. Nobody on Labor's opposition front bench, he thought, would be worthy of replacing any minister who had served in a cabinet that he led.

Hawke was also disappointed with the union movement. He thought union leaders too often showed a 'narrow' and 'limited' perspective that did not reflect the national interest. He said unions were no longer attracting the 'stream of outstanding talent' that they once had.[9] As membership levels plummeted – from 40 per cent when he left office in 1991 to just 14 per cent of the workforce by 2019 – he came to believe the unions had lost much of their authority and credibility.[10] He worried that union leaders were 'suffocating' Labor with their demands on policy, candidates and personnel. And he was utterly appalled by systemic criminality and corruption in sections of the union movement.[11]

—

Hawke often commented publicly on policy and political issues. He organised a letter co-signed by Gough Whitlam, Malcolm Fraser and Paul Keating to condemn the 'unmitigated evil' of racism following the establishment of Pauline Hanson's nativist and xenophobic One Nation party in August 1998.[12] His strongest intervention was to speak out against the invasion of Iraq in March 2003, a war he said was based on 'lies' and 'deceit'.[13] He organised for Whitlam, Fraser, Bill Hayden and John Hewson to join him in urging the Howard government not to commit forces to any attack that lacked United Nations backing. He also advocated nuclear power as a replacement energy source for fossil fuels, as a key step towards reducing carbon emissions, and Australia becoming a repository for nuclear waste.

Hawke supported constitutional recognition of Indigenous Australians and a treaty as a meaningful step towards reconciliation, even though he had failed to deliver it when he was prime minister. He joined with former prime ministers Keating, Fraser and Whitlam to witness Kevin Rudd's historic apology to the Stolen Generations in the House of Representatives on 14 February 2008. He called for better understanding between different faiths. And he became an advocate for voluntary euthanasia, or assisted dying, laws.

He campaigned vigorously for a republic ahead of the referendum on 6 November 1999. Malcolm Turnbull, Australia's pre-eminent republican, recalled that Hawke was 'an enthusiastic' and 'very effective' advocate. 'There was a view at the time that politicians should be kept away from the campaign, but it became obvious that the advocates with the best cut-through and credibility were, in fact, politicians,' Turnbull recalled. 'So we recruited Hawke and also Whitlam and Fraser. Hawke was especially important because the weakness in our vote was, in fact, in Labor seats.'[14]

It was on the evening of the failed referendum, Hawke recalled, that Turnbull approached him and said he wanted to become a Labor MP. 'He wanted to join the Labor Party,' Hawke recalled. 'He asked me and he asked Kim [Beazley].' Hawke said Turnbull approached him at the Marriott Hotel in Sydney and said: 'Bob, the only thing I can do now is join the Labor Party.'[15] Turnbull has always rejected this claim, even though Hawke stood by it. He said Labor was trying to recruit him, not that he wanted to join Labor. 'The bottom line was that I didn't feel I would be comfortable in the ALP, or the ALP comfortable with me,' Turnbull said.[16]

While Hawke was enthusiastic about a republic, he never made it a priority as prime minister and believed the best time to sever Australia's constitutional links with the United Kingdom was when the reign of Queen Elizabeth II ended. In July 2000, John Howard led a high-level delegation to London to mark the centenary of the passage of the Australian Constitution through the British parliament. The delegation included John Gorton, Whitlam, Fraser and Hawke. They met with British prime minister Tony Blair and the Queen.

Hawke took on several official roles. After supporting Sydney's bid for the Olympic Games in 2000, he became an Olympic attaché for the Malaysian Olympic team when the Games took place. In April 2010, he was appointed to the National Commission on the Commemoration of the Anzac Centenary, along with Fraser and RSL president Ken Doolan. This involved consulting with Australians about how best to commemorate the centenary and preparing a report for the government.

In December 2002, Hawke turned his mind to peace in the Middle East. He believed the West should invest in rebuilding the Palestinian economy – like the Marshall Plan for post-war Europe – as a foundation for a political solution between Israel and Palestine. This economic investment would be provided in return for an end to attacks on Israel. He named it the Powell Plan for Palestine, after the US secretary of state Colin Powell. Hawke enthusiastically promoted it to serving and former leaders around the world. While it was positively received by prime ministers and presidents in the United States, the United Kingdom and Europe, it went nowhere.

Hawke's business interests remained focused on China, where he developed close relationships with political, business and cultural leaders. He made more than 100 trips to China in his post–prime ministerial life, opening doors and arranging deals. 'I advise Chinese companies and Australian companies,' Hawke explained in 2015. 'I also engage in discussions with high-level think tanks, swap ideas with them, which is something I very highly value.'[17] He also did business in Japan and Indonesia, and elsewhere in the Asia-Pacific and parts of Europe.

Hawke's associations and deal-making continued to concern his friends and former colleagues, as they often skirted the bounds of propriety. Kevin Rudd recalled Hawke lobbying him as prime minister. 'Bob had been around to see me on a couple of occasions on matters which I was uncomfortable about – these were commercial matters relating to his business interests – and I basically did nothing about them because I thought it was wrong to,' Rudd recalled. 'There was some personal level of estrangement following that.'[18]

Hawke began each day by completing cryptic crosswords and other puzzles. 'It became an obsession,' recalled Jill Saunders. 'There were dozens of people who sat next to him on planes and would have loved to chat, but he would be totally focused on crosswords.'[19] He read several newspapers each day. Hawke liked to play blackjack in casinos while puffing on a cigar and drinking red wine. He indulged his love of horseracing and had part-ownership of several horses. He also played golf regularly and had a putting green installed on his roof at home. He went on fishing trips and occasionally dropped a line into Sailors Bay from his home jetty. He had a million mates but few genuine friends other than Peter Abeles (who died in June 1999) and Col Cunningham, but saw a steady stream of business partners, union and party figures, former staff, and family. There were adventure holidays with Blanche to Antarctica, to the Galápagos Islands and to Africa. And there were the legendary birthdays: a seventieth at home, where wine was funnelled from the breasts and penis of twin ice statues, and an eightieth at Guillaume At Bennelong at the Sydney Opera House, where a stripper dressed as John Howard burst out of a cake. It was tasteless.

In the final years of his life, Hawke returned to what he had been in the 1970s: a celebrity personality and larrikin superstar. His life became the stuff of legend, sweeping away the complexities, the light and the shade, as the myth almost overshadowed the real man. In truth, he remained exceptionally gifted but profoundly flawed.

In July 2010, a movie of Hawke's life was broadcast on the Ten Network, with Richard Roxburgh in the title role. Hawke was regularly profiled for television specials, including *Elders* with Andrew Denton (July 2008), Annabel Crabb's *Kitchen Cabinet* (October 2014), a two-part *Australian Story* (November 2014), a tacky episode of *60 Minutes* where he and Blanche again donned white bathrobes (January 2017), and the feature documentary *Hawke: The Larrikin & the Leader* (February 2018). Derek Rielly met Hawke at home for a weekly conversation over a year and spun it into a book, *Wednesdays with Bob*, published in November 2017. Hawke was a regular attendee at the summer Woodford Folk Festival, where he would ruminate on politics to a captivated audience.

When, as he sat in the Members' Stand at the Sydney Cricket Ground to watch a Test match, Hawke was shown on the big screen, the cheers from the crowd would prompt him to scull a beer, which would lead to further eruptions of applause. Hawke allowed his name to be used for a beer brand, Hawke's Brewing Co., founded by Nathan Lennon and David Gibson, which launched in April 2017. He had one proviso: that his royalty share be donated to Landcare Australia, which he had made a national, government-supported movement. By 2021, nearly $300,000 had been donated. Hawke joked that if he'd known how profitable it would be, he would never have agreed not to take a cent.

—

The ex-PMs' club swelled during Hawke's years out of politics. He initially did not get on well with the other members, predecessors Gorton, Whitlam and Fraser, and occasionally sparred with them over their respective legacies.[20] Hawke formed various relationships with his successors but had the highest professional regard for John Howard. The Labor and Liberal prime ministers who followed Hawke all speak highly of his prime ministership, and of his broader contribution to public life.

Scott Morrison was a teenager when Bob Hawke became prime minister. He remembered the contrast with Malcolm Fraser in terms of personality and style. 'Bob Hawke was larger than life – a true Australian character,' he recalled. 'Australians loved Bob Hawke and it was a romance played out in every part of this country. Bob and the Australian community knew each other well and that was because he was so deeply Australian, in character, temperament and outlook.' Morrison said he would never forget 'the joy' of *Australia II* winning the America's Cup and the Bicentenary as another reminder of those 'optimistic and positive times'.

The thirtieth prime minister judged Hawke to be Labor's greatest prime minister. 'He had wit, intellect, passion and courage,' Morrison said. 'He had a deep sense of Australia and the world – modernised the economy, kept the alliances strong and had a deep understanding that aspiration is in the heart of Australians.' Morrison also admired Hawke's 'disciplined commitment' to the cabinet process and respect for the public service. 'He sought to promote good people . . . and also ensure the discipline and oversight that was necessary with good decision making,' Morrison said. 'As a big personality, he didn't seem intimidated by others who also didn't struggle with self-confidence.'

Morrison said he learnt many lessons from how Hawke operated as prime minister. The esteem for Hawke is about more than prime-ministerial performance; it is about his visceral connection with Australians. 'He had a deep love of this country,'

Morrison said. 'He had his weaknesses and vanities. But he was a passionate Australian who left the place better than he found it. He also wasn't a perfect man – as the title of your book reflects – but no-one is.' This high praise is reflected in the assessments of all of Hawke's Labor and Liberal successors.[21]

When Hawke led Labor to power in 1983, Malcolm Turnbull was twenty-eight. 'I was impressed with his energy, charisma and zeal for reform,' Turnbull recalled. 'As a PM he was a great reformer. Now, to be fair, a lot of his reforms – for which Keating can take equal credit – were part of the zeitgeist. But they did accelerate reform beyond the inevitable or conventional. So full marks from my perspective.' During his prime ministership, Turnbull had friendly relations with Hawke despite the sporadic barbs.

Turnbull remembered that when Bill Leak was painting his portrait for the Archibald Prize, he was also painting the official portraits of Hawke and Hayden. '[Bill] described how, as each of the men came for their sittings, they would critique the portrait of the other,' Turnbull said. 'Hayden would look at Hawke's picture and say, "Not bad, Bill, but you haven't quite captured his mean little lips." And Hawke in his turn would survey Hayden's picture and say, "Ah, Bill, it's getting better but you need a bit more red in that boozer's nose." I have no idea whether this was a product of Bill Leak's imagination, but it's a good story.'[22]

Tony Abbott regards Hawke as an 'outstanding prime minister' and 'certainly the very best Labor prime minister in living memory'. As a young student, he recalled having 'the typical Liberal disdain' for Hawke but conceded, even at the time, that he thought Hawke 'did a very good job'. Abbott recalled meeting Hawke when he was president of the Sydney University Students' Representative Council in 1979 and found him 'irresistible as a personality'.

As prime minister, Abbott invited Hawke to Kirribilli House to share his thoughts about Australia–China relations. 'He was an absolutely delightful companion,' Abbott recalled. 'There is no doubt about the wisdom of people who have done a lot, lived through a lot and reflected a lot on important subjects. I was incredibly lucky and grateful for that meeting.' Abbott paid tribute to Hawke's authenticity. 'He was the quintessential Aussie bloke,' Abbott said. 'He loved a beer, he loved sport, he loved women – perhaps to excess. He was great fun to be with and he was comfortable in his own skin.'[23]

Julia Gillard remembered, as a school student, her father's interest in politics. He was 'a very strong Hawke supporter' who realised his promise as a future Labor leader. She too was an admirer. Gillard met Hawke occasionally at party and union events over the years, but it was not until she was in parliament and joined Labor's front bench that she got to know him personally. 'When I came to Sydney, I would go and see him from time to time,' she recalled. He never wanted to relive past glory days. 'He would prefer to discuss a live political issue of the day or something that was coming down the pipeline tomorrow,' Gillard said.

Gillard was influenced by how Hawke ran a collegiate cabinet process and prioritised efficiency in the administration of government. Gillard referred to this as 'a Hawke culture'. They talked occasionally about political strategy and issues such as climate change, industrial relations and China. 'A lot of it was more in the personal realm,' Gillard said. 'How are you going? How are you feeling?' There was a mutual regard between them. Hawke spoke at Labor's 2010 campaign launch. She invited Bob and Blanche to Kirribilli House. When Gillard lost the prime ministership, Hawke phoned to tell her that she had 'much to be proud of' and to 'look after yourself'. As an ex–prime minister, Gillard continued to visit Hawke occasionally at his office and at home.[24]

When Kevin Rudd became prime minister, he was mindful of his Labor predecessors and wanted to honour their legacy. He also wanted to try to mend any rifts between them. He invited Whitlam, Hawke and Keating to Labor's 2007 campaign launch, asked them to witness his apology to the Stolen Generations and had them over to Kirribilli House. Never before had four Labor prime ministers dined at the same table. 'I tried to rebuild the bridges between the three of them,' Rudd recalled. 'I listened to them and was interested in their reflections on political office. I remember Hawke and Keating, arm in arm, laughing, on the gravel outside Kirribilli House as they left.'[25]

John Howard praised the Hawke government's economic reforms and Hawke's ability to communicate complex and difficult decisions to voters. 'He was a highly intelligent man and he understood economics, which was a great virtue he brought to the prime ministership,' Howard said. 'He reaffirmed my belief that constantly communicating to the public what you were doing is very important. I respected his political skills enormously. He was the best Labor prime minister that Australia has had.'[26]

When in 2004 Howard surpassed Hawke to become the second-longest serving prime minister, he received a generous letter and phone call from the former Labor PM:

> I am writing to offer you my genuine congratulations on your achievement. I doubt there has been anyone in the history of federal politics who has shown greater resilience and determination to overcome setbacks than you displayed throughout your career; and very few who would match your skills as a political operator. You and I know that we have a number of deep differences on views of domestic and international politics, but I believe that, according to our lights, we have both been motivated by what we are convinced is in Australia's best interests.[27]

Howard replied with his own note of grace for history:

> Respect across the political divide in Australia has not been all that plentiful. Of our relationship it can, however, be said that each has always had a proper regard for the other's contribution to public life. It has long been my view – publicly and privately – that you have been the outstanding Labor figure of the post-World War II period. As history records, you have been Labor's most successful leader ever.[28]

In late 2018, as the end neared, Howard visited Hawke as a mark of respect for his contribution to public life.

—

These later years were the happiest of Hawke's post-prime ministerial life. He was deeply in love with Blanche. His eyes sparkled and he smiled whenever she entered a room. It was an intellectual, spiritual and physical love that never dimmed. 'You don't have all the demons chasing you that you do when you are less mature,' Blanche explained. 'That was all behind us. We were able to concentrate on love.' But the second marriage was not always smooth sailing. There were rows over Bob's renewed drinking and his jealousy, which led Blanche to temporarily leave him.[29]

He also strayed from the marital bed. Hawke had never been faithful to one woman, and he was not going to start now. When Hawke travelled overseas to China, he was offered the company of other women and usually indulged. D'Alpuget acknowledged this, albeit cryptically, in a combined edition of her two-volume biography of Hawke, published after his death. 'He vowed that in his second marriage he had honoured his oath of exclusive devotion,' she wrote. 'If his memory was at fault, his intention was not.'[30]

Susan, Stephen and Rosslyn were very unhappy when their father remarried. Their relationship with Blanche was hostile, and there were public clashes. In June 2011, it was reported that Blanche had slapped Susan several times in the face during a heated exchange in the Qantas Chairman's Lounge at Brisbane Airport.[31] But with the passage of time, these rifts healed. Both Susan and Rosslyn developed warm relationships with Blanche in the final years of Bob's life.

Hazel built a happy and fulfilling new life at Middle Cove. She enjoyed spending time with her children and grandchildren, tending to her garden and playing the piano. Hazel had a devoted group of friends. She contributed to several public organisations and charitable causes. She chaired the NSW Heritage Council, served on the NSW Centenary of Federation Committee and the board of the Australian Children's Television Foundation. Hazel was elected to the 1999 Constitutional Convention on the republican ticket. She was made a national living treasure – an honour denied to her ex-husband.

In November 2003, Hazel revealed that she had been diagnosed with Alzheimer's disease. She decided to speak about it publicly to raise awareness of the challenges faced by those living with the affliction. A few years later, she was moved to a residential care facility at Hammondville, in south-west Sydney. Wendy McCarthy recalled visiting Hazel and encouraging her to play piano for the other residents. On a return visit, McCarthy found her playing 'Under the Spreading Chestnut Tree', a song she had played for Bob when they were courting.[32]

Hazel died from complications of Alzheimer's on 23 May 2013. She was eighty-three. A fortnight before, on 11 May, Bob met with Hazel for the last time. Susan and Stephen, and the grandchildren, visited in the final weeks too. Hazel had had a stroke. Rosslyn urged her father to see her mother one final time. He agreed. The reunion was awkward at first, and Bob did not know what to say. Rosslyn suggested he sing a song. So he held Hazel's hand and sang 'Danny Boy', a favourite ballad of their youth. Hazel looked at Bob. It rekindled something. When Bob said his goodbye and walked to the door, Hazel looked at him and said in a soft voice, 'I love you.'[33]

Stephen reflected on his parents. 'Mum and Dad had a great romance that ran into trouble, and became fraught, particularly in the late 1970s and early 1980s, but they made a decision to stay together that served them both incredibly well,' he said. 'It wasn't an act. It wasn't a charade. It was a genuine partnership. There were periods of difficulty and periods of accommodation, and periods of being reasonably comfortable around each other. But for anyone to try and suggest that it was anything other than a great romance is just complete and utter nonsense.'[34]

A private service for Hazel's family and friends was held at the Eastern Suburbs Crematorium. A few years later, Stephen organised for his mother's ashes to be scattered in the West Australian bush, as she had stipulated in her will. Bob wanted to speak at Hazel's state memorial service, held at the Sydney Opera House on 25 June that year. This was deemed not appropriate by Hazel's family and friends, but he did speak at a private gathering afterwards, paying tribute to her as a mother and wife and expressing regret for the pain he had caused her. McCarthy said Australians felt a deep connection to Hazel. 'I can't think of a woman or Australian citizen who is more respected and loved by Australian people than Hazel,' she said.[35]

Hazel had made a will on 18 October 1999. She bequeathed $10,000 to the Brotherhood of St Laurence and $5000 for a scholarship to be established in her name at Curtin University. The rest of her estate was to be divided equally between Susan, Stephen and Rosslyn. The total estate was valued at $987,034.83.[36]

Bob made a deed of agreement on 22 December 2009. It made provision for Susan, Stephen, Rosslyn and his stepson Louis to each receive $750,000 from the sale of the Northbridge property.[37] He made a will on 11 April 2016, which gave Blanche 'absolute discretion' to distribute a range of personal items to his children and she would inherit the rest of the estate.[38] After Bob's death, Blanche wrote to Susan, Stephen, Rosslyn and Louis to inform them about the $750,000 payment. 'I hope you agree that Bob and I have provided what we believe will allow you to feel confident and happy – and that you will be kind and loving to each other,' she wrote. 'Bob's life was long. Ours may be much shorter – too short for any bitterness to spoil it.'[39]

Bob, according to Blanche, felt 'he had provided very well for them as children and in their adult life'.[40] Rosslyn acknowledged that her parents had supported her and her sons with housing, food, clothing and financial assistance, but nevertheless challenged her father's estate after his death.[41] Susan, Stephen and Louis were not a party to this. Bob and Blanche's palatial Northbridge home was sold for $14.5 million on 22 March 2019. They planned to downsize to an apartment in Sydney's CBD overlooking Hyde Park, which was purchased for $3.63 million off the plan in 2015. Blanche moved there after Hawke's death. Hawke's entire estate was reportedly valued at $18 million – a figure disputed by Blanche.[42]

The legal row between Rosslyn and Blanche was settled out of court on 21 May 2020, almost a year to the day since Bob's death. Rosslyn asked for $4.2 million but settled for the $750,000 already provided for in the deed of agreement and an additional sum of just $150,000. 'I paid Ros $50,000 to stop it going to court because I knew if it went to court, she would be torn to pieces and I wanted to save her from that,' Blanche explained. 'I also paid $100,000 towards her very high legal costs. So, I paid out $150,000 to Ros.'[43]

———

Paul Keating saw Bob Hawke for the last time on 7 November 2018. It was the second of two meetings in three months. The first took place on 15 August 2018, at Northbridge, and was the longer of the two. The idea of a meeting came from Craig Emerson. 'I told [Paul] that I did not think Bob was going to be around much longer and asked if he would consider coming to meet with him,' Emerson recalled. 'Paul said he would. I also asked Paul if he would speak at Bob's memorial service, and he agreed. I arranged the time and Paul and I went over to Northbridge together. It was a great meeting.'[44]

It was not a reconciliation, but rather an acknowledgement of their partnership, Keating thought. 'Bob and I had a hugely productive relationship,' Keating reflected. 'While our relationship had its ups and downs, the only real down was over the leadership in 1991. Before that, you would call it the odd tremor. By and large we found ourselves in agreement because we were both serious enough to put the country first. I never hated Bob. But I think he wanted to make some sort of peace with me before he died.'[45]

The Hawke–Keating relationship had indeed been a roller-coaster since Labor's election defeat in March 1996. They had disagreed publicly from time to time, mostly over who was responsible for certain policy initiatives, but slowly relations had improved. Keating dined at Hawke's home at Northbridge in 2008 and attended his eightieth birthday party in 2009. There was always respect, admiration and indeed affection between the two, but they did not see each other regularly.

The *Hawke* television movie and D'Alpuget's book *Hawke: The Prime Minister*, both of which appeared in July 2010, halted the rapprochement. Keating thought the movie presented a warped view of their relationship, portrayed him as a villain and painted a hagiographic portrait of Hawke. Hawke's ministerial colleagues also thought the carefully crafted, overly positive portrayal of Hawke's life in articles, books and television programs – which would continue until his death – was becoming nauseating. Gareth Evans, one of Hawke's closest supporters in government, called D'Alpuget's book 'a work of second-rate hagiography'.[46]

That book, launched by Gillard, incensed Keating. 'I let Bob get away with his first bitchy memoir,' Keating said, 'but I wouldn't let the Hawke family – him and Blanche – get away with a second one.'[47] Keating wrote to Hawke, a letter which he later made public, taking aim at several falsehoods in the book, such as that he opposed floating the dollar. He accused Hawke and D'Alpuget of a 'rewriting of history' to satisfy Hawke's 'Narcissus-like' need for praise. Keating said the book ignored Hawke's 'breakdown' in 1984 and his 'emotional and intellectual malaise' that cast a pall over the government until 1990.[48] This debate would be relitigated several times in subsequent years.

In the lead-up to the May 2019 election, Hawke and Keating issued a joint statement in support of the election of a Labor government. The reporting of the statement erroneously claimed that they had 'not spoken' for 'nearly three decades', and had only just overcome the 'bitterness in their relationship'.[49] In truth, the disagreements had long been put aside. They had seen each other from time to time and spoken occasionally on the phone over the previous decades.

In August 2018, Hawke and Keating shared tea and biscuits and reminisced about old times. They talked about contemporary politics. It was emotional for both of them. 'I won't see you again,' Hawke told Keating. 'I'll die before I see you again. I'm ready to go. I don't want to be around anymore. I've got nothing more to do or say.'

Keating tried to lighten the mood. 'Oh, you're tougher than that, Bob,' he replied. 'I'll come back, and you'll still be alive.' They shook hands and Keating departed.

They met again in November 2018. This time it was the last occasion they would be together. Tea was poured. They chatted. Photos were taken.

'Bob wanted to acknowledge our partnership,' Keating said. 'We completely changed the country. We gave Australia a new motor. It was a very sweet and generous moment.'[50]

34

THE GOLDEN
BOWL IS BROKEN

On Wednesday, 15 May 2019, Bob Hawke was at home at Northbridge. A few days earlier, he had travelled to Mount Wilson, a few hours out of Sydney, to watch stepson Louis Pratt marry Brianna Roberts in a garden setting. Meanwhile, the election campaign was entering its final days and hours. Hawke thought Scott Morrison had inherited a dysfunctional and divided government and this would disqualify the Coalition from securing another term. He thought Labor, led by Bill Shorten, would win the election. But he was concerned the party was often too beholden to unions and factions. He worried about Labor not understanding the importance of middle-class aspiration or how markets could produce better economic and social outcomes than regulation and intervention. He did not subscribe to class warfare or the politics of envy. But he remained staunchly Labor and wanted to see Shorten lead the party to victory.

In the afternoon, Hawke felt intense pain in his chest. He decided to lie down. Blanche phoned his doctor, Mark Haran. She feared this might be the end. For months, she had woken each morning wondering if the man next to her had breathed his last during the night. Hawke had had a stroke earlier that year. His body was weak and frail, and his speech had slowed. Blanche watched him fighting against the pain. 'Try to surrender to it,' she said. 'I can't surrender!' he replied. Bob had spoken about how he was willing to die, and wanted to die, and would not fight it when it came. He was not afraid of death. But when the end neared, he resisted.

Hawke's health had slowly deteriorated over the previous decade. He had chronic back aches and peripheral neuropathy in his feet, which often made it excruciatingly painful to walk. He was aided by a walking stick or walking frame, and then a wheelchair. He used a motorised golf cart but when he refused to abide by rules not to park in the middle of fairways or on the greens, he was banned from playing. He had a pacemaker and hearing aids, and suffered from glaucoma. He became deathly ill from a stomach bug on a visit to Saudi Arabia in 2015. He suffered two transient ischaemic attacks (similar to a minor stroke) in 2018, and a stroke in early 2019. He had several periods in hospital during these years.[1]

Blanche recalled Bob's final years: 'It was wonderful. Once his body armour had fallen away into desuetude and he was just a human being, just a soul and a spirit, and an intellect still, he was filled with love. He had that true warrior spirit that does not fear death. I would put him to bed, and we would say to each other, night after night, how lucky we were to have had this period of his frailty and fast-approaching death, together. It was enormously fulfilling for both of us.'[2]

Blanche called Craig Emerson and he arrived at the house with his partner, Tracey Winters. 'Bob's body had given up on him,' Emerson recalled. 'He was not fighting. He said, "I've done everything I want to do, and I have love in my life, and I am ready to go." He said that many times. There was no crying or sobbing.'[3]

They kept a bedside vigil over the next twenty-four hours as Bob slept, assisted by morphine, and continued to breathe heavily. At 5.04 pm on Thursday, 16 May, there was a sharp intake of breath, and then he was gone. Blanche issued a statement announcing her husband's death and paying tribute to his extraordinary life. It ended with words from the Bible: 'The golden bowl is broken.' These words were a fitting tribute to the son of the manse. They were also the words that Clem and Ellie had chosen when Neil died of meningitis at age seventeen in 1939.

The outpouring of public emotion towards Hawke was immense. Tributes were paid from across the political divide. Prime Minister Scott Morrison said: 'Bob Hawke was a great Australian who led and served our country with passion, courage and an intellectual horsepower that made our country stronger.'[4]

Opposition Leader Bill Shorten, who had been with Hawke ten days earlier, said: 'In Australian politics, there will always be B.H. and A.H.: Before Hawke and After Hawke. After Hawke, we were a different country. A kinder, better, bigger and bolder country.'[5]

Newspaper, television, radio and online coverage was extensive, and it ran for days and days. News of Hawke's death overshadowed the election campaign. It served as a reminder of what Labor once was and what it should be. But rather than boost Labor's chances, as some expected, Hawke's death probably served to diminish them. There was, after all, only one Hawke.

A private memorial service was held at the Macquarie Park Cemetery and Crematorium, in Sydney, at 12.30 pm on 27 May 2019. About fifty people – mainly friends and family – attended. Hawke's coffin was held aloft by his son Stephen, stepson Louis, and grandsons Paul, Ben, Sam and Kel. There were several speeches, readings and poems. Hawke's ashes would later be interred at the same cemetery, along with a plaque that said: 'He loved Australians and they loved him back.' On 9 December 2020, a plaque was installed on a rockface opposite Hawke's Northbridge home, noting that he had lived there for twenty-five years until his death. An initiative of the local Bushcare group, it was donated by Hawke's Brewery and Landcare Australia, and installed by Willoughby Council.

It was fitting that Hawke's public memorial service was held at the Sydney Opera House; where he had launched Labor's campaign in 1983 promising to bring Australians together.[6] At 11.30 am on 14 June 2019, Hawke brought the nation together one last time. This was his mission, and he fulfilled it in life and in death. Australians came in their thousands from across the political divide to pay tribute, offer thanks and bid farewell to Australia's most popular post-war prime minister. The Concert Hall was full. Thousands more were on the steps outside, watching on a large screen. Only Gough Whitlam's celebratory memorial service at the Sydney Town Hall in 2014 and Robert Menzies's more solemn state funeral at Scots Church in Melbourne in 1978 could rival it for public attention and attendees.

As Blanche said, the Opera House service marked the transition from mourning to celebrating Hawke's life. Those who assembled included governors and governors-general, prime ministers and premiers, ministers and opposition leaders, scores of state and federal MPs, plus former staff, ambassadors and bureaucrats. The oldest and youngest of the surviving Whitlam-era ministers were there: Doug McClelland and Paul Keating. There were fine eulogies from Scott Morrison and Anthony Albanese. But the trio of Keating, Kim Beazley and Bill Kelty had the audience captivated with well crafted, perfectly pitched and brilliantly delivered orations. Keating was poignant, Beazley erudite, Kelty rousing.

Hawke loved Sydney. He relished weekends at Kirribilli. He had taken his mum, Ellie, to the opening of the Opera House in 1973. He'd spoken at Labor's doomed launch there in 1977, and launched his own campaigns there in 1983, 1984 and 1987. He had been to countless concerts and plays, and many other events over the years. He had celebrated his eightieth birthday at Guillaume At Bennelong. He had even conducted the Sydney Philharmonia Choirs there. There was no better place for Hawke's final curtain call.

HAWKE
REFLECTS

B ob Hawke did not dwell on the past. He did not hold grudges. He did not have many regrets. He thought hate, envy and bitterness were destructive emotions. In his final interviews, he lamented that he had not been a better husband and father. He was ashamed of some of his behaviour earlier in his life when he had been possessed by the demon drink and unfaithful in his marriage. Asked what kind of father he was, Hawke replied, 'Oh, not a good one.' He said he had put his career in the union movement ahead of his marriage and family. He had caused the 'difficulties' in the marriage and was not 'faithful' to Hazel. He added that Hazel was 'an extraordinarily good mother' and 'a marvellous prime minister's wife', who was liked and respected by all Australians.[1]

In government, there were two areas in which Hawke wished he could have done better. The first was his misreading of the economy in the late 1980s and early 1990s, which deepened and lengthened the recession. The second was not doing more to advance land rights and reconciliation with Aboriginal and Torres Strait Islander Australians.

There were three achievements for which Hawke most wanted to be remembered. First, for 'bringing Australia together', which provided the 'reconciliation' that led to the 'fundamental transformation of the Australian economy'. That process began with the National Economic Summit in 1983, which provided the springboard for the milestone reforms: floating the dollar, deregulating the financial sector, overhauling the tax system with big reductions in personal and company tax rates, slashing tariffs and privatising government assets. The budget was structurally repaired and returned to surplus for the first time since the 1950s. These policies laid the basis for three decades of economic growth and prosperity.

Second, Hawke named the dramatic increase in high-school completion rates and his government's landmark university reforms, which provided greater access to education and therefore improved equality of opportunity. 'If you are going to have a decent, fair society, the opportunity for a child to develop his or her talents cannot be a function of the size of Mum or Dad's wallet but of their interests and capacities,' Hawke said. He was also proud of establishing Medicare and implementing the Prices and Incomes Accord, which moderated wage claims in return for social wage benefits. And the Hawke government's environmental legacy is substantial: stopping the Franklin Dam in Tasmania, setting up Landcare, saving the Daintree Rainforest in Queensland, preserving old-growth forests in Tasmania, protecting the Great Barrier Reef, safeguarding Kakadu National Park in the Northern Territory, and helping to keep Antarctica free of mining.

The third initiative that Hawke identified was his role in ending apartheid in South Africa. He had been one of the leaders for racial equality in South Africa since the 1970s. As prime minister, he had worked with other Commonwealth leaders to implement trade and investment sanctions. He also led the establishment of the Asia-Pacific Economic Cooperation trade forum. He strengthened the ANZUS alliance by developing good relations with Ronald Reagan and George H.W. Bush. Hawke was also proud to have acted as a mediator during the Cold War, between the Soviet Union and China in the East and the United States and the United Kingdom in the West.

The key to understanding Bob Hawke's life is to appreciate the unique bond he had with the Australian people. This 'special relationship' attracted sneers from colleagues and opponents, but it was inexorably linked with who Hawke was as a person and as a political figure. No other politician has come close to emulating this mutual affection, which crossed generations and was the bedrock of his success. Moreover, this bond sustained him in public life, motivated him to try to change the economy and society, and gave him faith in the Australian people and their country.

'The Australian people know that I love them and this country,' Hawke explained. 'I just love Australia and I love Australians. One of the strange things for me in politics was to see the way in which so many of my colleagues were frightened of people. I genuinely enjoyed moving among Australians, meeting with them, listening to them and sharing their interests.' He thought that it was his interest in sport and his background in the union movement that endeared him to Australians. 'The genuine love and respect I had for the Australian people was warmly reciprocated,' he said. Hawke believed that Australians looked at him and thought: 'Hawkey really is one of us.'[2]

—

Nobody is better equipped to judge a prime minister than another prime minister. They have carried the same burdens and stresses. They have managed the same giant workload. They have each wrestled with difficult decisions.

Hawke thought John Curtin was Australia's greatest prime minister. He respected Ben Chifley, although he believed his decision to nationalise the banks was a monumental blunder. Hawke personally knew four prime ministers before becoming prime minister himself. He liked John Gorton and admired the way he had tried to instil a new sense of Australian nationalism in public life. He thought Billy McMahon was out of his depth and regarded him as a fool. He admired what Gough Whitlam achieved in education, health and foreign policy, but judged his government poorly for economic management, public administration and political judgement. He thought Malcolm Fraser had recklessly pushed the political system to the brink to gain power and then floundered in office, but praised him highly for his record on matters concerning race and colour at home and abroad.

In his final years, Hawke lamented the standard of political leadership in Australia. He felt Australians had been let down by the quality of prime ministers. Hawke thought that Paul Keating led a 'good' government and made 'a great contribution to Australia' as both treasurer and prime minister. He regarded John Howard as the most substantial Liberal leader post-Menzies, even though they disagreed on issues such as the Iraq War and the introduction of the GST. 'He has more tenacity than any other Australian politician,' Hawke said of Howard.

Hawke disliked Kevin Rudd. 'I don't want to talk about him,' Hawke would routinely say. While he praised Rudd highly for the response to the global financial crisis and the apology to the Stolen Generations, he thought Rudd was inept at running a government, treated his ministerial colleagues and staff appallingly, and showed poor policy and political judgement. 'Rudd's method of government was one which just almost inevitably was going to lead to a [leadership] challenge because he wanted to run so much of things single-handedly,' Hawke said.

Hawke had a higher regard for Julia Gillard. 'History will treat Julia Gillard reasonably kindly,' he said. 'She made mistakes, but no prime minister has ever operated under more difficult parliamentary circumstances.' Hawke regarded Gillard as a leader with grace and dignity, and he liked her personally.

While Hawke remained committed to the Labor cause, he had a degree of personal regard for Tony Abbott. Hawke said Abbott was a 'decent' person and enjoyed his company, but judged him to be 'bloody hopeless' as prime minister because he kept 'making the same mistakes' and could not grow into the prime ministership.

Before his death, Hawke thought Scott Morrison was unlikely to win the May 2019 election because of the 'shenanigans' over the leadership of the Liberal Party. But he did not rule out a Coalition victory and judged Morrison to be a shrewd politician who should not be underestimated.

Hawke's strongest criticism was reserved for Malcolm Turnbull. He thought Turnbull was 'not interested in anyone but himself' and had sold out his principles to become prime minister in 2015. He was highly critical of Turnbull's approach to same-sex marriage, climate change and the republic, and thought he had failed to follow his convictions and show courage on these issues. Hawke assessed Turnbull to be the worst prime minister since McMahon. 'I think he has handled himself poorly,' he said.[3]

—

Bob Hawke worried about the future of Australian democracy, the deteriorating quality of politicians, the health of political parties, the effectiveness of the national parliament and quality of public debate. He wanted politicians to work more cooperatively across the political spectrum. He thought unions and business should be more willing to work together in the national interest. He wanted Australia to become a republic and a treaty to be forged with Indigenous Australians that could provide the basis for reconciliation.

Hawke thought social media was making politics dangerously tribal, combative and toxic. It was not only dumbing down debate and distracting politicians from focusing on more important issues, but it was also wrecking the ability of political parties to attract the best and brightest to public life. 'I would like to see, on both sides of politics, an improvement in the quality of candidates standing for parliament,' he said. 'I think people are disinclined to expose themselves and their families to the intrusiveness of the social media, and I think we have paid a high price for that.'

He believed one way to attract better quality ministers was to facilitate a referendum to allow people to serve in cabinet without having to be elected to parliament. 'You would have a limited number of people who could be called in to serve and be entitled to sit in parliament in respect of any issue concerning their portfolio,' he said. 'They wouldn't be a full member of parliament, but they would be members of the government.' Hawke said this would considerably improve the standard of ministers. It was an idea he had first raised in the 1970s.

Parliament itself also needed reform. Hawke suggested Australia would be better off with a four-year House of Representatives term and either a four-year or eight-year Senate term, which would allow difficult reforms to be explained and implemented over a longer period between elections. A referendum on four-year terms was put to voters and rejected in 1988. He also thought politicians should be more willing to debate issues and reach bipartisan agreement in parliament rather than in the party room. 'One of the reasons why people hold parliament and parliamentarians in contempt is because the process is a total charade,' he said. 'It would make a hell of a difference if the parties identified two or three policy areas where they could freely debate issues and allow MPs to vote with their conscience.'

He always believed that politicians underestimate the intelligence of voters, and too often choose the low road when the high road is available. He placed a premium on argument, advocacy and persuasion. 'We ought to treat the electorate more seriously and give them as much information as possible,' he argued. 'My thesis is that ignorance is the enemy of good policy, and that was the very foundation of my government right from the beginning.'

While he argued state governments should be abolished, Hawke saw an opportunity to reform the federation so that roles and responsibilities were better delineated to improve the efficiency of service delivery. 'We should get rid of the bloody states, but I think that's probably the counsel of perfection, so we should look at federalism anew and try to make it work as effectively as possible,' he said. He thought transport, education and health were areas ripe for reform, and he was open to giving states a share of national income tax, as he proposed in 1991.

In his final years, Hawke was also troubled about the state of leadership around the world – he could not identify one outstanding leader – and thought we were not doing enough to address climate change or the threat of weapons of mass destruction. These two things, he believed, threatened the survival of humankind. He argued that if we set aside petty differences, worked together and identified the national and international interest, then the future would indeed be bright. Hawke was always an optimist.

'We are at a unique point in human history,' Hawke said. 'For the first time, due to the technological genius of humankind, we can substantially lift the standard and quality of life of all or we can destroy life as we know it.' The two great threats we face, he argued, are the destruction of our planet to the point it is uninhabitable because of the failure to deal with climate change and the deployment of nuclear, chemical or biological weapons. It is up to all of us, not just politicians, to decide what kind of future we want. 'There are two awesomely important alternate paths for humankind,' Hawke said. 'We have got to make sure we go down the right one.'[4]

APPENDIX

Exchange of letters between Bob Hawke and Bill Hayden about the Labor leadership in 1983

Leader of the Opposition

3 February 1983

Mr R J Hawke, MHR
Parliament House
CANBERRA ACT 2600

Dear Bob

I wish to confirm our discussions of this morning in which I informed you that it is my intention to stand down as Leader of the Federal Parliamentary Labor Party.

I will today ask the Executive of the Federal Parliamentary Labor Party of convene a meeting of the Caucus for Tuesday next week, 8 February 1983 at which I will formally tender my resignation.

You have informed me of your intention to be a candidate for the Leader of the Federal Parliamentary Labor Party and this letter is written on the assumption that you be elected Leader. As I informed you this morning, in standing down as Leader I will be making a number of sacrifices. I have done this however for what I and some of my senior parliamentary colleagues believe to be the interests of the party.

I confirm our discussions and agreement on the following points:

1. That you will immediately arrange for appropriate employment for all members of my staff who are not currently permanently employed in the Australian Public Service.

2. That you guarantee the continuation in their existing Shadow Ministries or an alternate Shadow Ministry of equivalent status to be agreed upon with them of Messrs John Dawkins, Peter Walsh and Neal Blewett.

3. That I will be appointed as Shadow Minister for Foreign Affairs until the next federal election and thereafter in the event of Labor losing such election until such time as agreement is reached on any alternate position between us.

4. That I, as Shadow Minister may be allocated in addition to any staff entitlement I shall have a staff member of Assistant Private Secretary Grade II. entitlement.

../2

Parliament House, Canberra, A.C.T. 2600

-2-

5. That in the event of the Labor Party forming a
    government after the 1983 Federal election, I be
    appointed as Minister for Foreign Affairs, such
    appointment to be of such period as is required
    to enable me to be appointed Australian High
    Commissioner to London for a period of five years.

6. In the event of the Australian Labor Party not
    forming a government following the 1983 Federal
    election the arrangement referred to in the preceding
    paragraph is to apply immediately following the
    next succeeding election if at that election the
    Labor Party is elected to government.

I would be pleased if, as was agreed, you acknowledge
receipt of this letter and confirm the arrangements.

Yours sincerely

(Bill Hayden)

PARLIAMENT OF AUSTRALIA
HOUSE OF REPRESENTATIVES

Parliament House
CANBERRA   ACT   2600

3 February 1983

Mr W G Hayden, MHR
Leader of the Opposition
Parliament House
CANBERRA   ACT   2600

Dear Bill

I acknowledge receipt of your letter of 3 February 1983
in relation to your resignation as Leader of the Australian
Labor Party.

In that letter you set out certain terms and conditions
which have been the subject of discussion between us
in relation to your future.

On the assumption that at the Caucus Meeting on Tuesday
8 February 1983 I am elected Leader of the Australian
Labor Party I confirm that the matters set out in your
letter have been agreed between us and as indicated to you
verbally I undertake to abide by those conditions.

Yours sincerely

(Bob Hawke)

Paul Keating's note on the November 1988 Kirribilli Agreement, made in 1991

Note of Meeting at Kirribilli 25/11/88. given to Richardson 20/5/91 and read to Oakes of National 9 News Since 30/5/91

At the Prime Minister's initiative, and following a conversation
in the latter part of 1988 during which the Treasurer had told
him he was prepared to fight the 1990 Election with him, the
Prime Minister suggested that he take the Party into the fourth
election and then resign at some suitable time thereafter in
favour of the Treasurer.

The Treasurer said he agreed, but that such an agreement would
require formality unlike other such discussions in the past.

The Prime Minister accepted this and offered to convene a
meeting where an agreement would be made and witnessed.

He suggested Sir Peter Abeles be the witness. In response
the Treasurer put to the Prime Minister that somebody of
significance from the Labour movement should also be in
attendance for an occasion that would so materially affect
the Party and the movement's future. He suggested Bill Kelty,
and the Prime Minister agreed.

The meeting was arranged and held at Kirribilli House on
25 November 1988, with the Prime Minister, the Treasurer,
Sir Peter Abeles and Bill Kelty in attendance.

The meeting had only one item under discussion, namely the
leadership, which the Prime Minister came to directly.

He said he wished to lead the Party to a fourth election
and if won would serve some suitable time thereafter, and then
resign in favour of the Treasurer, giving the Treasurer the
time and opportunity to establish himself.

In return it was understood the Treasurer would serve and fight
the election with him. It was agreed by all that it would
be important to the Government's prospects for the
Prime Minister and the Treasurer to go to the election as
a fighting unit.

The Prime Minister's promise to resign during the fourth term
was unconditional, save for the fact that he said that if
the details of the agreement leaked, his commitment to the
arrangement would terminate.

The Treasurer accepted this codicil as did the other two
attendees.

Both the Prime Minister and the Treasurer agreed that this
arrangement would facilitate a smooth transition of power
and leadership within the Government which would enhance its
longer term electoral prospects.

The meeting finished and the visitors left Kirribilli House
for their respective destinations.

P.J. Keating Collection, Sydney. This was provided to the author by Paul Keating.

Bob Hawke's note on the November 1988 Kirribilli Agreement, made in 1991

1. Peter Abeles and Kelty believed independently of any Hawke/Keating discussions that there should be a meeting of friends to resolve the tensions.

2. PK independently asked whether Kelty would attend a meeting all been talking about

    -   PK had spoken to Peter and Bill K. And Peter himself spoke to PK and me

    -   Series of discussions.

3. Meeting not to witness some arrangement.

4. BK initiated meeting been talking about.

5. Never was a question of Abeles being there for me and Kelty for Paul

    -   always four mutual friends.

6. Nothing I've said does he dispute.

Personal Papers of Prime Minister Hawke, M3594/73, National Archives of Australia, Canberra.

SELECT
BIBLIOGRAPHY

Archives

Australian Labor Party (National Secretariat), National Library of Australia, Canberra

Australian National University Archives, Canberra

George H.W. Bush Papers, George Bush Presidential Library and Museum, College Station, Texas

John Button Papers, State Library of Victoria, Melbourne

Cabinet Papers and Cabinet Notebooks, National Archives of Australia, Canberra

Blanche d'Alpuget Papers, National Library of Australia, Canberra

Federal Parliamentary Labor Party (Caucus), National Library of Australia, Canberra

A.J. Forbes Papers, National Library of Australia, Canberra

Bob Hawke Personal Papers, Bob Hawke Prime Ministerial Library, Adelaide

Bob Hawke Prime Ministerial Papers, National Archives of Australia, Canberra

Hazel Hawke Papers, John Curtin Prime Ministerial Library, Perth

Bill Hayden Papers, National Library of Australia, Canberra

P.J. Keating Collection, Sydney (Private Collection)

Oxford University Archives, Oxford

Rhodes Trust Archives, Oxford

Ronald Reagan Papers, Ronald Reagan Presidential Library and Museum, Simi Valley, California

Perth Modernians Society Archives, Perth

Margaret Thatcher Papers, United Kingdom National Archives, Kew

University College Archives, Oxford

University of Western Australia Archives, Perth

Books

Stan Anson, *Hawke: An Emotional Life*, McPhee Gribble, Ringwood, 1991

Gerry Bloustien, Barbara Comber and Alison Mackinnon (eds), *The Hawke Legacy*, Wakefield Press, Kent Town, 2009

Troy Bramston, *Paul Keating: The Big-Picture Leader*, Scribe, Brunswick, 2016

—, *Rudd, Gillard and Beyond*, Penguin, Melbourne, 2014

—, *For the True Believers: Great Labor Speeches That Shaped History* (ed.), The Federation Press, Sydney, 2012

John Button, *As It Happened*, Text Publishing, Melbourne, 1998

Blanche d'Alpuget, *Bob Hawke: The Complete Biography*, Simon & Schuster, Cammeray, 2019

—, *Hawke: The Prime Minister*, Melbourne University Publishing, Carlton, 2010

—, *On Longing*, Melbourne University Publishing, Carlton, 2008

—, *Robert J. Hawke: A Biography*, Schwartz, Melbourne, 1982

Craig Emerson, *The Boy from Baradine*, Scribe, Brunswick, 2018

Gareth Evans, *Incorrigible Optimist*, Melbourne University Publishing, Carlton, 2017

—, *Inside the Hawke–Keating Government: A Cabinet Diary*, Melbourne University Publishing, Carlton, 2014

Malcolm Fraser and Margaret Simons, *Malcolm Fraser: The Political Memoirs*, Melbourne University Publishing (The Miegunyah Press), Carlton, 2010

Graham Freudenberg, *A Figure of Speech: A Political Memoir*, Wiley, Milton, 2005

Robert Haupt with Michelle Grattan, *31 Days to Power: Hawke's Victory*, George Allen & Unwin, Sydney, 1983

Bob Hawke, *The Hawke Memoirs*, William Heinemann Australia, Port Melbourne, 1994

Bob Hawke and Derek Rielly, *Wednesdays with Bob*, Pan Macmillan, Sydney, 2017

Bill Hayden, *Hayden: An Autobiography*, Angus & Robertson, Sydney, 1996

John Howard, *Lazarus Rising: A Personal and Political Autobiography*, HarperCollins, Sydney, 2010

John Hurst, *Hawke: The Definitive Biography*, Angus & Robertson, Sydney, 1979

Christine Jennett and Randal Stewart (eds), *Hawke and Australian Public Policy: Consensus and Restructuring*, Macmillan, South Melbourne, 1990

Barry Jones, *A Thinking Reed*, Allen & Unwin, Crows Nest, 2006

Paul Kelly, *The End of Certainty*, revised edition, Allen & Unwin, St Leonards, 1994

—, *The Hawke Ascendancy*, Angus & Robertson, Sydney, 1984

Paul Kelly and Troy Bramston, *The Dismissal: In the Queen's Name*, Penguin, Melbourne, 2015

Ros Kelly, *A Passionate Life*, Hardie Grant Books, Richmond, 2017

John Kerin, *The Way I Saw It; the Way It Was*, Analysis and Policy Observatory, Melbourne, 2017

Craig McGregor, *Time of Testing: The Bob Hawke Victory*, Penguin Books, Ringwood, 1983

Stephen Mills, *The Hawke Years: The Story from the Inside*, Viking, Ringwood, 1993

Sue Pieters-Hawke, *Remembering Bob* (ed.), Allen & Unwin, Crows Nest, 2019

—, *Hazel: My Mother's Story*, Pan Macmillan, Sydney, 2011

Robert Pullan, *Bob Hawke: A Portrait*, Methuen Australia, Sydney, 1980

Margaret Reynolds, *Living Politics*, University of Queensland Press, St Lucia, 2007

Graham Richardson, *Whatever It Takes*, Bantam Books, Sydney, 1994

Susan Ryan, *Catching the Waves: Life in and out of Politics*, HarperCollins, Pymble, 1999

Susan Ryan and Troy Bramston (eds), *The Hawke Government: A Critical Retrospective*, Pluto Press, Melbourne, 2003

Anne Summers, *Gamble for Power: How Bob Hawke Beat Malcolm Fraser*, Nelson, Melbourne, 1983

Robert Tickner, *Taking a Stand: Land Rights to Reconciliation*, Allen & Unwin, Crows Nest, 2001

Tom Uren, *Straight Left*, Random House, Milsons Point, 1994

Peter Walsh, *Confessions of a Failed Finance Minister*, Random House, Milsons Point, 1995

Gough Whitlam, *The Whitlam Government, 1972–1975*, Viking, Richmond, 1985

Documentaries and Movies

Five of a Kind, ABC TV, 1985
Labor in Power, ABC TV, 1993
The Liberals, ABC TV, 1994
Hawke, Ten Network, 2010
Hawke: The Larrikin & the Leader, ABC TV, 2018

NOTE TO READERS

This book draws on extensive interviews and conversations with Bob Hawke, which began in 2002. Almost all were recorded and transcribed; some were documented by hand. A few were conducted via email. These interviews, and those with others, have at times been edited for clarity or brevity. The book also makes use of Hawke's extensive personal papers, many of which were kept at his Sydney office and transferred after his death to the Bob Hawke Prime Ministerial Library at the University of South Australia. They have since been catalogued using a new records system.

NOTES

Preface
1   Interview with Bob Hawke, Sydney, 12 February 2019. See also Troy
     Bramston, 'Bob Hawke: Some regret, lots of love and plenty of memories',
     The Weekend Australian, 18 May 2019, p. 1.
2   Interview with Hawke, Sydney, 29 August 2018.
3   Labor Party Life Membership Presentation Dinner for Arthur and Dawn
     Gietzelt, Sutherland and District Trade Union Club (The Tradies),
     Gymea, 27 May 1994.

Prologue
1   While this deal has been known, the actual letters exchanged between the
     vanquished Bill Hayden and the victor Bob Hawke have not been revealed
     before.
2   Bill Hayden to Bob Hawke, 3 February 1983, Papers of Bill Hayden,
     MS 7624, Series 3/12, Folder 28, National Library of Australia (NLA),
     Canberra.
3   Bob Hawke to Bill Hayden, 3 February 1983, Hayden Papers, MS 7624,
     Series 3/12, Folder 28, NLA.
4   Interview with Alister Drysdale, via phone, 27 February 2021.
5   Bill Hayden, *Hayden: An Autobiography*, Angus & Robertson, Sydney, 1996,
     p. 362.
6   Paul Ellercamp and Russell Schneider, '"There's no blood on my
     hands . . ."', *The Australian*, 4 February 1983, p. 1.
7   Minutes of the Federal Parliamentary Labor Party, 8 February 1983,
     Records of the Federal Parliamentary Labor Party (FPLP), MS 6852,
     NLA.
8   Interview with Hawke, Sydney, 5 June 2014.
9   Interview with Hawke, Sydney, 12 February 2019.
10   Interview with Hawke, Sydney, 14 December 2017.

Chapter 1
1   Clem Hawke, *Yesterday, Today and Tomorrow*, unpublished, c. 1982, p. 49,
     Bob Hawke Personal Papers (ex-Sydney).

2 His father's name is listed as 'Clement Arthur' and his mother's middle name is spelt 'Emiley' on the Registration of Birth. See Robert James Lee Hawke, Registration of Birth, 31 December 1929, A-Z Files, Box 96, Bob Hawke Prime Ministerial Library (BHPML), University of South Australia, Adelaide.

3 'Births', *The Advertiser* and 14 December 1929, p. 24.

4 'Births', *The Chronicle*, 19 December 1929, p. 39. See also 'Births', *The Advertiser*, 21 December 1929, p. 18 and 'Births', *The Chronicle*, 26 December 1929, p. 35.

5 The Hawkes wrote either 'Bobbie' or 'Bobby' when referring to young Robert.

6 Blanche d'Alpuget, *Robert J. Hawke: A Biography*, Schwartz Publishing Group, East Melbourne, 1982, p. 1.

7 Hawke, *Yesterday, Today and Tomorrow*, p. 49.

8 Interview with Hawke, Sydney, 28 November 2017.

9 Bob Hawke, 'Bob Hawke', in Terry Lane (ed.), *As the Twig Is Bent*, Dove Communications, Melbourne, 1979, p. 58.

10 Interview with Hawke, Sydney, 29 August 2018.

11 Bob Hawke, *The Hawke Memoirs*, William Heinemann Australia, Port Melbourne, 1994, p. 4.

12 Blanche d'Alpuget argued that Hawke had 'to make a sort of peace' between his 'biological maleness' and 'the phantom Elizabeth' which manifested as 'a defiant masculinity' and 'displays of swashbuckling virility'. This is, to say the least, a highly speculative leap into psychoanalysis. It is an idea that Hawke himself never entertained. See D'Alpuget, *Robert J. Hawke*, p. 6.

13 Interview with Hawke, Sydney, 28 November 2017.

14 Birth certificate for Arthur Clarence Hawke, 5 March 1898, Births, Deaths and Marriages Registration Office, Adelaide.

15 'Bob Hawke mourns his father's death', *The Canberra Times*, 24 December 1989, p. 3.

16 Interview with Hawke, Sydney, 28 November 2017.

17 Ellie Hawke's death certificate lists Kadina as her place of birth. See Birth certificate for Edith Emily Lee, 1 October 1897, Births, Deaths and Marriages Registration Office, Adelaide and Death certificate for Edith Emily Lee, 8 September 1979, Births, Deaths and Marriages, Perth.

18 Hawke, *The Hawke Memoirs*, p. 3.

19 Interview with Hawke, Sydney, 8 December 2015.

20 The marriage certificate lists Clem as age 23 and Ellie as age 22 when they were in fact both 22 years old. Moreover, Clem's name is listed as 'Clement Arthur Hawke' whereas his birth certificate reads 'Arthur Clarence Hawke'. See Marriage certificate for Clement Arthur Hawke and Edith Emily Lee, 2 June 1920, Births, Deaths and Marriages Registration Office, Adelaide.

21 'Approaching Marriages', *The Chronicle*, 22 May 1920, p. 27.

22 Hawke, *Yesterday, Today and Tomorrow*, p. 49.

23 Scott Morrison, '$750,000 to preserve Hawke house', Media Release, 7 July 2019.

24 Hawke, *Yesterday, Today and Tomorrow*, p. 49.

25 Bob Hawke, 'Loyal Temperance Legion of Australasia', 27 October 1939, RH14, Box 3, Folder 38, BHPML.

26 Bob Hawke, 'Independent Order of Rechabites' and Essay, October 1939, RH14, Box 3, Folder 38, BHPML.

Chapter 2

1 Bob Hawke, 'RSPCA Certificate of Membership', 16 May 1939, RH14, Box 3, Folder 38, BHPML.

2 Maitland Primary School Admission Register, State Records of South Australia.

3 Jan Mayman, 'Bob Hawke – By His Mum & Dad', *Woman's Day*, 25 September 1978.

4 D'Alpuget, *Robert J. Hawke*, p. 16.

5 Bob Hawke, Maitland Primary School Report, 1937, BHPML.

6 Interview with Hawke, Sydney, 29 August 2018.

7 Maitland Primary School Admission Register, State Records of South Australia.

8 Hawke, 'Bob Hawke', p. 59.

9 Interview with Hawke, 28 November 2017, Sydney.

10 'Caught in a Few Yards', *News*, 27 February 1939, p. 5.

11 Oddly, Neil Hawke's gravestone records that he was eighteen years old when he died.

12 'Deaths', *The Advertiser*, 21 February 1939, p. 8.

13 Hawke, *The Hawke Memoirs*, p. 5.

14 Hawke, *Yesterday, Today and Tomorrow*, p. 54.

15 Hawke, *Yesterday, Today and Tomorrow*, p. 55.

16 Mark McGowan, 'Historic Bob Hawke family home to be preserved', Media Release, 27 December 2020.

17 Bob Hawke, West Leederville State School Report, December 1940, A-Z Files, Box 234, BHPML.

18 Letter from Bob Hawke to West Leederville Primary School, 15 June 1988. Provided by West Leederville Primary School.

19 Hawke, *The Hawke Memoirs*, p. 7.

20 Interview with Hawke, Sydney, 28 November 2017.

21 Hawke, Arthur Clarence, Personal Service Record, Second Australian Imperial Force, 1939–48, B884/W58, National Archives of Australia (NAA), Canberra.

22 Edith Emily Hawke, Record of Service Cards – Teaching Staff, 1944–61, S132 Cons3512, State Records Office of Western Australia.

23 Hawke, *Yesterday, Today and Tomorrow*, p. 56.

24 Interview with Hawke, Sydney, 5 June 2014.

25 Hawke, 'Bob Hawke', p. 62.

26 Interview with Hawke, Sydney, 5 June 2014.

27 Interview with Hawke, Sydney, 5 June 2014.

28 *Perth Modern School: The History and the Heritage*, B+G Resource Enterprises, Cottesloe, 2005, p. 71.

29 Interview with Hawke, Sydney, 28 November 2017.

30 Interview with Hawke, Sydney, 29 August 2018.

31 Paula Hamilton, interview with Bob Hawke, 13 March 2001, Sydney, Perth Modernian Society Museum Association.

32 Interview with John Stone, via phone, 16 December 2020.

33 Joe Poprzeczny, 'Prankster PM rekindles fiery schooldays', *The Australian*, 3 December 1986, p. 3.

34 Robert James Lee Hawke, Student Admission Card, 1942–46, S3117 Cons7151, State Records Office of Western Australia.

35 'Corridor Chatter', *The Sphinx*, vol. 10, no. 86, November 1945, p. 26.

36 'Corridor Chatter', *The Sphinx*, vol. 10, no. 89, November 1946, p. 25.

37 Noel Sampson, 26 November 1946, Student File, R.J. Hawke, University of Western Australia (UWA) Archives, Perth.

38 'The Junior – Examination Results', *The West Australian*, 16 January 1945, p. 3.

39 'Public Examinations – Leaving Certificate Results', *The West Australian*, 9 January 1947, p. 12.

40 John Hurst, *Hawke: The Definitive Biography*, Angus & Robertson, Sydney, 1979, pp. 12–13.

41 Hamilton, interview with Hawke, 13 March 2001.

Chapter 3

1 Interview with Hawke, Sydney, 28 November 2017.

2 Hawke, *The Hawke Memoirs*, p. 11.

3 D'Alpuget, *Robert J. Hawke*, p. 29.

4 'Youth injured', *The West Australian*, 12 August 1947, p. 14.

5 Interview with Hawke, via email, 23 April 2019.

6 See Troy Bramston, 'Hawke's fateful crash bike goes full cycle', *The Weekend Australian*, 27–28 April 2019, p. 5.

7 *A Celebration of Contribution*, Department of Education, Perth, 2016, p. 220.

8 Hackett Bursary Applications, 1947–50, Student File, R.J. Hawke, UWA Archives.

9 'Three contest Guild presidency,' *The Pelican*, UWA, Perth, 26 September 1950, p. 1.

10 Interview with Stone, via phone, 16 December 2020.

11 'Election results – Stone Guild president', *The Pelican*, UWA, Perth, 6 October 1950.

12 Robert Pullan, *Bob Hawke: A Portrait*, Methuen, Sydney, 1980, pp. 44–47.

13 'Close contest for presidency – Hawke swoops home,' *The Pelican*, UWA, Perth, 5 October 1951.

14 Bob Hawke, 'Introducing your Guild president', *The Pelican*, UWA, Perth, 4 April 1952.

15 Interview with Hawke, Sydney, 29 August 2018.

16 Interview with Neal Blewett, Leura, 16 November 2019.

17 'Cunderdin C.W.A. entertains Rhodes Scholar', *The Eastern Recorder*, 9 July 1953.

18 D'Alpuget, *Robert J. Hawke*, pp. 37–38.

19 The book is now located at the BHPML.

20 'Rhodes winner', *The Pelican*, UWA, Perth, 23 April 1953.

21 D'Alpuget, *Robert J. Hawke*, p. 41.

22 Interview with William Heseltine, Sydney, 22 June 2017.

23 Interview with Hawke, Sydney, 28 November 2017.

24 '3,000 attend W.A. youth festival', *The West Australian*, 8 October 1951.

25 Philip Ziegler, *Legacy: Cecil Rhodes, The Rhodes Trust and The Rhodes Scholarships*, Yale University Press, London, 2008, pp. 13–19.

26 Bob Hawke, Rhodes Scholarship Personal Statement, 27 September 1952, Rhodes Trust Archive (RTA), Rhodes House, Oxford University.

27 Frank Beasley to Secretary of the Committee of Selection, Rhodes Scholarships, 18 September 1951, RTA.

28 Mervyn Austin to Secretary of the Committee of Selection, Rhodes Scholarships, 11 November 1952, RTA.

29 Hawke, *The Hawke Memoirs*, p. 19.

30 Ziegler, *Legacy*, p. 288.

31 Charles Gairdner, 'Report on the Western Australian Rhodes Scholarship Selection Committee's Interview with Mr R.J.L. Hawke, the Successful Candidate for 1953', November 1952, RTA.

32 'Good wishes and packing occupy Rhodes Scholar', *The West Australian*, 29 November 1952, p. 3.

33 'Rhodes Scholar is selected', *The West Australian*, 29 November 1952, p. 6.

34 'Rhodes Scholar', *The Argus*, 29 November 1952, p. 7.

35 'Civic welcome to the New Zealand High Commissioner', *The Northam Advertiser*, 5 December 1952, p. 7.

36 Bob Hawke to Clem and Ellie Hawke, 22 December 1952, Hazel Hawke Collection, John Curtin Prime Ministerial Library (JCPML), Curtin University, Perth.

37 Interview with Hawke, Sydney, 28 November 2017.

38 Hawke, *Yesterday, Today and Tomorrow*, p. 68.

39 Interview with Hawke, Sydney, 28 November 2017.

40 Bob Hawke, Diary and Notebook, 1952, RH6, Box 2, Folder 8, BHPML.

41 'W.A. Rhodes Scholar – return from youth conference', *Kalgoorlie Miner*, 14 January 1953, p. 7.

42 Hawke, Diary and Notebook , 1952, BHPML.

Chapter 4

1 Hawke, *The Hawke Memoirs*, p. 17.

2 Hazel Hawke, Diary, 5–6 April 1947, Hazel Hawke Collection, JCPML. See also Sue Pieters-Hawke, *Hazel: My Mother's Story*, Pan Macmillan, Sydney, 2011, p. 39.

3 See Hazel Hawke, Diary, 9 April, 25 April, 3 May and 24 May 1947, JCPML.

4 Hazel Hawke, *My Own Life: An Autobiography*, Text Publishing, Melbourne, 1992, p. 26–27.

5 Hazel Hawke, Diary, 4 April 1948, JCPML.

6 Hazel Hawke, Diary, 5 April 1948, JCPML.

7 Hawke, *My Own Life*, pp. 6–7.

8 Hawke, *My Own Life*, p. 22.

9 Hazel Hawke, Diary, 23 April 1948, JCPML.

10 Hazel Hawke, Diary, 11 May 1948, JCPML.

11 Hawke, *My Own Life*, p. 34.

12 Interview with Hawke, Sydney, 29 August 2018.

13 Hawke, *My Own Life*, p. 34.

14 Pieters-Hawke, *Hazel*, p. 48.
15 Hawke, *My Own Life*, pp. 36–37.
16 Hawke, *My Own Life*, p. 38.
17 Blanche d'Alpuget writes that Hawke lost his virginity in 1949 – his third
    year of university. It is likely to have been in 1948, with Hazel Masterson.
    See D'Alpuget, *Robert J. Hawke*, p. 41.
18 Hawke, *My Own Life*, p. 40.

Chapter 5
1   'Rhodes Scholar farewelled', *The West Australian*, 6 August 1953, p. 13.
2   'Subiaco cleric praises scholar', *The West Australian*, 3 August 1953, p. 13.
3   The book is now located at the BHPML.
4   'Vice-regal tennis', *The West Australian*, 15 August 1953, p. 2.
5   'They are talking about . . .', *Western Mail*, 11 December 1952, p. 34.
6   'Rhodes Scholar farewelled', *The West Australian*, 6 August 1953, p. 13.
7   'W.A. Graduates get free passages', *The West Australian*, 23 July 1953, p. 10.
8   Bob Hawke to Clem and Ellie Hawke, 25 August 1953, JCPML.
9   Bob Hawke, Diary, 1953, Hawke Personal Papers (ex-Sydney).
10 Bob Hawke to Clem and Ellie Hawke, 10 September 1953, JCPML.
11 Bob Hawke to Clem and Ellie Hawke, 16 September 1953, JCPML.
12 Bob Hawke to Clem and Ellie Hawke, 8 November 1953, JCPML.
13 Bob Hawke to Clem and Ellie Hawke, 25 September 1953, JCPML.
14 Bob Hawke to Clem and Ellie Hawke, 6 October 1953, JCPML.
15 Bob Hawke to Clem and Ellie Hawke, 15 November 1953, JCPML.
16 Here, I draw on Deborah Manley and Philip Opher, *Oxford Town Trail:
    Presidents, Prime Ministers and other Political Persons*, Heritage Tours
    Publications, Oxford, 2001, pp. 8–10.
17 Bob Hawke to Hazel Masterson, 9 October 1953, JCPML.
18 Bob Hawke to Clem and Ellie Hawke, 12 October 1953, JCPML.
19 Bob Hawke to Clem and Ellie Hawke, 25 October 1953, JCPML.
20 Bob Hawke to Clem and Ellie Hawke, 12 October 1953, JCPML.
21 Bob Hawke to Clem and Ellie Hawke, 15 November 1953, JCPML.
22 Bob Hawke to Clem and Ellie Hawke, 19 October 1953, JCPML.
23 Bob Hawke to Clem and Ellie Hawke, 1 November 1953, JCPML.
24 Bob Hawke to Clem and Ellie Hawke, 8 November 1953, JCPML.
25 Bob Hawke to Clem and Ellie Hawke, 10 February 1954, JCPML.
26 Bob Hawke to Clem and Ellie Hawke, 9 December 1953, JCPML.
27 Bob Hawke, Application for Admission as a Probationer-Student for the
    Degree of Bachelor of Letters, 12 February 1954, Bob Hawke, Bachelor
    of Letters File, FA 10/2/15, Oxford University Archives (OUA), Bodleian
    Library, Oxford University.
28 Interview with Hawke, Sydney, 28 November 2017.
29 Colin Clark to University Registry, 18 March 1954, Hawke, Bachelor of
    Letters File, FA 10/2/15, OUA.
30 Bob Hawke to Clem and Ellie Hawke, 10 February 1954, JCPML.
31 Interview with Hawke, Sydney, 28 November 2017.
32 Colin Clark's son, David, broke Hawke's Oxford drinking record in 1972.
    Colin told David that it was 'the best thing you have done at Oxford'.
    See Alex Millmow, 'How Hawke's old antagonist had the last laugh', *The
    Sydney Morning Herald*, 22 March 2012.

33 Interview with Hawke, Sydney, 28 November 2017.

34 Imre Salusinszky, 'Two at Oxford', *The Age*, 24 July 1979, p. 9.

35 Bob Hawke, Probationer-Student for the Degree of Bachelor of Letters, 24 November 1954, Hawke, Bachelor of Letters File, FA 10/2/15, OUA.

36 Edgar Williams to The Trustees, 16 February 1955, RTA.

37 Kenneth Wheare to Edgar Williams, 31 January 1955, RTA.

38 Hawke, *The Hawke Memoirs*, pp. 26–27.

39 Edgar Williams, Warden's Notebook, 1953, RTA.

40 Dean's Card, Bob Hawke Student File, University College Archives (UCA), Oxford University.

41 Giles Alington, the dominant figure at University College during Hawke's time as a student, died the following year, 1956, at the age of 41. See Giles Alington to Edgar Williams, 1953-55, Bob Hawke Rhodes Scholar File, RTA.

42 Bob Hawke to Hazel Masterson, 12 October 1953. See also Hawke, *My Own Life*, pp. 41–42.

43 Bob Hawke to Hazel Masterson, 19 October 1953.

44 Bob Hawke to Hazel Masterson, 23 October 1953.

45 Bob Hawke to Clem and Ellie Hawke, 26 October 1953, JCPML.

46 Interview with Rawdon Dalrymple, Sydney, 18 December 2019.

47 Pieters-Hawke, *Hazel*, p. 75.

48 Bob Hawke to Hazel Masterson, 2 November 1953, JCPML.

49 Bob Hawke to Hazel Masterson, 9 November 1953, JCPML.

50 Bob Hawke to Hazel Masterson, 10 November 1953, JCPML.

51 Bob Hawke to Hazel Masterson, 29 October 1953, JCPML.

52 Paula Hamilton, interview with Bob Hawke, Sydney, 27 April 2000, JCPML.

53 Bob Hawke to Clem and Ellie Hawke, 16 December 1953, JCPML.

54 Bob Hawke to Clem and Ellie Hawke, 9 January 1954 and 1 February 1954, JCPML.

55 Bob Hawke to Clem and Ellie Hawke, 15 February 1954, JCPML.

56 Bob Hawke, Speech to the Oxford Union, 26 October 1993, A-Z Files, Box 202, BHPML.

57 Salusinszky, 'Two at Oxford', p. 9.

58 'Cricket Club', *University College Record*, 1953–54, UCA, p. 39.

59 'For Hawke, a painful ban', *The Australian*, 16 April 1971, p. 20.

60 Bob Hawke to Hazel Masterson, 16 November 1953, JCPML.

61 Interview with Dalrymple, Sydney, 18 December 2019.

62 'Student shouts "Shame!" in Oxford Car Court', *Oxford Mail*, 19 January 1955.

63 Hurst, *Hawke*, pp. 23–24.

64 D'Alpuget, *Robert J. Hawke*, pp. 60–61.

65 Norris McWhirter and Ross McWhirter, *The Guinness Book of Records*, Guinness Superlatives Ltd, London, 1965, p. 230. Hawke's Oxford drinking record was equalled by Clive Anderson, of Magdalen College, in 1967.

66 Interview with Hawke, Sydney, 28 November 2017.

67 Hazel Hawke, Diary, 'Oxford to Oxford, via France, Belgium, Luxembourg, Germany, Switzerland, Austria, Italy, France, Switzerland, France – 15th August to 18th September, 1954', Hazel Hawke Collection, JCPML.

68 R.J.L. Hawke, 'An Appraisal of the Role of the Australian Commonwealth Court of Conciliation and Arbitration with Special Reference to the Development of the Concept of a Basic Wage', Bachelor of Letters thesis, University of Oxford, December 1955, BHPML, p. 11.

69 Interview with Dalrymple, Sydney, 18 December 2019.

70 Interview with Stone, via phone, 16 December 2020.

71 W.K. Hancock, *Australia*, Ernest Benn, London, 1930, p. 194.

72 Bob Hawke, Application for Early Examination, 19 November 1955, Hawke, Bachelor of Letters File, FA 10/2/15, OUA.

73 K.G.J.C. Knowles and H.A. Clegg, Report of the Examiners, 7 January 1956, Hawke, Bachelor of Letters File, FA 10/2/15, OUA.

74 Bob Hawke, 'Arbitration today', *Weekend Mail*, 17 March 1956, p. 9.

75 Malcolm Fraser studied at Oxford from 1949 to 1952, and left with a third-class Bachelor of Arts in PPE, later converted to a Masters with a fee. He had gone straight to Oxford from Melbourne Grammar as a nineteen-year-old. See Bruce Elder, 'Oxford's worst PM', *National Review*, 8–14 March 1977, p. 11.

76 'Oxford honours Hawke', *The Age*, 4 July 2003.

77 The other former Rhodes Scholars awarded honorary degrees were John Brademas, Rex Nettleford and David Woods.

78 Peter Fray, 'Out of Africa', *The Sydney Morning Herald*, 2 July 2003, p. 14.

79 Ziegler, *Legacy*, p. 290.

80 Interview with Josh Frydenberg, via phone, 7 July 2021.

81 Josh Frydenberg to Bob Hawke, 26 May 1999, Hawke Personal Papers (ex-Sydney).

82 Interview with Robert Hannaford, via phone, 6 July 2021.

83 Interview with Frydenberg, via phone, 7 July 2021.

Chapter 6

1 Certificate of Marriage, 3 March 1956, A-Z Files, Box 96, BHPML.

2 Bob Hawke, Application for Scholarship – Australian National University, 6 August 1955, Student Files, R.J.L. Hawke, Australian National University Archives (ANUA), Canberra.

3 Ken Wheare to The Registrar, 9 August 1955; Edgar Williams to The Registrar, 11 August 1955; F.R. Beasley to The Registrar, 8 September 1955; Student Files, Hawke, ANUA.

4 'Canberra Diary', *The Canberra Times*, 21 March 1956, p. 4.

5 Peter Coleman, 'Mr. Inflation', *The Observer*, 30 April 1960, p. 5.

6 Geoffrey Sawer, Oral History Interview, 1990, ANUA.

7 Peter Coleman, *Memoirs of a Slow Learner* (revised edition), Connor Court, Ballarat, 2015, p. 85.

8 Coleman, 'Mr. Inflation', pp. 5–6.

9 Interview with Hawke, Sydney, 29 August 2018.

10 Michael Piggott and Maggie Shapley, *Prime Ministers at the Australian National University: An Archival Guide*, ANU eView, Canberra, 2011, pp. 60–61.

11 R.A. Hohnen to Bob Hawke, 27 February 1957, Student Files, Hawke, ANUA.

12 Interview with Hawke, Sydney, 28 November 2017.

13 Bob Hawke to Clem and Ellie Hawke, 24 October 1956, JCPML.
14 Bill Titterington to Bob Hawke, 17 October 1957, RH6, Box 15,
    Folder 149, BHPML.
15 Bob Hawke to Harold Souter, 26 September 1956, RH6, Box 14,
    Folder 141, BHPML.
16 Bob Hawke to Clem and Ellie Hawke, 18 November 1956, JCPML.
17 Interview with Hawke, Sydney, 29 August 2018.
18 Interview with Hawke, Sydney, 12 February 2018.
19 Coleman, *Memoirs of a Slow Learner*, pp. 85–86.

Chapter 7
1   Hawke, *The Hawke Memoirs*, p. 34.
2   Interview with Hawke, Sydney, 4 June 2014.
3   D'Alpuget, *Robert J. Hawke*, pp. 93–94.
4   Interview with Ralph Willis, Melbourne, 12 December 2018.
5   Hurst, *Hawke*, p. 28.
6   Pullan, *Bob Hawke*, p. 66.
7   Hurst, *Hawke*, p. 29.
8   Alan Trengove, 'The union advocate', *The Sun News-Pictorial*, 13 March
    1965.
9   'Judge Foster critical of wage adjustment suspension', *The Canberra Times*,
    25 February 1959, p. 3.
10 Interview with Hawke, Sydney, 28 November 2017.
11 Pullan, *Bob Hawke*, p. 70.
12 Irving Stone's *Clarence Darrow for the Defense* (1941) had a significant impact
    on Hawke. It was republished in 1958, shortly after he joined the ACTU.
13 Minutes, ACTU Executive Meeting, 9 June 1958, pp. 37–38, RH45,
    Box 18, BHPML. Hawke recalls this was a year's salary but it was half a
    year's salary. See Hawke, *The Hawke Memoirs*, p. 33.
14 Hawke, *My Own Life*, p. 64.
15 Hawke, *My Own Life*, pp. 62, 64, 68–69.
16 Pieters-Hawke, *Hazel*, p. 88.
17 D'Alpuget, *Robert J. Hawke*, p. 95.
18 Interview with Willis, Melbourne, 12 December 2018.
19 E.P. Thomas to Geoffrey Sawer, 5 April 1960, Student Files, Hawke,
    ANUA.
20 D'Alpuget, *Robert J. Hawke*, pp. 97–99.
21 Interview with Barrie Unsworth, Sydney, 21 August 2019.
22 LeVan Roberts to Bob Hawke, 30 April 1962, Hawke Personal Papers
    (ex-Sydney).
23 Hazel Hawke to Bob Hawke, 22 June 1962, Hawke Personal Papers
    (ex-Sydney).
24 Hazel Hawke to Bob Hawke, 5 August 1962, Hawke Personal Papers
    (ex-Sydney).
25 Hazel Hawke to Bob Hawke, 1 July 1962, Hawke Personal Papers
    (ex-Sydney).

Chapter 8
1   Cyril Wyndham to Bob Hawke, 23 October 1963, RH7, Box 12, Folder 77,
    BHPML.

2 'Poll plans discussed by parties', *The Canberra Times*, 22 October 1963, p. 3.

3 Interview with Hawke, Sydney, 29 November 2017.

4 Clyde Cameron to Bob Hawke, October 1963, RH7, Box 12, Folder 77, BHPML.

5 Interview with Willis, Melbourne, 12 December 2018.

6 *The Australian Labor Party Proudly Presents R.J. (Bob) Hawke, B.A., LL.B., B.Lit., ALP Candidate For Corio*, RH7, Box 12, Folder 77, BHPML.

7 *Australia Needs a Labor Government – Corio Needs a Labor Representative*, RH7, Box 12, Folder 77, BHPML.

8 D'Alpuget, *Robert J. Hawke*, p. 104.

9 D'Alpuget, *Robert J. Hawke*, p. 106.

10 Bob Hawke, Speech Notes, 12 November 1963, RH7, Box 12, Folder 77, BHPML.

11 'A.L.P. policy "burgled"', *The Canberra Times*, 13 November 1963, p. 9.

12 D'Alpuget, *Robert J. Hawke*, p. 103.

13 Daniel Oakman, *Oppy: The Life of Sir Hubert Opperman*, Melbourne Books, Melbourne, 2018, p. 265.

14 Pullan, *Bob Hawke*, p. 78.

15 Oakman, *Oppy*, p. 266.

16 Cyril Wyndham to Bob Hawke, 7 November 1963, RH7, Box 12, Folder 77, BHPML.

17 'Two days left: leaders confident', *The Canberra Times*, 28 November 1963, p. 1.

18 Bob Hawke, Speech to Geelong Plaza Theatre, 27 November 1963, RH7, Box 12, Folder 77, BHPML.

19 'Leaders confident in final poll messages', *The Canberra Times*, 30 November 1963, p. 1.

20 'Big guard for P.M. at factory', *The Canberra Times*, 30 November 1963, p. 3.

21 Interview with Willis, Melbourne, 12 December 2018.

22 Oakman, *Oppy*, p. 267.

23 Interview with Susan Pieters-Hawke, Sydney, 5 March 2020.

24 'Candidates express views on Corio poll', *Geelong Advertiser*, 12 December 1963, p. 1.

25 Clyde Cameron to Bob Hawke, 3 December 1963, RH7, Box 12, Folder 77, BHPML.

26 Labor's Gordon Scholes did, however, win Corio at a by-election in July 1967 when Hubert Opperman resigned to become High Commissioner to Malta.

27 F.E. Carr to Bob Hawke, 15 August 1965, RH6, Box 10, Folder 84, BHPML.

28 Interview with Hawke, Sydney, 5 June 2014.

29 Interview with Peter Barron, via phone, 7 July 2021.

30 Interview with Willis, Melbourne, 12 December 2018.

31. 'Unions end wage submission', *The Canberra Times*, 7 May 1964, p. 3.

32 'Basic wage "has an integral place"', *The Canberra Times*, 5 May 1964, p. 3.

33 Bob Hawke, Notice of Assessment 1962–63, Hawke Personal Papers (ex-Sydney).

34 Harold Souter to Bob Hawke, 13 April 1964, Hawke Personal Papers (ex-Sydney).

35 Bob Hawke, Group Certificate 1964–65, Hawke Personal Papers (ex-Sydney).

36 One of Bob Hawke's appalling colloquialisms was to tell Alan Trengove that, at Oxford, he had 'worked like a nigger'. Hawke regularly used the phrase into the 1960s. See Trengove, 'The Union Advocate'. Hawke's use of this racist language was referred to again in the 1970s. See Dennis Minogue, 'Hawke – the man on the white horse', *The Australian*, 18 October 1972, p. 7.

37 'Commission blamed for demands', *The Canberra Times*, 5 March 1965, p. 3.

38 'Government "policy on wages is dishonest"', *The Age*, 13 March 1965.

39 Hurst, *Hawke*, p. 43.

40 John Hurst, 'Hawke refuses safe Labor federal seat', *The Australian*, 2 October 1965.

41 Elaine McFarling, 'The man who works for the workers', *The Herald*, 20 October 1967, p. 21.

42 Hazel Hawke, Scrapbooks, Hazel Hawke Collection, JCPML.

43 Interview with Willis, Melbourne, 12 December 2018.

44 Interview with Pieters-Hawke, Sydney, 5 March 2020.

45 Blanche d'Alpuget, 'Beverley', Blanche d'Alpuget Papers, MS 7348, Box 2, File 12, NLA.

46 Hurst, *Hawke*, p. 49.

47 Brian Buckley, 'Hawke: "Hyde Park Cicero" or defender of the faith?', *The Bulletin*, 2 April 1966, p. 23.

48 Geoffrey Gleghorn, 'How high will he fly?', *The Australian Financial Review*, 6 June 1966.

49 Hawke, *The Hawke Memoirs*, p. 44.

50 Hawke, *The Hawke Memoirs*, p. 44.

51 Interview with Bill Kelty, Melbourne, 28 March 2019.

52 Interview with Paul Munro, via phone, 2 March 2021.

53 Bob Hawke to Paul Munro, 26 March 1968, Hawke Personal Papers (ex-Sydney).

54 Interview with Munro, via phone, 2 March 2021.

55 'Role of Hawke, R in the Papua New Guinea Local Officers case', Department of Territories, A452, 1967/3430, NAA.

56 John Hurst, 'It's not just a question of salaries, says Mr Hawke . . .', *The Australian*, 7 July 1967.

Chapter 9

1   Interview with Hawke, Sydney, 29 November 2017.

2   Jim Davies, 'Albert Monk to retire', *The Sun News-Pictorial*, 10 March 1969.

3   Hurst, *Hawke*, p. 65.

4   John Hurst, 'Two ACTU men will nominate for the top job', *The Australian*, 10 March 1969.

5   Hawke, *The Hawke Memoirs*, p. 46.

6   Harold Souter, Statement, 10 March 1969, RH7, Box 9, Folder 59, BHPML.

7   Bob Hawke, Statement, 11 March 1969, RH7, Box 9, Folder 59,
    BHPML.
8   Interview with Hawke, Sydney, 29 November 2017.
9   John Sorell, 'Contenders line up for union job', *The Herald*, 10 March
    1969.
10 Fred Wells, 'Hawke is ACTU's new leader,' *The Sydney Morning Herald*,
    11 September 1969, p. 1 and Fred Wells, 'Academic at the ACTU', *The
    Sydney Morning Herald*, 11 September 1969, p. 2.
11 The vote in the Services Group ballot was tied and Albert Monk used his
    authority as president to declare that Joe Riordan, the incumbent, should
    maintain his position on the ACTU executive.
12 Ray Gietzelt, *Worth Fighting For: The Memoirs of Ray Gietzelt*, The
    Federation Press, Leichhardt, 2004, p. 174.
13 Geoffrey Barker, 'Clues to the future', *The Age*, 20 October 1967, p. 5.
14 Fred Wells, 'Hawke ahead in ACTU leadership moves', *The Sydney
    Morning Herald*, 14 November 1967, p. 12.
15 Bob Hawke, Speech to ACTU Congress, 29 August 1967, RH5, Box 7,
    Folder 94, BHPML.
16 Hurst, *Hawke*, pp. 58–59.
17 'Moderates control TLC', *The Canberra Times*, 11 February 1969,
    p. 11.
18 Interview with Unsworth, Sydney, 21 August 2019.
19 Interview with Kelty, Melbourne, 28 March 2019.
20 Interview with Simon Crean, Melbourne, 1 February 2019.
21 Scott Henderson, 'The academic who aims to reach the ACTU's top post',
    Daily News, 30 July 1969, p. 10.
22 Interview with Bob Carr, Sydney, 31 October 2019.
23 Interview with Unsworth, Sydney, 21 August 2019.
24 Hurst, *Hawke*, p. 78.
25 Ray Turner, 'At home, just an average family man', *Daily News*, 6 August
    1970, p. 15.
26 Tony Stephens, 'At the head of 2 million, the whiz kid from Oxford',
    The Daily Mirror, 11 September 1969.
27 Interview with Kerry Sibraa, via phone, 4 November 2019.
28 John Hurst, 'Hawke elected ACTU president by 49 majority',
    The Australian, 11 September 1969, p. 1.
29 Bob Hawke, Acceptance Speech, 10 September 1969, RH45, Box 18,
    BHPML.
30 Ray Turner, 'A quiet start to Hawke's reign', *The Daily Mirror*, 1 January
    1970, p. 5.
31 Barry Donovan, 'Bringing unity to the unions', *The Age*, 1 January 1970,
    p. 1.
32 Alan Trengove, 'An Oxford scholar in Lygon St.', *The Sun News-Pictorial*,
    11 September 1969, p. 3.
33 Editorial, 'Hawke takes charge', *The Age*, 11 September 1969, p. 7.
34 Editorial, 'New leader', *The Sydney Morning Herald*, 11 September 1969,
    p. 2.
35 Editorial, 'Leading the ACTU in the 70s', *The Australian*, 11 September
    1969, p. 10.

36 In Hazel Hawke's memoir, she recalls being in Paddington and celebrating with Bob that evening. But this does not accord with the newspaper coverage at the time, which places her at home in Melbourne, where she was interviewed and photographed with the children. See Hawke, *My Own Life*, pp. 87–88.

37 John Sorrell, 'The white and blue collars mix . . .', *The Herald*, 11 September 1969, p. 2.

38 Christabel Hirst, 'The Hawkes at home', *The Sun News-Pictorial*, 18 September 1969.

Chapter 10

1 The 1969 ACTU Congress had extended Albert Monk's presidential term until 31 December 1969.

2 These figures were provided by Andrew Leigh and I also reviewed OECD, ABS and ACTU surveys. See also Alan Thornhill, 'A new look with Hawke', *The West Australian*, 11 September 1969, p. 5.

3 Interview with Hawke, Sydney, 5 June 2014.

4 In the Services Group ballot for the ACTU executive, Ray Gietzelt defeated Keith Clarke, the federal assistant secretary of the Health and Research Employees' Association, by eighty-nine votes to eighty-six.

5 Interview with Willis, Melbourne, 12 December 2018.

6 Interview with Unsworth, Sydney, 21 August 2019.

7 Hawke, *The Hawke Memoirs*, p. 96.

8 Barry Donovan, 'What drives a dynamo?', *The Sydney Morning Herald*, 25 July 1970, p. 13.

9 Jim Quirk, 'Battle to beat a bogy-man image', *The Daily Mirror*, 5 June 1972, p. 17.

10 Glennys Bell, 'Fem lib and unions: there's no revolution', *National Times*, 23–30 July 1971, p. 14.

11 '42pc give Hawke approval in poll', *The Sydney Morning Herald*, 5 May 1971, p. 3.

12 Richard Farmer, 'The people against Hawke', *The Sunday Australian*, 22 August 1971, p. 1.

13 'More approve of ACTU leader, poll shows', *The Canberra Times*, 7 March 1972, p. 9.

14 Quirk, 'Battle to beat a bogy-man image', p. 17.

15 Roger Collier, 'King Hawke: He's never been more popular as head of the ACTU', *The Daily Telegraph*, 27 September 1972, p. 8.

16 Interview with Hawke, Sydney, 28 November 2017.

17 Billy Snedden and Bernie Schedvin, *Billy Snedden: An Unlikely Liberal*, Macmillan, South Melbourne, 1980, p. 134.

18 Here, I draw on 'The siege of Sinatra', *The Sydney Morning Herald*, 22 April 2002.

19 Troy Bramston, 'ALP boss John Ducker a friend of the US', *The Weekend Australian*, 13 April 2013, p. 16.

20 Interview with Hawke, Sydney, 28 November 2017.

21 Neil McMahon, 'Frank Sinatra down under', *The Sydney Morning Herald*, 2 December 2015.

22 Milton Rudin to Bob Hawke, 23 March 1983, Personal Papers of Prime Minister Hawke, Personal Correspondence 1983, M3826/1, NAA.

23 John Hurst, 'The other side of unionism', *The Australian*, 16 June 1971, p. 13.

24 Peter Harvey, 'Hawke's eye view', *The Guardian*, 8 August 1972.

25 Hawke, *The Hawke Memoirs*, p. 56.

26 Fred Brenchley, 'McMahon spotlights Hawke at Liberal meeting', *The Australian Financial Review*, 1 June 1971, p. 5.

27 Hawke, *The Hawke Memoirs*, pp. 57–58.

28 Ian Hancock, *John Gorton: He Did It His Way*, Hodder Headline, Sydney, 2002, p. 295.

29 Interview with Hawke, Sydney, 28 November 2017.

30 Interview with Hawke, Sydney, 25 August 2015.

31 Interview with Hawke, Sydney, 28 November 2017.

32 Bob Hawke, 'Profiles', ABC TV, 27 September 1970, C100, 73/7/7, NAA, Sydney.

33 Owen Thomson, 'Hawke', *The Australian*, 25 July 1970, p. 15.

34 Donovan, 'What drives a dynamo?', p. 13.

35 Interview with Kelty, Melbourne, 28 March 2019.

36 Fred Wells, 'Hawke renews a waterfront link', *The Sydney Morning Herald*, 15 September 1972, p. 8.

37 Thomson, 'Hawke', p. 15.

38 David Frost, interview with Bob Hawke, *Frost Over Australia*, Seven Network, 13 September 1972.

39 'Watch your language, Hawke told', *The Courier-Mail*, 29 October 1975, p. 8.

40 George Negus, 'Hawke: ego, intellect and commitment', *The Weekend Australian Magazine*, 22 April 1978.

41 Cameron Stewart, 'US believed Hawke could have won in 72', *The Weekend Australian*, 30 November 1996, p. 8.

42 Interview with Rob Jolly, via phone, 20 December 2019.

43 Interview with Stone, via phone, 16 December 2020.

44 Interview with Stone, via phone, 16 December 2020.

45 Interview with Laurie Oakes, Canberra, 7 August 2019.

46 Interview with Gillian Appleton, via phone, 8 July 2021. See also Blanche d'Alpuget, interview with Gillian Appleton, 31 July 1980, D'Alpuget Papers, MS 7348, Box 2, File 12, NLA.

47 Tom Lewis to Troy Bramston, via email, June–July 2021. See also Tom Lewis, *Coverups & Copouts*, Hodder Moa Beckett, Auckland, 1998, pp. 139–40.

48 Thomson, 'Hawke', p. 15.

49 Interview with Willis, Melbourne, 12 December 2018.

50 'Mr Hawke is "Father of Year"', *The Canberra Times*, 2 September 1971, p. 3.

51 Interview with Hawke, Sydney, 29 August 2018.

52 Interview with Willis, Melbourne, 12 December 2018.

53 Here, I draw on Hurst, *Hawke*, pp. 159–60.

54 Interview with Pieters-Hawke, Sydney, 5 March 2020.

55 Interview with Stephen Hawke, Perth, 11 December 2019.

56 Interview with Meredith Burgmann, via email, 27 February 2021.

57 Rachel Baxendale, 'When Bob Hawke played a dead bat to the Don's bumper', *The Australian*, 28 April 2016.

58 Patrick Mullins, *Tiberius with a Telephone: The Life and Stories of William McMahon*, Scribe, Brunswick, 2018, pp. 418–19.

59 'Union attacks Mr Hawke over tour', *The Canberra Times*, 2 July 1971, p. 10.

60 Owen Thomson, 'A hitch for Hawke?', *The Australian*, 29 June 1971, p. 9.

61 Interview with Burgmann, via email, 27 February 2021.

Chapter 11

1   Paul Kelly, 'Hawke and PM get it together', *The Australian*, 6 September 1974, p. 9.

2   Daniel Connell, *The Confessions of Clyde Cameron 1913–1990*, ABC Enterprises, Crows Nest, 1990, p. 194.

3   'Mr Hawke on unions and control of ALP', *The Canberra Times*, 28 September 1970, p. 3.

4   'Move to dissolve state ALP', *The Canberra Times*, 14 September 1970, p. 3.

5   'Mr Hawke "possible PM"', *The Canberra Times*, 30 August 1971, p. 3.

6   Interview with Mary Elizabeth Calwell, via email, 9 February 2017.

7   Interview with Graham Richardson, Sydney, 3 September 2019.

8   Geoff Cahill to Bob Hawke, 4 December 1972, RH9, Box 2, Folder 12, BHPML.

9   David Solomon and Michael Jacobs, 'Big crowds hear party leaders', *The Canberra Times*, 1 December 1972, pp. 1, 11.

10 Gough Whitlam, *The Whitlam Government 1972–75*, Viking, Ringwood, 1985, p. 556.

11 Interview with Hawke, Sydney, 25 August 2015.

12 'Most against 2 Hawke roles', *The Sun News-Pictorial*, 11 December 1973, p. 7.

13 Interview with Hawke, via email, 6 October 2011.

14 Barry Donovan, 'Hawke's two hats', *The Sun News-Pictorial*, 11 July 1973, p. 8.

15 Hawke, *The Hawke Memoirs*, pp. 63–64.

16 Bob Hawke, Statement, 19 July 1973, RH10, Box 30, Folder 306, BHPML.

17 Hawke, *The Hawke Memoirs*, p. 64.

18 'Galston site decision "not irreversible"', *The Canberra Times*, 12 September 1973, p. 22.

19 'Parramatta held by Liberals – vote increased', *The Canberra Times*, 24 September 1973, p. 1.

20 Interview with Jim Spigelman, via email, 26 February 2021.

21 Terry Coleman, 'Hawke as MP? "I'd aim for the top"', *The Australian*, 8 January 1974, p. 7.

22 Hurst, *Hawke*, p. 142.

23 Alan Ramsey, 'Whitlam blasts Hawke: he's not speaking for me', *The Australian*, 9 November 1973, p. 1.

24 Hurst, *Hawke*, pp. 150–51.

25 Graham Freudenberg, *A Certain Grandeur: Gough Whitlam in Politics*, Macmillan, South Melbourne, 1977, p. 284.

26 David Combe, 'Report to Federal Executive on 1975 Double Dissolution Campaign', August 1974, RH9, Box 4, Folder 30, BHPML.

27 Here, I draw on John Hurst, 'Hawke: the showman on the go', *The Australian*, 16 May 1974, p. 15.

28 Neil Mitchell, 'Labor could lose next year: Hawke', *The Age*, 10 December 1974, p. 1.

29 Interview with Spigelman, via email, 26 February 2021.

30 Whitlam, *The Whitlam Government 1972–75*, p. 203.

31 Phil Somerset, '"I was Bob Hawke's lover"', *New Weekly*, 27 February 1995, pp. 18–19.

32 Jim Cairns confirmed the affair with Junie Morosi during an interview with John Cleary on ABC Radio on 15 September 2002.

33 'Resignation "act of stupidity"', *The Canberra Times*, 4 June 1975, p. 13.

34 Interview with John Mant, via phone, 26 February 2021.

35 Paul Kelly, 'Hawke on Hawke', 11 October 1975, *The Australian*, p. 24.

36 Hawke, *The Hawke Memoirs*, p. 68.

37 Interview with Hawke, Sydney, 25 August 2015.

38 Interview with Denise Darlow, via email, 26 February 2021.

39 Tom Uren, *Straight Left*, Random House, Milsons Point, 1994, p. 252.

40 Interview with Eric Walsh, Canberra, 1 May 2019.

41 Interview with Mant, via phone, 26 February 2021.

42 Interview with Hawke, Sydney, 25 August 2015.

43 Pullan, *Bob Hawke*, pp. 123–34.

44 Interview with Hawke, Sydney, 25 August 2015.

45 Hawke, *My Own Life*, p. 109.

46 Interview with Hawke, Sydney, 25 August 2015.

47 Hayden, *Hayden*, p. 286.

48 Interview with Hawke, Sydney, 25 August 2015.

49 Blanche d'Alpuget, interview with Don Dunstan, March 1980, D'Alpuget Papers, MS 7348, Box 3, Folder 15, NLA.

50 Warren Beeby, 'It's the end of Whitlam', *The Australian*, 1 March 1976, p. 1, RH7, Box 7, Folder 40, BHPML.

51 Jack Egerton to Bob Hawke, 8 March 1976, RH7, Box 7 Folder 40, BHPML.

52 Minutes of the FPLP, 17 March 1976, NLA.

53 Clyde Cameron, *The Cameron Diaries*, Allen & Unwin, North Sydney, 1990, p. 84.

54 Bob Hawke, A.A. Calwell Memorial Lecture, Monash University, Melbourne, 3 August 1976.

55 Blanche d'Alpuget, interview with Frederick Wheeler, 18 September 1980, D'Alpuget Papers, MS 7348, Box 3, Folder 15, NLA.

56 'Poll finds 50% back Hawke in ACTU', *The Sydney Morning Herald*, 8 November 1973, p. 8.

57 Neil Mitchell, 'Day of Hawke MP closer', *The Age*, 11 December 1974, p. 9.

58 'Hawke left his run too late – Gough', *The Australian*, 21 December 1979, p. 1.

59 Allan Barnes, 'Hawke MP, or high hopes R.I.P.?', *The Age*, 4 September 1975, p. 9.

60 Kelly, 'Hawke on Hawke', p. 23.

61 Coleman, 'Hawke as MP? "I'd aim for the top"', p. 7.

Chapter 12

1 Interview with Kelty, Melbourne, 28 March 2019.
2 Interview with Hawke, Sydney, 12 February 2019.
3 '150 faces for the future', *Time*, 15 July 1974, p. 130.
4 Brian Barder to John Hickman, 28 June 1974, FCO 24/1884, The National Archives (TNA), Kew. This was provided to the author by James Curran.
5 These cables, sent by US diplomats from Canberra, Sydney and Melbourne between 1973 and 1976, were declassified by the US State Department in 2006. They were published online by WikiLeaks in 2013.
6 For an account of Hawke's talks with US diplomats, see Cameron Coventry, 'The "Eloquence" of Robert J. Hawke: United States informer, 1973–79', *Australian Journal of Politics and History*, vol. 67, no. 1, March 2021, pp. 67–87.
7 John Blaxland, *The Protest Years: The Official History of ASIO 1963–1975*, Allen & Unwin, Sydney, 2015, p. 106.
8 Interview with Isi Leibler, via email, 4 March 2021.
9 Geoffrey Gleghorn, 'Hawke: from Jew-baiter as boy to passionate Israeli supporter', *The National Times*, 3–8 December 1973, pp. 42–43.
10 Hawke, *The Hawke Memoirs*, p. 75.
11 'Susan meets the PM', *The Sydney Morning Herald*, 8 July 1971, p. 3.
12 Hawke, *The Hawke Memoirs*, pp. 76–77.
13 D'Alpuget, *Robert J. Hawke*, p. 262.
14 Hawke, *The Hawke Memoirs*, p. 78.
15 Hurst, *Hawke*, p. 153.
16 Bob Hawke, *Bob Hawke Speaks on Israel*, Australia/Israel Publications, Melbourne, 1975.
17 Hawke, *Yesterday, Today and Tomorrow*, p. 76.
18 The book is now located at the BHPML.
19 Interview with Leibler, via email, 4 March 2021.
20 Max Blenkin, 'Assassination plot against Bob Hawke', *The Daily Telegraph*, 1 January 2007, p. 11.
21 'Bob Hawke death threat: family's ordeal', *The Sunday Telegraph*, 2 December 1973, p. 1.
22 Here, I draw on D'Alpuget, *Robert J. Hawke*, pp. 256–57.
23 Editorial, 'The making of Mr Hawke', *The Daily Telegraph*, 28 May 1979, p. 6.
24 Hawke, *The Hawke Memoirs*, p. 354.
25 Hawke, *The Hawke Memoirs*, p. 72.
26 Interview with Leibler, via email, 4 March 2021.
27 Interview with Dalrymple, Sydney, 18 December 2019.
28 John Mason to Francis Pym, 'Robert Hawke: Prime Minister of Australia', 7 March 1983, FCO 160/82/22, TNA.
29 Hawke, *The Hawke Memoirs*, pp. 87–88.
30 Barry Donovan, 'The path to world power this century', *The Sun News-Pictorial*, 9 October 1978, p. 8.

Chapter 13

1 Interview with John Howard, Sydney, 17 March 2021.

2 Tony Street, 'Conciliation and Arbitration Amendment Bill - Consultations with Peak Union and Employer Groups', Cabinet Submission, 16 May 1977, A12933/61, NAA.

3 Interview with Howard, Sydney, 17 March 2021.

4 Interview with David Barnett, via phone, 26 February 2021.

5 Hawke, *The Hawke Memoirs*, p. 84.

6 Interview with Howard, Sydney, 17 December 2014.

7 D'Alpuget, *Robert J. Hawke*, p. 304.

8 Interview with Hawke, Sydney, 5 June 2014.

9 Interview with Hawke, Sydney, 5 July 2010.

10 Interview with David Kemp, via email, 23 February 2021.

11 Michael Gordon, 'Hawke lashes out', *The Age*, 14 September 1979, p. 1.

12 Interview with Kelty, Melbourne, 28 March 2019.

13 Interview with Jolly, via phone, 20 December 2019.

14 Interview with Kelty, Melbourne, 28 March 2019.

15 Neil Mitchell, 'Hawke: mellow but not mollified', *The Age*, 5 October 1976, p. 9.

16 Jim Foley, 'Peter Nolan holds the fort', *The Herald*, 3 November 1977.

17 Interview with Kelty, Melbourne, 28 March 2019.

18 Interview with Jolly, via phone, 20 December 2019.

19 Here, I draw on Fiona Whitlock, 'Jan Marsh – the voice for Australia's 6.5 million workers', *The Australian Women's Weekly*, 2 June 1982, p. 13 and Carmel Egan and Deborah Gough, 'Polarising trailblazer leaves field of battle', *The Sydney Morning Herald*, 23 March 2008.

20 Interview with Jan Marsh, via phone, 20 August 2019.

21 Ian Warden, 'Labor's faithful sing as campaign opens', *The Canberra Times*, 18 November 1977, p. 3.

22 Morgan Gallup, July 1978.

23 Interview with John Kerin, via phone, 1 November 2019.

24 Interview with Sibraa, via phone, 4 November 2019.

25 Interview with Ros Kelly, Sydney, 27 November 2019.

26 Craig McGregor, 'Inside Bob Hawke', *The National Times*, 9–14 May 1977, p. 8.

27 Hawke, *My Own Life*, p. 96.

28 Interview with Stephen Loosley, Sydney, 6 November 2019.

29 Toni McRae, 'Trim, tough – but he's really a softie', *The Sun*, 20 March 1977, p. 25.

30 George Negus and Peter Meakin to Bob Hawke, 21 October 1980, RH7, Box 2, Folder 10, BHPML.

31 George Negus to Bob Hawke, 22 April 1980, RH7, Box 2, Folder 10, BHPML.

32 Mike Steketee, 'Hawke: top job or nothing', *The Sydney Morning Herald*, 2 July 1977, p. 1.

33 'Union hotel to be called R.J. Hawke', *The Canberra Times*, 21 December 1972, p. 10.

34 'Putting down a foot', *The Canberra Times*, 19 May 1973, p. 3.

35 'Sing-along with Bob, straight to the bar', *The Age*, 8 August 1975, p. 1.

36 'Hawke campaigns in pub crawl', *The Canberra Times*, 28 October 1975, p. 7.

37 Interview with Kelty, Melbourne, 28 March 2019.
38 Blanche d'Alpuget refers to Hawke's drinking benders. See D'Alpuget, *Robert J. Hawke*, p. 270. Hazel Hawke refers to Brian Woodward's property. See Hawke, *My Own Life*, p. 90.
39 Blanche d'Alpuget interview with Col Cunningham, 4 April 1981, D'Alpuget Papers, MS 7348, Box 2, File 12, NLA.
40 Interview with Kelty, Melbourne, 28 March 2019.
41 Paul Kelly, 'Hawke's curious campaign', *The National Times*, 5–10 July 1976, pp. 3, 11.
42 Interview with Unsworth, Sydney, 21 August 2019.
43 See Troy Bramston, *For the True Believers: Great Labor Speeches That Shaped History*, The Federation Press, Leichhardt, 2012, pp. 74–78.
44 Interview with Paul Kelly, Sydney, 10 November 2019.
45 Paul Kelly and Stuart Simson, 'How Bob Hawke blew it – again', *The National Times*, 22–28 July 1979, pp. 3–5.
46 Brett Bayly, 'Hawke's wings clipped?', *The Advertiser*, 19 July 1979, p. 5.
47 Bob Hawke, *The Resolution of Conflict: 1979 Boyer Lectures*, ABC, Sydney, 1979, p. 23.
48 Talbot Duckmanton to Bob Hawke, 19 December 1979, RH7, Box 2, Folder 8, BHPML.
49 David Smith to Bob Hawke, 22 January 1979, RH7, Box 13, Folder 88, BHPML.
50 Xavier Herbert to Bob Hawke, 26 January 1979, RH7, Box 13, Folder 88, BHPML.
51 Sue Arnold, 'Why Bob would be a good PM', *The Sun News-Pictorial*, 2 May 1980, p. 14.
52 Hawke, *My Own Life*, pp. 68, 141.
53 Hawke, *The Hawke Memoirs*, p. 103.
54 D'Alpuget, *Robert J. Hawke*, p. 335.
55 Interview with Blanche d'Alpuget, 20 February 2020, Sydney.
56 Neil Mitchell, 'Political power is a sobering influence, says Hawke', *The Age*, 30 July 1975, p. 1.
57 D'Alpuget, *Robert J. Hawke*, p. 285.
58 Interview with Bob Hogg, via phone, 25 November 2019.
59 Interview with Richardson, Sydney, 3 September 2019.
60 Interview with Carr, Sydney, 31 October 2019.
61 Pullan, *Bob Hawke*, pp. 163–64 and Mamie Smith, 'A man of all trades', *The Herald*, 18 October 1974, p. 25.
62 McGregor, 'Inside Bob Hawke', p. 12.
63 Interview with Carr, Sydney, 31 October 2019.
64 D'Alpuget, *Robert J. Hawke*, pp. 176, 198, 325.
65 Blanche d'Alpuget, 'Gay Davidson's comments on H.', 5 March 1980, D'Alpuget Papers, MS 7348, Box 2, File 12, NLA.
66 Interview with Carr, Sydney, 31 October 2019.
67 Blanche d'Alpuget, 'Treatment of women', D'Alpuget Papers, MS 7348, Box 2, File 12, NLA.
68 Interview with Susan Ryan, Sydney, 20 September 2019.
69 Smith, 'A man of all trades', p. 25.
70 Hawke, *My Own Life*, p. 119.

71 Heather Kennedy, 'I'm always seen as Bob Hawke's wife – never myself', *Woman's Day*, 8 March 1976, p. 6.

72 Pieters-Hawke, *Hazel*, p. 151.

73 Interview with Hawke, Perth, 11 December 2019.

74 Interview with Pieters-Hawke, Sydney, 5 March 2020.

75 Pieters-Hawke, *Hazel*, p. 185.

76 Interview with Hawke, Perth, 11 December 2019.

77 Interview with Crean, Melbourne, 1 February 2019.

78 Interview with Kelty, Melbourne, 28 March 2019.

79 Arnold Bloch to Bob Hawke, 22 July 1980, RH7, Box 2, Folder 9, BHPML.

80 Interview with Pieters-Hawke, Sydney, 5 March 2020. See also Hawke, *My Own Life*, p. 124.

81 D'Alpuget, *Robert J. Hawke*, p. 337.

82 Hawke, *Yesterday, Today and Tomorrow*, p. 81.

Chapter 14

1 Rawdon Dalrymple was a senior diplomat at the Australian Embassy in Jakarta between 1969 and 1972.

2 Interview with D'Alpuget, Sydney, 20 February 2020.

3 Interview with Hawke, Sydney, 29 August 2018.

4 Interview with D'Alpuget, Sydney, 20 February 2020.

5 Interview with D'Alpuget, Sydney, 20 February 2020.

6 Kate Legge, 'The secret life of Blanche', *The Weekend Australian Magazine*, 2 August 2008.

7 Interview with D'Alpuget, Sydney, 20 February 2020.

8 Blanche d'Alpuget, *On Longing*, Melbourne University Press, Carlton, 2008, p. 31.

9 Trent Dalton, 'Bob Hawke and Blanche d'Alpuget: Love, legacy and a secret brush with death', *The Weekend Australian Magazine*, 18 November 2017.

10 Interview with Hawke, Sydney, 29 August 2018.

11 Interview with D'Alpuget, Sydney, 20 February 2020.

12 Hawke, *My Own Life*, p. 126.

13 Interview with Pieters-Hawke, Sydney, 5 March 2020.

14 Interview with D'Alpuget, Sydney, 20 February 2020.

15 Hawke, *My Own Life*, p. 127.

16 Paul Kelly, 'Bob and Blanche: an affair for the ages', *The Weekend Australian*, 25 May 2019.

17 Bob Hawke to Blanche d'Alpuget, 30 April 1980, D'Alpuget Papers, MS 7348, Box 3, Folder 19, NLA.

18 Interview with D'Alpuget, Sydney, 20 February 2020.

19 Janet Hawley, 'The bliss of being Bob and Blanche . . . and how it all began', *The Good Weekend Magazine*, 21 February 1998.

20 For example, see Blanche d'Alpuget to Edgar Williams, 18 January 1980, RTA.

21 Interview with D'Alpuget, Sydney, 20 February 2020.

22 Hawke, *My Own Life*, p. 134.

23 Interview with Pieters-Hawke, Sydney, 5 March 2020.

24 Interview with D'Alpuget, Sydney, 20 February 2020.
25 Blanche d'Alpuget, 'Hazel Hawke, Interview Notes, June 1980', D'Alpuget Papers, MS 7348, Box 3, Folder 14, NLA and Blanche d'Alpuget, 'Hazel Hawke', D'Alpuget Papers, MS 7348, Box 3, Folder 16, NLA.
26 'Corrections', D'Alpuget Papers, MS 7348, Box 3, Folder 19, NLA.
27 It is not clear whether this letter, or this version of it, was sent. See Blanche d'Alpuget to Hazel Hawke, 10 January 1982, D'Alpuget Papers, MS 7348, Box 3, Folder 19, NLA.
28 Interview with D'Alpuget, 20 February 2020, Sydney.
29 'Corrections', D'Alpuget Papers, MS 7348, Box 2, Folder 6, NLA.
30 Michelle Grattan, 'Malcolm Fraser's secret fears', *The Age*, 27 September 1982.
31 Hawke, *My Own Life*, p. 134.
32 D'Alpuget, *Robert J. Hawke*, p. 353.

Chapter 15
1   Malcolm Colless, 'Biggest political event since Whitlam's fall', *The Australian*, 24 September 1979, p. 3.
2   Michael Gordon, 'The Beginning of Everything', in Susan Ryan and Troy Bramston (eds), *The Hawke Government: A Critical Retrospective*, Pluto Press, Melbourne, 2003, pp. 18–28.
3   Bob Hawke, Prime Ministers on Prime Ministers Address, 6 March 1998, Old Parliament House, Canberra.
4   F.S. Oliver, *The Endless Adventure*, Macmillan, London, 1930, p. 30.
5   D'Alpuget, *Robert J. Hawke*, p. 25.
6   Interview with Bill Hayden, Brisbane, 23 June 2017.
7   Michael Gordon, 'Hawke to stand for parliament', *The Age*, 24 September 1979, p. 1.
8   Interview with Kelty, Melbourne, 28 March 2019.
9   Here, I draw on Ann Harding and Richard L'Estrange, 'Hawke's profit and loss account with the ACTU', *The National Times*, 30 September–6 October 1979, p. 5.
10 Interview with Kelty, Melbourne, 28 March 2019.
11 Bob Hawke, Receipt of Nomination for Wills, 1 October 1979, RH9, Box 25, Folder 180, BHPML.
12 Bill Mellor, 'The quiet man who stands between Hawke and Canberra', *The Sun-Herald*, 30 September 1979.
13 Richard L'Estrange, 'Why the Left won't let Bob Hawke run', *The National Times*, 5–11 August 1979, p. 3.
14 Bob Hawke, Statement to Wills Preselection Panel, 14 October 1979 RH9, Box 25, Folder 180, BHPML.
15 Interview with Robert Ray, Melbourne, 19 November 2019.
16 Michael Doyle and Michael Gordon, 'Hawke wins, two lose', *The Age*, 15 October 1979, p. 1.
17 Interview with Mimi Tamburrino, via phone, 26 February 2021.
18 Interview with Gareth Evans, Canberra, 19 September 2019.
19 See Pru Goward, 'Morrison has chosen his Everest', *The Sydney Morning Herald*, 28 May 2020, p. 23.
20 See Blanche d'Alpuget, 'Hawke and Sir Peter Abeles', D'Alpuget Papers, MS 7348, Box 2, File 12, NLA.

21 Interview with Richardson, Sydney, 3 September 2019.
22 Blanche d'Alpuget, 'Libels', D'Alpuget Papers, MS 7348, Box 1, Folder 5, NLA.
23 This cable was declassified by the US State Department in 2006 and published online by WikiLeaks in 2013.
24 D'Alpuget, 'Hawke and Sir Peter Abeles', p. 2.
25 Trevor Kennedy, 'Rupert Murdoch tells: "Where I go now"', *The Bulletin*, 11 December 1979, p. 66.
26 Interview with Oakes, Canberra, 7 August 2019.
27 Interview with Michelle Grattan, Canberra, 7 August 2019.
28 Interview with Kelly, Sydney, 10 November 2019.
29 Andrew Clark, 'The Playboy interview: Bob Hawke', *Playboy*, May 1980, p. 43.
30 Interview with Hawke, Sydney, 28 November 2017.
31 Interview with Unsworth, Sydney, 29 December 2014.
32 Interview with Paul Keating, Sydney, 5 May 2016.
33 Interview with Carr, Sydney, 8 April 2014.
34 Bob Carr, 'Is Hawke finished?', *The Bulletin*, 25 April 1978, pp. 44–47, 50–51.
35 Bob Carr, 'Hurdles still face Hawke', *The Bulletin*, 19 June 1979, pp. 30, 33.
36 Bob Carr, 'Hawke loses ground inside the Labor Party', *The Bulletin*, 15 January 1980, pp. 14–15, 17–18.
37 Interview with Carr, Sydney, 8 April 2014.
38 Neil O'Reilly, 'He has time on his side – 30 years to become PM', *The Sun-Herald*, 23 September 1979, p. 61.
39 Paul Kelly, *The Hawke Ascendancy*, Angus & Robertson, Sydney, 1984, pp. 114–15.
40 Interview with Keating, Sydney, 5 May 2016.
41 Interview with Keating, Sydney, 17 December 2014.
42 Hawke, *The Hawke Memoirs*, p. 438.
43 Interview with Keating, Sydney, 17 December 2014.
44 Kelly, *The Hawke Ascendancy*, p. 115.
45 This was questionable under caucus rules, given that members of the parliamentary executive must be members of parliament, but Bill Hayden exercised his authority under Rule 24, which allowed the leader to make decisions when they cannot consult the party.
46 Bob Hawke to Peter Nolan, 21 August 1980, RH7, Box 2, Folder 9, BHPML.
47 David Combe, 'Report from National Secretary and Campaign Director, David Combe, on the 1980 Federal Election', RH18, Box 20, Folder 232, BHPML.
48 'In Wills, it's all go, go, go', *The Sunday Telegraph*, 2 December 1979, p. 11.
49 Combe, 'Report from National Secretary and Campaign Director, David Combe, on the 1980 Federal Election'.
50 Here, I draw on Troy Bramston, 'Peter Walsh: Labor's fiscal powerhouse', *The Australian*, 14 April 2015.
51 Bill Hayden to Bob Hawke, 17 October 1980, RH7, Box 2, Folder 10, BHPML.
52 Interview with Tamburrino, via phone, 26 February 2021.

53 Here, I draw on Kelly, *The Hawke Ascendancy*, p. 107.
54 Interview with Hawke, 14 December 2017, Sydney.
55 House of Representatives (HoR), *Hansard*, 26 November 1980, pp. 97–101.
56 Interview with Hawke, Sydney, 20 December 2013.
57 'Emotional defence by Hawke of Sinai stance', *The Sydney Morning Herald*, 30 October 1981, p. 1 and 'Bob Hawke tells – why I cried', *The News*, 30 October 1981.
58 Bob Hawke, Paul Keating and Ralph Willis, 'Discussion Paper', RH18, Box 21, Folder 240, BHPML.
59 Interview with Kim Beazley, Perth, 11 December 2019.
60 Jack Darmody, 'Hawke: Why I'd like to be PM', *The Daily Mirror*, 21 April 1981, pp. 1, 4–5.
61 'Herald survey', *The Sydney Morning Herald*, 18 May 1981, p. 1.
62 'How the public sees them', *The Age*, 9 July 1982, p. 1.
63 Interview with Rod Cameron, Sydney, 8 March 2020. See also Kelly, *The Hawke Ascendancy*, p. 173.
64 Hayden, *Hayden*, p. 333.
65 Interview with Cameron, Sydney, 8 March 2020.
66 Interview with Margaret Gibbs, Sydney, 8 March 2020.
67 Interviews with Cameron and Gibbs, Sydney, 8 March 2020.
68 Interview with Bob McMullan, Canberra, 9 December 2019.
69 Niki Savva, *So Greek: Confessions of a Conservative Leftie*, Scribe, Carlton North, 2010, p. 95.
70 Brian Toohey, 'Hawke's Indian joke', *The National Times*, 6–12 September 1981, p. 1. See also Barrie Cassidy, 'Politicians and fruit cakes: A tawdry tale', *The Drum*, ABC Online, 19 October 2012.
71 Interview with Brian Dale, via email, 28 February 2021.
72 Interview with Darlow, via email, 26 February 2021.
73 Interview with Loosley, Sydney, 14 May 2014.
74 Brian Toohey, 'US reassured by Mr Hawke on basing at Cockburn Sound', *The Australian Financial Review*, 2 July 1980.
75 'Hawke denies leadership claim', *The Australian*, 30 June 1980, p. 1.
76 Interview with Graham Evans, Melbourne, 25 June 2019.
77 Graham Evans to Bob Hawke, 28 June 1981, A-Z Files, Box 210, BHPML.
78 Bob Hawke to Graham Evans, circa July 1981, A-Z Files, Box 210, BHPML.
79 Interview with Evans, Melbourne, 25 June 2019.
80 Interview with Geoff Walsh, Melbourne, 10 October 2019.
81 Interview with Hogg, via phone, 25 November 2019.
82 Interview with Barron, via phone, 7 July 2021.
83 Tony Stephens, 'Labor's words man says this speech is vital', *The Sydney Morning Herald*, 23 June 1987, p. 7.
84 Interview with Hawke, Perth, 11 December 2019.
85 Hawke, *My Own Life*, p. 124.
86 Interview with D'Alpuget, Sydney, 20 February 2020.
87 Samantha Maiden, '"MP raped me but dad said I shouldn't tell police"', *The New Daily*, 7 December 2019.
88 Graham Richardson, *Whatever It Takes*, Bantam Books, Sydney, 1994, p. 94.

89 Interview with Ray, Melbourne, 19 November 2019.

90 Hawke, *The Hawke Memoirs*, pp. 111–12.

91 Michelle Grattan, '"ALP could win under me" – Hawke', *The Age*, 8 July 1982, p. 1.

92 Michelle Grattan, '7 days to showdown: Hayden and Hawke lobby for leadership votes', *The Age*, 9 July 1982, p. 1.

93 Hawke, *The Hawke Memoirs*, p. 113.

94 Interview with Blewett, Leura, 16 November 2019.

95 Interview with Richardson, Sydney, 14 March 2016.

96 Neal Blewett, Diary, 8 July 1982. This was provided to the author by Neal Blewett.

97 Interview with Ray, Melbourne, 19 November 2019.

98 Hawke, *The Hawke Memoirs*, p. 113.

99 Interview with Crean, Melbourne, 1 February 2019.

100 Interview with Ray, via phone, 8 June 2016.

101 Interview with Evans, Canberra, 6 June 2015.

102 Interview with Keating, Sydney, 5 May 2016.

103 Paul Keating, Statement, 14 July 1982.

104 'Numbers – Leadership Challenge – 1982', A-Z Files, Box 137, BHPML.

105 Kelly, *The Hawke Ascendancy*, p. 236.

106 Interview with Carr, Sydney, 31 October 2019.

107 Bob Carr, 'Bob Hawke – warts and all . . .', *The Bulletin*, 21 September 1982, p. 43.

108 Interview with John Dawkins, Sydney, 5 December 2019.

109 Minutes of the FPLP, 16 July 1982, NLA.

110 Russell Schneider, 'Cabinet claps Hayden's win', *The Australian*, 17 July 1982, p. 1.

111 Gough Whitlam to Bill Hayden, 16 July 1982, Hayden Papers, MS 7624, Series 3/12, Folder 9, NLA.

112 Interview with Ray, Melbourne, 19 November 2019.

113 Gallup Poll, August 1982.

114 Interview with Hawke, Sydney, 14 December 2017.

115 Interview with Hayden, Brisbane, 23 June 2017.

Chapter 16

1 Colin Brammall, 'Hawke denies planning challenge', *The Canberra Times*, 9 November 1982, p. 1.

2 Michelle Grattan, 'Libs warn PM against '82 poll', *The Age*, 28 October 1982, p. 1.

3 Tony Eggleton to Malcolm Fraser, 'Assessment of Seats', 26 October 1982, A.J. Forbes Papers, MS 9875, Series 7, Box 26, Folder 26, NLA.

4 Bill Hayden to Ralph Willis, 29 April 1982, RH18, Box 20, Folder 235, BHPML.

5 Interview with Marsh, via phone, 20 August 2019.

6 Interview with Loosley, via phone, 15 November 2019.

7 Interview with Hawke, Sydney, 28 November 2017.

8 Kelly, *The Hawke Ascendancy*, p. 337.

9 Minutes of the FPLP, 8 December 1982, NLA.

10 Lionel Bowen, Oral History Interview, 1990–91, ORAL TRC 4900/85, NLA, p. 372.

11 Gregory Hywood, '"Kingmaker" Button ponders Hayden's future', *The Australian Financial Review*, 24 December 1982.
12 John Button to Bill Hayden, 30 December 1982, Hayden Papers, MS 7624, Series 3/12, Folder 29, NLA.
13 Interview with Hogg, via phone, 25 November 2019.
14 Interview with Michael Duffy, Melbourne, 9 October 2019.
15 John Button, 'Memorandum of Discussion – January 6, 1983', John Button Papers, MS 13728, Box 9, Folder 12, State Library of Victoria (SLV).
16 Interview with Willis, Melbourne, 6 May 2015.
17 Bill Hayden to Troy Bramston, via email, 22 July 2015.
18 Interview with Hawke, Sydney, 5 June 2014. See also Kelly, *The Hawke Ascendancy*, p.352.
19 John Button, *As It Happened*, Text Publishing, Melbourne, 1998, p. 194.
20 Interview with Duffy, Melbourne, 9 October 2019.
21 John Button, 'Some political notes – 16 January 1983', Button Papers, MS 13728, Box 8, Folder 9, SLV.
22 Bowen, Oral History, p. 373.
23 John Button to Bill Hayden, 28 January 1983, Button Papers, MS 13728, Box 8, Folder 9, SLV.
24 Interview with Michael Costello, Canberra, 11 June 2021.
25 John Button, 'Rough notes of discussion with Bill Hayden – Feb or March 83', Button Papers, MS 13728, Box 9, Folder 4, SLV.
26 Interview with Dawkins, Sydney, 5 December 2019.
27 Interview with Don Grimes, via phone, 4 November 2019.
28 Malcolm Fraser, Statement, 28 January 1983.
29 Interview with Oakes, Canberra, 7 August 2019.
30 Interview with Costello, Canberra, 11 June 2021.
31 I have reconstructed the timeline based on contemporary media reports, later articles and books, and my interviews. There has been confusion in several accounts between Brisbane time which was one hour behind Canberra time. See 'The tale in two cities', *Canberra Times*, 4 February 1983.
32 Bowen, Oral History, p. 375.
33 Interview with Keating, Sydney, 4 May 2021.
34 Interview with Ryan, Sydney, 13 May 2016.
35 Interview with Kerin, via phone, 1 November 2019.
36 Interview with Blewett, Leura, 16 November 2019.
37 Interview with Chris Hurford, via phone, 8 November 2019.
38 Bowen, Oral History, p. 376.
39 Hawke, *The Hawke Memoirs*, p. 124.
40 Bowen, Oral History, p. 376.
41 Interview with Hawke, Sydney, 28 November 2017.
42 Susan Ryan, *Catching the Waves: Life in and out of Politics*, HarperCollins, Sydney, 1999, p. 206.
43 Interview with Ryan, Sydney, 20 September 2019.
44 Interview with Peter Beattie, Sydney, 4 November 2019.
45 'What Hayden said after quitting', *The Age*, 4 February 1983, p. 4.
46 'Statements from Hayden, Bowen, Hawke', *The Canberra Times*, 4 February 1983, p. 7.

47 Interview with Blewett, via email, 7 February 2013.
48 Button, *As It Happened*, p. 198.
49 Interview with Hayden, via phone, 26 June 2017.
50 Interview with Hawke, via phone, 14 February 2013.
51 Interview with Loosley, via phone, 15 November 2019.
52 Malcolm Fraser had learnt there were moves to replace Bill Hayden with Bob Hawke from 'a source close to Hayden' on 2 February 1983. See Philip Ayres, *Malcolm Fraser: A Biography*, William Heinemann Australia, Richmond, 1987, p. 427.
53 Ross McMullin, 'The great tip-off mystery', *The Age*, 30 November 1993. John Stubbs writes that Malcolm Fraser had spoken to 'a former Whitlam government minister'. See John Stubbs, *Hayden*, William Heinemann Australia, Port Melbourne, 1989, p. 247.
54 Paul Kelly writes that Fraser's information 'had come from the mouth of a member of Hayden's own staff'. See Kelly, *The Hawke Ascendancy*, p. 382.
55 Interview with Drysdale, via phone, 27 February 2021.
56 Interview with Dale, via phone, 15 July 2021.
57 Interview with Hayden, via phone, 5 August 2021.
58 Interview with Howard, Sydney, 17 March 2021.
59 Interview with Tony Eggleton, via email, 8 March 2021.
60 Interview with Drysdale, via phone, 27 February 2021.
61 Interview with Kemp, via email, 23 February 2021.
62 Susan Mitchell, *Stand By Your Man: Sonia, Tamie & Janette*, Random House, North Sydney, 2007, p. 91.
63 'Fraser's wife says Hawke is sexy', *The Canberra Times*, 9 February 1983, p. 14.
64 Interviews with Cameron and Gibbs, Sydney, 8 March 2020.
65 Interview with Malcolm Fraser, via phone, 28 May 2014.
66 Interview with Hawke, via phone, 14 February 2013.
67 Graham Richardson, '"A New Direction" versus "Australia Deserves Better"', 1982, RH35, Box 4, Folder 22, BHPML.
68 Clem Lloyd, 'Strategy Paper – 1983 Elections', 25 October 1982, RH35, Box 4, Folder 22, BHPML.
69 Bob Hawke, '"Reconciliation" Theme in Electoral Strategy', 20 January 1983, RH35, Box 4, Folder 23, BHPML.
70 Hawke, *The Hawke Memoirs*, p. 133.

Chapter 17

1 Peter Bowers, 'Hawke winds down as Fraser winds up', *The Sydney Morning Herald*, 17 February 1983, p. 1.
2 Interview with Hawke, Sydney, 5 July 2010.
3 Liberal Party Federal Secretariat, 'Analysis of Quantitative Research for 1983 Campaign', February 1983, Forbes Papers, MS 9875, Series 7, Box 26, Folder 26, NLA.
4 Interview with Cameron, Sydney, 8 March 2020.
5 Bob Hawke, Statement, 8 February 1983.
6 Bob Hawke, Statement, 8 February 1983.
7 Interview with Hogg, via phone, 25 November 2019.
8 Kelly, *The Hawke Ascendancy*, p. 402.

9   Kerry Sibraa, Diary, 8 February 1983 and 11 February 1983. This was provided to the author by Kerry Sibraa.
10 Interview with Walsh, Melbourne, 10 October 2019.
11 Interview with Sibraa, via phone, 4 November 2019.
12 Interview with Wendy Fatin, Perth, 12 December 2019.
13 Interview with Kelly, Sydney, 10 November 2019.
14 Interview with Kelty, Melbourne, 11 February 2014.
15 Hawke, *The Hawke Memoirs*, p. 135.
16 Paul Kelly, John Short and Jennifer Hewett, 'PM seizes on policy doubt', *The Sydney Morning Herald*, 25 February 1983, p. 1.
17 Sibraa, Diary, 24 February 1983.
18 Interview with McMullan, Canberra, 21 July 2016.
19 Interview with Barbara Ward, Sydney, 20 July 2014.
20 Hawke, *The Hawke Memoirs*, p. 135.
21 Interview with Bob Brown, via phone, 25 June 2021.
22 Hawke, *The Hawke Memoirs*, p. 138.
23 Interview with Howard, Sydney, 17 March 2021.
24 Interview with Richard Farmer, via phone, 26 August 2019.
25 Interview with Jill Saunders, Sydney, 5 December 2019.
26 Interview with Walsh, Melbourne, 10 October 2019.
27 Here, I draw on Craig McGregor, 'Prologue', in Ryan and Bramston (eds), *The Hawke Government*, pp. 7–17.
28 Bob McMullan, 'Report of the National Secretary on the 1983 Election Campaign', March 1983, RH18, Box 4, Folder 69, BHPML.
29 Tony Eggleton, 'The 1983 Election – Report by the Federal Director', 23 March 1983, Australian Labor Party National Secretariat Papers, MS 4985, 1997 Consignment, Box 434, Folder 'Federal Election 1983 Voting Patterns/Analysis/General', NLA.
30 Interview with Cameron, Sydney, 26 August 2014.
31 Interview with Cameron, Sydney, 8 March 2020. See also Rod Cameron, 'Post-Election Survey in Capital Cities', April 1983, ALP National Secretariat Papers, MS 4985, 1997 Consignment, Box 434, Folder 'Federal Election 1983 Voting Patterns/Analysis/General', NLA.
32 Bob Hawke, 'The complete text of Hawke's statement', *The Canberra Times*, 6 March 1983, p. 10.
33 Interview with Hawke, Sydney, 5 June 2014.

Chapter 18
1   Prince Philip to Bob Hawke, 20 March 1983, PM Hawke Personal Papers, M3855/152, NAA.
2   Geoff Yeend, 'Note for File: First Meeting with Prime Minister Designate', 9 March 1983, M4810/27, NAA.
3   Interview with Stone, Sydney, 6 October 2015.
4   John Stone to Paul Keating, 'Economic Assumptions Underlying the Fiscal Outlook', 7 March 1983, M3596/544, NAA.
5   Interview with Kelty, Melbourne, 11 February 2014.
6   Interview with Hawke, Sydney, 5 June 2014.
7   Paul Kelly, *The End of Certainty* (revised edition), Allen & Unwin, Sydney, 1994, p. 55.

8 Interview with Barron, 4 September 2015, Sydney.

9 Interview with Graham Freudenberg, 9 November 2015, Sydney.

10 Interview with Kelty, Melbourne, 11 February 2014.

11 John Stone, 'Paul Keating: A Memoir', *Quadrant*, March 2013, p. 44.

12 Interview with Richardson, Sydney, 14 March 2016.

13 Bob Hawke, 'First Hawke Ministry', PM Hawke Personal Papers, M3850/276, NAA.

14 Interview with Hawke, via phone, 20 December 2011.

15 John Hewson, 'Can a leopard change its pinstripes', *Business Review Weekly*, 15 May 1987, p. 128.

16 Interview with Freudenberg, Canberra, 26 August 2018.

17 Interview with Evans, Melbourne, 25 June 2019.

18 Interview with Chris Conybeare, Sydney, 1 August 2019.

19 Interview with Sandy Hollway, Sydney, 29 August 2019.

20 Interview with Dennis Richardson, Canberra, 23 August 2019.

21 Peter Barron and Bob Hogg were paid the same salary and allowance as Graham Evans ($59,350). See Graham Evans to Alan Rose, 16 March 1983, PM Hawke Personal Papers, M3855/68, NAA.

22 Interview with Barron, via phone, 7 July 2021.

23 Interview with Stephen Mills, Sydney, 20 February 2020.

24 Interview with Tamburrino, via phone, 26 February 2021.

25 Interview with Evans, Melbourne, 25 June 2019.

26 Interview with Hawke, via phone, 20 December 2011.

27 Bob Hawke, 'Challenges in public administration', The 1988 Sir Robert Garran Oration, *Australian Journal of Public Administration*, vol. 48, no. 1, March 1989, p. 10.

28 Interview with Dawkins, Sydney, 5 December 2019.

29 Harvey Barnett, 'Briefing – Prime Minister', 8 March 1983, ASIO Briefings and Documents, A6122/2914, NAA.

30 Harvey Barnett to Bob Hawke, 22 March 1983, ASIO Briefings and Documents, A6122/2914, NAA.

31 See Troy Bramston, 'Agent's true story better than memoir', *The Weekend Australian*, 9–10 August 2014, p. 20.

32 See Troy Bramston, '"Sympathiser" senator a risk: US', *The Weekend Australian*, 9–10 August 2014, p. 2.

33 Harvey Barnett, 'Record of Conversation', 8 March 1983, ASIO Briefings and Documents, A6122/2914, NAA.

34 Interview with Tom Uren, Sydney, 13 December 2013.

35 Interview with Hayden, 18 August 2015, via phone.

36 Interview with Hawke, Sydney, 20 December 2012.

37 Interview with Hawke, Sydney, 6 May 2004.

38 Interview with Ryan, Sydney, 20 September 2019.

39 Button, *As It Happened*, p. 215.

40 Interview with Hollway, Sydney, 29 August 2019.

41 Interview with Hawke, Sydney, 14 December 2017.

42 Interview with Hawke, Sydney, 12 February 2019.

43 Interview with Keating, Sydney, 4 May 2021.

44 Jim Shepherd and Keith Chatto, 'The Kings Cross Connection', *The Phantom*, No. 1000, Frew Publications, Sydney, 1992.

45 Hawke, Prime Ministers on Prime Ministers Address, 5 March 1998.
46 The EPAC sought the input of ministers, state premiers, captains of industry, and representatives of unions, community groups, local government and small business.
47 Interview with Hawke, Sydney, 20 December 2013.
48 Interview with Hawke, Sydney, 10 December 2014.
49 Interview with Wendy McCarthy, Sydney, 5 November 2019.
50 Interview with Pieters-Hawke, Sydney, 5 March 2020.
51 Interview with Hawke, Perth, 11 December 2019.

Chapter 19
1 Interview with Hawke, Sydney, 10 December 2014.
2 John Edwards has argued that Ross Garnaut wanted to sack John Stone. See John Edwards, *Keating: The Inside Story*, Viking, Melbourne, 1996, p. 182.
3 Interview with Ross Garnaut, Melbourne, 10 October 2019.
4 Interview with Keating, Sydney, 5 May 2016.
5 Interview with Stone, Sydney, 6 October 2015.
6 Interview with Andrew Peacock, via phone, 8 November 2016.
7 Interview with Hawke, Sydney, 6 May 2004.
8 See Bramston, *For the True Believers*, p. 80.
9 Bob Hawke, 'National Economic Summit Conference: Report and Further Action', Cabinet Submission, 18 April 1983, A13977/72, NAA.
10 Interview with Hawke, Sydney, 8 December 2015.
11 Interview with Barron, via phone, 7 July 2021.
12 Interview with Garnaut, Melbourne, 10 October 2019.
13 Paul Keating and John Dawkins, '1983–84 Budget – Economic Policy Considerations', Cabinet Submission, 29 March 1983, A13977/16, NAA.
14 Minutes of the FPLP, 19 May 1983, NLA.
15 Interview with Keating, Sydney, 4 May 2021.
16 HoR, *Hansard*, 23 August 1983, p. 44.
17 Interview with Hawke, Sydney, 20 December 2012.
18 See Bede Nairn, *Civilising Capitalism: The Beginnings of the Australian Labor Party*, Melbourne University Press, Carlton, 1989 and Carol Johnson, *The Labor Legacy: Curtin, Chifley, Whitlam, Hawke*, Allen & Unwin, North Sydney, 1989.
19 Interview with Mills, Sydney, 20 February 2020.
20 Interview with Crean, Melbourne, 2 September 2013.
21 Hawke, *The Hawke Memoirs*, p. 597.
22 Harvey Barnett, 'IVANOV Expulsion – Briefing of the Prime Minister and Subsequent Events', 26 April 1983, ASIO Briefings and Documents, A6122/2914, NAA.
23 Interview with Evans, Melbourne, 25 June 2019.
24 Interview with Jeff Townsend, Sydney, 8 August 2019.
25 Interview with Evans, Canberra, 19 September 2019.
26 Cabinet Minute, National and International Security Committee, Decision No. 321 (NIS), 'Without Submission – Expulsion of KGB Officer: Mr. V.N. Ivanov', 9 December 1983, A13979/321, NAA.
27 Interview with Hawke, Sydney, 14 December 2014.

28 Interview with Walsh, Melbourne, 10 October 2019.

29 Interview with Hogg, via phone, 25 November 2019.

30 Harvey Barnett, 'IVANOV/EPIC', 11 May 1983, ASIO Briefings and Documents, A6122/2914, NAA.

31 Harvey Barnett, 'Record of Conversation', 4 May 1983, ASIO Briefings and Documents, A6122/2914, NAA.

32 Hawke, *The Hawke Memoirs*, p. 199.

33 Interview with Hawke, Sydney, 14 December 2014.

34 Harvey Barnett, 'IVANOV Expulsion – Briefing of the Prime Minister and Subsequent Events', 7 June 1983, ASIO Briefings and Documents, A6122/2914, NAA.

35 Interview with Evans, Canberra, 19 September 2019.

36 Interview with David Combe, via phone, 29 August 2019. See also Troy Bramston and Simon Benson, 'Hawke, Russian spies and sad goodbyes to David Combe', *The Australian*, 25 September 2019, p. 1.

37 The officials were the governor of the Reserve Bank, the secretary of the Treasury and the deputy secretary of the Department of Prime Minister and Cabinet.

38 Interview with Hawke, Sydney, 5 June 2014.

39 Interview with Garnaut, Melbourne, 10 October 2019.

40 Interview with Bob Johnston, Sydney, 26 May 2016.

41 Interview with Stone, Sydney, 6 October 2015.

42 Don Sanders, 'Discussions with Treasury', 6 September 1983, RBA SD85-03520, Reserve Bank of Australia Archives (RBA), Sydney.

43 Interview with Ted Evans, Canberra, 6 May 2016.

44 Interview with David Morgan, via email, 15 June 2016.

45 Don Sanders, 'Meeting with the Treasurer', 14 October 1983, RBA SD85-03527, RBA.

46 John Stone, 'Part 1 – Floating the dollar: Facts and fiction', *Quadrant*, January 2012.

47 Hawke, *The Hawke Memoirs*, pp. 239–40.

48 Interview with Stone, via phone, 16 December 2020.

49 Interview with Keating, Sydney, 5 May 2016.

50 Interview with Garnaut, Melbourne, 10 October 2019.

51 Paul Keating, 'Monetary and Exchange Rate Policy', Cabinet Memorandum, 1 November 1983, A13977/504, NAA.

52 John Phillips, 'Discussions with the Treasurer', 30 November 1983, RBA D08/324228, RBA.

53 Dick Rye, 'The Float: Treasury Involvement', Note for File, 13 December 1983. This was provided to the author by Selwyn Cornish.

54 Interview with Hawke, Sydney, 5 June 2014.

55 Interview with Stone, via phone, 16 December 2020. See also John Stone, 'Part 2 – Floating the dollar: Facts and fiction', *Quadrant*, January 2012.

56 Cabinet Minute, Economic Policy Committee, Decision No. 2620 (EP), 'Cabinet Memorandum 323 – Intervention Under a Floating Rate System', 9 December 1983, A13978/323, NAA.

57 Geoff Yeend, Cabinet Notebook, 24 August 1983 – 9 December 1983, A11099/5/74, NAA.

58 Editorial, *The Australian*, 10 December 1983, pp. 1 and 14.

59 See Troy Bramston, *Paul Keating: The Big-Picture Leader*, Scribe, Melbourne, 2016, p. 220.

60 Interview with Howard, Sydney, 17 March 2021.

61 Bob Johnston, 'Commonwealth Treasurer', 10 March 1983, RBA GRJ-83-1, RBA.

62 Ross Gittins, 'Recovery via the half-way house', *The Sydney Morning Herald*, 4 April 1983, p. 7.

63 Interview with Keating, Sydney, 5 May 2016.

64 Rod Cameron, 'A Resume of Federal Voter Research – April–September 1983', ALP National Secretariat Papers, MS 4985, 1997 Consignment, Box 445, Folder 'Campaign Committee', NLA.

65 Interview with Townsend, Sydney, 8 August 2019.

66 Interview with Hawke, Sydney, 5 June 2014.

67 Ronald Reagan to Bob Hawke, 26 September 1983, Executive Head of State Files – Australia – Prime Minister Hawke, Box 002, Ronald Reagan Presidential Library and Museum (RRPL).

68 Richard Nixon to Bob Hawke, 29 September 1983, PM Hawke Personal Papers, Personal Correspondence 1983, M3826/2, NAA.

69 Interview with Townsend, Sydney, 8 August 2019.

Chapter 20

1 Les Hollings, 'Hawke is the man who is bringing us together', *The Weekend Australian*, 31 December 1983, p. 1.

2 Russell Barton and Simon Balderstone, 'Hawke himself wins the greatest accolade', *The Age*, 26 January 1984.

3 'Mister 78 P.C. – that's Bob', *The Sun News-Pictorial*, 29 March 1984, p. 1.

4 John Curtin's approval rating reached 82 per cent in December 1942, according to Gallup.

5 Ann Harding, *The Suffering Middle: Trends in Income Inequality in Australia 1982-94*, National Centre for Social and Economic Modelling, University of Canberra, June 1997.

6 Interview with Ryan, Sydney, 20 September 2019.

7 Interview with Blewett, via email, 30 January 2014.

8 Interview with Blewett, Leura, 16 November 2019.

9 Interview with Blewett, Leura, 16 November 2019.

10 Neal Blewett, Cabinet Submission 6567, Decision No. 13073, 'National HIV-AIDS Strategy Policy Information Paper', 1 August 1989, A14039/6567, NAA.

11 Interview with Grimes, via phone, 4 November 2019.

12 Interview with Ryan, via email, 27 December 2011.

13 Interview with Ryan, Sydney, 20 September 2019.

14 Interview with Anne Summers, via email, 12 July 2021.

15 The Hawke government also appointed John Toohey (1987) and Michael McHugh (1989) to the High Court. Anthony Mason was appointed Chief Justice in 1987. Hawke later regretted Mason's appointment after his secret role advising Sir John Kerr before, during and after the 1975 constitutional crisis was revealed. See Paul Kelly and Troy Bramston, *The Dismissal: In the Queen's Name*, Penguin, Melbourne, 2015, pp. 43–44.

16 Interview with Summers, via email, 12 July 2021.

17 Bob Hawke, Election Policy Speech, 13 November 1984.
18 Bob Hawke, Launch of National Women's Health Policy, 20 April 1989.
19 Bob Hawke, Speech to the Commonwealth/State Ministers' Conference on the Status of Women, 14 February 1991.
20 Cabinet Minute, Decision No. 3069, 'Without Submission – National Anthem and National Colours', 9 April 1984, A13979/3069, NAA.
21 Philip Moore to Bob Hawke, 14 March 1986, PM Hawke Personal Papers, M3855/63, NAA.
22 Interview with Evans, Canberra, 19 September 2019.
23 Bob Hawke, Speech to ALP National Conference, 10 July 1984, RH 18, Box 3, Folder 61, BHPML.
24 Neville Wran, 'Taking Power', *Labor in Power*, ABC TV, 8 June 1993.
25 Bramston, *Paul Keating*, pp. 230–32.
26 Morgan Gallup, *The Bulletin*, 2 October 1984, p. 40.
27 ANOP, Research Report, September 1984, ALP National Secretariat Papers, MS 4985, 1997 Consignment, Box 479, Folder '1985 Campaign Planning Group', NLA.
28 Brian Sweeney & Associates, 'A Research Report on Swinging Voters' Attitudes to Federal Politics', October 1984, Forbes Papers, MS 9875, Series 7, Box 32, Folder 34, NLA.
29 Michelle Grattan, 'December poll proper: Hawke', *The Age*, 9 October 1984, p. 1.
30 Interview with Beazley, Perth, 11 December 2019.
31 Alan Rose, Cabinet Notebook, 16 August 1983 – 20 October 1983, A11099/5/73, NAA.
32 Interview with Ray, Melbourne, 19 November 2019.
33 Hawke, *The Hawke Memoirs*, p. 272.
34 Interview with Barron, via phone, 7 July 2021.
35 Interview with Walsh, Melbourne, 10 October 2019.
36 'PM's wife tells of daughter's heroin addiction,' *The Canberra Times*, 25 September 1984, p. 1.
37 Interview with Hogg, via phone, 25 November 2019.
38 Interview with McMullan, Canberra, 9 December 2019.
39 In December 1984, Lionel Murphy was charged with attempting to pervert the course of justice. In July 1985, he was convicted, but this was overturned on appeal. In April 1986, he was acquitted after a retrial. In May 1986, a parliamentary inquiry was established to further examine his conduct. In July 1986, it was revealed that Murphy had inoperable cancer. He returned briefly to the High Court in August 1986 and died in October 1986.
40 Interview with Hawke, Sydney, 20 December 2012.
41 Interview with Roger Martindale, Sydney, 27 November 2019.
42 Campaign Committee Meeting, 27 September 1984, RH18, Box 2, Folder 44, BHPML.
43 'Voters prefer Labor's management by 2 to 1', *The Sydney Morning Herald*, 10 October 1984, p. 4.
44 Bob Hawke, Government Taxation Policy Statement, 31 October 1984.
45 Michelle Grattan, 'PM keeps pledges modest', *The Age*, 14 November 1984, p. 1.

46 Paul Malone, 'Peacock tops debate polls', *The Canberra Times*, 27 November 1984, p. 1.
47 Interview with Barron, via phone, 7 July 2021.
48 Hawke, *The Hawke Memoirs*, p. 275–76.
49 The referendum proposals were: simultaneous elections, four-year parliamentary terms, allowing jurisdictions to interchange powers, giving the High Court an advisory jurisdiction, and removing outmoded and expended provisions from the Constitution.
50 Interview with Evans, Canberra, 19 September 2019.
51 Interview with Cameron, Sydney, 26 August 2014.
52 Interview with McMullan, Canberra, 21 July 2016.
53 Bob McMullan, 'Campaign Director's Report 1984 Federal Election', RH18, Box 4, Folder 65, BHPML.
54 Tony Eggleton, '1984 Federal Election – Campaign Director's Report', Forbes Papers, MS 9875, Series 7, Box 35 Folder 97, NLA.
55 Interview with Peacock, via phone, 8 November 2016.
56 Interview with Hawke, Sydney, 20 December 2012.
57 Michelle Grattan, 'Real Prime Ministers can cry', *The Age*, 24 September 1984. See Hawke, Scrapbooks, JCPML.
58 Joan Marriott, 'Hazel Hawke: Her life at the Lodge', *Woman's Day*, 19 November 1984, p. 4.
59 Jerry Featherston, 'Hazel Hawke, a tower of strength', *Woman's Day*, 15 October 1984, p. 6.

Chapter 21

1 Chris Pritchard, 'Hawke eye', *Playboy*, August 1983, p. 44.
2 Interview with Hawke, Sydney, 6 May 2004.
3 Ronald Reagan to Bob Hawke, 5 March 1983, Executive Head of State Files – Australia – Prime Minister Hawke, Box 002, RRPL.
4 Bob Hawke to Ronald Reagan, 14 March 1983, Executive Head of State Files – Australia – Prime Minister Hawke, Box 002, RRPL.
5 Central Intelligence Agency (CIA), 'Australia's Labor Party: Implications of an Election Victory', 8 February 1983, United States State Department (DOS), Maryland.
6 Interview with George Shultz, via Zoom, 20 October 2020.
7 Interview with James Baker, via phone, 9 December 2020.
8 Interview with Hawke, Sydney, 12 February 2019.
9 Ronald Reagan, Diary, 13 June 1983, RRPL.
10 Interview with Hawke, Sydney, 17 December 2017.
11 Interview with George H.W. Bush, via email, 23 May 2018.
12 CIA, 'National Intelligence Daily', 8 June 1983, DOS.
13 Interview with Hayden, Brisbane, 23 June 2017.
14 CIA, 'Australia's Bill Hayden and the Centre-Left: A New Challenge for Hawke', 14 May 1985, DOS.
15 Interview with Hayden, Brisbane, 23 June 2017.
16 Interview with Costello, Canberra, 11 June 2021.
17 Interview with Hawke, Sydney, 28 November 2017.
18 Interview with Beazley, Perth, 11 December 2019.
19 Interview with Costello, Canberra, 11 June 2021.

20 Interview with Costello, Canberra, 11 June 2021.
21 Cabinet Minute, Decision No. 4613 (Sec), 'Without Submission – MX Missile Tests', 29 January 1985, A13979/4613/SEC, NAA.
22 Interview with Beazley, Perth, 11 December 2019.
23 Interview with Hawke, Sydney, 20 December 2012.
24 Cable from Washington to Canberra, 'Prime Minister's Visit: MX Tests', 6 February 1985, USA – Relations with Australia – Visit by Prime Minister of Australia', A1838, 250/9/10/3, PART 28, NAA.
25 Interview with Shultz, via Zoom, 20 October 2020.
26 Interview with Beazley, Perth, 11 December 2019.
27 Interview with Hayden, via phone, 17 August 2020.
28 Interview with Bush, via email, 23 May 2018.
29 Interview with Shultz, via Zoom, 20 October 2020.
30 A video of these exchanges is available at the RRPL and on YouTube.
31 Reagan, Diary, 7 February 1985, RRPL.
32 Interview with Beazley, Perth, 11 December 2019.
33 A video of these exchanges is available at the RRPL and on YouTube.
34 Reagan, Diary, 17 April 1986, RRPL.
35 Ronald Reagan and Bob Hawke, Memorandum of Conversation, 11 July 1987, WHORM Presidential Handwriting File – Telephone Calls – Call to Prime Minister Bob Hawke, Box 010, RRPL.
36 Interview with Dalrymple, Sydney, 18 December 2019.
37 Interview with Brian Mulroney, via phone, 2 October 2020.
38 Interview with Hawke, Sydney, 14 December 2017.
39 Interview with Garnaut, Melbourne, 10 October 2019.
40 Hawke, *The Hawke Memoirs*, p. 343.
41 Record of Conversation between Zhao Ziyang and Bob Hawke, 7 February 1984, Beijing, China – Relations with Australia – Mr Hawke's Visit to China 1984, A1838, 3107/38/12/27, PART 4, NAA.
42 Record of Conversations between Zhao Ziyang and Bob Hawke, 8–9 February 1984, Beijing, China – Relations with Australia – Mr Hawke's Visit to China 1984, A1838, 3107/38/12/27, PART 4, NAA.
43 Record of Conversation between Li Xiannian and Bob Hawke, 8 February 1984, Beijing, China – Relations with Australia – Mr Hawke's Visit to China 1984, A1838, 3107/38/12/27, PART 4, NAA.
44 Record of Conversation between Hu Yaobang and Bob Hawke, 11 February 1984, Beijing, China – Relations with Australia – Mr Hawke's Visit to China 1984, A1838, 3107/38/12/27, PART 4, NAA.
45 Record of Conversation between Zhao Ziyang and Bob Hawke, 19 May 1986, Beijing, A-Z Files, BHPML.
46 Bob Hawke, Press Conference, Beijing, 20 May 1986.
47 Record of Conversations between Hu Yaobang and Bob Hawke, 21 May, Chengdu, and 22 May, Nanjing, A-Z Files, BHPML.
48 J.E. Holmes to Tim Flesher, 'Visit of Australian Prime Minister', 6 June 1983, FCO 19/1675, TNA.
49 John Mason to Francis Pym, 'Robert Hawke: Prime Minister of Australia', 7 March 1983, FCO 160/82/22 TNA.
50 Margaret Thatcher and Bob Hawke, Memorandum of Conversation, 6 June 1983, FCO 19/1675, TNA.

51 A.J. Coles to Margaret Thatcher, 5 October 1983, PREM 19/0969, TNA.
52 A.J. Coles, 'Record of Conversation', 23 November 1983, PREM 19/0970, TNA.
53 Interview with Charles Powell, London, 19 March 2020.
54 Interview with Hawke, Sydney, 5 July 2010.
55 Margaret Thatcher to Bob Hawke, 10 October 1985, PREM 19/1644, TNA.
56 Charles Powell, 'Prime Minister's Meeting with the Prime Minister of Australia', 17 October 1985, PREM 19/1688, TNA.
57 See Bramston, *For the True Believers*, pp. 366–69.
58 Charles Powell to Antony Acland, 'CHOGM: Heads of Government Retreat at Lyford Cay', 21 October 1985, PREM 19/1688, TNA.
59 Interview with Powell, London, 19 March 2020.
60 Cabinet Minute, Decision No. 6748, 'Without Submission – Report on CHOGM', 28 October 1985, A13979/6748, NAA.
61 Interview with Drysdale, via phone, 27 February 2021.
62 Ninian Stephen, Commission of Appointment, 13 July 1983, The Whitlam Institute, Sydney.
63 Interview with Hawke, Sydney, 14 December 2017.
64 John Mason to Geoffrey Howe, 'Australia: Annual Review for 1983', FCO 160/221/25, TNA.
65 'Hawke, The Hon. Robert ("Bob") James Lee AC MP', PREM 19/1675, TNA.
66 Charles Powell to Tony Galsworthy, 'Prime Minister's Meeting with the Prime Minister of Australia', 21 April 1986, PREM 19/1675, TNA.
67 Hawke, *The Hawke Memoirs*, p. 327.
68 Interview with Powell, London, 19 March 2020.
69 Interview with Hawke, Sydney, 14 December 2017.
70 Hawke, *The Hawke Memoirs*, p. 329.
71 Interview with Heseltine, Sydney, 22 June 2017.
72 Interview with Hawke, Sydney, 14 December 2017.

Chapter 22

1 Minutes of the FPLP, 19 February 1985, NLA.
2 Minutes of the FPLP, 19 March 1985, NLA.
3 Paul Keating, 'The Main Economic Issues the Government Faces in 1985', Cabinet Submission, 13 December 1984, A14039/1977, NAA.
4 Cabinet Minute, Decision No. 4518, 'Endorsement of Budget Parameters Announced During the Election Campaign', 13 December 1984, A13979/4518, NAA.
5 Paul Keating, 'Participation in Banking – Applications for Banking Authorities', Cabinet Submission, 26 February 1985, A14039/2186, NAA.
6 John Short and Michael Lawrence, 'Keating's big victory', *The Sydney Morning Herald*, 28 February 1985, p. 1.
7 Paul Keating, 'Draft White Paper on Reform of the Australian Tax System', Cabinet Submission, 9 May 1985, A14039/2875, NAA.
8 Gareth Evans, *Inside the Hawke–Keating Government: A Cabinet Diary*, Melbourne University Publishing, Carlton, 2014, pp. 120–21.
9 Peter Walsh, *Confessions of a Failed Finance Minister*, Random House, Milsons Point, 1995, pp. 141–46.

10 John Short and Mike Steketee, 'Keating tax plan "political suicide"', *The Sydney Morning Herald*, 26 April 1985, p. 1.

11 Tom Burton, 'Walsh on Hawke: "he needs a spine transplant"', *The Sydney Morning Herald*, 11 May 1990. See also Paul Keating and Peter Walsh, 'Taxing Times', *Labor in Power*, ABC TV, 15 June 1993.

12 Edna Carew, *Keating: A Biography*, Allen & Unwin, Sydney, 1988, p. 127.

13 Hawke, *The Hawke Memoirs*, p. 310.

14 Evans, *Inside the Hawke–Keating Government*, p. 142.

15 Interview with Willis, Melbourne, 6 May 2015.

16 Interview with Hawke, Sydney, 20 December 2012.

17 Bob Hawke and Paul Keating, 'Tax Reform Measures', Cabinet Submission, 8 July 1985, A14039/3012, NAA.

18 Paul Kelly, 'Tax go-slow rebounds on PM', *The Sunday Telegraph*, 22 September 1985, p. 37. This was provided to the author by Paul Keating.

19 Neil O'Reilly, 'Good news for Hawke in tax poll', *The Sun-Herald*, 22 September 1985, p. 3. This was provided to the author by Paul Keating.

20 Interview with Hawke, Sydney, 20 December 2012.

21 Evans, *Inside the Hawke–Keating Government*, pp. 223–24.

22 Interview with Barron, via phone, 7 July 2021.

23 Kelly, *The End of Certainty*, p. 149.

24 Interview with Peacock, via phone, 8 November 2016.

25 Interview with Hawke, Sydney, 20 December 2013.

26 Interview with Paul Ellercamp, via phone, 8 July 2021.

27 Interview with Conybeare, Sydney, 1 August 2019.

28 Interview with Barron, via phone, 7 July 2021.

29 Interview with Hogg, Sydney, 10 June 2004.

30 David O'Reilly, 'Treasurer hits out at PM's "minders"', *The Australian*, 30 May 1986, p. 1.

31 Interview with Hawke, Sydney, 6 May 2004.

32 Interview with Grattan, Canberra, 7 August 2019.

33 Interview with Steve Sedgwick, Canberra, 10 December 2019.

34 Mike Steketee, 'PM puts Accord on the line', *The Sydney Morning Herald*, 12 June 1986, p. 1.

35 Mike Steketee, 'Bob a TV pro, even at 2.45 am', *The Sydney Morning Herald*, 12 June 1986, p. 1.

36 Paul Keating, '1986–87 Budget Strategy', Cabinet Submission, 2 March 1986, A14039/3647, NAA.

37 Interview with Sedgwick, Canberra, 10 December 2019.

38 See Bramston, 'Peter Walsh: Labor's fiscal powerhouse', 14 April 2015.

39 Interview with Ryan, Sydney, 13 May 2016.

40 Interview with Barry Jones, via phone, 27 October 2020.

41 Interview with Brian Howe, Melbourne, 9 October 2019.

42 Walsh, *Confessions of a Failed Finance Minister*, p. 151.

43 Bob Hawke, 'Work Program for Committee on Structural Adjustment (CSA)', Cabinet Submission, 17 August 1987, A14039/5089, NAA.

44 John Button, 'Textiles, Clothing and Footwear Industries – Post 1988 Assistance Issues', Cabinet Submission, 9 October 1986, A14039/4394, NAA.

45 Interview with Kerin, via phone, 1 November 2019.

46 Rupert Murdoch would later sell his two Channel Ten stations to Frank Lowy to fund his acquisition of the Herald & Weekly Times group.

47 Interview with Duffy, Melbourne, 9 October 2019. See also Paul Barry, *The Rise and Rise of Kerry Packer*, Bantam, Sydney, 1993, pp. 408–09.

48 Interview with Keating, Sydney, 19 December 2013.

49 Cabinet Minute, Decision No. 8809, 'Without Submission – Murdoch Takeover of Herald and Weekly Times', 8 December 1986, A13979/8809, NAA.

50 Interview with Hawke, Sydney, 5 June 2014.

51 Bob Hawke, Speech to ALP National Conference, 9 July 1986, RH18, Box 5, Folder 85, BHPML.

52 Anthony Albanese, a delegate to the national conference, was among those in the Left who voted to return to a regulated exchange rate. Albanese opposed many of the major reforms of the period, from fiscal consolidation and privatisation to cutting tariffs, exporting uranium and introducing HECS.

53 Paul Keating, Speech to ALP National Conference, 10 July 1986, RH18, Box 5, Folder 85, BHPML.

54 Interview with Ellercamp, via phone, 8 July 2021.

55 Interview with Kelly, Sydney, 10 November 2019.

Chapter 23

1 Rod Cameron, 'Developing a Position for the ALP in the Late 1980s – Some Further ANOP Thoughts', August 1985, RH18, Box 2, Folder 50, BHPML.

2 Rod Cameron, 'Government's Electoral Standing – Strategy for 1988 Election', October 1986, RH18, Box 2, Folder 52, BHPML.

3 Interviews with Cameron, Sydney, 8 March 2020 and McMullan, Canberra, 9 December 2019.

4 Interview with Cameron, Sydney, 26 August 2014.

5 Minutes of the FPLP, 24 February 1987, NLA.

6 Michelle Grattan, 'PM seizes on opposition disarray for 11 July poll', *The Age*, 28 May 1987, p. 1.

7 Newspoll, 'ALP gains after mini-budget', Media Release, 19 May 1987.

8 Interview with Bob Sorby, Sydney, 5 March 2020.

9 Graham Freudenberg to Jean Sinclair, 2 April 1987, PM Hawke Personal Papers, Personal Correspondence 1987, M3826/17, NAA.

10 'Hawke's statement', *The Canberra Times*, 28 May 1987, p. 10.

11 Interview with Conybeare, Sydney, 1 August 2019.

12 Interview with Barrie Cassidy, Melbourne, 10 October 2019.

13 Interview with Sorby, Sydney, 5 March 2020.

14 John Lyons, 'At the court of king Hawke', *The Weekend Australian*, 11–12 June 1988.

15 Interview with Sorby, Sydney, 5 March 2020.

16 Interview with Craig Emerson, via phone, 15 July 2021.

17 Anne Summers, 'The times will suit me, says John Howard', *The Australian Financial Review*, 7 July 1986, p. 1.

18 'Joh most popular conservative leader', *The Australian*, 10 February 1987, p. 1.

19 Interview with Howard, Sydney, 17 March 2021, Sydney.

20 Interview with Ian Sinclair, via phone, 18 June 2015.

21 Australian National Opinion Polls (ANOP), 'Phase Three Marginals', 30–31 May 1987, RH 16, Box 2, Folder 28, BHPML.

22 ANOP, 'Campaign Monitor', 7–8 June 1987, RH16, Box 2, Folder 28, BHPML.

23 ANOP, 'Campaign Monitor', 13–14 June 1987, RH16, Box 2, Folder 28, BHPML.

24 Stephen Hutcheon, 'Keating sees $7bn hole in Lib tax plan', *The Sydney Morning Herald*, 18 June 1987, p. 7.

25 Interview with Howard, Sydney, 22 February 2016.

26 ANOP, 'Campaign Midweek Survey', 7 July 1987, RH16, Box 2, Folder 28, BHPML.

27 Interview with Eggleton, via email, 13 February 2016.

28 Interview with Farmer, via phone, 26 August 2019.

29 Interview with Hawke, Sydney, 20 December 2013.

30 Interview with Loosley, Sydney, 6 November 2019.

31 Tony Stephens, 'Who's who parades for the message', *The Sydney Morning Herald*, 24 June 1987, p. 11.

32 Bob Hawke, Election Policy Speech, 23 June 1987.

33 Interview with Hawke, Sydney, 20 December 2013.

34 Interview with Sorby, Sydney, 5 March 2020.

35 Interview with Mills, Sydney, 20 February 2020.

36 Bob Hawke, 'Achievements, Alternatives and Prospects', June 1987. This was provided to the author by Craig Emerson.

37 Interview with Sorby, Sydney, 5 March 2020.

38 Interview with Howard, Sydney, 17 March 2021.

39 Interview with Hawke, Sydney, 20 December 2013.

40 Interview with Howard, Sydney, 17 March 2021.

41 Bob McMullan, 'Campaign Director's Report 1987 Election', RH18, Box 3, Folder 57, BHPML.

42 Paul Keating, 'Conserving Power', *Labor in Power*, ABC TV, 22 June 1993.

43 Interview with Peacock, via phone, 8 November 2016.

44 John Button to Bob Hawke, 3 June 1987, PM Hawke Personal Papers, 'Election 1987 – Miscellaneous Papers', M3830/77, NAA.

45 Interview with Mike Codd, Williamsdale, 22 July 2019.

46 Some lawyers argued that Section 64 of the Constitution held that only one minister could be responsible for a department. The new structure was upheld as constitutionally valid by the Federal Court on 16 September 1987.

47 Cabinet Minute, No. 9669 (M), 'Without Submission – Portfolio and Other Ministers', 24 July 1987, A13979/9669/M, NAA.

48 Craig Emerson to Bob Hawke, 28 March 1988, RH 34, Box 3, Folder 35, BHPML.

49 Interview with Rod Sims, Sydney, 17 December 2019.

50 Brian Howe, 'Confirmation of Election Commitments on Family Assistance Reform', Cabinet Submission, 7 August 1987, A14039/5012, NAA.

51 Hugh Lamberton, 'PM to archbishop: it's bloody unchristian', *The Canberra Times*, 23 June 1990, p. 1.

52 Cassandra Goldie, 'ACOSS tribute to Bob Hawke', Media Release, 17 May 2019. See also Peter Martin, 'Hawke, history and child poverty pledge', *The Sun-Herald*, 15 October 2017, p. 7.
53 Hawke, *The Hawke Memoirs*, p. 403.
54 Errol Simper, 'Tourism twins are no shrimps at promotion', *The Australian*, 1 January 1987, p. 1.
55 Cabinet Minute, No. 2197, 'Without Submission – The America's Cup 1983 – Successful Australia II Challenge', 27 September 1983, A13979/2197, NAA.
56 Interview with John Brown, Sydney, 7 November 2019.
57 International tourism visitors to Australia reached over 8 million a year by the end of 2019, with China being Australia's largest source market.
58 'Higher Education Students Assistance Schemes', 1985, PM Hawke Personal Papers, Subject Files, M3855/101, NAA.
59 Interview with Ryan, Sydney, 20 September 2019.
60 Interview with Hawke, Sydney, 10 December 2014.
61 Interview with Dawkins, Sydney, 5 December 2019.
62 Interview with Jones, via phone, 27 October 2020.
63 Interview with John Hewson, via phone, 7 July 2021.
64 Interview with Richardson, Sydney, 3 September 2019.
65 Interview with Hawke, Sydney, 10 December 2014.
66 Interview with Hawke, Sydney, 6 May 2004.
67 Interview with Richardson, Sydney, 3 September 2019.
68 Interview with Evans, Canberra, 19 September 2019.
69 Interview with Emerson, via phone, 15 July 2021.
70 Paul Keating to Bob Hawke, 27 April 1989. This was provided to the author by Paul Keating.
71 Ross Dunn, 'Hawke wavers on Antarctic treaty', *The Australian Financial Review*, 5 May 1989, p. 5.
72 Ian Anderson, 'Antarctic minerals deal heads for rocks', *New Scientist*, 20 May 1989, p. 21.
73 Don Russell, 'Meeting between the French Prime Minister and the Treasurer', 30 September 1988, RBA SD90-03786, RBA.
74 Interview with Keating, Sydney, 17 December 2014.
75 Interview with Hawke, Sydney, 10 December 2014.
76 Interview with Sorby, Sydney, 5 March 2020.
77 Interview with Grant Nihill, Canberra, 26 November 2019.
78 Interview with Martindale, Sydney, 27 November 2019.
79 Interview with Cassidy, Melbourne, 10 October 2019.
80 Interview with Martindale, Sydney, 27 November 2019.
81 Don Woolford, 'Still ebullient after five years', *The Canberra Times*, 5 March 1988.
82 Bob Carr, Diary, 15 April 1989. This was provided to the author by Bob Carr.
83 Interview with Farmer, via phone, 26 August 2019.
84 Interview with Sorby, Sydney, 5 March 2020.

Chapter 24

1   Interview with Jones, via phone, 27 October 2020.
2   Interview with Hawke, Sydney, 5 July 2010.

3   Interview with Freudenberg, via phone, 3 February 2017.
4   Interview with Mills, Sydney, 20 February 2020.
5   Interview with Colin Parks, Canberra, 26 November 2019.
6   'Grunter' was Nihill's nickname. Interview with Nihill, Canberra, 26 November 2019.
7   'Butch' was Cassidy's nickname. Hawke introduced Cassidy to George H.W. Bush as 'Butch Cassidy – my press bloke', which was met with a bemused look. Interview with Cassidy, Melbourne, 10 October 2019.
8   Interview with Cassidy, Melbourne, 10 October 2019.
9   Bob Hawke, Speech to the ALP National Conference, 8 June 1988, RH18, Box 6, Folder 96, BHPML.
10 Interview with Beattie, Sydney, 4 November 2019.
11 Interview with Hawke, Sydney, 5 July 2010.
12 Geoff Kitney, 'PM's judgement worries the ALP', *The Australian Financial Review*, 14 March 1988, p. 1.
13 Hayden, *Hayden*, pp. 481–86.
14 Richardson, *Whatever It Takes*, p. 200.
15 Gareth Evans, 'Conserving Power', *Labor in Power*.
16 Button, *As It Happened*, p. 233.
17 Keating's four budget surpluses were 1987–88, 1988–89, 1989–90 and 1990–91, according to the Budget Papers at the time. Under revised accounting measures adopted during the Howard government, which exclude net advances, Keating is now recorded as having delivered three budget surpluses.
18 Carr, Diary, 29 July 1988.
19 'Keating next PM: Hawke', *The Daily Mirror*, 27 August 1987, pp. 1–2.
20 Bruce Jones, 'Hawke picks next PM', *Sun-Herald*, 19 June 1988, p. 1.
21 Interview with Sorby, Sydney, 5 March 2020.
22 Hawke, *The Hawke Memoirs*, p. 446.
23 Interview with Seumas Dawes, Sydney, 29 July 2014.
24 Hawke, *The Hawke Memoirs*, p. 447.
25 Kelly, *The End of Certainty*, p. 444.
26 Edwards, *Keating*, p. 339.
27 Hawke, *The Hawke Memoirs*, p. 448.
28 Barrie Cassidy, 'Conserving Power', *Labor in Power*.
29 Hawke, *The Hawke Memoirs*, p. 449.
30 Barrie Cassidy, 'Conserving Power', *Labor in Power*.
31 Glenn Milne, 'Name the date, Button tells PM', *The Sydney Morning Herald*, 29 August 1988, p. 1.
32 Paul Keating, 'Notes of discussion with Hawke end of 1988', 28 August 1988. This was provided to the author by Paul Keating.
33 Bob Hawke, 'Conserving Power', *Labor in Power*.
34 Keating, 'Notes of discussion with Hawke end of 1988'.
35 Interview with Dawkins, via phone, 10 December 2014.
36 Hawke, *The Hawke Memoirs*, p. 450.
37 Interview with Dawkins, Adelaide, 5 March 2015.
38 Interview with Kelly, Sydney, 24 May 2016.
39 Interview with Dawkins, via phone, 10 December 2014.
40 Minutes of the FPLP, 30 August 1988, NLA.

41 Richardson, *Whatever It Takes*, pp. 249–50.

42 Mike Steketee, 'Keating vows loyalty, but doubts linger', *The Sydney Morning Herald*, 18 October 1988, p. 1.

43 Interview with Kelty, Melbourne, 11 February 2014.

44 Hawke, *The Hawke Memoirs*, pp. 452–53. See also Bob Hawke, 'Conserving Power', *Labor in Power*.

45 Paul Keating, 'Conserving Power', *Labor in Power*.

46 Interview with Kelty, Melbourne, 11 February 2014.

47 Peter Abeles, 'Conserving Power', *Labor in Power*.

48 Don Woolford, 'Hawke: I'll retire if I lose poll', *The Canberra Times*, 7 December 1989, p. 1.

49 Interview with Keating, Sydney, 4 May 2021.

Chapter 25

1   Interview with D'Alpuget, Sydney, 20 February 2020.

2   John Gorton had an affair with Lady Harrington, the widow of Vice Admiral Hastings 'Arch' Harrington. John Curtin was rumoured to have had an affair with Belle Southwell, manager of the Hotel Kurrajong in Canberra. It has been alleged that Robert Menzies had an affair with Elizabeth 'Betty' Fairfax. There is little evidence, however, for either claim.

3   Tony Stephens, 'Bob Hawke in tears: How I cheated on Hazel', *The Sydney Morning Herald*, 21 March 1989, p.1.

4   Interview with Brown, Sydney, 7 November 2019. See also Jan Murray, *Sheer Madness: Sex, Lies and Politics*, Mira Books, Chatswood, 2010, p. 230.

5   Interview with Brown, Sydney, 7 November 2019.

6   Michael Harvey, 'Yes, yes, oh yes Minister', *The Herald*, 30 July 1987, p. 1.

7   Interview with Evans, via phone, 28 July 2021.

8   Interview with Brown, Sydney, 7 November 2019.

9   Interview with Martindale, Sydney, 27 November 2019.

10 Interview with Cassidy, Melbourne, 10 October 2019.

11 Interview with Sorby, Sydney, 5 March 2020.

12 Interview with Hogg, via phone, 25 November 2019.

13 Interview with Martindale, Sydney, 27 November 2019.

14 Alan Ramsey, 'Jean Sinclair: Hawke loses his right-hand', *The Sydney Morning Herald*, 14 September 1991, p. 25.

15 Interview with D'Alpuget, Sydney, 20 February 2020.

16 Interview with Ellercamp, via phone, 8 July 2021.

17 Interview with D'Alpuget, Sydney, 20 February 2020.

18 Blanche d'Alpuget, 'Bob Hawke and the burden of office', *The Age*, 15 March 1986.

19 Blanche d'Alpuget admitted: 'He had shrunken in my life, in my mind, so I was probably projecting on to him, which we all too often do, project our own feelings into other people – and they're inaccurate.' See Kelly, 'Bob and Blanche'.

20 Blanche d'Alpuget, *Hawke: The Prime Minister*, Melbourne University Publishing, Carlton, 2010, p. 232.

21 D'Alpuget, *On Longing*, p. 59.

22 Interview with D'Alpuget, Sydney, 20 February 2020.

23 Interview with Nihill, Canberra, 26 November 2019.

24 Blanche d'Alpuget, 'Hawke: A Sentimental Journey', *The Weekend Australian Magazine*, 2 December 1989, pp. 8–24.
25 Rhys Blakely, 'Sex on the brain? Love hormone is to blame', *The Times*, 23 September 2019.
26 Interview with D'Alpuget, Sydney, 20 February 2020.
27 Interview with McCarthy, Sydney, 5 November 2019.
28 Interview with Evans, Canberra, 19 September 2019.
29 Interview with Howe, Melbourne, 9 October 2019.
30 Interview with Evans, Canberra, 19 September 2019.

Chapter 26
1 See Troy Bramston, 'In from the cold', *The Australian*, 12 October 2020, p. 12.
2 Interview with Mulroney, via phone, 2 October 2020.
3 Hawke had visited New Zealand, Papua New Guinea, Indonesia, China, Japan, Malaysia, Thailand, the Philippines, Singapore and India.
4 Hawke had visited Ireland, Switzerland, France, Germany, Italy, Belgium, Hungary, Turkey, Yugoslavia, Cyprus and Greece.
5 Interview with Shultz, via Zoom, 20 October 2020.
6 Interview with Hawke, Sydney, 14 December 2017.
7 Bob Hawke also wrote that Zhao Ziyang assured him the capitalist system in Hong Kong would remain until at least 2047, the existing legal system would remain unchanged and China would not interfere in Hong Kong's internal affairs. See Bob Hawke to Margaret Thatcher, 10 February 1984, PREM 19/1263, TNA.
8 Margaret Thatcher to Bob Hawke, 23 February 1984, PREM 19/1263, TNA.
9 Margaret Thatcher to Bob Hawke, 25 September 1984, PREM 19/1267, TNA.
10 Hawke had visited the USSR, as ACTU president, in 1970, 1971, 1973 and 1979.
11 Department of Prime Minister and Cabinet, Prime Minister's Brief – Visit to the USSR – 29 November – 2 December 1987, Stephen Mills Papers, Box 218, BHPML.
12 Bob Hawke, Toast at Lunch in Leningrad, 29 November 1987.
13 Interview with Hawke, Sydney, 14 December 2017.
14 Interview with Hawke, Sydney, 14 December 2017.
15 Interview with Hawke, Sydney, 12 February 2019.
16 Hawke, *The Hawke Memoirs*, pp. 358–59.
17 Bob Hawke to Ronald Reagan, 4 December 1987, Mills Papers, Box 218, BHPML.
18 Interview with Hayden, via phone, 18 September 2020.
19 Interview with Leibler, via email, 4 March 2021.
20 Bob Hawke to John Major, 22 March 1991, PM Hawke Personal Papers, International Leaders – President Gorbachev, USSR, M3571/191, NAA.
21 Miles Kupa, Record of Conversation, 10 May 1991, PM Hawke Personal Papers, Briefing Papers, M3571, 344 Part 2, NAA.
22 Hugh White, Record of Phone Conversation, 22 August 1991, PM Hawke Personal Papers, International Leaders – President Gorbachev, USSR, M3571/191, NAA.

23 Interview with John Bowan, Sydney, 15 August 2019.

24 Interview with Bowan, Sydney, 15 August 2019.

25 Philip Green, Record of Conversation, 27 March 1991, PM Hawke Personal Papers, M3571, 344 Part 1, NAA.

26 Interview with Leibler, via email, 4 March 2021.

27 Reagan, Diary, 23 June 1988, RRPL.

28 Robert Menzies addressed the US House of Representatives on 1 August 1950.

29 Ronald Reagan to Bob Hawke, 9 January 1989, PM Hawke Personal Papers, Personal Correspondence 1989, M3826/22, NAA.

30 George H.W. Bush, Diary, 2 January 1989, George Bush Presidential Library (GBPL). This was provided to the author with permission from the George & Barbara Bush Foundation and the GBPL.

31 Interview with Hawke, Sydney, 14 December 2017.

32 Interview with Bush, via email, 23 May 2018.

33 Interview with Baker, via phone, 9 December 2020.

34 Interview with Bush, via email, 23 May 2018.

35 Bush, Diary, 25 June 1989, GBPL.

36 George Bush and Bob Hawke, Record of Conversation, 27 June 1989, Presidential Correspondence – Presidential Memcons, GBPL.

37 Bob Hawke to George Bush, 5 March 1991, PM Hawke Personal Papers, M3571/189, NAA.

38 George Bush to Bob Hawke, 25 March 1991, PM Hawke Personal Papers, M3571/344 PART 2, NAA.

39 George Bush and Bob Hawke, Record of Conversation, 5 July 1989, Presidential Correspondence – Presidential Telcons, GBPL.

40 George Bush and Bob Hawke, 19 July 1989, Presidential Telcon, GBPL.

41 George Bush and Bob Hawke, 20 December 1989, Presidential Telcon, GBPL.

42 George Bush and Bob Hawke, 29 March 1990, Presidential Telcon, GBPL.

43 John Coles to Geoffrey Howe, 'Visit by the Prime Minister to Australia', 9 August 1988, FCO 160/262/6, TNA.

44 Charles Powell, 'Commonwealth of Australia Constitution Act', 4 July 1988, PREM 19/2588, TNA.

45 Department of Prime Minister and Cabinet, Briefing for Overseas Visit to France, UK, US, Germany, Hungary, 16 June – 3 July 1989, A-Z Files, Box 209, BHPML.

46 Interview with Hawke, Sydney, 12 February 2019.

47 Charles Powell to Stephen Wall, 'Prime Minister's Meeting with the Australian Prime Minister', 21 June 1989, PREM 19/3218, TNA.

48 Bob Hawke to Margaret Thatcher, 23 June 1989, PREM 19/3218, TNA.

49 Interview with Neil Kinnock, London, 19 March 2020.

50 Interview with Kinnock, London, 19 March 2020.

51 Interview with Doug McClelland, Sydney, 1 November 2019.

52 Interview with McClelland, Sydney, 1 November 2019.

53 Interview with Mulroney, via phone, 2 October 2020.

54 Interview with Powell, London, 19 March 2020.

55 Bernard Ingham, *The Slow Downfall of Margaret Thatcher: The Diaries of Bernard Ingham*, Biteback Publishing, London, 2019, p. 124.

56 Interview with Bernard Ingham, via phone, 2 July 2019.

57 Malcolm Fraser to Bob Hawke, 14 November 1989, PM Hawke Personal Papers, Personal Correspondence 1989, M3826/23, NAA.

58 Interview with Tamie Fraser, via email, 23 February 2021.

59 Margaret Thatcher to Bob Hawke, 22 November 1990, PREM 19/3213, TNA.

60 Bob Hawke to Margaret Thatcher, 23 November 1990, PREM 19/3213, TNA.

61 D'Alpuget, *Hawke*, p. 207.

62 Interview with Mulroney, via phone, 2 October 2020.

63 Interview with Powell, London, 19 March 2020.

64 HoR, *Hansard*, 21 August 1986, p. 453.

65 R.N. Peirce, 'Prime Minister's Meeting with the Leader of the Australian Liberal Party', 26 July 1988, PREM 19/3219, TNA.

66 Interview with John Major, via email, 3 November 2020.

67 'Brief: United Kingdom', United Kingdom-Australia Relations, A9737, 1991/1788, PART 7, NAA.

68 'Record of Conversation between the Prime Minister and Prime Minister Major', 21 August 1991, United Kingdom-Australia Relations, A9737, 1991/1788, PART 7, NAA.

69 John Major to Bob Hawke, 11 September 1991, United Kingdom–Australia Relations, A9737, 1991/1788, PART 7, NAA.

70 Interview with Major, via email, 3 November 2020.

71 J.D. Anderson to Mike Codd, 11 October 1990 and Allan Gyngell to Mike Codd, 10 October 1990, Visit to Australia by Nelson Mandela, A463, 1990/3181 PART 1, NAA.

72 'Nelson Mandela – A Profile', 2 October 1990, Visit to Australia by Nelson Mandela, A463, 1990/3181 PART 1, NAA.

73 Gareth Evans to Nelson Mandela, 5 September 1990, PM Hawke Personal Papers, M3571/207, NAA.

74 Tony Wright, 'Mandela accepts invitation to visit Australia', *The Canberra Times*, 28 September 1990, p. 3.

75 'Mandela – Personal Characteristics', 22 October 1990, PM Hawke Personal Papers, M3571/207, NAA.

76 Hugh White, 'Record of Discussion Between Bob Hawke and Nelson Mandela', 24 October 1990, PM Hawke Personal Papers, M3571/207, NAA.

77 'Record of Discussions in Cabinet with Nelson Mandela', 24 October 1990, PM Hawke Personal Papers, M3571/207, NAA.

78 Nelson Mandela, Speech at Luncheon Hosted by Bob Hawke, 23 October 1990, Visit to Australia by Nelson Mandela, A463, 1990/3181 PART 2, NAA.

79 The cost of Mandela's visit, charged to the Australian government, was $177,762. Frank Leverett, 'Report on the Visit to Australia by Nelson Mandela', 5 November 1990, Visit to Australia by Nelson Mandela, A463, 1990/3181 PART 4, NAA.

80 Interview with Hawke, Sydney, 14 December 2017.

81 Hawke often claimed that when Mandela walked into his office, he said, 'I am here today because of you.' However, the official meeting record, taken by Hugh White, does not confirm this.

82 Interview with Richardson, Canberra, 23 August 2019.
83 Hawke visited Fiji, Samoa, Tonga, Tuvalu, Kiribati, Noumea, Cook Islands, New Caledonia, Vanuatu and New Zealand. These visits often coincided with meetings of the South Pacific Forum.
84 Interview with Dawkins, Sydney, 5 December 2019.
85 See Bramston, *For the True Believers*, pp. 370–73.
86 Cabinet Minute, No. 12301, 'Discussion paper – Asia Pacific Economic Cooperation – Intergovernmental Forum Proposal, 6 March 1989, A14039/6276, NAA.
87 Interview with Codd, Williamsdale, 22 July 2019.
88 Interview with Baker, via phone, 9 December 2020.
89 Interview with Evans, Canberra, 19 September 2019.
90 Interview with Richard Woolcott, Sydney, 15 November 2018.
91 Interview with Hawke, Sydney, 14 December 2017.
92 Here I draw on Troy Bramston, 'Tiananmen Square broke Bob Hawke's heart', *The Australian*, 4 June 2019.
93 Interview with Hawke, Sydney, 12 February 2019.
94 Interview with Woolcott, Sydney, 15 November 2018.
95 Cable from Beijing to Canberra, 'China: Political Crisis', 7 June 1989, A-Z Files, BHPML. See also 'Speaking notes, speeches etc – 12 May to 26 July 1989', PM Hawke Personal Papers, M3851/129, NAA.
96 Interview with Hollway, Sydney, 29 August 2019.
97 Interview with Richardson, Canberra, 23 August 2019.
98 Interview with Nihill, Canberra, 26 November 2019.
99 Cabinet Minute, No. 12812, 'Australia's Relations with China', 13 July 1989, A14039/6571, NAA.
100 Interview with Hawke, Sydney, 12 February 2019.
101 Cabinet Minute, No. 12813, 'Immigration Consequences of People's Republic of China Nationals Seeking to Enter and/or Remain in Australia', 13 July 1989, A14039/6588, NAA.
102 Interview with Bowan, Sydney, 15 August 2019.
103 Hawke, *The Hawke Memoirs*, pp. 51–52.
104 Interview with Hawke, Sydney, 12 February 2019.

Chapter 27

1 Interview with Keating, Sydney, 17 December 2014.
2 Interview with Hawke, Sydney, 8 December 2015.
3 Paul Keating, 'Economic and Fiscal Policy Strategy', Cabinet Submission, 1 March 1989, A14039/6227, NAA.
4 Interview with Sims, Sydney, 17 December 2019.
5 Cabinet Minute, No. 13202, 'Without Submission – Domestic Airline Pilots' Dispute', 12 September 1989, A13979/13202, NAA.
6 Interview with Sims, Sydney, 17 December 2019.
7 Interview with Hawke, Sydney, 10 December 2014.
8 Michael Gordon, 'And they said it wouldn't last', *The Sunday Age*, 20 August 1989, p. 1.
9 Ray Martin, *Ray: Stories of My Life*, William Heinemann Australia, North Sydney, 2009, pp. 242–43. See also Ray Martin, *Ray Martin's Favourites: The Stories Behind the Legends*, Victory Books, Carlton, 2011, pp. 107–29.

10 David O'Reilly, 'Mr 18%: What makes Johnny run?' *The Bulletin*, 20 December 1988, pp. 48–54.

11 John Schauble, 'Peacock seen as a plus', *The Sydney Morning Herald*, 19 May 1989, p. 6.

12 Interview with Howard, Sydney, 17 December 2014.

13 Interview with Hawke, Sydney, 10 December 2014.

14 Geoff Walsh to Bob Hawke, 15 May 1989, ALP National Secretariat Papers, MS 4985, 2005 Consignment, Box 52, Folder 'Elections – Federal Election – Strategy (2), NLA.

15 Geoff Walsh to Bob Hawke, 12 July 1989, ALP National Secretariat Papers, MS 4985, 2005 Consignment, Box 52, Folder 'Elections – Federal Election – Strategy (2), NLA.

16 Geoff Walsh to Bob Hawke, 25 October 1989, ALP National Secretariat Papers, MS 4985, 2005 Consignment, Box 52, Folder 'Elections – Federal Election – Strategy (2)', NLA.

17 Bob Bell confronted Hawke over the disparity between politicians' salaries and those living on the pension. Hawke also called him a 'silly old man'. See 'Hawke apologises to pensioner', *The Canberra Times*, 28 September 1989, p. 3.

18 ANOP, 'Voter Research – Campaign Lead-Up Monitors', RH16, Box 5, Folder 54, BHPML.

19 Hawke Personal Papers, (ex-Sydney).

20 Hawke Personal Papers, (ex-Sydney).

21 Glenn Milne, 'Hawke rebukes Button over leadership gaffe', *The Australian*, 8 February 1990, p. 2.

22 Milton Cockburn, 'They're off to a March 24 poll', *The Sydney Morning Herald*, 17 February 1990, p. 1.

23 ANOP, 'ALP Themes and Election Position: ANOP Strategy Note for the 1990 Federal Election', RH16, Box 5, Folder 54, BHPML.

24 Interviews with Cameron and Gibbs, Sydney, 8 March 2020.

25 Simon Balderstone to Bob Hogg, 'Environment Statement', 2 November 1988, ALP National Secretariat Papers, MS 4985, 2005 Consignment, Box 52, Folder 'Elections – Federal Election – Strategy (2)', NLA.

26 Cabinet Minute, 'Submission 6363 – Australian Response to the Greenhouse Effect and Related Climate Change', 3 April 1989, A14039/6363, NAA.

27 Bob Hawke to Paul Keating, 9 July 1990, A14039/7399, NAA.

28 Cabinet Memorandum, 'Negotiations for a Convention on Climate Change – Progress Report', 16 December 1991, A14039/8486, NAA.

29 Interview with Kelly, Sydney, 27 November 2019.

30 Interview with Brown, via phone, 25 June 2021.

31 Interview with Cassidy, Melbourne, 10 October 2019.

32 Paul Kelly, 'Peacock a "danger in the Lodge"', *The Australian*, 9 March 1990, p. 1.

33 Interview with Kelly, Sydney, 10 November 2019.

34 Tony Wright, 'Hawke: no false hopes', *The Canberra Times*, 9 March 1990, p. 1.

35 Margaret Gibbs, 'Groups: 18–19 December 1989, Sydney', ALP National Secretariat Papers, MS 4985, 2005 Consignment, Box 51, Folder 'Elections – Federal Election – Research', NLA.

36 Margaret Gibbs, 'Groups: Melbourne, Brisbane, Sydney, 19–21 March 1990', ALP National Secretariat Papers, MS 4985, 2005 Consignment, Box 51, Folder 'Elections – Federal Election – Research', NLA.

37 Paul Keating to Bob Hawke, 23 March 1990, RH16, Box 5, Folder 58, BHPML.

38 Interview with Peacock, via phone, 8 November 2016.

39 Interview with Eggleton, via email, 8 March 2021.

40 Bob Hogg, 'Campaign Director's Report 1990 Federal Election', 6 July 1990, RH18, Box 9, Folder 124, BHPML.

41 Interview with Cameron, Sydney, 8 March 2020.

42 Minutes of the FPLP, 3 April 1990, NLA.

43 Interview with Richardson, Sydney, 3 September 2019.

44 Bob Hawke, Media Briefing on the 1990–91 Cabinet Papers, Sydney, 4 December 2015. The author was present.

45 Brendan Nicholson, 'Graham Richardson fires up at Bob Hawke barb', *The Australian*, 2 January 2016.

46 Interview with Richardson, Sydney, 3 September 2019.

47 Richardson, *Whatever It Takes*, p. 283.

48 Carr, Diary, 9 April 1990.

49 Interview with Hawke, Sydney, 8 December 2015.

50 Interview with Willis, Melbourne, 12 December 2018.

51 Interview with Ray, Melbourne, 19 November 2019.

52 Interview with Kerin, via phone, 1 November 2019.

53 Interview with Peacock, via phone, 8 November 2016.

54 Interview with Hawke, Sydney, 8 December 2015.

55 Mike Codd to Bob Hawke, 'Commonwealth-State Rationalisation', 7 August 1987. This was provided to the author by Mike Codd.

56 Mike Codd to Bob Hawke, 'The Federal System', 20 April 1990. This was provided to the author by Mike Codd.

57 Departments of Treasury, Finance, Prime Minister and Cabinet, Industrial Relations, 'Furthering State Involvement in Microeconomic Reform', Cabinet Memorandum, 2 June 1990, A14039/7152, NAA.

58 Interview with Codd, Williamsdale, 22 July 2019.

59 Interview with Nick Greiner, Sydney, 4 June 2018.

60 Interview with Sims, Sydney, 17 December 2019.

61 Interview with Fatin, Perth, 12 December 2019.

62 Bob Hawke, *Building a Competitive Australia*, Parliamentary Statement, HoR, 12 March 1991.

63 Cabinet Minute, 'Submission 7327 – Structural Relationship Among the Three Telecommunications Carriers', 'Submission 7329 – Public Mobile Phone Services', 'Submission 7330 – AUSTEL Funding and Cost Recovery', 10 September 1990, A14039/7327, NAA.

64 Kelly, *The End of Certainty*, p. 617.

65 Interview with Beazley, Sydney, 30 June 2016. See also Robert Ray, 'The Recession We Had to Have', *Labor in Power*, ABC TV, 29 June 1993.

66 Richardson, *Whatever It Takes*, p. 307.

67 Bob Hawke, Speech to ALP Special National Conference, 24 September 1990, RH 18, Box 9, Folder 128, BHPML.

68 Interview with Hurford, via phone, 8 November 2019.

69 See Bramston, *For the True Believers*, pp. 90–94.

70 Katharine Betts, 'Immigration Policy Under the Howard Government', *Australian Journal of Social Issues*, vol. 38, no. 2, May 2003, p. 173.

71 Interview with Gerry Hand, via phone, 28 February 2021.

72 Interview with Patrick Dodson, via phone, 21 July 2021.

73 Interview with Hand, via phone, 28 February 2021.

74 Interview with Dodson, via phone, 21 July 2021.

75 Tony Wright, 'Message "very fitting" last act for Hawke', *The Canberra Times*, 21 December 1991, p. 1.

76 Interview with Simon Balderstone, Sydney, 23 September 2019.

77 Charles Perkins was the first Indigenous Australian to become a permanent head of a federal government department. He had a prickly relationship with Hawke. He resigned as secretary of the Department of Aboriginal Affairs in November 1988 after allegations of maladministration were made against him, which were never substantiated.

78 Charles Perkins, 'Conserving Power', *Labor in Power*.

79 Interview with Hand, via phone, 28 February 2021.

80 Interview with Dodson, via phone, 21 July 2021.

81 Interview with Hawke, Sydney, 20 December 2012.

82 Paul Keating, 'Economic Situation and Outlook', Cabinet Submission, 11 May 1990, A14039/7054, NAA.

83 Interview with Willis, Melbourne, 12 December 2018.

84 Minutes of the FPLP, 28 August 1990, NLA.

85 Interview with Mark Ryan, Sydney, 6 August 2014.

86 Bob Hawke, 'The Recession We Had to Have', *Labor in Power*.

87 Liz Hickson, 'Bob and Hazel: "This is a very happy time for us"', *The Australian Women's Weekly*, October 1989, pp. 6–7.

88 Paul Mann, 'Bob Hawke: "I'm a better grandfather than I was father"', *New Idea*, 11 July 1987, p. 10.

89 Glenn Milne, 'Hero Hazel or just another media Hawke?', *The Australian*, 15 February 1990, p. 15.

Chapter 28

1 Cabinet Minute, Decision No. 76 11989, 'Submission No. 6060 – New Parliament House – Report No. 15 77 and Minute 11974(GA) – March to May 1988', 7 November 1988, A14039/6060, NAA.

2 Interview with Hawke, Sydney, 10 December 2014.

3 Interview with Hollway, Sydney, 29 August 2019.

4 Interview with Hawke, Sydney, 14 December 2017.

5 Interview with Heseltine, Sydney, 22 June 2017.

6 Interview with Hawke, Sydney, 14 December 2017.

7 Ninian Stephen to Bob Hawke, 9 March 1989, PM Hawke Personal Papers, M3855/18, NAA.

8 Interview with Hawke, Sydney, 10 December 2014.

9 Interview with Hayden, Brisbane, 30 October 2014.

10 Interview with Hayden, Brisbane, 23 June 2017.

11 'Hayden "must give up" after royal snub', *The Canberra Times*, 7 August 1988, p. 3.

12 'Hawke and Howard discussed Hayden for G-G', *The Canberra Times*, 1 July 1988, p. 1.

13 William Heseltine, Diary, 10 May 1988. This was provided to the author by William Heseltine.

14 Cabinet Minute, Decision No. 11753 (M), 'Without Submission – Appointment of Governor-General', 17 August 1988, A13979/11753/M, NAA.

15 Interview with Heseltine, via email, 10 December 2020.

16 Interview with Hayden, via phone, 17 August 2020.

17 Access to these letters was provided to the author by Bill Hayden. They were designated as personal correspondence and closed until 16 February 2046. The High Court in *Hocking v Director-General of the National Archives of Australia* on 29 May 2020 judged vice-regal letters to be official records, meaning they should be released after twenty years. These letters should now be available for public access.

18 Bill Hayden to Queen Elizabeth II, 6 October 1989, Hayden Papers, MS 7624, Series 5/10, NLA.

19 William Heseltine to Bill Hayden, 23 October 1989, Hayden Papers, MS 7624, Series 5/10, NLA.

20 Bill Hayden to Queen Elizabeth II, 11 December 1989, Hayden Papers, MS 7624, Series 5/10, NLA.

21 Bill Hayden to Queen Elizabeth II, 10 April 1990, Hayden Papers, MS 7624, Series 5/10, NLA.

22 Bill Hayden to Queen Elizabeth II, 25 July 1990, Hayden Papers, MS 7624, Series 5/10, NLA.

23 William Heseltine to Bill Hayden, 12 January 1990, Hayden Papers, MS 7624, Series 5/10, NLA.

24 Bill Hayden to William Heseltine, 15 February 1990, Hayden Papers, MS 7624, Series 5/10, NLA.

25 Bill Hayden to William Heseltine, 18 April 1990, Hayden Papers, MS 7624, Series 5/10, NLA.

26 Bill Hayden to Queen Elizabeth II, 25 July and 2 November 1990, Hayden Papers, MS 7624, Series 5/10, NLA.

27 Robert Fellowes to Bill Hayden, 20 November 1990, Hayden Papers, MS 7624, Series 5/10, NLA.

28 Bill Hayden to Queen Elizabeth II, 5 March 1991, Hayden Papers, MS 7624, Series 5/10, NLA.

29 Bill Hayden to Queen Elizabeth II, 11 June 1991, Hayden Papers, MS 7624, Series 5/10, NLA.

30 Bill Hayden to Queen Elizabeth II, 8 July 1991, Hayden Papers, MS 7624, Series 5/10, NLA.

31 Robert Fellowes to Bill Hayden, 23 July 1991, Hayden Papers, MS 7624, Series 5/10, NLA.

32 Bill Hayden to Queen Elizabeth II, 13 September 1991, Hayden Papers, MS 7624, Series 5/10, NLA.

33 Bill Hayden to Queen Elizabeth II, 24 December 1991, Hayden Papers, MS 7624, Series 5/10, NLA.

34 Hayden, *Hayden*, p. 499.

35 Interview with Hayden, via phone, 26 June 2017.

Chapter 29

1 Interview with Ingham, via phone, 2 July 2019.
2 See Troy Bramston, 'Power of words', *The Weekend Australian*, 4 August 2018.
3 Interview with Hawke, Sydney, 5 July 2010.
4 George Bush and Bob Hawke, 9 August 1990, Presidential Telcon, GBPL.
5 It was reported at the time that Australia had proposed contributing to the naval blockade. However, the details of the Hawke–Bush phone call were not then known. See Paul Grigson, 'How we begged to go to the Gulf', *Sydney Morning Herald*, 1 September 1990, p. 1.
6 Bob Hawke, Transcript of Press Conference, Parliament House, Canberra, 10 August 1990.
7 HMAS *Sydney* and HMAS *Brisbane* relieved HMAS *Adelaide* and HMAS *Darwin* in December 1990, and HMAS *Westralia* relieved HMAS *Success* in January 1991.
8 Cabinet Minute, 'Middle East Deployment', 14 August 1990, A14039/7387, NAA.
9 Interview with Hawke, Sydney, 14 December 2017.
10 Interview with Bush, via email, 23 May 2018.
11 Interview with Hugh White, Canberra, 19 July 2019.
12 Interview with Keating, Sydney, 4 May 2021.
13 Interview with Hawke, 14 December 2017, Sydney. See also Hawke, *The Hawke Memoirs*, p. 512.
14 George Bush and Brian Mulroney, 9 August 1990, Presidential Telcon, GBPL.
15 Interview with Mulroney, via phone, 2 October 2020.
16 Interview with White, Canberra, 19 July 2019.
17 George Bush and Bob Hawke, 15 November 1990, Presidential Telcon, GBPL.
18 Paul Keating attended as deputy prime minister and John Button as the government's Senate leader.
19 Hawke, *The Hawke Memoirs*, p. 517.
20 Paul Keating, Statement, 12 October 1994.
21 Tony Wright, 'Keating crazy and a liar, says Hawke', *The Sydney Morning Herald*, 13 October 1994, p. 3.
22 John Button, Press Release, 13 October 1994.
23 Grigson, 'How we begged to go to the Gulf', p. 1.
24 The note says: 'Keating started arguing that we should not do anything: "What has the US ever done for us?"' See A-Z Files, Box 121, BHPML.
25 Interview with White, Canberra, 19 July 2019.
26 George Bush and Bob Hawke, 9 January 1991, Presidential Telcon, GBPL.
27 Bush, Diary, 16 January 1991, GBPL.
28 The record of this conversation is not available. George Bush and Bob Hawke, 16 January 1991, Presidential Telcon, GBPL.
29 Interview with Baker, via phone, 9 December 2020.
30 Interview with Evans, Canberra, 19 September 2019.
31 Interview with Ray, Melbourne, 19 November 2019.
32 Interview with Hand, via phone, 28 February 2021.
33 Glenn Milne, 'Retribution urged for ALP Senate rebels', *The Australian*, 24 January 1991, p. 4.

34 Bob Hogg to Mary Crawford, 11 February 1991, ALP National Secretariat Papers, MS 4985, 1997 Consignment, Box 559, NLA.
35 George Bush and Bob Hawke, 7 February 1991, Presidential Telcon, GBPL.
36 Bush, Diary, 7 February 1991, GBPL.
37 George Bush and Bob Hawke, 23 February 1991, Presidential Telcon, GBPL.
38 George Bush and Bob Hawke, 28 February 1991, Presidential Telcon, GBPL.
39 ASIO, 'ASIO Response to Gulf Crisis', 10 January 1991, ASIO Briefings and Documents, A6122/2914, NAA.
40 Interview with Hawke, Sydney, 14 December 2017. See also Hawke, *The Hawke Memoirs*, p. 525.
41 Interview with Bush, via email, 23 May 2018.
42 Interview with Baker, via phone, 9 December 2020.
43 Interview with Keating, Sydney, 4 May 2021.
44 Paul Keating to Bob Hawke, 24 September 2002, A-Z Files, Box 86, BHPML.
45 Hawke, *The Hawke Memoirs*, p. 526.
46 Peter Gration to Bob Hawke, 5 March 1991, PM Hawke Personal Papers, Personal Correspondence 1991, M3826/29, NAA.
47 'War lifts Hawke's approval rating', *The Australian*, 27 February 1991, p. 1.
48 'Hewson topples Hawke in poll', *The Australian*, 1 November 1990, p. 1.

Chapter 30
1   'Days in Office – Fraser and Hawke', PM Hawke Personal Papers, M3596/486, NAA.
2   Hawke, *The Hawke Memoirs*, pp. 497–98.
3   Interview with Evans, Canberra, 19 September 2019.
4   Richardson, *Whatever It Takes*, pp. 295–96.
5   Interview with Keating, Sydney, 4 May 2021.
6   Michael Gordon, *A True Believer: Paul Keating*, University of Queensland Press, St Lucia, 1996, pp. 3–11.
7   Don Russell said it was not an attack on Hawke. But Tom Mockridge, the only Keating staff member present, said it was. See Bramston, *Paul Keating*, pp. 356–57.
8   Interview with Grattan, Canberra, 7 August 2019.
9   Gordon, *A True Believer*, pp. 3–11.
10 Interview with Nihill, Canberra, 26 November 2019.
11 Bob Hawke, 'The Recession We Had to Have', *Labor in Power*.
12 Bob Hawke, Transcript of Doorstop, Sydney, 10 December 1990.
13 Interview with Cassidy, Melbourne, 10 October 2019.
14 Bob Hawke, 'The Recession We Had to Have', *Labor in Power*.
15 Interview with Cassidy, Melbourne, 10 October 2019.
16 Bob Hawke and Paul Keating, Joint Statement, 10 December 1990.
17 Bob Hawke, Transcript of Press Conference, Canberra, 11 December 1990.
18 Bob Hawke suggests there were two meetings with Paul Keating in this period – 31 January and 4 February – but recollections of what was said when seem to have become blurred with the passage of time.
19 Paul Keating, 'The Recession We Had to Have', *Labor in Power*.

20 Hawke, *The Hawke Memoirs*, p. 501.
21 Amanda Buckley, 'Keating keeps his Paris dream on the back-burner', *The Australian Financial Review*, 29 June 1987, p. 6.
22 Evans, *Inside the Hawke–Keating Government*, p. 51.
23 Bob Hawke recalled that this conversation took place at the Lodge. Interview with Hawke, Sydney, 10 December 2014.
24 Kelly, *The End of Certainty*, p. 626.
25 Interview with Keating, Sydney, 4 May 2021.
26 Interview with Parks, Canberra, 26 November 2019.
27 'Beazley seen as preferred option', *The Canberra Times*, 24 November 1990, p. 9.
28 'Hawke support stalls as Coalition holds lead', *The Australian*, 19 March 1991, p. 2.
29 'Keating's approval rating slips to record low', *The Australian*, 7 March 1991, p. 2.
30 Laurie Oakes, 'A very laborious coup', *The Bulletin*, 30 April 1991, p. 24.
31 Interview with Ray, via phone, 8 June 2016.
32 Interview with Beazley, Perth, 11 December 2019.
33 Interview with Evans, Canberra, 19 September 2019.
34 Gordon, *A True Believer*, p. 157.
35 Interview with Richardson, Sydney, 14 March 2016.
36 Bob Hawke recalled it was 'just before 6 pm' but most accounts place the initial discussions earlier, between 4.30 pm and 5.30 pm. Hawke's meeting with Wayne Goss, Kevin Rudd and Bill Ludwig was scheduled for 4.30 pm. See Hawke, *The Hawke Memoirs*, p. 503.
37 Interview with Richardson, Canberra, 23 August 2019.
38 Colin Parks to Troy Bramston, via email, 6 August 2021.
39 Bob Hawke recalled saying to Paul Keating: 'As you can see, I've got people here, and when I've finished with them, I'll see you.' But this is disputed by Parks. See Bob Hawke, 'The Sweetest Victory', *Labor in Power*, ABC TV, 6 July 1993.
40 Interview with Keating, Sydney, 17 December 2014.
41 Bob Hawke, 'The Sweetest Victory', *Labor in Power*.
42 Interview with Parks, Canberra, 26 November 2019. See also Colin Parks, 'Hawke: the verdict', *The Sunday Age*, 21 August 1994, p. 13.
43 Interview with Kevin Rudd, via phone, 24 April 2020.
44 Parks to Bramston, via email, 6 August 2021.
45 Edwards, *Keating*, p. 432.
46 Interview with Oakes, via phone, 10 December 2015.
47 Paul Keating, Note of Meeting at Kirribilli, 29 May 1991. This was provided to the author by Paul Keating.
48 Paul Keating, Note Given to Richardson, 29 May 1991. This was provided to the author by Paul Keating.
49 Parks to Bramston, via email, 6 August 2021.
50 Interview with Kelty, Melbourne, 11 February 2014.
51 Interview with Kelty, Melbourne, 28 March 2019.
52 Interview with Crean, Melbourne, 1 February 2019.
53 Bob Hawke, Special Caucus Meeting, 31 May 1991, PM Hawke Personal Papers, M3594/74, NAA. See also Minutes of the FPLP, 31 May 1991, NLA.

54 Interview with Michael Lee, Sydney, 11 May 2014.
55 Minutes of the FPLP, 31 May 1991, NLA.
56 Kelly, *The End of Certainty*, p. 633.
57 Interview with Lee, Sydney, 11 May 2014.
58 Richardson, *Whatever It Takes*, p. 318.
59 Paul Keating, Statement – Caucus Meeting, 31 May 1991.
60 Minutes of the FPLP, 31 May 1991, NLA.
61 Interview with Gary Punch, Sydney, 21 June 2016.
62 Hawke, *The Hawke Memoirs*, p. 505.
63 Interview with Hewson, Sydney, 10 June 2014.
64 Interview with Peacock, via phone, 26 June 2015.
65 Interview with Howard, Sydney, 17 December 2014.
66 Editorial, 'Hawke should stand aside', *The Sydney Morning Herald*, 1 June 1991, p. 22.
67 Editorial, 'It should be Keating', *The Age*, 3 June 1991, p. 13.
68 Editorial, 'It's time, Mr Hawke', *The Australian Financial Review*, 3 June 1991, p. 16.
69 Christine Wallace, 'Newspapers drop PM over fears of Left', *The Australian*, 3 June 1991, p. 4.
70 'What the papers say', *The Sydney Morning Herald*, 3 June 1991, p. 5.
71 Editorial, 'Whatever the outcome, Hawke's leadership is done', *The Courier-Mail*, 1 June 1991, p. 30.
72 'Bad news for Keating in poll', *The Sunday Telegraph*, 2 June 1991, p. 4.
73 Denis Muller, 'Hawke preferred to Keating, poll shows', *The Age*, 1 June 1991, p. 1.
74 Minutes of the FPLP, 3 June 1991, NLA.
75 Bob Hawke, Transcript of News Conference, 3 June 1991, Canberra.
76 Bob Hawke, Handwritten Note, 19 December 1991, PM Hawke Personal Papers, M3594/73, NAA.
77 Interview with Keating, Sydney, 4 May 2021.
78 Paul Keating did not attend the caucus meeting.
79 Bob Hawke could not appoint an acting treasurer because there was no treasurer. He was advised that he had to appoint a treasurer, so he appointed himself while caucus elections were held and he consulted about the make-up of the new ministry.
80 Interview with Willis, Melbourne, 12 December 2018.
81 Interview with Keating, Sydney, 21 December 2015.
82 Interview with Cassidy, Melbourne, 10 October 2019.

Chapter 31
1 Bob Hawke, Speech to ALP Centenary Conference, 26 June 1991.
2 Nick Bolkus, Ros Kelly, Robert Tickner, Alan Griffiths, 'Cabinet Submission 7994 – Response to the Resource Assessment Commission (RAC) Inquiry into Use of Resources of Kakadu Conservation Zone', 24 May, A14039/7994, NAA.
3 Interview with Balderstone, Sydney, 23 September 2019.
4 Interview with Nick Bolkus, via phone, 7 July 2021.
5 Interview with Kelly, Sydney, 27 November 2019.
6 Bob Hawke, Cabinet Notes, 18 June 1991, A-Z Files, BHPML.

7   Interview with Kelly, Sydney, 27 November 2019.
8   Robert Ray, 'The Sweetest Victory', *Labor in Power.*
9   Bob Collins on Kim Beazley, 'The Sweetest Victory', *Labor in Power.*
10 Bob Collins, 'The Sweetest Victory', *Labor in Power.*
11 Cabinet Minute, 'Response to the Resource Assessment Commission (RAC) Inquiry into Use of Resources of Kakadu Conservation Zone', 18 June 1991, A14039/7994, NAA.
12 Hawke, *The Hawke Memoirs*, p. 510.
13 Interview with Howe, 9 October 2019, Melbourne.
14 Bob Hawke, Caucus Notes, 20 June 1991, A-Z Files, BHPML.
15 Minutes of the FPLP, 20 June 1991, NLA.
16 Transcript, *The Midday Show*, Nine Network, 17 July 1991.
17 Transcript, *Four Corners*, ABC TV, 19 August 1991.
18 Denis Muller, 'Hawke preferred to Keating, poll shows', *The Age*, 1 June 1991, p. 1.
19 Peter Hartcher, 'Keating creeps up on PM', *The Sydney Morning Herald*, 17 August 1991, p. 1.
20 Glenn Milne, 'Keating anti-PM plan put on hold', *The Weekend Australian*, 9 November 1991, p. 1.
21 Interview with Hewson, Sydney, 10 June 2014.
22 Minutes of the FPLP, 26 November 1991, NLA.
23 Philip McIntosh, 'Coalition support surges after package', *The Sydney Morning Herald*, 27 November 1991, p. 4.
24 Interview with Andrew Robb, Sydney, 8 July 2015.
25 Interview with Hewson, Sydney, 10 June 2014.
26 The deficit blew out to $12.6 billion.
27 Interview with Kerin, via email, 18 December 2015.
28 John Fraser to John Kerin, 'Timing of the Budget Speech', Treasury Minute Paper, 25 July 1991. This was provided to the author with John Kerin's permission.
29 Minutes of the FPLP, 10 October 1991, NLA.
30 Interview with Howe, via email, 17 June 2016.
31 Bob Hawke, Statement of the Economy and Employment, HoR, 14 November 1991.
32 Interview with Parks, Canberra, 26 November 2019.
33 Interview with Kerin, via phone, 1 November 2019.
34 Interview with Kerin, via email, 18 December 2015.
35 Interview with Howe, Melbourne, 9 October 2019.
36 Interview with Terry Sheahan, Sydney, 15 March 2016.
37 Interview with Freudenberg, Sydney, 9 November 2015.
38 Interview with Carr, Sydney, 31 October 2019.
39 'Australians give thumbs down to Hawke', *The Canberra Times*, 14 December 1991, p. 11.
40 Geoff Kitney, 'Looking for a revitalised Prime Minister', *The Australian Financial Review*, 9 December 1991, p. 1.
41 Peter Hartcher, Tom Burton and Pilita Clark, 'Hawke's last days', *The Sydney Morning Herald*, 12 December 1991, p. 1.
42 Alan Ramsey, 'They come to bury Caesar', *The Sydney Morning Herald*, 12 December 1991, p. 1.

43 Robert Ray, 'The Sweetest Victory', *Labor in Power*.

44 Interview with Beazley, Perth, 11 December 2019.

45 Interview with Duffy, Melbourne, 9 October 2019.

46 Interview with Hand, via phone, 28 February 2021.

47 Interview with Bolkus, Adelaide, 18 August 2016.

48 Gareth Evans, 'The Sweetest Victory', *Labor in Power*.

49 Hawke, *The Hawke Memoirs*, p. 555.

50 Interview with Ray, via phone, 8 June 2016.

51 Amanda Buckley, 'Hawke refuses to quit', *The Daily Telegraph Mirror*, 13 December 1991, pp. 1–2.

52 Interview with Ray, via phone, 8 June 2016.

53 Interview with Bolkus, Adelaide, 18 August 2016.

54 Cheryl Critchley, 'Bob's bad day ends with a shout', *The Daily Telegraph Mirror*, 13 December 1991, p. 2.

55 Interview with Keating, Sydney, 21 December 2015.

56 Interview with Beazley, Sydney, 30 June 2016.

57 John Button, 'Notes of Discussion with RJ Hawke re Leadership', 17 December 1991, Button Papers, MS 13728, Box 9, Folder 4, SLV. See also Button, *As It Happened*, p. 237.

58 Interview with Beazley, Sydney, 30 June 2016.

59 Interview with McMullan, Canberra, 21 July 2016.

60 Interview with Ray, via phone, 8 June 2016.

61 Interview with Nihill, Canberra, 26 November 2019.

62 'Hawke's approval drops to all-time low', *The Bulletin*, 17 December 1991, p. 16.

63 'Keating closing fast in new poll', *The Sydney Morning Herald*, 14 December 1991, p. 1.

64 Ben Humphreys joined the cabinet in May 1992 but was dumped from the ministry altogether after the March 1993 election.

65 Interview with Fatin, Perth, 12 December 2019.

66 Peter Baldwin to Troy Bramston, via email, 12 December 2019.

67 Interview with Kerin, via phone, 1 November 2019.

68 Interview with Jennie George, via email, 13 September 2021.

69 Interview with Martin Ferguson, via phone, 17 September 2021.

70 Interview with Richardson, Canberra, 23 August 2019.

71 Interview with Saunders, Sydney, 5 December 2019.

72 HoR, *Hansard*, 19 December 1991, p. 3769.

73 Minutes of the FPLP, 19 December 1991, NLA.

74 Interview with Ray, via phone, 8 June 2016.

75 Interview with Punch, Sydney, 21 June 2016.

76 Minutes of the FPLP, 19 December 1991, NLA.

77 Minutes of the FPLP, 19 December 1991, NLA.

78 Interview with Hawke, Sydney, 5 May 2004.

79 Interview with Nihill, Canberra, 26 November 2019.

80 Interview with Parks, Canberra, 26 November 2019.

81 Interview with Richardson, Canberra, 23 August 2019.

82 Interview with Howard, Sydney, 19 February 2016.

83 Bob Hawke, Press Conference, 19 December 1991.

84 Bill Hayden to Troy Bramston, via email, 5 November 2014.

85 Bill Hayden to Queen Elizabeth II, 24 December 1991, Hayden Papers, MS 7624, Series 5/10, NLA.
86 Interview with Beazley, Perth, 11 December 2019.
87 Interview with Ray, Melbourne, 19 November 2019.
88 Neal Blewett told me that he would not have resigned from cabinet, nor does he believe that John Button and Peter Cook would have resigned either. Neal Blewett to Troy Bramston, via email, 11 March 2021.
89 Ros Kelly told me she would not have resigned from cabinet. Ros Kelly to Troy Bramston, via email, 20 March 2021.
90 Interview with Freudenberg, via phone, 3 February 2017.
91 Interview with Hawke, Sydney, 8 December 2015.
92 Interview with Keating, Sydney, 21 December 2015.
93 Interview with Keating, Sydney, 22 October 2019.
94 HoR, *Hansard*, 19 December 1991, p. 3867.
95 Interview with Hewson, via phone, 7 July 2021.
96 Interview with Richardson, Canberra, 23 August 2019.
97 Walter Bagehot, 'The Character of Sir Robert Peel', in Mrs Russell Barrington (ed), *The Works and Life of Walter Bagehot*, Longmans, Green, and Co., London, 1915, pp. 179–81.

Chapter 32

1   Interview with Bolkus, Adelaide, 18 August 2016.
2   Joanne Gray, 'Hawke v media: battle goes on', *The Australian Financial Review*, 11 August 1992, p. 12.
3   Deborah Cameron, 'Spare a room for an old PM?', *The Sydney Morning Herald*, 15 February 1992.
4   Bush, Diary, 3 January 1992, GBPL.
5   Paul Keating, Statement, 20 February 1992.
6   Joanne Gray, 'Hawke hits cash-dash hurdle', *The Australian Financial Review*, 10 August 1992, p. 16.
7   Interview with Tamburrino, via phone, 26 February 2021.
8   Interview with Aaron Rule, via phone, 20 September 2021.
9   Marian Wilkinson, 'Life after the Lodge', *The Weekend Australian*, 30–31 July 1994, p. 25.
10 Paul Keating to Bob Hawke, 10 January 1992, A-Z Files, BHPML.
11 Interview with James Erskine, via phone, 9 August 2021.
12 Gray, 'Hawke hits cash-dash hurdle', p. 16.
13 Hawke donated his $35,000 fee for the Somalia program to World Vision. See Anne McKendry to Richard Super, 6 October 1992, A-Z Files, Box 160, BHPML.
14 BBC Contract, 30 June 1993, A-Z Files, Box 214, BHPML.
15 Bob Hawke to Don Bradman, 29 October 1992, A-Z Files, Box 213, BHPML.
16 Don Bradman to Bob Hawke, 25 October 1992, A-Z Files, Box 213, BHPML.
17 Don Bradman to Bob Hawke, 4 November 1992, A-Z Files, Box 213, BHPML.
18 Don Bradman to Bob Hawke, 2 December 1992, A-Z Files, Box 213, BHPML.

19 Don Bradman to Bob Hawke, 25 December 1992, A-Z Files, Box 213, BHPML.
20 The Martin–Bradman interview, *87 Not Out*, aired in May 1996. See Martin, *Ray*, pp. 338–40.
21 Dennis Grant to Bob Hawke, 18 October 1995, A-Z Files, Box 76, BHPML.
22 The publishing agreement was signed with Reed International Books Australia, with William Heinemann as the imprint. Reed was sold to Random House in 1997.
23 Craig Emerson to Bob Hawke, 10 January 1994, RH45, Box 15, BHPML.
24 Ross Garnaut to Bob Hawke, 2 May 1994, RH45, Box 12, BHPML.
25 Interview with Saunders, Sydney, 5 December 2019.
26 Interview with Erskine, via phone, 9 August 2021.
27 Memo from Mark McCormack to James Erskine, 23 August 1993 and Memo from James Erskine to Mark McCormack, 25 August 1993, Mark McCormack Papers, MS700, University of Massachusetts Amherst Libraries.
28 Interview with Erskine, via phone, 9 August 2021.
29 Cameron Forbes, Gary Hughes and Tony Parkinson, 'Past PMs agree on winner', *The Weekend Australian*, 13 March 1993, p. 8.
30 Philip Chubb to Bob Hawke, 28 October 1991, A-Z Files, Box 78, BHPML.
31 Joshua Black, 'A Life Triumphantly Written: Producing the Hawke Legacy, 1979–2019', *ANU Historical Journal II: Number 2*, ANU Press, Canberra, 2020, p. 91.
32 Paul Chamberlain, 'ALP fury as Hawke tips Downer to be next PM', *The Sydney Morning Herald*, 27 June 1994, p. 1.
33 Tony Wright, 'Bob's shout at the Mandela inauguration', *The Sydney Morning Herald*, 1 July 1994, p. 1.
34 Sally Loane, 'Bob gives rancour a rest for the day', *The Sydney Morning Herald*, 17 August 1994, p. 1.
35 Geoffrey Barker and Innes Willox, 'PM hits back at Hawke', *The Age*, 24 June 1994, p. 1.
36 Bob Hawke, Press Statement, 24 June 1994, RH45, Box 2, BHPML.
37 David Humphries, 'PM's unpopularity a problem: Hawke', *The Australian*, 16 August 1994, p. 1.
38 This calculation is based on sales figures, royalty statements and the publishing contract. See Memoirs File, RH45, Box 18, BHPML.
39 Interview with Erskine, via phone, 9 August 2021.
40 Sandy Grant to Troy Bramston, via text, 26 October 2021.
41 Hawke, *My Own Life*, p. 232.
42 D'Alpuget, *Hawke*, p. 371.
43 'Affairs of the heart', *The 7.30 Report*, ABC TV, 13 July 2010.
44 Interview with McCarthy, Sydney, 5 November 2019.
45 Pieters-Hawke, *Hazel*, pp. 320, 348–50.
46 Interview with Pieters-Hawke, Sydney, 5 March 2020.
47 'Hawkes to split up after 38 years', *The Canberra Times*, 30 November 1994.
48 Interview with Pieters-Hawke, Sydney, 5 March 2020.
49 D.D. McNicoll, 'Nothing but tears for Bob without Hazel', *The Australian*, 1 December 1994, p. 1.
50 Lisa Carty, 'Bob's new love', *Illawarra Mercury*, 2 January 1995, p. 1.

51 Sue Williams, 'Hawke, d'Alpuget sell story for $200,000', *The Australian*, 2 February 1995, p. 1.

52 Neil Chenoweth, 'Hawke Inc: the silver bodgie's midas touch', *The Australian Financial Review*, 30 March 1994, p. 1.

53 Interview with Beattie, Sydney, 4 November 2019.

54 Neal Blewett, 'Robert James Lee Hawke', in Michelle Grattan (ed.), *Australian Prime Ministers (revised edition)*, New Holland Publishers, Sydney, 2016, p. 405.

55 Interview with Kelty, Melbourne, 28 March 2019.

56 Interview with George, via email, 13 September 2021.

57 Gordon, *A True Believer*, p. 316.

58 Martin Chulov, 'Hawke the peacemaker', *The Sun-Herald*, 19 November 1995, p. 1. This was provided to the author by Paul Keating.

59 Michael Gordon, 'Bizarre slap in the face for Keating', *The Australian*, 20 November 1995, p. 1.

60 Interview with Kelty, Melbourne, 28 March 2019.

Chapter 33

1 Mike Steketee, 'All is forgiven: Bob did a fine job', *The Weekend Australian*, 29–30 November 1997, pp. 1–2.

2 Interview with Keating, Sydney, 13 August 2016.

3 Nicholas Way and David Forman, 'Labor buries Keating', *Business Review Weekly*, 3 March 1997, pp. 41–45.

4 Interview with Beazley, Sydney, 30 June 2016.

5 Interview with Hawke, Sydney, 29 August 2018.

6 Interview with Keating, Sydney, 27 August 2016.

7 Interview with Hawke, Sydney, 20 December 2013.

8 Bob Hawke, Life Membership Presentation Speech, 1 August 2009, ALP National Conference, Sydney.

9 Interviews with Hawke, Sydney, 5 June 2014 and 29 August 2018.

10 During Hawke's prime ministership, union membership fell from 50 per cent of the workforce in 1983 to a still sizeable 40 per cent by 1991.

11 Interviews with Hawke, Sydney, 20 December 2013 and 8 December 2015.

12 'Australian elder statesmen attack racism', BBC News Online, 31 August 1998.

13 Bob Hawke, 'Lies and deceit litter road to war', *The Australian*, 19 March 2003, p. 13.

14 Interview with Malcolm Turnbull, via email, 13 July 2021.

15 Interview with Hawke, Sydney, 29 August 2018. See also Glenn Milne, 'Malcolm Turnbull wanted to join Labor', *The Sunday Telegraph*, 23 August 2009.

16 Interview with Turnbull, via email, 13 July 2021.

17 Interview with Hawke, Sydney, 25 August 2015.

18 Interview with Rudd, via phone, 24 April 2020.

19 Interview with Saunders, Sydney, 5 December 2019.

20 In 1992, Gough Whitlam said of Bob Hawke: 'He had one objective in public life and that was to become prime minister and when he got there, he had no purpose.' Hawke called Whitlam a 'sour old man'. See Errol Simper, 'The battle for history', *The Weekend Australian*, 5–6 September 1992, p. 18.

21 Interview with Scott Morrison, via email, 26 October 2021.

22 Interview with Turnbull, via email, 13 July 2021.

23 Interview with Tony Abbott, via phone, 8 July 2021.

24 Interview with Julia Gillard, Sydney, 7 February 2020.

25 Interview with Rudd, via phone, 24 April 2020.

26 Interview with Howard, Sydney, 17 March 2021.

27 Bob Hawke to John Howard, 16 December 2004, A-Z Files, Box 11, BHPML.

28 John Howard to Bob Hawke, 19 December 2004, A-Z Files, Box 11, BHPML.

29 Interview with D'Alpuget, Sydney, 20 February 2020.

30 Blanche d'Alpuget, *Bob Hawke: The Complete Biography*, Simon & Schuster, Cammeray, 2019, p. 916.

31 Susan Pieters-Hawke was unhappy with Blanche d'Alpuget's portrayal of Hazel in her book *Hawke: The Prime Minister*. See Rachel Browne, 'Hawke's daughter tells more', *The Sydney Morning Herald*, 23 October 2011.

32 Interview with McCarthy, Sydney, 5 November 2019.

33 Kate Legge, 'Moment of peace as Bob sang for Hazel, but first lady had last word', *The Weekend Australian*, 25 May 2013.

34 Interview with Hawke, Perth, 11 December 2019.

35 Natasha Robinson, '"Generosity of spirit" in Hazel Hawke's lifetime of memories', *The Australian*, 26 June 2013.

36 Last Will and Testament of Hazel Hawke, 18 October 1999.

37 Robert James Lee Hawke and Blanche d'Alpuget, Deed of Agreement, 22 December 2009.

38 Will of Robert James Lee Hawke, 11 April 2016.

39 Blanche d'Alpuget to Susan Pieters-Hawke, Stephen Hawke, Rosslyn Dillon and Louis Pratt, 18 June 2019.

40 Interview with D'Alpuget, Sydney, 20 February 2020.

41 Affidavit of Rosslyn Dillon, 6 December 2019.

42 Samantha Maiden, 'Bob Hawke's daughter Rosslyn Dillon settles multi-million dollar claim against his will', news.com.au, 22 May 2020.

43 Interview with D'Alpuget, via phone, 17 September 2021.

44 Interview with Emerson, via phone, 15 July 2021.

45 Interview with Keating, Sydney, 4 May 2021.

46 Bob Hawke & Derek Rielly, *Wednesdays with Bob*, Pan Macmillan, Sydney, 2017, pp. 144–45.

47 Interview with Keating, Sydney, 17 December 2014.

48 Paul Keating to Bob Hawke, 12 July 2010. This was provided to the author by Paul Keating.

49 Peter Hartcher, 'Bob Hawke and Paul Keating reunite for the first time in 28 years to endorse Labor's economic plan', *The Sydney Morning Herald*, 7 May 2019, p. 1.

50 Interview with Keating, Sydney, 4 May 2021.

Chapter 34

1   Here, I draw on D'Alpuget, *Bob Hawke*, pp. 919–21.

2   Interview with D'Alpuget, Sydney, 20 February 2020.

3 Interview with Emerson, via phone, 15 July 2021.
4 Scott Morrison, Media Statement, 16 May 2019.
5 Bill Shorten, Statement, 16 May 2019.
6 Here, I draw on Troy Bramston, 'Perfect setting for Bob Hawke final bow', *The Weekend Australian*, 15 June 2019, p. 6.

Epilogue
1 Interview with Hawke, Sydney, 29 August 2018.
2 Interview with Hawke, Sydney, 8 December 2015.
3 Interviews with Hawke, Sydney, 20 December 2013 and 29 August 2018.
4 Interviews with Hawke, Sydney, 20 December 2013, 8 December 2015 and 29 August 2018.

ACKNOWLEDGEMENTS

A fortnight after Bob Hawke's death, I visited his thirteenth-floor office at 100 William Street in Sydney. I was invited by Jill Saunders, his long-time executive assistant and office manager, to look over a few files as the office was being packed up. The best place to sit was, somewhat uncomfortably, at Hawke's vacant desk. His corner office overlooked Sydney's Domain and Royal Botanic Garden out to Sydney Harbour. There were several landscape paintings on the walls and a frame of Indigenous artefacts. A photo of Hawke with Nelson Mandela sat atop a shelf next to one of John Curtin. Volumes of *Hansard* framed a television and video player. Another bookshelf held tomes on history, politics and policy. A copy of the 1991 Budget Papers and the *Building a Competitive Australia* statement were perpetual reminders of his final year as prime minister. I turned over the yellowed pages of Hazel Hawke's scrapbooks, looked at family letters and drawings that Susan, Stephen and Rosslyn had sent to their father in the 1960s, and read Clem Hawke's unpublished memoir, loosely bound in a brown leather folder. There were files from Hawke's union and early parliamentary days, including lists drawn up for the challenge against Bill Hayden in mid-1982. This was an immense privilege.

Writing a biography about Bob Hawke has been challenging but also rewarding. It is an honour to be trusted by Hawke to write his unauthorised full-life biography with his cooperation. This would not have been possible without Jill, who served Hawke devotedly for more than thirty-five years. I owe her a debt of gratitude for scheduling my interviews with Hawke and providing access to his papers. Graham Evans, who ran Hawke's prime ministerial office, offered me much encouragement while I was writing this book. He answered many queries and asked others to talk to me, and I shall always be thankful for this. Jeff Townsend, who was Hawke's senior private secretary, also gave me encouragement and assistance, including over an unforgettable long lunch at Potts Point. Jane Angel and her team at the Bob Hawke Prime Ministerial Library, including Karen Mattingly, Kate Sergeant and Gillian Yeend, were very helpful in facilitating my visits and responding to requests for archival material.

I interviewed Hawke's family and friends, ministers, staff, party and union colleagues, senior public servants, journalists and business associates. Some have never given interviews before. Some remained off the record. I especially thank Blanche d'Alpuget, Susan Pieters-Hawke and Stephen Hawke for agreeing to interviews. This was not easy for them, and I appreciate their frankness. Paul Keating has never been interviewed for a book about Hawke before, so I am grateful that he agreed for this one. Bill Hayden offered his complete backing for this project, and it has been a pleasure to interview him and receive his occasional phone calls. It has been an honour to conduct new interviews with Scott Morrison and former prime ministers John Howard, Kevin Rudd, Julia Gillard, Tony Abbott and Malcolm Turnbull. Sadly, several people who were interviewed for this book are no longer with us. A number remain vivid in my memory: my friends Graham Freudenberg and Susan Ryan, the inimitable Bob Sorby, the incomparable Andrew Peacock and the remarkable George Shultz, who spoke to me via Zoom as he approached the age of 100. And, of course, Hawke himself.

I conducted new interviews with 115 people for this book. For their insights and reflections, I acknowledge and thank: Tony Abbott, Gillian Appleton, James Baker, Simon Balderstone, David Barnett, Peter Barron, Peter Beattie, Kim Beazley, Neal Blewett, Nick Bolkus, John Bowan, Bob Brown, John Brown, Meredith Burgmann, George H.W. Bush, Mary Elizabeth Calwell, Rod

Cameron, Bob Carr, Barrie Cassidy, Mike Codd, David Combe, Chris Conybeare, Michael Costello, Simon Crean, Blanche d'Alpuget, Brian Dale, Rawdon Dalrymple, Denise Darlow, John Dawkins, Patrick Dodson, Alister Drysdale, Michael Duffy, Tony Eggleton, Paul Ellercamp, Craig Emerson, James Erskine, Gareth Evans, Graham Evans, Richard Farmer, Wendy Fatin, Martin Ferguson, Tamie Fraser, Graham Freudenberg, Josh Frydenberg, Ross Garnaut, Jennie George, Margaret Gibbs, Julia Gillard, Michelle Grattan, Don Grimes, Gerry Hand, Robert Hannaford, Bob Hawke, Stephen Hawke, Bill Hayden, William Heseltine, John Hewson, Bob Hogg, Sandy Hollway, John Howard, Brian Howe, Chris Hurford, Bernard Ingham, Rob Jolly, Barry Jones, Paul Keating, Paul Kelly, Ros Kelly, Bill Kelty, David Kemp, John Kerin, Neil Kinnock, Isi Leibler, Stephen Loosley, John Major, John Mant, Jan Marsh, Roger Martindale, Wendy McCarthy, Doug McClelland, Bob McMullan, Stephen Mills, Scott Morrison, Brian Mulroney, Paul Munro, Grant Nihill, Laurie Oakes, Col Parks, Andrew Peacock, Susan Pieters-Hawke, Charles Powell, Robert Ray, Dennis Richardson, Graham Richardson, Kevin Rudd, Aaron Rule, Susan Ryan, Jill Saunders, Steve Sedgwick, George Shultz, Kerry Sibraa, Rod Sims, Bob Sorby, Jim Spigelman, John Stone, Anne Summers, Mimi Tamburrino, Jeff Townsend, Malcolm Turnbull, Barrie Unsworth, Eric Walsh, Geoff Walsh, Hugh White, Ralph Willis and Richard Woolcott. I also drew on previous interviews I have undertaken for other books and articles in *The Australian*.

For organising access to archival material, I particularly thank: Sebastian Zwalf and Sandy Rippingale (Australian Labor Party); Catherine Ziegler and Beth Lonergan (Australian National University Archives); Zachary Roberts (George H.W. Bush Presidential Library and Museum); Sally Laming and Debbie Williamson (John Curtin Prime Ministerial Library); Edwina Jans, Daryl Karp, Nanette Louchart-Fletcher and Campbell Rhodes (Museum of Australian Democracy, Old Parliament House); Andrew Cairns, Louise Doyle and Anne McLean (National Archives of Australia); Catriona Anderson (National Library of Australia); Flora Chatt (Oxford University Archives); Sallie Davies (Perth Modernian Society Museum Association);

Antonia White (Rhodes Trust Archives, Oxford); Robin Darwall-Smith, The Master and Fellows (University College Archives, Oxford); and Paivi Lindsay (The Whitlam Institute).

For responding to my queries and providing assistance, I acknowledge: Louise Adler, Peter Baldwin, Joshua Black, John Blaxland, Chris Brown, Dale Budd, Kim Carr, Brenton Carson, Jim Chalmers, Greg Combet, Cameron Coventry, Annabel Crabb, Paul Dalgleish, Maggie Dawkins, Alexander Downer, Malcolm Farnsworth, Michael Fullilove, David Gibson, Patrick Gorman, John Graham, Sandy Grant, Simon Grose, Susan Grusovin, Ed Husic, Josh Klenbort, Cass Lawry, Chip Le Grand, Andrew Leigh, Nathan Lennon, Tom Lewis, Samantha Maiden, Gino Mandarino, Shane Mattiske, Robert McClelland, Daphne McKenzie, Ross McMullin, John Nethercote, Peter Nixon, Ben Oquist, Chris Patten, Tanya Plibersek, Nicholas Reece, Derek Rielly, Paul Ritchie, Ian Robertson, Jill Rowbotham, Basil Scaffidi, Linda Scott, Rosa Silvestro, Helen Smith, Paul Smith, Cameron Stewart, Paul Strangio, Garry Sturgess, Louise Swinn, Remy Varga, Felicity Wade, Christine Wallace, Denis White and Bruce Wolpe.

I am indebted to Ben Ball, a terrific publisher, who contracted this book for Penguin in 2017. The team at Penguin Random House, led by the brilliant Nikki Christer, have been wonderful to work with. Patrick Mangan has managed the book, and its author, with the utmost care, understanding and professionalism. I am very grateful to Julian Welch, who edited the manuscript and made many fine suggestions that improved the book.

I could not ask more of my colleagues at *The Australian*, who have been enthusiastic about this book and enabled me to take periods of leave to work on it without question. I especially acknowledge Chris Dore, Michelle Gunn, Helen Trinca, Jennifer Campbell, Georgina Windsor and Alan Howe. Milan Scepanovic went above and beyond to source photos for this book and has my deep appreciation.

Paul Kelly, my friend, colleague and collaborator, was a regular sounding board while I wrote this book, and his insights and judgements were invaluable. Paul, along with Stephen Loosley, read the manuscript and provided feedback, which was warmly welcomed.

This book is dedicated to my close friends John Degen, Kate Degen and Ben Heraghty. They have been steadfast in the loyalty and support they have given to me over many years. It is impossible to repay them. John and Kate also read the manuscript and their comments were highly valued.

This has been something of a family project. It has been rewarding to talk to my father, Jeff Bramston, and my mother, Michele Bramston, about the many issues I had to resolve in my mind about Hawke's life. My mother transcribed most of the interviews and offered useful suggestions on the manuscript. My daughter, Madison, and my son, Angus, helped with organising my papers and selecting photographs for this book. Madison also helped with fact-checking and transcribed several interviews, and it was fun to talk to her about these. With my wife, Nicky Seaby, the four of us travelled to Bordertown in January 2019 to see where Hawke was born, to visit the church manse where he lived and to quiz locals for stories about the Hawke family. Nicky, Madison and Angus put up with my absences and distractions as deadlines neared. My gratitude to the three of you is beyond words.

My beautiful and devoted wife, Nicky, was with me every step of the way as I researched and wrote this book. Whether it was on our walks, during Covid lockdowns or over the dinner table, she listened as my latest discoveries, ideas, judgements and challenges spooled out again and again. She was, as ever, reassuring and provided wise advice. I have not met anybody who is so kind, generous and loving. I consider myself the luckiest of men to be married to her.

PHOTOGRAPHY
CREDITS

p.1:   Baby Bob Hawke: News Corp Australia
p.1:   Young Bob Hawke: News Corp Australia
p.1:   Hawke Family: News Corp Australia
p.2:   Bob Hawke with Clem Hawke, circa 1941: News Corp Australia
p.2:   Bob Hawke in India in 1952: John Curtin Prime Ministerial Library
p.2:   Bob Hawke with Ellie Hawke in 1952: John Curtin Prime Ministerial Library
p.3:   Bob Hawke with Hazel Masterson on Panther motorbike in 1947–48: John Curtin Prime Ministerial Library
p.3:   Bob Hawke with Hazel Masterson and their van in England, 1953–54: Bob Hawke Prime Ministerial Library
p.3:   Bob Hawke and Hazel Masterson's wedding in 1956: John Curtin Prime Ministerial Library
p.4:   The Hawke Family in 1963: News Corp Australia
p.4:   Bob Hawke with Gough Whitlam in 1970: News Corp Australia
p.4:   Bob Hawke at his desk at the ACTU: News Corp Australia
p.5:   Bob Hawke and daughter Susan with Golda Meir in 1971: News Corp Australia
p.5:   Bob Hawke with Gough Whitlam and Clyde Holding: News Corp Australia
p.5:   Bob Hawke with Peter Abeles: Ray Strange/News Corp Australia
p.6:   Bob Hawke with Glenda Bowden in 1975: News Corp Australia
p.6:   Bob Hawke with Gough Whitlam in 1975: News Corp Australia
p.6:   Bob Hawke with John Moore, Harold Souter, George Polites, Gough Whitlam and Richard Kirby in 1977: News Corp Australia
p.7:   Bob Hawke with Blanche d'Alpuget and Richard Kirby in 1982: Graeme Thomson/News Corp Australia
p.7:   Bob Hawke campaigning in Wills in 1980: Stephen Cooper/News Corp Australia
p.7:   Bob Hawke with Hazel, Stephen, Rosslyn and Susan in 1982: Bob Hawke Prime Ministerial Library

657

p.7:   'Give Bob the Job' badge: Museum of Australian Democracy, Old Parliament House

p.8:   Bob Hawke with Bill Hayden in 1982: News Corp Australia

p.8:   'Bringing Australia Together' badge: Museum of Australian Democracy, Old Parliament House

p.8:   Bob Hawke at the National Tally Room in 1983: News Corp Australia

p.9:   Bob Hawke blazing a cigar in 1983: Ray Strange/News Corp Australia

p.9:   Bob Hawke with Paul Keating and Neville Wran in 1984: David Hickson/News Corp Australia

p.9:   Bob Hawke with Hazel Hawke at the piano in 1990: News Corp Australia

p.10: Graham Evans in 1983: Graham Evans

p.10: Bob Hawke with Lionel Bowen in 1983: News Corp Australia

p.10: Hawke Ministry in 1983: Bob Hawke Personal Collection

p.11: Bob Hawke with Malcolm Fraser in 1978: Graeme Thomson/News Corp Australia

p.11: Bob Hawke with Andrew Peacock in 1988: News Corp Australia

p.11: Bob Hawke with John Howard in 1988: Hugh Hartshorne/News Corp Australia

p.12: Bob Hawke after the America's Cup victory in 1983: News Corp Australia

p.12: Bob Hawke shedding tears after the Tiananmen Square crackdown in 1989: Graeme Thomson/News Corp Australia

p.12: Bob Hawke being hit in the face by a cricket ball in 1984: Graeme Thomson/News Corp Australia

p.13: Bob Hawke with Ronald Reagan in 1983: Bob Hawke Prime Ministerial Library

p.13: Bob Hawke with George H.W. Bush in 1986: Bob Hawke Prime Ministerial Library

p.13: Bob Hawke with Margaret Thatcher in 1986: Hulton Archive/News Corp Australia

p.14: Bob Hawke with Hu Yaobang in 1985: News Corp Australia

p.14: Bob Hawke with Mikhail Gorbachev in 1987: Bob Hawke Prime Ministerial Library

p.14: Bob Hawke with Nelson Mandela in 1990: Paul Johns/News Corp Australia

p.15: Bob Hawke with Blanche d'Alpuget on their wedding day in 1995: Nick Cubbin/News Corp Australia

p.15: Bob Hawke with Bill Kelty and Jennie George in 1995: Bob Finlayson/News Corp Australia

p.15: Bob Hawke with Kim Beazley in 2006: John Feder/News Corp Australia

p.16: Bob Hawke at the Woodford Folk Festival in 2014: Megan Slade/News Corp Australia

p.16: Bob Hawke at The Clock Hotel in 2017: Justin Lloyd/News Corp Australia

p.16: Bob Hawke with Paul Keating in 2018: Craig Emerson

INDEX

7.30 Report 404, 550
60 Minutes 411, 550, 552, 562
  Hawke guest reporter role 545
1929 Federal election 4
1943 Federal election 21
1958 Federal election 74
1961 Federal election 93
1963 Federal election 96, 99
1966 Federal election 151
1969 Federal election 126, 152
1972 Federal election 236
  campaign 153–5
  results 155
1974 Federal election 159, 160
1975 Federal election 166, 173
1977 Federal election 192, 193
  Labor campaign 194–5, 675
1980 Federal election 225, 226, 227
1983 Federal election 254
  election night 272–3, 274–5
  Fraser calling xviii, xxi–xxii, 254, 256, 257, 260, 262
  Labor campaign 25, 263–4, 265, 267–8, 272, 274
  Labor economic policy 270
  Labor landslide win xiv, xxiii, 273–4, 281
  Liberal campaign 268
1984 Federal election 327, 329

Labor campaign 330, 331, 332
  Liberal campaign 332, 334
  results 332–3
  televised debate 331–2, 385
1987 Federal election 379
  Hawke vision 385
  Labor campaign 380, 381, 382, 383
  Liberal campaign 382
  refusal to debate Howard 385
  results 385–6
1987 global stock market crash 448
1988 Bicentenary 290, 378, 563
1990 Federal election 453, 454
  Labor campaign 455, 458, 459
  Liberal campaign 458, 459
  results 460
  televised debate 459
1990 recession 448–9, 471–2
1991 (May–June) Keating leadership challenge 484, 504–5, 507–12
  Hawke lack of media support 511
  Hawke supporters 508, 509
  Keating supporters 509
  Kirribilli Agreement 407–9, 415, 451, 484, 498–9, 501–8, 511–13
1991 (December) Keating leadership challenge 527–31
  Hawke supporters 529

  Keating reflections on leadership battle 534–5
  Keating supporters 529
  Morgan Gallup poll 528
1993 Federal election xiv, 549
1996 Federal election 556
1998 Federal election 557
2001 Federal election 557, 558
2004 Federal election 557
2007 Federal election 557
2013 Federal election 558
2016 Federal election 558
2019 Federal election 558, 572

A Current Affair 203, 404, 543, 550
Abbott, Tony 67, 564–5, 579
ABC 372
Abeles, Peter 138, 221, 222, 236, 237, 461, 544, 553, 562
  Kirribilli Agreement 407–9, 506
  Reserve Bank board 360, 407
Aboriginal and Torres Strait Islander Commission (ATSIC) 468–9
Aboriginal and Torres Strait Islander people 468–70
ATSIC 468–9
Barunga Statement 470
Council for Aboriginal Reconciliation 469
native title rights 469, 470–1
Royal Commission into Black Deaths in Custody 468
Uluru, handing back 468

Aboriginal and Torres Strait Islander Heritage Protection Act 1984 516
Aboriginal Reconciliation Unit 290
Aboriginal Tent Embassy 286
Adler, Louise 547
'Advance Australia Fair' 324
The Advertiser 3, 454
The Age 120, 125, 190, 332, 379, 414, 511
agriculture, trade in 441–2
Cairns Group 441
Aird, Drew 85
al-Rifai, Zaid 426
Albanese, Anthony 558, 575
Albers, Joy (née Woods) 41
Alington, Giles 55–6
Allan, Jimmy 62
Amalgamated Engineering Union 83, 84, 120
Amalgamated Metal Workers' and Shipwrights Union 129, 190
America's Cup yacht race 1983 316–18, 563
Anderson, Joe 119
Antarctica xxvi, 290, 536
ban on mining 393–5, 419, 432, 456
CRAMRA Convention 393–4
Madrid Protocol 395
Anthony, Doug 315
Anthony, Julie 383
Anyaoku, Emeka 434
ANZUS Treaty 97, 98, 176, 239, 337, 339, 344, 345, 577
apartheid xxvi, 49, 148–9, 336, 346, 353–4, 356, 419, 434, 435, 536, 577
Eminent Persons Group (EPG) 354, 355, 356
Langkawi Accord 434
sanctions against South Africa 356, 357, 434, 435, 439
Springboks tour 1971 148–9, 174
Appleton, Gillian 144
affair with Hawke 144
Arbitration Act 14
archival material drawn upon xv–xvii
Armitage, John 234
Arthur Calwell Memorial Lecture 170

Ashburner, Richard 90
Ashdown, Paddy 545
Asia Pacific 440
Asia-Pacific Economic Cooperation (APEC) 290, 336, 419, 536, 577
Hawke proposal for 442
members 443
US and 443
Asia-Pacific nations, cooperation xxvi
Association of Southeast Asian Nations (ASEAN) 340, 443
Attlee, Clement 51, 52
Austin, Mervyn 35
Australia II 316, 317, 563
Australia-Overseas Club 31, 47
Australia Acts 324
Australia and New Zealand Passenger Conference 48
Australia Card 388
The Australian 105, 112, 126, 163, 315, 332, 407, 511, 550
Australian Conservation Foundation 382–3, 456
Australian Council of Employers' Federation 100
Australian Council of Trade Unions (ACTU)
1957 Basic Wage Case 75
1958 Basic Wage Case 75
1959 Basic Wage Case 81, 83–6, 88
1959 Margins Case 86
1960 Basic Wage Case 88, 89
1961 Wage and Hour Case 90
1964 Basic Wage Case 100–2, 103
1965 Basic Wage Case 103–5
1965 Congress 119
1966 Basic Wage, Margins and Total Wage Case 107–10
1967 Basic Wage Case 113–14
1967 Congress 115, 119, 120, 121
1968 Basic Wage Case 114
1969 Basic Wage Case 114
1969 Congress 114, 118, 120, 122, 123–4

1971 Congress 150
1973 Congress 139
1975 Congress 162
1977 Congress 188, 197
1979 Congress 189, 207
1982–3 wage accord policy 246, 247, 269
ACTU Executive 119–20, 123, 129
annual income 218
establishment 82
letters and briefing papers xv
media reaction to election as president 125–6
president *see* ACTU presidency
representation 105, 128, 218
research officer and advocate xxiv, 76–7, 82
Special Congress 1957 74
ACTU-Bourke's 137–8, 218–19
ACTU presidency xxiv, 105, 124, 125, 128, 130–1
ACTU Executive 129, 190–1
approval ratings 131, 140
campaign for presidency 117–23
candidacy for president 116
dispute resolution 132–3, 190
overview 127, 217–18
petrol tanker drivers disputes 133
political strikes 149–50, 173–4
private sector, partnerships with 136–8
retail price maintenance 137, 138, 219
social policy, contribution to debate 139
vision for the ACTU 128–9
ACTU-Jetset 138, 219
ACTU-Solo 138, 219
Australian Defence Force 344–5
Collins-class submarines 345
Australian Democrats 274, 453, 458, 460
Australian Electoral Commission 333
Australian Federation of Air Pilots 450–1

*The Australian Financial
    Review* 109, 287, 332,
    511, 523
Australian Journalists'
    Association 169
Australian Labor Advisory
    Council (ALAC) 165,
    297
    January 1974 meeting 159
Australian Manufacturing
    Workers Union 190
Australian National
    University (ANU) xxiv,
    70–1
    adjunct professor
        appointment 548
    behaviour, indiscretions
        73
    doctorate 72, 76, 89
    Student Representative
        Council 72
    teaching position 73–4
Australian Population and
    Immigration Council
    170
Australian Refugee
    Advisory Council 170
Australian Republican
    Movement 484
Australian Security
    Intelligence
    Organisation (ASIO)
    xvi, 176, 291
    Combe-Ivanov scandal
        305–11
    Gulf War and 496
    Hawke file 176–7
    Operation Bushfowl
        306–8
    Whitlam and 291
Australian Story 562
Australian system of
    honours 325, 482, 483
Australian Tramway
    and Motor Omnibus
    Employees' Association
    114
Australian War Memorial
    286
Australian Women's Weekly
    473
Australian Workers' Union
    84, 119, 190, 505
Aziz, Tariq 493

Bagehot, Walter 536
Baker, James xvi, 338, 429,
    443, 493
Balderstone, Simon 289,
    456–7, 470, 516

Baldwin, Peter 402, 529
Bannon, John 363
Barblett, Alan 22, 28, 29, 70
Barder, Brian 175
Barker, Geoffrey 120
Barnard, Lance 155, 160,
    162
Barnes, Allan 171
Barnett, David 186
Barnett, Harvey 291–2,
    306–10
Barron, Peter 236, 267–8,
    282, 288–89, 302, 308,
    328–9, 332, 362, 366,
    368–9, 373, 376
Barwick, Garfield 228
basic wage
    Oxford thesis,
        considerations in 64–6
    Royal Commission on the
        Basic Wage 1920 64
Basic Wage Case 1953
    cost-of-living adjustments,
        abolition 74, 84, 86, 89
Basic Wage Case 1957 75
Basic Wage Case 1958 75
Basic Wage Case 1959 81,
    83–6, 88
Basic Wage Case 1960 88,
    89
Basic Wage Case 1961 90
Basic Wage Case 1964
    100–2, 103
Basic Wage Case 1965
    103–5
Basic Wage, Margins and
    Total Wage Case 1966
    107–10
Basic Wage Case 1967
    113–14
Basic Wage Case 1968 114
Basic Wage Case 1969 114
Batt, Neil 226
Baume, Peter 468
Bavadra, Timoci 357
Beasley, Frank 34, 35, 71
Beattie, Peter 257, 402, 554
Beazley, Kim 231, 239, 284,
    285, 327–8, 357, 361, 393,
    406, 433, 502, 508, 509,
    510, 517, 524, 525, 528,
    529, 533, 554, 575
    advice to Hawke to resign
        524, 526–7
    Hayden-Hawke
        relationship 340
    Hawke's preferred
        successor 403, 534
    Kirribilli Agreement, view
        of 503–4

Labor Party leader 556,
    557
Minister for Aviation 282
Minister for Defence 359,
    433
Minister for Finance 522
MX missile 342–3
telecommunications
    reform 466
Beck, Joy 58
Beecham, Sir Thomas 52
Belle Du Jour (racehorse)
    68
Benaud, Richie 50
Bennett, Ken 168
Benson, Sam 98
Berinson, Joe 22
Bertrand, John 317
Beveridge, William 51
BHP 515
Bhutto, Benazir 419
Birney, Jack 230
Bjelke-Petersen, Joh 302
    'Joh for Canberra'
        campaign 380, 381
Blair, Tony 432, 433, 560
Blanchard, Francis 336
Blewett, Neal xvi, xix, 30–1,
    240, 253, 256, 258, 509,
    529, 533, 554
    diary 241
    Hayden downfall 258
    HIV/AIDS response 321,
        321–2
    Medicare 320, 321
    Minister for Health 282
Bloch, Arnold 207
Blunt, Charles 452
Boao Forum of Asia 548
Bob Hawke Gallery,
    Bordertown 27
Bob Hawke Prime
    Ministerial Centre 548
Bob Hawke Prime
    Ministerial Library xv,
    69, 548
Boilermakers' Union 88
Bolkus, Nick 296, 508, 509,
    516, 517, 525, 527, 528,
    529
Bolte, Henry 81
Bond, Alan 317, 374, 461
Bordertown xvii, xxiii, 3,
    9–10
    Bob Hawke Gallery 27
    Congregational Church 9
    manse 8, 10
Botha, P.W. 357, 435
Boulton, Alan 199
Bowan, John 287, 289, 426,
    445

Bowden, Bob 288
Bowden, Glenda 162
    affair with Hawke 162
Bowen, Lionel xviii, xx,
    xxi, 169, 193, 226, 233,
    239, 244, 248, 267, 307,
    368, 553
    Attorney-General 333,
    359, 392
    Deputy Prime Minister
    282
    Hawke and 295
    Hayden, leadership
    resignation 252, 255, 256
    retirement 461
Bowen, Nigel 157
Bowers, Peter 265, 302
Boyer Lectures 201, 222
Bradman, Sir Donald 149
    proposed interview by
    Hawke 545–6
Bradshaw, Bill 250
Brereton, Laurie 462, 528
Brezhnev, Leonid 182
British-Australian Summit
    1989 432
Broadbent, Dr Eric 3
Broadby, Reg 83
Brodney, Bob 75
'brotherhood of man' 6, 7,
    67–8, 454
Brown, Bill 120, 153
Brown, Bob 271, 458
Brown, Gordon 433
Brown, H.P. 'Horrie' 75, 83
Brown, John 242, 389, 390,
    411, 412
    Expo '88 contracts 416
    Hawke chasing women
    411–12
Brown, Neil 367
Bruce, Stanley 4
Bryant, Gordon 192, 229
Bryant, John 70
Buckley, Brian 108
budget deficits
    1982–3 272
    1983–4 272, 281, 299
budget surpluses 371, 577
    1987–8 371, 403, 449
    1988–9 403, 405, 449
    1989–90 449
    1990–1 471
Building Workers' Industrial
    Union 129, 190
Bull, Hedley 61
The Bulletin 108, 222, 224,
    240, 503, 523, 528
Burgmann, Meredith
    148–9

Burke, Brian 363, 469
Burnham, Paul 317, 318
Burns, Tom 152, 156
Burton, Tom 373
Bury, Les 114
Bush, Barbara 429
Bush, George H.W. xvi,
    xxvi, 336–7, 339, 343,
    346, 418, 419, 577
    1989 meeting 429
    Antarctica 394
    Australian visit 1991–2
    525, 542–3
    diary 428, 429, 493, 496,
    542
    Gulf War 487–97
    Hawke relationship with
    428–31
bushfires 1983 262
Business Review Weekly 284
Butler, Lord 67
Butler, Richard 341
Button, John xviii, 193, 205,
    233, 243, 295, 386, 392,
    406, 439, 461, 509, 514,
    522, 529, 533
    advice to Hawke to resign
    526–7
    Hayden, view of 251
    Minister for Industry and
    Commerce 282
    role in Hayden resigning
    xx–xxi, 248–9, 251–2,
    255, 258, 260
Buttrose, Ita 322

Cahill, Geoff 154
Cain, John 363
Cairns, Jim 148, 160, 161,
    162, 171, 192
Cairns Group 441
Calwell, Arthur 93, 97, 98,
    151, 244, 534
Calwell, Mary Elizabeth
    153
Cambodia 290, 340, 341,
    348, 349
    Khmer Rouge 341, 348
Cameron, Clyde 94, 100,
    152, 157, 161, 169, 260
Cameron, Rod 232, 243,
    262, 267, 274, 288, 333,
    377, 378, 453, 455
Campbell, George 375
Campbell, Graeme 509, 513
Campbell, Keith 315
Campbell inquiry 315
Canberra
    1956 move to 71
    The Lodge 102, 285

The Canberra Times 93
Cape Town 49, 149
Cape York 456
Carleton, Jim 367
Carleton, Richard xxii, 268
Carmichael, Laurie 242
Carnegie, Roderick 221
Carr, Bob xvi, 123, 204,
    205, 224, 242, 397, 403
    NSW Labor leader 462
    diary 403, 462
Carter, Jimmy 182
Cassidy, Barrie 288, 376,
    380, 387–8, 396–7, 401,
    412–13, 500, 507
    advice to Hawke to resign
    514
Central Intelligence Agency
    (CIA) 337
Chamber of Manufacturers
    86
Cheney, Fred 452
Chifley, Ben 399, 406, 410
Chifley government
    post-war immigration
    policy 31
Child, Joan 233, 323
child poverty pledge 384–5,
    388–9
Child Support Agency 388
childcare funding 324
Childs, Bruce 291, 292, 495
China 155, 419, 437
    1978 trip 183, 346
    1984 trip 346–8, 419
    1986 trip 349–51, 419
    1993 trip 447
    China-US intermediary,
    as 420, 577
    Chinese students in
    Australia 444
    economic relationship
    with 348, 444
    hosting Chinese leaders
    419
    joint ventures with 348,
    349
    post-prime ministerial
    business dealings/
    consultancies 553–4, 561
    temporary entry visa
    extension 446, 468
    Tiananmen Square
    protests 351, 432, 444–6
Christianity 4
The Chronicle 3, 8
Chubb, Philip xvi, 549
Churchill, Winston 50, 490
Clancy, Pat 129, 190, 191
Clark, Dr Colin 53–4, 84

Clark, Manning 72
Cleary, Phil 544
Clegg, Hugh 66
Clinton, Bill 67
Coates, John 495
Codd, Mike 288, 290, 386,
    387, 482, 531
'New Federalism' 463–5
Cohen, Barry 233, 242
    Minister for Home Affairs
    and Environment 282–3
Cohen, Ian 383
Cohen, Judith 177
Cohen, Sam 177
Cold War xxvi, 60, 418, 577
Cole, Tony 313, 520
Coleman, Peter 71, 72, 76
Coleman, Verna 72
Colless, Malcolm 216
Collins, Bob 517, 533
Combe, David 159, 167,
    169, 197, 226, 233
    career 310–11
    Combe-Ivanov scandal
    283, 305–311, 416
Combe-Ivanov scandal 283,
    305–311
Combet, Greg 558
Commonwealth Heads of
    Government Meeting
    (CHOGM) 336, 353, 419
    1983 352
    1985 346, 353
    1986 356
    1987 357–8
    1989 433–4
    1991 436–7
communism 60, 81, 98
Communist Party, Australia
    60, 292–3
Conciliation and Arbitration
    Act 157, 185
Congregational Youth
    Fellowship 41
    conference 1951 33
    Easter Camps 41, 42
    Subiaco 47
Connor, Rex 163, 164
Constitutional Conventions
    290
Conybeare, Chris 287, 368,
    376, 380, 387, 395
Cook, Peter 190, 296, 509,
    529, 533
Coombs, H.C. 'Nugget'
    202
Copland, Sir Douglas 90
Corbett, Kel 298, 454, 473,
    574
Corbett, Lesley 298, 473

Corbett, Sam 298, 454,
    473, 574
Corio seat 94, 100, 151
    1963 preselection 93
    campaign 94–8
    result 99
Cornford, Phil 169
cost-of-living adjustments
    1953 abolition 74, 84,
    86, 89
Costello, Michael 252, 254,
    340–1
Costigan Royal
    Commission 246, 329
Council for Aboriginal
    Reconciliation 469
Council of Australian
    Governments (COAG)
    290, 464
The Courier-Mail 332, 511
Court, Charles 197
Court of Conciliation and
    Arbitration
    1953 cost-of-living
    adjustments, abolition
    74, 84, 86, 89
    1959 Basic Wage Case
    84–6
    1973 appointment of
    president 157
    Oxford thesis 64–6

Cousteau, Jacques 394
Cowdrey, Colin 61
Cowen, Sir Zelman 202
Crabb, Annabel 562
Crawford, George 152
Crawford, John 171
Crean, Frank 142, 153, 168,
    171, 192
Crean, Simon 122, 207, 239,
    241, 242, 305, 360, 361,
    363, 508, 529, 556
    ACTU president 304
    Kirribilli Agreement, view
    of 508
    Labor Party leader 557
    Minister for Primary
    Industries and Energy
    513
Crellin, Chris 180
cricket
    ACT first grade 71
    Melbourne Cricket Club
    thirds 95
    Oxford XI 61
    Perth Modern School
    21, 22
    University College Cricket
    Club 61

University of Western
    Australia 28
West Leederville State
    School 17–18
Crisp, Fin 72
Crown Prince Hassan bin
    Talal 426
Cunningham, Col 198, 221,
    272, 562
currency
    'crawling peg' 311
    devaluation 1983 299–300
    floating the Australian
    dollar 311–15, 326, 375,
    453, 536
Currie, Dr George 34
Curtin, John 20–1, 217, 273,
    319, 399, 410, 578
    Keating assessment 499
Curtin government
    post-war immigration
    policy 31
Cyclone Tracy 161

Daily Mirror 231
Daily News (Perth) 122
The Daily Telegraph 97, 181
Daintree Rainforest 382,
    536, 577
Dale, Brian 234, 260
D'Alpuget, Blanche xii, xiii,
    xvi, 566–7
    1986 interviews with Bob
    414
    1989 interview with Bob
    415
    affair with Bob 210,
    212–13, 413–14, 415
    Bob wedding proposal 552
    Bob's drinking 202, 203
    Bob's womanising 410,
    416
    divorce 415
    first meeting 209
    Hawke biography 212
    Hawke: The Prime Minister
    xv, 570
    Hazel, interview with 213
    marriage to Bob 541, 553
    Mediator 212
    plane crash 552
    relationships with Bob's
    children 567
    Robert J. Hawke: A
    Biography xv, 214–15
    separation from Tony 211
    Turtle Beach 211
Dalrymple, Rawdon 58, 62,
    64, 182, 209
    Israel ambassador 182

United States ambassador 346

Dalrymple, Rossie 209

Daly, Fred 98, 383

Daly, Lieutenant-General Thomas 139

Darling, Elaine 495

Darlow, Denise 165, 234

Darrow, Clarence 87

Davidson, Gay 205

Dawes, Seumas 404

Dawkins, John xix, 243, 253, 283, 393, 509, 529, 533
Hawke-Keating leadership 406–7
Minister for Education 391
Minister for Finance 282
Minister for Trade 359

de Klerk, F.W. 357, 435, 439

decimal currency 107

Dedman, Jim 94

Defence White Paper 1985 344

Democratic Labor Party (DLP) 81, 96, 99, 152

Deng, Xiaoping 183, 350, 351, 418, 444

Denton, Andrew 562

Department of Prime Minister and Cabinet 280, 290

Deverall, Ed 84, 85

Devereux, Jack 119

Deutscher Gewerkschaftsbund (DGB) West Germany 136

Dibb, Paul 344

Dillon, David 329, 335

Dillon, Matt 329, 334

Dillon, Paul 329, 335, 574

discrimination against women 322–3
the dismissal 164, 165–6, 167, 285

Docker, Norman 84

Dodson, Patrick 469, 470

Doig, R.H. 47

Dolan, Cliff 159, 186, 191, 225, 247, 251

Donnelly, Phyllis 410

Donovan, Barry 125

Doolan, Ken 560

Downer, Alexander 550

Drysdale, Alister xxii, 260, 261, 355

du Plessis, Barend 356, 435

Ducker, John 121, 124–5, 129, 134, 156, 186, 190, 193, 224

Dudley, Robert 51

Duffy, Michael xx–xxi, 68, 249, 251, 393, 509, 524, 529
Minister for Communications 282
television network licences 373

Duke of Edinburgh Study Conference, Canada 91, 279–80

Duncan, Peter 495, 509, 527

Dunstan, Don 167–8, 171, 199, 383

East Timor 326

Economic Planning Advisory Council (EPAC) 290, 296, 302

education
AUSTUDY 390
'Dawkins Revolution' 391–2
Hawke reforms 319, 320, 390–2
HECS Scheme 391
Whitlam, abolition of university fees 390

Egerton, Jack 156, 168, 191, 204

Eggleston, Richard 75, 84, 85, 89, 166

Eggleton, Tony 246, 261, 274, 460

Elders 562

Eldon, Lord 51

Electrical Trades Union 90

Ellercamp, Paul 288, 368, 376, 414

Elliott, John 380

Emerson, Craig 289, 380, 385, 387, 388, 394, 547, 569, 570, 573

environmental achievements 456–8, 460, 577
Antarctica, ban on mining 393–5
Franklin Dam 271, 325, 382, 456, 577
Helsham report 392–3
Lemonthyme and Tasmanian Southern forests 392, 456, 577
National Greenhouse Advisory Committee 457
Our Country, Our Future statement 456, 457

Erskine, James 544, 547, 548, 551

European Economic Community 91

Evans, Gareth 221, 241, 280, 307, 308, 310, 325, 341, 361, 393, 438, 508, 509, 514, 522, 524, 529, 533, 556
Antarctica 393, 394
Attorney-General 282
Gulf War 493–4
Hazel, view of 416
Kirribilli Agreement, view of 504
Minister for Resources and Energy 359
Tasmania logging 393

Evans, Geoff 267

Evans, Graham 235–6, 280, 306, 376, 411–12
principal private secretary 287

Evans, John 52

Evans, Ted 290, 312

Evatt, H.V. 'Doc' 73, 228, 244

Expenditure Review Committee 283, 294, 370–1

Face to Face 406

Fadden, Arthur 50

Faiman, Peter 369

Family Allowance Supplement 385, 388, 389

Farmer, Richard 267, 272, 379, 383, 397–8, 500

Fatin, Wendy 269, 529, 533

Federal elections see by year date

Federated Clerks' Union 83, 119, 129, 149

Federated Ironworkers' Association 84, 129, 149, 190

Federated Miscellaneous Workers' Union 118, 119, 129, 190

Fellowes, Robert 483, 484

Ferguson, Martin 529

Fightback! manifesto 484, 519, 520
Hawke critique 519

Fiji coups 357, 358

financial deregulation 315, 316, 326

Fischer, Henri 168

Fitzgibbon, Charlie 118, 119, 129, 190, 191
Reserve Bank board 360

Flinders
  1982 by-election xx, 247,
    248
floating the Australian
  dollar 311–15, 326, 375,
  453, 536
Foot, Michael 352
For the True Believers xv
Forbes, Dr Jim 246
Forbes MacFie Hansen 267,
  331
Forde, Frank xxiii, 253
foreign affairs 336–40,
  419–31
  Bush-Hawke relationship
    428–31
  Cairns Group 441
  China-US intermediary,
    as 420, 577
  Middle East trip 1987
    426–7
  Soviet-US intermediary,
    as 423–4
foreign banks 316, 326, 360
Foster, Alf 84, 85
Four Corners 518, 550
  'Republic of Oz' program
    545
Frąckiewicz, Ryszard xxii
Franklin Dam 271, 325, 382,
  456, 536, 577
Fraser, Bernie 326, 520
Fraser, John 471, 521
Fraser, Malcolm 67, 180,
  184, 341, 346, 406, 462,
  475, 491, 498, 549, 559,
  560, 563, 578
  1975 Federal election 166
  1977 Federal election 192,
    193, 260
  1980 Federal election 225,
    227
  1983 Federal election 254,
    275, 279
  approval ratings 194, 243,
    319, 331, 556
  back issues 246
  calling 1983 election xviii,
    xxi–xxii, 254, 256, 257,
    260, 262
  Commonwealth secretary-
    general bid 434–5
  Eminent Persons Group
    (EPG) 355
  Gorton and 139, 262
  government of, divisions
    xxv
  Hawke and 185, 186, 187,
    197, 534, 550
  Howard and 186, 261,
    272, 315

Liberal leader 164
  Margaret Thatcher and
    352, 353–4
  Minister for Defence 127
Fraser, Tamie 186, 262, 435
Fraser government 171,
  245–6, 261
  1982–3 budget 261, 272
  industrial matters,
    approach to 184, 185
Fraser Island 505, 506
Free, Ross 513, 514
French nuclear testing,
  South Pacific 148, 174
Freudenberg, Graham 159,
  236, 265, 267, 282, 284,
  285–6, 289, 379, 383,
  400, 413, 523, 534
Frost, David 141
Frydenberg, Josh 68

Gairdner, Sir Charles 31,
  35, 36, 47
Gallagher, Frank 84, 86,
  102, 103, 104, 107, 108,
  109, 110
Gallipoli, 75th anniversary
  commemorations 486–7
Gandhi, Indira 353
Gandhi, Rajiv 419
Ganilau, Sir Penaia 358
Garnaut, Ross 287, 289,
  300, 303, 312, 347, 376,
  547
  *Australia and the North
  East Asian Ascendancy*
    440–1
  Garran Oration 1988 290
Gaudron, Mary 323
Geelong Trades Hall
  Council 95
George, Jennie 529, 555
Gibbs, Margaret 232, 262,
  288, 377, 378, 455, 460
Gibson, David 563
Gietzelt, Arthur 156, 197,
  365
  dual member of
    Communist Party 291–3
  Minister for Veterans'
    Affairs 283
Gietzelt, Ray 118, 119, 129,
  190, 191
Gillard, Julia 557, 565, 579
Gillespie, Margaret 410
Gillies, Max 296
Gittins, Ross 315
Gleghorn, Geoffrey
  109–10, 131
Goldberger, David 138

Gorbachev, Mikhail 420–5,
  432
  Hawke meeting 1987 421,
    422
  Major meeting 1991
    424–5
Gordon, Michael 216, 451
Gorman, Russ 510
Gorton, John 126, 132, 139,
  262, 319, 410, 560, 578
Goss, Wayne 505
Grant, Sandy 547, 551
Gration, Peter 494, 497
Grattan, Michelle 215, 223,
  334–5, 369, 400, 499,
  521
Gray, Malcolm 289
Great Barrier Reef 147, 204,
  382, 456, 577
Great Depression 3, 10, 501
'greenhouse effect' 457
Greens Party 458, 460
Greenwood, Ivor 132
Gregory, Bob 190
Greiner, Nick 464
Griffiths, Alan 516, 517
Grimes, Don xviii, xxi,
  253, 322
  Minister for Social
    Security 282
Guild of Undergraduates
  28, 29–30, 47
Guinness Book of Records 63
Gulf War 418, 437, 483,
  487–96
  Australian commitments
    487, 489, 494
  Bush-Hawke dialogue
    487–9, 491–2, 495, 497
  Canadian commitment
    490–1
  counter-terrorism alert,
    raising 496
  media coverage 495
  MPs opposed 495
  Operation Desert Shield
    491, 497
  Operation Desert Storm
    494, 497

Halfpenny, John 139, 242
Hall, Fred 119
Hamer, David 171
Hamer, Dick 260
Hancock, Keith 75
  Australia 65
Hand, Gerry 219, 220, 296,
  468, 508, 509, 524, 527,
  528, 529
  Gulf War 494–5

Minister for Aboriginal
Affairs 469
Hannaford, Robert 68, 69
Hannah, Norman 134
Hanson, Pauline 559
Haran, Mark 572
Harare Declaration 1991
436
Hardy, Graham 131
Harris, Rolf 22
Hartley, William (Bill) 82,
152, 153, 168, 179, 188,
192, 291
Harvey, Neil 50
Hawke, Albert 6, 7, 17, 21,
47, 70
mentor to Bob, as 19–20,
74
political career 20, 217
Hawke, Arthur Clarence
(Clem) xxiii, 3, 573
1976 Israel trip 179, 180
1983 Federal election 265,
272, 273, 275–6
Army Chaplaincy 18, 19
background and career
5–6, 8
Bob, relationship with
xxii, 4, 5, 6–7, 10
Bordertown life 9–10
death and funeral 454
freemasonry 19
marriage 8
personality and nature 5
post-War church positions
19
Subiaco Congregational
Church 19
wedding, officiating at 70
*Yesterday, Today and
Tomorrow* 4
Hawke, Edith Emily (Ellie)
xxiii, 3, 573
1976 Israel trip 179, 180
alcohol, views about 5, 11,
19, 33
Bordertown life 9–10
death and funeral 207–8,
211
love for Bob xxii, 4
marriage 8
personality and nature 5,
7, 11
teaching 7, 9, 11, 18
Hawke, Elizabeth Ann (née
Pascoe) 5, 13
Hawke, Hazel Susan (née
Masterson) xii, xiii, 41,
297, 526
60th birthday party 473

abortion 1952 45
activism and public life
473–4
Alzheimer's disease 567–8
background and childhood
43–4
Blanche, interview with
213
Bob's affairs 416
Brotherhood of St
Laurence 237
career 43
charity work 473
children xxiv, 46
collapse of marriage 541,
551–2
dementia 46
early relationship with
Bob 44–6
employment in Oxford 60
engagement 38, 44
European tour 1954 63–4
family life 145, 146
friendship with Bob 45
life after divorce 567
loyalty to Bob 46, 88, 335,
416
marriage xxiv
marriage difficulties 202,
206–7, 211
meeting Bob 41–2
Melbourne 77, 81, 87–8,
106
My Own Life 551
Oxford 58, 59–60
Papua New Guinea 112
personal papers xv
personal qualities 46,
106, 335
respect felt towards 568
Robert, death 94
Rosslyn's heroin addiction
329, 334, 414
Sandringham house 102,
474
wedding 70
Hawke, James Renfrey 5,
6, 13
Hawke, John Neil 5, 8, 9, 15
boarding school 5, 10,
13, 15
death 16, 573
Hawke, Robert (Jnr) 94
Hawke, Robert James Lee
10th anniversary of
coming to power 541
20th anniversary of
coming to power 541
60th birthday party 473
70th birthday party 562

80th birthday party 562
1952 student conference,
India xxiii, 36–9
1962 scholarship and
travels 91
1982 leadership challenge
240, 242, 243
ABC Radio lectures on
thesis 71
Albert Hawke, influence
of 19–20
alcohol and xxiv, xxv, 32,
33, 41, 46, 88, 197–8,
200–1, 202, 203
alcohol, giving up 223,
410
alcohol poisoning 94
alcoholic, highly
functioning 202–3
ANU *see* Australian
National University
(ANU)
appearances and
consultancies 553
appointments accepted
548
approval ratings 194, 319
Arts degree 28, 53
Australian of the Year 319
back issues 395
beer drinking record 63,
67, 197
behaviour when drunk 88,
89, 142, 144, 198–9, 205
birth 3
bodyguard, need for 180
campus life 32
Canberra, move to 1956
70–1
casinos 397–8
charisma xiv, 4, 262
childhood 10, 13–15, 20
childhood ill-health 24
Clem, relationship with
xxii, 4, 5, 6–7, 10
collapse of marriage 541
Companion of the Order
of Australia 201
Corio seat *see* Corio seat
D'Alpuget biography 212
death and memorial
services 573–4
death threats 180
defamation suits 102, 222
depression over family
issues 328, 366
destined for greatness 4
detox spells 198
education 14, 17–18, 21–4,
25–8

election night
commentaries, paid 196,
546
election victories xxvi
elocution 24
European tour 1954 63–4
exhibitionism and nudity
195–6, 285, 397, 485
family life 145, 146
farewells, pre-Oxford 47
Father of the Year award
1971 146
foreign trips as PM
336–40, 419, 421–2, 426,
429, 432–3, 440, 441
Fraser and 185, 186, 187,
197
golf 354, 395
grandchildren 473
guest television
interviewer 545
Guild of Undergraduates
28, 29–30, 47
Hayden and 259, 340, 478
health in later years 573
honorary doctorate
Oxford University 67
income 102, 130
Industrial Relations,
shadow Minister for
228, 231
Junior and Leaving
Certificates 23–4
Keating, relationship
see Hawke-Keating
relationship
Kirribilli House 285
Labor Party, Western
Australia 27
last interview xi–xiii
last will and testament
568–9
Law degree 26–7
the Lodge 285
London 1953–4 49–50,
59–60
maiden speech 229–30
media see media
Melbourne 1958 move to
77, 81, 87–8
motor cycle accident at 17
xxiii, 26, 27
'Mr Inflation' 86
newspaper columns 546
Northbridge purchase
474, 542
other ex-PMs, relationship
with 563
Oxford University see
Oxford University

paid interviews 546
papers and personal papers
xv–xvi
Papua New Guinea 1966
111–12
parenting 92, 145, 146
parents, influences of 4
personality and behaviour
xxiv–xxv
physical appearance
140–1
physicality 7
pilot's licence 61–2
post-prime ministerial life
541, 542–67
post-prime ministerial
benefits and pension 544
press conferences 401
punting 112, 285, 396–7
religion 33, 38, 40
Reserve Bank of Australia
board 170
resignation press
conference 532
Rhodes Scholarship see
Rhodes Scholarship
Robert, death 94
sailing boat 147
Sandringham house 102,
129, 474
'self-destruct syndrome'
223
sex addiction 38, 40, 46,
58, 59, 62, 142, 162, 416
speaking style 160
speeches 400, 401–2
sports 17–18, 21, 22, 28, 61
sustained high approval
ratings xxvi
tears 141–2, 179, 230, 265,
328, 365, 445, 470, 530
television, use of medium
xxv
University of Western
Australia 25–32, 53
wedding to Hazel 70
Whitlam and 152, 155–6,
157–8, 162–3, 175–6, 544
womanising xxiv, 41, 46,
88, 106, 107, 142, 196,
203–5, 215, 410, 411–13,
415
work ethic 88, 131, 141,
287, 288, 545
World Jewish Congress
award 1988 427
Hawke, Rosslyn xii, xxiv,
146, 329, 473, 474, 526,
553
Blanche, relationship with
567

Bob's estate, claim against
238, 569
childhood 126, 147
heroin addiction 211, 237,
328, 334
sexual abuse allegations
238
Hawke, Stephen xii, xvi,
xxiv, 146, 297–8, 335,
553, 574
Bob and Hazel's marriage,
views on 206–7, 568
childhood 95, 126, 147
Noonkanbah dispute 237
Noonkanbah: Whose Land,
Whose Law 473
Hawke government
1983 budget 303–4
education reforms 319,
320, 390–2
environment see
environmental
achievements
overview xxv–xxvii, 304,
536, 576–7
welfare sector reforms
319–20, 374
Hawke-Keating relationship
295, 365, 399, 451
1984, Keating views on
Hawke 366
1988 confrontation over
leadership 404–5, 406
'banana republic'
comments 368–9
final meetings 569–70,
571
Keating, leadership
transition 403–4
Keating 'Plácido
Domingo' speech
499–500
Kirribilli Agreement
407–9, 484, 498–9, 501,
503
leadership challenges
see 1991 (May–June)
Keating leadership
challenge; 1991
(December)
Keating leadership
challenge
meeting after 'Plácido
Domingo' speech 500–1
reneging on Kirribilli
Agreement 501–2, 505
Hawke television movie
570
The Hawke Memoirs xiv,
492, 547
Keating reaction to 550–1

money earned from 551
promotion of 550
*Hawke: The Larrikin &
Leader* 562
Hawke: The Prime Minister
xv, 570
Keating reaction to 570–1
Hawke's Brewing Co. 563,
574
Hawley, Janet 212
Hayden, Bill xvi, 126, 167,
174, 217, 233, 238–9,
524, 532
1977 leadership votes 193
1979 national conference
200
1980 Federal election 226
1987 Soviet trip 423, 424
approval ratings 194, 244
autobiography 1996 485–6
conditions for resigning
xix–xx, 253, 256
David Smith KCVO 482,
483
Governor-General
appointment 477–9
Hawke and 340
leadership challenges
1982–3 240, 242, 243,
249–51
1983 letters exchanged
with Hawke xix–xx,
256–7
letters to Queen while
Governor-General
479–82, 483–4, 533
Minister for Foreign
Affairs 282, 478
preferred leader polls 232
resignation of leadership
xviii–xix–xxi, xxii, 252,
253–9, 509
shadow Minister for
Foreign Affairs xix
Treasurer 1975 162
United States, view of
339–40
Healy, Jim 82, 140
Helsham, Michael 392
Helsham report 392–3
Henderson, Scott 122
The Herald 106, 332
Herbert, Xavier 202
Heseltine, Michael 435
Heseltine, Sir William xvi,
32, 325, 358–9, 476,
478–9, 482
diary 478–9
Hewson, John xvi, 284,
463–4, 483–4, 511, 534

Fightback! manifesto 484,
519, 520
Gallipoli 1990 486
Liberal party leader 463
preferred prime minister
polls 497, 502, 528
Hieser, Ron 72
Higgins, Chris 326, 499
Higgins, Roy 221
Histadrut (General
Federation of Labour in
Israel) 136
HIV/AIDS response 321–2
Hogan, Paul 389, 390
Hogg, Bob 203, 236, 249,
267, 268, 288, 289, 308,
309, 329, 362, 376, 456,
460
leadership advice to
Hawke 504
Hogg, Don 112
Hogue, Cavan 425
Holding, Clyde 192, 233,
239, 241
Minister for Aboriginal
Affairs 283, 469
Hollingworth, Archbishop
Peter 388
Hollway, Sandy 287, 288,
294, 387, 395, 445, 476
Hollywood Repatriation
General Hospital, Perth
19
Holmes à Court, Robert 373
Holt, Harold 126, 151, 410
Hong Kong 348, 420, 437
Hope, Robert 309, 310
Horne, Donald 484
Howard, John xvi, 127, 268,
301, 315, 436, 452, 563,
565–6, 578–9
1983 Federal election 261,
270
1987 Federal election 380,
381, 382, 385
1987 leadership challenge
by Peacock 386
1989 Peacock leadership
coup 452
commiserating Hawke
531–2
Kirribilli Agreement, view
of 511
2004 letters exchanged
with Hawke 566
Minister for Business and
Consumer Affairs 184–5
opposition to Hayden
Governor-General
appointment 478

party leader 1980s 367,
452
satisfaction rating 1987
379
Treasurer 186, 300
Howe, Brian 371, 383, 416,
509, 514, 521, 522–3, 529
deputy leader 513
Minister for Defence
Support 283
Minister for Social
Security 383
Hu, Qili 349
Hu, Yaobang 347, 349, 350,
351, 420, 446
Hughes, Barry 281
Human Rights
Commissioner 322
Humphreys, Ben 528, 533
Hun Sen 341
Hurford, Chris 256
Minister for Housing and
Construction 282
Minister for Immigration
359, 467
Hurst, John 105–6, 121, 212
*Hawke: The Definitive
Biography* xv
Hussein, Saddam 487, 491,
492, 493, 496, 497

Illawarra Mercury 552
immigration
Hawke government 467,
468
Hawke views on 31, 48,
467
illegal immigrants 468
post-War immigration
31, 467
refugee processing centre
468
skilled immigrants 467,
468
Tiananmen Square, visa
extensions 446, 468
Immigration Planning and
Advisory Committee
170
India
1952 Christian student
conference xxiii, 36–9
Indochina 337, 340, 350
Industrial Court 74
penal powers 114
industrial disputes
air traffic controllers 190
live sheep exports 190
metal trades industry
1966–7 114

nationwide general strike
1976 173
petrol tanker divers, 1972
133, 190
State Electricity
Commission 190
Telecom 190
Industrial Relations Bureau
184, 185
inflation
1973 158
1974–5 160, 161
1983–4 281
Ingham, Bernard xvi, 434,
486
Ingham, Bob 553
Innes, Ted 122
interest rates
1988–9 448
deregulation 326
International Club 31
International House Appeal
31, 36, 47
International Labour
Organization (ILO) 83,
116, 174, 223, 336
1970 conference 174
Hawke, possible director-
general appointment
174, 508
Governing Body
appointment 174
International Management
Group (IMG) 544, 545,
548
Iraq Ba'ath Socialist Party
168, 310
Iraq invasion 2003 559
Israel 141, 145, 175, 177–80,
230–1, 427
Arab states and,
negotiations 182–3
Labor's official stance
179, 188
Refuseniks, negotiations
for 180–1, 334
Ivanov, Valery 283, 305–11

Jackson, Gordon 170
Jackson Committee 170–1
Jakobsen, Carolyn 495, 528
Japan 348
Hawke visits 441
Jawoyn people
Coronation Hill mining
516, 517
Jenkins, Harry 171
Jiang, Zemin 447
John Curtin Prime
Ministerial Library xv

Johns, Gary 518
Johnson, Johno 406
Johnson, Les 242
Johnson, Lyndon 542
Johnston, Bob 299, 311, 312
Jolly, Rob 142, 190, 191
Jones, Barry 370–1, 392,
399
Minister for Science and
Technology 282
Jones, Reverend C. Gordon
47
Jordan 426

Kakadu National Park 382,
517, 536, 577
Jawoyn people 516, 517
mining at Coronation Hill
515–18
Kaunda, Kenneth 354
Keating, Annita 295, 336
Keating, Paul xii, 168,
223–4, 226, 286, 575
1982 Hawke leadership
challenge 241, 242
1983 budget 303–4
1983 Federal election 275
1983 overseas tour with
Hawke 336–9
1983 wage accord 269–70
1984 budget 305, 326
1986 budget 370, 378
1987 budget 378, 403
1988 budget 403, 404
1989 budget 451
1990 budget 471
1990 recession 472
1991 Prime Minister xiv
1993 Federal election win
549
1996 Federal election 556
Antarctica 394–5
backbencher 1991 518
'banana republic' remarks
367, 368, 375
Blaxland seat 126
deputy prime minister
461
early meetings with
Hawke 224–5
floating the Australian
dollar 311–15, 375
Gulf War and 492, 497
Hawke, relationship with
see Hawke–Keating
relationship
Hayden leadership
resignation 255
Iraqi 'loan' 169

Kirribilli Agreement
407–9, 484, 498–9, 501,
503
Kirribilli Committee 360
leadership challenge
see 1991 (May–June)
Keating leadership
challenge; 1991
(December Keating
leadership challenge
media and television
appearances 1991 518
net satisfaction rating 1991
503
NSW Labor president
224
piggery investment 526
'Plácido Domingo' speech
499–500, 501
press gallery, Canberra
400, 511, 518
Question Time 399–400
relationship with xiii
shadow Treasurer 250,
270
Tasmanian logging 393
taxation white paper
361–2
telecommunications
reforms 1990 466
Treasurer 280, 281, 282,
326, 364
uranium mining 188
Kelly, Paul 152, 163, 223,
269, 376, 400, 407, 459
Kelly, Raymond 84
Kelly, Ros 195, 233, 283,
387, 457, 509, 516, 517,
529
Kelty, Bill 110, 122, 140,
175, 189, 190, 198, 217,
281–2, 305, 363, 507, 529,
554, 575
1995 asking Hawke to act
as ACTU advocate 555
ACTU assistant secretary
191
advice to Hawke on
leadership 508
background 191
Kirribilli Agreement
407–9, 506
Reserve Bank board 360,
407
Kemp, David 187, 261
Kennedy, John F.
assassination 97
Kennedy, Trevor 222
Kennett, Jeff 381
Kenny, Jim 120

Kerin, John 194, 255, 372, 392, 462, 509, 529, 533
  1991 budget 520–2
  Treasurer 484, 513, 514, 520, 522
Kerr, John 86, 103, 109, 114, 166
  the dismissal 164, 165
Keynes, John Maynard
  The General Theory of Employment, Interest and Money 49
Khemlani, Tirath 164
Khemlani loans affair 163–4
Kiek, Dr Edward S. 4
Kiki, Albert Maori 112
King Hussein 426
King's College, Adelaide 5
Kinnock, Neil xvi, 432, 433, 545
Kirby, Richard 84, 85, 86, 90, 102, 103, 104, 105, 107, 108, 114, 553
  D'Alpuget biography 212
Kirribilli Agreement 407–9, 484, 498–9, 501, 503, 513
  Hawke interpretation of 513
  Keating interpretation of 513
Kitchen Cabinet 562
Kitney, Geoff 523–4
Klenbort, Josh 553
Klugman, Dick 234
Knight, John 28, 72
Knowles, K.G.J.C. 66
Kohl, Helmut 418
Kornhauser, Eddie 165, 221
Kornhauser, Jack 165
Kuwait *see* Gulf War

Labatt, Edward 222
Labor in Power documentary 549
Labor Party (Federal)
  1963 federal conference 97
  1972 campaign 153–4
  1975 federal conference 161–2
  1976 leadership vote 168
  1977 federal conference 188
  1977 leadership votes 193
  1977 National Committee of Inquiry 193
  1979 national conference 200

1983 Hayden resignation xviii–xix–xxi, xxii, 252, 253–8
1984 national conference 325
1986 national conference 375
1988 national conference 401, 402
1990 national conference 466
1991 national conference 484, 515
  Canberra, 1950s 73
  Hawke life membership 558
  junior vice president 153
  leader of xxv
  president 1973–1978 xxv, 156
  senior vice president 153
  upheavals 1958 81
  Victorian branch 83, 93, 152, 153, 188
  Western Australia branch 27
Labor Party National Secretariat
  archival papers xvi
Labor Party NSW branch 224, 225
  1991 annual conference 523
Landcare 456, 562, 577
Landeryou, Bill 122, 192, 217, 236, 239
  sexual abuse allegations 238
Lang, Jack 501
Langmore, John 281
Latham, Mark 557
Laws, John 270, 367
Leak, Bill 564
Lee Kuan Yew 299, 346
Lee, Lily 8
Lee, Matilda (née Broster) 7, 13
Lee, Michael 510, 518
Lee, William 'Will' 7, 13
Leibler, Isi 138, 180, 181, 182, 221, 424, 426
Lennon, Nathan 562
Leonard, Walter 'Mac' 133
Lerner, Alexander 181
Leschen, Bob 29
Lewis, Tom 144, 145
Li, Peng 419, 444, 446
Li, Xiannian 348–9
Liberal Party
  Federal elections *see* by year date

Fightback! manifesto 484, 519, 520
  leadership issues 1985 366–7
Lipski, Sam 180
Lloyd, Clem 263
Logue, Peter 500
Loosley, Stephen 235, 247, 259, 383
Loyal Temperance Legion of Australasia 11
Ludwig, Bill 505
Lynch, Phillip 133, 184
Lyneham, Paul 404, 404
Lyons, John 380

McAlpine, Jenny 82
McCarthy, Wendy 297, 416, 551, 567, 568
McCarthyism 60
McClelland, Doug 242, 433, 575
McClelland, Jim 144, 162
McCormack, Mark 548
McDonald, Alec 82
McEwen, John 126
McFarling, Elaine 106
McGowan, Mark 17
McGregor, Craig 195, 204
McHugh, Jeanette 495
McKenzie, David 228
McKiernan, Jim 512, 530, 531
McLean, Gary 32
McLeay, Leo 528, 543
McMahon, Billy 126, 132, 138, 234, 578
  approval rating 319
  relationship with 139–40
  Springboks 1971 tour 149
McMullan, Bob 232–3, 267, 274, 288, 329, 333, 377, 378, 527
McNolty, Albert 93
Macphee, Ian 231, 468
McRae, Toni 162, 196
Madgwick, Rod 111
Mahathir, Dr Mohamed 328, 346
Maher, Michael 234
Mahoney, James 94, 96, 99
Maitland 13–15
Maitland Primary School 14
Major, John xvi, xxvi, 418, 437, 545
  Gorbachev meeting 1991 424–5
  Hawke-Major dialogue 436–7

Malaysia-Indonesia
  confrontation 1963 97
Malone, Frank 28
Manchester, William 490
Mandela, Nelson xxvi, 355,
  418, 550
  Australia visit 1990
    438–40
  freeing of 435
Mant, John 162, 163, 165
Markson, Max 552
Marylebone Cricket Club 61
Marsh, Jan 131, 191–2, 247
Marsh, Ralph 121, 129, 159
Martin, Ray 405, 451, 452,
  518, 546
Martin, Vic 316
Martindale, Roger 330, 396,
  397, 412
Mason, John 182
Masterson, Edith Laura
  43, 70
Masterson, James (Jim) 43,
  44
maternity leave 192, 218
Matthews, L.G. 111, 112
Matthews, Peter 27, 131
Maumill, Bob 330
Mauroy, Pierre 336
Maynes, John 121, 139
Meat Industry Employees'
  Union 82, 119
media
  ACTU presidency
    campaign 122
  cross-media ownership
    laws 374
  press conferences 401–2
  relationships with 105,
    141, 399, 400, 511, 511
  television appearances
    141, 400
Medibank 159, 160, 173–4,
  175, 239, 320
Medicare 320–1, 374, 378,
  453, 460, 536
Meir, Golda 178, 180, 181
  My Life 180
Melbourne
  1958 move to 77, 81, 87–8
  Lygon Hotel 89, 106, 145
  Sandringham house 102,
    129
Melville, Sir Leslie 73
Meneghello, Osvaldo 284,
  294, 395
Menzies, Robert 98, 151,
  228, 410
Menzies government 81, 93,
  97, 109
  1963 policy speech 96

Meshel, Yeruham 179
Metal Trade Employers'
  Association 101
Metal Trades Federation of
  Unions 119
The Midday Show 451, 518
Middle East
  1987 trip 426–7
  Powell Plan for peace 561
Millane, Corinne 131
Miller, Rod 95–6
Mills, Stephen 285, 289,
  383–4, 400
Milne, Glenn 474, 518
Mirages, sale of 433
Mitchell, Alex 500
Mitchell, Neil 171
Mitterrand, François 336,
  394, 418
Monash University Council
  170
Monk, Albert 75, 76, 82, 85,
  88, 105, 115, 116, 151
  1967 ACTU Congress 115
  background and career
    82–3
  International Labour
    Organization (ILO) 83,
    116
  retirement as ACTU
    president 115–16
Monsarrat, Nicholas
  The Cruel Sea 48
Moore, John 90, 102, 103,
  104, 107, 108, 110, 157,
  367
Moore, Sir Philip 324–5
Morgan, David 312
Morgan Gallup polls 452,
  497, 523, 528
Morosi, Junie 160, 162
Morris, Alan 510
Morris, John 190
Morris, Peter
  Minister for Transport
    282
Morrison, Scott 10, 563–4,
  572, 573, 575
The Movement 81
Mubarak, Hosni 426
Mulroney, Brian xvi, xxvi,
  346, 418, 434, 435, 488,
  490–1
Munich Olympics 1972 180
Munro, Paul 111, 112–13
Murdoch, Rupert 222, 373,
  374
Murphy, Denis 257
Murphy, Lionel 156, 329
Murray, Jan 411

Murray, John 6
MX missile test program
  341–3, 359

Nakasone, Yasuhiro 346,
  418
National and International
  Security Committee
  (NISC) 307
National Archives of
  Australia xv
National Competition
  Policy 465
National Crime Authority
  329
National Economic Summit
  1983 290, 296, 300,
  301–2, 576
National Farmers'
  Federation 456
National Gallery 406
National Press Club
  July 1976 address 199
  January 1983 272
National Taxation Summit
  1985 290, 360, 363–4,
  365, 377
  Keating white paper
    361–2
The National Times 219, 234
National Union of
  Australian University
  Students 30, 33
Nationwide 262
native title land rights 469,
  470–1, 576
Negus, George 141
New Idea 473
NSW Labor Council 121,
  129, 223
New Scientist 394
New Zealand 344
  1975 trip 144–5
News Limited 374
Newsworld 410–11
Newton, Maxwell 22, 29,
  72
Nihill, Grant 288, 380,
  396, 401, 415, 500, 507,
  528, 531
Nimmo, John 102, 103,
  104, 107
Nixon, Peter 132
Nixon, Richard 317
Nolan, Peter 191
Noonkanbah dispute 237,
  469
Noriega, Manuel 431
Norman, Greg 545
North, Lindsay 124

nuclear disarmament 337,
    341
  French nuclear testing,
    South Pacific 148, 174
Nuclear Disarmament Party
    342

Oakes, Laurie xxi, 142,
    168, 223, 254, 259, 400,
    503, 511
  Kirribilli Agreement story,
    breaking 506–7
O'Donoghue, Lowitja 469
Office of Chief Scientist
    290
Office of Multicultural
    Affairs 290
Office of the Status of
    Women 290, 323
oil industry, industrial
    disputes 1970s 133, 134
O'Keefe, Neil 367, 508
Oliver, Frederick Scott
    The Endless Adventure 216
Olympic Games, Sydney
    2000
O'Neill, Garry 330
Operative Painters' and
    Decorators' Union 119
Opperman, Hubert 93, 94,
    96, 97, 98, 99, 151
O'Shea, Clarrie 114
Our Country, Our Future
    statement 456, 457
Oxford 58
  arrival of Hazel 59
Oxford University xxiv,
    47–8, 50, 51–6, 62
  Bachelor of Letters 53–4,
    66
  course work 52, 53
  honorary doctorate 67
  journey to Oxford 48
  liberalism 60
  loneliness 56–7
  Oxford XI 61
  police charges 62–3
  return visits to give talks
    and lectures 68
  thesis 54–5, 62, 64–6
  University College 50–1,
    61
Oxford University Air
    Squadron 61–2
Oxford University Archives
    xvi

Packer, Kerry 222, 373, 374,
    461, 546
Painters' and Dockers'
    Union 246

Palestine 426, 427
Palestine Liberation
    Organization (PLO)
    178, 426
Panama, US invasion 430–1
Papua New Guinea 440
    1966–7 111–12
    1983 336
    1985 365
Parks, Colin 288, 400–1,
    502, 505, 506, 524, 531
Parliament House 228, 286,
    475
  Hawke's office 285–6
  new building 286, 475
  opening new Parliament
    House 475, 476
  sexual liaisons 411
Parramatta
    1973 by-election 157–8
Peacock, Andrew xvi, 127,
    174, 243, 275, 301, 511
    1984 Federal election
    331–2, 334, 385
    1987 leadership challenge
    386
    1989 leadership coup 452
    1990 Federal election 454,
    455, 458, 460
  Kennett, car conversation
    381
  Minister for Foreign
    Affairs 327
  opposition leader 301,
    316, 327
  resignations as party
    leader 367, 462
Peres, Shimon 180, 426
Perkins, Charles 470
Perth Modern School 21–4
  scholarship 21
  school reports 22–3
Peterson, Fred 190
Petrie, Jack 122, 129
Phillips, Hazel 154
Phillips, John 313
Pieters-Hawke, Susan xii,
    xvi, xxiv, 76, 146, 335,
    553
  birth 71
  Blanche, relationship with
    567
  Bob and Hazel marriage,
    views on 107, 146–7, 297
  childhood 95, 99, 126, 147
  Israel trip 1971 178
  Jakarta trip 1970 209
  marijuana use 211
  uranium mining protests
    189

pilots' strike 1989–90
    450–1, 456
Pimenov, Piotr 182
Plibersek, Tanya 558
PM radio program 519
Pol Pot 350
Polites, George 100, 101,
    291
Pollard, Reg 98
Pope John Paul II 174, 419
Popplewell, Oliver 63
Powell, Charles xvi, 353,
    354–5, 434, 436
Poyser, George 95, 96
Pratt, Louis 211, 568, 569,
    572, 574
Pratt, Richard 553
Pratt, Tony 209
press gallery 400, 511, 518,
    521, 525
Price, Roger 514
Prices and Income Accord
    296, 304, 305, 374, 450,
    536
Prime Minister
    see also Hawke government
  chiefs of staff 286
  committees 294
  consensus-style leadership
    287, 293, 295, 296
  daily routine 284–5
  duration 284
  election victories 498
  foreign affairs 336–40,
    419–31
  outer ministry 282, 295
  private secretaries 287
  staff and advisers 287–9
Prime Minister, first term
    1983–4
  approval rating 319, 327
  factions 283, 295–6
  Ministers 282–4
Prime Minister, second
    term 1984–87
  cabinet and ministry
    changes 359
  changes in office 376
  microeconomic reforms
    371–2
  private industry reform
    372
  satisfaction rating 379
Prime Minister, third term
    1987–89
  factions 387, 402, 527
  'Glee Club' 395
  ministerial structure
    changes 386–7

personal office changes
387–8
referendums 392
tariff reductions 389
Prime Minister, fourth term
1990–91
approval rating during
Gulf War 497
*Building a Competitive
Australia* 465
factions 467, 527
'Gang of Six' meeting
December 1991 524–5
last House of
Representatives address
535
leadership challenges
see 1991 (May–June)
Keating leadership
challenge; 1991
(December) Keating
leadership challenge
microeconomic reform
465–6
ministerial changes,
mishandling 461–2
Morgan Gallup poll
December 1991 523
net satisfaction rating 1991
503
'New Federalism' 463–5
preferred prime minister
polls 497, 502, 511, 523,
528
resignation press
conference 532
Statement on the
Economy and
Employment 522
Prime Minister's XI
1984 eye injury 330
Prince Charles 280
Prince Hassan 183
Prince Philip 91, 279–80
Prince Sihanouk 348
Princess Diana 280
public service, relationship
with 290, 291
Public Service Association
111
*Public Service Reform Act
1984* 291
Pullan, Robert 204, 212
Bob Hawke: A Portrait xv
Punch, Gary 310, 510, 528

Queen Elizabeth II 279,
324–5, 336, 476, 560
Queensland Trades and
Labour Council 82

Rabin, Yitzhak 180
Rabuka, Colonel Sitiveni
357
Ramphal, Sonny 355
Ramsey, Alan 139, 234, 250,
260, 524
Randall, Ken 331
Rattigan, Alf 157
Ray, Robert 220, 242, 244,
296, 462, 507, 508, 509,
517, 527, 528, 529
'Gang of Six' 524–5
Gulf War 487, 494
Kirribilli Agreement, view
of 503
Minister for Defence 462,
487
Minister for Immigration
467
Reagan, Ronald xvi, xxvi,
254, 317, 418, 577
1983 meeting 336, 337,
338–9
1985 meeting 344–5
1986 meeting 345–6
1988 meeting 427–8
diary 338, 344, 345, 427
Gorbachev and 420–1,
422–3
recessions 472–3
1990 448–9, 471–2, 503
Reddall, Ruth 220
Redlich, Peter xvi, 192, 222,
236, 549
refugee processing centre
468
Regan, Donald 336, 339
Reid, Alan 73, 97
Reith, Peter 247, 452
republic referendum 1999
560
Reserve Bank of Australia
1988–9 interest rates 448
board 170, 360
Resource Assessment
Commission 515, 516
resources boom 1980s 231
retail price maintenance
137, 138
Bourke's-ACTU store
137–8, 218–19
Revelman, George 137
Revelman, Lionel 137, 138
Reynolds, Margaret 387,
495
Rhodes, Cecil Memorial,
Cape Town 49
Rhodes House, Milner
Hall 69
Rhodes Scholarship xxiv,
33, 34–6, 45, 67

see also Oxford University
allowance paid 60
application and interview
34–6, 45
centenary commemoration
2003 67
journey to Oxford 48
thesis 54–5, 62, 64–6
The Rhodes Trust 69
Rhodes Trust Archive xvi
Richards, Beverley 107
affair with Hawke 107
Richardson, Dennis 287,
440, 445, 504, 505, 507,
529–30
Richardson, Graham 154,
203, 224, 232, 239, 241,
282, 286, 296, 529
Antarctica 393, 394
brief to Oakes about
Kirribilli Agreement
506–7
Hawke, falling out with
461–2
Hawke-Keating leadership
498, 504, 509, 528, 533
Kirribilli Agreement 498,
503, 506
Tasmanian logging 392,
393
Rielly, Derek
Wednesdays with Bob 562
Riordan, Joe 119, 149
Rivkin, Rene 553
RJL Hawke & Associates
553
Robertson, Clive 410
Robertson, Ian 547, 553
Robinson, Jim 100–1, 103,
109
Rocard, Michel 394
Rockey, George 221
Ross, David 84
Rossiter, Dr James 34
Roulston, Jim 190
Roxburgh, Richard 562
Roxby Downs 240, 283
Royal Air Force Volunteer
Reserve 61, 95
Royal Commission into
Black Deaths in Custody
468
Royal Commission on
Australia's Security and
Intelligence Agencies
309, 310
Royal Society for the
Prevention of Cruelty to
Animals (RSPCA) 13
Rudd, Kevin 505, 557, 565,
579

apology to Stolen
    Generations 559, 579
Rudd/Gillard government
    557–8
Ruddock, Philip 158, 468
Rudin, Milton 'Mickey'
    134, 135, 136
Rule, Aaron 544
Russell, Bertrand
    *A History of Western
    Philosophy* 47
Russell, Eric 83
Ryan, Morgan 329
Ryan, Susan xiv, 205, 255,
    257, 283, 293, 320, 322,
    361, 370, 553
    Minister for Education
    and Youth Affairs 282,
    391
Rye, Dick 281

Sadleir, David 444
Salter, Wilfred 83
Sampson, Noel 21, 22, 23
Santamaria, B.A. 81, 84
Saulwick Poll 511, 528
Saunders, Jill 272–3, 288,
    543, 547, 561
Savva, Niki 234
Sawer, Geoffrey 72, 74,
    76, 89
SBS 372
Schacht, Chris 509
Scharansky, Anatoli 181
Schildberger, Michael 203
Schoenmaker, Mario 553
Scholes, Gordon 283, 307,
    509
    Minister for Defence 282
    Minister for Territories
    359
Schwarzkopf, Norman 495
Sciacca, Con 533
Scott, Dick 190
Scott, John 495
Scowcroft, Brent 495
Sedgewick, Steve 289, 369,
    376, 387
Sedky, Atef 426
Seelaf, George 82
Sex Discrimination Act 1984
    322
Sex Discrimination
    Commissioner 322
Shamir, Yitzhak 426
Shannon, Jim 120
Shaw, George Bernard
    Pygmalion 52

Sheahan, Terry 523
Sheet Metal Workers'
    Union 93
Shelepin, Alexander 181
Shibaev, Alexei 181
Short, John 363
Short, Laurie 149
Shorten, Bill 558, 572, 574
Shultz, George xvi, 336,
    337–8, 342, 343, 419
Sibraa, Kerry xvi, 124, 194,
    268–9, 270
    Diary 268–9, 270
Simmonds, Peter 267
Sims, Rod 289, 388,
    449–50, 464
Sinatra, Frank 136
    1974 Australia tour 134–5
Sinclair, Angus 413
Sinclair, Ian 381, 407, 452
Sinclair, Jean 132, 165, 212,
    227, 267, 268, 280, 288,
    289, 379, 413
    affair with Hawke 132,
    212, 413
Singleton, John 68, 542, 553
Skase, Christopher 373
Slatyer, Ralph 22
Smith, David
    Knight Commander in the
    Royal Victorian Order
    482–3
Smith, Mamie 204, 206
Smith, Richard 179
Snedden, Billy 22, 132, 164,
    171, 262, 347
Snow, Jim 533
social media 580
Solomon, David 165
Somare, Michael 112, 336
Sorby, Bob 288, 376, 379,
    380, 383, 387, 395, 413
Souter, Harold 75, 82, 83,
    88, 159
    ACTU candidacy for
    president 116, 117, 118,
    121, 122
    background 83
    post-1969 ACTU work
    130, 131, 132
    retirement 191
South Africa xxvi, 49,
    148–9, 336, 346, 353–4,
    356, 419
South Melbourne Football
    Club 171
South Pacific 440
South Pacific Forum 419
    1983 290
South Pacific Nuclear Free
    Zone 341

Soviet-Afghan War 418
Soviet Union 419, 437
    collapse 418, 425
    Gorbachev and Hawke
    421, 422, 424–5
    Jews emigrating from 181,
    424
    KGB and GRU in
    Australia 291, 305
    Refuseniks, negotiations
    for 180, 181, 334, 424
Sparkes, Robert 381
Special Premiers'
    Conferences 1990, 1991
    463–4
Spigelman, Jim 158, 161
The Sportsman 396
Springboks tour 1971
    148–9, 174
Stop the Tours campaign
    148
Stanford University 548
Staples, Peter 508
State Bank of Victoria 471
State Electricity
    Commission dispute 190
Staunton, Pat 529
Stephen, Sir Ninian xxii,
    260–1, 279, 477, 550
Stewart, Don 515–16
Stokes, Kerry 373
Stone, John 22, 29, 64,
    142–3, 280, 281, 287, 299,
    300, 326
    floating of Australian
    dollar 313, 314
Stone, Ken 190
Storemen and Packers'
    Union 122, 129
    Phoenix Hotel, Brunswick
    197
Stowell, Lord 51
Strategic Defense Initiative
    (SDI) 341
Street, Tony 184, 185
Structural Adjustment
    Committee 371
Student Christian
    Movement 27, 29
Sturgess, Garry 547
Subiaco Congregational
    Church 19
Suharto, President 336
Summers, Anne 290, 323
Sun 411
Sun News-Pictorial 142, 332
Sunday 511
The Sunday Age 451, 546
Super, Richard 553
Superannuation Guarantee
    520

Sweeney, Charles 103, 104, 107, 157
The Sydney Morning Herald 126, 332, 363, 511

Taiwan 351
Tamburrino, Mimi 220, 227, 289, 543
Tanner, Lindsay 375
tariff reductions
  Hawke government 389, 452, 465, 536
  Whitlam government 157, 158
Tate, Michael 387
Tatiara district, South Australia 9
tax file number system 388
taxation reforms 331
  1985 364–5
  capital gains tax 362
  consumption tax 361, 362, 363, 364
  fringe benefits tax 361
taxation summit *see* National Taxation Summit 1985
telecommunications reforms 1990 466–7
television network licences 373
The Telegraph Mirror 511
Telstra 466
Terry Willesee Tonight 329
Thatcher, Margaret xvi, xxvi, 352–3, 355, 357, 418, 433
  1988 Australian visit 431
  Antarctica 394
  apartheid 353–5, 356, 357, 433–4, 436
  Falklands War 433
  Gallipoli 1990 486
  Hong Kong 420
  resignation 435
Thomson, Owen 140
Tiananmen Square protests 351, 432, 444–6
  temporary entry visa extension 446, 468
Tickner, Robert 516, 517
Time 174–5
Tinsulanonda, Prem 346
Tiparra West School 15
Titterington, Bill 74
TNT (Thomas Nationwide Transport) 138
Tolmer, Alexander 9
Toohey, Brian 234
Toohey, John 27, 70
tourism industry

Hogan ad campaign 1983 389, 390
Townsend, Jeff 288, 307, 317–18
Transport Workers' Union 82, 149
Trengove, Alan 102–3, 125
Trudeau, Pierre 336
'True Believers' dinner 1993 549
Truman, Ronald 85–6
Turnbull, Malcolm 560, 564, 579
  wanting to be a Labor MP 560
Turner, Ray 124, 125

Uluru, handing back 468
unemployment
  1974 161
  1983 266, 281
  1991 448, 503, 522
United Nations 419, 494
  sanctions on Iraq 487, 488, 492
  Security Council 487, 491, 492
United States
  Export Enhancement Program (EEP) 441, 442
  Joint Session of Congress address 428
  McCarthyism 60
  MX missile test program 341–3, 359
  National Security Council report 1971 141
  Panama invasion 430–1
  Strategic Defense Initiative (SDI) 341
University College 50–1, 61
  Cricket Club 61
  Hawke portrait 68
University College Archive (Oxford) xvi
  student file 55
University College Record 61
University of Sydney
  visiting professor appointment 548
University of Western Australia 25–8, 53
  ALP Club 28
  Arts degree 28, 53
  International House Appeal 31, 36, 47
  John Norman Baker Prize for Law 27
  Law degree 26–7

overseas students 31
Student Christian Movement 27, 29
Unley Crystal Pool, Adelaide 15
Unsworth, Barrie 90–1, 121–2, 123, 124, 199–200, 223–4
uranium mining 188–9, 239, 326
  Nabarlek mine 240
  Non-Proliferation Treaty 189
  Ranger mine 240
  Roxby Downs 240
Uren, Tom 165, 168, 188, 197, 233, 240, 241, 260, 291, 292, 365
  Gietzelt as dual member of the Communist Party 292
  Minister for Territories and Local Government 283

Vassiliou, George 524, 525
Vaughn, F.S. 62
Vernon, Sir James 109–10
Vernon Committee of Economic Inquiry 109, 110
Victoria
  State election 1958 81
  State election 1963 93
Victorian Trades Hall Council 83, 190
Vietnam 340, 341, 348, 349
Vietnam War 148
  moratorium marches 149
  withdrawal of Australian troops 155
Viner, Ian 231
voluntary euthanasia advocate 559

WA Inc. scandal 503
Walker, Frank 375, 402, 495, 509, 527
Wall Street Crash 4
Walpole, Sir Robert 216
Walsh, Eric 165, 309
Walsh, Geoff 236, 267, 269, 288, 289, 308, 376, 387, 453
Walsh, Peter xix, 227, 243, 253, 320, 370, 392, 509
  Minister for Finance 370
  Minister for Resources and Energy 282
Ward, Barbara 270, 281

Ward, Phillip 144, 145
Ward, Roger 247
Warden, Ian 192–3
Warne, Brigitte 145
Warne, Jason 145
Warne, Shane 145
Waterhouse, Gai 553
Waterhouse, Robbie 553
Waterside Workers' Union
  82, 84, 118, 119, 190
Watts, Barry 169
Webb, Leicester 73
Weekend Mail 66
Weinberger, Caspar 336,
  343
welfare sector reforms
  319–20, 374
  child poverty pledge
    384–5, 388–9
  Family Allowance
    Supplement 385, 388,
    389
  pension assets tests 330
Wells, Fred 118, 120
Wells, H.G.
  A Short History of the World
    48–9
Wendt, Jana 543
West, Stewart 267, 283, 495,
  509, 527
  Minister for Immigration
    and Ethnic Affairs 282
The West Australian 36, 332
West Leederville, Perth 16,
  17, 18
  101 Tate Street 17, 18
West Leederville, State
  School 17–18
Wheare, Kenneth 54, 71
Wheeldon, John 22
Wheeler, Sir Fredrick 143,
  170
Whitby, Fred 119
White, Hugh 289, 490, 491
White, Jan *see* Marsh, Jan
White, Patrick 202
White Australia Policy 91
Whitlam, Gough 96, 97,
  126, 134, 139, 141, 142,
  148, 233, 243, 244, 262,
  534, 560, 578
  1972 campaign 153–5

1975–6 budget 162
1977 election 192, 193
approval rating 319
Hawke and 152, 155–6,
  157–8, 162–3, 544
Iraqi 'loan' 168–9
Khemlani loans affair
  163–4
Labor leader 151
UNESCO ambassador
  355
Whitlam, Margaret 155,
  233, 355
Whitlam government xxvi,
  160–2
  dismissal 164, 165–6, 167,
    285
  policy blunders 160–1
  reforms, landmark 159
  tariffs, removal of 157
  uranium mining 188
Wilderness Society 383
Williams, Edgar 54, 55,
  71, 190
Williams, Helen 324
Willis, Ralph 88, 89, 94,
  101, 129, 131, 146, 239,
  281, 462, 509, 514, 529
  Minister for Employment
    and Industrial Relations
    282
  recession 1990 471
  shadow Treasurer, removal
    from 250
  Treasurer 522
Willis, Stan 88
Wills electorate 226, 289
  1980 election xxv, 227, 228
  1992 by-election 544
  preselection 216–17, 219,
    220
  resignation as member
    for 543
Wilson, Harold 51
Winter, Terry 107, 114
Winters, Tracey 573
Wolfensohn, Jim 356
Woman's Day 552
Women's Christian
  Temperance Movement
  11, 18

Women's Liberation group
  130
Wood, Bill 190
Woodward, Brian 198
Woolcott, Richard 443
Wootten, Hal 111, 112
World Health Organization
  321
World Heritage Listing
  nominations 382
World Jewish Congress
  award 1988 427
World War I 6
World War II 18
Wran, Neville xxii, 171,
  222, 234–5, 260, 326,
  363, 383
  1980 Federal election 226
  1983 Federal election 264,
    265
Wran Committee 391
Wright, Syd 107, 109, 110

Yeend, Sir Geoffrey 280,
  287, 288, 301, 306, 315,
  412
Yeltsin, Boris 437
Young, Mick 152, 192, 197,
  199, 226, 229, 233, 239,
  241, 267, 361
  1983 Federal election 275
  1987 Federal election 383
  Combe-Ivanov scandal
    283
  Paddington Bear affair
    329, 416
  resignation from cabinet
    309
  Special Minister of State
    282
Yunupingu, Galarrwuy 470

Zampatti, Lloyd 22
Zanetti, Terry 70
Zhao, Ziyang 280, 346,
  347–8, 350, 351, 420, 432,
  444, 446
Zionist Federation of
  Sydney 179